LEGAL METHOD
AND WRITING

LEGAL METHOD AND WRITING

CHARLES R. CALLEROS

PROFESSOR OF LAW AND ASSOCIATE DEAN
ARIZONA STATE UNIVERSITY

LITTLE, BROWN AND COMPANY
BOSTON   TORONTO   LONDON

LIBRARY OF CONGRESS CATALOG CARD No. 90-60107

ISBN 0-316-12502-4

Fifth Printing

EB

Published simultaneously in Canada
by Little, Brown & Company (Canada) Limited

PRINTED IN THE UNITED STATES OF AMERICA

To Deborah, Alexander, and Benjamin,
con cariño

‖ SUMMARY of CONTENTS ‖

‖ PART I

INTRODUCTION to the LEGAL SYSTEM   1

‖ PART II

WRITING in LAW SCHOOL—FROM CASE BRIEFS to EXAMINATIONS   77

‖ CONTENTS ‖

‖ PART

I

INTRODUCTION TO THE LEGAL SYSTEM   1

‖ CHAPTER ‖

1

Statutory and Common Law Analysis   5

‖ C H A P T E R ‖

2

The Role of Precedent   29

‖ C H A P T E R ‖

3

An Approach to Legal Method   45

CHAPTER

4

Introduction to Writing Style · 71

PART

II

WRITING IN LAW SCHOOL—FROM CASE BRIEFS TO EXAMINATIONS · 77

CHAPTER

5

Case Analysis · 79

CHAPTER 6

Reorganization, Summary, and Inductive Reasoning in Outline Form   105

CHAPTER 7

Essay Examinations   119

PART

III

WRITING IN THE LAW OFFICE—NEUTRAL ANALYSIS

137

CHAPTER

8

The Office Memorandum of Law

139

‖ C H A P T E R ‖
9

Organization of Office Memoranda and Briefs   169

‖ C H A P T E R ‖
10

Legal Writing Style in the Office Memorandum   197

PART

IV

ADVOCACY 249

CHAPTER

11

Introduction to Advocacy 251

‖ CHAPTER ‖
12

Pleadings

‖ CHAPTER ‖
13

Motion for Summary Judgment

CHAPTER

14

Motion to Exclude Evidence Before Trial   323

CHAPTER

15

Appellate Briefs   333

PART V

WRITING to PARTIES: CONTRACTS and CORRESPONDENCE

397

CHAPTER 16

Contracts

399

‖ CHAPTER ‖
17

Advice and Demand Letters — 413

TABLE OF CHARTS AND SAMPLE DOCUMENTS

‖ PREFACE ‖

We legal educators strive primarily to develop analytical skills through classroom discussion of statutes and appellate judicial opinions. Secondarily, we teach substantive rules of law in the subjects that provide the context for the development of analytical skills. We typically devote even less attention to developing verbal skills, perhaps on the assumption that college and private practice are the best places for training in oral and written expression.

The activities of practicing attorneys, however, suggest that legal writing classes are important in disproportion to the emphasis given to them in law school. Although analytical skills and a general knowledge of legal principles form the intellectual foundation of your practice of law, legal analysis is only as effective as the quality with which it is expressed. In your practice, you undoubtedly will devote a substantial proportion of your time and effort to drafting legal documents such as office memoranda, letters, pleadings, motions, briefs, contracts, and wills. Moreover, techniques of expression are closely linked to the underlying substantive analysis; indeed, problems in writing style often betray confusion in the analysis.

Unfortunately, as a first-semester law student, you may have difficulty seeing the relationship between your efforts in legal writing classes and your short-term objectives for success in law school. You will rationally measure your success in law school by the grades you earn on final exams. On the other hand, you will be tempted to view your first-year writing courses, which may be ungraded, as a means of achieving a wholly distinct goal of preparing for successful performance in summer clerkships and in post-graduate practice. The extreme academic pressures of law school may stimulate you to place primary emphasis on your short-term goals of success on final examinations in graded courses and perhaps to resent an ungraded legal writing course as an inconvenient distraction.

With this book, I hope to reassure you that your work in your first-year legal writing courses will directly contribute to your success with law school exams as well as with legal documents that you draft in a summer clerking position or in post-graduate employment. I attempt to achieve that objective in two ways. First, I hope to eliminate any mystery in the study of law by comprehensively examining the three critical components for success in law school: (1) briefing and synthesizing cases, (2) reorganizing and summarizing course materials in course outlines, and (3) analyzing and answering essay examinations. Second, I demonstrate in Parts I-III that the skills you develop in analyzing a client's legal problem and drafting an office memorandum are directly transferable to your task of analyzing an essay exam and writing the exam answer.

Additionally, this book examines techniques of advocacy and client representation that should appeal to a broad spectrum of readers: participants in a first-year moot-court program, students in an advanced writing seminar, student law clerks and practicing attorneys. For example, Part IV examines written advocacy in the context of pleadings, pretrial motions, and appellate briefs. Moreover, it thoroughly examines principles of writing and persuasion that apply generally to any litigation document. Part V provides a step-by-step approach to drafting simple contracts, advice letters and demand letters. Finally, the extensive citations in footnotes, most of which first-year law students can pass over, will provide attorneys with a valuable source of authorities.

Chapters 4 and 9-11 of this book address matters of style. They use problems and examples to outline a general approach to style that focuses on the policies underlying conventions of composition and presentation of legal authority. In these chapters, I encourage you to adopt the following philosophy: we should not memorize and mechanically apply rules of composition any more than we would mechanically apply "black-letter" rules of law. Instead, we must understand the goals and purposes of the conventions of legal writing, and we should apply them flexibly to satisfy those goals and purposes.

Of course, this book reflects my own style quirks and biases: I freely split infinitives but always use the serial comma, and I dislike sexism in language. The problem of sexism in language arose most often in this book in the form of personal pronouns in the third person. If I constantly resorted to an ostensibly generic pronoun normally associated with the male gender, such as "his" or "him," I would offend those readers who do not view the pronoun as gender generic and who believe that the increasing numbers of female attorneys and judges deserve specific recognition. On the other hand, multiple pronouns, such as "his or her," often needlessly clutter already complex sentences, and plural pronouns, such as "they," are not always consistent with content. As a provocative response to the problem, I have alternated between male and female pronouns, for example by referring to an associate in a law firm with the pronoun "he" and to his supervising attorney with the pronoun "she." This approach may distract or even offend nearly all readers at one time or another, but it at least dramatizes the need for truly gender-neutral singular pronouns in our language. Perhaps writers should coin the terms "hes" and "hem."

Charles R. Calleros

March 1990

‖ ACKNOWLEDGMENTS ‖

Although my courses in contracts and civil rights legislation consume a substantial portion of my time and energy, I have always managed to maintain a role in legal writing programs at the College of Law and in Phoenix law firms. My interest and enthusiasm for legal writing stem largely from the inspiration and training that I received as a court law clerk at the Office of Central Staff Attorneys for the United States Court of Appeals for the Ninth Circuit. In particular, I owe a continuing debt of gratitude to my primary supervisors, Peter Shaw, now practicing in San Francisco, and Gregory Hughes, now practicing in Sacramento. I am equally grateful to United States Court of Appeals Judge Procter Hug, Jr., who sowed the seeds of my current views on flexible, policy-oriented approaches to legal writing.

Other attorneys, judges, and colleagues contributed to my manuscript with their comments on early drafts. In particular, I thank Thomas Gordon, who is a staff attorney for the Arizona Court of Appeals, fellow legal writing instructor, and former classmate at University of California at Davis School of Law. Mr. Gordon's keen analytical insights into the art of legal writing have contributed greatly to this book. Other important contributors include the rigorous reviewers for Little, Brown and Company, who strongly influenced the organization and content of the book; my marvelous manuscript editor, Barbara Rappaport; and Janet Wagner, a recent graduate who skillfully and artfully critiqued my writing style. Several colleagues contributed to selected portions of the book. They include Fred Cole, Amy Gittler, Mark Hielman, William Monahan, Roger Perry, Frank Placenti, Thomas Quarelli, Paul Ulrich, Judge Noel Fidel, and Professors Jane Aiken, Betsy Grey, Mark Hall, David Kader, Robert Misner, Mary Richards, Bonnie Tucker, James Weinstein, and Larry Winer.

The truly indispensable contributors to this book, however, are the students and attorneys who accepted my instruction and used the early versions of the teaching materials from which this book is derived. I especially acknowledge the Phoenix law firm of Streich, Lang, Weeks & Cardon for its exceptional dedication to continuing education in legal writing. I also thank the hard-working student writing instructors who helped me direct an experimental first-year writing program at the College of Law in the 1985-1986 academic year. The continuing success of that program is a tribute to their early efforts.

I must also thank staff and student research assistants for their contributions: Donna Blair provided word-processing, Janice Fuller checked citations, Virginia Vasquez evaluated the manuscript for readability from the perspective of a first-year student, and Toby Schmich and Victoria Stevens provided other editorial work.

Finally, I am indebted to Arizona State University College of Law, and especially to Deans Paul Bender and Alan Matheson. The college provided me with financial support, partial release time, and moral support, without which this book could not have been completed.

LEGAL METHOD
AND WRITING

INTRODUCTION TO THE LEGAL SYSTEM

In your first-year contracts course, you probably will study the case of *Hadley and Another v. Baxendale and Others*.[1] By examining the history of this case now, you can become acquainted with the methods by which you will study law in most of your classes.

The dispute between the Hadleys and Baxendale began as a business transaction during an economic boom in the midst of England's industrial revolution: operators of a flour mill in Gloucester entered into a contract with a carrier for the transportation of a broken engine shaft to a manufacturer in Greenwich, on the other side of England.

The operators of the mill, the Hadleys, were anxious to transport the broken shaft to the manufacturer as quickly as possible; the failure of the shaft had halted the milling of corn, and the broken shaft would serve as a model for the manufacture of a new shaft. An employee of the carrier, Pickford and Co., promised that the shaft would be delivered to the manufacturer within two days after the date that the carrier took possession of the shaft. For this, the mill operators paid £2 4s. The carrier could have transported the shaft as promptly as promised had it immediately used available means of land transportation. Presumably to reduce costs, however, it held the shaft for several days in London before loading it onto a canal barge along with a shipment of iron that was bound for the same manufacturer. As a consequence, the carrier delivered the shaft to the manufacturer on the seventh day after the carrier received it, resulting in an additional delay of five days during which the mill was stopped.

The mill operators demanded that the carrier compensate for an estimated £300 in lost profits that the mill suffered because of the additional delay. The carrier refused, and the mill operators sued the carrier's managing director, Baxendale, in a trial court in Gloucester, claiming approximately £200 in dam-

---

1. 9 Ex. 341, 156 Eng. Rep. 145 (1854).

ages. Although the carrier offered to settle the dispute for £25, the mill operators rejected the offer, and the case went to trial before a jury. The mill operators presented witnesses who testified to £120 in damages, and the jury awarded the mill operators £50 in a compromise verdict that became the judgment of the trial court.

The carrier appealed to the Court of Exchequer, an appellate court. It ultimately persuaded a panel of three judges on this court to reverse the judgment of the trial court and to grant a new trial on the ground that the trial judge had given the jury excessive latitude in awarding damages for lost profits.

The appellate court reversed the judgment of the trial court and ordered a new trial. In the appellate court's written opinion, the authoring judge explained that a jury may award only those damages that would flow naturally from the breach of such a contract or that would be reasonably within the contemplation of the parties because of special circumstances communicated at the time of contracting. Because the appellate judges assumed that the mill would ordinarily have spare shafts with which to keep running, they concluded that lost profits stemming from an idle mill would not be the natural consequence of the breach of the contract for prompt carriage. Whether the possibility of lost profits would nonetheless have been in the contemplation of the parties would depend on whether, at the time of contracting, the mill operators had communicated to the carrier the special circumstances that the broken shaft was the mill's only shaft and that the mill would be idle in its absence.

The appellate court concluded that the mill operators had informed the carrier only that they operated a mill and that the article to be transported was the broken shaft of a mill.[2] On this premise, the appellate court held that the trial judge should not have allowed the jury to consider any lost profits in its calculation of damages.

The case of *Hadley v. Baxendale* illustrates both how a case makes its way through the legal system and how you typically will join the case only at its destination in its legal journey. Reacting to a pressing commercial need, the mill operators entered into an agreement with the carrier to exchange money for certain services. Disappointed with the services rendered, the mill operators demanded compensation. Failing to secure the compensation through informal means, they ultimately filed an action in a trial court to obtain a judgment compelling the carrier to pay compensation.

At trial, the parties discovered that their claims and defenses were limited by their ability to present credible supporting evidence to the jury, to whom the court had delegated the task of finding facts. Hence, the mill operator's original demand dropped first from £300 to £200, and then to the £120 of losses for which it could produce testimony. Relying on centuries of development of law and custom, the court recognized the contractual relationship as one deserving of the protection of the Queen's courts, and it permitted the jury to award damages for the carrier's breach of the contract. The jury awarded less in damages than the trial court's instructions and the testimony would have

---

2. Interestingly, this represents a departure from the summary of the trial proceedings prepared by the court reporter, who had reported at the beginning of the appellate opinion that the mill operators had informed the carrier that the mill was stopped. See R. Danzig, The Capability Problem in Contract Law 80 (1978) (characterizing the finding of the Court of Exchequer as "remarkable").

allowed, but more than the carrier thought the law should permit. Accordingly, the carrier took the dispute before a court of higher authority, which ordered a new trial that would exclude lost profits from any recovery, and which explained its decision in a written judicial opinion.

It is primarily to this final action of the appellate court that law school courses will direct your attention. In nearly all first-year courses in law school, students encounter the law in casebooks, each of which presents judicial opinions on various topics that relate to a general field of law such as property, contracts, criminal law, procedure, or torts.

The "cases" in a casebook are the disputes that parties bring to courts for resolution. Most of the judicial opinions that analyze the cases are the opinions of appellate courts. The edited appellate opinions published in casebooks often summarize the facts of the dispute and the proceedings in lower courts in the most economical way possible,[3] sometimes providing no more than a bare outline of the human drama that has preceded the appellate litigation. Most appellate opinions focus instead on using the cases before them as vehicles for developing and articulating general legal rules or principles. These rules not only resolve the dispute before the court, they also provide guidance to courts and litigants in future disputes of a similar nature, as well as to persons who desire to conform their actions to the law so as to avoid disputes.

Judicial opinions may mystify you in your first weeks at law school. They are peppered with legal terminology that will incrementally become part of your working vocabulary only after weeks and months of study. Moreover, the opinions assume a knowledge of the legal system and of the legal method that courts use when working within that system. For example, you might wonder how an early English decision such as *Hadley v. Baxendale* is relevant to your study of American law. Also confusing to some new law students is the relationship between "common law" and "statutory law," both of which may be addressed in the same judicial opinion.

Part I of this book seeks to answer these and many other questions by introducing you to our legal system and to fundamental principles of legal method. This foundation should better prepare you to develop skills in studying law in first-year courses, in analyzing legal problems in a law office or judge's chambers, and in advocating a client's position to a court, all of which are discussed in Parts II-V. Chapter 1 begins building the foundation with an introduction to the American legal system.

You undoubtedly must prepare cases for class discussion beginning with the first day of class. Accordingly, before your first day of classes, you may wish to glance through Sections I and III of Chapter 5, the introduction and conclusion, which provide an overview to the process of briefing cases for class discussion. After completing Part I, you can then study Chapters 5-7 more thoroughly to develop a comprehensive, three-point plan for success in your substantive courses: (1) briefing and synthesizing cases, (2) outlining course materials, and (3) applying effective examination techniques.

---

3. Indeed, many of the details of Hadley v. Baxendale described in this book do not appear in the report of the Court of the Exchequer, much less in a casebook's edited version of that report. The source of this book's more detailed recounting of the case is R. Danzig, The Capability Problem in Contract Law 68-105 (1978).

1

Statutory and Common Law Analysis

I. SOURCES OF LAWMAKING POWERS

The United States Constitution allocates powers between the state and national governments and thus establishes the framework for our federal system of government. In turn, each state's constitution establishes the framework for that state's government. A fundamental tenet of these state and federal constitutions is the separation of powers between the legislative, judicial, and executive branches of government. Although lawmaking functions rest primarily with the legislative branch, all three branches exercise some form of lawmaking power.

The state and federal legislatures create law by enacting statutes within the authority granted to them by the state and federal constitutions. The legislatures may delegate some of this lawmaking power to the executive branch by statutorily authorizing an executive agency to issue rules and regulations designed to help implement a statutory scheme.

For example, in the exercise of its federal constitutional authority to regulate commerce, the United States Congress has enacted comprehensive labor relations statutes, such as the National Labor Relations Act.[1] It has also created the National Labor Relations Board, an agency of the United States, and it has authorized the board to issue administrative rules and regulations necessary to help the board enforce the labor relations statutes.

Legislatures cannot amend a constitution in the same way that they enact statutes. For example, Article V of the United States Constitution authorizes Congress to propose constitutional amendments, but such proposals do not become effective until ratified by the legislatures or constitutional conventions of three-fourths of the states.

---

1. 49 Stat. 449 (1935).

The judicial branch of government develops law in two ways, both of them in the context of particular disputes. First, state and federal courts contribute to the development of constitutional and statutory law by interpreting the necessarily general terms of such law and applying those terms to the facts of disputes. Second, as an offspring of the English judicial system, American courts have adopted and continue to develop a substantial body of common law, judge-made law that applies to issues not addressed by constitutional or statutory law. State courts are the primary source of common law, because federal courts no longer create and develop "federal general common law."[2] Nonetheless, the federal courts retain the power in a few restricted fields, such as admiralty law, to develop "specialized federal common law."[3]

An example of the interplay between statutory law and common law is provided in the first-year contracts course. Many principles of contract law, such as consideration, offer and acceptance, performance and breach, and remedies, find their source in a substantial body of common law, developed by judges, first in England and later in America. This common law forms a backdrop against which state legislatures have enacted statutes, such as commercial codes, that supersede some of the common law rules. In the resulting hybrid system, the statutes provide the rule of law on issues to which they apply, while common law applies to gaps within and between statutes.

These fundamental principles of state and federal lawmaking apply only in limited fashion to two other kinds of governments in the United States: (1) local governments of political subdivisions of the states, such as cities and counties, and (2) American Indian tribal governments.

Local governments come in a variety of models. Although many of them exercise legislative, executive, and judicial powers, they do not always practice the same degree of separation of these powers as do state and federal governments. In many states, the state constitution and statutes at least partially define the legal structure that a local government can adopt and the powers that it can exercise.

More nearly autonomous are American Indian tribes. Although their powers may be limited by federal law, they are otherwise sovereign governments with inherent powers to exercise tribal authority. Not all of the tribes have chosen to adopt every fundamental tenet of the state and federal governments. For example, the Navajo Nation of the Southwestern United States has no constitution, and it has not always recognized complete separation of legislative, judicial, and executive powers. Nonetheless, its legal system is similar to the Anglo-American system in several important respects. The tribe elects the members of the Navajo Tribal Council, which enacts statutory law in the form of tribal codes. The executive power rests primarily in the Tribal Chair, an elected official. Finally, the Navajo tribal trial courts and the Navajo Supreme Court apply federal law and tribal codes, and they develop and apply a tribal common law based on tribal custom and cultural values.

This book primarily addresses state and federal common law and statutes. This chapter separately discusses first common law analysis and then statutory analysis before further addressing the relationship between the two.

---

2. Erie R.R. v. Tompkins, 304 U.S. 64, 78 (1938).
3. Friendly, In Praise of Erie—And of the New Federal Common Law, 39 N.Y.U.L. Rev. 383, 405 (1964).

II. COMMON LAW

The common law that American courts develop and apply has its roots in the English common law, which was dispensed in the courts of the English king. This English law came to be known as the "common law" because it applied generally throughout medieval England and thus replaced a less uniform system of customary law dispensed in local or regional courts and in the private courts of feudal lords. The English Court of Chancery, representing a separate system of law, competed with the early common law courts for jurisdiction by applying a system of "equity law" that provided relief when common law remedies were inadequate.

Distinctions between some common law and equitable claims, defenses, and remedies continue to have substantive significance.[4] Most American jurisdictions, however, have eliminated the dual court system by merging law and equity procedure.[5] Accordingly, this book will use the term "common law" to refer generally to legal principles created and developed by the courts independent of legislative enactments, regardless whether the principles have their roots in early common law or equity law.

Oliver Wendell Holmes traced the origins of some English and American common law to early Germanic and Roman law.[6] Other common law principles simply reflect judicial recognition of community needs, habits, or customs, and are "accounted for by their manifest good sense."[7] More generally, common law is "the embodiment of broad and comprehensive unwritten principles . . . inspired by natural reason and an innate sense of justice."[8]

The term "common" may be misleading when applied to American common law: the courts in each state are free to develop the common law of that state in a manner that reflects local policies; therefore, variations in common law among the states are inevitable. Nonetheless, to a surprising degree, courts in different states share common views on general principles of law. For example, a federal appellate court has noted that "the principles of contract law do not differ greatly from one jurisdiction to another."[9] Perhaps more important for law students and practitioners, the legal method employed by courts in deciding disputes and developing common law does not vary substantially among the states.

The early common law crime of burglary, which was punishable by death, illustrates the judicial development of common law rules to serve particular needs of the community. In imposing capital punishment for this crime, the common law courts sought to deter a serious invasion of the right of habitation during hours of darkness, when the inhabitants were most vulnerable to attack

---

4. D. Dobbs, Remedies § 2.6 (1973); cf. 5A A. Corbin, Corbin on Contracts § 1136 (1964) (procedural merger of law and equity has resulted in partial substantive merger of legal and equitable principles of remedies).

5. See, e.g., Fed. R. Civ. P. 2 ("There shall be one form of action to be known as 'civil action'."); D. Dobbs, Remedies § 2.6 app., at 81-82 (1973).

6. O. Holmes, Jr., The Common Law 2, 18, 34, 340-344, 360 (1923).

7. Id. at 2, 337-339.

8. Mosk, The Common Law and the Judicial Decision-Making Process, 11 Harv. J.L. & Pub. Pol. 35 (1988) (citing Rodriguez v. Bethlehem Steel Co., 12 Cal. 3d 382, 398, 525 P.2d 669, 682-683 (1974)).

9. E.g., Hall v. Perry (In re Cochise Park, Inc.), 703 F.2d 1339, 1348 n.4 (9th Cir. 1983).

and the invader most likely to escape recognition. Efforts by the common law courts to narrowly address that evil are reflected in the general definition of common law burglary, which separates the crime into distinct elements: (1) the breaking and (2) entering (3) of the dwelling house (4) of another (5) in the night (6) with the intent to commit a felony.

In defining and applying these elements of common law burglary in the context of successive cases, the courts exhibited a reluctance to extend the crime beyond the minimum reach necessary to achieve the underlying purposes of the crime, probably because of the severity of punishment. For example, the courts viewed an intruder as less culpable if the occupant of a dwelling encouraged the intrusion by failing to properly secure the dwelling. Accordingly, many courts held that a trespasser who gained entry by further opening a partially open door or window had not committed the "breaking" necessary for a burglary.[10]

The history of another common law crime, murder, illustrates the manner in which courts gradually developed common law doctrine "over several centuries of time as a parade of cases, involving different fact situations, came before the judges for decision."[11] The common law decisions generally define murder as the unlawful killing of another human being with malice aforethought. Early decisions defined "malice aforethought" narrowly by requiring proof of a premeditated intent to kill. As subsequent cases presented unpremeditated or even unintentional killings that warranted classification as murder, courts effectively expanded the definition of "malice aforethought" by recognizing other circumstances that would justify conviction for murder: intentional but unpremeditated killing without sufficient provocation; unintentional killing during the commission of another felony; unintentional killing through conduct that reflects a reckless disregard for the lives of others; and killing during the course of conduct engaged in with the intent to do serious bodily harm short of death.[12]

This process of incremental development of the common law does not always proceed in an unbroken line. Courts sometimes abandon previously adopted lines of authority to chart new courses that better reflect current social, economic, and technological realities:

> The inherent capacity of the common law for growth and change is its most significant feature. It is constantly expanding and developing to keep up with the advancement of civilization and the new conditions and progress of society, and adapting itself to the gradual changes in trade, commerce, arts, inventions, and the needs of the country. . . . The vitality of the common law can flourish if the courts remain alert to their obligation and have the opportunity to change it when reason and equity so demand. The common law requires that each time a rule of law is applied, it must be carefully scrutinized to make sure that the conditions and needs of the times have not so changed as to make further application of the rule an instrument of injustice. Although the legislature may speak to the subject, in the common law system the primary instruments of legal evolution are the courts.[13]

---

10. W. LaFave & A. Scott, Jr., Criminal Law § 8.13, at 792-793 (2d ed. 1986).
11. Id. § 7.1, at 605.
12. Id. at 605-606.
13. Mosk, supra note 8, at 36.

A change in conditions is not the only possible inspiration for abandonment of existing common law. A court will occasionally conclude that a previous decision was flawed from its inception. Hindsight may show that the previous court premised its decision on erroneous factual assumptions about conditions existing at that time. Alternatively, the current court, which itself may have changed in political or intellectual composition, may simply reject the reasoning of the previous decision.[14] This process of evolution, however, is restricted by the doctrine of stare decisis, explored in Chapter 2.

EXERCISE 1-1

1. *Wrongful Conception, Wrongful Life*

In general, the common law of torts imposes civil liability upon a physician who breaches a duty of care to a patient. By applying this general common law rule to new medical procedures, courts and juries necessarily refine the content of the rule. In the following problem, you should assume that the common law of the jurisdiction has not previously addressed the issues that are raised by the facts. You must decide how you would fashion the common law that applies to the issues if you were a judge preparing to instruct a jury on the applicable legal rules. Specifically, you must decide to what extent you think the common law should impose liability on a physician for negligently permitting a child to be conceived.

Problem

When Sandra Gonzalez and her husband, Miguel, had their third child, they agreed that they desired no further children and that Sandra should undergo sterilization. They consulted Dr. Leonard, who performed surgery designed to tie off Sandra's fallopian tubes and thus to prevent her ova from entering her uterus. Although Dr. Leonard pronounced the operation a success, he in fact performed the operation carelessly, leaving Sandra capable of conceiving further children. Sandra became pregnant within two months after the failed sterilization procedure.

a. In the process of developing the state's common law of torts, should a state court permit Sandra and Miguel to sue Dr. Leonard on a negligence theory of "wrongful conception"? If so, should the damages include only the medical expenses and other costs associated with the childbirth, or should they more broadly include the costs of raising the fourth child?

b. Suppose that the fourth child was born with severe mental retardation, but that the failed sterilization procedure did not contribute to the retardation. Should these facts affect the court's evaluation of the parent's claim based on wrongful conception? Should the court recognize a cause of action on the behalf of the fourth child for "wrongful life," permitting the child herself to collect damages on the theory that she would have been better off had she not been conceived?

---

14. See generally Stone, Precedent, the Amendment Process, and Evolution in Constitutional Doctrine, 11 Harv. J.L. & Pub. Pol. 67, 71 (1988).

c. Should the analysis of any of these questions be affected by the fact that Sandra could have legally aborted her fetus soon after discovering her pregnancy?

2. *Punitive Damages for Breach of a Marriage Agreement*

A contract may be partially defined as a legally enforceable private agreement in which parties have exchanged promises to engage in some performance in the future. The law of contracts governs the formation, interpretation, and enforcement of contracts. A party to a contract who fails to perform its contractual promise is said to have "breached" the contract. The victim of such a breach may bring an action in court to enforce the contract. In most cases, a court will remedy a breach with an award of money damages. Specifically, it will order the breaching party to pay to the victim of the breach "compensatory damages" in the amount of the value of the expected performance.

As a general principle of the common law of contracts, an award of damages for breach of contract is limited to such compensatory damages. Absent proof of an independent civil wrong known as a "tort," most courts will not grant additional "punitive damages" designed to punish the breaching party and to discourage other parties from breaching contracts.

An early exception to this general rule is the traditional willingness to award punitive damages for breach of a contract to marry. Contracts scholar Arthur L. Corbin discussed the kinds of jury instructions that might permit a jury in such cases to award damages that have punitive elements:

> Thus, where, under promise of marriage, *A* is seduced by *B* and then cast off in disgrace, it is proper to tell the jury that they may consider these facts and may increase the damages even though there is no evidence of pecuniary loss. Again, where *A* is jilted by *B,* who marries another without first notifying *A* that the engagement is broken and denies that there has been an engagement, *A*'s hurt feelings, wounded pride, the length of the engagement, the loss of opportunity to marry others, *B*'s wealth and social standing may all be considered by the jury in awarding damages.[15]

Assume that an 1898 decision of a state's highest court permits an award of punitive damages for breach of any marriage agreement, regardless of whether it is accompanied by an independent tort or elements of a tort. Does such a "marriage contract" exception find support in contemporary public policy and social mores?

Those who doubt the continued vitality of actions for breach of marriage agreements should consult the complaint in Assignment 1 of Chapter 6 of the assignment book. Drafted in 1984, it alleges breach of a promise to marry. In reviewing proposed instructions to a jury on the proper measure of damages in such an action, should a court today abandon this traditional exception to the rule against awarding punitive damages? Conversely, can you think of other kinds of contracts of more recent origin that are so exceptional in nature that they should inspire a new exception to the general rule against punitive damages for breach of contract?

---

15. 5 A. Corbin, Corbin on Contracts § 1077, at 440-441 (1964).

3. *Economic Analysis*

Read the following problem and use it to construct an economic rationale for a general rule disallowing punitive damages for even intentional breaches of commercial contracts. If a policy supports application of a general rule in most cases, should courts apply the rule without exception to promote certainty in the law, or should they recognize exceptions to the general rule to reach a fair result in exceptional cases? Consider the ethical problems, if any, of advising a client to intentionally breach a clearly binding contract.

Problem

Uptown, Inc., is a chain of department stores with a store in Bonneville that employs 100 Bonneville residents. As the population of Bonneville grew over the years, business increased at the local Uptown store, putting pressure on the store's ground-level parking lot during peak hours. In January, the Board of Directors of Uptown committed funds to construct a three-level underground parking facility at the Bonneville store. On January 25, Uptown contracted with the largest excavator in Bonneville, Pierce Excavation Co., to excavate the site for the new parking facility. In the written contract, Pierce Excavation Co. promised to begin excavation on July 1 and to complete the work by August 15, and Uptown promised to pay Pierce Excavation Co. $30,000. John Pierce, owner of Pierce Excavation Co., estimated that he would earn about $4,500 profit from the project and that it would use about half the capacity of his firm; he did not have any other offers for work beyond the last week of May.

On June 10, the City Council of Bonneville unexpectedly broke a year-long deadlock and approved the plans of a developer, Lynn Mullins, to construct a lavish convention center near the Bonneville airport. The convention center will employ 800 Bonneville residents and contribute millions of dollars annually to the Bonneville economy. Pierce Construction Co. is the only excavator in Bonneville with sufficient equipment to efficiently excavate the convention center site. Anxious to begin construction of the long-delayed project, Mullins offered to pay Pierce Construction Co. $115,000 to perform excavation and other earth moving at the convention center site if Pierce agreed to begin work immediately and complete work sometime in August. Pierce estimated that he would earn $40,000 profit from the project and that it would use the full capacity of his firm for approximately eight weeks beginning in mid-June.

On June 11, John Pierce met with officers of Uptown and discussed the possibility of modifying their contract to delay excavation until mid-August. The Uptown officers refused to modify the contract; a six-week delay in excavation would extend the construction period into the holiday shopping season, disrupting even the existing ground-level parking. Another Bonneville excavator was available to perform the Uptown work in July, either as an independent contractor or as a subcontractor to Pierce Construction Co. However, in light of market conditions caused by the approval of the convention center plans, the substitute excavator insisted on a price of $35,000 for the Uptown project. Moreover, even if the substitute excavator acted nominally as Pierce's subcontractor, Pierce would not have the capacity during the month of July to supervise the Uptown project. Uptown had hired Pierce Construction Co. partly for its reputation for high quality work, and it was reluctant to replace it with a substitute. Uptown represented that it would suffer $10,000 to $15,000 in damages if it were forced to hire a substitute excavator or delay excavation until mid August.

On March 5, John Pierce met with his attorney, Patricia Ruiz, to discuss his options. Ruiz advised Pierce to repudiate the Uptown contract, accept Mullins's offer, and pay the consequences of his breach of the Uptown contract. Ruiz knew that Pierce would not be liable for punitive damages, and she was confident that she could negotiate a $5,000 to $10,000 settlement of Uptown's claim. Do you approve of Ruiz's advice?

III. STATUTORY ANALYSIS

A. ROLE OF CONSTITUTIONAL AND STATUTORY LAW

"The Constitution states the framework for all our law. Legislation is one great tool of legal change and readaptation."[16] As expressed by a state supreme court, constitutional and statutory law reflect collective expressions of public policy, or social values:

> As the expressions of our founders and those we have elected to our legislature, our state's constitution and statutes embody the public conscience of the people of this state.[17]

Consistent with its role as the paramount policymaking body, a legislature often enacts statutes to address problems that it concludes are not adequately addressed by the common law. For example, the early common law crime of theft was defined as a trespassory taking and carrying away of personal property of another with intent to steal.[18] The requirement of a trespassory taking excluded the conduct of one who took possession of another's property lawfully, but who subsequently converted the property to his own use with the intent to permanently deprive the owner of it. Because the common law did not impose criminal liability for such a misappropriation, the English Parliament and American legislatures created the statutory crime of embezzlement, generally defined as the fraudulent conversion of another's property by one who is already in lawful possession of it.[19] Had the legislatures not acted, the courts might have eventually achieved the same result through further development

---

16. K. Llewellyn, The Bramble Bush 18 (1978).
17. Wagenseller v. Scottsdale Mem. Hosp., 147 Ariz. 370, 378, 710 P.2d 1025, 1033 (1985).
18. W. LaFave & A. Scott, Jr., Criminal Law § 8.2, at 706 (2d ed. 1986).
19. Id. at § 8.6.

of the common law, but legislative action sometimes provides a quicker and more certain means of "social readjustment."[20]

A more contemporary example deals with the process of reaching a legally binding agreement through the process of offer and acceptance. Under the common law of contracts, a department store's newspaper advertisement typically amounts to an invitation to negotiate rather than an offer to enter into a binding contract; in most cases, a customer makes the first offer by entering the store and requesting to purchase the advertised good. Under common law, the store owner is free to reject the customer's offer without incurring any contractual liability.[21] Unfortunately, this allocation of legal rights and obligations has encouraged some sellers to use "bait and switch" tactics: they lure customers into their stores with the "bait" of goods advertised at spectacularly reduced prices; then they "switch" goods by resisting the customer's desire to purchase the advertised goods and by persuading the customer to purchase a more expensive item. In response, state legislatures have promoted public policy favoring consumer protection by enacting legislation that restricts or prohibits such bait-and-switch tactics.[22] These state laws have altered rights and obligations as defined under the common law of contracts.

Early English and American legislatures tended not to replace common law wholesale with a comprehensive system of statutes. Instead, they typically enacted statutes to correct specific defects or fill gaps in a well-developed body of common law. Thus, until this century, statutory law assumed a role of secondary importance in American law, inspiring one scholar to characterize them as "warts on the body of the common law."[23] However, state and federal legislation has so proliferated in this century that "most American jurisdictions now are Code states."[24] This new prominence of statutory law in the American legal system warrants an examination of methods of statutory analysis.

B. JUDICIAL INTERPRETATION AND APPLICATION OF STATUTES

A statute imposes liability on certain employers for discrimination against any individual in the "terms" or "conditions" of employment "because of such individual's . . . sex." Would the statute impose liability on an employer who fired your clients, male and female homosexuals, because of their sexual orientation? Would it impose liability on an employer who made sexual advances toward only female employees, thus adversely affecting their working environment, but who did not condition tangible job benefits on acquiescence to his demands? The answers to these questions depend on the intended meaning of

---

20. K. Llewellyn, supra note 16, at 18.
21. 1 A. Corbin, Corbin on Contracts § 25 (1963); J. Calamari & J. Perillo, Contracts § 2-8 (1977).
22. See, e.g., Uniform Consumer Sales Practices Act § 3(b)(6); Cal. Bus. & Prof. Code § 12024.6 (West Supp. 1987); Note, State Control of Bait Advertising, 69 Yale L.J. 830 (1960).
23. K. Llewellyn, The Bramble Bush 79 (1978); see also Pound, Common Law and Legislation, 21 Harv. L. Rev. 383 (1908).
24. Mosk, The Common Law and the Judicial Decision-Making Process, 11 Harv. J.L. & Pub. Pol. 35 (1988).

the statutory language "because of . . . sex" and "terms" or "conditions" of employment.

The questions arise because statutory language sometimes is vague or ambiguous. An ambiguous term has multiple meanings, although each of the meanings may be precise and all of the meanings may be easily identified. A vague term is uncertain in its meaning and indefinite in its scope, making it difficult to identify the meaning or meanings that it encompasses.[25]

As discussed more fully below, statutory language sometimes is necessarily vague because of deliberate generality or is avoidably ambiguous because of unintended imprecision. Consequently, the way in which statutory language applies to the facts of a particular dispute may be subject to reasonable dispute. Courts give greater specificity and precision to the statutory language by interpreting and applying the statute in the context of the dispute. A court does not engage in a wholly creative process when it interprets a vague or ambiguous statute. Rather, it seeks to determine and to give effect to the intent of the enacting legislature by analyzing the statutory language, the stated or apparent purpose of the statute, and the legislative activities related to enactment of the bill.[26]

This search for the intended meaning of a statute is governed by a separate layer of judicially developed rules of interpretation and construction. Although the terms "interpretation" and "construction" are often used interchangeably, this book will recognize the following distinction: "interpretation" refers to the process of determining legislative intent, and "construction" refers to the process of reconciling statutory language with public policy in the absence of conclusive evidence of legislative intent.

Evidence of legislative intent may be intrinsic to the statute, extrinsic to it, or both. Intrinsic evidence of legislative intent is the statutory text itself. This includes the statutory language in question and other portions of the statute that state or imply the statutory purpose or otherwise provide a context within which to interpret the language in question. Some statutes include a section of defined terms, which may provide partial guidance even when it does not conclusively resolve a dispute over the proper interpretation of the language in question.

The primary source of extrinsic evidence of legislative intent is legislative history, such as the text of legislative debates, preliminary drafts of the legislation, and hearings or reports of legislative committees. Under the "plain meaning" rule of interpretation, if the statutory language in question has a plain meaning on its face, a court may be reluctant to consider legislative history supporting a less obvious interpretation.[27] However, it is not precluded from doing so,[28] as when a federal court of appeals engaged in an exhaustive analysis of legislative history and statutory policy to interpret the statutory term "or" to mean the conjunction "and," rather than the disjunctive "either/or."[29]

---

25. See generally W. Quine, Word and Object 85, 129 (1960).

26. E.g., Jackson Transit Auth. v. Local Div. 1285, Amalgamated Transit Union, 457 U.S. 15, 22-29 (1982); Mohasco v. Silver, 447 U.S. 807, 815 (1980).

27. See, e.g., Maine v. Thiboutot, 448 U.S. 1, 4 (1980) (suggesting that analysis of legislative history is unnecessary or inappropriate if language is unambiguous).

28. See id. at 13-14 (Powell, J., dissenting).

29. Unification Church v. Immigration & Naturalization Serv., 762 F.2d 1077, 1083-1090

Unfortunately, misuse of legislative history may mislead more than enlighten. The search for legislative intent is an attempt to reconstruct the collective intent of numerous legislators whose views on the wisdom or scope of the statute may conflict. Opposing advocates often can draw on different portions of legislative history to support conflicting views on the proper interpretation of a statute: they simply invoke isolated statements of legislators taken out of the context of the complete debate on a bill. Indeed, a court may then justify the result that it wants to reach by selectively drawing on portions of legislative history that support that result. These and other pitfalls have led one Supreme Court Justice to decry the "level of unreality that our unrestrained use of legislative history has attained."[30]

If a court cannot obtain clear evidence of legislative intent through intrinsic or extrinsic evidence, it may use other means to resolve vagueness or ambiguity in statutory language. For example, if an administrative agency has developed expertise in administering the statute, the court may simply defer to that agency's interpretation of the statutory language.[31] Otherwise, the court may resort to a judicial rule of construction, such as the general rule that ambiguities in criminal statutes "should be resolved in favor of lenity."[32] Such a rule may reflect general policies with which the legislature is likely to agree, but it does not necessarily reflect the legislative purpose of the particular statute in question.[33] Accordingly, a court will resort to a general rule of construction only if a "statute's language, structure, purpose, and legislative history leave its meaning genuinely in doubt."[34]

In the following subsections, analyses of two kinds of uncertainty in statutory language provide vehicles for examining techniques that the courts use to clarify the scope and effect of statutes. First, an analysis of ambiguous statutory language illustrates general rules of statutory interpretation and construction. Second, an analysis of vague statutory language illustrates the manner in which courts gradually give concrete meaning to abstract statutory language by applying general terms to particular disputes.

1. Imprecision Leading to Ambiguity

Ambiguity may result from avoidable imprecision in the words or phrases selected by the drafter. The question raised at the beginning of section B above addresses the proper interpretation of a federal statute popularly known as Title VII of the Civil Rights Act of 1964. Section 703(a) of the Act prohibits certain kinds of employment discrimination:

(D.C. Cir. 1985); see also The Mountain States Tel. & Tel. Co. v. Arizona Corp. Comm'n, 160 Ariz. 350, 360, 773 P.2d 455, 465 (1989) (supp. opinion) (courts have consulted legislative history to determine whether "shall" means "must" or "may" in various statutes).

30. Blanchard v. Bergeron, 109 S. Ct. 939, 947 (1989) (Scalia, J., concurring).

31. See, e.g., Young v. Community Nutrition Inst., 476 U.S. 974, 979-984 (1986).

32. Bell v. United States, 349 U.S. 81, 83 (1955); see W. LaFave & A. Scott, Jr., Criminal Law § 2.2, at 77-80 (2d ed. 1986).

33. See, e.g., Bell, supra, at 83-84.

34. United States v. Otherson, 637 F.2d 1276, 1285 (9th Cir. 1981).

> It shall be an unlawful employment practice for an employer . . . to discriminate against any individual with respect to his compensation, terms, conditions, or privileges of employment, because of such individual's race, color, religion, sex, or national origin. . . .[35]

It is unclear from the quoted language whether section 703(a) prohibits an employer from discriminating against male and female homosexual employees because of their sexual orientation. Title VII's reference to "sex" as a protected classification might prohibit such an employment policy, but only if Congress used the term "sex" to refer broadly to any characteristic related to sexual activity, including an individual's sexual preference or orientation, rather than only to the characteristic of being male or female.

Judicial interpretation of a statute should start with the most direct intrinsic evidence of legislative intent: the statutory language in question.[36] An analysis of the language of Title VII § 703(a), however, provides only limited guidance. Dictionaries commonly define "sex" as, among other things, either (1) the division of species between male and female or (2) more general sexual behavior and characteristics:

> 1: either of two divisions of organisms distinguished respectively as male or female   2: the sum of the structural, functional, and behavioral peculiarities of living beings that subserve reproduction by two interacting parents and distinguish males and females   3a: sexually motivated phenomena or behavior b: SEXUAL INTERCOURSE.[37]

Other provisions of Title VII may provide intrinsic evidence of the intended meaning of "sex" in section 703(a). In subsection h of section 703, Congress probably used the term in the narrow sense of the division of species between male and female.[38] There it used "sex" in a reference to the Equal Pay Act of 1963, which more clearly prohibits only certain kinds of discrimination based on the status of an employee as male or female.[39] If Congress consciously used "sex" in that sense in section 703(h), the obvious virtues of consistency in statutory drafting suggest the likelihood, though not certainty, that Congress ascribed the same meaning to "sex" when it used that term in section 703(a) of the same act.

---

35. 42 U.S.C. § 2000e-2(a) (1982).

36. See, e.g., Tribe, Judicial Interpretation of Statutes: Three Axioms, 11 Harv. J.L. & Pub. Pol'y 51 (1988) ("Axiom one is: *Language first.*"); Unification Church v. INS, 762 F.2d 1077, 1083 (D.C. Cir. 1985).

37. Webster's Seventh New Collegiate Dictionary 347 (1970) (as quoted in Holloway v. Arthur Andersen & Co., 566 F.2d 659, 662 n.4 (9th Cir. 1977)).

38. Section 703(h) incorporates limitation set forth in the Equal Pay Act:

> . . . It shall not be . . . unlawful . . . to differentiate upon the basis of *sex* . . . if such differentiation is authorized by the provisions of [the Equal Pay Act].

42 U.S.C. § 2000e-2(h) (1982) (emphasis added).

39. The Equal Pay Act refers to members of the "opposite sex":

> No employer . . . shall discriminate . . . between employees on the basis of *sex* by paying wages to employees . . . at a rate less than the rate at which he pays wages to employees of the *opposite sex* . . . for equal work. . . .

29 U.S.C. § 206(d) (1982) (emphasis added). The phrase "opposite sex" is commonly used to refer only to distinctions between males and females. Therefore the Equal Pay Act is nearly unambiguous in its classifying only on the basis of employees being male or female.

Thus, intrinsic evidence of Congress's intended meaning in §703(a) of the word "sex" is helpful but inconclusive. Therefore, a court interpreting "sex" would likely seek guidance from extrinsic evidence, such as legislative history. The original House bill did not include sex as a prohibited basis of discrimination. Instead, Southern Democrat and Chair of the House Rules Committee Howard Smith proposed the addition of "sex" as a protected classification in a last-minute amendment on the House floor. He apparently hoped that the amendment would spark sufficient controversy to cause the defeat of the entire bill.[40]

Smith's unsuccessful strategy left the courts with "little legislative history to guide us in interpreting the Act's prohibition against discrimination based on 'sex'."[41] However, the few statements made on the House floor about the proposed amendment, both by Smith and by Representatives who more sincerely favored equality of the sexes, suggest that the speakers interpreted "sex" to refer narrowly to the characteristic of being male or female.[42] That interpretation is supported by post-enactment evidence of congressional intent. First, the House report on the 1972 Amendments to Title VII clearly reflects that Congress was primarily concerned with putting women on equal economic footing with men. Second, successive congressional rejections of several bills proposing to amend Title VII by adding "sexual preference" as a protected classification suggest that members of Congress probably had never collectively intended the statutory term "sex" to encompass sexual preference.[43]

Relying on this legislative history, courts have interpreted the word "sex" in section 703(a) to refer only to male or female status and not also to characteristics that relate more generally to sexual activities or preferences.[44] Interpreted in that way, Title VII does not prohibit an employer from discriminating against employees because of their homosexuality, provided that the employer treats male and female homosexuals equally.[45]

Had the evidence of specific congressional intent been less convincing, the interpreting court might have applied the general rule of construction that "remedial" statutes should be liberally construed. Title VII is remedial in its purpose of redressing the pervasive social and economic problem of employment discrimination.[46] Therefore, the rule of construction would favor a liberal construction of the term "sex," which might encompass characteristics relating to sexual preference or activity. However, this general rule of construction is subordinate to evidence of more specific congressional intent relating to the statute in question.[47]

Congress might have avoided the ambiguity in section 703(a) by selecting a more precise term, such as "gender," which more clearly refers only to clas-

---

40. C. Whalen & B. Whalen, The Longest Debate 84, 115-116 (1985).
41. Meritor Sav. Bank, FSB v. Vinson, 447 U.S. 57, 64 (1986).
42. Whalen, supra note 40, at 116-117.
43. Holloway v. Arthur Andersen & Co., 566 F.2d 659, 662 (9th Cir. 1977).
44. E.g., id. at 662-663.
45. E.g., DeSantis v. Pacific Tel. & Tel. Co., 608 F.2d 327 (9th Cir. 1979). But cf. Gay Law Students v. Pacific Tel. & Tel. Co., 24 Cal. 3d 458, 156 Cal. Rptr. 14, 595 P.2d 592 (1979) (different result under California constitutional and statutory law).
46. E.g., Bell v. Brown, 557 F.2d 849, 853 (D.C. Cir. 1977).
47. See Mohasco v. Silver, 447 U.S. 807, 818-819 (1980) (Title VII is remedial legislation, but also is the product of legislative compromise).

sifications based on one's status as male or female. Although "gender" refers to classifications in grammar as well as in animal species, that ambiguity would not likely cause confusion in the context of section 703(a).

2. Generality Resulting in Vagueness

Even if the legislature chooses its words carefully, most statutory language is necessarily general, because almost all legislation addresses broad categories of activities or disputes rather than particular cases. Legislators simply do not possess the stamina and prescience required to consider every potential dispute within the scope of legislation and to provide a specific resolution for each. Instead, courts provide greater specificity in statutory language by applying the general terms of the statute to the facts of particular disputes, thus adding precision to statutory law in much the same way that they develop common law: gradually and in the context of successive disputes.

For example, section 703(a) of Title VII of the Civil Rights Act of 1964 prohibits discrimination only with respect to an individual's "compensation, terms, conditions, or privileges of employment."[48] That statutory phrase is necessarily general, because Congress could not practicably describe in more specific terms all of the possible kinds of discrimination that have a sufficient relationship to employment to trigger congressional concern about equal opportunity in the workplace. That generality results in a vagueness that promotes disputes over the interpretation and application of the statute in particular cases.

For instance, parties may reasonably dispute whether sexual advances made by an employer's agent to an employee affect the employee's "terms, conditions, or privileges of employment" if the agent does not make tangible benefits of employment contingent on acquiescence to the demands.[49] Courts have given more specific meaning to the statutory phrase by adopting a more specific legal standard for determining the circumstances in which the statute is satisfied: to give effect to Title VII's remedial purpose, they have decided that sexual advances by an employer's agent may affect "terms, conditions, or privileges of employment" if they create "a substantially discriminatory work *environment,* regardless of whether the complaining employees lost any tangible job benefits as a result of the discrimination."[50]

Although the "discriminatory work environment" standard adds a judicial gloss to the statutory language by identifying a specific subset of employment relations within the scope of the statute, the judicial standard is itself abstract and suffers from its own problems of vagueness. The precise parameters of the judicial standard, and thus of the statutory language that it seeks to effectuate,

---

48. 42 U.S.C. § 2000e-2(a) (1982).

49. Such conduct constitutes sex discrimination if the harasser would not have engaged in the conduct but for the employee's gender; that requirement normally is satisfied in the case of a heterosexual or homosexual harasser, but not necessarily in the case of a bisexual supervisor. See Barnes v. Costle, 561 F.2d 983, 990 n.55 (D.C. Cir. 1977). That analysis, however, does not answer the question whether the discrimination satisfies Title VII's requirement of a nexus to employment.

50. Bundy v. Jackson, 641 F.2d 934, 943-944 (D.C. Cir. 1981); *accord* Meritor Sav. Bank v. Vinson, 106 S. Ct. 2399 (1986).

will take form only when courts repeatedly apply the standard to the facts of different disputes.

In one case, for example, a federal appellate court held that male supervisors' repeated sexual propositions and inquiries directed to a female employee created a discriminatory work environment in violation of Title VII.[51] In another case, a federal trial court held that an isolated lewd comment combined with invitations to meet at a restaurant and other "flirtations" did not create an illegally discriminatory work environment.[52] If you examine those and other decisions addressing the same issue in different factual contexts, you can gain a better understanding of the intended reach of the statute than is provided by the general statutory language, "terms, conditions, or privileges of employment," or even the more specific judicial interpretation, "discriminatory work environment."

═══════ E X E R C I S E 1 - 2 ═══════

1. Statutory Policy and Classification

The Highway Patrol of State X informed legislators of State X that motorists were causing accidents by consuming soft drinks while driving. The Highway Patrol was not overly concerned that drivers could keep only one hand on the wheel while consuming soft drinks. Instead, they were concerned that drivers often obstructed their vision, and thus lost partial control of their automobiles, when they tilted their heads back and tipped their soft drink containers upward to consume the last of their soft drinks. In response, state legislators enacted a new section to the State X Vehicle Code that makes it a misdemeanor "to operate a motor vehicle while consuming any beverage from a can or bottle." Should the new law apply to:

a. a driver who tilts her head back to drink water from a metal, canvass-covered canteen?

b. a driver who keeps his head level while he sips a soft drink through a straw from a bottle?

c. a driver who eats a submarine sandwich in a way that distracts her and obstructs her vision?

2. Legislative History

The current codification of a Reconstruction era civil rights act prohibits certain kinds of discrimination:

> *All persons* within the jurisdiction of the United States shall have the same right in every State and Territory to make and enforce contracts . . . *as is enjoyed by white citizens.* . . .

---

51. Bundy v. Jackson, 641 F.2d 934 (D.C. Cir. 1981); see also Hall v. Gus Constr. Co., 842 F.2d 1010 (1988) (employer had notice of persistent verbal and physical abuse of female road construction workers by their male coworkers).

52. Scott v. Sears, Roebuck & Co., 605 F. Supp. 1047, 1055-1056 (D. Ill. 1985), aff'd, 798 F.2d 210 (7th Cir. 1986). As an alternative ground for its judgment, the court also held that the employer's supervisors did not have notice of the allegedly harassing conduct and that the employer therefore could not be liable for the conduct. Id. at 1054-1055.

42 U.S.C. § 1981 (emphasis added). The original predecessor to this statute contained similar language:

> [C]itizens of the United States . . . , of every race and color, without regard to any previous condition of slavery or involuntary servitude, . . . shall have the same right, in every State and Territory in the United States, to make and enforce contracts . . . *as is enjoyed by white citizens.* . . .

Civil Rights Act of 1866 § 1, 14 Stat. 27 (1866) (emphasis added); see also Civil Rights Act of 1870 §§ 16, 18, 16 Stat. 144 (1870). The "immediate impetus" for the original statute was "the necessity for further relief of the constitutionally emancipated former Negro slaves."[53] However, to allay fears among some legislators that the proposed bill would favor nonwhites, proponents of the bill defended it at several stages of the legislative process as one that would protect *all* citizens.[54] More than a century after the initial enactment, the United States Supreme Court applied the modern version of this statute to prohibit private, commercially operated, nonsectarian schools from discriminating against African-Americans in admission to the schools.[55]

a. Should a court apply the statute to protect nonwhites other than African-Americans from race discrimination in contractual relations?

b. Should a court apply the statute to protect white citizens from race discrimination? See *McDonald v. Santa Fe Trail Transportation Co.,* 427 U.S. 273 (1976).

c. If the statute applies to protect racial groups other than African-Americans, how does one define race for purposes of finding prohibited discrimination? Would the statute apply to prohibit discrimination against a person because he is Arab rather than Anglo-American? See *Saint Francis College v. Al-Khazraji,* 481 U.S. 604 (1987) (looking to racial classifications recognized at time of enactment of predecessors to section 1981). Would it apply to discrimination because one is Jewish? See *Shaare Tefila Congregation v. Cobb,* 481 U.S. 615 (1987) (same analysis under companion statute, 42 U.S.C. § 1982).

C. LEGISLATIVE CHANGE

As a serious student of the law, you should not be content with an interpretive analysis of statutory law but should reflect on the political wisdom of the legislative purpose. A legislature that has the power to enact legislation also has the power to repeal or amend it, and a constant critique of statutory law helps to fuel the dynamic process of the growth and development of legislation.

For example, the discussion in the previous section shows that Congress intended Title VII's prohibition of "sex" discrimination to apply to discrimination on the basis of gender but not on the basis of sexual preference. The first exercise below asks you to consider whether the policies underlying Title

---

53. McDonald v. Santa Fe Trail Transp. Co., 427 U.S. 273, 289 (1976).
54. Id. at 289-295.
55. Runyon v. McCrary, 427 U.S. 160 (1976), *reaff'd in part,* Patterson v. Mclean Credit Union, 109 S. Ct. 2363 (1989).

VII's current prohibitions apply as well to discrimination because of sexual orientation or preference, and whether Congress should amend Title VII to prohibit such discrimination.

You may question some statutes not for the policies they reflect but for the manner in which they express them. You are nearly certain to do this when you struggle with alternative interpretations of Uniform Commercial Code § 2-207 in your contracts class. The first of three subsections of § 2-207 provides that a response to an offer may be an acceptance even though it varies the terms of the offer:

> (1) A definite and seasonable expression of acceptance or a written confirmation which is sent within a reasonable time operates as an acceptance even though it states terms additional to or different from those offered or agreed upon, unless acceptance is expressly made conditional on assent to the additional or different terms.

The second subsection provides that, between merchants, some of the new terms in the acceptance may be added to the contract without the express assent of the original offeror:

> (2) The additional terms are to be construed as proposals for addition to the contract. Between merchants such terms become part of the contract unless:
> (a) the offer expressly limits acceptance to the terms of the offer;
> (b) they materially alter it; or
> (c) notification of objection to them has already been given or is given within a reasonable time after notice of them is received.

After studying section 2-207 in your contracts class, you may be ready to agree with one commentator that

> the section is a mess. It is confusing, susceptible to different and inconsistent interpretations, and nigh well impossible to apply to solve a specific fact situation.[56]

The third exercise below asks you to consider how you would redraft this statute to eliminate its ambiguities.

════════ E X E R C I S E   1 - 3 ════════

1. *Invidious Discrimination*

Consider the bases of discrimination covered by Title VII of the Civil Rights Act of 1964: race, color, religion, sex, and national origin. Other federal statutes prohibit discrimination based on age or handicap. What characteristics do these classifications have in common? Why are these classes entitled to special protection? Does the class of homosexuals deserve similar protection against

---

56. Shanker, Contract by Disagreement!? (Reflections on UCC 2-207), 81 Comm. L.J. 453 (1976).

employment discrimination? Should Congress amend Title VII to include sexual orientation or preference as a protected characteristic? Do you support legislation banning discrimination on the basis of positive testing for the AIDS virus?

2. *Mandatory Safety Rules*

Do you support state legislation requiring a person to wear a protective helmet while driving or riding as a passenger on a motorcycle on a public street or highway? What policies arguments support or oppose such legislation?

3. *Drafting for Clarity*

After you study U.C.C. § 2-207 in your contracts class, attempt to redraft all or part of that statute to achieve the primary statutory purposes while reducing problems of interpretation.

4. *Surrogate Motherhood*

a. Legislative Authorization or Prohibition

Many states have recently enacted legislation specifically addressing "surrogate mother contracts." Pursuant to such contracts, a woman charges a fee to carry to full term a fetus that either is the product of artificial insemination of the woman's own ovum or is the implanted, fertilized ovum of another woman. Technically, the woman bearing the child is a "surrogate mother" only if she is carrying the fertilized ovum of another woman. If she is carrying her own artificially inseminated ovum, she is the biological mother. However, the term "surrogate mother" is frequently used to refer to both roles. In either case, on birth of the child, the "surrogate mother" is obligated under the contract to relinquish custody of the child to the biological parent or parents who contracted with her.

(1) What public policies are implicated in a legislative decision to approve, prohibit, or otherwise regulate such contracts?

(2) If called on to draft legislation on the subject, how would you balance the conflicting policies?

b. Specific Enforcement and Punitive Damages

In enforcing ordinary commercial contracts, a court may in limited circumstances remedy a breach of promise by "specifically enforcing" the promise, or ordering the breaching party to perform precisely as promised. In most cases, however, specific enforcement is impracticable or otherwise inappropriate, and the court will award "substitutional relief" by ordering the breaching party to pay money damages.

(1) As a legislator, would you vote for a statute that would authorize or mandate specific enforcement of a surrogate mother contract, thus compelling the surrogate mother to relinquish custody of her newborn child, as promised in the contract?

(2) After reviewing Exercise 1-1(2), page 10, would you vote for a statute that would authorize a court to award punitive damages against a surrogate mother who failed to relinquish custody?

IV. INTERPLAY BETWEEN STATUTORY AND COMMON LAW ANALYSIS

A. RELATIONSHIP BETWEEN STATUTORY LAW AND COMMON LAW

Although the legislature and the judiciary each exercise lawmaking powers, the legislature is the paramount lawmaking authority, and legislative enactments supersede inconsistent common law. The Supreme Court's following statement about the federal system applies as well to the state governments:

> [W]e consistently have emphasized that the federal lawmaking power is vested in the legislative, not the judicial, branch of government; therefore, federal common law is "subject to the paramount authority of Congress."[57]

Accordingly, the legislature may enact statutes that modify, overrule, or codify existing common law. For example, under the common law of contracts, parties may form a contract through a process of agreement that culminates in an offer and an acceptance. A recipient who is dissatisfied with an offer may decline to accept it and may instead convey a counteroffer to the other party. Indeed, under the traditional common law "mirror-image rule," a party who significantly varies the terms of an offer in a purported acceptance conveys a counteroffer rather than an effective acceptance.[58] However, all states have enacted some version of Article 2 of the Uniform Commercial Code, which rejects and supersedes this common law rule for transactions in goods. As set forth in the immediately preceding Section III(C), section 2-207 of the Code recognizes, in some circumstances, an acceptance that includes a nontrivial variance of the terms of the offer.

Even if no statute currently applies to a dispute, a court may decline to extend common law principles to the area if it concludes that the matter is better left to legislative action.[59] Moreover, if the court decides to develop and apply the common law, it nonetheless may look to statutory law for expressions of public policy that help the court formulate the common law rule. In one case, for example, a court addressed the question whether, under the common law of torts, retailers should assume liability for injuries stemming from their sales of guns without regard to the care that they exercised in the sales. The

---

57. Northwest Airlines, Inc. v. Transport Workers, 451 U.S. 77, 95 (1981) (quoting New Jersey v. New York, 283 U.S. 336, 348 (1931)).

58. E.g., 1 A. Corbin, Corbin on Contracts § 82 (1963).

59. E.g., City & County of San Francisco v. United Ass'n of Journeymen & Apprentices of the Plumbing & Pipefitting Indus., Local 38, 42 Cal. 3d 810, 230 Cal. Rptr. 856, 726 P.2d 538 (Cal. 1986).

court looked to the policy of federal and state gun control legislation to apply this doctrine of "strict liability" to the sale of some, but not all, kinds of guns.[60] Another court drew guidance from an enacted, but not yet effective, commercial code to develop a common law doctrine of unconscionability in sales contracts.[61]

Although statutory law supersedes common law, the common law at the time of a statute's enactment may provide contextual background that is helpful in analyzing legislative intent.[62] If a statute overrules a common law rule or seeks to address a problem left untouched by the common law, a court can better understand the statute's intended scope if it appreciates the deficiencies of the common law to which the legislature responded.[63] Conversely, if a statute codifies existing common law, cases that developed the common law rule obviously will provide guidance in interpreting the enactment.

For example, under the common law of contracts an offeror is the "master of his offer" and, with some limitations, is free to prescribe the manner in which the offeree can accept his offer.[64] Even in the absence of an express limitation by the offeror on the means of accepting his offer, some courts adopted relatively technical rules of common law that required the offeree to communicate acceptance in the same mode in which the offeror had communicated the offer, such as by telegram.[65] The Uniform Commercial Code has embraced the first common law principle and rejected the second:

> Unless otherwise unambiguously indicated by the language or circumstances
> (a) An offer to make a contract shall be construed as inviting acceptance in any manner and by any medium reasonable in the circumstances.[66]

Although subsection (a) substitutes a more flexible standard for some of the more technical common law rules of acceptance, the clause preceding this subsection retains the common law principle that the offeror is the master of the offer and may restrict the means of acceptance, so long as the restriction is clearly indicated. If a court is sensitive to the arbitrariness of the common law rules rejected by the Code, and if it is familiar with the common law principle embraced by the Code, it can better appreciate the intended scope of the Code.[67]

Moreover, a statute often addresses only selected issues within the general subject matter touched by the statute, thereby creating gaps that common law may fill. In some cases the statute itself provides for reference to common law, as in the Uniform Commercial Code:

---

60. Kelly v. R.G. Indus., 304 Md. 124, 497 A.2d 1143 (1985).
61. Williams v. Walker Thomas Furniture Co., 350 F.2d 445 (D.C. Cir. 1965).
62. See 2A C. Sands, Sutherland Statutory Construction, § 50.01 (4th ed. 1984); W. LaFave & A. Scott, Jr., Criminal Law § 2.2, at 79-80 (2d ed. 1986) (interpretation of criminal statutes in light of common law); City of Oklahoma City v. Tuttle, 471 U.S. 808, 835-838 (1985) (Stevens, J., dissenting).
63. See, e.g., Heydon's Case, 76 Eng. Rep. 637, 638 (1584) (quoted in C. Sands, supra, § 45-05, at 21); K. Llewellyn, The Bramble Bush 79-80 (1978).
64. See, e.g., J. Calamari & J. Perillo, Contracts § 2-10, at 69 (3d ed. 1977).
65. See, e.g., U.C.C. § 2-206 comment 1.
66. U.C.C. § 2-206(1)(a).
67. See Empire Mach. Co. v. Litton Business Tel. Sys., 115 Ariz. 568, 572, 566 P.2d 1044, 1048 (App. 1977).

> Unless displaced by the particular provisions of this Act, the principles of law and equity, including the law merchant and the law relative to capacity to contract, principal and agent, estoppel, fraud, misrepresentation, duress, coercion, mistake, . . . or other validating or invalidating cause shall supplement its provisions.[68]

In other cases, statutes only implicitly incorporate common law principles. For example, a federal statute imposes liability for certain conduct without any express qualifications or limitations. Yet, courts have assumed that Congress intended the statute to implicitly incorporate common law defenses of immunity from liability for money damages:

> It is by now well settled that the tort liability created by [42 U.S.C.] § 1983 cannot be understood in a historical vacuum. In the Civil Rights Act of 1871, Congress created a federal remedy against a person who, acting under color of state law, deprives another of constitutional rights. . . . One important assumption underlying the Court's decisions in this area is that members of the 42d Congress were familiar with common-law principles, including defenses previously recognized in ordinary tort litigation, and that they likely intended these common-law principles to obtain, absent specific provisions to the contrary.[69]

B. JUDICIAL POWER AND LIMITATIONS REGARDING LEGISLATION

Although the legislature can modify or overrule common law principles developed by the court, the courts retain an important role in the development of statutory law. Courts may review statutes for consistency with constitutional requirements and will refuse to enforce unconstitutional legislation.[70] Additionally, as discussed in section III above, courts determine the scope and effect of legislation by interpreting statutes and applying them to particular disputes.

Nonetheless, courts have less flexibility in interpreting statutory law than in developing common law. If a court changes its previous analysis of legislative intent, it may overrule its earlier interpretation of a statute, just as it sometimes overrules its previous application of a principle of common law.[71] However, the court may not ignore a statute or modify its terms to reflect judicial views that are inconsistent with legislative intent. In contrast, a court may directly reject the substance and reasoning of a common law principle that is announced and applied in a prior decision: "we have not hesitated to change the common law . . . where . . . such course was justified."[72]

Interestingly, some American Indian tribal court judges have boldly hinted that they may challenge the conventional hierarchy of laws in tribal governments. Under Anglo-American assumptions, tribal codes should have priority

---

68. U.C.C. § 1-103.
69. City of Newport v. Fact Concerts, Inc., 453 U.S. 247, 258 (1981).
70. Marbury v. Madison, 5 U.S. (1 Cranch) 137 (1803) (federal system).
71. E.g., Monell v. Department of Social Serv., 436 U.S. 658 (1978) (overruling the Court's previous decision that the term "person" in 42 U.S.C. § 1983 does not include municipalities); W. LaFave & A. Scott, Jr., Criminal Law § 2.2, at 88-90 (2d ed. 1986); see also Chapter 2 § III.
72. Kelley v. R.G. Indus., 304 Md. 124, 140, 497 A.2d 1143, 1150-1151 (1985).

over tribal common law, because the tribal council has adopted the codes, just as a federal or state legislature enacts statutes. However, even though tribal codes are formally enacted by tribal councils, many were conceived and drafted by Anglo-Americans and may reflect a poor understanding of tribal culture. In contrast, some tribal courts more consciously seek to promote tribal culture and policies when they develop and apply tribal common law.

This phenomenon may justify a departure from Anglo-American legal method in tribal courts. For example, the Navajo Supreme Court has hinted that it may simply refuse to give effect to outdated tribal code sections that fail to promote tribal values or are inconsistent with longstanding Navajo custom. In gestures acknowledging the role of the legislative branch of government, it has explicitly recommended in its opinions that the Navajo Tribal Council amend tribal codes that do not promote tribal culture and policies.[73] This kind of communication between branches of government is not foreign to the Anglo-American legal system. However, not content to wait for action from its legislative branch, the Navajo Supreme Court has considered a more radical legal method. When necessary to preserve important values of tribal culture or sovereignty, the Navajo Supreme Court appears willing to elevate Navajo common law or custom above otherwise applicable tribal codes.[74]

That such legal method is generally viewed as remarkable[75] simply illustrates the rigidity of the Anglo-American hierarchy of laws: a constitution defines the reach of statutory authority, and statutes can limit the application of common law.

V. SUMMARY

Legislatures enact statutes within the authority granted to them by state and federal constitutions. Courts create case law in the context of individual disputes by (1) interpreting and applying the provisions of constitutions and statutes and (2) developing and applying a separate body of judge-made common law. A state or federal legislature is the primary policy-making body within a jurisdiction, and it can modify or overrule common law by enacting a superseding statute.

---

73. See, e.g., In re: Validation of Marriage of Francisco, 16 Indian L. Rep. 6113, 6115 (Navajo S. Ct. 1989).

74. See id. ("This court . . . does not rely on [the tribal code], but instead on Navajo custom."); see also Transcript of Proceedings, Legal Method and Opinion-Writing Workshop for Tribal Court Judges 40-45 (Ariz. State Univ. Nov. 18, 1989).

75. But see G. Calabresi, A Common Law for the Age of Statutes 163-166 (1982) (recommending that Anglo-American courts refuse to enforce outdated statutes unless reaffirmed by the legislature).

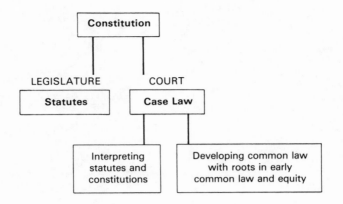

2

The Role of Precedent

I. INTRODUCTION TO STARE DECISIS

In American law, previous court decisions may influence, or even dictate, the result in a dispute currently before a court. The legal effect of the previous decisions is governed by a complex set of conventions for which the Latin phrase "stare decisis" is often used as convenient shorthand.

As defined in Black's Law Dictionary, "stare decisis" means "[t]o abide by, or adhere to, decided cases." Under the doctrine of stare decisis, a court endeavors to decide each case consistently with its own previous decisions, sometimes called "precedent." Moreover, the court is strictly bound by the precedent of a higher court that reviews the decisions of the subject court.

Judicial adherence to the doctrine of stare decisis serves several significant goals:

(1) it promotes efficiency in judicial administration;

(2) it facilitates private and commercial transactions by assuring a degree of certainty and predictability in the law that regulates such transactions; and

(3) it satisfies the common moral belief that persons in like circumstances should be treated alike.[1]

You can explore the third justification for stare decisis on a simple level by examining familiar decisions such as parental decisions on simple family matters. Imagine that two parents, Gerald and Janice, formulated rules to impose on their two children, Tanya and William, both of whom were excellent students. When the children entered their teen years, Gerald and Janice required them to "use good sense" in restricting their hours away from home at night.

---

1. E. Bodenheimer, Jurisprudence: The Philosophy and Method of the Law 425-428 (rev. ed. 1974); Wachtler, Stare Decisis and a Changing New York Court of Appeals, 59 St. John's L. Rev. 445, 447-452 (1985).

When William, the older child, entered his junior year of high school, he began to attend evening social and athletic events frequently. After he had stayed out past 11:00 P.M. three nights in a single week, his parents admonished him. In justifying their admonishment, Gerald and Janice explained that William had not used the requisite good sense for a student of his age and responsibilities. The parents worried that excessively late hours would hamper their son's studies and even endanger his health. To avoid such evils, they announced a refinement of their previous "good sense" rule: William can stay out at night on nonfamily outings no more than twice in a week. Furthermore, despite William's arguments that midnight was a more reasonable curfew, Gerald and Janice announced that William must come home by 11:00 P.M. on such occasions.

A year later, Tanya entered her junior year of high school and also began to attend evening social and athletic events frequently. When Tanya stayed out one night past 10:30 P.M., Gerald and Janice admonished her about her hours. Both parents initially held the opinion that Tanya should not stay out at night on nonfamily outings more than once in a week and that she must come home by 10:00 P.M. on such occasions. Asked for her reaction to these restrictions, Tanya protested that the proposed rule would treat her unfairly: although she and William were engaged in nearly identical activities, she would be subject to greater restrictions than those that her parents had imposed on William.

At first, Gerald and Janice considered whether they could justify the difference in treatment by distinguishing between their two children on the basis of gender: perhaps Tanya needed extra protection because she is female. On reflection, however, Gerald and Janice concluded that William and Tanya were indeed similarly situated because of their activities and that gender was not relevant to the policies and purposes of their curfew rule. Accordingly, they applied the same restrictions to Tanya that they had earlier devised for William.

Throughout months of applying their general curfew rule to William and Tanya, Gerald and Janice developed exceptions to meet special circumstances. For example, both Tanya and William were members of high school basketball teams, both of which occasionally travelled by bus to night games at competing schools in a neighboring county. On such nights, the team bus often did not return the team members to school in time to enable them to return home before 11:00 P.M. Because they valued their children's participation in athletic events, Gerald and Janice permitted late hours on such nights pursuant to one of a growing number of special exceptions to their general rule.

Midway through William's senior year at high school, Gerald and Janice concluded that their general curfew rule was unworkable for two reasons. First, their rule had been excessively mechanical and inflexible from its inception: it required the formulation of numerous exceptions to meet special circumstances, and it completely failed to address questions about activities that should be prohibited rather than merely restricted in their hours and frequency. Second, circumstances had changed: both Tanya and William had increased their participation in worthy organizations and activities that occasionally required late hours or even overnight stays. The general rule now required so many exceptions to meet legitimate needs that it ceased to have significant meaning.

Gerald and Janice were initially reluctant to abandon a rule that they had so thoughtfully developed and applied. After a year and a half, however, they abandoned their original curfew rule and substituted a new, more flexible one. They announced that they would evaluate any proposed activity primarily on the basis of the nature of the activity rather than solely on the frequency and degree to which it required late hours.

Thus, Gerald and Janice strove for consistency in applying their rules to specific events, but they departed from past practice when new information or changes in circumstances suggested that their previous decisions no longer provided the best guide for satisfying their policy objectives. Specifically, they initially announced a general rule for William that satisfied general policy concerns about William's health and academic performance. They applied the same rule to Tanya, rather than a more restrictive rule, because Tanya persuaded them that her case was indistinguishable from that of William. Gerald and Janice later developed special exceptions to their general rule to meet the needs of specific events. Eventually, they grew dissatisfied with their general rule, and they abandoned it. They replaced it with a new rule that used different criteria for evaluating their children's activities.

This parental decisionmaking illustrates some of the ways in which courts develop case law within and without the framework of stare decisis. However, most courts would not be quite as casual as were Gerald and Janice in departing from stare decisis and abandoning their original rules in favor of new ones. Separate opinions by different Justices in a decision of the United States Supreme Court illustrate judicial concern for at least the appearance of adherence to the doctrine of stare decisis. In *Pennhurst State School & Hospital v. Halderman,*[2] the Supreme Court held that the eleventh amendment to the United States Constitution prohibited a federal trial court from exercising a certain kind of "jurisdiction," or judicial power. In reaching that result, a majority of the Court found a way to avoid the decisionmaking restrictions imposed by stare decisis. It concluded that its prior decisions reaching a contrary result had not specifically addressed the issue and therefore created no precedent on the issue:

> These cases thus did not directly confront the question before us. "[W]hen questions of jurisdiction have been passed on in prior decisions *sub silentio,*[3] this Court has never considered itself bound when a subsequent case finally brings the jurisdictional issue before us." [Citation omitted] We therefore view the question as an open one.[4]

Other Justices on the Supreme Court complained in a separate "dissenting opinion" that the majority had mischaracterized the holdings of the prior decisions and thus had failed to accord them the deference demanded by stare decisis:

> None of these cases contain only "implicit" or *sub silentio* holdings; all of them explicitly consider and reject the claim that the Eleventh Amendment prohibits federal courts from issuing injunctive relief based on state law. There is

---

2. 465 U.S. 89 (1984).
3. "Sub silentio" is a Latin phrase meaning "[u]nder silence; without any notice being taken." Black's Law Dictionary 1281 (5th ed. 1979).
4. *Pennhurst,* 465 U.S. at 119.

therefore no basis for the majority's assertion that the issue presented by this case is an open one. . . .[5]

Indeed, the dissenters implicitly accused the majority of analyzing the prior decisions disingenuously:

> The majority incredibly claims that *Greene* contains only an implicit holding on the Eleventh Amendment question the Court decides today. . . . In plain words, the *Greene* Court held that the Eleventh Amendment did not bar consideration of the pendent state-law claims advanced in that case. The Court then considered and sustained those claims on their merits.[6]

Similarly sharp comments punctuated the 1987 hearings of the Senate Judiciary Committee on Judge Robert Bork's unsuccessful bid for confirmation to the United States Supreme Court. Judge Bork's nomination sparked heated debate about the extent to which Bork would adhere to stare decisis if confirmed.[7]

Any governing principle that engenders such controversy is worth further exploration. The strength of an authority as precedent depends in part on the relationship between the court that created the precedent and the court that may subsequently apply it. Therefore, our exploration should begin with an introduction to the court system.

II. THE COURT SYSTEM

A. STRUCTURE OF STATE AND FEDERAL COURTS

Most state court systems include courts of "limited jurisdiction," which hear disputes on limited matters, such as domestic relations, traffic violations, or civil suits with a small amount in controversy. All other disputes are tried in branches of a trial court of "general jurisdiction," typically named "Superior Court," "Circuit Court," or "District Court."

In most states, final decisions of this trial court may be reviewed in appellate courts at two different levels: a disappointed litigant may appeal from a trial court judgment to an intermediate court of appeals; further appeals are taken to a court of last resort, often known as the "Supreme Court" of the state. Some court systems have no intermediate appellate court. Instead, a single

---

5. Id. at 137 (Stevens, J., dissenting).
6. Id. at 137 n.14.
7. Compare The White House Report: Information on Judge Bork's Qualifications, Judicial Record & Related Subjects (July 31, 1987) (Statement on "General Judicial Philosophy" of Judge Bork), reprinted in 9 Cardozo L. Rev. 187, 191 (1987) with The United States Senate Judiciary Committee Chairman's Consultants, Response Prepared to White House Analysis of Judge Bork's Record § VI (Sept. 2, 1987), reprinted in 9 Cardozo L. Rev. 219, 287-296 (1987).

court of last resort routinely hears appeals directly from judgments of the trial courts of general jurisdiction.[8]

The state court system in Arizona is representative of the four-tier model:

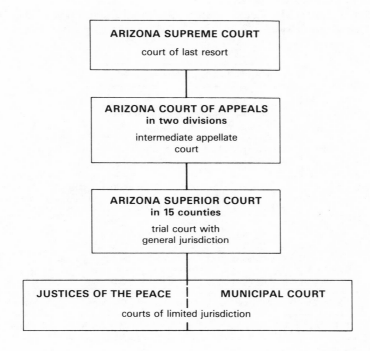

In Arizona, two courts of limited jurisdiction, justices of the peace and the municipal court, hear restricted classes of cases in courthouses serving precincts, cities, and towns. The trial court of general jurisdiction is the Superior Court, which serves each of 15 counties throughout the state.[9] The Superior Court hears appeals from the courts of limited jurisdiction, and it entertains original actions in a wide variety of civil and criminal cases. Disappointed litigants in a criminal or civil case may appeal from a judgment of the Superior Court to the Arizona Court of Appeals. The Court of Appeals is divided into two divisions, each of which hears civil and criminal appeals from departments of the Superior Court in counties assigned to that division. A disappointed litigant in either division of the Court of Appeals may petition the Arizona Supreme Court for discretionary review. The Arizona Supreme Court will exercise its discretion to review a decision of the Court of Appeals only if the

8. In 1986, those states included Delaware, Maine, Mississippi, Montana, Nebraska, Nevada, New Hampshire, North Dakota, Rhode Island, South Dakota, Vermont, West Virginia, and Wyoming. The District of Columbia also uses a two-tier system. See A Uniform System of Citation 177-216 (14th ed. 1986).

9. In November 1989, the Arizona Supreme Court approved a proposal by its Commission

appeal presents important or novel questions of law, or if review is necessary to resolve a conflict within the Court of Appeals.[10] The California court system is similar to that of Arizona, except that it has six intermediate courts of appeals assigned to different districts, and its trial court of general jurisdiction has branches in each of 58 counties.

The structure of the federal court system is similar to those of the Arizona and California court systems:

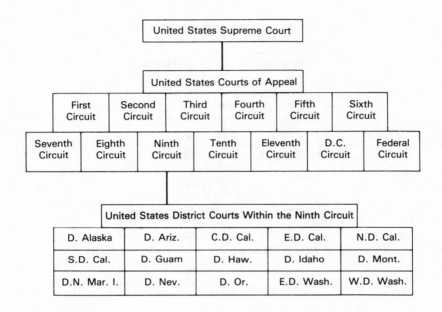

The primary federal trial courts are the United States District Courts. With few exceptions, disappointed litigants appeal from a judgment of a district court to the appropriate one of 13 United States Circuit Courts of Appeals. Further appeals, most of them discretionary, are taken to the United States Supreme Court. The chart above shows the line of review from judgments of the United States District Courts that serve the geographical area within the jurisdiction of the United States Court of Appeals for the Ninth Circuit.

The Ninth Circuit encompasses the states and territories of Alaska, Arizona, California, Guam, Hawaii, Idaho, Montana, Nevada, the Northern Mariana Islands, Oregon, and Washington. Each of those states and territories has at least one district court; California and Washington have more. For example, California is divided into four district courts: the United States District Courts for the Central, Eastern, Northern, and Southern Districts of California.

---

on the Courts to combine the Superior Court with the courts of limited jurisdiction in two counties. The consolidated court would be known as the District Court. This proposal will become effective, however, only with an amendment to the state constitution.

10. See Ariz. R. Crim. P. § 31.19(c)(4) (West 1988); Ariz. R. Civ. App. P. § 23(c)(4) (West 1988).

B. COURT STRUCTURE AND STARE DECISIS

Precedent has only limited stare decisis effect on the decisionmaking of the court that created the precedent: although it will do so only in unusual circumstances, a court can depart from its own prior rulings. For lower courts within the same court system, stare decisis is less flexible: precedent is binding on the lower courts for which the creating court acts as a court of review. As discussed further in section III below, the lower court must either distinguish the precedent or apply it as controlling authority.

Stare decisis generally does not require a court to follow the precedent of coequal, autonomous courts, of lower courts within the same court system, or of any courts outside that system, although the court may consider such nonbinding precedent as persuasive authority. For example, the Arizona Supreme Court is not bound by the decisions of the other Arizona courts or by those of the California Supreme Court. Similarly, the United States Court of Appeals for the First Circuit is not bound by the decisions of either the United States Court of Appeals for the Second Circuit or any United States District Courts. Precedent of the United States Supreme Court, however, is binding on all federal courts and, on matters of federal law, on all state courts.

In some courts, a judicial unit of fewer than all members of the court may create precedent for the entire court. For example, the United States Court of Appeals for the Ninth Circuit has more than two dozen judges, but most appeals in the circuit are heard by panels of three judges each. Each three-judge panel creates precedent that must be followed by all other three-judge panels in the circuit. Within the circuit, a decision of a three-judge panel can be overruled only by a limited en banc panel of eleven members of the court.[11]

Defining the scope of stare decisis in the Arizona Court of Appeals has created greater controversy. A judge in Division One of the Court of Appeals has argued that, because the divisions are separated geographically, and because they review the decisions of different departments of the trial court, the law developed by either division is not entitled to deference from the other.[12] The Arizona Supreme Court subsequently held, however, that the two divisions of the Court of Appeals create precedent as a single court, so that each division must give to the decisions of the other division the deference required by stare decisis.[13] Interestingly, either division may depart from a decision of the other,

---

11. See, e.g., United States v. Seawell, 583 F.2d 416, 419 (9th Cir. 1978) (Hug, J., concurring); *cert. denied,* 439 U.S. 991 (1978); United States v. McLennan, 563 F.2d 943, 948 (9th Cir. 1977); U.S. Ct. App. Ninth Cir. R. 35-3 (West 1988). Ninth Circuit Chief Judge Alfred T. Goodwin has stated that "failure to follow precedent will almost always result in a call for an *en banc* hearing." The Maricopa Lawyer 6 (March 1989) (quoting address to Federal and Maricopa County Public Lawyers, February 7, 1989).

12. Señor T's Restaurant v. Industrial Comm'n, 131 Ariz. 389, 393-394, 641 P.2d 877, 881-882 (App. 1981) (Froeb, J., specially concurring), *vacated,* 131 Ariz. 360, 641 P.2d 848 (1982) (en banc). Judge Froeb's discussion of the relationship between divisions of the Court of Appeals is probably dictum; the dispute in *Señor T's* concerned the relationship among departments within Division One. See id. at 392-393, 641 P.2d at 880-881.

13. Scappaticci v. Southwest Sav. & Loan Ass'n, 135 Ariz. 456, 461, 662 P.2d 131, 136 (1983).

but neither has the power to overrule a decision of the other. Consequently, if one division departs from the decision of the other after according it the deference demanded by stare decisis, it simply creates conflicting decisions within the Court of Appeals that must be resolved by the state Supreme Court.

III. SCOPE AND APPLICATION OF STARE DECISIS

Some form of stare decisis is justified in any society that values efficiency, certainty, and at least those notions of fairness predicated on equal treatment for similarly situated parties. On the other hand, unquestioning adherence to precedent may extend the rule of previous decisions beyond the rationale and policy of the original decision, or it may retain outdated or otherwise unsound precedent.

Two limits to stare decisis help to strike the proper balance between consistency and rigidity in the law:

(1) A court may distinguish a prior decision if it concludes that the prior decision addressed a significantly different dispute from the one presently before the court. If so, even under stare decisis, the prior decision does not dictate the result in the case before the court.

(2) Alternatively, even though a prior decision of a court would otherwise be binding in a dispute presently before the same court, the court may reject its own precedent as authority for the present dispute. Specifically, it can directly depart from its previous decision after giving it the deference required by stare decisis.

A. ANALOGIZING AND DISTINGUISHING PRECEDENT

Few disputes are so similar in their facts and legal issues that resolution of the first dispute provides a clear basis for resolving the second. In those relatively rare cases, the prior decision is "controlling" precedent in the sense that it dictates the result of the subsequent case under stare decisis.[14]

More often, differences between two cases in the facts and in the nature of the legal claims and defenses raised by the litigants are sufficiently substantial that the prior decision does not clearly dictate the resolution of the second. Whether the differences meet this standard often is a question of degree on which reasonable jurists may disagree.[15]

Assuming that the precedent is not strictly controlling, the differences between the cases may be such that the reasons for the result in the prior

---

14. See generally Hutto v. Davis, 454 U.S. 370 (1982).

15. E.g., id. Compare the majority opinion in Hutto v. Davis at 372-375 and Justice Powell's concurrence at 375-381 with Justice Brennan's dissent at 381-388.

decision do not apply to the current case. If so, the distinctions between the two cases justify a different result in the current case, or at least an analysis free of deference to the prior decision. Conversely, even though a prior decision does not provide a clear resolution of the current case because of differences between the two cases, the reasons for the legal result in the prior decision may apply equally to the current case. If so, the prior case is analogous to the current case in a way that justifies the same legal result in both.

Of course, this process of either restricting or extending the application of precedent in relation to a new dispute is far from an exact science. The determination whether a prior decision supports a proposed outcome in a new case may implicate the most deeply held values of those who must interpret and apply the precedent:

> Like the antebellum judges who denied relief to fugitive slaves . . . the Court today claims that its decision, however harsh, is compelled by existing legal doctrine. On the contrary, the question presented by this case is an open one, and our Fourteenth Amendment precedents may be read more broadly or narrowly depending upon how one chooses to read them. Faced with the choice, I would adopt a "sympathetic" reading, one which comports with dictates of fundamental justice and recognizes that compassion need not be exiled from the province of judging.[16]

Although uncertainty about the reasons for a prior decision often complicates the analysis, courts regularly engage in the processes of distinction and analogy to limit, extend, refine, and clarify the rules of prior decisions. Indeed, the precise parameters of the rule of a decision typically do not become clear until courts analyze the decision in subsequent decisions in the context of other disputes. This analytical inquiry is largely one of defining, limiting, and extending the "holdings" of prior decisions; you will revisit it when you study the discussion in Chapter 5 of techniques of briefing cases.

Supreme Court decisions interpreting and applying the fourth amendment to the United States Constitution[17] illustrate the techniques of analogy and distinction. In *Carroll v. United States*,[18] the Supreme Court held that the fourth amendment permitted federal officers to search an automobile without first obtaining a warrant. The Court reasoned that, although a suspect may have privacy interests in the contents of an automobile, the ready mobility of the automobile makes it impracticable for officers to obtain a warrant before searching.[19] Seven months later, in *Agnello v. United States*,[20] the Supreme

---

16. DeShaney v. Winnebago County Dep't of Soc. Serv., 109 S. Ct. 998, 1012 (1989) (Blackmun, J., dissenting).

17. The fourth amendment prohibits unreasonable searches and seizures by government officials:

> The right of the people to be secure in their persons, houses, papers, and effects, against unreasonable searches and seizures, shall not be violated, and no Warrants shall issue, but upon probable cause, supported by Oath or affirmation, and particularly describing the place to be searched, and the persons or things to be seized.

U.S. Const. amend. IV.

18. 267 U.S. 132 (1925).

19. Id. at 153; California v. Carney, 471 U.S. 386, 390 (1985) (quoting and interpreting *Carroll*). Under *Carroll*, even if a warrant is not required, the searching officers must have probable cause to believe that the car contains contraband before they can search it. *Carroll*, 267 U.S. at

Court held that the fourth amendment prohibited the warrantless search of the home of a suspect who had been arrested in another location.[21] In disapproving the warrantless search, the *Agnello* Court distinguished *Carroll* on the bases of the immobility of the house and the particularly great privacy interests the owner has in the contents of a house.[22]

Sixty years after *Carroll* and *Agnello,* in *California v. Carney,*[23] the Court considered whether the fourth amendment prohibited law enforcement officers from engaging in a warrantless search of a fully mobile motor home. Neither *Carroll* nor *Agnello* clearly controlled, because a motor home arguably combines the mobility of an automobile and the privacy interests associated with a house.[24] Consequently, the result in *Carney* under the doctrine of stare decisis depended on whether the Court found the facts of the case to be more nearly analogous to those of *Carroll* or to those of cases like *Agnello.*

The California Supreme Court had disapproved the search on two grounds. First, it analogized *Carney* to cases like *Agnello,* reasoning that the nature of the contents of a motor home creates similarly high expectations of privacy in those contents as the privacy expectations that one has in the contents of a house. Second, it distinguished *Carroll* on the basis of the comparatively low expectation of privacy that an owner has in the contents of an automobile.[25]

On review, the United States Supreme Court reversed the decision of the California Supreme Court. It analogized the case to *Carroll,* reasoning that an automobile and a motor home are not only similarly mobile but are similar in the reduced expectations of privacy in their contents. The expectations of privacy in a motor home are low partly because of the pervasive governmental regulation applicable to all licensed motor vehicles.[26] The two appellate courts applied the precedent differently because they differed in their analyses, primarily factual, of the expectations of privacy that one has in the contents of a motor home.

The processes of analogy and distinction may be applied to the selection or refinement of legal rules as well as to factual analysis. For example, suppose that you represent the plaintiff in an action against a tailor who agreed to make gowns for a wedding ceremony and who misrepresented the state of readiness of the gowns at the time of delivery. To prevail on a claim under a state consumer fraud statute, you must establish that the statute applies to fraud during the delivery of goods under a preexisting agreement and is not limited to fraud during bargaining, fraud that induces the contract. The statute itself

---

153-162. Discussion of the issue of probable cause, however, is not necessary to the analysis in the text above.

20. 269 U.S. 20 (1925).

21. Long before Carroll v. United States, the Supreme Court had assumed that police generally could not search a house without a warrant, unless the search was incidental to a lawful arrest in the house. *Agnello,* 269 U.S. at 32 (interpreting Boyd v. United States, 116 U.S. 616 (1886)). The Court did not directly decide that question, however, until *Agnello,* a few months after *Carroll. Agnello,* 269 U.S. at 32.

22. *Agnello,* 269 U.S. at 31-33; see also Payton v. New York, 445 U.S. 573, 585-590 (1980).

23. 471 U.S. 386 (1985).

24. See id. at 395 (Stevens, J., dissenting).

25. People v. Carney, 34 Cal. 3d 597, 604-610, 668 P.2d 807, 810-814 (1983).

26. *Carney,* 471 U.S. at 390-394; see also New York v. Class, 475 U.S. 106 (1986).

prohibits various kinds of fraud during the "advertisement or sale" of goods. The term "advertisement" does not help you on this question, because it normally refers to representations made before an agreement is reached. Although the term "sale" might refer to performance of an existing contract, the statute doesn't specifically define "sale" in a way that resolves the question whether "sale" refers to the moment of contracting or to the subsequent transfer of goods. A commercial statute of the same state, however, specifically defines sale as "the passing of title from the seller to the buyer for a price," an event that could coincide with the delivery of goods under a preexisting contract. The remedial purposes of the consumer fraud statute suggest that it should have at least the breadth of application of the state's commercial statutes. Therefore, as counsel for the plaintiff in the fraud action, you could argue by analogy to the commercial statute that the consumer fraud statute prohibits fraud during the delivery of goods under a preexisting contract.[27]

In contrast, the common law requirement of proof of fraud by the elevated standard of "clear and convincing evidence" may not apply by analogy to an action under the consumer fraud statute. In enacting the statute, the legislature intended to increase consumer protection beyond that afforded by an action for common law fraud. Therefore, the statute should require proof by the normal standard of a "preponderance of the evidence" rather than the more demanding common law standard.[28]

Although these examples involve interpretation and application of constitutional and statutory law, they also illustrate the manner in which common law develops, case by case, through analogy and distinction in the context of stare decisis.

B. OVERRULING PRECEDENT

Precedent that is indistinguishable in any material way from the dispute before the court is "controlling." In most court systems, a lower court is absolutely bound by the controlling precedent of the appellate courts that review its decisions.[29] However, the doctrine of stare decisis is more flexible in the courts that created the precedent.[30] In exceptional circumstances, a court may depart from a strict application of stare decisis and refuse to follow its own controlling precedent. In so doing, it "overrules" the prior decision and substitutes new precedent in its place.[31]

---

27. Cf. Schmidt v. American Leasco, 139 Ariz. 509, 512, 679 P.2d 532, 535 (App. 1983) (fraud during performance of lease).

28. See, e.g., Dunlap v. Jimmy GMC of Tucson, Inc., 136 Ariz. 338, 343-344, 666 P.2d 83 (App. 1983) (applying Arizona consumer fraud statute).

29. E.g., Hutto v. Davis, 454 U.S. 370, 375 (1982).

30. E.g., Jaffree v. Wallace, 705 F.2d 1526, 1532 (11th Cir. 1983), aff'd 472 U.S. 38 (1985).

31. In some circumstances, a branch of a court may be bound to accord deference to the precedent of a coequal branch, yet it may lack the power to overrule that precedent if it decides to depart from the precedent after giving it the deference required by stare decisis. In those circumstances, the latest decision creates conflicting precedent within the court, conflict that may be resolved only by a higher court or by a special panel of the same court. See supra section II(B).

An early Supreme Court decision was surprisingly liberal in its approval of such departures from stare decisis:

> The rule of *stare decisis,* though one tending to consistency and uniformity of decision, is not inflexible. Whether it shall be followed or departed from is a question entirely within the discretion of the court, which is again called upon to consider a question once decided.[32]

A more recent statement of the Court is more cautious: "any departure from the doctrine of stare decisis demands special justification."[33]

A court may overrule a previous decision that was sensible in light of its original social, economic, technological, and legal context but that fails to serve important policies in current conditions.[34] Under the early English common law, for example, an employment contract that provided for an annual salary was interpreted as providing a one-year term of employment absent a clear expression of contrary intent. The original impetus for the one-year rule was a desire to protect seasonal farm workers from the insecurity of shorter and unpredictable terms of employment. Nonetheless, English courts extended the rule to a new population of factory workers created by the industrial revolution.

Some American jurisdictions adopted a form of the English one-year rule, perhaps because of the early American tradition that a master was responsible for the well-being of his servants. Employer paternalism, however, declined with the industrialization of the United States in the late nineteenth century. Partly to facilitate efficient allocation of resources in developing industries subject to business cycles, American courts abandoned the English rule. In its place, they created the "at will" doctrine, which raised a presumption that an employment contract for an indefinite term was terminable by either party at any time and for any reason or no reason at all.

The at-will rule was consistent with developing contract doctrine, which imposed obligations based on voluntary agreement rather than on status such as that of an employer in the master-servant relationship.[35] In this century, however, American industry has outgrown its need for protection from labor costs that cannot vary perfectly with business needs. Concern has shifted to the need for greater security for nonunion employees, whose bargaining power is typically much inferior to that of their employers. As a reflection of this shift in concern, courts have begun to depart from their traditionally rigid application of the at-will rule and have recognized exceptions to the rule in the form of new tort and contract theories.[36]

---

32. Hertz v. Woodman, 218 U.S. 205, 212 (1910).

33. Arizona v. Rumsey, 467 U.S. 203, 212 (1984); see also Patterson v. McLean Credit Union, 109 S. Ct. 2363, 2370 (1989).

34. See, e.g., Amadio v. Levin, 509 Pa. 199, 501 A.2d 1085 (1985) (to recognize right on behalf of deceased fetus under wrongful death and survival statutes, court relied partly on intervening advances in medical knowledge and on changes in the laws of other states to overrule precedent).

35. Murg & Scharman, Employment at Will: Do the Exceptions Overwhelm the Rule?, 23 B.C.L. Rev. 329, 332-336 (1982).

36. See, e.g., Wagenseller v. Scottsdale Memorial Hosp., 147 Ariz. 370, 375-386, 710 P.2d 1025, 1030-1041 (1985); Petermann v. International Bhd. of Teamsters Local 396, 174 Cal. App. 2d 184, 344 P.2d 25 (1959); Annot., 12 A.L.R. 4th 544 (1982).

Even absent an intervening change in conditions, a court may overrule one of its prior decisions simply because it thinks that the prior decision was poorly reasoned at the outset or has proved to be unworkable in light of experience.[37] For example, in *Maryland v. Wirtz*,[38] the Supreme Court held that the principles of state sovereignty in the tenth amendment[39] did not prohibit Congress from regulating the compensation of state employees by applying the Fair Labor Standards Act of 1938 to selected state institutions. The Court relied heavily on dicta[40] from a previous decision of the Court, *United States v. California*.[41] Eight years later, in *National League of Cities v. Usery*,[42] a closely divided Supreme Court overruled *Maryland v. Wirtz:* a plurality of four Justices explained that the dicta from *United States v. California* on which the *Maryland* Court had relied was "simply wrong."[43] Eight years after *National League of Cities,* the Supreme Court in a 5-4 decision overruled *National League of Cities* on the ground that *it* was wrongly decided:

> We do not lightly overrule recent precedent. We have not hesitated, however, when it has become apparent that a prior decision has departed from a proper understanding of congressional power under the Commerce Clause.[44]

The Supreme Court's double reverse on the proper interpretation of the tenth amendment may simply exemplify a more general relationship between the Supreme Court and the United States Constitution. Article V of the Constitution provides that an amendment to the Constitution is not effective unless approved by two-thirds of each house of Congress and ratified by three-fourths of the states. Thus, Congress cannot easily amend the Constitution to reflect changing social or economic conditions or to overrule judicial interpretations with which Congress disagrees. In recent history, for example, Congress marshalled sufficient votes to propose the Equal Rights Amendment and even to extend the time within which the states could ratify it, but fewer than the requisite number of states ratified.[45] Consequently, some scholars and judges

---

36. See, e.g., Wagenseller v. Scottsdale Memorial Hosp., 147 Ariz. 370, 375-386, 710 P.2d 1025, 1030-1041 (1985); Petermann v. International Bhd. of Teamsters Local 396, 174 Cal. App. 2d 184, 344 P.2d 25 (1959); Annot., 12 A.L.R. 4th 544 (1982).

37. Stone, Precedent, the Amendment Process, and Evolution in Constitutional Doctrine, 11 Harv. J.L. & Pub. Pol'y 67, 71 (1988).

38. 392 U.S. 183 (1968).

39. The tenth amendment to the United States Constitution reserves power to the states:

The powers not delegated to the United States by the Constitution, nor prohibited by it to the States, are reserved to the States respectively, or to the people.

40. "Dicta" are statements in a judicial opinion that are not necessary to the court's resolution of the dispute before it. Dicta may give some insight into the court's views about the proper resolution of other disputes, but they do not form part of the decision's binding precedent.

41. 297 U.S. 175, 184-185 (1936) (quoted in *Wirtz,* 392 U.S. at 198).

42. 426 U.S. 833 (1976).

43. *National League of Cities,* 426 U.S. 854-855. Justice Blackmun wrote a separate opinion concurring with the plurality opinion and providing the fifth vote necessary to overrule Maryland v. Wirtz. Id. at 856.

44. Garcia v. San Antonio Metro. Transit Auth., 469 U.S. 528, 557 (1985).

45. J. Nowak, R. Rotunda, & N. Young, Constitutional Law App. B, at 1105-1106 (2d ed. 1983). In an exceptional reaction to a particular ruling of the Supreme Court, Congress proposed, and the states ratified, the eleventh amendment as a way of overruling Chisholm v. Georgia, 2 U.S. (2 Dall.) 419 (1793). Nowak, Rotunda, & Young, at 52-53.

believe that the Supreme Court should "keep [constitutional] law in accord with the dynamic flow of the social order," with less than the normal restraints of stare decisis,[46] and with less than complete deference to the immediate concerns of Congress when it enacted the constitutional provision or amendment in question.[47]

IV. SUMMARY

Under the doctrine of stare decisis, a court endeavors to decide each case consistently with its previous decisions, sometimes called precedent. This policy of consistency permits a court to depart from precedent if the precedent is distinguishable from the current dispute. Even if the precedent is not distinguishable, a court may depart from stare decisis and overrule its own prior case law if a different rule of law would better respond to current social and economic conditions. Stare decisis is less flexible with respect to the precedent of a higher court in the same jurisdiction: a trial court or intermediate court of appeals is strictly bound to apply the precedent of a higher court. A court is never bound to apply the precedent of a lower court or any court in another jurisdiction.

════════ E X E R C I S E   2 - 1 ════════

Review Exercise 1-1(2) on page 10 and analyze the following problems based on decisions of the fictitious Calzona Supreme Court:

PRECEDENT: *Smith v. Collier,* 47 Calz. 78 (1891).

On February 1, Smith and Collier agreed to marry before the end of the year. They later set a wedding date of December 1. In November, Smith complained about Collier's habit of playing poker on Saturday nights. In retaliation, Collier announced that Collier would not marry Smith. Smith sued Collier for breach of contract, requesting compensatory and punitive damages. Smith did not allege that Collier committed a tort.

The opinion of the Calzona Supreme Court includes the following excerpt:

> We affirm the trial court's factual findings that Collier breached the marriage contract with the malicious intent to cause Smith injury. Although the courts of this state recognize a general rule against punitive damages for breach of contract,

46. E. Bodenheimer, Jurisprudence: The Philosophy and Method of the Law 430 (rev. ed. 1974); see also Patterson v. McLean Credit Union, 109 S. Ct. 2363, 2370 (1989).

47. See generally J. Nowak, R. Rotunda, & J.N. Young, Constitutional Law 14 n.13 (2d ed. 1983) (comparing value-oriented theory of judicial review to others); Berger, New Theories of "Interpretation": The Activist Flight from the Constitution, 47 Ohio St. L.J. 1 (1986).

the trial court correctly instructed the jury that it could award punitive damages as well as compensatory damages in this case.

1. Distinguishing *Smith v. Collier*

In the following cases, you represent the defendant. Identify the facts in *Smith v. Collier* that appear to have motivated the court to permit an award of punitive damages. Identify factual differences in your case that might motivate the Calzona Supreme Court to distinguish *Smith v. Collier* and to rule that punitive damages cannot be awarded against your client. Explain why those factual differences justify a different result from the ruling in *Smith v. Collier*. Identify any factual similarities between your case and *Smith v. Collier*. Explain why those similarities do not justify the same result as in *Smith v. Collier*. Which of the following cases is easiest to distinguish from *Smith v. Collier*?

a. *White v. Strunk*

White agreed to pay Strunk $100,000 for construction of a house on White's property. Strunk agreed to complete construction by August 1, regardless of weather or labor conditions. Unfortunately, abnormally frequent rainfall and faulty workmanship by subcontractors delayed Strunk's work. Despite Strunk's best efforts, he failed to complete construction by August 1, causing White to suffer economic losses.

b. *Roget v. Webster*

Roget agreed to pay Webster $100,000 in exchange for Webster's promise to construct a house on Roget's property. Before either Roget or Webster began performance, Ballentine offered to pay Webster $150,000 to build a similar house on Ballentine's property. Because he could not perform both jobs at once, and because a contract with Ballentine was more profitable, Webster repudiated his contract with Roget and accepted Ballentine's offer.

c. *White v. Benkowski*

White's property had no water supply. White agreed to pay Benkowski a monthly fee in exchange for fresh water supplied through pipes from Benkowski's well. After personal animosity developed between White and Benkowski, Benkowski maliciously shut off the water supply to the White's property.

2. Overruling *Smith v. Collier*

You represent the defendant in *Statler v. Corbin*, a case that is factually and procedurally indistinguishable from Smith v. Collier. Explain why the Calzona Supreme Court should overrule *Smith v. Collier* and disallow punitive damages for breach of a marriage agreement.

3. Distinguishing *Statler v. Corbin*, 305 Calz. 219 (1990).

In *Statler v. Corbin*, the Calzona Supreme Court overruled *Smith v. Collier* and held that punitive damages are not available to remedy even a malicious breach of a marriage contract. In the following case, you represent the plaintiff.

Identify factual or procedural differences between *Statler v. Corbin* and your case, and explain why those differences justify an award of punitive damages in your case.

Jones v. Marsh

In July, Jones and Marsh agreed to marry on November 1. At a family reunion in August, Marsh broke off the engagement in a public statement in which he cruelly humiliated Jones. In addition to proving breach of contract, you have alleged and proved that Marsh intentionally inflicted emotional distress on Jones, conduct that is actionable as a tort in Calzona. In opposing Jones's request for punitive damages, Marsh relies on *Statler v. Corbin*.

3

An Approach to Legal Method

I. OVERVIEW—SOLVING LEGAL PROBLEMS

Attorneys perform many tasks for clients that may not directly relate to litigation of legal disputes, including estate and tax planning, business counseling, and legislative lobbying. Even these tasks, however, may be inspired partly by the desire to avoid or influence future litigation. Moreover, relatively few clients seek legal counseling to avoid legal problems; instead, most consult an attorney only after they have become embroiled in a legal dispute in which litigation has commenced or is imminent. Consequently, legal method relating to litigation of legal disputes is an important component of nearly every attorney's practice.

As explored in detail in Chapter 12, a lawsuit is formally commenced with the filing of "pleadings": the plaintiff brings suit by filing a "complaint" against the defendant, and the defendant responds by filing an "answer." If you represent a party in the early stages of such litigation, you must evaluate the strengths and weaknesses of your client's claims or defenses to help you prepare for various stages of advocacy, from the pleadings and settlement negotiations to trial and appeal. In a large or medium-sized law firm, the typical means of communicating your evaluation to other members of the firm is an office memorandum of law, discussed in detail in Part III of this book. The principal means of persuading a judge or other adjudicatory body to accept your client's legal claims or defenses is a written brief, discussed in detail in Part IV. To prepare either kind of document, you must apply fundamental skills of legal method that you develop in the first year of law school, as discussed in Part II.

This chapter will examine methods of legal problem-solving in the context of litigation of legal disputes. It builds on the groundwork laid in Chapters 1 and 2, and it provides an overview for more detailed discussions of legal method found throughout the remaining chapters.

II. IDENTIFYING ISSUES FOR ANALYSIS

A. DEFINING ISSUES

A legal issue is a question that a judge, jury, agency hearing officer, arbitrator, or other adjudicator must resolve to determine the outcome of a legal dispute. You can identify potential legal issues immediately on the occurrence of an event that gives rise to a legal dispute, even though no party has yet begun to litigate a claim or has even made any demands on another. Constitutions, statutes, case law, and perhaps even the private law of an agreement between the parties impose duties on some parties and correlative rights on others in the context of the event. Armed with at least a general knowledge of the law and of the facts of the event, you can address the question whether any party is liable to another for breach of a legal duty. At the least, you can advance arguments in support of either a potentially liable party or a potentially wronged victim. If the arguments for both parties have potential merit, you have identified a legal issue.

1. Issues and Subissues

A general issue may encompass discrete subissues. For example, case law establishes that a defendant generally will be liable to the plaintiff for damages caused by breach of contract if (1) the parties formed an enforceable contract; and (2) the defendant failed to perform his contractual promises, thus breaching the contract. At the broadest level, the facts of a dispute might raise the general issue of whether the defendant is liable for breach of contract. More specifically, the facts may raise separate subissues about (1) contract formation, and (2) performance and breach.

You may want to further subdivide these subissues to recognize multiple legal elements associated with each. For example, case law establishes two primary requirements for contract formation: (1) an agreement reached through a process of offer and acceptance and (2) "consideration" in the form of a mutually induced exchange. These elements are distinct, because parties are capable of agreeing to a transaction that does not satisfy the consideration requirement. Depending on the circumstances of the dispute, the facts may raise separate subissues regarding (1) offer and acceptance and (2) consideration. Similarly, within the subissue of performance and breach, the law and the facts may raise a second level of subissues regarding, for example, (1) interpretation of the defendant's contractual promises and (2) possible discharge of the defendant's obligations because unforeseen circumstances made his performance impossible.

2. Continuing Development of Issues

At the inception of a dispute, incomplete knowledge of the facts and vagueness or ambiguity in the arguably applicable legal rules make the eventual outcome of the dispute particularly uncertain. At that stage, you can identify the issues only tentatively. As the dispute proceeds through stages of litigation, the issues will become increasingly well defined.

For example, a demand letter or complaint may reveal which of numerous potential legal claims a claimant has decided to advance, thus raising some questions of liability and eliminating others. Under modern rules of civil procedure, parties to a civil lawsuit may use various "discovery" devices to obtain certain kinds of information from witnesses and from the opposing party.[1] This court-supervised discovery process or other investigation may reveal that some claims or defenses are meritless and may raise new questions about others. Moreover, as explored in Chapters 13 and 14, a litigant may request the court to rule before trial that certain evidence will be excluded from trial or even that the litigant is entitled to judgment without trial. Thus, pretrial motions could raise issues under applicable rules of evidence or procedure concerning the admissibility of evidence or the proper application of standards for summary disposition. Finally, if the dispute goes to trial, the nature of the disposition in the trial court and the factual record developed in the trial court will help determine which issues the losing party might reasonably raise on appeal.

As illustrated by these examples, the parties help to define the issues by making strategic decisions about what claims and defenses to assert and about which procedural vehicles should be used to assert them. With few exceptions, courts do not address questions that are not raised by either party to a dispute.[2]

3. Materiality

Not every potential disagreement about the facts or the law amounts to a legal issue. Even a hotly disputed question of fact or law would not be "in issue" if it were immaterial. A disputed point is immaterial if it could not affect the outcome of the lawsuit in light of other facts and rules of law.

To take an obvious example, suppose that evidence shows that the defendant drove his car through an intersection and struck the plaintiff in a pedestrian crosswalk. The defendant's liability for negligence would not be affected by even a heated disagreement over the color of the socks that the defendant wore that day. Assuming that the identity of the driver of the car is conclusively established through some means other than the color of the socks

---

1. See, e.g., Fed. R. Civ. P. 26-37.
2. E.g., Jones v. City of Somerville, 735 F.2d 5, 7 (1st Cir. 1984) (appellate waiver of legal theory for failure to present it to trial court); Hershinow v. Bonamarte, 735 F.2d 264, 266 (7th Cir. 1984) (waiver of claim presented to appellate court in perfunctory manner). But cf. Giannakos v. M/V Bravo Trader, 762 F.2d 1295, 1297 (5th Cir. 1985) (federal trial and appellate courts must address questions of federal subject-matter jurisdiction on their own motions); In re Pizza of Hawaii, Inc., 761 F.2d 1374, 1377-1378 (9th Cir. 1985) (appellate court must determine appellate jurisdiction on its own motion); In re Pacific Trencher & Equipment, Inc., 735 F.2d 362, 364 (9th Cir. 1984) (discretionary appellate consideration of pure question of law not raised in the trial court).

he wore, the issues of law and fact would include such material questions as the following:

(1) Which party had the green light?

(2) What injuries did the plaintiff sustain?

(3) Does the law permit the jury to reduce the plaintiff's recovery if her own negligence combined with that of the defendant to cause her injuries?

Of course, many cases raise closer questions of materiality than that in the example above. As discussed in the next section, some questions of materiality may be a matter of degree requiring the exercise of judgment in selecting issues for discussion or argument in a legal document.

════ E X E R C I S E   3 - 1 ════

Although American jurisdictions have enacted criminal codes that largely supersede the early criminal common law, imagine a state that still applies the common law definition of the crime of burglary: the breaking and entering of a dwelling of another at night with the intent to commit a felony. As stated in Chapter 1, the law relating to this crime reflected a concern about a serious invasion of the right of habitation during hours of darkness, when the inhabitants were most vulnerable to attack and the invader most likely to escape recognition.

Armed only with this general knowledge of the law, identify the issues relating to the common law crime of burglary raised by the following facts:

> In June, Leona Rosal left her San Francisco apartment and drove her VW bus down the coast for a three-week vacation in Monterey Bay. Although she occasionally ate at restaurants or stayed with friends, she mostly slept in the back of the bus and prepared simple meals in the bus with groceries that she purchased at local stores.
>
> On the evening of June 20, Leona parked her bus in an overnight recreational-vehicle parking space at Seacliff State Beach. She prepared dinner from an ice chest in the back of the bus, leaving the driver's window in the cab completely open and an expensive portable stereo radio and cassette player on the driver's seat. She fell asleep in the back of her bus at 11:00 P.M. A curtain separated the sleeping area of the bus from the driver's cab. At 5:15 A.M., just as the first hints of a sunrise glowed from the hilltops opposite the ocean, Michael Glass, a local surfer, approached Leona's van. Through the open window next to the driver's seat, Michael spied the stereo equipment lying on the seat. Hoping to add it permanently to his own home system, Michael opened the closed but unlocked driver's door and placed his hand on the stereo equipment. At that moment, a patrolling police officer drove up to Leona's VW bus and arrested Michael for burglary and attempted larceny. Leona awoke only when the officer knocked on her bus after the arrest.

You may assume that theft of the stereo equipment would constitute felony larceny in the jurisdiction. In the prosecution of Michael Glass on the burglary charge, what elements of the common law crime of burglary would the prosecutor and defense attorney likely dispute? What elements of burglary are not reasonably in dispute? Would further facts help define or resolve the issues? Would case law that refines the law of burglary help define or resolve the issues? If you were assigned the task of preparing an office memorandum on this problem, what facts or law would you desire to investigate further?

B. SCOPE OF ANALYSIS

Any dispute of at least moderate complexity presents a range of potential legal theories and arguments that you might raise in litigation. At the near end of the spectrum are persuasive and conventional legal theories or arguments that a court would almost certainly address in analyzing the dispute. At the far end are legal theories or factual analogies of such doubtful merit or applicability that a court might view them as frivolous or immaterial to the outcome of the dispute.

The extent to which you discuss topics toward the far end of the spectrum is a question of "scope of analysis" and depends partly on the nature of your document. The scope of analysis typically is quite broad in a law school essay examination answer, somewhat narrower in an office memorandum addressed to a supervising attorney, and narrower still in a good brief addressed to a judge.

You will often touch on a broad range of issues in an examination answer because most law professors will specifically test your ability to spot issues. Indeed, on many examinations, you will earn a higher grade if you identify and briefly discuss all possible issues, including the less obvious and more exotic ones, than if you thoroughly analyze only the most obvious.

In comparison, your supervising attorney may expect a slightly narrower scope of analysis in your office memorandum. She probably will want detailed discussion of significant issues, and she will generally encourage creative and aggressive analysis, but she may not have time to thoroughly examine more exotic theories or approaches if they are unlikely to have a practical effect on the outcome of the dispute. Unfortunately, you may be tempted to convey to your supervisor the long hours that you have spent in the library by describing in detail every legal theory or authority that made its way into your library notes. Your supervisor will not be impressed. She realizes that you will regularly follow research leads that bear no useful fruit, and she expects the final draft of your memorandum to shield her from the burden of retracing your steps down paths that led only to distracting tangents.

On the other hand, the materiality of a fact or theory may be difficult to assess in the early stages of litigation and fact investigation. Accordingly, if you draft an office memorandum at the early stages of a dispute, you should consider discussing close questions of scope of analysis with your supervising attorney before beginning to write. Absent specific direction from your supervisor, you probably should at least mention any argument of potential significance, even if only in a sentence or two. You can distinguish between a major theory and a less significant one in the depth of your analysis of each. Then, if later developments in the litigation establish the significance of an issue of previously questionable importance, you can analyze that issue in greater depth in a supplemental memorandum.

When drafting a brief, you often must exercise even stricter control on the scope of analysis. Although creative and novel arguments often win appeals by inspiring changes in the law, some arguments are so clearly marginal that they may simply detract from the cumulative persuasiveness of the entire brief. If you add a nearly frivolous argument to one with greater merit, you reduce the number of pages within the maximum allowed that you can devote to the meritorious argument. Even worse, you may lose credibility on the whole brief.

III. DEDUCTIVE REASONING

A. THE LEGAL SYLLOGISM—ORIENTATION AND LIMITATIONS

Once you have identified legal issues and have determined the appropriate scope of analysis, you must analyze the issues. Most essay examinations, office memoranda, and briefs require more than purely abstract legal analysis: they require you to apply legal standards to specific facts to reach a conclusion. In many cases, the analysis follows a pattern of deductive reasoning known as the syllogism, which derives a conclusion from a major premise and a minor premise:

Major Premise:	All men are mortal.
Minor Premise:	Socrates is a man.
Conclusion:	Therefore, Socrates is mortal.[3]

In a legal argument, the major premise is a legal rule. It may represent the terms of a statute, the holding of a single judicial decision that acts as precedent, or a general principle derived from a series of previous decisions. The minor premise of a legal argument generally is a set of facts taken from the dispute that you are analyzing. The conclusion represents your resolution of the question whether the facts stated in the minor premise satisfy the legal standard stated in the major premise.

A deductive argument is valid if its conclusion follows necessarily from its premises; the correctness or truth of the conclusion of a valid argument depends on the truth of its premises.[4] For example, the fourth amendment to the United States Constitution ordinarily requires a police officer to obtain a search warrant from a judicial officer before searching an enclosed structure such as a house. However, under the "automobile exception," an officer may search an automobile without a warrant if he has probable cause to believe that it contains evidence of a crime. Suppose that a police officer searched Jack Greenberg's motor home without a warrant and found illegal drugs. In the state's criminal prosecution of Greenberg for possession of the illegal drugs, the state might advance the following valid deductive argument:

---

3. See generally I. Copi, Introduction to Logic § 1.4, at 23-24 (4th ed. 1972).
4. Id. at 23.

Major Premise—The automobile exception to the fourth amendment's warrant requirement applies to all vehicles with mobility similar to that of an automobile on a street or highway.

Minor Premise—Even while parked in Greenberg's backyard, Greenberg's motor home was a vehicle with mobility similar to that of an automobile on a street or highway.

Conclusion—The automobile exception to the fourth amendment's warrant requirement applied to Greenberg's motor home while it was parked in Greenberg's backyard.

Although the conclusion of this valid argument follows necessarily from the premises, the conclusion is not true if either of the premises is untrue. The attorney for each party will attempt to persuade the judge to reach a certain conclusion by accepting particular formulations of the major and minor premises and by rejecting others. For example, Greenberg's attorney could raise the fourth amendment issue by asking the judge to exclude the evidence obtained in the warrantless search of Greenberg's motor home. In response, the state prosecutor would advance the deductive argument above to demonstrate that the fourth amendment did not require the police to obtain a warrant to search Greenberg's motor home. Greenberg's attorney could attack this argument either by arguing as a matter of law that the prosecutor's major premise exaggerates the scope of the automobile exception or by establishing as a matter of fact that the prosecutor's minor premise exaggerates the mobility of the motor home parked in Greenberg's backyard.

A deductive argument is not valid if its conclusion does not follow necessarily from its premises. For example, if Greenberg's attorney proved that Greenberg's motor home was significantly less mobile than an automobile on the street or highway, the judge would undoubtedly replace the prosecutor's untrue minor premise with the minor premise established by Greenberg's attorney. As reconstructed, the deductive argument would no longer be valid, because the prosecutor's conclusion would not follow from the original major premise and the new minor premise.

Deductive reasoning provides at least a rough organizational framework for most legal analyses in office memoranda, answers to essay examinations, and briefs. The usefulness of the syllogism in legal reasoning, however, is limited by the flexibility and uncertainty inherent in legal analysis. For example, to establish the major premise of your argument, you may state your interpretation of the holding of a previous decision or your synthesis of the holdings of a series of decisions. Until a judge expresses her opinion on the matter, however, you cannot be certain whether she will agree with your interpretation of previous decisions and thus with your statement of the major premise.

Indeed, the dominant description of legal method in this century, known as "legal realism," rejects the notion that the law is external to the judges and other officials who apply and enforce it. Instead, the law is simply a prediction about what such officials will do in the face of a dispute. Moreover, their decisions will be based on a complex set of motivations, including personal values and prejudices not explicitly accounted for in the formal abstract rule of law. Thus, judges or juries can take advantage of uncertainty in law or facts by manipulating them to justify results that they reach on other than purely logical grounds.[5]

In short, legal disputes cannot be analyzed with mathematical certainty:

> The life of the law has not been logic: it has been experience. The felt necessities of the time, the prevalent moral and political theories, intuitions of public policy, avowed or unconscious, even the prejudices which judges share with their fellow-men, have had a good deal more to do than the syllogism in determining the rules by which men should be governed.[6]

Nonetheless, the syllogism provides a useful starting point for discussing general techniques of presenting legal analyses.

B. IRAC

Most law students use the acronym IRAC to help them remember the elements of deductive reasoning. IRAC stands for **I**ssue, **R**ule, **A**pplication, and **C**onclusion. Thus, after identifying an **I**ssue, you should

(1) state the legal **R**ule that will help resolve the issue,

(2) **A**pply the rule to the relevant facts, and

(3) reach a **C**onclusion on the question of whether the facts satisfy the legal rule.

For example, the following excerpt of an answer to an essay examination discusses the availability of punitive damages in a tort action. Although the examination answer itself should not explicitly refer to IRAC, the margin notes below represent the elements that a student should keep in mind when formulating a complete response. In this example, after raising an issue about punitive damages, the student has summarized general legal rules regarding the availability of punitive damages, has applied them to the facts of the examination, and has reached a conclusion:

Issue	*Punitive Damages*—In addition to compensation for his actual losses, Ling may request punitive damages, designed to punish the tortfeasor and to deter others from engaging in similar wrongdoing.
Rules	A jury has the discretion to award punitive damages if the tortfeasor acted with the malicious intent to cause harm. In many jurisdictions, punitive damages are also permitted if the tortfeasor acted with

---

5. See J. Harris, Legal Philosophies 93-98 (1980). The more recent Critical Legal Studies movement goes beyond legal realism to broadly attack contemporary legal method, scholarship, and education as a system that legitimizes and perpetuates an oppressive socio-economic order. See generally Critical Legal Studies Symposium, 36 Stan. L. Rev. 1 (1984); M. Kelman, A Guide to Critical Legal Studies (1987); R. Unger, The Critical Legal Studies Movement (1986). Some feminist scholars challenge traditional legal reasoning as reflecting a male perspective. E.g., Women in Legal Education—Pedagogy, Law, Theory, and Practice, 38 J. Legal Educ. Nos. 1 & 2 (1988).

6. O. Holmes, Jr., The Common Law 1 (1923); see also id. at 312 ("The distinctions of the law are founded on experience, not on logic. It therefore does not make the dealings of men dependent on a mathematical accuracy."); N. MacCormick, Legal Reasoning and Legal Theory 65-72 (1978) (discussing "the limits of deductive justification").

reckless disregard for the risk of harm to others. Unless exceptional circumstances justify the risky conduct, a person acts recklessly if he consciously engages in conduct that he knows or should know poses a great risk of harm to others.

    In this case, Con Motor Co. did not maliciously intend to cause injury when it designed its Firebird sports car. In fact, the discussion at the May meeting shows that the board of directors genuinely hoped that the risky design would not cause accidents. However, Con's chief engineer informed the board of directors of her opinion that placement of the gas tank near the rear exterior of the car would create a risk of deadly explosion in even minor rear-end collisions. Yet, the directors approved that design solely because it would save production costs of $100/car. In so doing, Con's directors knowingly created a great risk of death or terrible injury to consumers without any socially significant justification.

    Con Motor Co. thus acted recklessly, permitting a jury in many jurisdictions to assess punitive damages against it. Indeed, in a jurisdiction that requires proof of malicious intent to injure, this case would be a good vehicle for arguing for a liberalization of the standards to include recklessness as a basis for an award of punitive damages.

Application to facts

Conclusion

    To help you avoid the oversimplification that may result from an excessively mechanical application of IRAC, later chapters of this book explore some sophisticated techniques of analysis that build on the general framework of deductive reasoning. Chapter 6 section II introduces two variations of inductive reasoning, and Chapter 9 section III(E) tackles problems of organization that arise when an issue or subissue presents different layers or levels of syllogisms.

IV. DEVELOPMENT OF LEGAL PRINCIPLES

A. OVERVIEW—SOURCES OF AUTHORITY

    Consistent with the general pattern of deductive reasoning, your first step in discussing a legal issue is to identify and analyze applicable legal rules. You will seldom find these rules clearly set forth in a single source of authority; the law that an adjudicator will apply to resolve a legal issue may be a combination of rules, any one of which may represent a synthesis of several sources of law. The relative importance of legal authorities to the analysis of the issue depends on such factors as

(1) the primary or secondary nature of the authority;

(2) the jurisdiction, in the sense of the political or geographical body, in which primary authority is controlling; and

(3) if the primary authority is case law, the strength of the case law as precedent.

1. Primary and Secondary Authority

So far, this book has addressed only "primary" legal authority: direct statements of law issued by lawmaking bodies. Primary authority includes constitutions, statutes, administrative rules and regulations, and case law. Subject to limitations discussed in sections 2 and 3 below, a primary authority or combination of primary authorities will supply the applicable rule in any legal dispute.

"Secondary" authorities, such as treatises, restatements of the law, and articles, do not directly supply the rule of law in a legal dispute. Instead, they express a commentator's explanation of the law or her opinions about what the law should be. A secondary authority has persuasive value only: it may influence a court or legislature to act in a particular way, but it has no mandatory or binding effect.

An example of a popular treatise is Prosser and Keeton on Torts. This secondary authority generally describes tort law in American jurisdictions and examines the relevant policies supporting competing approaches in the tort law of different states.

Another frequently cited example of secondary authority is the collection of Restatements of Law issued by the American Law Institute. The institute has drafted two restatements of contract law, the Restatement of Contracts (1932) and the Restatement (Second) of Contracts (1979). Each of these is divided into numerous sections and subsections, most of which attempt to summarize rules of the common law of contracts generally accepted when the restatement was drafted. A few sections, however, are meant to influence the law by promoting trends that had not yet been widely accepted at the time of drafting. Section 90 of each restatement, for example, represents an innovative view of a theory of recovery based on reliance, commonly known as promissory estoppel. Although no court is required to follow the approach of either restatement, section 90 has in fact influenced many courts. Indeed, some courts have quoted approvingly the precise language of section 90 of the first restatement, thus incorporating it into its own case law and giving it the quality of primary authority.[7]

Unless a secondary authority has been thus incorporated into primary authority, you should use it only as a starting point in your analysis. You may use secondary authorities to help you locate and understand primary authority or to help develop an argument not fully addressed or supported by primary authority. However, you should not base your legal analysis or argument on a secondary authority when supporting primary authority is available.

---

7. See e.g., Corbit v. J. I. Case Co., 70 Wash. 2d 522, 538-539, 424 P.2d 290, 300-301 (1967) (en banc) (quoting § 90 as a "useful guideline").

2. Jurisdiction in Which Authority Controls

Some federal constitutional, statutory, and special common laws apply broadly to all jurisdictions. For example, the thirteenth amendment to the United States Constitution abolishes the institution of slavery, whether practiced by a government or private entity, within the United States.

In contrast, the constitutional, statutory, and common laws of a state apply only within that state. For example, the Civil Code of California and the case law of the California courts interpreting that code do not have any binding effect on the law of torts or contracts in New York. Similarly, the courts of one state are free to develop the common law of that state independently of the judicial development of common law in other states.

Even though the laws of one state do not directly apply to activities in another state, in some circumstances those laws may have at least persuasive influence in the other state. For example, in developing the Arizona common law tort of wrongful discharge of an employee, the Arizona Supreme Court has drawn guidance from the emerging common law of California and of other states.[8]

Indeed, even case law from one state interpreting a statute of that state could have persuasive effect on the application of a statute of a different state, if the statutes in both states have similar or identical language and purposes. For example, the New York and New Hampshire legislatures have adopted identical versions of Uniform Commercial Code § 2-302, which authorizes a court to deny enforcement of a contract provision that is "unconscionable."[9] A New York trial court interpreting section 2-302 of New York's commercial code drew support from, though was not bound by, a decision of the New Hampshire Supreme Court interpreting the identical language in section 2-302 of New Hampshire's commercial code.[10]

3. Strength of Case Law as Precedent

The binding or persuasive force of case law will depend on its strength as precedent under the doctrine of stare decisis. Section 2 above has already examined one aspect of this relationship: the relationship of the authority to the forum jurisdiction. The strength of case law as precedent also depends on

(1) the relative levels of the court that created the precedent and the one applying it; and

(2) the degree to which the precedent is directly applicable, rather than merely analogous, to the current dispute.

---

8. Wagenseller v. Scottsdale Memorial Hosp., 147 Ariz. 370, 375-376, 710 P.2d 1025, 1030-1031 (1985).

9. N.H. Rev. Stat. Ann. § 382-A: 2-302 (1961); N.Y. [U.C.C.] Law § 2-302 (McKinney 1964).

10. Jones v. Star Credit Corp., 59 Misc. 2d 189, 298 N.Y.S.2d 264 (1969) (citing to American Home Improvement, Inc. v. MacIver, 105 N.H. 435, 201 A.2d 886 (1964) for the proposition that § 2-302 applies to "price unconscionability").

a. Level of Court

A trial court or intermediate court of appeals is bound by squarely applicable precedent of a higher court within its court system. Moreover, although a court can overrule its own precedent, it will do so only in exceptional circumstances warranting departure from the doctrine of stare decisis. On the other hand, it need not defer at all to the decisions of a lower court within the same state; at most, those decisions would have persuasive effect.

Thus, whenever possible, you obviously should support your analyses or arguments with case law from an appellate court in your jurisdiction that is higher than the court in which your dispute is currently being adjudicated. The basis for a helpful illustration is provided by the chart of the courts on page 34 and the discussion of the United States Courts of Appeals for the Ninth Circuit on pages 34-35. When writing a brief to that Court of Appeals, you should try to support your argument with United States Supreme Court precedent, which is binding on the Court of Appeals. If no Supreme Court authority applies, you can strongly support your argument with a previous decision of the Ninth Circuit Court of Appeals itself. Although a special 11-member panel of the Court can overrule such precedent, it will do so only in unusual circumstances. If no higher authority is available, you can derive some support for your argument from a published decision of the United States District Court for the Northern District of California, a federal trial court. However, because decisions of the District Court have only persuasive value in the Court of Appeals, you will then assume the burden of persuading the Court of Appeals that the District Court's decision represents the best legal approach, the approach that the Court of Appeals should adopt as its own.

b. Controlling, Analogous, and Distinguishable Authority

The strength of case law as binding or persuasive authority also depends on the degree to which it squarely applies to the current dispute. Even precedent of a higher court within the jurisdiction will not control the outcome of the dispute if it is distinguishable; the more significant the distinctions, the less nearly analogous is the precedent, thus decreasing the likelihood that the precedent will influence the outcome. Similarly, the persuasiveness of nonbinding authority from lower courts within the jurisdiction or from courts of other jurisdictions will depend in part on the degree of similarity between the precedent and the current dispute.

When evaluating the legally significant similarities or distinctions between precedent and the current dispute, you should resist the temptation to overemphasize superficial factual similarities that appear in legally distinct contexts. Consider, for example, a current dispute in which the plaintiff's new television set spontaneously generated an electrical fire, causing major damage to the plaintiff's home. In this dispute, the parties may raise the issue of whether the retailer is liable to the plaintiff on a claim of breach of the warranty of merchantability implied in the sales contract under the state's version of the Uniform Commercial Code (UCC).[11] Suppose further that an appellate opinion

---

11. The UCC's warranty of merchantability implies a promise on the part of a merchant that goods are generally nondefective. U.C.C. § 2-314.

in the state, decided in 1957, decides only that the plaintiff in that action, a consumer, failed to file his complaint within the time prescribed by the state's statute of limitations, thus barring his action for negligent manufacture of a television set that spontaneously burst into flames, setting fire to the plaintiff's home.

At first glance, the prior decision might appear significant because of the factual similarities of the events giving rise to the actions. In fact, however, the prior decision may be completely inapplicable. It does not interpret the UCC's warranty of merchantability in a contract for a sale of goods because it addresses a legally distinct cause of action in tort; indeed, the prior decision was issued before state enactment of the UCC and before the widespread adoption of more contemporary tort doctrines of products liability. Most important, the prior decision discusses only the bar of the statute of limitations; it does not directly address the elements of any claim for relief other than timely filing. More helpful to the current dispute would be analogous precedent that addresses the scope of the warranty of merchantability, even if in the context of different goods causing different kinds of accidents and injuries.

4. Summary

Only primary authority within the forum jurisdiction is potentially binding. Primary authority from other jurisdictions and secondary authority are persuasive only.

If the primary authority is case law within the forum jurisdiction, its strength as precedent will depend partly on the relative levels of the court that created the precedent and the court that will apply it. It will depend also on how closely analogous the precedent is to the current dispute.

════ E X E R C I S E   3 - 2 ════

The Hazardous Materials Transportation Act (HMTA) of State X makes it a criminal offense to transport certain hazardous materials, such as toxic chemicals, except with statutorily specified safeguards. For example, the statute requires a transporter of regulated materials to first confine the materials in steel drums and then secure the drums within a cargo bay that is enclosed on all sides with material of specified strength. Leek Chemical Co. violated the HMTA by transporting highly toxic chemicals in steel drums secured to an open flatbed truck. The truck overturned on a slick highway, causing several of the barrels to roll across lanes of oncoming traffic. An automobile driven by Daniel Stein collided with one of the barrels, bursting the barrel and spreading the toxic chemical onto and into Stein's automobile. Stein was not seriously injured by the initial impact with the barrel; however, he was permanently injured by contact with the toxic chemical.

Stein sues Leek Chemical Co. in tort for damages. In State X, Leek Chemical Co. will be liable for negligence if it engaged in a negligent act or omission through breach of a duty of care owed to Stein, causing Stein to suffer injury. Stein hopes to establish the element of negligent act through the doctrine of negligence per se, which other states recognize but which the Supreme Court of State *X* has never squarely adopted. Under the strongest version of the doctrine of negligence per se, proof of Leek Chemical Co.'s violation of the HMTA, a safety statute, would conclusively establish the element of negligent act.

To help her evaluate proposed jury instructions at the close of the trial in Stein's lawsuit, the trial judge requests briefing and oral argument on the question of whether State *X* recognizes the doctrine of negligence per se. Stein has the following authority at his disposal:

1. abundant case law from other states recognizing the doctrine of negligence per se in a variety of contexts;

2. an opinion from the highest appellate court of neighboring State *Υ* approving application of the doctrine of negligence per se to a violation of a similar hazardous materials transportation statute in State *Υ;*

3. an opinion of the State *X* intermediate court of appeals holding that evidence of violation of the State *X* speed limit laws, proximately causing injury, supported a jury verdict of negligence, even in the absence of any other evidence of lack of due care;

4. an opinion of the Supreme Court of State *X* holding that a transporter of regulated hazardous materials may be criminally liable under the HMTA for violations of that act, even if the illegal transportation does not result in any accident or injury.

Discuss the relative strength of these authorities to Stein's position. How should Stein's attorney use each authority, if at all?

B. ANALYSIS OF LEGAL STANDARDS

In some legal disputes, formulation of the applicable legal rules is a simple task: the applicable laws are easily identified, and their general content is clear, at least in the abstract. For example, a dispute over the jury's authority to grant punitive damages in a tort action may be governed by clearly defined rules in the forum state's case law. If so, you could summarize those rules directly and concisely in an office memorandum:

> In this state, a jury may award punitive damages against a person who has committed a tort with either (1) intent to cause injury or (2) reckless disregard for the risk of harm to others. Unless exceptional circumstances justify the risky conduct, a person acts recklessly if he consciously engages in conduct that he knows or should know poses a great risk of harm to others. *Ray v. Bradbury* . . .

In such a dispute, once the facts are found, any significant uncertainty about the outcome of the dispute typically derives from the mixed question of fact and law whether the particular facts of the case satisfy the legal rule. Although analysis of such a mixed question necessarily involves refinement of the content of the legal rule, it also requires careful evaluation of the facts. Thus, assuming that *Ray v. Bradbury* reflects current policy in the jurisdiction, the tortfeasor will not likely dispute the abstract rule governing the availability of punitive damages. More substantially in issue is a mixed question of fact and law: do the facts of the case reflect recklessness or an intent to injure and thus satisfy the legal rule?

In other disputes, however, the parties may raise substantial issues about the fundamental content of applicable legal rules, such as the issue of whether the word "sex" in Title VII refers narrowly to gender or more broadly to any activity related to sexual relations. Compared to the dispute described in the preceding paragraph, resolution of this question requires less comprehensive fact analysis and more thorough analysis of the content of the rule at a fairly general level. An even more extreme example is provided by the question of whether a court should change the course of the common law by adopting a new theory of tort liability for wrongful discharge of an employee. Although such a question would arise in the context of the facts of a particular dispute, the question of whether to adopt a new common law theory of liability would be analyzed as a nearly pure question of law.

If an issue in a brief, office memorandum, or answer to a law school essay examination raises a question about the fundamental content of a legal rule at a general level, you should analyze the legal rule thoroughly before engaging in substantial fact analysis. The discussion of common law and statutory law in Chapter 1 provides a foundation for the development of techniques of legal analysis. Three techniques are particularly important: (1) recognition of the hierarchical nature of authority, (2) consideration of policy concerns, and (3) synthesis of incremental authority.

1. Hierarchy of Authority

Constitutional law, statutory law, and common law form a hierarchy in descending order of priority: assuming that the applicable state or federal constitution authorizes the exercise of state or federal power, a legislature can overrule or modify the common law by enacting statutory law. Accordingly, rather than assume that an issue is governed by common law, you should first consider the possible applicability of constitutional or statutory law.

If a statute applies, you should begin your research and analysis with the relevant language of the statute, even though it may be insufficiently narrow to clearly resolve the issue by itself. Only after you have studied the letter of the statute and its context within an act or a code system can you fully appreciate interpretive case law on the matter. The following passage from an office memorandum illustrates the hierarchy of authority and the focus on statutory language.

The Arizona Constitution grants municipalities the right to engage in industrial activities:

The State of Arizona and each municipal corporation within the State of Arizona shall have the right to engage in industrial pursuits.	**Constitution**

Ariz. Const. art. 2, § 24. The Arizona Public Utilities statute more specifically grants municipal corporations the power to acquire water utility corporations "within or without its corporate limits":

Statute

[Municipal corporations may] engage in any business or enterprise which may be engaged in by persons by virtue of a franchise from the municipal corporation, and may construct, purchase, acquire, own and maintain within or without its corporate limits any such business or enterprise.

Ariz. Rev. Stat. § 9-511.

The statutory reference to corporate limits appears without qualification to permit a municipal corporation to acquire utilities that provide service outside the municipality's corporate limits. Arizona case law, however, hints at a narrower interpretation that recognizes two limitations on the acquisition power.

Interpretive case law

First, it is unclear whether a city may acquire a water company's property outside the city corporate limits unless the city has shown that it genuinely and reasonably anticipates future growth into that area. See *Sende Vista Water Co. v. City of Phoenix,* 127 Ariz. 42, 617 P.2d 1158 (App. 1980). In *Sende,* . . .

In theory, the principle of analyzing statutory language before turning to interpretive case law also applies to constitutional provisions, as illustrated in the example above. As a practical matter, however, some constitutional provisions are so general that their actual language may provide quite limited guidance, and interpretive case law takes on special significance. For example, the reference to "equal protection" in the fourteenth amendment to the United States Constitution is purposefully vague; its generality invites the courts to shape its contours in a way that best satisfies its underlying policies. The mass of case law interpreting the Equal Protection Clause has embellished this simple clause with rich detail. Accordingly, when researching and analyzing an equal protection problem, you should not begin with a grammatical analysis of the words "equal protection." Instead, after identifying the fourteenth amendment as the source of the clause, you could appropriately turn immediately to interpretive case law.

Conversely, the eleventh amendment to the Constitution is actually too specific to provide a good starting point for analysis. The actual language of the eleventh amendment appears to bar federal suits against a state, but only if brought by a noncitizen of that state:

> The Judicial power of the United States shall not be construed to extend to any suit in law or equity, commenced or prosecuted against one of the United States by Citizens of another State, or by Citizens or Subjects of any Foreign State.

Many scholars and court decisions, however, interpret this amendment to simply express part of a more general common law principle of sovereign immunity that applies with equal force to a suit against a state brought by a citizen.[12]

---

12. See, e.g., Hans v. Louisiana, 134 U.S. 1 (1980); T. Eisenberg, Civil Rights Legislation, Cases and Materials 224 (1981).

Thus, your analysis of state sovereign immunity in federal courts should not dwell too long on the language of the eleventh amendment, but should turn quickly to interpretive case law.[13]

2. Policy Analysis

Almost by definition, policy analysis lies at the heart of most lawmaking. A legislature pronounces public policy when it enacts public legislation within the framework of applicable constitutions. Any such enactment represents elected officials' choice among alternative means to address the socioeconomic needs of the jurisdiction. Not surprisingly, the search for legislative intent typically does not end with a conclusive grammatical analysis of language or with a reference to specific and definitive legislative history. Instead, statutory interpretation most often takes the form of a multifaceted analysis reconciling the statutory language, legislative history, and general rules of construction with the apparent policies or purposes on which the legislation is based. Constitutions are less specific than most statutes and are not so easily amended; consequently, analysis of policy and general purpose often is even more important in constitutional interpretation.

Similarly, because common law rules are largely a reflection of judicial recognition of community needs, habits, or customs, they constitute the judiciary's pronouncement of public policy within the framework of constitutional and statutory law. Any question about further development of the common law, such as adoption of a new theory of common law liability or elimination of a common law basis for damages, necessarily raises policy questions about the effect that the new rule will have on the community and about the relationship of the new rule to legislative policies.

The arguments and conclusions that you develop in response to a policy question depend in part on the values that you apply to the problem. A policy argument may be based on moral, economic, political, institutional, or other social values.[14] When developing or evaluating a legal argument, you should identify the values underlying the legislative purpose and judicial policy of applicable authorities, and you should determine which policy arguments would best advance your client's position.[15]

═══════ E X E R C I S E   3 - 3 ═══════

1. Surrogate Motherhood and Baby Selling

State *X* has a criminal "baby selling" statute making it a felony to "to relinquish custody of one's child to another for payment, or to pay or offer to

---

13. One author has warned:

> Although the eleventh amendment provides something to read when contemplating a state's immunity from suit in federal court . . . , it is a trap for those who dig no further.

T. Eisenberg, supra note 12, at 221 (1981).

14. P. Atiyah & R. Summers, Form and Substance in Anglo-American Law 5 (1987) (defining "substantive reasons" for legal decisions); see also R. Summers, Two Types of Substantive Reasons: the Core of a Theory of Common-Law Justification, 63 Cornell L. Rev. (1978).

15. See generally J. M. Balkin, The Crystalline Structure of Legal Thought, 39 Rutgers L. Rev. 1 (1986).

pay another to relinquish custody of the other's child." What is the likely policy behind this statute, and what kind of conduct should be its primary concern? In light of your understanding of the statutory policy, should a court interpret the statute to prohibit a surrogate mother from charging a fee for carrying the fertilized ovum of another couple to full term and surrendering custody of the child to the couple after birth? Does the analysis change if the one charging the fee agrees to artificial insemination of her own ovum, thus making her the biological mother? Should the state enact new legislation more specifically addressing surrogate mother contracts?

2. Job Security

State X has long recognized the common law "at will" rule, which permits an employer to discharge an employee for any reason, or for no reason at all, so long as the employment contract does not provide the employee with job security. Unionized employees in State X have used the collective bargaining process to negotiate labor agreements that include a promise by the employer not to fire any employee except for "just cause." Almost all nonunion employees, however, lack the bargaining power to negotiate such agreements; their employment contracts are terminable at the will of either party and therefore do not restrict the employer's discretion to discharge employees. Most employers' discretion to discharge is limited by labor and nondiscrimination statutes, but those laws prohibit a fairly narrow range of conduct.

What are the policy implications of a new law that would further restrict the right of an employer to discharge employees, even in the absence of a contractual provision for job security? Assume that two laws are under consideration: one would prohibit an employer from discharging any employee except for "good cause"; the other would prohibit an employer more narrowly from discharging an employee for a reason that contravenes an important public policy reflected in existing legislation or case law. Does either proposed law express a desirable public policy? Should a court adopt one of these standards as a new theory of common law tort liability? Should such lawmaking be left to the legislature? Which of the laws is the best vindication of public policy? If the first law is adopted, how should "good cause" be defined? If the second law is adopted, how would it expand existing legal rights and duties?

3. Synthesis of Incremental Law

In few research problems is the legal standard set forth in a single, clearly controlling authority. More often, the legal rules that apply to a dispute are the products of a synthesis of multiple authorities. For example, a Reconstruction era civil rights statute imposes liability for racial discrimination in private contractual relations,[16] but its application is tempered by constitutional interests in privacy and free association.[17] Thus, the true reach of the statute is

---

16. 42 U.S.C. § 1981 (as interpreted in Runyon v. McCrary, 427 U.S. 160 (1976)); see also Patterson v. Mclean Credit Union, 109 S. Ct. 2363 (1989).

17. See *Runyon,* supra note 16; cf. Board of Directors of Rotary Int'l v. Rotary Club of Duarte, 481 U.S. 537 (1987) (application of state antidiscrimination statute to Rotary Club did not violate club members' rights to free association).

defined both by the statute and by the first amendment to the federal Constitution.

Synthesis of authority is particularly important in case analysis. Whether it interprets statutory law or develops common law, case law is inherently incremental. Courts express their legal analyses in the context of individual controversies, and an isolated holding in a judicial opinion is often too narrow to support an accurate prediction about how the decision will influence subsequent cases. Instead, a series of cases addressing a topic in a variety of factual contexts will support a generalization about the case law that can be applied more broadly to a wide range of cases.

4. Developing Arguments for Both Sides

With few exceptions, essay examinations and office memorandum assignments call on you to present a balanced discussion of legal issues. Although one party may be identified as your client, your professor or supervising attorney expects you to explore the weaknesses of the client's claims and defenses as well as the strengths.

When writing a brief, you should not take such a balanced approach; instead, you must advocate your client's position and discredit your opponent's arguments. Nonetheless, to maximize your own advocacy, you must anticipate and evaluate the arguments of your opponent. You might express that more balanced analysis in an office memorandum, or you might simply contemplate it as you outline the arguments for your brief.

Thus, to analyze a legal dispute effectively, you must develop arguments for both sides of the dispute. In synthesizing case law, you should consider alternative formulations of the general principles that emerge from individual holdings. Similarly, in analyzing statutory language, you should consider intrinsic and extrinsic aids that support alternative interpretations.

For example, the common law of negligence imposes tort liability on a person who proximately causes injury to another by breaching a duty of care owed to the injured person. As a specific application of this tort law, physicians in most circumstances are liable for injuries caused by their failure to exercise reasonable skill and care in their practices. The courts of State X have also developed a common law doctrine of strict liability for injuries resulting from ultrahazardous activities, but they have refused to apply this doctrine even to experimental medical practices. Against this background of common law, State X might enact a statute that makes any "commercial enterprise strictly liable" for injuries caused by its use "of any toxic material."

Now suppose that a medical patient in this state died from a reaction to general anesthesia triggered by the patient's rare disorder of the nervous system. Much of the legal dispute in a malpractice action brought by the patient's estate might center around the applicability of the statute. Assuming that anesthesiology is "a commercial enterprise," if the anesthetic is "a toxic material" within the meaning of the statute, the anesthesiologist or her employer would be statutorily liable without regard to the care that she exercised. In contrast, a companion claim based on common law negligence would require an inquiry into the duty of care that the anesthesiologist owed and the degree of care she actually exercised.

In preparing for advocacy, counsel for either side of this dispute would want to evaluate arguments for both sides on the question of the applicability of the statute. For example, without going beyond the face of the statute, counsel for the estate could argue that the statutory requirement of "toxic materials" is satisfied in this case because the ordinary meaning of "toxic" is "poisonous," and the anesthetic acted like a poison on the nervous system of the patient. Counsel for the estate would also want to anticipate a strong counterargument: it is doubtful that the legislature intended to inhibit physicians' use of substances that produce medically beneficial results in almost all cases in which they are administered; rather, the statutory term "toxic materials" is likely intended to apply only to materials that are generally harmful to all persons, such as potent acids or pesticides. After formulating and evaluating the anesthesiologist's probable counterargument, counsel for the estate should try to present the estate's argument in a way that will reduce the counterargument's impact.

V. FACT ANALYSIS—APPLICATION OF LAW TO FACTS

A. BASIC PATTERNS

At trial, the critical issues often are questions of purely historical fact, such as the question whether the party with the burden of persuasion has proved that an employer exclaimed "women can't perform this job" when he rejected a woman's application for employment. As explored in later chapters, appellate courts will defer to some degree to the factual findings of a jury or trial judge; therefore, issues on appeal inevitably contain a more substantial element of law. However, even nearly pure questions of law are developed in the context of particular disputes and with an appreciation for the probable facts of future disputes. More important, most disputes present nontrivial questions about whether the facts satisfy the applicable legal standards, such as whether certain acts of preparation leading up to a murder satisfy the "premeditation" requirement of a first-degree murder statute.

A pattern should emerge from your treatment of facts in an office memorandum or brief. First, you will state all the important facts of the dispute at or near the beginning of the document. Second, you will separately analyze groups of facts as the minor premises of deductive arguments in the discussion section of a memorandum or the argument section of a brief. In that section, after discussing the legal rule applicable to a particular issue, you will discuss or argue whether the relevant facts satisfy the legal rule. You and your professor will follow a similar pattern in an essay examination: your professor will state all the facts in the essay question, and you will analyze groups of facts as the minor premises of deductive arguments in your examination answer.

If your assignment does not call for great depth of analysis, you might directly explain why particular facts support or undermine the application of a legal rule. Suppose, for example, that you are writing an office memorandum analyzing the claims of a client seeking punitive damages, as introduced in previous examples in this chapter. After stating the legal rule that a malicious or reckless tortfeasor may be liable for punitive damages, you could identify the facts relevant to this issue and explain how each supports or defeats application of the legal rule:

> We have no evidence that Con Motor Co. maliciously intended to cause injury when it designed the Firebird sports car. In fact, our notes of the May meeting of the board of directors shows that the board members genuinely hoped that the risky design would not cause accidents.
>
> **Facts showing no intent**
>
> However, we do have evidence of recklessness. Con's Chief Engineer informed the board of directors of her opinion that placement of the gas tank near the rear exterior of the car would create a risk of deadly explosion in even minor rear-end collisions. Yet, the directors approved that design solely because it would save production costs of $100/car. In so doing, Con's directors knowingly created a great risk of death or terrible injury to consumers without any socially significant justification.
>
> **Facts showing recklessness**

B. DEVELOPING ARGUMENTS FOR BOTH SIDES

As with your analysis of more abstract legal rules, your fact analysis in an essay examination answer or in an office memorandum ought to explore arguments for both sides of the dispute. Similarly, when writing a brief, you should consider your opponent's factual arguments as you develop your own. In the typical dispute, some facts will support application of the legal rule and others will suggest that the legal rule is not satisfied. Still other facts may be used in different ways to support both positions. By balancing and weighing the facts, you can reach at least a qualified conclusion about whether the legal rule is satisfied.

This can be illustrated by extending one of the examples in the previous section on analysis of legal rules. If the parties dispute an anesthesiologist's liability on a claim of common law negligence, an office memorandum might call for analysis of the following facts:

1. The anesthesiologist informed a patient scheduled for heart surgery of the advantages and risks associated with the three most appropriate anesthetics. On the basis of relative costs, the patient rejected the safest anesthetic in favor of a generally safe and more widely used anesthetic.

2. The anesthesiologist administered general anesthesia without assistance, before the surgical team had arrived and while the circulating nurse was occupied with another patient.

3. While administering general anesthesia, the anesthesiologist concentrated intensely on gauges on her equipment that measured the patient's intake of the anesthetic.

4. The anesthesiologist did not maintain visual contact with the patient or with equipment monitoring the patient's vital signs; as a consequence, she failed to terminate the intake of anesthetic until ten seconds after the first visible signs of an adverse reaction.

5. The patient suffered from a rare disorder of the nervous system that produced the fatal reaction to the anesthetic.

6. The patient died within a minute of the administration of general anesthesia.

The facts in the first paragraph suggest that the anesthesiologist followed a reasonable procedure in prescribing the anesthetic. Indeed, the facts in paragraph 5 suggest that the patient's unusual disorder, rather than the anesthesiologist's conduct, precipitated the fatal reaction. Moreover, the facts in paragraph 3 support an argument that the anesthesiologist used at least reasonable care in administering the anesthetic, because she concentrated intensely on an obviously important function.

In addition to providing some support for a finding of reasonable care, however, the facts of paragraph 5 emphasize the need for special care in administering the anesthetic. Moreover, the facts of paragraph 2 support an argument that the anesthesiologist breached a duty of care in administering the anesthetic without assistance. Although the facts of paragraph 3 reflect the anesthesiologist's genuine concern about the patient's potential sensitivity to anesthesia, they also raise a question about the appropriate focus of the anesthesiologist's attention. Finally, the facts of paragraph 4 support an argument that the anesthesiologist acted carelessly in focusing her attention so narrowly on the intake gauge.

To complete your deductive reasoning in an office memorandum, you must discuss whether the facts establish a breach of the applicable duty of care, thus satisfying the legal rule that defines an element of the cause of action. Because the facts in this case support opposing arguments, different legal analysts might reasonably reach different conclusions, depending on the significance the analysts assign to particular facts. Of course, an advocate writing a brief would emphasize the facts supporting her argument and would develop her argument in a way that lessened the impact of anticipated counterarguments.

VI. REACHING CONCLUSIONS

The final element of deductive reasoning is a conclusion derived from the law of your major premise and the facts of your minor premise. When writing a brief, you obviously must state a firm conclusion for each argument that you present. Your conclusions represent the critical points that the court must accept before granting your client the relief that he seeks.

You may hesitate to state conclusions in the more nearly neutral analysis of an office memorandum or essay examination answer, particularly if the dispute presents close questions. Nonetheless, most supervising attorneys and professors will want you to take a position and to reveal your best judgment about the probable outcome of each issue. If necessary, you may hedge your conclusions with qualifiers such as "probably," but you should remember to complete your deductive reasoning by stating a conclusion for each issue:

On these facts, a jury likely will find that Con Motor Co. acted recklessly, permitting the jury to award punitive damages. ‖

In some cases, you may find it appropriate to make your conclusion contingent on your ability to establish critical facts or law:

Assuming that we can prove that most hospitals require a team of at ‖ least two personnel to administer anesthesia, a jury will almost certainly find ‖ that Humana Hospital was negligent in this case. ‖

VII. SUMMARY

To analyze a legal problem, you should
(1) identify the **issue;**
(2) state the legal **rule** or rules that will help you resolve the issue;
(3) **apply** the rule to the relevant **facts;** and
(4) reach a **conclusion** on the question of whether the facts satisfy the legal rule.
A single dispute between two parties may present several issues. To achieve an appropriate scope of analysis, you should exercise judgment to determine which issues and subissues are sufficiently significant and material to warrant discussion and which are sufficiently tangential to warrant exclusion or summary treatment.
Whenever the law or fact analysis is in doubt, you must evaluate arguments for both sides of the dispute. To evaluate arguments about the applicable legal rules, you should consider
(1) the hierarchy of primary authority,
(2) synthesis of authorities,
(3) policy analysis, and
(4) the relative strength of different kinds of case law as precedent.
Always state a conclusion for each issue, even in the analysis in an office memorandum or examination answer.

══════ E X E R C I S E   3 - 4 ══════

Cheryl Watkins, an expert pilot, retained Flight Ready, a private aircraft service, to maintain her single-engine private plane based at Palm City International Airport in Calzona. While flying from Palm City to a nearby town on a business trip, Watkins noticed that the passenger door of the cabin had sprung partially open. She knew that the partially open door would destabilize the aircraft under certain conditions and that flying for more than a few minutes with the door open would be hazardous. She rejected the idea of making an emergency landing on the busy highway below or on the desert dotted with massive saguaro cacti. Instead, Watkins leaned across the passenger's seat to close the passenger door. At that moment, the plane abruptly rolled to the right and spiraled into a sharp dive. Watkins was not in position to take control of the aircraft, and it crashed into the desert seconds later, killing Watkins instantly. A tape recorder found in the wreckage had recorded Watkins's comments during the emergency, allowing investigators to reconstruct the events.

In a wrongful death action brought by Watkins' survivors in Calzona, the jury answered several specific questions, called "special interrogatories," submitted to it by the court. Specifically, the jury found that personnel for Flight Ready had negligently repaired a latch on the passenger door of Watkins' aircraft, which had previously stuck in the closed position. The negligent repair caused it to spring open during the flight. The jury also found that the partially open door had destabilized the aircraft, causing it to roll and dive when Watkins shifted her position in the aircraft. Finally, the jury found that, had Watkins remained in the pilot's seat, she likely could have maintained control of the plane and survived an emergency landing on the desert. Following an instruction based on the doctrine of "contributory negligence," the jury denied Watkins's survivors any recovery.

Under the traditional common law doctrine of contributory negligence, a victim of a tort is precluded from recovering damages from the tortfeasor if the victim negligently contributed to her own injuries. At the time of trial, Calzona courts still applied the doctrine of contributory negligence as a defense in a tort action brought either by the victim or by her survivors. Accordingly, the trial court had rejected a jury instruction proposed by counsel for the plaintiffs that would have permitted the jury to apply one form of the doctrine of "comparative negligence." Under the proposed instruction, Watkins's own negligence would not preclude the plaintiffs from all recovery; instead, their recovery would simply be diminished in proportion to which Watkins's own negligence contributed to her death.

On appeal from the judgment denying recovery, Watkins' survivors want to (1) challenge the sufficiency of the evidence supporting the jury's finding of contributory negligence, and (2) argue that the Calzona Supreme Court ought to abandon the doctrine of contributory negligence and adopt a comparative negligence standard. Discuss the following issues, taking care to develop arguments for both sides of each issue:

1. *Formulation of Legal Rule*

Should Calzona reject the contributory negligence standard in favor of the comparative negligence standard proposed by the plaintiffs' counsel? What policy considerations support each standard? How important is stare decisis?

2. *Application of Law to Facts*

If the Calzona Supreme Court adopts a comparative negligence standard, how will that standard likely apply to the facts on remand?

3. *Review of Jury's Findings*

If the Calzona Supreme Court retains the contributory negligence standard, will it approve the jury's finding that Watkins was contributorily negligent? Should the Supreme Court evaluate the evidence as if it were in the position of the jury, or should it defer to the jury's weighing of the evidence to some extent?

CHAPTER

4

Introduction to Writing Style

I. GENERAL APPROACH

The two most important characteristics of good legal writing style are clarity and conciseness. The importance of clarity in legal writing should be obvious: your legal memorandum will not enlighten, nor will your brief persuade, unless the reader of each can understand it. To appreciate the significance of conciseness, you need only consider the time pressures that a supervising attorney or a judge faces; neither has time to glean from 20 pages ideas that you could have clearly expressed in ten.[1]

The dual goals of clarity and conciseness are often compatible: making a draft more concise by omitting surplus words and by creating a more efficient organization likely will enhance clarity as well. At the margin, however, further conciseness may come only at the expense of clarity; in those circumstances, you must give priority to clarity.

II. THE PERSPECTIVE OF THE LEGAL WRITER

Law students often complain that the emphasis on clarity and conciseness in legal writing courses compels them to abandon the literary eloquence that

---

1. See, e.g., Reliance Ins. Corp. v. Sweeney Corp., Maryland, 792 F.2d 1137, 1139 (D.C. Cir. 1986) ("this court encourages short, tightly argued briefs in all cases, regardless of their complexity"); Morgan v. South Bend Community School Corp., 797 F.2d 471, 480 (7th Cir. 1986) ("A [page] limitation induces the advocate to write tight prose, which helps his client's cause."); Westinghouse Elec. Corp. v. National Labor Relations Board, 809 F.2d 419, 424-425 (7th Cir. 1987) (imposing $1,000 penalty on counsel for evading federal rule limiting the number of pages of its opening brief).

they strove so hard to develop in college and to replace it with a dry, uniform style. They may overstate their complaint; effective legal writing reflects application of principles of good writing generally. Nonetheless, as an inevitable consequence of the substance and purpose of legal documents, the substance and style of legal writing does indeed differ from other kinds of writing.

For example, consider how different writers might treat the subject of a male employer's sexual harassment of a female subordinate. A poet might try to create an image of the pain and frustration of the victim of the harassment, so vivid an image that readers who had never experienced sexual harassment could appreciate the victim's plight.[2] A writer for a political journal might describe the specific incident as a symptom of more general oppression within a sexist society. A novelist might describe the harassment in particularly dramatic prose, perhaps as a vehicle of character development or perhaps purely to engage or shock the reader.

On the other hand, an associate for the firm representing the victim of the harassment is understandably preoccupied with the legal significance of the employer's actions. In preparing an office memorandum, the associate will analyze whether the harassment constituted "extreme and outrageous conduct," thus satisfying an element of a claim under the tort of intentional infliction of emotional distress. The extent of the injury suffered by the victim will interest the associate mainly as an indication of the damages that the victim can recover. Moreover, the associate may discuss events or circumstances that other writers would ignore completely. For example, the associate may note that the employer employs only 12 employees and therefore is not a covered "employer" for purposes of Title VII of the Civil Rights Act of 1964.[3]

The different perspectives of these writers necessarily influence their writing styles. The poet's meaning may be obscured in the interest of "avoiding dull exposition" and of gaining dramatic effect through rhythm and metaphor.[4] Similarly, the novelist may seek to entertain or stimulate the reader by resorting to elegant variation or other deliberate ambiguity.[5] But the legal writer can seldom afford to entertain at the expense of communicating clearly. On occasion, legal writers may have legitimate reasons for ambiguity, but deliberate ambiguity should be the exception, not the rule. A supervising attorney is not interested in dwelling on each sentence of an office memorandum to divine its meaning as he might dwell on each line of a poem. Similarly, a judge will not likely be persuaded by a brief that she doesn't fully comprehend, even though it entertains her.

This does not mean that lawyers must always write from a legal perspective. If you desire to retain or develop literary eloquence, you may write poetry by night and easily adapt your writing style to the requirements of the law office by day. Nor does it mean that legal writing must be dull and dry. Clear, concrete, concise writing can and should be active, vivid, and engaging. Indeed,

---

2. Cf. E. Schneider, Poems and Poetry 3 (1964) (discussing the difficulty of transferring an "experience whole and alive into the mind, emotions, and sensations of another person").

3. See 42 U.S.C. § 2000e(b).

4. See E. Schneider, supra note 2, at 25-26.

5. See W. Strunk, Jr., & E. White, The Elements of Style 79 (3d ed. 1979) ("There are occasions when obscurity serves a literary yearning, if not a literary purpose . . .").

the persuasive effect of a brief may be enhanced with a telling metaphor or an unusually dramatic phrase.

Moreover, the legal perspective does not doom legal writers to absolute uniformity of style. The goals of clear communication or persuasion leave room for individuality. Indeed, you should approach rules of writing style in much the same way that you approach legal rules: you should extend the application of the rules no further than necessary to serve the policies that support the rules. Even seemingly inflexible conventions of punctuation or sentence structure may simply reflect a desire for clarity or proper emphasis, leaving room for writers' discretion in how best to achieve those objectives.

For example, many writers believe that they may never start a sentence with "however," because teachers or editors told them of a rule against such placement. But it is difficult to justify an inflexible rule to that effect; instead, the placement of transitional words such as "however" likely is influenced by considerations of emphasis and flow in the sentence. Those considerations often call for placement of "however" at a natural breaking point in mid-sentence, because it subordinates "however" as a parenthetic transition guide, and it permits more substantive parts of the sentence to enjoy the prominence of the position at the beginning of the sentence:

> The statute of frauds does not apply, however, because Vasquez could have performed the contract within one year.

However, if you wish to draw immediate attention to the change of direction signaled by the transition word or phrase, placement at the beginning of the sentence, as in this one, is perfectly appropriate.

Many other rules of composition are nothing more than conventions that reflect generalities about the best way to achieve clear, concise writing with effective emphasis and flow. Even the traditional rule against splitting infinitives appears to have given way to a more flexible discretionary approach: "Some infinitives seem to improve on being split, just as a stick of round stovewood does."[6] You will do well to familiarize yourself with rules of composition, including the recommendations summarized in Chapter 10, as general guides to achieving the objectives of clarity and conciseness rather than as ends in themselves.

III. AUDIENCE AND PURPOSE

In every legal document, you should adapt your writing style to achieve the purpose of the document and to suit the needs of your intended audience. Many of the chapters in this book thoroughly examine this feature of writing style in the context of essay examinations, office memoranda, briefs, and letters. An overview here will serve to introduce some fundamental principles.

---

6. Id. at 58, 78.

A. PURPOSE

Many legal documents can be classified as having either of two essential purposes: (1) to communicate a balanced analysis, or (2) to persuade. With few exceptions, essay examination answers, office memoranda, and advice letters to clients fall into the first category. Ordinarily, the purpose of each is to help your reader understand the strengths and the weaknesses of a legal claim or defense. Briefs to a court and demand letters to an opposing party, on the other hand, fall into the second category. The purpose of a brief is to persuade a judge or panel of judges to make a ruling that favors your client. The purpose of a demand letter is to persuade another party to take some practical action, such as pay a debt, drop a claim, or cease some activity that is causing injury to your client.

You should adapt the content and style of the writing in each of your documents to suit these distinct purposes. For example, in an office memorandum and an advice letter, you must communicate to your supervising attorney and to your client the strengths as well as the weaknesses of your client's claims or defenses. Thus, if your client seeks to prove that her employer breached an employment contract by discharging her without good cause, you should candidly reveal to her and to your supervisor that the contract language is ambiguous on that point:

> Each of the five grounds for discharge specifically listed in section IX of the employment contract describes some kind of misconduct or unsatisfactory performance by the employee. However, the prefatory phrase "such as" suggests that the list is not exhaustive, but illustrative. If so, the employer may argue that he retained the right to fire an employee for any reason and that he listed only the most obvious reasons in the contract.
>
> To establish that the contract requires just cause for dismissal, we should . . .

In contrast, in your brief to a court, you will attempt to persuade a judge or panel of judges to interpret the contract language in a way that limits grounds for discharge. Accordingly, you should adopt a writing style that reflects confidence in your client's position:

> Section IX of the contract limits grounds for discharge to employee misconduct or poor performance. Even if the five grounds listed in section IX are illustrative rather than exhaustive, as argued by the defendant, they all illustrate cases in which the employer has good cause for terminating the employment contract. Thus, section IX describes a limited category of grounds for discharge that does not justify the arbitrary discharge in this case. . . .

B. AUDIENCE

Even when you seek to achieve similar purposes with different documents, you may need to adapt your writing style to the needs of each audience. For example, in both an office memorandum and an advice letter, your purpose is to present a balanced analysis of your client's claims and defenses. However, the readers of each document may vary greatly in legal sophistication. The experienced attorney who reads your office memorandum will appreciate your use of fundamental legal terminology and legal authority, as in this excerpt from an analysis of a client's defense in a civil rights action:

> Even if the district court denies Officer Tippett's motion for summary judgment, he can file an interlocutory appeal on the issue of qualified immunity. See *Mitchell v. Forsyth,* 472 U.S. 511, 524-530 (1985).

On the other hand, your client, Police Officer Tippett, presumably has little or no legal training in pretrial and appellate procedure. Accordingly, in an advice letter to Officer Tippett on the same issue, you should explain your analysis in nonlegal terms:

> Even if the trial court denies your request to dismiss the action against you before trial, you need not face a trial immediately. Under federal law, you can immediately appeal the trial court's rejection of your immunity defense. In the meantime, the trial will be delayed while the appellate court determines whether your asserted conduct was indeed sufficiently reasonable to warrant granting you immunity from liability for damages.

In some cases, your task is complicated by the presence of multiple purposes and audiences. You can best explore these matters further in later chapters, in the context of thorough examination of particular documents.

IV. CONCLUSION

This introduction to writing style completes the discussion in Part I of method in legal analysis and writing. This chapter and Chapters 9-11 develop and describe a method of approaching and resolving problems of composition, much as Chapters 1-3 describe a method of approaching legal problems.

Chapters 9-11 thoroughly examine problems of organization and writing style in the context of office memoranda and briefs. You may benefit by glancing at selected topics in those chapters before moving on to Part II of this book. However, because problems in writing style are often closely linked with problems in legal method and analysis, you can profitably delay close examination of Chapters 9-11 until you have studied both Parts I and II.

═══════ E X E R C I S E 4 - 1 ═══════

Examine your previous education and experiences in writing. Consider whether the special characteristics of legal writing will require you to depart from writing styles that you have successfully used in other contexts. Use this self-examination to help prepare you for constructive criticism from your writing instructors.

WRITING IN LAW SCHOOL—FROM CASE BRIEFS TO EXAMINATIONS

5

Case Analysis

I. STUDY OF CASES

When preparing for law school classes or researching an office memorandum, you must engage in case analysis: the study of judicial decisions, mostly appellate, that resolve particular disputes. Although you will encounter case law differently in a law firm than in law school, you ultimately will perform similar analytic functions with it.

In a law firm, your supervising attorney typically will request a memorandum that addresses the rights and liabilities of parties to an actual pending dispute, and you will research and analyze case law with the dispute in mind. The reported judicial decisions that you find in the library are unedited opinions that often address multiple issues, some of which may be irrelevant to the dispute that is the subject of your office memorandum.

In one way, your task at law school is simpler: rather than search for unedited opinions in the library, you will read opinions that are grouped in some logical fashion in a casebook and that are edited to isolate selected issues. Just as you typically will analyze case law in a law firm to determine its applicability to a new dispute, you should analyze case law in law school with a view toward applying newly discovered legal principles to facts other than those presented in the opinions. Professors will routinely test that facility with classroom hypotheticals and essay examinations.

II. PREPARING A CASE BRIEF

A. GENERAL APPROACH AND FORMAT

Both when researching a memorandum problem and when preparing for class, you should prepare "case briefs," written, analytic summaries of appellate opinions. Although you will eventually develop shorthand techniques for taking notes on cases that you find in the library or that are assigned in a casebook, you should prepare formal, thorough case briefs in the first semester to ensure that you develop skills of case analysis.

You should not be troubled if your instructors and textbooks recommend a variety of different formats for case briefs. All the formats include essentially the same information; they vary chiefly in emphasis and organization. Below are outlines of two sample formats. If necessary, you can modify either one of them to suit the particular requirements of a classroom instructor who might ask students to recite parts of a case in a different order.

A	B
1. Identification	1. Identification
2. Issue(s) and Holding(s)	2. Facts
3. Facts	3. Procedural History
4. Procedural History	4. Issue(s) and Holding(s)
5. Reasoning	5. Reasoning
6. Evaluation	6. Evaluation
7. Synthesis	7. Synthesis

Although format B is probably the more conventional of the two, format A has the advantage of forcing you to frame the legal issue before stating the facts, thus ensuring that you state the facts with an appreciation for their legal significance. The issue and holding also provide an effective overview of the case brief.

Whatever format you select, your first step in briefing a case is to read it completely before beginning to write. Statement of some elements of a case brief may require an understanding of other elements, and the organization of an appellate opinion may differ from that of either case brief format outlined above. Indeed, some elements of the case brief may not appear explicitly anywhere in the opinion. Instead, the precise issue and holding of a decision may be only implicit in the court's statement of the facts, legal reasoning, and disposition. Consequently, before beginning to brief a case, you should read the entire opinion as many times as is necessary to understand all the elements of the case.

B. ELEMENTS OF A CASE BRIEF

1. *Identification of the Case*

Your case brief should begin with

(1) the name of the case, which is usually taken from the names of two adversary parties;[1]

(2) the jurisdiction, in the sense of the geographical and political body, within which the court sits;

(3) the level of the deciding court; and

(4) the date of decision.

For example, the following notes identify a 1904 decision of the Supreme Court of the State of Rhode Island:

Davis v. Smith (R.I. S. Ct. 1904)   ‖

You may also wish to jot down

(5) the citation to the reporters in which the full opinion appears in the library, to develop familiarity with citation form, and

(6) the page on which the case appears in the casebook (CB), to facilitate quick cross-reference between notes and casebook:

Davis v. Smith, 26 R.I. 129, 58 A. 630 (S. Ct. 1904), CB 387   ‖

These examples all identify the authoring court in *Davis v. Smith* as the court of last resort in Rhode Island. That information shows that the court is not bound by lower court decisions within Rhode Island or by decisions in other states, although such decisions might provide persuasive authority.

The early date of the *Davis v. Smith* decision, 1904, helps explain the decision's place in Rhode Island law: in light of changes in economic conditions, political and social attitudes, and the legal context in the intervening years, the Rhode Island Supreme Court overruled *Davis v. Smith* in 1967.[2]

The name of a case does not always clearly identify the original parties to the underlying dispute. A named party may be a representative of one of the original disputants or an assignee of its rights and obligations. For example, the dispute in *Hamer v. Sidway*[3] concerned the contract rights and obligations of William E. Story, Sr., and his nephew, William E. Story, 2d. The case name is taken from the parties to the lawsuit: the executor of the senior Story's estate and an assignee of the nephew's contract rights.

---

1. In some *in rem* actions, a named party may be an object, such as money, a plot of land, or a ship. E.g., United States v. $129,374 in U.S. Currency, 769 F.2d 583 (9th Cir. 1985); Winooski Hydroelectric Co. v. Five Acres of Land in East Montpelier and Berlin, Vermont, 769 F.2d 79 (2d Cir. 1985); Giannakos v. M/V Bravo Trader, 762 F.2d 1295 (5th Cir. 1985); see O. Holmes, Jr., The Common Law 28-30 (1923). In other cases, the case name will refer not to adversary parties but to events, relationships, or other subjects of proceedings. E.g., In re Garland Corp., 6 Bankr. 456 (Bankr. D. Mass. 1980) (bankruptcy proceeding); In re: Validation of Marriage of Francisco, 16 Indian L. Rep. 6113 (Navajo S. Ct. 1989) (marriage validation proceeding).

2. Rampone v. Wanskuck Bldgs., Inc., 102 R.I. 30, 227 A.2d 586 (1967).

3. 124 N.Y. 538, 27 N.E. 256 (1891).

Identifying the court may be problematic as well. *Hamer v. Sidway* is a decision of the Court of Appeals of New York, the court of last resort in New York. "Court of Appeals" is a label more commonly associated with an intermediate court of appeals, rather than the court of last resort. To add to the confusion, the decision in *Hamer v. Sidway* indicates that the Court of Appeals reviewed the judgment of the "general term" of the New York "Supreme Court," which had reversed the judgment of the "special term" of the Supreme Court. "Supreme Court" is a name that in most states would signify the court of last resort. In fact, the opening paragraph of its opinion in *Hamer v. Sidway* reveals that different terms of the New York Supreme Court acted as the trial court and the intermediate appellate court.[4] Fortunately, most court systems use the more familiar labels "Court of Appeals" to refer to the intermediate appellate court and "Supreme Court" to refer to the court of last resort.

2. Issue and Holding

a. Issue

An "issue" is a material question of fact or law that arises from the claims, defenses, and arguments of the parties. An issue may be a question of law, such as whether Congress intended the term "sex" in section 703(a) of Title VII of the Civil Rights Act of 1964 to encompass sexual preference as well as gender. Except at the trial level, an issue rarely presents only a question of fact, such as whether the evidence shows that an employer exclaimed "women can't perform this job" when he rejected a woman's application for employment.

Perhaps most commonly, the issue before a trial or appellate court requires a combination of legal and factual analysis in the determination of whether the facts of a dispute satisfy a general legal rule. An example of such a question is whether certain conduct by an employer in fact created a discriminatory work environment, thus satisfying Title VII's rule regarding discrimination in "conditions . . . of employment." By applying the rule to the facts and reaching a conclusion, the court not only resolves the immediate dispute before it, it also refines the rule by adding more concrete substance to its abstract terms.

If you look for a concise statement of the issues in an appellate opinion, you may find only frustration. Courts do not always state the issues in simple terms before resolving them. When a court does formally state the issues, it may not state them with the narrowness and specificity required for development of analytic skills in the first semester. You may find clues to the precise question addressed by the court in the court's description of the trial court decision that it is reviewing, in its summary of the parties' arguments on appeal, in the emphasis it places on particular facts, and in its discussion of the law.

At a minimum, you should state an issue sufficiently narrowly that it identifies a substantive legal question that distinguishes the case from the bulk

---

4. A recent guide identifies the current structure of the New York court system: The trial courts of general jurisdiction are the Supreme Court and the County Court. The intermediate appellate courts are the Appellate Divisions of Supreme Court and the Appellate Terms of Supreme Court. The Court of Appeals is the court of last resort. K. King & J. Springberg, BNA's Directory of State Courts, Judges, and Clerks 216 (2d ed. 1988).

of case law in the casebook. In addition, you should specifically incorporate the facts of the case that are critical to the court's analysis and that therefore help to define the precedential effect of its decision.

For example, consider the following case summary, which is loosely based on the procedural history and appellate disposition of a tort claim in *Wagenseller v. Scottsdale Memorial Hospital*:[5]

> Catherine Wagenseller (the employee) worked for Scottsdale Memorial Hospital (the employer) as a staff nurse under an employment contract of indefinite term. She alleged that her supervisor discharged her partly because she refused to participate in a humorous skit in which the participants "mooned" fellow hospital employees. The trial court found that the parties did not dispute any material facts and that the employer was entitled to summary judgment, which is judgment before trial, because the indefinite term of the employment contract made it terminable at the will of either party. Such a contract is terminable at any time and for any reason, or for no reason at all. The intermediate court of appeals affirmed.
>
> The state supreme court reversed and remanded to the trial court, deciding that an employer is liable in tort to an employee that it discharges for a reason that contravenes a clear mandate of public policy. The state supreme court found such a mandate in a state criminal statute that prohibited certain acts of "indecent exposure." In discussing the sources of public policy, the court compared criminal statutes to other sources, such as common law: "Although we do not limit our recognition of the public policy exception to cases involving a violation of a criminal statute, we do believe that our duty will seldom be clearer than when such a violation is involved."

The following statement of the issue in *Wagenseller* is obviously too general:

Did the trial court correctly grant summary judgment for the defendant? ||

This issue statement describes the trial court's disposition and the stage of the proceedings at which it made the disposition, facts that are within the procedural history of the case. Unfortunately, if your statement of the issue does no more than identify elements of the procedural history, you will not distinguish the case from hundreds of others in first-year casebooks. The procedural facts will certainly help you understand the decision. Moreover, the standards for summary judgment may even be the central issue in a case raising a dispute about rules of civil procedure. However, this case presents substantive questions of tort and perhaps contract law, and the issue statement should identify them.

The following statement of the issue is an improvement, because it identifies a substantive legal dispute:

Is an employer liable in tort for discharging an at-will employee for a reason ||
that violates public policy?

---

5. 147 Ariz. 370, 710 P.2d 1025 (1985).

This statement of the issue identifies (1) a legally significant relationship between the parties (employer/employee), (2) the nature of the claim (tort),
(3) the basis for the claim (public policy), and (4) the obstacle to relief on a
contract claim (the at-will nature of the employment contract).

Though the second statement of the issue is much more informative, it
still leaves room for improvement. Your issue statement will better define the
effect of the decision as precedent if you more specifically refer to the critical
facts of the case.

For example, the court discusses the sources of public policy. That discussion suggests that a subsequent case may raise the question of the legal significance of public policy that is expressed in a judicial opinion analyzing common
law, rather than in a criminal statute. To help determine whether *Wagenseller*
would be controlling on, distinguishable from, or persuasively analogous to
the subsequent dispute, your statement of the issue in *Wagenseller* could incorporate material facts that provide a potential basis for analogy and distinction:

> Is the employer liable in tort for discharging an at-will employee because of
> her refusal to participate in a public "mooning," a discharge that contra-
> vened the public policy against indecent exposure reflected in a criminal
> statute?

This statement of the issue identifies the source of public policy, and it gives
sufficient factual details to permit an assessment of the importance of that
policy.

The point at which the disadvantages of increased complexity begin to
outweigh the benefits of enhanced specificity in the issue statement is a matter
for your judgment and personal style. As discussed in subsection b below, you
can reduce the complexity of the issue statement by transferring some of the
critical information to the statement of the holding.

Finally, although you should incorporate facts into your issue statement,
you should not assume matters that are in dispute and that are thus themselves
issues considered by the court. For example, the previous statement of the issue
assumes that (1) the employment contract was terminable at will, and (2) the
criminal statute reflected a public policy against compelled "mooning" and
therefore against an employer's discharging an at-will employee for refusing to
engage in "mooning." The statement questions only whether state law recognizes a claim in tort for such retaliation against an at-will employee. Suppose
instead that the employee had alleged breach of contract and had disputed that
the employment contract was terminable at will. Suppose further that the employer had disputed that the criminal statute reflected a public policy against
compelled "mooning." In those circumstances, you should add an issue relating
to contract law and should divide the tort issue into two subissues:

> 1. Did the employee establish a genuine factual dispute on the question
> of whether the employer made a binding promise in its personnel manual
> to give the employee job security, thus entitling the employee to a trial on
> her contract claim?

2. Even if the employment contract was terminable at will, is the employer liable to the employee for discharging her for a reason that violates public policy?

     a. Should the court recognize a new exception to the at-will rule by imposing tort liability for such a discharge?

     b. Does a state criminal statute prohibiting public exposure of one's anus or genitalia reflect a public policy against compelled public exposure of bare buttocks?[6]

Issue #1 achieves specificity in procedural facts, as well as historical facts, by identifying the employee's burden on a motion for summary judgment.

b. Holding

The "holding" is simply the court's answer to the question presented in the issue. If you state the issue sufficiently narrowly and specifically to provide a basis for evaluating the effect of the decision as precedent, you may state the holding with a simple "yes" or "no." Of course, if a professor asks you during class discussion for the holding of a case without first asking for the issue, she expects you to offer more than "yes" or "no." In those circumstances, you should transform the issue into a detailed holding in the form of a statement:

The employee was entitled to a trial on her contract claim because she established a genuine factual dispute on the question of whether the employer made a binding promise in its personnel manual to give the employee job security.

Even when coupling the holding to a detailed statement of the issue, you may wish the holding to convey further information than "yes" or "no." For example, if a fully descriptive statement of the issue would be unwieldy, you can move supplementary information to the holding:

Issue: Did the employer discharge the employee for a reason that violates public policy, thus rendering the employer liable in tort for wrongful discharge?

Holding: Yes. By discharging the employee because she refused to participate in public "mooning," the employer violated public policy reflected in a criminal statute prohibiting indecent exposure.

The holding and the issue obviously are simply the opposite sides of the same coin. Therefore, the following examination of the appropriate scope of statements of holding is simply a continuation and refinement of the preceding discussion of narrowness and specificity in issues.

---

6. See id., 147 Ariz. at 380 n.5, 710 P.2d at 1035 n.5 (admitting to "little expertise in the techniques of mooning").

Because narrowly drafted statements of the issue and holding represent an attempt to identify the effect of the decision under stare decisis, from a practical standpoint the precise contours of the issue and holding may not become clear until subsequent decisions interpret and apply them as precedent. Through that process of determining whether the prior decision is controlling, analogous, or distinguishable, subsequent decisions can refine the judicial understanding of the relative importance of various facts and policies to the prior decision and consequently to the resolution of subsequent disputes as well.

For example, in *Monge v. Beebe Rubber Co.*[7] the New Hampshire Supreme Court held an employer liable for discharging a female employee because she had engendered hostility in her foreman by refusing his sexual advances. The court's own statement of its holding is reasonably consistent with a broad theory of liability that encompasses a wide range of employer actions:

> We hold that a termination by the employer of a contract of employment at will which is motivated by bad faith or malice or based on retaliation is not in the best interest of the economic system or the public good and constitutes a breach of the employment contract.[8]

Six years later, in *Howard v. Dorr Woolen Co.,*[9] however, the same court adopted one of the narrowest of the possible interpretations of *Monge*'s holding. The *Howard* court clearly required (1) a link to public policy beyond a general interest in good faith and fair play in a private employment relationship, and (2) retaliation for a specific act or refusal to act on the part of the employee:

> We construe *Monge* to apply only to a situation where an employee is discharged because he performed an act that public policy would encourage, or refused to do that which public policy would condemn.[10]

Without explaining which of the two requirements was missing, the *Howard* court applied its view of the holding in *Monge* to refuse to impose liability for an employer's discharging an employee because of sickness and age.[11]

This process of refining the holding of a prior decision may permit a court to interpret precedent in a way that was not intended by the court establishing that precedent. In most subsequent decisions, however, courts more faithfully attempt to identify the considerations that were essential to the decision that acts as precedent and to evaluate the precedent's effect on the subsequent disputes.

If the holding of a decision is thus defined in terms of the way in which courts make use of the decision as precedent in subsequent cases, the issue and holding of the decision cannot be identified with perfect certainty when analyzing that decision in isolation. Rather, each decision presents a range of

---

7. 114 N.H. 130, 316 A.2d 549 (1974).
8. Id. at 133, 316 A.2d at 551 (the unofficial reporter omits the word "in" in the quoted passage).
9. 120 N.H. 295, 414 A.2d 1273 (1980).
10. Id. at 297, 414 A.2d at 1274.
11. Id. (interpreted in Wagenseller v. Scottsdale Memorial Hosp., 147 Ariz. 370, 377 n.3, 710 P.2d 1025, 1032 n.3 (1985)).

possible statements of the issue and holding.[12] When preparing for class, you should try to state an issue and holding that falls somewhere within a plausible range and to appreciate how other statements nearer to either end of the plausible range would aid in the advocacy of either side of a subsequent dispute.

3. Facts

Pressed for time, you may be tempted to skim over the facts of cases and rush instead to the middle of the opinion, searching for succinct statements of law that you can preserve in your notes. In the final analysis, however, legal rules are nothing more than statements of the legal consequences of special facts:

> Wherever the law gives special rights to one, or imposes special burdens on another, it does so on the ground that certain special facts are true of those individuals. In all such cases, therefore, there is a twofold task. First, to determine what are the facts to which the special consequences are attached; second, to ascertain the consequences. The first is the main field of legal argument.[13]

Whether case law is based on statutory interpretation or common law, it generally develops gradually, with each new opinion adding refinements in the law through its application of legal standards to the facts of a new dispute. A court's statements about the law are fully meaningful only when read in light of the facts of the dispute that the court's decision resolves. Consequently, you should master the facts of a case with the same intensity that you devote to appreciating the court's discussion of legal principles.

Your statement of facts should include all "material" facts, facts that have legal significance and therefore directly influence the court's holding and reasoning. Identification of material facts is not an exact science; rather, it is a matter of judgment that requires an appreciation of the factors that the court considered in reaching its decision. In your statement of facts, you should also refer in general terms to any additional background facts that, although legally unimportant, are helpful to a full understanding of the dispute and to class discussion. At the least, your statement of facts should identify

(1) the principal parties to the dispute that precipitated the legal proceedings,

(2) the relationships among those parties, and

(3) the events that led to the dispute.

You may wish to refer to such facts as "historical facts" to distinguish them from "procedural facts," which are discussed in subsection 4 below.

For purposes of discussion, this book will often use the procedural term "plaintiff" to refer to the party who initiates a lawsuit, and the term "defendant" to refer to the one against whom suit is brought. You can create a more concrete image of the underlying dispute, however, if you identify the parties with their more specific, formal names.

---

12. See K. Llewellyn, The Bramble Bush 69 (1978).
13. O. Holmes, Jr., The Common Law 289 (1923).

In addition, you should consider supplementing the formal names with labels that have substantive, rather than merely procedural, significance. Because statutes generally address broad categories of activities rather than individual cases, they often create rights and obligations in broad but carefully defined classifications of persons, such as "employers" and "employees," or "buyers" and "sellers."[14] Similarly, although courts interpret statutes and develop common law in the context of individual disputes, a series of judicial decisions on closely related points may create case law that allocates rights and obligations according to membership within general classes of persons, such as "landowners" and "trespassers."[15] Therefore, you can more clearly reveal the legal significance of material facts in your case brief if you identify the named parties or other important actors with labels that reflect undisputed and legally significant classifications, such as employer, buyer, seller, merchant, landlord, tenant, landowner, or invitee.

When you assign a label to a party or otherwise characterize a factual matter, you should not prematurely state a conclusion on an issue that is disputed by the parties and that is later analyzed in the opinion. For example, your statement of facts should not refer to a seller as a "merchant" if the parties dispute whether the seller is a merchant for purposes of determining the seller's warranty obligations under the Uniform Commercial Code.[16] Similarly, your statement of facts should not state that the defendant in a criminal burglary prosecution "broke into" a "dwelling" if "breaking" and "dwelling" are elements of the charged offense and if the parties dispute those elements.[17]

Rather than state disputed legal conclusions in your statement of facts, you should summarize the subsidiary facts that the court analyzes in reaching its conclusion on the issue. For example, in the first case in the preceding paragraph, you might state that the seller of a computer system did not normally buy or sell goods, and that her sale of the computer system was an isolated transaction, but that the seller's occupation as a computer repairperson led the buyer to believe that the seller had special knowledge of the performance capabilities of different computer systems. In other parts of your case brief, you can discuss whether those subsidiary facts satisfy the legal definition of "merchant."[18]

In most cases the appellate judge who wrote the opinion has already sifted and condensed the facts that were presented to the trial court. Nonetheless, you should try to be even more discriminating in your identification of material facts and helpful background facts, and you should try to summarize them

---

14. See, e.g., Title VII of the Civil Rights Act of 1964, 42 U.S.C. §§ 2000e(b), 2000e-2(a) (1982) (defining and imposing obligations on "employers").

15. See, e.g., Prosser and Keeton on Torts § 58, at 393 (W. Keeton gen. ed. 1984) (duties owed by landowner to trespassers, licensees, and invitees).

16. See U.C.C. § 2-314 (implying a warranty of merchantability in a contract for the sale of goods "if the seller is a merchant with respect to goods of that kind").

17. See W. LaFave & A. Scott, Jr., Criminal Law § 8.13 (2d ed. 1986).

18. The U.C.C. definition focuses on regular practices and on representations of expertise:

Merchant means a person who deals in goods of the kind or otherwise by his occupation holds himself out as having knowledge or skill peculiar to the practices or goods involved in the transaction . . .

U.C.C. § 2-104.

further. You should also reorganize the opinion's facts if their organization is not satisfactory; chronological order is often the most logical.

To truly master the facts, however, you should go beyond simply summarizing or reorganizing the opinion's fact statement. Instead, you should seek a conceptual understanding of the facts, one that creates concrete images of the parties and transactions. If necessary to attain that goal, you should prepare charts, time lines, or other graphics that vividly represent the relationships among multiple parties and events.

4. *Procedural History*

In your statement of the procedural history of a case on appeal, you should identify

(1) which party or parties initiated legal action against which others;

(2) the legal claims and defenses and the relief sought;

(3) the trial court's disposition along with the stage of the proceedings at which the trial court rendered its decision;

(4) the dispositions of any intermediate courts below the authoring court;

(5) and the authoring court's disposition.

In some cases, it may also be helpful to summarize the arguments that the parties made to the trial or appellate courts.

The case name on appeal does not always reveal which party initiated the legal action in the trial court. Although the case name as it appears in the trial court begins with the plaintiff's name, the case name in the appellate courts of some jurisdictions begins with the name of the party who is dissatisfied with the trial court's decision and has thus appealed (the "appellant") or petitioned for review (the "petitioner").[19]

The nature of the plaintiff's legal claim and request for relief in the trial court may provide a key to the appellate court's analysis. For example, classification of a plaintiff's legal claim as one in tort rather than in contract may determine whether the claim is barred by a statute of limitations[20] or whether the plaintiff is entitled to punitive damages.[21] Similarly, whether a contract is sufficiently definite to enforce may depend on whether the plaintiff seeks enforcement through an award of damages or through injunctive relief granting specific enforcement.[22]

As with the statement of facts, you should not reach a premature conclusion in your statement of the procedural history regarding the nature of a legal claim if that is one of the issues disputed by the parties and analyzed by the court. For example, the parties may dispute whether a claim is properly clas-

---

19. See e.g., Fiege v. Boehm, 210 Md. 352, 123 A.2d 316 (App. 1956) (Hilda Boehm had sued Louis Fiege in the trial court).

20. See, e.g., Salmon Rivers Sportsman Camps v. Cessna Aircraft Co., 97 Idaho 348, 352, 544 P.2d 306, 310 (1975).

21. J. Calamari & J. Perillo, Contracts § 14-3 (1979).

22. See E. Farnsworth, Contracts § 12.7, at 832-833 (1982); Restatement (Second) of Contracts § 33 comment b (1981); cf. 5A A. Corbin, Corbin on Contracts § 1174, at 278-279 (1964) ("It is believed, however, that the required degree of definiteness and certainty [for specific enforcement] is seldom much greater than is required for enforcement by other remedies.").

sified as tort or contract, because that classification may determine the applicable statute of limitations or the availability of punitive damages.[23] In many cases, however, the nature of the legal claim will be undisputed and easily identifiable.

By stating the dispositions of all the courts that rendered decisions in the case, you can identify precisely the ruling that the authoring court has reviewed. The "disposition" is the practical, procedural effect of the court's holding on the litigation. In an opinion of a trial court, it might be "action dismissed," "summary judgment for the plaintiff," or "judgment on the jury verdict for the defendant." In an opinion of an appellate court, it might be "affirmed," "reversed," or "reversed and remanded for further proceedings."

In stating the trial court's disposition, you should try to identify the stage of the proceedings at which the trial court rendered judgment. An appellate court gives varying degrees of deference to different kinds of trial court decisions. Therefore, the likelihood of reversal by an appellate court depends partly on the stage of the proceedings at which judgment is rendered and, in some cases, on the classification of critical issues as ones of fact or law.[24]

For example, although appellate courts review without restriction the legal rules formulated by trial courts, they restrict their review of the factual findings made by a trial judge or jury after a full trial, overturning such findings only in unusual circumstances.[25] On the other hand, a trial judge makes no formal findings of fact when he uses summary judgment to dispose of claims before trial, and an appellate court will reverse summary judgment if it determines, without deference to the analysis of the trial court, that the parties genuinely dispute material facts.[26] Further, on a motion to dismiss an action for failure of the complaint to state a claim for relief, both the trial court and appellate courts simply assume the truth of the allegations of fact in the complaint and analyze the legal significance of those allegations.[27]

5. Reasoning

a. Rule and Rationale

In part, published appellate judicial decisions serve the function of ensuring the "correct" result in a particular case. However, their primary purpose is

---

23. See, e.g., Woodward v. Chirco Constr. Co., 141 Ariz. 520, 523, 687 P.2d 1275, 1278 (App. 1984), *approved as supplemented*, 141 Ariz. 514, 687 P.2d 1269 (1984) (implied warranty claim arose out of a written contract and therefore was governed by six-year limitations period rather than by shorter limitations period for tort claims); Gates v. Life of Montana Ins. Co., 668 P.2d 213, 215 (Mont. 1983) (breach of implied duty of good faith and fair dealing in employment contract gives rise to a tort, thus permitting award of punitive damages).

24. See Chapter 15 Section II.

25. See, e.g., Fed. R. Civ. P. 52(a) (federal appellate court may not set aside trial judge's findings of fact unless they are "clearly erroneous"); 2 Fed. Proc., L. Ed. § 2:233, at 195-196 (1981) (reviewing court cannot overturn the fact findings of a jury unless they are not supported by substantial evidence).

26. See Fed. R. Civ. P. 56 (summary judgment standards); Heiniger v. City of Phoenix, 625 F.2d 842, 843-844 (9th Cir. 1980) (standards for appellate review of summary judgment).

27. See, e.g., Experimental Engineering, Inc. v. United Technologies Corp., 614 F.2d 1244, 1246 (9th Cir. 1980) (dismissal is appropriate only if court is convinced that the plaintiff can prove no set of facts in support of a claim that would warrant relief).

to serve the "institutional function" of "developing and declaring legal principles that will have application beyond the case that serves as the vehicle for expression of the principles."[28] The reasoning set forth in a judicial opinion should provide guidance in determining how the court will apply its decision to subsequent, analogous cases. Because certainty in the law is not the only criterion for judicial rulemaking, courts should hesitate to extend a previous decision beyond the reasons that supported it.

By carefully studying the reasoning of opinions, you will gradually develop a "feel" for the way in which judges decide cases. With that acquired knowledge, you can develop the ability not only to analyze a problem and predict its likely outcome in court, but also to persuade a court to reach a conclusion favorable to your client.

Unfortunately, published opinions provide only an imperfect guide to the decision-making process. The reasons for an individual judge's vote on an appellate panel may be complex, and some reasons may be subconscious.[29] Of the reasons on which the judge consciously relies, the judge may not express all of them to fellow panel members in panel discussions and memoranda. Finally, the published opinion of the panel may exclude some of the more pragmatic reasons privately expressed by panel members to one another and may focus instead on more conventional legal analysis. Because an opinion thus only imperfectly communicates a court's actual reasoning, you should not hesitate to "read between the lines" and attempt to identify facts or policy considerations that likely contributed to the court's decision, even though the court did not expressly identify them as critical factors.

On the most fundamental level, when stating a court's reasoning, you should note whether the court is interpreting and applying a statute or is developing common law. Many judicial opinions deal with both. Beyond that, you should summarize the court's reliance on precedent, its analysis of policy considerations, its explanation of the significance of critical facts, and its adoption or recognition of a legal rule of general application.

Some opinions do not formulate or restate a general legal rule that controls the analysis. Instead, they simply define a dispute on particular facts, reach a decision, and provide a justification that is fairly narrowly tailored to the dispute before the court. Such an opinion leaves you only with a "holding" in the narrowest sense. Using techniques described in the next chapter, however, you can synthesize several such cases addressing similar issues and derive your own rule of general application.

b. Holding and Dictum

One of your most challenging tasks is to distinguish the holding of a decision from dicta. Narrowly defined, a "holding" is the court's resolution of an issue before it, limited to the particular facts of the dispute. It does not include statements in the opinion about the probable outcome of disputes not before the court.

---

28. Calleros, Title VII and Rule 52(a): Standards of Appellate Review in Disparate Impact Cases—Limiting the Reach of *Pullman-Standard v. Swint,* 58 Tulane L. Rev. 403, 420-421 (1983).

29. See generally id., at 424 & n.97.

"Dictum," on the other hand, is a statement in the opinion that helps explain the court's reasoning but that addresses questions not squarely presented in the dispute before the court. Courts make and apply law in the context of individual disputes; however, as a natural consequence of the uniformity of treatment demanded by stare decisis, courts have developed general rules that apply to whole categories of disputes.[30] As a means of explaining the reasons supporting its holding, a court may in dicta compare its rule of decision with other rules that it does not apply to the dispute, or it may discuss in dicta how its rule of decision would apply to facts other than those presented in the dispute before it.

As illustrated by the following excerpt, the issue and holding of a previous decision limits its effect as precedent under stare decisis. Even a lower court that is absolutely bound by the holdings of the previous decision may choose not to follow the dicta of the decision. In this example from civil rights litigation, a U.S. Court of Appeals extended the same immunity defense to judges of limited jurisdiction state courts, such as traffic courts, as had been applied to judges of general jurisdiction state courts, such as general trial courts. In doing so, it departed from U.S. Supreme Court dictum:

> The district court held that judges of courts of limited jurisdiction may be sued for judicial acts done merely in excess of jurisdiction. . . . Although the Supreme Court cases relied upon by the district court contain language supporting such a view, . . . we hold that judges of courts of limited jurisdiction are entitled to absolute immunity for their judicial acts unless they act in the clear absence of all jurisdiction.
>
> First, we emphasize that since the [Supreme Court] cases involved suits against judges of courts having general jurisdiction, any statements made by the Supreme Court about judges of courts having only limited or inferior jurisdiction were *dicta*.[31]

Dictum in an opinion is not meaningless; it may in fact help you accurately predict the authoring court's action in a subsequent case that squarely presents the issue addressed in the dictum.[32] Nonetheless, because dictum does not have the force of precedent, you should take care to read all of the court's reasoning in light of its narrow, fact-specific holding. You should not confuse what a court *says*, or even what it *says it is doing*, with what it actually *does* in a case.

6. Evaluation

You should resist any tendency to defer to the reasoning of a judicial decision as the expression of the single "correct" analysis of a dispute. Many disputes present close questions that are reasonably susceptible to alternative, inconsistent resolutions. You should read a decision critically to determine whether you agree with the result and the reasoning. Constant practice in critical examination of judicial opinions will help you develop the ability later

---

30. See generally K. Llewellyn, The Bramble Bush 42-43 (1978).
31. 766 F.2d 962, 966 (6th Cir. 1985), *cert. denied*, 474 U.S. 971 (1985).
32. R. Keeton, Venturing to Do Justice 30-31 (1969).

to persuade a court to adopt or reject the rule or reasoning of nonbinding authority.

On one level, you should examine an opinion for doctrinal integrity by asking such questions as

(1) whether the court analogized or distinguished precedent in a convincing manner,

(2) whether it applied the appropriate standard of review,

(3) whether it analyzed a statute under accepted principles of statutory interpretation and construction, or

(4) whether the court placed excessive emphasis on certainty in a general rule at the expense of equitable considerations in the context of peculiar facts.

On another, closely related level, you should examine the policy and practical implications of an opinion. For example, you might ask such questions as

(1) whether a decision that promotes economic security for employees unwisely reduces economic efficiency at the expense of producers and consumers, or

(2) whether a court-developed tort standard allocates risks among parties in a way that encourages them to conduct themselves in a manner that avoids harm to others yet encourages socially productive ventures.

7. Synthesis

Perhaps the most important and the most challenging element of a case brief is the "synthesis," in which you explore the relationships among two or more cases that address the same issue or closely related ones. After comparing the critical elements of each in a series of cases, you can refine your view of the holding of each case in the series. With synthesis, you can either (1) formulate a general principle that explains each decision or (2) compare and evaluate the inconsistent approaches of different courts or of the same court over time. By synthesizing cases, you take a critical step in legal analysis that will have special significance when you look ahead to final examinations: synthesis forms a bridge between daily briefing of isolated cases and periodic preparation of course outlines.

The process of synthesizing cases reveals that the study of case law is analogous in some ways to the study of a foreign language. After a brief introduction to the basic structure of a language and its rules of pronunciation, you typically proceed to study the language by gaining familiarity with a succession of words and phrases that gradually grow into a working vocabulary. The learning process is complicated by the relationship of parts to the whole: you cannot fully appreciate the nuances of meaning of a word or phrase without a working knowledge of its role in a larger body of the language; yet you cannot attain a working knowledge of the larger body of the language without first gaining at least a preliminary understanding of individual words and phrases. As you gradually add to your vocabulary and to your understanding of the relationship of words and phrases to one another, you continually refine your understanding of the individual words and phrases that you studied earlier, and you come closer to attaining fluency in the whole language.

Similarly, when studying law, you cannot fully appreciate the legal significance of a single judicial decision without examining its role within a larger body of case law; yet, you cannot master the larger body of case law without first gaining at least an imperfect grasp of its parts, first one case in isolation and then a growing group of cases. As you brief a series of cases, you will gain new insights by examining the cases' relationships to one another. Those insights may cause you to modify your early, less sophisticated understanding of a case standing alone or standing with fewer cases in the series. Additionally, they may enable you to identify a general legal principle, or at least a set of accepted criteria, that helps to explain the decisions.[33]

The first step in synthesizing cases is to compare the cases' substantive results as conveyed by their holdings, regardless of the procedural dispositions of the appellate courts. For example, assume that two appellate decisions from different jurisdictions have addressed the question of whether a particular newspaper advertisement meets the following definition of an offer: an "offer" is an expression of willingness to enter into a contract that empowers the offeree to create a contract by accepting the offer. One of the decisions, Case A, affirmed a trial court judgment that a particular newspaper advertisement amounted to an offer to sell the advertised goods. The other, Case B, affirmed a trial court judgment that another newspaper advertisement communicated only an invitation to negotiate rather than an offer to sell.[34] If you are not yet prepared to abandon hope of finding at least limited uniformity among the states in their application of common law, you should be curious about the reasons for the difference in results.

In the next step of the synthesis, you should determine whether Cases A and B are materially distinguishable and therefore warrant different results on application of the same legal principles, or whether they are legally inconsistent and simply represent different views of the law adopted by courts in different states. As a general approach, you should first attempt to reconcile the cases by searching for distinctions in facts, procedure, or both that support a conclusion that the cases are legally consistent. For example, unusually specific and detailed language of commitment in the advertisement in Case A might clearly communicate a willingness to conclude a contract for sale on a customer's assent. In contrast, more general language in the advertisement in Case B might leave important terms of sale unaddressed, suggesting a need for further bargaining before the advertiser is willing to commit itself to a contract for sale.

In these circumstances, you could compose a single, narrow legal rule that is consistent with the reasoning of each case and that produces different results on application to the facts of both cases:

|| A newspaper advertisement is an offer only if it is so clear and definite that it leaves no important detail for future negotiation.

---

33. For a critical evaluation of the method with which case synthesis is taught in American law schools, see Greenstein, Teaching Case Synthesis, 2 Ga. St. U.L. Rev. 1 (1985-1986).

34. Compare Lefkowitz v. Great Minneapolis Surplus Store, 251 Minn. 188, 86 N.W.2d 689 (1957) (offer) and Craft v. Elder and Johnston Co., 38 N.E.2d 416 (Ohio 1941) (no offer), reprinted in part in E. Farnsworth & W. Young, Cases and Materials on Contracts 145-148 (4th ed. 1988).

With such a synthesis, you will better understand the holdings of Cases A and B, more firmly grasp otherwise abstract legal principles, and improve your ability to predict the outcome of a new case that presents the same issue on novel facts.

If you fail to find material distinctions in facts or procedure between Cases A and B, you can safely conclude that the appellate decisions are legally inconsistent. In that event, you should analyze the reasons for the different views of the law. Such a synthesis helps you to put conflicting case law into perspective and to develop the ability to persuade a court in a future case to adopt one line of conflicting authority over another.

Different results in cases decided by the same court present particularly interesting questions of synthesis, because the court cannot depart from a prior decision without departing also from stare decisis and overruling the prior decision. If the cases are not obviously distinguishable but the court does not explicitly overrule the prior decision, you should search with particular care for possible distinguishing features before concluding that the court has implicitly overruled the prior decision. Of course, the proper synthesis may lie in middle ground: a decision may limit the range of possible interpretations of a prior holding without completing overruling it.

If two cases reach the same result, a synthesis should compare the facts and reasoning of the two cases to determine whether the courts were influenced by similar factors. For example, suppose that, in Case A, a court in State X held that a particular newspaper advertisement constituted an offer to sell the advertised goods. Suppose further that, in Case C, a court in State Z found a different newspaper advertisement to constitute an offer. Although both decisions find offers, a comparison of the facts may suggest that Case C represents a significant extension of the holding of Case A. Similarly, the reasoning of Case A might suggest that the court in State X would not have reached the same result if presented with the facts on which the court in State Z found an offer in Case C.

When you synthesize, you compare two or more cases, of course. Therefore, when you prepare a single case brief in isolation, you will not include a synthesis, except perhaps in the form of a prediction of the questions that may arise later from uncertainty in the breadth of the holding of the case. The late Professor Llewellyn went so far as to state that

> a case read by itself is meaningless, is nil, is blank, is blah. Briefing should begin *at the earliest* with the second case of an assignment. Only *after* you have read the second case have you any idea what to do with the first.[35]

Thus, in a perfect world, you could read all in a series of cases relating to a particular problem area before briefing any of them, then brief each case with an eye to the problems raised in the others, and finally prepare a single synthesis of the entire series of cases.

Unfortunately, class assignments and library research techniques seldom permit that luxury. As a more practical procedure, you should prepare a syn-

---

35. K. Llewellyn, The Bramble Bush 54 (1978).

thesis for each case in a series beginning with the second case. Each succeeding synthesis will reflect the addition of a case to the group of cases that may be compared to one another, thus adding additional insights to previous syntheses.

III. SUMMARY

After thoroughly reading the entire case at least once, follow these steps:

(1) Identify the case. Include details that help identify the case's place in the overall jurisdiction and the case's value as precedent.

(2) State the issue and the holding as narrowly as possible without making your question cumbersome and unwieldy; tailor your statement of the issue to the facts.

(3) Summarize the material facts and the helpful background facts.

(4) Summarize the procedural history, including the dispositions in the trial court and on appeal.

(5) Summarize the reasoning of the court. Distinguish holding from dictum. Identify general rules recognized by the court, and pay particular attention to the authority, policy analysis, and logic on which the court relies.

(6) Critically evaluate the court's holding and reasoning.

(7) Synthesize the case with others that present the same or a similar issue. Attempt to explain apparently conflicting results among the cases.

======= E X E R C I S E   5 - 1 =======

1. *Case Brief*

Using the techniques described in this chapter, read the following excerpt of the appellate opinion in *White v. Benkowski,* and prepare a case brief. Do not be satisfied with the court's statement of the issue; try to improve on it. Critically evaluate the court's holding and dicta regarding the availability of punitive damages; ask yourself whether you can defend the court's views on the grounds of economic efficiency, certainty in legal rules, equity in individual cases, the proper roles of compensation and deterrence, or any other policy considerations. You should not yet attempt to synthesize this case with any others, although you may comment on possible extensions of, or limitations on, its holding that subsequent cases could introduce. After completing your case brief, compare it with the sample set forth in Exercise 5-1(2) below.

WHITE v. BENKOWSKI
Supreme Court of Wisconsin
37 Wis. 2d 285, 155 N.W.2d 74 (1967)

This case involves a neighborhood squabble between two adjacent property owners.

Prior to November 28, 1962, Virgil and Gwynneth White, the plaintiffs, were desirous of purchasing a home in Oak Creek. Unfortunately, the particular home that the Whites were interested in was without a water supply. Despite this fact, the Whites purchased the home.

The adjacent home was owned and occupied by Paul and Ruth Benkowski, the defendants. The Benkowskis had a well in their yard which had piping that connected with the Whites' home.

On November 28, 1962, the Whites and Benkowskis entered into a written agreement wherein the Benkowskis promised to supply water to the White home for ten years or until an earlier date when either water was supplied by the municipality, the well became inadequate, or the Whites drilled their own well. The Whites promised to pay $3 a month for the water and one-half the cost of any future repairs or maintenance that the Benkowski well might require. As part of the transaction, but not included in the written agreement, the Whites gave the Benkowskis $400 which was used to purchase and install a new pump and an additional tank that would increase the capacity of the well.

Initially, the relationship between the new neighbors was friendly. With the passing of time, however, their friendship deteriorated and the neighbors actually became hostile. In 1964, the water supply, which was controlled by the Benkowskis, was intermittently shut off. Mrs. White kept a record of the dates and durations that her water supply was not operative. Her record showed that the water was shut off on the following occasions:

(1) March 5, 1964, from 7:10 P.M. to 7:25 P.M.
(2) March 9, 1964, from 3:40 P.M. to 4:00 P.M.
(3) March 11, 1964, from 6:00 P.M. to 6:15 P.M.
(4) June 10, 1964, from 6:20 P.M. to 7:03 P.M.

The record also discloses that the water was shut off completely or partially for varying lengths of time on July 1, 6, 7, and 17, 1964, and on November 25, 1964.

Mr. Benkowski claimed that the water was shut off either to allow accumulated sand in the pipes to settle or to remind the Whites that their use of the water was excessive. Mr. White claimed that the Benkowskis breached their contract by shutting off the water.

Following the date when the water was last shut off (November 25, 1964), the Whites commenced an action to recover compensatory and punitive damages for an alleged violation of the agreement to supply water. . . .

The jury returned a verdict which found that the Benkowskis maliciously shut off the Whites' water supply for harassment purposes. Compensatory damages were set at $10 and punitive damages at $2,000. On motions after verdict, the court reduced the compensatory award to $1 and granted defendants' motion to strike the punitive-damage question and answer.

Judgment for plaintiffs of $1 was entered and they appeal.

WILKIE, Justice.
Two issues are raised on this appeal. . . .
2. Are punitive damages available in actions for breach of contract? . . .

PUNITIVE DAMAGES

"If a man shall steal an ox, or a sheep, and kill it, or sell it; he shall restore five oxen for an ox, and four sheep for a sheep."[3]

Over one hundred years ago this court held that, under proper circumstances, a plaintiff was entitled to recover . . . punitive damages.[4]

Kink v. Combs[5] is the most recent case in this state which deals with the practice of permitting punitive damages. In *Kink* the court relied on Fuchs v. Kupper[6] and reaffirmed its adherence to the rule of punitive damages.

In Wisconsin compensatory damages are given to make whole the damage or injury suffered by the injured party.[7] On the other hand, punitive damages are given

". . . on the basis of punishment to the injured party not because he has been injured, which injury has been compensated with compensatory damages, but to punish the wrongdoer for his malice and to deter others from like conduct."[8]

Thus we reach the question of whether the plaintiffs are entitled to punitive damages for a breach of the water agreement.

The overwhelming weight of authority supports the proposition that punitive damages are not recoverable in actions for breach of contract.[9] In Chitty on Contracts, the author states that the right to receive punitive damages for breach of contract is now confined to the single case of damages for breach of a promise to marry.[10]

Simpson States:

"Although damages in excess of compensation for loss are in some instances permitted in tort actions by way of punishment . . . in contract actions the damages recoverable are limited to compensation for pecuniary loss sustained by the breach."[11]

Corbin states that as a general rule punitive damages are not recoverable for breach of contract.[12]

In Wisconsin, the early case of Gordon v. Brewster[13] involved the breach of an employment contract. The trial court instructed the jury that if the nonperformance of the contract was attributable to the defendant's wrongful act of discharging the plaintiff, then that would go to increase the damages sustained. On appeal, this court said that the instruction was unfortunate and

---

3. Exodus 22:1
4. McWilliams v. Bragg (1854), 3 Wis. 377 (*424).
5. (1965), 28 Wis. 2d 65, 135 N.W.2d 789.
6. (1963) 22 Wis. 2d 107, 125 N.W.2d 360.
7. Malco, Inc. v. Midwest Aluminum Sales (1961), 14 Wis. 2d 57, 66, 109 N.W.2d 516, 521.
8. Id.
9. Annot. (1933), 84 A.L.R. 1345, 1346.
10. 1 Chitty, Contracts, (22d ed. 1961), p.1339.
11. Simpson, Contracts, (2nd ed. hornbook series), p.394, sec. 195.
12. 5 Corbin, Contracts, p.438, sec. 1077.
13. (1858), 7 Wis. 309 (*355).

might have led the jurors to suppose that they could give something more than actual compensation in a breach of contract case. We find no Wisconsin case in which breach of contract (other than breach of promise to marry)[14] has led to the award of punitive damages.

Persuasive authority from other jurisdictions supports the proposition (without exception) that punitive damages are not available in breach of contract actions.[15] This is true even if the breach, as in the instant case, is willful.[16]

Although it is well recognized that breach of a contractual duty may be a tort,[17] in such situations the contract creates the relation out of which grows the duty to use care in the performance of a responsibility prescribed by the contract.[18] Not so here. No tort was pleaded or proved.

Reversed in part by reinstating the jury verdict relating to compensatory damages and otherwise affirmed.

2. Sample Case Brief

Compare the case brief that you prepared in Exercise 1 with the following sample. Remember that the sample is only an example of a reasonable reaction to the opinion; it is not necessarily the best interpretation and evaluation of the opinion, and it certainly is not the only reasonable one. In particular, the "evaluation" is a matter of individual opinion.

White v. Benkowski,   37 Wis. 2d 285, 155 N.W.2d 74 (1967), CB 14.

Issue and Holding: Is Buyer entitled to an award of punitive damages for Supplier's malicious breach of a contract to supply water, even though Buyer established no independent tort? No.

Facts: The Whites (Buyer) and Benkowskis (Supplier) are neighbors. By written agreement Supplier promised to supply Buyer's house with water from Supplier's well for ten years, unless the well became inadequate or unnecessary. The relationship deteriorated, and Supplier maliciously shut off Buyer's water supply partially or completely on nine occasions for the purpose of harassing Buyer.

Procedural History: Buyer sued Supplier for compensatory and punitive damages, alleging only breach of contract. On a finding of malicious breach of

---

14. Simpson v. Black (1870), 27 Wis. 206.

15. White, Inc. v. Metropolitan Merchandise Mart (1954), 48 Del. 526, 9 Terry 526, 107 A.2d 892; Thompson v. Mutual Ben. Health & Acc. Ass'n of Omaha, Neb. (D.C. Iowa 1949), 83 F. Supp. 656; Cain v. Tuten (1950), 82 Ga. App. 102, 60 S.E.2d 485; Mabery v. Western Casualty & Surety Co. (1952), 173 Kan. 586, 250 P.2d 824; Bland v. Smith (1955), 197 Tenn. 683, 277 S.W.2d 377, 49 A.L.R.2d 1212.

16. McDonough v. Zamora (Tex. Civ. App. 1960), 338 S.W.2d 507; Holt v. Holt (Tex. Civ. App. 1954), 271 S.W.2d 477; Chelini v. Nieri (Cal. App. 1948), 188 P.2d 564.

17. Colton v. Foulkes (1951), 259 Wis. 142, 47 N.W.2d 901; Presser v. Siesel Construction Co. (1963), 19 Wis. 2d 54, 119 N.W.2d 405; Peterson v. Sinclair Refining Co. (1963), 20 Wis. 2d 576, 123 N.W.2d 479.

18. 38 Am. Jur., Negligence, p.661, sec. 20.

contract, the jury awarded Buyer $10 in compensatory damages and $2,000 in punitive damages. On motions after verdict, the trial court disallowed punitive damages and reduced the compensatory-damage award from $10 to $1. Buyer appealed. The appellate court reversed the trial court's reduction of the award for compensatory damages, and it affirmed the trial court's elimination of the award for punitive damages.

Reasoning: Prior Wisconsin case law, persuasive authority from other jurisdictions, and the views of three commentators support the following common law principle: even an intentional and malicious breach of contract will not support an award of punitive damages. In dictum, the court suggests that punitive damages could be awarded if the breach of contract also constituted an independent tort; however, Buyer failed to plead and prove an independent tort. The court did not explicitly overrule a 19th century decision in which it had approved punitive damages for breach of a marriage contract, thus leaving open the possibility of exceptions from the rule of the current case for breaches of extraordinary contracts.

Evaluation: In light of the maliciousness of Supplier's behavior, this decision is too restrictive. To deter such egregious conduct, I would allow punitive damages for any breach of contract that is accompanied by fraudulent or malicious intent, even though not all the independent elements of a tort are established.

3. *Case Briefs with Synthesis*

Contracts are formed through a process of offer and acceptance. An offer is an expression of a willingness to enter into a contract. It gives to the party to whom it is addressed, the "offeree," the power to create the contract by assenting to the offer in a manner authorized by the offer. To constitute an offer, an expression must lead a reasonable person in the position of the offeree to understand that she has such power.

With that background, prepare a case brief for each of the following two cases. End the second case brief with a synthesis of the two cases.

CRAFT v. ELDER & JOHNSTON CO.
38 N.E.2d 416 (Ohio Ct. App. 1941)

BARNES, Judge. . . .
. . . On or about January 31, 1940, the defendant, the Elder & Johnston Company, carried an advertisement in the Dayton Shopping News, an offer for sale of a certain all electric sewing machine for the sum of $26 as a "Thursday Only Special." Plaintiff . . . alleges that the above publication is an advertising paper distributed in Montgomery County and throughout the city of Dayton; that on Thursday, February 1, 1940, she tendered to the defendant company $26 in payment for one of the machines offered in the advertisement, but that defendant refused to fulfill the offer and has continued to so refuse. The petition further alleges that the value of the machine offered was $175

and she asks damages in the sum of $149 plus interest from February 1, 1940. . . .

The trial court dismissed plaintiff's petition as evidenced by a journal entry, the pertinent portion of which reads as follows: "Upon consideration the court finds that said advertisement was not an offer which could be accepted by plaintiff to form a contract, and this case is therefore dismissed with prejudice to a new action, at costs of plaintiff." . . .

We will now briefly make reference to some of the authorities.

"It is clear that in the absence of special circumstances an ordinary newspaper advertisement is not an offer, but is an offer to negotiate—an offer to receive offers—or, as it is sometimes called, an offer to chaffer." Restatement of the Law of Contracts, Par. 25, Page 31.

Under the above paragraph the following illustration is given, " 'A', a clothing merchant, advertises overcoats of a certain kind for sale at $50. This is not an offer but an invitation to the public to come and purchase."

"Thus, if goods are advertised for sale at a certain price, it is not an offer and no contract is formed by the statement of an intending purchaser that he will take a specified quantity of the goods at that price. The construction is rather favored that such an advertisement is a mere invitation to enter into a bargain rather than an offer. So a published price list is not an offer to sell the goods listed at the published price." Williston on Contracts, Revised Edition, Vol. 1, Par. 27, Page 54.

"The commonest example of offers meant to open negotiations and to call forth offers in the technical sense are advertisements, circulars and trade letters sent out by business houses. While it is possible that the offers made by such means may be in such form as to become contracts, they are often merely expressions of a willingness to negotiate." Page on the Law Contracts, 2d Ed., Vol. 1, Page 112, Par. 84. . . .

"But generally a newspaper advertisement or circular couched in general language and proper to be sent to all persons interested in a particular trade or business, or a prospectus of a general and descriptive nature, will be construed as an invitation to make an offer." 17 Corpus Juris Secundum, Contracts, page 389, § 46, Column 2. . . .

We are constrained to the view that the trial court committed no prejudicial error in dismissing plaintiff's petition.

The judgment of the trial court will be affirmed and costs adjudged against the plaintiff-appellant.

Entry may be prepared in accordance with this opinion.

GEIGER, P. J., and HORNBECK, J., concur.

LEFKOWITZ v. GREAT MINNEAPOLIS SURPLUS STORE
251 Minn. 188, 86 N.W.2d 689 (1957)

MURPHY, Justice

This is an appeal from an order of the Municipal Court of Minneapolis. . . . The order for judgment awarded the plaintiff the sum of $138.50 as damages for breach of contract.

This case grows out of the alleged refusal of the defendant to sell to the plaintiff a certain fur piece which it had offered for sale in a newspaper advertisement. It appears from the record that on April 6, 1956, the defendant published the following advertisement in a Minneapolis newspaper:

> "Saturday 9 A.M. Sharp
> 3 Brand New
> Fur
> Coats
> Worth to $100.00
> First Come
> First Served
> $1
> Each"

On April 13, the defendant again published an advertisement in the same newspaper as follows:

> "Saturday 9 A.M.
> 2 Brand New Pastel
> Mink 3-Skin Scarfs
> Selling for $89.50
> Out they go
> Saturday, Each. . . . $1.00
> 1 Black Lapin Stole
> Beautiful,
> worth $139.50. . . . $1.00
> First Come
> First Served"

The record supports the findings of the court that on each of the Saturdays following the publication of the above-described ads the plaintiff was the first to present himself at the appropriate counter in the defendant's store and on each occasion demanded the coat and the stole so advertised and indicated his readiness to pay the sale price of $1. On both occasions, the defendant refused to sell the merchandise to the plaintiff . . .

The defendant relies principally on Craft v. Elder & Johnston Co. . . . On the facts before us we are concerned with whether the advertisement constituted an offer, and, if so, whether the plaintiff's conduct constituted an acceptance.

There are numerous authorities which hold that a particular advertisement in a newspaper or circular letter relating to a sale of articles may be construed by the court as constituting an offer, acceptance of which would complete a contract. [citations omitted]. . . .

The authorities above cited emphasize that, where the offer is clear, definite, and explicit, and leaves nothing open for negotiation, it constitutes an offer, acceptance of which will complete the contract. The most recent case on the subject is Johnson v. Capital City Ford Co., La. App., 85 So. 2d 75, in which the court pointed out that a newspaper advertisement relating to the purchase and sale of automobiles may constitute an offer, acceptance of which will consummate a contract and create an obligation in the offeror to perform according to the terms of the published offer.

Whether in any individual instance a newspaper advertisement is an offer rather than an invitation to make an offer depends on the legal intention of the parties and the surrounding circumstances. Annotation, 157 A.L.R. 744, 751; 77 C.J.S., Sales, § 25b; 17 C.J.S., Contracts, § 389. We are of the view on the facts before us that the offer by the defendant of the sale of the Lapin fur was clear, definite, and explicit, and left nothing open for negotiation. The plaintiff having successfully managed to be the first one to appear at the seller's place of business to be served, as requested by the advertisement, and having offered the stated purchase price of the article, he was entitled to performance on the part of the defendant. . . .

Affirmed.

Reorganization, Summary, and Inductive Reasoning in Outline Form

I. REORGANIZATION—MAPPING THE FOREST

When preparing for final examinations or preparing to write a legal memorandum, a law student or an associate in a law firm must make a significant transition from analysis of individual cases to the final expression of a completed legal analysis of the assigned problem. That transition begins with the synthesis of cases and continues with further analysis and reorganization, often leading to a transfer of the information in library notes or class notes to outline form.

An associate researching and analyzing a simple problem may not need to reorganize her modest library notes before expressing her analysis in a short memorandum. Long hours of researching a complex, multiple-issue problem, however, may produce a massive stack of disorganized notes dealing with several issues and lines of authority. In those circumstances, the associate may need to summarize and reorganize the notes in some manner before writing or even outlining the memorandum, and perhaps even before completely analyzing the problem.

Such a process is facilitated by taking library notes on note cards and limiting the notes on each card to discussion of a single statute or case. Indeed, if a single case separately discusses more than one issue relating to the assignment, the associate should make multiple copies of the note card or note the discussion of each issue on separate note cards. The associate can then devise categories for the note cards that identify distinct legal problems, assign each card to one of the groups, and summarize the fruits of her research in a short outline.

If the associate has used a note pad rather than note cards, she may wish to prepare an index of the cases, and perhaps even of distinct issues within a case, by assigning consecutive numbers to her case briefs. When reorganizing the product of her research in an outline, she can refer to her notes on a case by its number to facilitate cross-reference to her notes. With either technique, the associate can more easily analyze her notes because she has divided them into manageable portions, each of which relates to a distinct legal problem.

A law student preparing for final examinations has a special need to summarize, reorganize, and reanalyze his notes in outline form. In the course of a semester, a typical law student will amass several notebooks full of case briefs and notes of class discussion. Although these notes represent a summary of the thousands of pages of reading and hundreds of hours of class discussion and lecture, they are still too massive and disorganized to permit effective review and analysis for exam preparation. A well organized summary of those notes in outline form can enable the student to stand back from the trees formed by cases and to see the broad outline of the legal forest.

The real value of a course outline, however, is not in the final product as a study aid, but in the student's activities of reviewing and synthesizing material and of drafting the outline. These tasks develop important skills of organization, analysis, and expression. A method of reasoning essential to the entire process of outlining is inductive reasoning.

II. INDUCTIVE REASONING

Through two variations of inductive reasoning, you can use information from a series of specific cases to reach a conclusion about either:
  (1) the outcome of another specific case, or
  (2) the likelihood of the truth of a general proposition.

A. ANALOGY

The process of using inductive reasoning to predict the outcome of a specific case by comparing it to other cases is one of analogy. For example, a series of cases has permitted warrantless searches of various kinds of automobiles if the searches were supported by probable cause because (1) the mobility of the automobiles created exigent circumstances that made it impracticable to obtain a warrant before searching, and (2) the owner of each automobile had only limited expectations of privacy in its contents. From those cases, you could use inductive reasoning to conclude that police may search a motor home without a warrant because (1) the motor home is similar in mobility to the automobiles that were the subjects of the prior cases, and (2) government regulation of all licensed motor vehicles gives the owner of the motor home reduced expectations of privacy similar to those of the owner of an automobile.

As with all inductive reasoning, this conclusion about the motor home does not necessarily follow from the outcomes of the previous cases. Rather, the strength of the supporting cases simply makes the truth of the conclusion more or less likely. Indeed, you might argue that government regulation of licensed vehicles is less significant to the scope of privacy expectations than is the range and nature of activities for which a vehicle is designed. If that argument were accepted, you might use inductive reasoning to generalize from a series of cases, each of which have held that police could not search a house without a warrant even if they had probable cause to search. From those cases, you could conclude that the occupant of a motor home would enjoy protection from warrantless searches similar to that enjoyed by the occupant of a house, because each structure is designed for residential uses such as sleeping, eating, and storing personal effects.

B. GENERALIZING FROM PARTICULARS

With the second variation of inductive reasoning, you can construct a general proposition from specific cases. By using this process to prepare a course outline, you take a critical step toward the transition from daily briefing of cases to solving problems on a final examination. With this type of reasoning, you attempt to construct a general rule that is consistent with the facts and outcomes of past cases and that will apply to other cases with similar facts.

For example, you may have briefed four cases in which courts denied punitive damages on claims for various breaches of contract: innocent breach of a construction contract, intentional breach of a contract for the sale of real estate, malicious breach of a contract to supply water, and intentional breach of an employment contract. Although the rule would not necessarily follow from the cases, you could reasonably induce from the cases a general rule that punitive damages are not available for breach of contract. You could then apply that rule to a new case, such as the intentional breach of a lease, that is not identical to any of the prior cases but is nonetheless encompassed by the general rule arrived at from the prior cases through inductive reasoning.

The degree of confidence that you have in the general rule will depend on the strength of the supporting cases. If one of the previous decisions had awarded punitive damages for breach of a marriage contract, the general rule stated above would be a less reliable guide to the outcome of other kinds of disputes within its terms, and you would apply the rule with caution. You could improve the reliability of the rule by modifying it to achieve consistency with all the previous cases: punitive damages are not available for breach of contract, except for breach of marriage contracts.

═══════ **E X E R C I S E   6 - 1** ═══════

Review the illustration in Chapter 2, pages 29-31, regarding the family rules developed by Gerald and Janice for their children, Tanya and William. Assume that Gerald and Janice did not clearly articulate their rules but provided guidance to William simply by admonishing him when they disapproved of his actions. Imagine how William might use inductive reasoning to infer those rules from the following events:

1. On Friday, October 1, William attended a high school football game, which ended at 9:45 P.M. He then joined some friends for pizza and arrived home at 11:30 P.M. Gerald and Janice scolded him for being late, saying "next time, come home right after the game."

2. On Friday, October 8, William attended a high school football game, which ended at 9:45 P.M. He then joined some friends for pizza and arrived home at 10:55 P.M. His parents greeted him at the door cheerfully and asked, "how was your evening?"

3. On Saturday, October 9, William took a friend out to a movie and returned home by 11:00 P.M. His parents expressed no disapproval of his actions.

4. During the Week of October 11-17, William attended a special meeting of the high school debate club on Tuesday night, a football game on Friday night, and a high school musical production on Saturday night, returning home by 11:00 P.M. on each night. On Sunday morning, Gerald and Janice admonished him that he was "taking too much time away from his studies" and that he should not go out at night so often.

5. During the week of December 1-7, William went to a musical concert on Thursday night and saw a movie on Friday night, returning home by 11:00 P.M. on each night. On Saturday night, Gerald and Janice took Tanya and William to a relative's wedding and reception, returning home with the family by 10:45 P.M. Gerald and Janice expressed no disapproval of William's actions during that week.

C. RELATIONSHIP TO DEDUCTIVE REASONING

Both forms of inductive reasoning described in sections A and B above can be applied to the broad framework of deductive reasoning described in Chapter 3, pages 50-53. In that framework, after identifying an issue, you state the applicable rule and apply it to the relevant facts to reach a conclusion:

Issue
Rule   {Major Premise}
Application to Facts   {Minor Premise}
Conclusion

1. Formulating the Rule

Through the inductive process of constructing a general proposition from a series of cases, you can identify the rule that forms the major premise of your deductive analysis. In an office memorandum or a brief, you could represent this process comprehensively in several paragraphs or pages of in-depth analysis of case law that shows how you arrived at your understanding of the current form of a developing legal principle. The discussion of law in the first sample memorandum in Chapter 8, pages 157-158, illustrates such analysis.

Alternatively, you could state the rule as simply as a proposition in a single sentence, followed by citation to a couple of cases from which you derived the rule:

A promise does not satisfy the consideration requirement if it leaves the promisor free to perform not at all, subject only to his unfettered discretion rather than to external constraints. *See Strong v. Sheffield,* 144 N.Y. 392, 39 N.E. 330 (1895); *see also Di Benedetto v. Di Rocco,* 372 Pa. 302, 93 A.2d 474 (1953).

Because of time limitations and other constraints, when you state a rule in an examination answer, you will tend toward this simpler example, almost always without any citation to authority.

2. Applying the Rule to the Facts

To help you apply the legal rule to the facts of your dispute, you can invoke the inductive process of analogizing between previous cases and your own. In an office memorandum or brief, you may represent this process comprehensively in several paragraphs or pages in which you compare the facts and reasoning of previous cases to the facts of your own case. Again, the fact analysis in the first sample memorandum in Chapter 8, page 158, illustrates such explicit analogy and distinction.

Alternatively, you could analyze the facts more simply by directly explaining why the facts of your case do not satisfy the legal rule:

In this case, the lender's promise to forbear until he "needs" the money appears to condition the length of his forbearance on financial events that are at least partly outside his control. As long as his income and expenses create no need for the money, the lender has committed himself to forbear from demanding payment. Therefore, the lender's promise satisfies the consideration requirement, and the guarantor's promise is enforceable.

As with the statement of the legal rule, your fact analysis in an exam answer will often tend toward this simpler example. In developing even a simple fact analysis, however, you may implicitly compare the facts of your case with the facts and reasoning of the cases that you have earlier analyzed. Thus, although you may not always have time during an examination to express the details of your comparison, the inductive process of analogizing and distinguishing cases nonetheless informs your fact analysis.

3. Role of the Course Outline

By preparing a course outline, you can use inductive reasoning to help bridge the gap between your case briefs and the deductive analysis called for in a law school examination. As discussed more fully below, your outline should be organized around general legal rules, some of which you have constructed through inductive reasoning from groups of cases. These are rules that you can later recall and restate in an examination answer.

Moreover, your outline should illustrate these rules with brief summaries of the cases from which you derived the rules. Your familiarity with the facts and reasoning of these cases will help you apply the general rules to the facts of your exam questions, even if you do not always have time during the exam to fully express your process of analogizing and distinguishing cases.

III. TECHNIQUES OF OUTLINING COURSE MATERIALS

To transform your case briefs and class notes to a useful outline, you must reorganize, analyze, and summarize. The finished product will be an infinitely more useful study guide than your original notes, but the real value of a course outline is in the process of constructing it rather than in the finished product. Expressing your understanding of the law in outline form forces you to identify and resolve lingering areas of confusion that a less rigorous form of review might conceal. Moreover, outlining develops skills of organization and expression that you must summon and apply in the exam room and the law office. A commercial outline might contain information that you can understand and even remember, but it does not provide an effective means of developing important skills.

A. FUNDAMENTAL PRINCIPLES OF OUTLINING

The format for a course outline is largely a matter of personal style for each student. The techniques of outlining described in this chapter are not the only ones that you might find helpful. The techniques described here, however, have the benefit of developing skills that can be readily employed in drafting office memoranda and briefs, as well as exam answers. These outlining techniques require you to

(1) classify cases to facilitate a reorganization that focuses on general principles rather than on individual cases, and

(2) display the proper relationships among points in the outline.

1. Classification

Your course outline should not simply present a series of case briefs or even of summaries of case briefs. Instead, it should emphasize general rules of law and should relegate the case briefs to the role of illustrating the rules.

The first step in organizing such a course outline is to classify the kinds of problems or rules addressed in the case briefs and class notes and to recognize which kinds of problems are subsets of more general topics. Depending on the volume and complexity of the material to be outlined, you may identify several levels of classifications of problem areas or principles. If so, the most logical way to proceed is first to identify the classifications that have the broadest scope, and then to identify the subsidiary classifications that form subsets of the major classifications.

For example, the remedies portion of a contracts course might encompass two broad categories of relief: (1) specific relief, in the form of an injunction to perform as promised; and (2) substitutional relief, or money damages. Within each of those two major topics, the course material would undoubtedly present subsidiary problem areas, each of which encompasses another set of subsidiary problem areas, and so on. The following sequence of headings traces a single, descending line of such classifications leading to the topic of the availability of punitive damages in tort and contract actions.

    I. Specific Relief
       • • • •
   II. Substitutional Relief—Money Damages
      A. Nominal Damages
         • • • •
      B. Compensatory Damages
         • • • •
      C. Punitive Damages
        1. Purpose and Measure
           • • • •
        2. Availability
          a. Torts
            • • • •
          b. Contracts
            • • • •

Each of the classifications in this outline identifies a subset of the area of law encompassed by the subject of remedies and identifies the subject matter of disputes that have required the application of legal rules to facts. Moreover, each major classification in the outline first addresses a topic at the most general level and then separately examines more specific problems within the topic.

To clearly signal the organizational procession from the general to the specific, you may wish to begin each significant section and subsection with a brief paragraph or a separate introductory section that presents an overview of the subsections that follow:

    I. Overview
      A successful claimant may be entitled to either or both of two basic kinds of relief: (1) specific relief, in the form of an injunction that orders the defendant to take, or refrain from taking, some action; (2) substitutional relief, in the form of an award of money damages.
    II. Specific/Injunctive Relief
       • • • •
   III. Substitutional Relief
      Depending on the circumstances, courts may award any of three kinds of money damages: nominal, compensatory, or punitive.

A. Nominal Damages
   • • • •
B. Compensatory Damages
   • • • •
C. Punitive Damages
   • • • •

2. Proper Relationships Among Points

By displaying the proper relationships among points in your outline, you demonstrate a full understanding of its analytic content. For example, the excerpts presented above accurately identify some topics as subsets of more general topics. In contrast, the following outline erroneously classifies compensatory damages as an element of specific relief. It also misleadingly suggests that the topics of the availability and measure of punitive damages are no more closely related to one another than either is to questions about nominal damages:

I. Specific Relief
  A. Compensatory Damages
    • • • •
II. Substitutional Relief—Money Damages
  A. Nominal Damages
  B. Availability of Punitive Damages
  C. Measure of Punitive Damages

If you have trouble getting your outline started, you might set organizational considerations aside until you clearly identify the points that you later will display in logical structure. For example, you might start by glancing through your notes and the table of contents of your coursebook and by making a "laundry list" of rules or problem areas that the cases have presented:

injunctions   expectation interest   nominal damages
adequacy of remedy at law   compensatory damages
mitigation of damages   punitive damages   unique goods
specific performance of personal services

Once you have identified the topics that you want to address in the outline, you can classify the problems presented in the list and can determine their proper relationships to one another. The organizational structure of your casebook might provide a helpful starting point, but you should not hesitate to depart from it. A casebook will occasionally adopt an unusual organizational structure for pedagogical purposes, and you may prefer a more straightforward structure that will translate more readily to a guide for problem-solving.

Organizing an outline of legal points is not an exact science. The flexibility and uncertainty inherent in the analysis of much of the material that you encounter in the first year of law school make it impossible to identify a single "correct" method of organizing an outline of that material. Nonetheless, your diligent efforts leading to a reasonable outline will develop skills of organization that you can transfer directly to more formal legal documents such as briefs, memoranda, and contracts.

B. CONTENT OF THE OUTLINE

1. Identifying, Constructing, and Stating Rules

As a means of preparing to apply general legal rules to the facts of an exam problem, you should identify or even construct legal rules from the statutes and cases that you have studied. This process needn't suggest an unduly simplistic and mechanical approach to the law. The legal rules are simply shorthand representations of more complex sets of information that are explored in greater detail in references to the case law from which the rules are drawn. Consider, for example, one scholar's views on identifying and stating general principles relating to the doctrine of consideration in contract law:

> Here, as elsewhere, it is our function to construct working rules and definitions. The process and the result are made no different by the admission that the rules and definitions are not absolute but relative, not eternal but changeable. They will be useful if they are based on judicial history down to date, if they clearly indicate the facts and transactions to which they apply, and if they are in accord with the prevailing judicial action of modern time. At the least, we can review and classify the facts that have been held to be (or not to be) a "sufficient consideration" to make an informal promise enforceable. If we find a high degree of uniformity and agreement, rules can be stated and definitions attempted. We can consider the rules and definitions of the past, show the extent to which they have worked, and indicate the variation and progress that require a new restatement.[1]

On some topics, a legislature supplies a statutory rule, or a court states a general rule derived from earlier case law. Even dictum from a judicial opinion may provide a reliable guide to a tentative statement of a general rule. Although you must identify the narrow holding of a decision to evaluate the effect of the case as precedent, you may safely look to dictum for aid in constructing general rules that you can profitably apply in an exam.

In many instances, however, you will not find concise statements of general rules on a particular legal topic in statutes or in the holdings or dicta of judicial decisions. Instead, you must identify the cases that address issues related to the topic, and you must use synthesis and inductive reasoning to construct a general rule from the individual cases. To use the example presented in the previous section, you might study the holdings in a series of decisions denying punitive damages in different kinds of contracts cases and construct a general rule that punitive damages are not available for breach of contract, even though none of the decisions stated such a rule of general application. Indeed, your synthesis and inductive reasoning at the outline stage may lead you to revise your earlier, more tentative generalizations about a series of cases.

---

1. 1 A. Corbin, Corbin on Contracts § 109, at 489-490 (1963).

2. *Illustrating Rules with Examples*

Regardless of the method that you use to identify a general legal rule, your statement of the rule should not stand alone. You should illustrate and give more definite shape to the rule by summarizing the case law from which the rule was derived and by identifying competing rules or exceptions to the rule:

> V. Punitive Damages
>   A. Purpose and Measure
>   • • • •
>   B. Availability
>   1. Torts— . . .
>   2. Contracts—Courts generally do not award punitive damages for breach of contract.
>   a. Example: In *White v. Benkowski,* CB at 14, the court affirmed a trial court's denial of punitive damages for even a malicious breach of an agreement to supply water.
>   b. Exception to Rule: In dictum, the *White* court suggested that it might retain a traditional exception allowing punitive damages for breach of a marriage agreement.
>   c. Minority Approach: A few jurisdictions have followed the lead of *Jordan v. Ash,* CB at 21, which granted punitive damages for an employer's "malicious and oppressive" breach of an employment agreement, even though the employee had not proved all the elements of an independent tort.

The concise statement of the general rule in subsection 2 of the outline above represents the kind of information that you must recall and express on a law school exam. To apply that rule to the facts of an exam question, however, you must have a more concrete understanding of the law than is reflected in the abstract statement of the general rule. For this, you must analyze individual cases, as illustrated in subsections a, b, and c in the above example.

Subsections a and b illustrate a student's understanding of the parameters of the rule in most jurisdictions: some courts might award punitive damages in the exceptional case of breach of a marriage agreement; otherwise, even a finding of malice on the part of the breaching party will not move a court to depart from the general rule. Subsection c reflects the student's judgment that *Jordan* represents a minority approach that departs from the general view that malice is not significant to the availability of punitive damages for breach of contract. By identifying the factual context of *Jordan,* the student can remain sensitive to the possibility that the minority approach is limited to employment contracts or other contracts in which the parties have disparate bargaining power.

A more sophisticated outline of the same material might incorporate a policy analysis of the rule and the cases that illustrate it, perhaps reflecting the student's evaluation, as well as her synthesis, of the cases:

> 2. Contracts—Courts generally do not award punitive damages for breach of contract.

        a. Possible policy justifications—A breach of a private contract may not injure community interests as much as would a tort or a crime. Indeed, in some instances a breach may benefit the community by permitting reallocation of the freed resources to more productive uses. Compensatory damages would permit this reallocation while making the victim of the breach whole, but punitive damages would discourage the reallocation.

        b. Example: In *White v. Benkowski,* CB at 14, the court affirmed denial of punitive damages for even a malicious breach of a contract to supply water. This decision doesn't seem to further any important policy, because the supplier did not reallocate the water to a more urgent use.

        c. Exception: In dictum, the *White* Court suggested that it might retain a traditional exception allowing punitive damages for breach of a marriage agreement, presumably because, according to Corbin, "community resentment" may once have been greater in such cases.

        d. Minority Approach: In *Jordan v. Ash,* CB at 21, the court approved punitive damages for an employer's "malicious and oppressive" breach of an employment agreement, even though the employee had not proved all the elements of an independent tort. Deterrence through punitive damages is appropriate in such cases, because the injurious conduct is designed to harm others rather than to reallocate resources or serve any other business needs.

In this example, illustration c does more than simply identify possible limitations to the rule. It also implicitly raises questions about the continued viability of an exception that arguably is rooted in outdated values. Similarly, illustration d does more than identify a minority approach as a different kind of qualification to the general rule. In conjunction with illustration b, it implicitly compares the merits of maintaining certainty in a broad rule of general application (illustration b) with the case-specific fairness achieved by narrowly shaping rules so that they apply no further than the reasons that support them (illustration d).

The policy analysis may be suggested in the opinions themselves, may be the topic of class discussion, or may be the product of your original analysis. If time permits, you may wish on occasion to consult a treatise for information and ideas with which to enrich your outline. However, you will develop skills best by preparing outlines from course materials and class notes with little or no reference to study aids and with only occasional reference to respected treatises to help clear up areas of confusion.

In either example of outlining, the single-sentence summaries of the cases should represent a substantial condensation of your case briefs and notes of class discussion. Nonetheless, they include a sufficient reference to the facts of those cases to bring each case to life and to place statements about the legal results of the cases in their factual context. Indeed, you may find that you can analyze some exam questions best by directly analogizing the exam problem to, or distinguishing it from, a particular case summarized in your outline rather than by recalling a general and abstract principle that you have constructed from several cases.

In preparing the outline, however, you should maintain a basic structure that organizes the subject matter around legal rules and that subordinates the cases to illustrations of those rules. For example, a case that addresses distinct issues relating to the proper measure of compensatory damages and to the availability of punitive damages might appear in summarized form in two places in the outline: (1) a summary of the court's first holding would illustrate a rule about compensatory damages, and (2) a summary of the second holding would illustrate a rule about punitive damages stated in a different section of the outline.

Often, you can best illustrate the parameters of a rule by comparing two factually distinguishable, legally consistent cases that reach different results. By identifying a set of facts that satisfies the legal rule and by contrasting them with a set of facts that does not, the outline helps to bring concrete meaning to an otherwise abstract rule.

For example, an outline of statutory liability for civil rights violations might address the subtopic of the defense of absolute immunity from money damages that is enjoyed by state court judges when performing a judicial, rather than an administrative, function:

VI. Immunity Defenses
[overview]
A. Absolute Immunities—Legislators, judges, and prosecutors must make sensitive policy decisions on controversial matters and are conspicuous targets for retaliatory suits. Absolute immunity allows them to exercise discretion without fear of reprisal.
1. Legislators— . . .
2. Judges—A state judge is absolutely immune from liability for money damages, even for allegedly malicious unconstitutional acts, if the judge (i) had subject-matter jurisdiction, and (ii) was acting in a judicial function.
a. Subject-matter Jurisdiction— . . .

Rule

b. Judicial Function—A judge enjoys immunity only for actions taken within a judicial function, as contrasted with the judge's administrative function.

Facts that satisfy the rule

(1) Example: In *Forrester v. White*, CB 423 (7th Cir. 1986) a judge enjoyed absolute immunity from liability for alleged discrimination in firing a probation officer. Because the probation officer's duties included advising the judge on substantive matters, hiring or firing the officer was a judicial function that "directly implicated the exercise of the judge's discretionary judgment."

Facts that do not satisfy the rule

(2) Example: In *McMillan v. Svetanoff*, CB 425 (7th Cir. 1986), a judge was not absolutely immune from liability for alleged race discrimination in firing a court reporter, who recorded proceedings but did not perform legal analysis. Hiring and firing such employees was an administrative task because it did not require exercise of the judge's legal knowledge or experience.

In this outline, subsections b(1) and b(2) give concrete meaning to the abstract rule stated in subsection b by providing examples of (1) facts that satisfy the rule stated in subsection b and (2) facts that fail to satisfy the rule.

C. THE OUTLINE AS A STUDY TOOL

Although the process of preparing an outline is more valuable than the finished product, a thoughtful outline makes an excellent study tool. When reviewing for exams, you can put your voluminous notes aside and use the brief references to cases in the outline to trigger your memory about the fuller case analysis that you performed earlier in the semester.

In the few hours before an exam, you may want to take a broader view of the course by skimming the legal rules stated in the major sections and subsections of your outline. The factual context provided by case summaries will easily come to mind if you have earlier analyzed those cases, expressed the analysis in the outline, and read the entire outline once or twice after preparing it. Indeed, you may find it helpful to prepare a brief outline of the outline by writing down the major headings of the outline on a separate sheet of paper.

IV. SUMMARY

To outline course material,

(1) Analyze and synthesize by briefing the cases and reflecting on class discussion.

(2) Identify topics that you intend to address in the outline. You should identify significant general rules that are stated in the course materials or that you can construct from the course materials through a process of synthesis and inductive reasoning.

(3) State those rules in an organized fashion that shows the proper relationships among the rules.

(4) Finally, illustrate the general rules with brief summaries of the cases from which the rules are derived.

======= **E X E R C I S E   6 - 2** =======

1. *Outlining Exercise—Rules of the House*

Imagine that parents, Gerald and Janice, are teaching their younger son, Reggie, good habits and behavior. Reggie can't fully understand abstract rules, so Gerald and Janice teach him through positive or negative feedback in specific situations. In the last few weeks, Reggie remembers the following experiences for which he received praise or admonishment:

The case of the Hand in the Cookie Jar: Reggie reached into a cookie jar and helped himself to a cookie shortly before dinner. Janice and Gerald admonished Reggie that the cookie would spoil his appetite for dinner.

The case of the Broken Vase: Reggie climbed onto a chair, reached a vase on a table top, and threw the vase to the floor, breaking it. Janice and Gerald sent Reggie to his room, admonishing him that he should not play with his parent's possessions.

The case of the Chocolate Ice Cream: After dinner one night, Reggie asked for some chocolate ice cream. To his surprise, his parents served him a dish of ice cream, praising him for having finished his vegetables.

The case of the Mistreated Teddy Bear: Anxious to test his parents' limits one evening, Reggie climbed onto a chair with his favorite teddy bear and threw the teddy bear onto the living room carpet. Reggie's parents saw this event but had no reaction; they continued reading the newspaper and watching TV.

The case of the Bouncing Ball: Emboldened by the teddy bear incident, Reggie brought out his favorite rubber ball and began kicking it around the living room, causing it to bounce off the TV set and to narrowly miss Janice's glass of wine sitting on the coffee table. Janice flashed Reggie an angry glance, and Gerald sternly said, "Outside with that ball, young man!"

Assignment: From these cases, derive at least two general rules governing Reggie's behavior in his home. Illustrate each of your rules with brief summaries that show what kinds of behavior either satisfy or violate the rules. If appropriate, draft an overview statement that captures the essence of all the rules and examples. When you have completed your outline, compare it with the sample outline in Chapter 7, pages 129-130.

2. *Outlining Exercise—Advertisements as Offers*

Review the case briefs that you prepared for Exercise 5-1(3), page 100. Prepare an excerpt of a contracts outline that addresses the question of whether a store's newspaper advertisement amounts to an offer. Derive a general legal rule from the two cases, and use summaries of the cases as illustrations of the rule.

7

Essay Examinations

I. OVERVIEW—PERSPECTIVE AND GENERAL FORMAT

The answer to a law school essay examination is generally similar to the discussion section of an office memorandum, which is discussed in detail in Chapter 8. When you reach Chapter 8, you should reflect on these parallels. To better prepare you for the comparison, this chapter will occasionally pause briefly to note which facets of examination answers have counterparts in office memoranda and to point out the differences in styles appropriate to each document.

A. PERSPECTIVE

Most essay examinations ask for a balanced analysis of a problem with a direction such as the following: "Discuss the claims and defenses that the parties may reasonably assert. Be sure to discuss arguments on both sides of each issue." Like an actual office memorandum assignment, the exam problem may identify one of the parties as your client. Nonetheless, the exam obviously requests that you take a nearly neutral perspective rather than advocate only your client's claims and defenses. In addition to developing arguments for your own client, you must anticipate and demonstrate an understanding of the counterarguments that the opposing party likely will raise.

Indeed, many exam problems do not even identify one of the parties as your client. Your perspective then will be even more strictly neutral than it would be for an office memorandum, which at least anticipates advocacy on behalf of an identified client.

Finally, a few exam problems may ask you to advocate only the claims and defenses of an identified client. If so, your answer will take the partisan approach of a brief to a court. Such exams, however, are rare.

B. GENERAL FORMAT

As introduced in Chapter 3, an answer to an essay examination and the discussion section of an office memorandum typically share a general structure: after (1) identifying the issue, you should (2) summarize the applicable legal rule or rules, (3) apply the rule to the relevant facts to determine whether the facts satisfy the legal rule, and (4) state a reasonable conclusion.

Some of the more formal components of other legal documents are notably missing from a good exam answer. For example, professors normally do not require you to formally state all the issues at or near the beginning of your answer, as you would in an office memorandum or in some briefs. Even more important, you should never waste time drafting an introduction that separately restates all the facts of the problem. In all but the most unusual examinations, the problem will state the facts in a summarized, well-organized fashion. Accordingly, your professor will test your ability to analyze groups of those facts in the context of specific issues, but not your ability to restate all the facts in isolation.

II. ELEMENTS OF THE ANSWER

A. ISSUES

1. Identifying Issues

Occasionally, a professor will identify examination issues by asking you to respond to specific questions, such as "did Seller make an offer to Buyer?". More commonly, the exam problem will end with a very general question about the rights and obligations of the party, and it requires you to identify the relevant issues.

To identify the issues, you must apply the skills and knowledge that you have acquired from briefing cases and outlining course material throughout the semester. By briefing countless cases, you have learned to sift through complicated fact patterns and to recognize the kinds of facts that have potential legal significance. Moreover, by briefing and synthesizing cases and by outlining the course material, you have armed yourself with a general knowledge of relevant legal rules and policies. With this preparation, by carefully studying the facts of the exam problem, you can determine what claims and defenses the parties can reasonably assert and which elements of those claims and defenses are placed in doubt.

For example, suppose that an exam problem asks you to assume that the relevant jurisdiction has retained the common law definition of burglary. Part of the problem describes Michael Glass just before dawn opening the door of the cab of a VW van and reaching inside to steal stereo equipment lying on the driver's seat. It also states that the owner of the van, Leona Rosal, is sleeping in the back of the van while on a road trip, with curtains drawn between her and the cab of the van. The problem also asks you to assume that theft of the stereo equipment would constitute felony larceny in the jurisdiction.

You know from your studies that the common law crime of burglary requires proof of the breaking and entering of a dwelling of another at night with the intent to commit a felony. Armed with this knowledge, you can see that the facts provide a nonfrivolous basis for prosecuting Michael Glass for common law burglary but that some elements of the crime are in doubt. Specifically, Michael's opening the cab door and reaching into the van to steal the stereo equipment are almost certainly a "breaking and entering" with an "intent to commit a felony." However, the moments "just before dawn" are only arguably "during the night," and the cab of Leona's van is not clearly part of "a dwelling." Thus, whether Michael committed a burglary is subject to some debate and is a general issue in the problem.

Moreover, each element of the crime that is in doubt forms the basis of a subissue. For example, the VW van may be unlike the more conventional houses that satisfied the "dwelling" requirement in the common law cases that you have studied. Although Leona is temporarily using the van as sleeping quarters, the van is arguably primarily a means of transportation, and the cab is physically separated from the sleeping quarters. Because you can reasonably argue either side of this topic, whether Leona's van is a "dwelling" for purposes of common law burglary is a subissue warranting discussion. Other elements of the crime and possible defenses may be placed in issue by the facts summarized above or by other facts in the problem.

2. Scope of Analysis

Because this process of identifying issues requires you to exercise judgment, you can never determine with complete certainty which questions your professor thinks are sufficiently clearly raised by the facts to warrant discussion. Moreover, some professors directly examine your ability to identify as many issues as possible, including those related to novel or particularly creative legal theories. In case of doubt, therefore, you should identify and at least briefly discuss even marginal issues. If the professor expects some discussion of a marginal issue, you will earn valuable points even with a conclusory discussion. On the other hand, if the professor disagrees that a particular matter warrants analysis, you will have minimized the lost time by keeping the discussion brief.

3. Expressing Your Identification of Issues

You need not state each of the issues and subissues of an examination problem in polished detail. However, your answer should leave no doubt about which issue you are analyzing in any passage in the answer. To guide your reader through your analysis, you can use the same techniques that help convey organization to the reader of an office memorandum. You should discuss major issues in separate sections and should precede each discussion with a section heading that generally identifies the issue analyzed in that section.

If your analysis of the issue is lengthy or complex, you may want to use subsection headings to identify your discussions of subissues. In many cases, however, subtler guides to the reader often will be sufficient for subissues: you can separate your discussions of distinct subissues into separate paragraphs, and you can use a topic sentence to identify the subissue addressed in each paragraph.

A section heading introducing an issue or subissue can simply be a brief word or phrase that refers to a claim, a defense, or one element of a claim or defense. Unless the question raises the possibility of claims of only one party against one other, section headings also should identify which party is bringing a claim against which other in each section.

For example, an examination problem might raise issues about various tort claims among three parties: Smith, Jones, and King. A student might display the general organization of his answer with section headings such as the following:

I. Smith v. Jones
  A. Battery
    • • • •
  B. Infliction of Emotional Distress
    • • • •
II. Smith v. King
  A. Negligence
    • • • •
  B. Strict Products Liability
    • • • •
III. Jones v. Smith—Defamation
    • • • •

In some cases, you may wish to illuminate the issue that is cryptically identified in a section heading by referring briefly to a potential argument of one of the parties, to facts that raise the issue, or to a preliminary legal conclusion that sets up the issue. For example, under section II(A) above, you might provide this orientation: "Smith may claim that King negligently hired Jones, proximately causing Smith's injuries at Jones's hands."

Alternatively, you can replace the word or phrase in the section heading with a question stated in a full sentence: "Is King liable to Smith for negligently hiring Jones, proximately causing Smith to suffer injury at Jones's hands?" If you adopt this approach, however, remember that the professor reading the examination answer typically will not expect the precision and specificity appropriate for the formal statement of issues in a case brief, office memorandum, or brief to a court. Therefore, you should not waste valuable time trying to meet those standards in framing your issue.

In response to a complex essay question that raises multiple issues, you may help orient the reader by beginning your response with an introductory paragraph that briefly identifies all the major issues that you plan to discuss. However, you should not compose a lengthy introduction that makes the subsequent discussion redundant.

B. LEGAL RULE

1. Presentation of Legal Rules

At the broadest level, the statement of a legal rule may be a summary of the elements of a claim that a party in the examination problem may reasonably pursue:

Intentional Infliction of Emotional Distress

Principal Jones may be liable to Schoolboy Smith for intentional infliction of emotional distress if he engaged in extreme and outrageous conduct that caused Smith severe emotional distress, and if Jones either intended to cause such distress or recklessly disregarded the near certainty of causing such distress.

If you divide the discussion of this claim into subsections or paragraphs to address separate subissues, you might state a subrule in the form of a definition or other illumination of one of the elements of the claim:

"Extreme and outrageous" conduct is limited to shocking conduct that is beyond all possible bounds of decency. The defendant's conduct is more likely to satisfy this standard if he occupies a position of power or authority over the plaintiff.

Some examination problems may raise questions about choice of law or the precise formulation of the applicable rule. For example, a problem in a contracts examination may raise the question of whether the Uniform Commercial Code or the common law applies to a transaction.[1] Other examination problems may raise questions about the choice between traditional rules and progressive trends, or between majority rules and minority approaches. If you have time to discuss such problems, you should consider briefly discussing each of the competing rules. Then, in the fact analysis that follows, you can discuss the likelihood of success of a claim or defense under each legal rule.

2. Depth and Formality of Analysis

When writing an office memorandum, you normally must discuss specific statutes and case law from a particular jurisdiction that apply to the dispute, and you must carefully cite to the authority on which you rely. Moreover, you often will express the in-depth case analysis and synthesis from which you derive a legal rule.

---

1. Article 2 of the Uniform Commercial Code applies "[u]nless the context otherwise requires . . . to transactions in goods." U.C.C. § 2-102.

In contrast, most law school examinations will require you to discuss general legal principles, primarily common law rules, that you must memorize for a closed-book examination. Additionally, you ordinarily will not have time to describe the process of synthesizing cases from which you have derived legal rules. Instead, you may simply present the kind of concise statements of law that you have constructed for your outlines.

Moreover, in an examination answer, you ordinarily need not cite to authority in your discussion of legal rules. You may earn an extra point or two by identifying the names of particular cases that illustrate issues or rules, but that practice is productive only if you remember the case name quickly and with certainty. The extra point or two is not worth a significant investment of time, and the possibility of losing points by naming an irrelevant case reduces the appeal of guessing.

Your professor's expectations may be greater if she gives an open-book examination or provides statutory materials for the examination. If you have legal authority at your disposal during the examination, you can more easily cite to statutes and cases, quote relevant portions of statutes, and explain how two or more cases combine to contribute to the development of a legal principle.

C. FACT ANALYSIS—APPLICATION OF LAW TO FACTS

1. Presentation of Fact Analysis

In each section or subsection devoted to an issue or subissue, you should identify facts relevant to the issue and should briefly explain whether the facts satisfy the legal rule that you have summarized. In most cases, you have identified a matter as an issue because the facts of the problem suggest uncertainty whether a legal rule is satisfied. Therefore, you usually can find some facts that support each side of the dispute, and you should take care to argue both sides:

> *Intentional Infliction of Emotional Distress*
>
> Principal Jones may be liable . . . Viewed in isolation, Principal Jones's method of questioning Schoolboy Smith about illegal drugs probably was not "extreme and outrageous" in itself, because Jones "addressed Smith politely" and "never raised his voice." On the other hand, Jones was inherently intimidating to Smith, a 10-year-old child, because of Jones's status as an adult and as the highest authority at the elementary school. Moreover, it was common knowledge in the school that Jones had suspended two other students that semester for forging false notes excusing absences. By asking Smith to empty his pockets and to reveal the contents of his desk and locker, Jones implicitly accused Smith of lying when Smith denied any involvement with illegal drugs. In light of Jones's position of authority, his request to search Smith may have been unusually shocking and intimidating, particularly because the request immediately followed Smith's sincere denials.

2. Depth and Formality of Analysis

In an office memorandum, you will explore in depth the application of legal rules to facts by carefully comparing the facts and reasoning of previous cases to the facts of your own case. Through this process of analogizing and distinguishing precedent, you can engage in a sophisticated analysis of whether the facts of your case satisfy the applicable legal rules.

In contrast, few professors will expect you to describe particular cases studied in class and to expressly analogize them to, or distinguish them from, the dispute presented in an exam problem. If you have conscientiously briefed your cases throughout the semester, you will recall cases that help you to spot issues and to analyze the problem, and you may mentally draw direct distinctions and analogies. However, you will seldom have sufficient time to express those distinctions and analogies in thorough case analysis in your examination answer. Instead, you should directly explain how relevant facts support or undermine the application of a legal rule.

Again, those professors who give open-book examinations may have higher expectations. If class materials are readily available to you during the exam, you may be expected to compare cases in your fact analysis. This may be true also for a closed-book exam in an exceptional area of law dominated by a manageable number of conspicuous cases, such as the Supreme Court case law governing personal jurisdiction. If you have mastered a relatively small number of important cases that define an area of law, you can feasibly refer to them by name and develop analogies and distinctions, even if you do not have access to your course materials during the examination.

D. THE CONCLUSION

1. Taking a Position

Just as your supervising attorney will expect you to reach conclusions on even close questions in an office memorandum, most law professors will expect you to state a conclusion for each issue that you discuss in an examination answer. On close questions, you can hedge the conclusion with qualifying terms, such as "probably." More important, the professor may accept any of several reasonable positions as an acceptable conclusion. Nonetheless, she will expect some resolution of each issue and subissue:

Intentional Infliction of Emotional Distress
Principal Jones may be liable to Schoolboy Smith for . . .

Extreme Conduct—
• • • •

Principal Jones's questioning and request to search constituted extreme and outrageous conduct.

Subsidiary conclusion

	Severe Distress—
	• • • •
Subsidiary conclusion	Schoolboy Smith's transitory fear probably did not amount to severe emotional distress.
	Conclusion—
General conclusion	Because Schoolboy Smith probably did not suffer extreme emotional distress, I conclude that Principal Jones is not liable for intentional infliction of emotional distress.

2. Subsidiary and Comprehensive Conclusions

In an office memorandum, you should not only state conclusions at the end of your discussion of each issue or subissue, you should also summarize and evaluate all your major conclusions in a separate "Conclusion" section.

In contrast, few law professors will expect you to summarize all previous major conclusions in a general summary of claims and defenses at the end of your answer to an exam problem. Such a consolidated restatement of conclusions ordinarily will score few points in an examination unless it adds new information or enhances the clarity of the discussion that precedes it. Accordingly, in most cases you will benefit by using the last few minutes allocated to a problem to look for additional issues that you might have missed rather than to summarize subsidiary conclusions that you have already clearly communicated.

III. TECHNIQUES FOR WRITING EXAM RESPONSES

A. EFFECTIVE USE OF TIME

At the beginning of the examination, you should determine how much time you will allocate to each problem, and you should adhere to that schedule. Adequate discussions of all the problems in an examination will score more points than unusually thorough discussions of some of the problems at the cost of inadequate treatment of others. The same holds true for treatment of issues within a problem: adequate discussions of all the major issues will score more points than an unusually thorough discussion of only half the issues. Thus, if an exam problem raises an unusual number of issues, the professor may expect only superficial discussion of each.

Although law school examinations require quick thinking, uninterrupted concentration, and rapid writing, you should not begin writing prematurely. You are more likely to write sensible responses and to avoid wasted effort if you spend up to a quarter or even half of the time allotted for each problem in mastering the assignment and "prewriting."

B. MASTERING THE ASSIGNMENT

You should read an exam problem once at a moderately quick pace to get a general picture of the events described, to classify the general nature of the probable claims and defenses, and to discover the particular question or questions stated by the professor, usually at the end of the problem. You should then read the problem at least once again, this time at a much more deliberate pace, to spot specific issues and to make marks or margin notes that highlight important facts.

C. PREWRITING

A few students have such well-developed skills of organization, such good memories, and such powers of concentration that they can write their examination answers without first outlining their analyses. The rest of us, however, will benefit greatly if we devote a few minutes to analysis and outlining before beginning to write.

The outline on scratch paper should be nothing more than a cryptic, skeletal construction of the issues that you intend to address and the significant facts relating to each of those issues. The outline becomes the primary vehicle for analysis and organization. Before you begin writing, you can use it to decide which issues you will address, what order of presentation is most logical or efficient, and what facts support each side of the dispute in each section:

Q1—
Smith v. Jones

   I. Intent. Inflic. of Emot. Distress
Extreme Conduct—Jones—polite & subdued, but great authority.—Request to search suggests disbelief and possibility of discipline
Intent or Reckless— . . .
  II. Defamation
     • • • •

If the legal rules associated with an issue are unusually complex, or if you desire to discuss alternative legal theories, you may wish to include some reference to the law in the outline as well.

By scribbling a quick outline, you can examine your complete analysis at a glance and can determine whether it makes sense. If the analysis appears to be faulty, incomplete, or illogically organized, you can easily change your plans at the outlining stage. Changing your approach after writing half of your response would be much more difficult.

Finally, after completing your outline, you should quickly read the problem once again before beginning to write. Because you have fully analyzed the problem in the outline, you can then more effectively recognize the legal significance of facts in the problem. Indeed, facts that appeared to be insignificant in early readings may now reveal themselves as material.

D. WRITING THE ANSWER

If you have prepared an outline of your answer, writing the answer in the answer booklet should be a fairly mechanical process. Your task is simply that of expressing in full sentences the ideas that are cryptically represented in your examination outline, taking care to cover all the elements discussed in section C above: issue, rule of law, application of law to facts, and conclusion. The outline provides a guide that will keep you on track even when you momentarily lose sight of the main issues because of nervousness or temporary devotion to the details of a subissue.

Because of the intense time pressures of most exams, law professors do not expect polished writing or perfect organization, and you should not waste precious time thinking about the best possible way to express your ideas. Nonetheless, you will have an advantage if you have developed skills of organization and clear, concise writing: you will score more points by clearly expressing a greater number of material ideas than will students whose writing is verbose and repetitious or is so unclear that the professor simply cannot understand it.

If you discover near the end of an exam that you have insufficient time to complete your analysis in full prose, you should simply outline the remainder of your response in your examination answer booklet. Most professors will give more points for a clear overview of all the remaining issues than for a fuller development of only one of several remaining issues.

IV. SUMMARY AND REVIEW

The three critical steps for success in the first semester of law school are to

(1) brief and synthesize cases;

(2) prepare a course outline by further synthesizing cases, reorganizing materials to highlight legal principles, and illustrating the principles with summaries of the case briefs; and

(3) analyze examination problems and express the answer in a clear, well organized fashion.

Below is a progression of study and exam materials that illustrate the process of studying law, from briefing cases to taking an exam. Because this example is taken from a family setting, the summary of cases is much less formal than a series of briefs of judicial opinions. With a bit of imagination, however, you can draw an analogy between these sample materials and those that you will prepare in law school.

Notice that the legal rules stated in the exam answer are taken directly from the student's outline, which the student has committed to memory. Moreover, the student's knowledge of the case illustrations in the outline help the student engage in the fact analysis in the examination answer. Finally, one issue in the exam requires the student to develop new rules by extrapolating from the familiar rules and the policies that support them.

CASE SUMMARIES WITH SYNTHESES

The case of the Hand in the Cookie Jar: Baby Reggie reached into a cookie jar and helped himself to a cookie shortly before dinner. Janice and Gerald admonished Reggie that the cookie would spoil his appetite for dinner.

The case of the Broken Vase: Reggie climbed onto a chair, reached a vase on a table top, and threw the vase to the floor, breaking it. Janice and Gerald sent Reggie to his room, admonishing him that he should not play with his parent's possessions.

The case of the Chocolate Ice Cream: After dinner one night, Reggie asked for some chocolate ice cream. To his surprise, his parents served him a dish of ice cream, praising him for having finished his vegetables. Unlike in the cookie jar case, Reggie did not spoil his appetite by eating the ice cream.

The case of the Mistreated Teddy Bear: Anxious to test his parents' limits one evening, Reggie climbed onto a chair with his favorite teddy bear and threw the teddy bear onto the living room carpet. Reggie's parents saw this event but had no reaction; they continued reading the newspaper and watching TV. Unlike in the broken vase case, Reggie's actions here did not jeopardize his parents' possessions.

The case of the Bouncing Ball: Emboldened by the teddy bear incident, Reggie brought out his favorite rubber ball and began kicking it around the living room, causing it to bounce off the TV set and to narrowly miss Janice's glass of wine sitting on the coffee table. Janice flashed Reggie an angry glance, and Gerald sternly said, "Outside with that ball, young man!" This is more similar to the broken vase case than to the teddy bear case, because Reggie's bouncing ball threatened to cause harm to his parents' television set and wine glass.

OUTLINE

Rules for Reggie

I. Overview—Reggie's parents try to restrict Reggie's activities to those that are beneficial to his health and that protect his parents' possessions from harm.

II. Dietary Rules—Reggie is permitted to eat sweets, but only at times that won't spoil his appetite for more healthful foods.

A. Example: In *the case of the Chocolate Ice Cream,* Reggie's parents gladly served him ice cream after dinner, because he had eaten all his vegetables.

B. Example: In *the case of the Hand in the Cookie Jar,* Reggie was not permitted to eat a cookie shortly before dinner, because it would ruin his appetite for dinner.

III. Rules about Toys—Reggie is permitted to play only with his own toys, and not in a way that will endanger his parents' possessions.

A. Example: In *the case of the Broken Vase,* Reggie was disciplined for breaking his parents' vase.

B. Example: In *the case of the Bouncing Ball*, Reggie was admonished for playing with his own rubber ball in a way that endangered his parents' possessions, such as the TV set and a wine glass.

C. Example: In *the case of the Mistreated Teddy Bear*, Reggie was permitted to play with his own teddy bear, even by throwing it onto the floor, apparently because such conduct did not harm any of his parents' possessions.

EXAMINATION PROBLEM

On Saturday morning, Reggie began coloring in his coloring book with a box of crayons. He soon expanded his artistic activity to drawing a multicolored mural on one of the walls of his room. Displeased with the quality of his drawing, Reggie broke each of his 24 crayons in half and threw them into his waste basket. Indeed, he was so displeased with his artistry that he decided to wash his drawing off the wall. To that end, Reggie opened the cupboard under the kitchen sink and took a bottle of liquid drain cleaner, which he thought was a form of soap but was in fact a toxic chemical capable of burning his eyes and skin. At that moment, Reggie's parents intercepted him and discovered each of his activities during the day. Fully discuss whether Reggie has violated any rules of his house.

EXAMINATION ANSWER

Issue[2]	*I. Harm to Parents' Possessions*
Rule	Reggie's parents permit him to use and even abuse his own toys, but they do not allow Reggie to harm their possessions.
Application	Reggie did not harm his parents' property by drawing in his coloring book. Nor did he harm their property by breaking his crayons, because those presumably were his own toys. However, Reggie almost certainly violated his parents' rules by drawing on his bedroom wall. Although the wall was in his room, his parents probably view it as part of their possessions, because they undoubtedly are responsible for maintaining it. Reggie did not physically break the surface of the wall as he might break a vase. However, a crayon drawing on the wall might require vigorous scrubbing or even repainting. Therefore, it probably represents actual harm to the wall.
Conclusion	Reggie has violated his parents' rule against harming their possessions.

---

2. The labels are designed to remind you that a complete legal analysis should include four basic elements. Those labels should not appear in the margins of an actual examination answer; some professors may be offended by such a mechanical approach.

II. Promotion of Reggie's Health and Safety of Parents' Possessions

Issue

Rule

In addition to prohibiting Reggie from harming their possessions, Reggie's parents forbid him to eat sweets if they will spoil his appetite for more healthful foods.

Application

Reggie has not tried to eat sweets at an inappropriate time. However, he has endangered his health by carrying a dangerous chemical, the drain cleaner, with the intention of opening the bottle and using the chemical to clean his wall. The policy behind the dietary rule is apparently to help maintain Reggie's health. Therefore, Reggie's parents likely would disapprove of other activities that endanger his health, particularly activities that would cause more serious harm than simply eating unhealthful foods.

Similarly, Reggie's parents may admonish him under an extension of their rule prohibiting harm to their possessions. Reggie is unlikely to do any harm to the drain cleaner. On the other hand, the drain cleaner is one of his parents' possessions rather than one of Reggie's toys. Moreover, if Reggie spilled the drain cleaner, he might harm other possessions of his parents that came in contact with the chemical. Therefore, Reggie's parents are likely to disapprove of Reggie's taking the drain cleaner out of concern for their possessions as well as concern for Reggie's safety.

Conclusion

Because the chemical could cause serious harm to Reggie and to his parents' possessions, I conclude that his parents will admonish him and will adopt a general rule prohibiting him from taking bottles from cupboards.

══════ S A M P L E S ══════

1. *Sample Examination Answer*

Read the Sample Memorandum 1 on page 156. Imagine that an exam problem raises several issues, one of which is similar to the consideration issue discussed in that sample memorandum. The general structure of the discussion of that issue in the examination answer would be similar to that of the Discussion section of the sample memorandum. Nonetheless, even a thorough examination answer would be less formal than the memorandum. For example, the examination answer would omit citations and in-depth case analysis:

Q1

Lender v. Borrower

• • • •

Lender v. Guarantor

• • • •

Issue

Consideration—Illusory Promise

The lender's promise to refrain from asserting his claim and demanding payment until he "needs the money" arguably is illusory, thus creating doubt whether the Guarantor's promise is enforceable.

Rule

An enforceable contract requires a bargained-for exchange in which a promisor exchanges his own promise for a return promise or performance. The requirement of an exchange is not satisfied if one party gives only an illusory promise, which does not commit the promisor to any future performance. Even if a promise leaves open the possibility that the promisor will escape obligation, however, the promise is valid if the promisor does not have complete control over the events on which the promisor's obligation is conditioned.

Application

The lender's promise to forbear until he "needs" the money appears to condition the length of his forbearance on financial events that are at least partly outside his control: as long as his income and expenses created no need for the money, the lender had a commitment to forbear from demanding payment. In an effort to escape obligations, the guarantor could argue that the word "need" refers to a subjective perception of deprivation that is inseparable from one's desires, which are subject to the promisor's unfettered discretion. However, "need" is distinguishable from "want."

Conclusion

Because the formality of the written agreement suggests that the parties must have intended to create binding obligations, a court probably would interpret the word "need" to impose objective restrictions on the lender's rights and conduct, thereby satisfying the consideration requirement and making the Guarantor's promise enforceable.

2. *Sample Examination Problem and Response*

Examine the following contracts problem and response. Although the fact analysis is fairly simple, the internal organization is more complex than that in the sample answer in problem 1 above, because the issue of recovery under quasi-contract invites discussion of two subissues in separate paragraphs, each with its own subrule, fact analysis, and preliminary conclusion.

Problem

While jogging one morning, realtor Maria Reyes came upon the victim of an auto accident that had occurred a few minutes earlier. The victim was unconscious and was bleeding profusely from a severed artery. Reyes easily saved the victim's life by applying direct pressure to the severed artery and by flagging down a passing motorist, a service for which a paramedic unit would have charged $300. Reyes later demanded compensation from the victim. What result, and why?

Sample Answer

Liability for unjust enrichment[3]

The unconscious victim could not expressly or through conduct communicate a promise to pay Reyes. Therefore, Reyes cannot recover on the basis of contract or promissory estoppel.[4]

Reyes likely will bring an action in quasi-contract for restitution of the reasonable value of the benefit that she conferred on the victim. To recover on this theory, she must prove that she unjustly enriched the victim.[5]

Enrichment is a measurable benefit. Reyes enriched the victim by rendering tangible first aid services and summoning help, thus saving the victim's life.[6]

Reyes must prove that it would be unjust for the victim to retain the benefits of the first-aid services without compensating Reyes for them. Reyes could prove this by showing that she had some relationship with the victim that led Reyes reasonably to expect compensation. The courts ordinarily presume that emergency services at the scene of an accident are provided gratuitously. Reyes could overcome that presumption if she could show that she acted in a professional capacity when rendering the services or that the services she rendered were unusually burdensome or hazardous. She likely will not succeed, because she is a realtor and is not in the business of charging for

---

3. This heading reflects the exam writer's decision to discuss issues of liability separately from those of remedies. Within the section addressing liability, the writer introduces the elements of quasi-contract and unjust enrichment, and she analyzes each separately. She could have begun each of those analyses with a subsection heading, but good paragraphing appears to be a sufficient guide to organization within the two major sections.

4. This paragraph makes an introductory point by stating the facts and conclusion and leaving the rule implicit. It is not absolutely necessary for a good answer, but it might be good for an extra point or two because it explains how the student selected issues for discussion.

5. This paragraph identifies the main issue and states the applicable rule on the broadest, most general level.

6. This paragraph introduces a subissue, "enrichment," states the applicable rule, and reaches a conclusion on that subissue by applying the rule to the facts.

medical services, and because she "easily saved the victim's life" without risk to herself.[7]

Because the facts suggest that Reyes could not reasonably have expected compensation for her emergency services, I conclude that Reyes cannot recover.[8]

Remedies

Assuming that Reyes could prove a claim for quasi-contract, she would be entitled to restitution measured by the reasonable value of the benefit that she bestowed on the victim. The purpose of such relief would be to deny the unjust enrichment to the recipient of the benefit; therefore, whenever feasible, damages ought to be measured by the value that the recipient places on the benefit. If that is not feasible, a court may award damages based on the general market value of the benefit or on the out-of-pocket costs incurred by the provider of the benefit.[9]

In this case, from the perspective of the victim, the value of the benefit bestowed by Reyes is the value of the victim's life. A court would not likely use this value as the measure of the restitutionary relief, because it is relatively difficult to fix and because it is disproportionally greater than the effort expended by Reyes. Instead, the court probably would award the damages based on the general market value of Reyes's services: that measure is more nearly proportionate to Reyes's efforts, and it can be easily established by reference to the $200 fee that would have been charged by a paramedic unit. Alternatively, a court might award damages based on the actual costs incurred by Reyes, as measured by such things as inconvenience to Reyes and possible damage to her jogging clothes. However, because the market-value remedy is more consistent with restitution, I conclude that a court would award $100 in damages if Reyes could establish a claim based on quasi-contract.[10]

EXERCISE 7-1

1. The Bait

Review the case briefs that you prepared for Exercise 5-1(3), page 100, and the outline that you prepared for Exercise 6-2(3), page 118. Then, put away your notes, treat the following problem as a closed-book examination question, and write a response in essay form that identifies the issue, summarizes the law, applies the law to the facts relevant to the issue, and arrives at a conclusion on the issue.

---

7. Like the preceding paragraph, this one identifies a subissue, states the law applicable to that subissue, and reaches a conclusion on that subissue by applying the law to the facts.

8. This paragraph states a conclusion on the entire issue of liability.

9. This paragraph discusses the legal standards for computing damages.

10. This paragraph reaches a conclusion on the question of damages by applying the legal standards to the facts.

Problem

Billy Anaya read the following advertisement for Matt's Bedroom Furniture Mart in his town's primary newspaper:

THIS SATURDAY ONLY—NOON TO 9 PM

Specially marked floor models up to ½ off! Beds, headboards, dressers, and lamp tables, in all styles, sizes, finishes. Come in and browse around. But hurry, all items are subject to prior sale.

Billy visited Matt's Bedroom Furniture Mart at 8 P.M. on Saturday and saw a beautiful hardwood bedframe and headboard marked ½ off from $600 to $300. He told a saleswoman that he wanted to purchase it, but the saleswoman replied: "I'm sorry, but my manager just informed me that we are ending the sale early. I'm afraid that we cannot take any further purchases at the sales prices. However, you really ought to consider purchasing this at the regular price; it's more than worth it."

Does Billy have an enforceable contract with Matt's Bedroom Furniture Mart for sale of the bedframe and headboard for $300? You can assume that the saleswoman is an authorized representative for the store. Also assume that no statutes apply to the facts; analyze this problem under the common law of contracts only.

2. *The Surfing Burglar*

Review Exercise 3-1 on page 48. Treat it as a closed-book examination question and write a response in essay form that identifies the issues, summarizes the law, applies the law to the facts relevant to each issue, and arrives at a conclusion on each issue. You may supplement the statements of law in Exercise 3-1 with any common law of burglary that you have studied in your criminal law course. Otherwise, base your analysis on the general legal rules provided in Exercise 3-1. In this introductory exercise, permit yourself 45 minutes to complete your examination response; be prepared for greater time pressures later in the semester.

WRITING IN THE LAW OFFICE— NEUTRAL ANALYSIS

The Office Memorandum of Law

I. PURPOSE AND PERSPECTIVE

An office memorandum of law is one of the most effective means with which a new associate or a summer law clerk can directly help a supervising attorney represent a client. The supervising attorney may be preparing to draft a more formal document, such as a pleading or brief to a court, an opinion letter to a client, or a demand letter to an opposing party. She may use the office memorandum as a source of information, or even as a partial rough draft. In other cases, the supervising attorney may use the information in an office memorandum to develop a tax strategy for a business client or a settlement strategy for negotiations on behalf of a litigation client.

An office memorandum informs rather than advocates. To effectively represent the client, the supervising attorney must know both the weaknesses and the strengths of the client's claims and defenses. If you present a balanced analysis of the dispute in your office memorandum, you will enable your supervising attorney to focus her attention on her strongest arguments, to anticipate the counterarguments of the opposing party, and to develop an effective strategy. On the other hand, if you selectively bear only good news to your supervising attorney, you will mislead her and perhaps cause her embarrassment when further proceedings expose holes in her client's case that might have caused less damage had the law firm studied them at an earlier stage.

On the other hand, an office memorandum is not entirely neutral; in most cases, it anticipates advocacy on behalf of a client. Therefore, even though you explore arguments on both sides of a dispute in your memorandum, you should not convey a detached indifference to the outcome.

Many supervising attorneys complain that student law clerks and recent graduates of law school tend to treat office memoranda as purely academic exercises and to abandon a client's cause too readily after identifying obstacles to the client's claims or defenses. Accordingly, you should not only identify weaknesses in a client's case, you should recommend the best means of overcoming them. You must neither conceal such weaknesses nor surrender to despair over them. Instead, you should identify the best means to exploit the strengths of the client's case, and you should suggest creative solutions to the problems raised by the weaknesses.

II. GENERAL FORMAT FOR AN OFFICE MEMORANDUM

Like alternative formats for student case briefs, a number of formats for office memoranda have earned popularity. If your law firm or individual supervising attorney expresses a preference for a particular format, you should respect the wishes of your intended audience. Otherwise, you can choose any reasonable format, such as any of the following:

Format A	**Format B**	**Format C**
Heading	Heading	Heading
I. Issue(s)	I. Overview	I. Issue(s)
II. Brief Answer(s)	II. Facts	II. Conclusion
III. Facts	III. Issue(s) & Brief Answer(s)	III. Facts
IV. Discussion	IV. Discussion	IV. Discussion
V. Conclusion	V. Conclusion	

Format A presents the issues before the facts so that the reader can appreciate the legal significance of the facts when she reads them. It follows the statement of issues with brief answers that tersely preview the final conclusion. As discussed below, the brief answers and the conclusion serve different purposes.

In some cases, complex multiple transactions and confusing relationships between multiple parties may make the statement of the issues incomprehensible to one who has not first read the facts. Format B provides an alternative format for such cases: in a paragraph or two, a brief overview identifies the general nature of the dispute and the issues, and it summarizes the writer's conclusions. Such an introduction enables the reader to appreciate the legal significance of the facts, and it may eliminate the need for anything more than one or two words in the brief answers. In turn, the statement of facts gives the reader sufficient information to comprehend a detailed statement of the issues, permitting the author of the memorandum to follow the facts with a more formal, specific statement of the issues than was feasible in the overview.

Format C is quite common in law offices. Its replacement of the brief answers with the main conclusion, however, makes it less effective than the other formats for two reasons. First, a full conclusion that summarizes the analysis and offers strategic recommendations may be premature if placed before the discussion section: the reader is better able to appreciate a sophisticated conclusion after first digesting the discussion. Second, a multi-issue memorandum that ends with the discussion of a single issue tends to produce a feeling of anticlimax: the reader typically feels much more satisfied if the memorandum concludes with a section that ties all of the issues together.

III. ELEMENTS OF AN OFFICE MEMORANDUM

The following subsections examine the content of the substantive elements of Format A.

A. ISSUES—IDENTIFICATION AND EXPRESSION

Your task of identifying issues for analysis in an office memorandum is similar to that of identifying issues on a law school examination: you must have at least a general knowledge of the law governing the dispute so that you can recognize the legal problems raised by the facts. In many cases, courses that you have taken in law school will enable you to identify the general nature of the issues and to direct your research efforts; if not, a secondary source such as a good treatise may provide the necessary background information.

You should not finally identify and express the issues until the final stages of drafting. When you prepare a case brief for class discussion, you ordinarily cannot state with particularity the issues discussed in the judicial decision until you have completed your analysis of the entire opinion. Similarly, when preparing an office memorandum, you ordinarily cannot state with particularity the issues raised by the facts of the dispute until you have finished your research and have fully analyzed the problem. At that time, you must decide which elements of a claim or defense are sufficiently in doubt that they warrant identification and discussion as issues.

For example, Title VII of the Civil Rights Act of 1964 imposes liability on employers for engaging in "unlawful employment practices," and it defines "employer" in part as "a person engaged in an industry affecting commerce."[1] Although engagement "in an industry affecting commerce" is always an element of employer liability, in many cases the facts known to all parties leave no doubt that the employer's activities satisfy the statutory rule under any reasonable interpretation. In such a case, the party charged with discrimination could not credibly dispute its status as an "employer" on grounds relating to commerce, and you should not identify that matter as an issue in your memorandum. At most, you might briefly state this conclusion in an introduction to the discussion of a substantial issue.

In the same case, however, unusual facts and uncertainty in the applicable legal standards might create doubt whether the employer has committed an

---

1. 42 U.S.C. §§ 2000e(b) (definition of "employer"), 2000e-2(a) (unlawful employer practices); see also id. at 2000e(g) and (h) (definitions of "commerce" and "industry affecting commerce").

"unlawful employment practice." Because the employer likely will deny committing an unlawful employment practice, and because the parties can reasonably dispute that matter, you should identify it as an issue and discuss it.

Once you have identified and analyzed issues for discussion in your memorandum, you should state them with the same specificity and attention to facts that would be appropriate in the statement of issues in a case brief prepared for class discussion. To review these techniques, you may want to return briefly to Chapter 5, pages 82-85.

For example, you should not state the issue described in the previous paragraph in such general terms as whether the employer committed an unlawful employment practice. Instead, after researching the law and analyzing the facts, you can more precisely identify the contours of the dispute likely to be raised by the parties:

> Did Salerno create a hostile or offensive working environment for his female employees by repeatedly asking them for dates, thus making Salerno liable for sex discrimination with respect to terms or conditions of employment?

B. BRIEF ANSWER

Each brief answer should be a succinct response to the question presented in each issue. The precise form of the answer may depend on the degree of specificity that you have achieved in the statement of the issue, just as the appropriate form for the statement of the holding in a case brief may depend on the degree of specificity of the issue statement.

In some cases, the issue may be sufficiently simple and the statement of the issue sufficiently specific to justify limiting the brief answer to a word or two, such as "yes," "no," "probably yes," or "probably no." If so, each brief answer can appear immediately after the statement of the corresponding issue without any separate section heading.

In many cases, however, you may find it difficult to state all the elements of a complex issue in a single, graceful sentence. In those cases, you can supply additional information in a brief answer of one or more sentences under a separate section heading. Even so, you should not use the brief answer to explore analytic justifications in great depth; the reader can more easily absorb a complex summary of the analysis after she has read the discussion section of the memorandum. For example, the medical malpractice dispute discussed on pages 63-66 might raise the following issues and brief answers:

> I. ISSUES
>
> A. Does the phrase "any toxic material" in New Maine's strict liability statute encompass a generally safe anesthetic that produced a fatal reaction in a patient with a rare nerve disorder?
> B. Is Humana Hospital liable to Souza's estate for negligent administration of the anesthetic?
> 1. Did Humana's anesthesiologist breach a duty of care by administering the anesthetic without assistance and by failing to monitor Souza's reactions to anesthesia?

2. Did Souza's nerve disorder constitute a supervening cause that broke the chain of causation between the anesthesiologist's conduct and Souza's death?

II. BRIEF ANSWERS

A. Probably not. A restrictive interpretation is supported by the legislative history and by a general public policy in New Maine encouraging the provision of affordable medical services. The legislature probably did not intend the statutory phrase "toxic material" to include medically prescribed substances that ordinarily produce a beneficial result or otherwise facilitate medical treatment.

B. Probably yes.

1. Probably yes. Under generally accepted hospital procedures, at least two trained medical personnel must monitor the administration of anesthesia, with at least one person monitoring the patient's reactions. A jury likely will find that the anesthesiologist breached a duty of care to the patient by administering the anesthesia alone.

2. No. The jury likely will also find that the patient's nerve disorder was not a supervening cause and that the anesthesiologist's negligence proximately caused the patient's death.

C. FACTS

Some new associates in a law firm regularly omit statements of facts in their legal memoranda. The associates often explain that a supervising attorney obviously knows the facts of an assigned case because she gives the facts to the associate in some oral or written form when she assigns the memorandum.

For several reasons, however, you should include at least a brief statement of facts in a legal memorandum unless your supervising attorney specifically authorizes you to omit it. The supervising attorney may have been familiar with the facts when she assigned the memorandum, but she may need a brief review to refresh her memory when she later reads your memorandum. Alternatively, she may simply want reassurance that you share her understanding of the facts. Furthermore, the memorandum should be a self-contained document that is helpful to any member of the firm who may be called on to take over the file, including an attorney who knows nothing about the case and does not have time to glean the facts from the file. Finally, a statement of the factual premises on which you based your legal analysis protects you from criticism if that analysis later becomes obsolete or misleading in light of newly discovered facts.

In selecting facts for statement, you should state material facts and background facts with attention to the considerations that you would apply in preparing a case brief for class. However, you should hesitate less in an office memorandum than in a case brief to mention a marginally significant fact. When briefing a case, you must rely on the court's summary of the facts as a complete record on which the court based its decision; moreover, you can test your analytic abilities by attempting to isolate the material facts and helpful background facts and by omitting the others. In contrast, when preparing an office memorandum at an early stage of a dispute, you know that the facts on which you rely for your analysis are incomplete. Subsequent proceedings may reveal other facts that support new claims, defenses, or arguments. Moreover, previously known facts that appeared to be unimportant when you drafted the memorandum may take on new legal significance as a consequence. In your statement of facts, therefore, you should recite all material facts in detail, and you should summarize any other information either that provides helpful background material or that appears to have the potential to take on new significance as the litigation proceeds.

D. DISCUSSION

1. Introducing Your Analysis

In the discussion section of your legal memorandum, you will express your complete legal analysis of each issue stated at the beginning of the memorandum. If your memorandum addresses a single issue that you have formally stated at or near the beginning of the memorandum, your discussion of the issue need not begin with any descriptive heading beyond the major section heading "Discussion."

However, if you address multiple issues, you should separately analyze each issue under a descriptive section heading. Although the heading need not restate the issue in full detail, it should link your analysis to an issue that is more formally and narrowly stated earlier in the memorandum:

> IV. Discussion
>   A. Strict Liability for Use of Toxic Materials
>   • • • •
>   B. Negligence
>   • • • •
>   1. Negligent Act
>   • • • •
>   2. Proximate Cause
>   • • • •

Immediately after you identify an issue with a section heading, you may want to illuminate the issue in an introductory sentence or two that refers briefly to facts, arguments, or theories that help to explain the significance of the issue. For example, the following opening sentence expands on the section heading by explaining the significance of the theory of strict liability:

> A. Strict Liability for Use of Toxic Materials
>
> If a statute or the common law imposes strict liability for Souza's death, then Souza's estate can establish liability without proving negligence.

In some cases, the opening paragraph of a section may even draw subsidiary legal conclusions as a means of pinpointing the narrow question in dispute:

A. Choice of Law—U.C.C. or Common Law

Whether Maldonado accepted Weinstein's offer depends in part on whether the common law of contracts or the Uniform Commercial Code (U.C.C.) applies to the transaction. The U.C.C. applies only to "transactions in goods." U.C.C. § 2-102. Weinstein's offer to supply specifically identified, separately priced, movable plumbing parts clearly contemplates a sale of goods as part of the transaction. *See* U.C.C. § 2-105(1). His proposed transaction, however, also involves the service of installing the fixtures, raising a question about the applicability of the U.C.C. to mixed transactions for both services and the sale of goods.

The U.C.C. applies to such a mixed transaction only if . . .

Of course, if an issue is adequately represented in a section heading and needs no further elaboration, the discussion can proceed immediately to an analysis of the legal standards:

A. Applicability and Satisfaction of the Statute of Frauds

The Arizona statute of frauds bars enforcement of "an agreement which is not to be performed within one year from the making thereof," unless it, "or some memorandum thereof, is in writing and signed by the party to be charged." Ariz. Rev. Stat. § 44-101(5) (West 1967) (copy of full text attached). . . .

2. Analyzing the Law and the Facts

After you have drafted the section heading and the optional elaboration of the issue, you ordinarily should follow the pattern of deductive reasoning developed in Chapter 3: analyze the law and apply the law to the facts to reach a conclusion. The nature of the analysis in a discussion section obviously will vary with each issue. If the clearly applicable abstract legal rule is simple, you can present the rule and supporting authority directly and concisely, permitting you to direct most of your attention to fact analysis. Other issues may require a choice among competing rules or a clarification of the content of the applicable legal rule. If so, you may need to discuss the abstract legal rule in depth before applying it to the facts. Of course, determining the content of the rule and applying it to the facts are often related tasks: your discussion of the question of whether particular facts satisfy the legal standard may help to clarify the content of a vague or uncertain rule.

a. Example: Statutory Analysis

Below is a portion of the discussion section of a sample office memorandum set in the fictitious state of New Maine. It analyzes the issue of statutory liability for administering anesthesia. The statutory analysis in the passage focuses on defining the legal rule in a simple factual context, thus requiring relatively little independent fact analysis. After refining the issue in an introduction, the author of the discussion presents the statutory analysis on three levels in descending order of priority: the language of the statute, its legislative history, and general policy considerations. In this example, the author has applied the law to the relevant facts at each level of the statutory analysis rather than in a single consolidated fact analysis at the end of the discussion.

IV. DISCUSSION

A. *Strict Liability for Use of Toxic Materials*

Introduction

If a statute or the common law imposes strict liability for Souza's death, then Souza's estate can establish liability without proving negligence. New Maine's common law doctrine of strict liability for injuries caused by ultrahazardous activities does not apply to noncriminal medical practices engaged in by licensed physicians. *Stanislaus v. Good Samaritan Hospital,* 212 N. Me. 113, 115 (1979). New Maine has recently enacted a statute, however, that imposes strict liability for injuries stemming from the use of "any toxic material":

> A commercial enterprise is liable for injuries proximately caused by its use of any toxic material, without regard to the degree of care exercised by the enterprise.

12 N. Me. Rev. Stat. § 242 (1988). As a profit-making hospital, Humana presumably is a "commercial enterprise" within the meaning of the statute. It is less certain, however, that the anesthetic administered to Souza would qualify as a "toxic" material.

Narrow issue

Analysis of statutory language

The common meaning of the word "toxic" is "poisonous." *See e.g., The Random House Dictionary of the English Language,* 1500 (unabridged) (1970). Souza's estate might plausibly argue that the anesthetic was a toxic material because it was poisonous to Souza, even though it would not have been poisonous to most others. The word "toxic," however, applies more naturally to substances that are universally harmful to humans, such as cyanide, DDT, or sulfuric acid. It strains the common meaning of "toxic" to apply it to an anesthetic that might occasionally be harmful to persons with unusual allergies or other extraordinary conditions.

Fact analysis

Legislative history

Legislative history also supports a restrictive interpretation of the statutory term "any toxic material." The report of the New Maine Senate Committee on Health and Welfare suggests that the legislature was concerned only with the most deadly of substances:

> The purpose of this bill is to reallocate the cost of unavoidable accidents from victims to industry and its consumers, to discourage unnecessary use of deadly chemicals and other hazardous materials, and to encourage the development and use of substitute materials that are generally safe for human contact.

N. Me. Sen. Rep. No. 112, 1987-88 Sess. 2 (1988). The anesthetic in this case probably is closer to the materials "generally safe for human contact" condoned by the legislature than it is to the "deadly chemicals and other hazardous materials" condemned by it.

    Finally, general state policy appears to support an interpretation that excludes medically prescribed substances from the reach of the statute. The legislature and judiciary of New Maine have recognized a policy of restricting the liability of physicians to encourage the ready availability of affordable medical services. For example, under the New Maine "Good Samaritan" statute, physicians who provide certain emergency medical services are not liable for adverse consequences unless they engage in culpable conduct amounting to at least gross negligence. 12 N. Me. Rev. Stat. § 229 (1985). This protective policy is also reflected in the courts' refusal to extend common law strict liability for ultrahazardous activities to even experimental medical practices. *Stanislaus,* 212 N. Me. at 115. The legislature presumably was aware of these legal developments when it enacted the toxic materials statute in 1988. Souza's estate may argue that the legislature intended to partially overrule *Stanislaus* by imposing strict liability on a limited segment of the activities of commercial medical practices. However, absent more specific evidence of legislative intent to alter the course of existing common law, it is probably more likely that the legislature retained its protective attitude and assumed that the term "toxic material" would not include routinely prescribed medicines or anesthetics.

    In this case, the prescribed anesthetic, ethane, was not the safest available at the time of Souza's operation. Nonetheless, it is a frequently prescribed substance that produces beneficial results with only minor side effects in all but the most unusual cases. The strict liability statute almost certainly does not apply to Souza's death.

Margin annotations:

Fact analysis

Policy analysis

Fact analysis

Conclusion

b. Example: Established Common Law

In contrast to the previous example, the sample discussion below briefly summarizes noncontroversial legal standards and places greater emphasis on fact analysis. After illuminating the issue of negligence and summarizing general principles, the discussion separately addresses distinct subissues in different subsections. Within the first of those subsections, devoted to "negligent act," the author has consolidated the relatively simple legal standards in a single paragraph, leading to a single, uninterrupted line of fact analysis. He has divided the fact analysis itself into two paragraphs, presenting opposing factual arguments.

IV. DISCUSSION

A. *Strict Liability for Use of Toxic Materials*

• • • •

B. *Negligence*

Introduction

Assuming that Humana is not strictly liable for Souza's death, it may nonetheless be liable to Souza's estate if its agent caused the death through negligence. *See Kityama v. Mercy Hospital,* 183 N. Me. 752, 759-60 (1974) (hospital liable for negligence of its nurse). An action for negligence requires proof of a negligent act or omission that proximately causes injury. *Baker v. Bruce,* 153 N. Me. 817, 820 (1967).

Narrow issues

In our case, the injury to Souza is obvious. In greater doubt are the elements of negligent act and proximate cause.

1. Negligent Act

Legal rules

A negligent act or omission consists of the breach of a duty of care owed to another. *Id.* at 821. A medical specialist owes a duty to patients to exercise at least the ordinary skill and care that is reasonable and customary nationwide in that medical specialty. *Kityama,* 183 N. Me. at 760. Furthermore, under the "thin-skulled plaintiff rule," that duty of care encompasses the special care necessary to address increased risks created by a patient's unusual susceptibility to injury. *Id.* In this case, Humana's anesthesiologist, Unger, may have breached duties of care in her unassisted administration of general anesthesia in the face of Souza's known nervous condition.

Fact analysis favoring Humana

Unger exercised care in determining Souza's disorder of the nervous system and in informing her of the risks presented by each of the most suitable anesthetics. Moreover, when administering the anesthetic selected by Souza, Unger took care to provide the prescribed dosage by monitoring the anesthetic intake gauge.

However, Unger's intense concentration on the anesthetic intake gauge may have been an act of carelessness, rather than enhanced care, because it diverted Unger's attention from Souza and from equipment monitoring Souza's vital signs. Faced with Souza's known nervous disorder, Unger probably had a duty to follow the standard medical practice of summoning a nurse to assist her in administering the anesthesia. Had she done so, the team could have monitored both Souza's vital signs and the intake gauge, and a team member undoubtedly would have detected signs of distress at least ten seconds before death, arguably enough time to cease anesthesia and take corrective measures.

Fact analysis favoring Souza's estate

On these facts, a jury could find that Unger was negligent in her administration of the anesthetic.

Conclusion

2. Proximate Cause

• • • •

E. THE CONCLUSION

Even though the questions addressed in an office memorandum may be close, and even though your supervising attorney will not feel bound by your advice, she will expect you to take a position by stating your conclusions. A thorough memorandum will include both (1) a brief resolution of each issue within the part of the discussion section devoted to that issue and (2) a more general summary of conclusions in a separate section at the end of the memorandum.

In the conclusion section, you can summarize the individual conclusions that you have reached in the discussion section of the memorandum. In addition, you may wish to summarize the analytic support for the conclusions in a depth that would have been inappropriate in the brief answers stated earlier.

Finally, you should use the conclusion section to express any strategic recommendations that your analysis inspires. For example, you may recommend that the law firm file a complaint, settle a weak case, investigate certain facts, or concentrate its efforts on a particular legal theory.

Although you may express more information in the conclusion section than in the brief answers, your conclusion should nonetheless represent a selective summary of your analysis and recommendations. In a simple case, a few sentences may suffice; even moderately complex cases require no more than a few paragraphs.

For example, the following passage concisely synthesizes the conclusions previewed above in section B as brief answers, and it adds strategic recommendations:

V. CONCLUSION

Summary of analyses

In light of legislative and judicial policies favoring limits on physicians' liability, the strict liability statute regulating toxic materials probably will not apply to the administering of the anesthetic in this case. The courts will be even less likely to retreat from precedent to apply the common law doctrine of strict liability for ultrahazardous activities. A jury may find, however, that Humana's anesthesiologist was negligent in failing to summon assistance to administer the anesthesia or to monitor the patient closely. We can try to characterize Souza's nervous condition as a supervening cause, but *Rainbow Landscaping* will not be easy to distinguish.

Strategic recommendation

Because the risk of substantial liability is great, I recommend that we advise Humana to settle. Souza's estate may be willing to compromise: their negligence claim is not appropriate for summary disposition, and they may want to avoid the unpredictability of a jury.

IV. TECHNIQUES FOR PREPARING OFFICE MEMORANDA

The techniques you use to master an assignment, research the problem, and prepare a memorandum for a supervising attorney are partly a matter of office politics and your personal style. The following suggestions provide a foundation on which you may build to suit your particular needs.

A. MASTERING THE ASSIGNMENT

The surest way to disappoint a supervising attorney is to misunderstand the assignment. Even a thoroughly researched and beautifully written memorandum will fall flat if it fails to address the matters that the supervisor wanted the associate to analyze.

Unfortunately, many supervising attorneys are too busy to communicate their assignments clearly and thoroughly. Even worse, most will not accept blame for confusion about the assignment. Instead, they expect you to assume responsibility for clarifying vague or confusing points. Consequently, you should not be shy about demanding additional information from the supervising attorney. Indeed, you should aggressively dig out the information that you need to master your assignment so that you can draft a memorandum that precisely meets the needs of your supervising attorney.

Confusion about the topics that your supervising attorney expects you to address may take various forms. In some cases, your inability to identify narrow, precise issues may stem from necessary abstractness in the assignment that is only partially avoidable. Supervising attorneys occasionally request office memoranda on general, abstract questions of law, such as the likely scope and effect of a new statute. Although they are not yet working on any disputes relating to the assigned issues, they expect that the general legal analyses developed in such memoranda will help them counsel clients when potential disputes do arise. You can tailor such a memorandum to your supervisor's needs by requesting clarification on (1) the kinds of topics that your supervisor deems to be essential and on (2) the kinds of disputes in which the firm's clients likely would become embroiled.

In many cases, the assignment is unnecessarily abstract because the supervising attorney intends to use the legal analysis in the memorandum to help represent a client in a currently active, concrete dispute. In such a case, if your supervising attorney does not provide you with sufficient information to enable you to thoroughly understand the factual context, you should take steps to acquire that information. By anticipating the application of legal standards to facts, you can frame the issues precisely and narrowly, and you can tailor the research and analysis to your supervisor's real needs.

Vagueness in an assignment often is attributable to precisely the analytic uncertainty on which the memorandum is intended to shed light. Therefore, you may benefit from secondary meetings with the supervising attorney after the initial assignment but before writing the memorandum. In some cases, your supervising attorney will not even attempt to identify issues but will instead supply factual context and ask you to define and analyze the issues. At most, the supervisor may provide a broad outline of the issues, expecting you to refine and supplement it. With a thorough knowledge of the factual context, you can clarify the essential issues as your research deepens your understanding of the legal standards.

As you do so, questions may arise about appropriate limits on the range of topics that you should address or about the depth to which the supervisor would like you to analyze a tangential issue. If so, you should determine whether the supervisor can conveniently give brief guidance on these questions before you begin writing. Although you should not become dependent on such guidance, neither should you give credence to a popular assumption on the part of clerks and associates that supervisors are universally hostile to such contacts. Most supervisors will recognize the benefit of a brief follow-up meeting, and many will make the time for it.

B. RESEARCH STRATEGY

Effective research skills are the product of long hours in the library, for which no primer on research techniques can substitute. Nonetheless, a few tips on research strategy may help you avoid duplicative or unproductive activity. The following discussion assumes that you are familiar with basic library resources.

First, you should acquire a general grasp of the fundamental legal principles in the relevant fields of research so that you can more effectively identify issues and exclude unproductive lines of inquiry. A general survey course on the subject in law school should be sufficient to enable you to define issues and to delve immediately into specific, primary authority such as statutes or case law. If you have not taken a course on the subject matter of the assignment, you should consider beginning your research with a secondary source, such as a reputable treatise, that provides necessary general background information. As their labels suggest, primary authority within the relevant jurisdiction takes analytic precedence over secondary authority. Nonetheless, you will often find and use the primary authority more effectively if you first consult a secondary source to enhance your understanding of the broad outlines of the subject.

Once you have begun to explore primary authority, you should look for relevant legislation before digging too deeply into case law. A single statute can diminish or even destroy the authoritative value of a whole line of case law that developed common law doctrines or interpreted previously effective legislation. Thus, you can avoid hours of marginally productive reading by immediately finding the latest applicable legislation.

Even when you know that a body of case law interprets currently effective legislation, you should turn first to the statute itself. At least a glance at the statutory language will provide valuable context for the interpretive case law. Moreover, annotated codebooks provide not only the statutory text but a means of finding interpretive case law as well.

Of course, if you find no statute or constitutional provision on point, you may safely turn to case law as primary authority for applicable common law. In the absence of any relevant primary authority in the jurisdiction, you can rely on the persuasive authority provided by secondary sources or by primary authority from other jurisdictions.

C. USE OF THE LIBRARY

1. Taking Notes

You should take thorough notes on any authority that may be helpful. Even marginally applicable cases may warrant note; their relevance may become clear only after further research and analysis. To avoid the need for frequent returns to the library, your notes should include any information that you may later need in drafting the office memorandum, including

(1) the full citation,

(2) the specific page on which relevant material appears,

(3) a sufficient summary of the facts to provide necessary context and to define the holding, and

(4) the verbatim language of any passage that you think might be worth quoting. You may want to photocopy any part of an opinion that warrants special or extended study.

Moreover, to facilitate further research, you should record data provided by the publisher designed to be used with formal research tools. For example, an opinion that is reproduced in a reporter published by West Publishing Company will begin with West "headnotes," serially numbered paragraphs that summarize the discussion of topics in the opinion. Each headnote includes at least one West "key number," which classifies the issue addressed in the passage of the opinion corresponding to the headnote. The following library notes incorporate these West features:

> *Osterholt v. St. Charles Drilling Co.,* 500 F. Supp. 529 (E.D. Mo. 1980).
>
> pp. 530-32. Landowner sued drilling company for damages stemming from installation of defective well and water system. pp. 534-35—Judgment for P on K.
>
> pg. 536 [9] (Fraud 61)—punitive damages denied for alleged misrepresentation, because of absence of "aggravating circumstances" such as willful, wanton, reckless, or malicious conduct.
>   See 582 F.2d at 1087

In this example, the researcher is particularly interested in the passage on page 536 discussing punitive damages. The short-hand citation at the end of the notes refers to an opinion cited in *Osterholt* that the researcher will examine. The phrase "(Fraud 61)" refers to a West key number that will help the researcher use the West digest system to find other cases discussing the same issue. Indeed, that key number may lead to other cases reported in the West system that will supply the researcher with other West key numbers that are productive on the topic of punitive damages. The number nine in brackets refers to the headnote number associated with the relevant passage. That headnote number will help the researcher use Shepard's citation service as a tool for finding subsequent cases that cite *Osterholt* on the issue of punitive damages for tort.

Of course, a reported opinion has little value if a higher court has vacated or reversed it; conversely, its authoritative value is enhanced by affirmance on appeal. Therefore, you should use the Shepard's citation service or a computer service to check the subsequent history of any case on which you intend to rely for your analysis.

2. Library Courtesy

In light of the scarcity of resources in any law library, discourtesy in the library can lead to frustration and wasted time for all. Rather than pile three dozen books on a table for an afternoon's reading, you should take only one or two books off the shelves at a time, take notes, and immediately reshelve the books. If you follow a methodical approach, you can efficiently exhaust the research possibilities with minimum duplication of effort.

For example, after finding an applicable statute in an annotated codebook, you may use the annotations to find interpretive case law. Because the descriptive paragraphs in the annotations provide only general guides, you may not be able to determine whether a reported opinion contains noteworthy information until you have glanced at the opinion itself. You can do that while standing at the stacks. If the opinion warrants close reading, you can take the reporter to a library carrel for note-taking. If the opinion appears to be unhelpful, you can return the reporter to the shelves without having taken it from the vicinity.

D. REORGANIZATION AND OUTLINING

As summarized at the beginning of Chapter 6, the process of transforming library notes into a well-organized office memorandum is similar to that of summarizing and reorganizing case briefs in a student course outline. Either process requires you to (1) synthesize cases to arrive at general principles and (2) classify cases to show which of them illustrates each principle. With this synthesis and reorganization, you can highlight ideas and illuminate them with illustrative cases, rather than simply present a laundry list of individual cases whose relationships to one another are unclear.

If you produce voluminous library notes for a complex assignment, you may wish to begin the process of reorganization by indexing your notes. For example, the author of the two sample memoranda in the Appendix in the accompanying Assignment Book assigned a number to each authority summarized in his library notes:

> 1. Statute of frauds—A.R.S. § 44-101 (West 1967)
> "No action shall be brought in any court in the following cases unless the promise or agreement upon which the action is brought . . . is in writing and signed by the party to be charged . . . . 5. Upon an agreement which is not to be performed within one year from the making thereof."
>
> 2. *Tiffany Incorporated v. W.M.K. Transit Mix, Inc.,* 16 Ariz. App. 415, 493 P.2d 1220 (1972).
> P.2d at 1221-22—Tiffany prepared a bid to state agency to complete work on highway project; before bidding, it received oral price quote from Transit Mix for the supply of sealcoat chips for the project. Tiffany used that quote in its bid, the state awarded the bid to Tiffany, Transit refused to perform, Tiffany sues, and Transit raises statute of frauds as defense.
>
> 1222-23—UCC statute of frauds applies
> 1224-25 [5-7] (Estoppel 52, 85, 99)—distinction between equitable and promissory estoppel: Equitable—reliance on misrepresentation of fact; used as a "shield" or defense against some claim. Promissory—reliance on a promise; used as a defense or as basis for cause of action for damages.
>
> 1225 [8,9] (Estoppel 85)—If proved at trial, following facts would support application of promissory estoppel: Transit promised to supply sealcoat chips at certain price in event that Tiffany got the main bid; Tiffany relied by using quote in its own bid; Transit should have foreseen that Tiffany would use its quote if it were the lowest. (dictum?)
>
> 1225-26 [10] (Frauds, stat. of 144)—nonetheless, statute of frauds bars enforcement of promise. Court recognizes estoppel to avoid statute if promissee relies on misrepresentation about requirements of statute (equitable estoppel?) or on promise to satisfy or not to rely on statute—but can't avoid statute by relying on other party's underlying oral promise to perform.
>
> 3. *Mac Enterprises v. Del E. Webb Development Co.,* 132 Ariz. 331, 645 P.2d 1245 (App. 1982).
> P.2d at 1250 [6] (Frauds, stat. of 144)—no estoppel to avoid statute of frauds, because Webb made no promise upon which Mac could reasonably rely.

4. *Kiely v. St. Germain*, 670 P.2d 764 (Colo. 1983) (en banc)
768-69—good discussion of liberal Rest. 2d use of promissory estoppel to avoid statute of frauds and case law that prompted it—*Tiffany* cited as example of narrower approach

· · · ·

After analyzing the problem, the author of the sample memoranda then developed a rough outline to express a proposed organization for each office memorandum. The outline of the discussion section is organized around legal principles and identifies which authority supports and illustrates each principle:

III. DISCUSSION

A. Applicability and Satisfaction of Statute of Frauds

Rules: requires writing signed by party to be charged if can't be performed in 1 year [ARS 44-101(5), #1]

Facts: K is for 2 years, and no writing at all

Conclusion: statute applies & is not satisfied

B. Estoppel to Avoid Statute

1. Misrep. or Promise about Statute's Requirements

Rules: equitable estoppel and promissory estoppel relating to requirements of statute [*Cress*, #6; and *Johnson*, #10, or *Tiffany*, #2]

Facts: no representation or promise about statute's requirements

Conclusion: trad. forms of avoidance through estoppel not available

2. Reliance on Underlying Promise to Perform

Rules: Introduce liberal doctrine [Rest. 2d, #5, *Kiely*, #4]. Discuss whether AZ likely to adopt liberal rule [*Cf. Fremming*, #9, with *Tiffany*, #2]
—Some cases have assumed theory, but found elements not satisfied [*Trollope*, #8, and *Mac*, #3]
—Distinguish *Tiffany*? [Wallach, #13 and UCC sections it cites; *Trollop*, #8; *Dean*, #7, and *Johnson*, #10]

Facts: Williams' posing probably constitutes detrimental, foreseeable reliance

Conclusion: If AZ court adopts liberal view of avoidance of statute through promissory estoppel, facts probably support claim for damages

Some authorities appear more than once and in different parts of the outline because those authorities contain information relevant to more than one topic or subtopic in the discussion. Each shorthand reference to an authority is followed by the index number to the place in the author's library notes where that authority is summarized. The index number helped the author quickly locate the authority in his notes when he drafted the memoranda.

When researching a problem, you should avoid the temptation to include every idea and authority that you have encountered in the library. The outlining stage provides a good opportunity to exclude marginally relevant material as well as to reorganize and analyze.

E. WRITING THE MEMORANDUM

Once you are satisfied with the organization and analysis reflected in your outline, you can use the outline as a general guide when writing the memorandum. Many law firms encourage their attorneys to dictate their first drafts into hand-held tape recorders, but many new associates find it difficult to display good style in dictation. Consequently, if you dictate the first draft, you may want to work from a particularly detailed written outline so that you can focus your attention on sentence structure rather than on organizational matters.

=========== S A M P L E S ===========

1. *Sample Memorandum 1*

[handwritten: Bad memo, compare to #2 which is good]

Imagine that an attorney from the fictitious state of Calzona drafted the following office memorandum using only authority from the Calzona Supreme Court. Study the memorandum and consider the questions that follow it.

MEMORANDUM
TO: Susan Elias
FROM: James Nelson
RE: Enforceability of Julie Week's Promise to Act as Guarantor for her Cousin's Loan Obligation; File 85-87
DATE: September 16, 1985

I. ISSUE AND BRIEF ANSWER

By stating that he would refrain from demanding payment from the Borrower on a loan obligation until he "needs the money," did the Lender state a promise that bound him to a future performance, thus providing consideration for the Guarantor's promise to pay the obligation in the event that the Borrower failed to pay on demand? Probably yes.

II. FACTS

One of our regular business clients, Julie Week (Guarantor), asserted the following facts in an interview:

On December 15, 1984, the Guarantor's cousin, Don Caslin (Borrower), purchased a used Mercedes Benz sports coupe from a private owner, Thomas Beatty (Lender), for $20,000. In a self-financing arrangement, the Borrower paid $8,000 on delivery and agreed in writing to pay the remainder of the purchase price in 12 monthly installments of $1,000 each, beginning January 1, 1985.

From January to June 1985, Borrower timely paid the Lender a total of $6,000 in monthly installments. In late June, however, Borrower suffered unusual losses in his private business, and he failed to pay the installments due on July 1 and August 1. After Lender threatened to sue for the return of the automobile, Guarantor negotiated a written agreement (the Guarantee Agreement) with Lender designed to give Borrower time to recover from his temporary financial difficulties. Dated August 5, 1985, the Guarantee Agreement refers to the agreement between Lender and Borrower as the "CREDIT/SALE AGREEMENT," and it contains the following statement of mutual obligations:

> 1. LENDER will refrain from asserting his claim against BORROWER and from demanding payment on the CREDIT/SALE AGREEMENT until LENDER needs the money.
> 2. In the event that BORROWER fails to pay all amounts due under the CREDIT/SALE AGREEMENT upon demand by LENDER, GUARANTOR will pay those amounts immediately and will pay further installments as they become due under the CREDIT/SALE AGREEMENT.

On August 25, 1985, Lender demanded payment from Borrower, and Borrower explained that he could not yet pay. On September 2, 1985, Lender demanded immediate payment of $3,000 from Guarantor; he also stated that he expects either Borrower or Guarantor to pay the remaining three installments as they become due on the first of each month.

We do not yet have any evidence that Lender engaged in fraud during formation of the Guarantee Agreement or that he did not in fact have a "need" for the money on August 25. You have asked me to analyze the question whether the Guarantee Contract is unenforceable on its face for lack of consideration.

III. DISCUSSION

Lender's promise to refrain from asserting his claim and demanding payment until he "needs the money" arguably is illusory. If so, Guarantor's promise is not supported by consideration and is unenforceable.

An enforceable contract requires a bargained-for exchange in which a promisor exchanges his own promise for a return promise or performance. *Smith v. Newman,* 161 Calz. 443, 447, 667 P.2d 81, 84 (1984); *Barney v. Johnson,* 93 Calz. 127, 312 P.2d 550 (1961); *see also* Restatement (Second) of Contracts § 71 (1981). The requirement of an exchange is not satisfied if one party gives only an illusory promise, which does not commit the promisor to any future performance. *See Atco Corp. v Johnson,* 155 Calz. 1211, 627 P.2d 781 (1980).

In *Atco Corp.*, the manager of an automobile repair shop promised to forbear "until I want the money" from asserting a claim against the owner of an automobile for $900 in repairs; in exchange, a friend of the owner promised to act as guarantor of the owner's obligation. *Id.* at 1212, 627 P.2d at 782. The word "want" stated no legally recognizable commitment because it permitted the manager at his own discretion to refuse to perform any forbearance at all. Because the manager incurred no obligation, the guarantor's promise was gratuitous and unenforceable. *Id.* at 1213-14, 627 P.2d at 782-84.

On the other hand, even if a promise leaves open the possibility that the promisor will escape obligation, the promise is valid if the promisor does not have complete control over the events on which the promisor's obligation is conditioned. *See Bonnie v. DeLaney,* 158 Calz. 212, 645 P.2d 887 (1982). In *Bonnie,* an agreement for the sale of a house provided that the buyer could cancel the agreement if the buyer "cannot qualify for a 30-year mortgage loan for 90% of the sales price" with any of several banks listed in the agreement. *Id.* at 213, 645 P.2d at 888. In enforcing the agreement against the seller, the court distinguished *Atco Corp.* on the ground that the word "cannot" referred to the buyer's *ability* to obtain a loan rather than to his *desire*. Because his ability to obtain a loan was partly controlled by events and decisions outside his control, the promises in the sale agreement were nonillusory and binding. *Id.* at 214-15, 645 P.2d at 889-91.

Our client's case probably is more nearly analogous to *Bonnie* than it is to *Atco Corp.* Lender's promise to forbear until he "needs" the money appears to condition the length of his forbearance on financial events that are at least partly outside his control: as long as his income and expenses create no need for the money, Lender has a commitment to forbear from demanding payment. To convince a court to draw an analogy to *Atco Corp.* rather than to *Bonnie,* we must argue that the word "need" refers to a subjective perception of deprivation that is inseparable from one's desires, which are subject to the promisor's unfettered discretion. Unfortunately, the analogy to *Bonnie* is stronger: Lender's promise probably is not illusory.

IV. CONCLUSION

The promises stated in the Guarantee Agreement appear to satisfy the consideration requirement because Lender assumed a legally recognizable obligation by promising to refrain from asserting his claim and demanding payment until he "needs" the money. Unless we discover other serious defects in the Guarantee Agreement, the Guarantor's defenses will not be worth litigating. We should urge Guarantor to settle the claim, and we should try to persuade Borrower to indemnify Guarantor and to assume responsibility for further payments.

Questions on Sample Memorandum 1

a. Did the substantive labels assigned to the parties serve as helpful reminders of the respective roles of the parties, or would you have retained the parties' last names as less distracting references?

b. Is the statement of the issue sufficiently detailed to justify a brief answer of only two words, or would you have preferred a more detailed brief answer under a separate heading?

c. Does the statement of facts include any facts that you would omit or summarize further? Does it omit any important facts to which the author likely had access?

d. Identify the parts of the discussion section that illuminate the issue, discuss the legal standards, analyze the facts, and state a conclusion.

e. Do you agree with the author's analysis? Does it adequately explore both sides of the dispute? Is it too pessimistic?

2. *Sample Memorandum 2*

The following memorandum, which is set in a fictitious jurisdiction, borrows from examples set forth in previous sections of this chapter addressing individual elements of office memoranda.

MEMORANDUM
TO: James Clapton
FROM: Ginger Jackson
RE: *Souza v. Humana;* strict liability and negligence—File No. 88-117
DATE: September 10, 1988

I. ISSUES

A. Does the phrase "any toxic material" in New Maine's strict liability statute encompass a generally safe anesthetic that produced a fatal reaction in a patient with a rare nerve disorder?

B. Is Humana Hospital liable to Souza's estate for negligent administration of the anesthetic?

1. Did Humana's anesthesiologist breach a duty of care by administering the anesthetic without assistance and by failing to monitor Souza's reactions to anesthesia?

2. Did Souza's nerve disorder constitute a supervening cause that broke the chain of causation between the anesthesiologist's conduct and Souza's death?

II. BRIEF ANSWERS

A. Probably not. A restrictive interpretation is supported by the legislative history and by a general public policy in New Maine encouraging the provision of affordable medical services. The legislature probably did not intend the statutory term "toxic material" to include medically prescribed substances that ordinarily produce a beneficial result or otherwise facilitate medical treatment.

B. Probably yes:

1. Probably yes. Under generally accepted hospital procedures, at least two trained medical personnel must monitor the administration of anesthesia, with at least one person monitoring the patient's reactions. A jury likely will

find that the anesthesiologist breached a duty of care to the patient by administering the anesthesia alone.

2. No. The jury likely will also find that the patient's nerve disorder was not a supervening cause and that the anesthesiologist's negligence proximately caused the patient's death.

III. FACTS

On February 17, 1988, our client, Humana Hospital, Inc. (Humana), admitted 22-year-old Teresa Souza to its facility in Greenville, New Maine, for surgery to correct a bone deformity in her foot. Souza's bone deformity was not life-threatening, but it severely hampered her mobility. The planned surgery required general anesthesia.

Dr. Roberta Unger, an anesthesiologist for Humana, studied Souza's medical history and discovered that she suffered from a rare nerve disorder that slightly increased the risk that she would suffer an adverse reaction from anesthesia. Unger carefully informed Souza of the advantages and risks associated with each of the three safest and most effective general anesthetics. Souza decided to proceed with the operation and with the administration of general anesthesia. Unger and Souza ultimately agreed that Unger would administer ethane, a widely used and generally safe form of ether. Unger had initially recommended Forane, a potent muscle relaxant that maintains a stable heart rate. Souza, however, rejected Forane because of its greater cost.

At 10:00 A.M. on February 18, Souza was prepared for surgery. While the circulating nurse was occupied with another patient, and before the surgical team arrived, Unger began administering the prescribed anesthetic to Souza. Unger and Souza were alone in the room. Apparently because she was concerned that an overdose might trigger an adverse reaction, Unger concentrated intensely on the anesthetic intake gauge, which monitored the flow of anesthetic. As a consequence, she failed to watch either Souza or equipment monitoring Souza's reactions. Approximately one minute after Unger began administering the anesthetic, the monitoring equipment sounded an alarm, and Souza died. Efforts to revive her failed. According to computer records, the monitoring equipment reflected growing signs of distress in Souza beginning approximately ten seconds before her death and before the alarm sounded.

An autopsy showed that the anesthetic combined with Souza's nerve disorder to trigger a reaction that caused cardiac arrest. Mary L. Richards, Ph.D., a professor at the University of New Maine School of Nursing, has told us that hospitals throughout the nation ordinarily require the anesthesiologist to be accompanied by a nurse during the administration of anesthesia. Both the nurse and the anesthesiologist are expected to continuously assess the patient's reaction to anesthesia by reading monitoring equipment and by observing the patient directly. Although she cannot be certain, Richards guesses that the fatal reaction was triggered largely by the final ten seconds of Unger's administration of anesthesia.

Souza's estate has sued Humana in tort for wrongful death. It advances two theories of tort liability: (1) statutory strict liability for use of toxic materials and (2) negligence in the administration of the anesthetic.

IV. DISCUSSION

A. Strict Liability for Use of Toxic Materials

If a statute or the common law imposes strict liability for Souza's death, then Souza's estate can establish liability without proving negligence. New Maine's common law doctrine of strict liability for injuries caused by ultrahazardous activities does not apply to noncriminal medical practices engaged in by licensed physicians. *Stanislaus v. Good Samaritan Hospital,* 212 N. Me. 113, 115 (1979). New Maine has recently enacted a statute, however, that imposes strict liability for injuries stemming from the use of "any toxic material":

> A commercial enterprise is liable for injuries proximately caused by its use of any toxic material, without regard to the degree of care exercised by the enterprise.

12 N. Me. Rev. Stat. § 242 (1987) (effective Jan. 1, 1988).

The New Maine courts have not yet had an opportunity to interpret the strict liability statute in a published opinion. As a profit-making hospital, Humana presumably is a "commercial enterprise" within the meaning of the statute. It is less certain, however, that the anesthetic administered to Souza would qualify as a "toxic" material.

The common meaning of the word "toxic" is "poisonous." *See e.g., The Random House Dictionary of the English Language,* 1500 (unabridged) (1970). Souza's estate might plausibly argue that the anesthetic was a toxic material because it was poisonous to Souza, even though it would not have been poisonous to most others. The word "toxic," however, applies more naturally to substances that are universally harmful to humans, such as cyanide, DDT, or sulfuric acid. It strains the common meaning of "toxic" to apply it to an anesthetic that might occasionally be harmful to persons with unusual allergies or other extraordinary conditions.

Legislative history also supports a restrictive interpretation of the statutory term "any toxic material." The report of the New Maine Senate Committee on Health and Welfare suggests that the legislature was concerned only with the most deadly of substances:

> The purpose of this bill is to reallocate the cost of unavoidable accidents from victims to industry and its consumers, to discourage unnecessary use of deadly chemicals and other hazardous materials, and to encourage the development and use of substitute materials that are generally safe for human contact.

N. Me. Sen. Rep. No. 112, 1987-88 Sess. 2 (1988). The anesthetic in this case probably is closer to the materials "generally safe for human contact" condoned by the legislature than it is to the "deadly chemicals and other hazardous materials" condemned by it.

Finally, general state policy appears to support an interpretation that excludes medically prescribed substances from the reach of the statute. The legislature and judiciary of New Maine have recognized a policy of restricting the liability of physicians to encourage the ready availability of affordable medical services. For example, under the New Maine "Good Samaritan" statute, physicians who provide certain emergency medical services are not liable for adverse consequences unless they engage in culpable conduct amounting to at least gross negligence. 12 N. Me. Rev. Stat. § 229 (1985). This protective policy is also reflected in the courts' refusal to extend common law strict liability for ultrahazardous activities to even experimental medical practices. *Stanislaus,* 212 N. Me. at 115. The legislature presumably was aware of these legal developments when it enacted the toxic materials statute in 1988. Souza's estate may argue that the legislature intended to partially overrule *Stanislaus* by imposing strict liability on a limited segment of the activities of commercial medical practices. However, absent more specific evidence of legislative intent to alter the course of existing common law, it is probably more likely that the legislature retained its protective attitude and assumed that the term "any toxic material" would not include routinely prescribed medicines or anesthetics.

In this case, the prescribed anesthetic, ethane, was not the safest available at the time of Souza's operation. Nonetheless, it is a frequently prescribed substance that produces beneficial results with only minor side effects in all but the most unusual cases. The strict liability statute probably does not apply to Souza's death.

B. Negligence

Assuming that Humana is not strictly liable for Souza's death, it may nonetheless be liable to Souza's estate if its agent caused the death through negligence. *See Kityama v. Mercy Hospital,* 183 N. Me. 752, 759-60 (1974) (hospital liable for negligence of its nurse). An action for negligence requires proof of a negligent act or omission that proximately causes injury. *Baker v. Bruce,* 153 N. Me. 817, 820 (1967).

In our case, the injury to Souza is obvious. In greater doubt are the elements of negligent act and proximate cause.

1. Negligent Act

A negligent act or omission consists of the breach of a duty of care owed to another. *Id.* at 821. A medical specialist owes a duty to patients to exercise at least the ordinary skill and care that is reasonable and customary nationwide in that medical specialty. *Kityama,* 183 N. Me. at 760. Furthermore, under the "thin-skulled-plaintiff rule," that duty of care encompasses the special care necessary to address increased risks created by a patient's unusual susceptibility to injury. *Id.* In this case, Humana's anesthesiologist, Unger, may have breached duties of care in her unassisted administration of general anesthesia in the face of Souza's known nervous condition.

Unger exercised care in determining Souza's disorder of the nervous system and in informing her of the risks presented by each of the most suitable anesthetics. Moreover, when administering the anesthetic selected by Souza, Unger took care to provide the prescribed dosage by monitoring the anesthetic intake gauge.

However, Unger's intense concentration on the anesthetic intake gauge may have been an act of carelessness, rather than enhanced care, because it diverted Unger's attention from Souza and from equipment monitoring Souza's vital signs. Faced with Souza's known nervous disorder, Unger probably had a duty to follow the standard medical practice of summoning a nurse to assist her in administering the anesthesia. Had she done so, the team could have monitored both Souza's vital signs and the intake gauge, and a team member undoubtedly would have detected signs of distress at least ten seconds before death, arguably enough time to cease anesthesia and take corrective measures.

On these facts, a jury could find that Unger was negligent in her administration of the anesthetic.

2. Proximate Cause

Even if its agent was negligent, Humana will not be liable to Souza's estate unless the negligence proximately caused Souza's death. *See, e.g., Baker v. Bruce,* 153 N. Me. 817, 821 (1967). Proximate cause is a flexible doctrine that precludes liability if the relationship between negligence and an injury is so attenuated that it would be unfair to hold the negligent party responsible for the injury. *Id.* at 821-22.

In this case, we can argue that the ten-second warning appearing on the monitoring equipment would not have given even two observant medical personnel sufficient time to reverse Souza's fatal reaction. If so, even careful administration of anesthesia would have resulted in death, suggesting that Souza's reaction was truly an unforeseeable accident rather than the proximate result of any negligent act. Unfortunately, the factual premise of this argument may be unsound: according to our own expert, the marginal effects of the final ten seconds of anesthesia probably were critical. We may want to investigate this further with other experts.

As a fall-back position on proximate cause, we could try to characterize Souza's rare nervous condition as a supervening cause. Such an intervening cause may break the chain of causation between the negligence and the injury, particularly if the intervening event was unexpected. *Safehouse Insurance Co. v. Rainbow Landscaping Co.,* 223 N. Me. 29, 31, 35 (1987) (dictum). Unfortunately, a court may be reluctant to analyze this issue within the framework of supervening cause. Under the more conventional approach, a court would simply apply the "thin-skulled-plaintiff" rule to expand Unger's duty of care to encompass responsibility for increased risks of injury created by Souza's known nervous condition. However, if we can persuade the court to depart from the conventional approach and to analyze the increased risk within the less clearly applicable framework of supervening cause, we will gain the opportunity to develop an additional argument to avoid liability.

To develop a supervening-cause argument, we must distinguish *Rainbow Landscaping,* which liberally allocates the risks of some intervening causes to the tortfeasor. In *Rainbow Landscaping,* a landscaping company agreed in writing with a general contractor to install a sprinkler system in the yards surrounding a new house in its final stages of construction. The written contract specifically obligated the landscaper to perform its work "in a manner that does not interfere with the ongoing work of other subcontractors or deface their finished product." *Id.* at 32. On the day that the landscaper began its work, its employees knew that another subcontractor was painting the interior of the house. While welding a sprinkler pipe to a house water line, an employee of the landscaper ignited paint fumes that had accumulated in a room recently painted by the painting subcontractor. The resulting fire completely destroyed the nearly completed house.

In a suit brought against the landscaper by the owner's insurer, the landscaper argued on its motion for a directed verdict that, even if the landscaper had acted negligently, the paint fumes constituted an intervening cause that precluded a finding of proximate cause. The trial court denied the motion, and the jury returned a verdict for the insurer. The New Maine Supreme Court affirmed. The Supreme Court held that the landscaper was responsible for the consequences of the combustion of paint fumes that it had triggered because its employee should have been aware of the paint fumes and the danger they posed. *Id.* at 35. In dictum, the court stated that it might have reached a different result had the landscaper reasonably failed to foresee that the welding could trigger such a blaze. *Id.*

We can try to distinguish our case from *Rainbow Landscaping* by arguing that the landscaper's agreement to accommodate the work of other subcontractors justified the finding that the landscaper should have known of the hazard. Under this reasoning, the agreement was critical to the allocation of responsibility to the landscaper for the consequences of igniting the paint. That contract has no direct counterpart in this case. Moreover, in light of New Maine's policy of limiting the liability of medical care providers, a court might be willing to apply the doctrine of proximate cause more stringently in a hospital setting than in a construction setting.

On the other hand, although Souza's adverse reaction to the anesthetic was not highly probable, it was certainly foreseeable as a possible consequence; Unger's intense concentration on the intake gauge shows that she indeed specifically anticipated such a reaction. The absence of a contract such as the one in *Rainbow Landscaping* might be viewed as a technical and only marginally material distinction.

Therefore, even if we can persuade a court to analyze Souza's nervous condition within the framework of supervening cause, the court probably will not find the doctrine satisfied on the facts of this case. If Souza can prove that Unger was negligent, she can probably show proximate cause as well.

V. CONCLUSION

In light of legislative and judicial policies favoring limits on physicians' liability, the strict liability statute regulating toxic materials probably will not apply to the administration of the anesthetic in this case. The courts will be even less likely to retreat from precedent to apply the common law doctrine imposing strict liability for ultrahazardous activities. A jury may find, however, that Humana's anesthesiologist was negligent in failing to summon assistance for the administration of the anesthesia and to monitor Souza more closely. We can try to characterize Souza's nervous condition as a supervening cause, but *Rainbow Landscaping* will not be easy to distinguish.

Because the risk of substantial liability is great, I recommend that we advise Humana to settle. Souza's estate may be willing to compromise; their negligence claim is not appropriate for summary disposition, and they may want to avoid the unpredictability of a jury.

Questions on Sample Memorandum 2

a. Distinguish between the statutory and common law claims discussed in Sample Memorandum 2. How does the legal method of analyzing one claim differ from that of the other?

b. Review the subsection discussing the element of proximate cause in a negligence action. Note how the author of the memorandum seeks to manipulate the analytic framework within which to address the legal consequences of Souza's unusual nervous condition. Is this a fair method of argument? Can it be used in other contexts? Most professors of tort law readily conclude that a court would analyze Souza's nervous condition within the "thin-skulled-plaintiff" rule regarding the scope of duties, and not within the framework of proximate cause. In that light, is the argument in the memorandum a welcome exercise in creative argument, or is it a misleading waste of time for the reader?

c. Notice the frequent use of the word "we" in the section on proximate cause. Should the author of a memorandum avoid using such first-person pronouns in a legal analysis? Are first-person pronouns appropriate when referring to the law firm's development of facts or legal theories? Are they better than passive voice or other abstractions?

3. *Review—Sample Examination Answer*

Review Sample Memorandum 1 above. The following single-issue examination problem is roughly based on the dispute analyzed in that memorandum. Study the sample answer that follows the problem and compare its sparer, leaner style with the more thorough analysis in the memorandum. Note also the function of each of the four paragraphs in the answer:

¶ 1 identifies the issue and explains why other matters are not in issue;
¶ 2 discusses the applicable legal rule;
¶ 3 applies the rule to the facts; and
¶ 4 states a conclusion.

Problem

On December 15, pursuant to an enforceable agreement, Lender sold his used Mercedes Benz car to Borrower for $20,000. Under the terms of the agreement, Borrower paid $8,000 in cash and agreed to pay the remaining $12,000 to Lender in 12 monthly installments of $1,000 each, beginning January 1.

Borrower paid the first six monthly installments, but failed to pay the next two installments on July 1 and August 1. When Lender threatened to sue Borrower, Borrower's cousin (Guarantor) entered into the following Guarantee Agreement with Lender to give Borrower time to recover from temporary financial difficulties. This Guarantee Agreement refers to the original contract between Lender and Borrower as the "CREDIT/SALE AGREEMENT."

GUARANTEE AGREEMENT

Parties . . .

Recitals . . .

Mutual Rights and Obligations
 The parties agree to the following exchange:
 1. LENDER will refrain from asserting his claim against BORROWER and from demanding payment on the CREDIT/SALE AGREEMENT until LENDER needs the money.
 2. In the event that BORROWER fails to pay all amounts due under the CREDIT/SALE AGREEMENT upon demand by LENDER, GUARANTOR will pay those amounts immediately and will pay further installments as they become due under the CREDIT/SALE AGREEMENT.

Guarantor and Lender signed this agreement on August 15. On August 25, Lender demanded payment of past due installments from Borrower. Borrower responded that he couldn't pay. Accordingly, on August 26, Lender demanded payment of past due installments from Guarantor and stated that he expected either Borrower or Guarantor to pay the remaining installments as they came due.

You represent Guarantor, who does not want to perform on her promise to pay Borrower's debt. In a balanced discussion addressed to your supervising attorney, fully address the rights and liabilities of Lender and Guarantor under the Guarantee Agreement. Do not discuss promissory estoppel, quasi-contract, or other theories of liability aside from conventional contract.

Sample Answer

 Guarantor's performance under section 2 of the Guarantee Agreement is due because Borrower has failed to pay on Lender's demand. The issue is whether the Guarantee Agreement is enforceable. The Guarantee Agreement appears to be reasonably definite and to have resulted from a valid offer and acceptance. Moreover, Lender had a perfectly valid claim under the original sale agreement; therefore, a promise by him to forbear from filing suit on that claim could be good consideration for Guarantor's conditional promise to pay. However, Lender's promise to refrain from asserting his claim and demanding payment only until he "needs the money" arguably is illusory, thus creating doubt whether Guarantor's promise is supported by consideration.

 An enforceable contract requires a bargained-for exchange in which a promisor exchanges his own promise for a return promise or performance. The requirement of an exchange is not satisfied if one party gives only an illusory promise, which does not commit the promisor to any future performance. A promise is illusory if it leaves the promisor free to perform or not according to his unfettered whim or discretion, such as a promise to refrain from asserting a claim "until I want the money." On the other hand, even if a promise leaves open the possibility that the promisor will escape obligation, the promise is valid if the promisor does not have complete control over the events on which the promisor's obligation is conditioned, such as a promise to buy land "if I can qualify for a loan."

Guarantor should argue that Lender's promise to forbear until he "needs" the money permits Lender to decide at his own whim and unfettered discretion when to demand payment, because he has some control of his own needs. However, that argument would prevail only if the word "need" refers to a subjective perception of deprivation that is inseparable from Lender's purely personal wants or desires. Lender can argue that the word "need" conditions the length of his forbearance on financial events that are at least partly outside his control: as long as his income and expenses create no need for the money, Lender has a commitment to forbear from demanding payment.

Unfortunately for our client, Lender's promise in the Guarantee Agreement probably is not illusory, because the word "need" provides some substance to Lender's commitment to forbear. Therefore, Guarantor's promise probably is supported by consideration and is enforceable.

4. *Advanced Samples*

The Appendix in the accompanying Assignment Book contains two alternative memoranda and an examination answer, all based on roughly the same problem. Working through these examples will help you to (1) continue to compare the general style of writing and analysis in a legal memorandum with that in an examination answer and (2) on an advanced level, critically evaluate specific writing techniques for legal memoranda.

V. SUMMARY

Before drafting an office memorandum,
   (1) master the assignment,
   (2) research and analyze the problem,
   (3) outline your memorandum, and
   (4) choose a suitable format.

Before writing your answer to a law school examination, reflect on the parallels between an essay exam answer and the discussion section of an office memorandum.

9

Organization of Office Memoranda and Briefs

One of the most important features of effective legal analysis and writing is good organization. Techniques of organization are also among the most difficult to develop and to teach. However, you can steadily improve your skills with a few months of practice. Regular outlining of course material in law school is an excellent way to build basic skills.

Although the focus of Part III is neutral analysis in office memoranda, the techniques of organization described in this chapter apply directly to both office memoranda and legal briefs. Accordingly, this chapter uses examples from both memoranda and briefs. The following sections explore organizational problems on four different levels, progressing from broader problems of (1) format and (2) relationships among multiple issues, to narrower problems of (3) progression within sections and (4) effective paragraphing.

I. FORMAT

Before drafting any legal document, you must select an appropriate format for the document. The format will determine the essential content of the document and the order in which you present the different parts of that content.

Rules of procedure and local court rules prescribe formats for appellate briefs; with somewhat less detail, they also prescribe or suggest formats for trial pleadings, motions, and briefs. You should take care to follow these rules, because they presumably reflect the court's views about effective content and administrative efficiency. If you depart from the prescribed format, you may irritate the judge or judges who must read the document. Indeed, you may even lead the judge or the clerk's office to reject the document for filing or to impose other sanctions.[1]

The most appropriate format for other documents, such as a contract or office memorandum, is more nearly a matter of judgment or style for you or your law firm. For example, Chapter 8, page 140, outlines three different formats for an office memorandum; whether one is more appropriate to an assignment than another will depend on such factors as the complexity of the memorandum, the preferences of your supervising attorney, and your own personal style. Before beginning to write such a document, you should take a few moments to determine which format will best suit your audience, your personal style, and the purposes of the document.

II. RELATIONSHIPS AMONG MULTIPLE ISSUES AND SUBISSUES

Your statement of the issues and your discussion or argument section of an office memorandum or legal brief should reflect the proper relationships among multiple issues and subissues. Good organization at this broad level requires a thorough understanding of the substantive analysis as well as attention to techniques of effective writing. Therefore, if you experience unusual difficulty with this level of organization, you may wish to supplement your research before proceeding further. By reviewing basic principles in a secondary source, you can gain a broad perspective that will help you organize your material.

A. PROPER RELATIONSHIPS AMONG TOPICS

Stated most simply, the section headings of the discussion or argument section of a document should show which topics are distinct and independent, and which are subsets of a more general topic. The statement of the issues should show the same relationships. These relationships are a function of the elements of the legal claims or defenses in question.

For example, suppose that you are preparing an office memorandum to discuss the following theories of employer liability for the discharge of an employee: (1) sex discrimination in violation of Title VII of the Civil Rights Act of 1964, using a disparate treatment theory; (2) sex discrimination in violation of Title VII, using a disparate impact theory; (3) violation of a contractual duty, expressed in the company policy manual, to invoke specified hearing procedures before terminating any employee; (4) wrongful discharge for a reason that violates public policy; and (5) intentional infliction of emotional distress.

---

1. See, e.g., McGoldrick Oil Co. v. Campbell, Athey & Zukowski, 793 F.2d 649, 653 (5th cir. 1986) (ordering a brief "stricken"); Westinghouse Elec. Corp. v. National Labor Relations Bd., 809 F.2d 419, 424-425 (7th Cir. 1987) (imposing $1,000 penalty on counsel for evading federal rule limiting the number of pages of its opening brief).

The following information about the legal content of these claims will help you devise an appropriate organizational structure. To establish a disparate treatment claim under Title VII, you must prove that the employer adversely affected the terms or conditions of a person's employment with the intent to discriminate on the basis of sex or other protected classification.[2] In disparate impact analysis, you may base Title VII liability on proof that a facially neutral employment practice adversely affected a disproportionate number of members of a protected class and was not justified by business necessity; specific proof of discriminatory intent is unnecessary.[3] The elements of a contract action for breach of promise in a policy manual are (1) a promise in the manual by the employer to restrict the circumstances justifying discharge of the employee; (2) a basis for enforcing the promise, such as incorporation of the manual into the employment contract; and (3) breach of the promise.[4] The elements of the tort of wrongful discharge of an at-will employee in violation of public policy are (1) discharge of the employee (2) for a reason that contravenes a public policy that is clearly mandated by statute or case law.[5] Finally, the elements of the tort of intentional infliction of emotional distress are (1) extreme and outrageous conduct (2) that is taken with the intent to cause emotional distress or with reckless disregard for the possibility of those consequences, and (3) that causes (4) severe emotional distress.[6]

Although organization of these topics is a matter of judgment rather than an exact science, most legal writers will agree that the following section headings of the discussion section of the memorandum leave some room for improvement:

IV. DISCUSSION
    A. Sex Discrimination—Disparate Treatment
    B. Sex Discrimination—Disparate Impact
    C. Tort
        1. Wrongful Discharge—Violation of Public Policy or Breach of Promise in Employee Manual
        2. Intentional Infliction of Emotional Distress
    D. Remedies

First, sections A and B simply discuss different means of proving discrimination under section 703 of Title VII, and these are the only theories of direct statutory liability discussed in the memo. Therefore, sections A and B have much more in common with one another than either has with any of the other sections or subsections. Indeed, in your memorandum, you likely would include background discussion of Title VII that would be common to both theories. For these reasons, you should combine sections A and B into a single section. Whether you should formally divide that section into subsections cor-

---

2. See, e.g., McDonnell Douglas Corp. v. Green, 411 U.S. 792 (1973).
3. See, e.g., Griggs v. Duke Power Co., 401 U.S. 424 (1971).
4. E.g., Wagenseller v. Scottsdale Memorial Hosp., 147 Ariz. 370, 381-383, 710 P.2d 1025, 1036-1038 (1985); Leikvold v. Valley View Community Hosp., 141 Ariz. 544, 688 P.2d 170 (1984).
5. *Wagenseller,* supra note 4, at 376-381, 710 P.2d at 1031-1036.
6. E.g., Watts v. Golden Age Nursing Home, 127 Ariz. 255, 619 P.2d 1032 (1980).

responding to the two theories of discrimination is a matter of judgment that would depend on such things as the depth of analysis in that section.

Second, the subsections of section C do not belong together in the same section. True, both subsections present common law theories of liability in an emerging field known generically as wrongful discharge, and two of those theories are classified as torts. Nonetheless, none of the theories has any important elements in common with either of the others. Therefore, subsections C(1) and C(2) have less in common than do sections A and B. Moreover, subsection C(1) addresses two distinct theories of wrongful discharge that should not be lumped together in the same subsection: wrongful discharge in violation of public policy is a tort whose elements have little in common with those of a claim for breach of a contractual promise to restrict the circumstances of terminating the employment contract. Finally, the heading of Section C, "Tort," is insufficiently broad to encompass all the theories discussed in that section, because subsection C(1) examines a contract theory as well as a tort theory.

These considerations suggest an improved organizational structure such as the following:

> A. Title VII—Sex Discrimination [general statutory standards, policies, and background]
>   1. Disparate Treatment
>   2. Disparate Impact
> B. Breach of Contract
> C. Wrongful Discharge in Violation of Public Policy
> D. Intentional Infliction of Emotional Distress
> E. Remedies

Of course, this sample outline represents only one of many reasonable organizational structures for the memorandum in question. Other organizational structures may reflect different ways of presenting the analyses of remedies. For example, you might recognize that sections A through D present various theories of liability and could be consolidated in a section that is on the same level as the separate topic of remedies:

> A. Theories of Liability
>   1. Title VII—Sex Discrimination
>   • • • •
>   4. Intentional Infliction of Emotional Distress
> B. Remedies
>   1. Title VII
>   2. Contract
>   3. Tort

Alternatively, you might decide to discuss remedies within each of the sections that introduces a theory of liability, rather than in a separate comprehensive section devoted to remedies. If so, you could consolidate the two tort theories into a single section, because the remedies for each would be governed by the same tort principles. Depending on the depth of discussion in the memorandum, you could discuss remedies either in a paragraph at the end of each major section or, as shown below, in separate subsections.

A. Title VII—Sex Discrimination
   [general statutory standards, policies, and background]
   1. Disparate Treatment
   2. Disparate Impact
   3. Remedies
B. Breach of Contract
   1. Breach of Promise in an Employee Manual
   2. Remedies
C. Tort
   1. Wrongful Discharge in Violation of Public Policy
   2. Intentional Infliction of Emotional Distress
   3. Remedies

B. ORDER OF TOPICS

In an office memorandum, you should organize your topics in a logical order that permits early topics to build a foundation for subsequent topics. The clearest example of this is a multiple-issue discussion in which some issues are "threshold issues" in the sense that the resolution of those issues affects the analysis of other issues. Logically, you should discuss the threshold issues before you discuss the issues that are dependent on the outcome of the threshold issues.

For example, suppose that Maya Tortilla Co. alleges that Bakeway Supermarkets (1) formed a contract with Maya; (2) breached its contractual obligations, at least under Maya's interpretation of the contract; (3) and is liable to Maya for $20,000 in damages. If Bakeway disputes each of these allegations, the parties have raised three entirely separate issues.

Logically, you should discuss issue 1 first because contract formation is a threshold issue: Bakeway did not assume any contractual obligations and consequent potential liability if it did not form a contract with Maya. Similarly, you should discuss issue 2 before issue 3 for two reasons: first, Bakeway is not liable in damages unless it breached; second, to determine whether Bakeway breached, you must interpret the contract and define Bakeway's obligation. In turn, the scope of Bakeway's obligation will determine Maya's expectation interest, on which damages will be based.

If you are drafting a brief rather than an office memorandum, you might organize your arguments differently: strategic considerations may lead you to depart from a purely logical ordering of arguments. In many cases, the first arguments in a brief influence the judge more strongly than later ones. Like other people, judges are strongly influenced by first impressions. Also, if pressed for time, a busy trial judge may not reach the last few pages of a pretrial motions brief before oral argument. Accordingly, if one of your arguments is much stronger than the others, you might exercise discretion to present it first in your brief, even though another issue is logically prior.

Finally, you should apply all these considerations only to order your topics effectively, not to cut off discussion of any of the issues. In a close case, you cannot predict with certainty how a court will resolve a threshold issue. Accordingly, if a threshold issue raises a question sufficiently doubtful to warrant full discussion in an office memorandum or a brief, you should address all of the other substantial issues, even if you tentatively resolve the threshold issue in a way that logically would cut off discussion. In an office memorandum, for example, if you conclude that Bakeway did not breach the contract, you should nonetheless discuss the question of the amount of damages for which Bakeway would be liable if it had breached.

C. TECHNIQUE

By far the most efficient way to organize the topics of a memorandum or brief is to outline them after you have researched and analyzed the problem but before you begin to write. Even when you are working under severe time pressure, you should take a few minutes to organize your notes, think deeply and creatively about the analysis, and explore the relationships among topics by comparing different outlines of the discussion or argument. You can much more easily modify your analytic approach and writing strategy at the outline stage than you can midway through the first draft.

If you do not prepare an outline before writing the first draft, and if the first draft appears hopelessly disorganized, you can still derive benefits from outlining techniques, albeit with less efficiency than at the prewriting stage. By writing out the section and subsection headings of your first draft in outline form, you can expose and evaluate the organization of your draft and can improve the organization by modifying the outline.

Finally, once you have chosen an organizational structure, you should clearly communicate that structure to the reader with descriptive section and subsection headings that are at least roughly parallel to the structure of the statement of issues. In an answer to a law school examination, such headings may even take the place of more formal statements of the issues.

III. PROGRESSION WITHIN SECTION OR SUBSECTION

Once you have divided your topics into separate sections, you are ready to organize the discussion or argument within sections. At the most general level, your analysis should follow the familiar pattern of deductive reasoning: after introducing the issue or argument with a heading and perhaps with a brief introduction in the text, you should discuss or argue the law, apply that law to the facts, and reach a conclusion.

Effective progression within a section also requires attention to one or more of five considerations:

(1) hierarchy of authority,
(2) progression from general to specific,
(3) progression from fundamental to uncertain,
(4) historical development, and
(5) separation or consolidation of logical discussions or arguments.

The first four of these considerations deal mainly with the development of legal standards. The fifth deals with methods of combining legal and factual analysis.

A. HIERARCHY OF AUTHORITY

In statutory analysis, the hierarchy of authority leads to a convention of organization. You should analyze, or at least present, the language in question before analyzing cases that either interpret the statute or that discuss supplemental common law:

> C. *Commercial Impracticability*
>
> The Uniform Commercial Code (U.C.C.) provides that, in limited circumstances, a seller's failure to deliver goods is not a breach of contract
>
> > if performance as agreed has been made impracticable by the occurrence of a contingency the non-occurrence of which was a basic assumption on which the contract was made . . .
>
> U.C.C. § 2-615(a). The U.C.C.'s use of the term "impracticable" suggests a more liberal standard for discharging obligations than the traditional common law standard of "impossibility of performance." *See Bjorn v. Borg* . . .

The normal convention of starting with the statutory language will occasionally apply with less force in the analysis of some of the more commonly litigated provisions of a constitution. Because constitutional provisions are typically even more general than statutory provisions, the enormous body of case law interpreting some provisions may take on a life of its own, overshadowing the actual words of the provision. Thus, you need not quote the language of the fourth amendment before asserting a well-established proposition about the need to obtain a warrant before searching a dwelling; reference to case law interpreting the fourth amendment in most cases will be sufficient. Nonetheless, you should begin the analysis by at least identifying the fourth amendment as the source of the restriction on searches. Moreover, some constitutional issues, like most issues of statutory interpretation, will be sufficiently novel to require original analysis, in which case you should begin the analysis with the language of the constitutional provision.

B. PROGRESSION FROM GENERAL TO SPECIFIC

Reading a legal analysis or argument should be like viewing a large painting that covers a third of the wall of a museum exhibit room. As the viewer enters, he sees the general outlines of the whole painting, and he becomes curious about a few provocative parts of the whole. He then moves closer to the painting to separately examine each of these parts. Finally, when he steps back to view the painting again as a whole, he may appreciate it more fully than he did before he had an opportunity to explore some of the details. Similarly, a legal document should

(1) provide an overview to the document,

(2) separately explore important matters in some detail, and

(3) conclude with a summary or with general insights that are easier to appreciate after the discussion of details.

On a broad level, a memorandum or brief performs these functions with (1) the statement of issues or other introduction, (2) the discussion or argument, and (3) the conclusion. On a narrower level, this kind of progression is often appropriate within a section of the discussion or argument.

For an example of progression within a section, suppose that the plaintiff in a tort action alleges that the defendant intentionally inflicted emotional distress. If the defendant, your client, contends that the facts in the record fail to satisfy two of the elements of that tort, your brief for the defendant might address each of those elements separately, either in separate paragraphs or separate subsections of the argument. If so, you can orient the reader by beginning with a paragraph that introduces each of the elements:

II. ARGUMENT

A. Lew's Allegations in Count II Fail to State a Claim for Intentional Infliction of Emotional Distress.

General overview

To establish a right to relief for intentional infliction of emotional distress, Lew must plead and prove that (1) Smith engaged in extreme and outrageous conduct (2) with the intent to cause severe emotional distress or with reckless disregard for the possibility of those consequences, and that (3) his actions caused Lew to suffer (4) severe emotional distress. *See Watts v. Golden Age Nursing Home,* 127 Ariz. 255, 619 P.2d 1032 (1980). Even assuming the truth of Lew's allegations about the manner in which Smith terminated Lew's employment contract, the complaint does not properly allege either the extreme conduct or the severe distress required for liability. Therefore, Lew has failed to state a claim for relief in Count II.

Specific argument

1. Smith's Alleged Conduct Was Not "Extreme and Outrageous."

Only the most deplorable and shocking conduct satisfies the narrow definition of "extreme and outrageous conduct." *See* . . .

In this case, the allegations that Smith . . .

2. Lew's Alleged "Depression" Does Not Amount to Severe Emotional Distress.

Proof of severe emotional distress . . .

The introduction in the first paragraph above not only provides an overview of the legal standards, it summarizes the overall argument of the section. That argument appears elsewhere as well: (1) it is stated concisely in the heading for section A; (2) it is developed in greater detail in each of the subsections; and (3) it should be repeated in general terms at the end of section A, in a separate conclusion section at the end of the document, or both.

At a different level within a section, you might introduce a general principle in a topic sentence before exploring it in greater detail within the same paragraph:

Even if a promise leaves open the possibility that the promisor will escape obligation, however, the promise is valid if the promisor does not have complete control over the events on which the promisor's obligation is conditioned. *See Bonnie v. DeLaney,* 158 Calz. 212, 645 P.2d 887 (1982). In *Bonnie,* an agreement for the sale of a house provided that the buyer could cancel the agreement if the buyer "cannot qualify for a 30-year mortgage loan for 90% of the sales price" with any of several banks listed in the agreement. *Id.* at 213, 645 P.2d at 888. In enforcing the agreement against the seller, the court distinguished *Atco Corp.* on the ground that the word "cannot" referred to the buyer's ability to obtain a loan rather than to his desire. Because his ability to obtain a loan was partly controlled by events and decisions outside his control, the promises in the sale agreement were nonillusory and binding. *Id.* at 214-15, 645 P.2d 889-91.	**Topic sentence** **Specific case analysis**

In the preceding example, the opening sentence of the paragraph summarizes the general point that the *Bonnie* decision illustrates. That introduction prepares the reader for the detailed analysis of *Bonnie* that follows.

C. PROGRESSION FROM FUNDAMENTAL TO COMPLEX POINTS

Some legal discussions or arguments may lend themselves to a related method of organization within a section or subsection: progression from fundamental or undisputed points to complex or disputed points. In some cases, the preliminary points may address matters that are not even ultimately in issue; they may simply provide helpful background information or establish legal premises to the main topic of discussion.

For example, the following passage from a brief provides background information about statutory policies that helps support the ultimate argument that a contractual provision attempting to fix damages for breach is not enforceable:

C. The Liquidated Damages Clause Is Void as a Penalty

Fundamental premises

    The contract for the sale of the engine parts is a "transaction in goods" and thus is covered by the Uniform Commercial Code. U.C.C. §§ 2-102, 2-105. U.C.C. remedies for breach of contract are designed to compensate the victim of the breach for the loss of the value of the expected performance. *See* U.C.C. § 1-106. They do not permit imposition of a penalty that is designed to discourage breach or to punish the breaching party. *Id.;* U.C.C. § 2-718(1).

Transition to disputed point

    Within limited parameters, the U.C.C. permits parties to agree to fix damages for breach in advance in their sales contract by including a provision for "liquidated damages." However, such damages must be limited to

> an amount which is reasonable in the light of the anticipated or actual harm caused by the breach, the difficulties of proof of loss, and the inconvenience or nonfeasibility of otherwise obtaining an adequate remedy. A term fixing unreasonably large liquidated damages is void as a penalty.

U.C.C. § 2-718(1). In this case, section 5.4 of the contract is a penalty clause, which is unenforceable because it attempts to fix damages at an amount that is disproportionate to any anticipated or actual harm.

    The first paragraph of the preceding passage addresses fundamental matters of statutory policy that the opposing party will not dispute and thus that are not technically in issue. It provides a general orientation, however, that will help to place in perspective the argument relating to the matter that will be hotly disputed: does the liquidated damages clause constitute an impermissible penalty under the U.C.C.?

D. HISTORICAL DEVELOPMENT

    You may help your audience understand the current contours of a legal rule by outlining the historical context from which the rule emerged. In rare cases, by chronologically describing the metamorphosis of a rule, you can help your reader appreciate the current state of the law without distracting her from the issue at hand. In most cases, however, you will develop your points more efficiently and gracefully if you (1) adopt one or more of the methods of organization discussed in sections A-C above, (2) begin your analysis with current authority, and (3) incorporate the historical analysis into the discussion of that authority.

1. *Chronological Development*

A strictly chronological account of the development of a legal rule might be helpful if the current rule arguably retains vestiges of earlier forms of the rule:

A. *Tippet's Qualified Immunity Defense*

Federal civil rights legislation imposes liability for deprivation of constitutional rights by agents of the state:

> Every person who . . .

42 U.S.C. § 1983.

Although section 1983 does not expressly limit its remedies, it implicitly incorporates a variety of traditional immunity defenses. *E.g., Tenney v. Brandhove,* 341 U.S. 367, 376 (1951) (absolute immunity for state legislators). The Supreme Court has recognized a qualified immunity for executive officials, such as police officers, acting in discretionary functions. *Pierson v. Ray,* 386 U.S. 547 (1967). In *Pierson,* the Court held that police officers who illegally arrested protesting clergymen could escape liability for money damages under section 1983 if "they reasonably believed in good faith that the arrest was constitutional." *Id.* at 557.

In an action under section 1983 alleging constitutional deprivations by school board officials, the Supreme Court further developed its test for qualified immunity. *Wood v. Strickland,* 420 U.S. 308 (1975). In *Wood,* the court emphasized that the test for qualified immunity included both objective and subjective elements:

> The official himself must be acting sincerely and with a belief that he is doing right, but an act violating a student's constitutional rights can be no more justified by ignorance or disregard of settled, indisputable law on the part of one entrusted with supervision of students' daily lives than by the presence of actual malice. . . . [A] school board member . . . must be held to a standard of conduct based not only on permissible intentions, but also on knowledge of the basic, unquestioned constitutional rights of his charges.

Id. at 321-22.

The qualified immunity doctrine took an abrupt turn in *Harlow v. Fitzgerald,* 457 U.S. 800 (1982). To facilitate summary judgment on a defense of qual-

---

Statute

Chronology of interpretive case law
1951

1967

1975

1982

ified immunity, the Court abandoned much of the subjective element of the test, increasing its reliance on objective reasonableness. The *Harlow* test protects government officials if "their conduct does not violate clearly established constitutional rights of which a reasonable person would have known." *Id.* at 818. *Harlow* involved a suit against federal officials, but courts have extended the *Harlow* modifications of the qualified immunity test to section 1983 actions. *E.g.,* . . .

Although the *Harlow* test contemplates that qualified immunity defenses in many cases will present questions only of objective reasonableness, the test arguably retains some remnants of the subjective element of *Wood v. Strickland. See Harlow* 457 U.S. at 821 (Brennan, J., concurring). . . .

Unfortunately, you may be tempted to overuse chronological development of the law as a method of organization. Every legal rule has a history, and most have steadily changed shape over time as courts and legislatures have modified, supplemented, and refined them. When writing a comprehensive law review article, you might choose to trace the chronological development of every significant legal rule in your scholarly analysis. Such a deliberate approach, however, may tend to impede the swifter flow of a legal memorandum or brief. Therefore, when writing a memorandum or brief, you ordinarily should adopt a method of organization that emphasizes the current state of the law. You should chronologically trace the development of a legal rule only when other methods of organization would inadequately convey the current form of the rule.

2. Current State of the Law as Focal Point

Even when the current law is comprehensible only in the context of earlier developments, you often can focus on current case law and can explore the historical context within your analysis of contemporary cases:

B. *Interlocutory Appeal*

Federal law vests the federal courts of appeals with jurisdiction over appeals only from "final decisions" of the federal district courts. 28 U.S.C. § 1291. Nonetheless, Officer Tippett probably can immediately appeal the district court's denial of his motion for summary judgment based on the defense of qualified immunity. *See Mitchell v. Forsyth,* 472 U.S. 511, 524-30 (1985).

In *Mitchell,* a person whose conversation had been intercepted in an illegal F.B.I. wiretap sued the U.S. Attorney General for authorizing the warrantless

Currently applicable case law

wiretap. The trial court denied the attorney general's motion for summary judgment based on absolute and qualified immunity, and the attorney general filed an interlocutory appeal. *Id.* at 513-17. The Supreme Court held that the court of appeals had jurisdiction over the interlocutory appeal under the "collateral order" doctrine established in *Cohen v. Beneficial Industrial Loan Corp.,* 337 U.S. 541 (1949).

Earlier source of controlling principle

In applying the collateral-order doctrine to a qualified immunity defense, the *Mitchell* Court considered two attributes of the defense, each of which stems from the objective nature of the test as established in *Harlow v. Fitzgerald,* 457 U.S. 800, 815-19 (1982). First, the test fashioned in *Harlow* is designed to permit the dismissal of insubstantial claims on summary judgment, thus protecting government officials from the burdens of trial. *Mitchell,* 472 U.S. at 526. Second, the *Harlow* test normally permits the appellate court to decide the interlocutory appeal as a matter of law. *Id.* at 528.

Earlier source of related principles

In our case, Crawford has asserted that Tippett maliciously . . .

Under this approach, you can focus your discussion on the current authority, *Mitchell,* and you can convey the historical significance of *Harlow* within your discussion of *Mitchell.* This approach permits you to present much of the analysis of *Mitchell* within one or more of the organizational structures discussed in sections A-C above.

E. SEPARATION OR CONSOLIDATION OF ANALYSES

1. Overview

In analyzing an issue in a memorandum or a brief, you ordinarily should follow the general structure of the syllogism of deductive reasoning:

(1) major premise—rule of law
(2) minor premise—application of law to facts
(3) conclusion

At the simplest level, you can present all the elements of a single syllogism in a single, undivided section of your discussion or argument:

A. Topic
Introduction
Legal Rule
Application to Facts
Conclusion

Many topics of discussion or argument, however, are not so simple. If a topic is unusually complex, you might separately present the elements of a single syllogism in several subsections:

> A. *Topic*
>   Introduction
>   1. Legal Rule
>   a. Analysis of Persuasive Authority
>   b. Policy Analysis
>   2. Application to Facts
>   a. Analysis of Category A Facts
>   b. Analysis of Category B Facts
>   3. Conclusion

Conversely, if your main topic of discussion or argument encompasses closely related subtopics that do not warrant separation into formal subsections, you might exercise discretion to discuss more than one topic within an undivided section or subsection. If so, you can present your analysis in either of two ways. First, you can separate the topics into several smaller syllogisms within the section, each syllogism with its own legal and factual analyses:

> B. *Topic*
>   Introduction
>   Legal Rule 1
>   Facts 1
>   Conclusion 1
>   Legal Rule 2
>   Facts 2
>   Conclusion 2

Alternatively, you can consolidate the related topics into a single syllogism:

> A. *Topic*
>   Introduction
>   Legal Rules 1 & 2
>   Application to Facts 1 & 2
>   Conclusions

Most writers tend to react to these problems on a subconscious, intuitive level. However, the decision to separate or consolidate is sufficiently important to warrant conscious analysis.

2. Single Syllogism in Undivided Section

At the broadest level, if a topic or argument is sufficiently important and discrete to warrant a separate section or subsection heading, you ordinarily should develop it completely and resolve it within that section or subsection. In the following excerpts from a brief, for example, an advocate divides the arguments about two elements of a tort into subsections. In each of these subsections, the advocate analyzes an element in a single, complete syllogism. Specifically, he presents his view of the law for that element, applies the law to the facts relating to that element, and states a conclusion about the sufficiency of the allegations relating to that element:

II. ARGUMENT

    A. *Lew's Allegations in Count II Fail to State a Claim for Intentional Infliction of Emotional Distress.*

            Major argument

To establish a right to relief . . .

    1. Smith's Alleged Conduct Was Not "Extreme and Outrageous."

            First subargument
            General rules of law

Only the most deplorable and shocking conduct satisfies the narrow definition of "extreme and outrageous conduct." *See* . . . . Conduct that simply reflects normal social and economic adversities is not extreme or outrageous. *See, e.g., Frank v. Boswell,* . . .

In *Frank,* a landlord's eviction notice did not reflect extreme and outrageous conduct, even though it was "rude, threatening, and intimidating." *Id.* at 289. The court reasoned that . . .

            In-depth analysis of case law

In this case, Lew's complaint alleges conduct that is even less extreme than the conduct in *Frank.* It alleges that Smith "fired Lew without severance pay and with full knowledge that Lew's family was facing a desperate financial crisis." Plaintiff's Second Amended Complaint ¶ 7. It further alleges that Smith communicated his decision in a "terse, unfriendly and unsympathetic conversation, without advance notice." *Id.* at ¶ 8.

            Facts of current dispute

These allegations state only that Lew was the victim of his own economic distress and that Smith acted to protect the interests of his business. Although some business owners might take it upon themselves to offer personal counseling and financial aid to their employees or ex-employees, Smith has no legal duty to do so.

            Analysis of facts

Thus, the complaint does not allege circumstances that could establish the requisite "extreme and outrageous conduct."

            Conclusion

    2. Lew's Alleged "Depression" Does Not Amount to Severe Emotional Distress.

            Second subargument

Proof of severe emotional distress . . .

3. Separation of Elements of Single Syllogism into Multiple Subsections

In a particularly complex analysis, you might depart from the most basic organizational structure by developing only one element of a complete analysis within a section or subsection. For example, you could develop the legal rules in one section and analyze the facts in a separate section, perhaps dividing the fact analysis into subsections:

Legal rules

A. Officer Bates Could Not Lawfully Arrest Jones Without Probable Cause to Believe That Jones Had Committed a Felony.

Although a police officer may arrest a suspect without a warrant in some circumstances, he may not place a suspect under full arrest without probable cause to believe that the suspect has committed a crime. *See* . . . A police officer does not have probable cause unless . . .

Application to facts

B. Officer Bates Did Not Have Probable Cause.

At the suppression hearing, Officer Jones asserted that Jones matched the description of the burglar and that Jones volunteered incriminating statements. Whether taken separately or together, however, these factors did not create probable cause.

First subset of facts

1. Jones Did Not Match the Description of the Burglar.

A written transcript of the radio report shows that Officer Bates received the following description of the burglary suspect: white male, six feet tall, 180 lbs., short brown hair, wearing a navy blue windbreaker. . . .

Second subset of facts

2. Jones's Statements Did Not Create Probable Cause.

The combined testimony of Jones and Officer Bates creates a clear and consistent picture of their conversation on Washington Street. . . .

Under this approach, the discussion of the law appears primarily in section A of the brief, and section B addresses the fact analysis. It would not be uncommon, however, for the author of such a passage to refer briefly to legal authority within section B when helpful to support the fact analysis.

4. *Multiple Syllogisms Within Single, Undivided Section*

Conversely, you may have occasion to present more than one complete analysis in a discrete section or subsection. If so, you can either (1) fully develop and resolve one syllogism before analyzing the next, or (2) combine the related legal rules of arguably distinct syllogisms and apply them to all the relevant facts.

a. Separation of Multiple Syllogisms

Within an undivided section, you may occasionally address several closely related topics, none of which is sufficiently important and discrete to warrant further subdivision into subsections. In many such cases, you can develop these related topics separately within the section or subsection.

For example, you can completely develop and resolve an introductory analysis before moving on to the main topic, as in the following excerpt from a legal memorandum:

I. OPTION CONTRACT UNDER UCC

In some circumstances, a merchant's promise not to revoke an offer to buy or sell goods is enforceable even if gratuitous:

> An offer by a merchant to buy or sell goods in a signed writing which by its terms gives assurance that it will be held open is not revocable, for lack of consideration . . . ; but any such term of assurance on a form supplied by the offeree must be separately signed by the offeror.

General statutory rules

U.C.C. § 2-205.

"Merchant" includes "a person who deals in goods of the kind." U.C.C. § 2-104. Stillwell regularly sells computers as part of her wholesale office supply business. Therefore, she is a merchant of the goods that she offered to supply to Azoulay, and § 2-205 thus governs the revocability of her offer.

Complete syllogism on preliminary matter

A more difficult question is whether Stillwell "separately signed" the promise not to revoke contained in the form supplied by Azoulay, the offeree. The purpose of the statutory requirement for a separate signing is . . .

Transition to main topic of discussion

The second paragraph of this example quickly resolves the question of merchant status in a complete syllogism, with a statement of the law, an analysis of the facts, and a conclusion. Because that issue is simple and noncontroversial, it does not warrant presentation in a separate subsection with its own heading.

On the other hand, it is sufficiently independent from the analysis of the requirement for a separate signing that you should develop and resolve it in a separate paragraph before analyzing other topics raised by the general standards in the first paragraph.

Some legal writers strain this form of separation when using it within a section that features in-depth case analyses of a series of cases. Rather than synthesize these cases and apply the synthesized law in consolidated form to the facts, the writer pauses briefly after each case analysis and applies the holding of that case to the relevant facts. Although this is a popular form of argument, it sometimes results in repetition and a rambling, piecemeal effect. You should not use it as a substitute for effective expression of synthesis of authority.

b. Consolidation of Multiple Syllogisms

In other cases, you may prefer to combine closely related legal standards and apply them as a group to all the relevant facts. This approach is illustrated by the second and third paragraphs of the following excerpt of a brief:

II. ARGUMENT

A. Bennett Will Prove That Tippett Is Liable Under 42 U.S.C. § 1983 for Violating Bennett's Civil Rights.

General statutory rules

Federal law imposes civil liability on a person who acts under the color of state law to deprive another of a federal right:

> Every person who, under the color of any [state law or custom], subjects, or causes to be subjected, any citizen of the United States or other person within the jurisdiction thereof to the deprivation of any rights, privileges or immunities secured by the Constitution and laws, shall be liable to the party injured . . .

42 U.S.C. § 1983.

Consolidated discussion of rules for three subarguments

A private party acts "under the color of state law" if he acts in concert with a state official acting in his official capacity. *Dennis v. Sparks,* 449 U.S. 24, 27-29 (1980). State action denying a litigant a fair and impartial hearing in civil litigation constitutes a deprivation of due process under the Fourteenth Amendment. *Cf. Cross v. Georgia,* 581 F.2d 102, 104 (5th Cir. 1978) (criminal prosecution). Although section 1983 implicitly incorporates the common law doctrine of absolute immunity for judges, that immunity does not protect private parties who conspire with the judge. *Dennis,* 449 U.S. at 29-32.

In this case, Bennett will prove all the elements

of his claim under section 1983. First, the evidence will show that Tippett conspired with Judge Bell by bribing Judge Bell to rule against Bennett on his motion for a preliminary injunction; Tippett therefore acted under the color of state law. Second, Tippett's bribe denied Bennett an impartial hearing and therefore deprived Bennett of his federal right to due process. Finally, even though Tippett acted under the color of state law, he has no official state function and therefore does not enjoy the protection of any official immunity.

Consolidated application of three rules to facts

Thus, the evidence will show that Tippett is liable to Bennett for violating Bennett's due process rights.

Conclusion

c. Discretion to Separate or Consolidate

The decision to separate or consolidate legal analyses often is a matter of judgment on which reasonable writers can disagree. As a general rule, a more superficial treatment of the topics lends itself to consolidation, as in the example above. On the other hand, if you analyze closely related topics in greater depth, you could divide the same discussion section of a brief into separate syllogisms that are fully developed and resolved in separate paragraphs within the section:

II. ARGUMENT

A. *Bennett Will Prove That Tippett Is Liable Under 42 U.S.C. § 1983 for Violating Bennett's Civil Rights.*

Federal law imposes civil liability on a person who acts under the color of state law to deprive another of a federal right:

General statutory rules

> Every person who, under the color of any . . .

42 U.S.C. § 1983. In this case, Bennett will prove all the elements of his claim under section 1983.

A private party acts "under the color of state law" if he acts in concert with a state official acting in his official capacity. *Dennis v. Sparks,* 449 U.S. 24, 27-29 (1980). In *Dennis,* a state judge . . . Similarly, the evidence in this case will show that Tippett conspired with Judge Bell by bribing Judge Bell to rule against Bennett on his motion for a preliminary injunction. Therefore, Tippett acted under the color of state law.

Full syllogism on first subargument

The fourteenth amendment's guarantee of due process in state proceedings is a federal substantive right, the deprivation of which is remediable under

Full syllogism on second subargument

Full syllogism on third subargument

section 1983. *See* generally *Carey v. Piphus,* 435 U.S. 247 (1978). State conduct denying a litigant a fair and impartial hearing in civil litigation constitutes a deprivation of due process under the fourteenth amendment. *Cf. Cross v. Georgia,* 581 F.2d 102, 104 (5th Cir. 1978) (criminal prosecution). In this case, Tippett's bribing the judge directly affected the outcome of the hearing on Bennett's request for a preliminary injunction; therefore, Tippett caused a deprivation of Bennett's right to due process.

Finally, Tippett is not immune from liability for money damages. Bennett agrees that state judges are absolutely immune from liability for damages for their judicial acts taken within their jurisdiction. *Stump v. Sparkman,* 435 U.S. 349 (1978). However, such immunity does not extend to a private party who conspires with a state judge, even though by so conspiring the private party acts under the color of state law. *Dennis,* 449 U.S. at 29-32 (1980). In this case, Tippett has no official status as an officer of the court; instead, he is a private party who therefore enjoys no official immunity.

General conclusion

Thus, the evidence will show that Tippett is liable to Bennett for violating Bennett's due process rights.

Of course, if the topics are truly independent and warrant extended discussion, you may wish to adopt the conventional approach of presenting each analysis in a separate subsection and under a separate heading:

II. ARGUMENT

A. Bennett Will Prove That Tippett Is Liable Under 42 U.S.C. § 1983 for Violating Bennett's Civil Rights.

General statutory rules

Federal law imposes civil liability . . . 42 U.S.C. § 1983. In this case, Bennett will prove all the elements of his claim under section 1983.

1. Tippett Acted Under the Color of State Law.

Full syllogism in several paragraphs within first subsection

A private party acts "under the color of state law" if he acts in concert . . .
In *Dennis,* . . .
In this case, the evidence will show that Tippett conspired with Judge Bell . . .
Therefore, Tippett acted under the color of state law.

2. Tippett Denied Bennett Due Process.

The Fourteenth Amendment's guarantee of due process in state proceedings is a federal substantive . . .

In *Cross,* . . .

In this case, Bennett will prove that Tippett bribed Judge Bell to rule against Bennett on his motion for a preliminary injunction. . . .

Therefore, Tippett violated Bennett's rights to due process.

Full syllogism in several paragraphs within second subsection

3. Tippett Is Not Immune From Suit.

Bennett agrees that . . .

Third subsection

d. Separate Analysis of Adverse Authority in Responsive Brief

A special organizational structure is sometimes appropriate for responsive briefs. In the ordinary three-stage briefing procedure, the answering brief will respond directly to the opening brief, and the reply brief will respond to the answering brief. In responding to an argument in a preceding brief, you can affirmatively develop a legal theory and apply it to the facts, and you can then separately address authority on which the preceding brief relies. You should analyze each adverse authority and discredit or distinguish it. You can use the same technique in an opening brief that anticipates a counterargument.

For example, in the following sample passage, the brief writer has affirmatively and confidently argued that Tippett denied Bennett due process under a mainstream legal theory. Only after completing that argument does he seek to persuade the judge to reject an approach based on *Parratt v. Taylor,* which the opposing party relied on in a previous motion:

II. ARGUMENT

A. Bennett Will Prove That Tippett Is Liable Under 42 U.S.C. § 1983 for Violating Bennett's Civil Rights Under . . .

1. Tippett Acted . . .

2. Tippett Denied Bennett Due Process.

The Fourteenth Amendment's guarantee of due process in state proceedings is a federal substantive . . .

In *Cross,* . . .

In this case, Bennett will prove that Tippett bribed Judge Bell to rule against Bennett on his motion for a preliminary injunction. . . . Therefore, Tippett violated Bennett's rights to due process.

Full syllogism in several paragraphs within second subargument

Separate paragraphs distinguishing adverse authority	Tippett argued in the reply brief to his motion to dismiss that Bennett has an adequate remedy under state tort law and that section 1983 therefore affords him no relief, citing *Parratt v. Taylor*, 452 U.S. 527 (1981). *Parratt* is distinguishable . . .

In this example, *Parratt v. Taylor* does not clearly address a distinct topic; instead, it helps define the limits of due process in certain contexts. Thus, in a neutral analysis, you might consolidate your discussion of *Parratt* with your discussion of other authorities that establish the legal rule, even though you ultimately distinguish *Parratt* from your case.

In a responsive brief, however, you should invite the judge to analyze your case initially without the distraction of distinguishable adverse authority. By delaying your analysis of the adverse case law in this manner, you are free to develop the initial argument strongly and positively, without the qualifications inherent in the subsequent discussion of adverse authority.

5. Summary

These examples have primarily illustrated two issues of organization: (1) whether to present topics in separate sections or within a single, undivided section and (2) whether to separate or consolidate analyses within a section. These issues illustrate the role of judgment in legal writing and particularly in developing organizational structures. Many problems of this nature have no single, clearly correct solution; your resolution will depend on the nature and the depth of the analyses or arguments and on your personal style preferences.

IV. PARAGRAPHS

Some scholars of legal method and writing use the topic heading "paragraphs" to classify a surprisingly broad range of writing techniques, from topic sentences to more general techniques of presenting a legal discussion or argument. This book addresses all such topics in substantial detail, but not all of them under the heading "paragraphs." More narrowly, this section on paragraphs introduces techniques of (1) using paragraphing to signal changes of topics within a discussion, (2) analyzing the appropriate content of paragraphs, and (3) effectively ordering sentences within a paragraph.

A. THE ROLE OF PARAGRAPHS WITHIN A SECTION

Just as descriptive headings and subheadings communicate the division of a discussion or argument into sections or subsections, good paragraphing helps to communicate the organizational structure within a section or subsection.

For instance, the paragraphing in the following passage signals the transition from (1) an analysis of the statutory requirements of conduct "under the color of" state law to (2) an analysis of fourteenth amendment guarantees:

A private party acts "under the color of state law" if he acts in concert with a state official acting in his official capacity. *Dennis v. Sparks,* 449 U.S. 24, 27-29 (1980). In *Dennis,* a state judge . . . Similarly, the evidence in this case will show that Tippett conspired with Judge Bell. . . .	**Statute**
The fourteenth amendment's guarantee of due process in state proceedings is a federal substantive right. . . .	**Constitution**

A second presentation of the same arguments assumes a greater depth of analysis. The five topic sentences represented by the phrases and clauses in the following example signal the transitions between (1) general legal rules, (2) in-depth case analysis, (3) fact analysis, (4) conclusion, and (5) analysis of potentially adverse authority.

The fourteenth amendment's guarantee of due process in state proceedings is a federal substantive right . . . *Cf. Cross v. Georgia,* . . .	**Law**
In *Cross,* . . .	
In this case, Bennett will prove . . .	**Facts**
Thus, Tippett is liable to Bennett . . .	**Conclusion**
Tippett has argued . . . , citing *Parratt v. Taylor,* 451 U.S. 527 (1981). *Parratt* is distinguishable . . .	**Adverse authority**

B. PARAGRAPH CONTENT AND DEVELOPMENT

To say that each paragraph should present a single topic or idea oversimplifies the matter, for the appropriate scope of the subject matter of each paragraph may depend on the relationship between the paragraph and the remainder of the discussion. For example, the following analysis of merchant status is superficial, conclusory, and preliminary to the main topic for discussion. Accordingly, you could combine the legal standard, fact analysis, and conclusion in a single paragraph:

"Merchant" includes "a person who deals in goods of the kind." U.C.C. § 2-104. Jones regularly sells computers as part of her wholesale office supply business. Therefore, she is a merchant of the goods that she offered to supply to Azoulay, and section 2-205 thus governs the revocability of her offer.

In contrast, the reader can most easily absorb the typically more thorough analysis of the main topic if you divide the statement of legal rules and the fact analysis into at least two separate paragraphs. At the simplest level, each paragraph could correspond to one of the three elements of deductive reasoning. For example, after it explains the issue, a sample exam answer analyzes a problem in three paragraphs that (1) summarize the applicable legal rules, (2) apply the rules to the facts, and (3) state a conclusion:

Legal rules

An enforceable contract requires a bargained-for exchange in which a promisor exchanges his own promise for a return promise or performance. The requirement of an exchange is not satisfied if one party gives only an illusory promise, which does not commit the promisor to any future performance. A promise is illusory if it leaves the promisor free to perform or not according to his unfettered whim or discretion, such as . . .

Application to facts

Guarantor should argue that Lender's promise to forbear until he "needs" the money permits Lender to decide at his own whim and unfettered discretion when to demand payment, because he has some control of his own needs. However, that argument would prevail only if the word "need" refers to a subjective perception of deprivation that is inseparable from Lender's purely personal wants or desires. Lender can argue . . .

Conclusion

Unfortunately for our client, Lender's promise in the guarantee agreement probably is not illusory, because the word "need" provides some substance to Lender's commitment to forbear. Therefore, Guarantor's promise probably is supported by consideration and is enforceable.

In more complex analyses, the development of legal standards alone may progress through several paragraphs, perhaps beginning with an overview of general standards in one paragraph, followed by two or more additional paragraphs, each of which explores a significant case or a policy argument. Similarly, the fact analysis may progress through several paragraphs, perhaps displaying different levels of fact analysis or different categories of facts. For example, the five paragraphs represented by the following phrases and clauses help to signal the transitions between (1) general legal standards, (2) in-depth case analysis, (3) identification of relevant facts, (4) analysis of those facts, and (5) conclusion:

A. Smith's Alleged Conduct Was Not "Extreme and Outrageous."

Law

. . . Conduct that simply reflects normal social and economic adversities is not extreme or outrageous. *See, e.g., Frank v. Boswell,* . . .
In *Frank,* . . .

In this case, Lew's complaint alleges conduct that is even less extreme than the conduct in *Frank*. . . .	**Facts**
These allegations state only that . . .	
Thus, the complaint does not allege circumstances that could establish the requisite "extreme and outrageous conduct."	**Conclusion**

C. THE ROLE OF SENTENCES WITHIN A PARAGRAPH

A paragraph need not contain some magic number of sentences. The appropriate number of sentences may depend in part on the relationship between the paragraph and the topics addressed in surrounding paragraphs.

Of course, if you find that you have set off a single sentence as a separate paragraph, you should always question whether the isolated sentence would better serve as the concluding sentence of the previous paragraph or the topic sentence of the next one. However, as illustrated by the concluding paragraph of the previous section, a single sentence may stand by itself as a separate paragraph if it completely addresses a discrete topic or if presentation in a separate paragraph achieves important goals of clarity or emphasis. If you blindly adhere to a "rule" against single-sentence paragraphs, you may find yourself composing an unnecessary, empty sentence to accompany an informative sentence that could have stood alone.

Whenever possible, your first sentence in a multiple-sentence paragraph should communicate your strategy by introducing the topic of the paragraph, expressing a transition, or both. For example, the first sentence in the following example signals the transition from the analysis of precedent to the identification of the relevant facts of the current dispute, and it provides an overview of the case comparison:

> In this case, Lew's complaint alleges conduct that is even less extreme than the conduct in *Frank*. It alleges that Smith "fired Lew without severance pay and with full knowledge that Lew's family was facing a desperate financial crisis." Plaintiff's Second Amended Complaint ¶ 7. It further alleges . . .

In this sample paragraph, the topic sentence introduces fact analysis. Topic sentences or thesis statements are at least as important in introducing discussions of legal authority. To effectively present authority, you must use such topic or transition sentences or paragraphs to introduce statutes and case law and to express your syntheses of authority.

After you have composed an effective topic sentence, you should organize other sentences within a paragraph to develop information in a logical, organized fashion. For example, the paragraph below is designed to define the limits of the scope of the Uniform Commercial Code and to raise a question about the applicability of the Code to a particular transaction. The awkward placement of the second and third sentences of the paragraph disrupts continuity by stating an intermediate conclusion before establishing its premise:

General issue	Whether Maldonado accepted Weinstein's offer depends in part on whether the common law of contracts or the Uniform Commercial Code (U.C.C.) applies to the transaction. Weinstein's offer to supply specifically identified, separately priced, movable plumbing parts clearly contemplates a sale of goods as part of the transaction. *See* U.C.C. § 2-105(1). The U.C.C. applies only to "transactions in goods." U.C.C. § 2-102. His proposed transaction, however, also involves the service of installing the fixtures, raising a question about the applicability of the U.C.C. to mixed transactions for both services and the sale of goods.
Application to facts	
Legal premise	
Specific issue	

Reversing the order of the second and third sentences develops points in a more logical order and retains the coherence of transitions:

General issue	. . . whether the common law of contracts or the Uniform Commercial Code (U.C.C.) applies to the transaction. The U.C.C. applies only to "transactions in goods." U.C.C. § 2-102. Weinstein's offer to supply specifically identified, separately priced, movable plumbing parts clearly contemplates a sale of goods as part of the transaction. *See* U.C.C. § 2-105(1). His proposed transaction, however, also involves the service of installing the fixtures, raising a question about . . .
Legal premise	
Application to facts	
Specific issue	

Many organizational approaches may result in a logical and coherent presentation of information in a paragraph. Nonetheless, one simple technique is worth highlighting: you can lead a reader from familiar to new information in a paragraph by beginning each sentence with a previously established idea and linking it to a new idea. For example, the phrases in bold typeface in the following passage represent new information, and the italicized phrases represent previously introduced information. In each sentence after the first one, previously introduced information is linked to a new idea.

An enforceable contract requires a **bargained-for exchange** in which a promisor **exchanges** his own promise for a return promise or performance. The requirement of an *exchange* is not satisfied if one party gives only an **illusory promise,** which does not commit the promisor to any future performance. A *promise is illusory* if it leaves the promisor free to perform or not according to his **unfettered whim or discretion,** such as . . .

This technique of consistently linking a familiar idea with a new one is only one of innumerable approaches that you may use in developing a paragraph. You should always retain maximum flexibility to adapt your organizational approach to the particular characteristics of a passage. The next chapter provides further guidance. It (1) continues to explore paragraphing and paragraph content in the context of presentation of authority and (2) addresses good organization of words and clauses within a sentence to enhance the clarity or persuasive force of the sentence.

V. SUMMARY

When organizing the topics or arguments in an office memorandum or brief, you should:

(1) with few exceptions, discuss separate issues in separate sections or subsections;

(2) arrange your sections and subsections so that they reflect the proper relationships among topics and subtopics; and

(3) present your topics or arguments in a logical order, subject to considerations of strategy.

Within a section or subsection, you should

(1) explain the legal rule,

(2) apply the rule to the facts, and

(3) reach a conclusion.

If the topic or argument within a section or subsection is governed by several closely related rules, you should exercise judgment to either

(1) consolidate your statement of all the rules before applying them to all the relevant facts or

(2) separately apply some preliminary legal rules to facts before progressing to other rules within the section or subsection.

When organizing material within a section or subsection, you should consider:

(1) the hierarchy of authority and

(2) progression from general to specific and from fundamental to uncertain.

You should not describe the chronological development of a legal rule unless an explanation is necessary to the reader's understanding of the current state of the law.

10

Legal Writing Style in the Office Memorandum

Chapter 4's introduction to writing style identified clarity and conciseness as the principal characteristics of effective legal writing. This chapter more comprehensively examines those topics as well as special problems of using authority and quotations.

This chapter uses selected writing problems as vehicles for developing a method for legal writing, a flexible approach that provides general guidance in any legal writing assignment. It seeks to show you that effective legal writing style to a great extent is simply a reflection of the sound practices of legal method and analysis discussed in the preceding chapters. More than that, it invites you to treat rules and conventions of writing very much like legal rules: to use them well, you must understand their purposes and policies.

Although this chapter primarily addresses writing style for office memoranda, most of the principles discussed apply equally to briefs, and some of the examples are taken from briefs. Special techniques of persuasive writing are explored in the next chapter.

I. CLARITY

You cannot write clearly unless you first develop clear ideas. In many cases, muddled legal writing reflects an incomplete understanding of the substantive legal analysis and suggests the need for further research and reflection. Only when you have fully mastered your analysis can you clearly communicate the analysis to a comprehending reader.

Beyond sound analysis, an important element of clarity in any legal document is effective organization on all the levels discussed in Chapter 9. Other elements of clarity, discussed below, are simplicity, effective sentence structure, and precision in word selection.

A. SIMPLICITY AND PLAIN ENGLISH

For centuries, the public has complained about lawyers' fondness for legal jargon: stuffy, peculiar, archaic legal terminology. People have good reason to complain. For example, some lawyers still refuse to end a witness's sworn and notarized written statement with the perfectly descriptive word "signed." Instead, they insist on inserting the archaic phrase "Further affiant sayeth not."

Although the extent to which you stray from plain and simple terms is partly a matter of personal style, you should tend toward simplicity. If a simple, familiar word will clearly express your idea, your reader may find that a peculiar, complex, or unfamiliar word or phrase in its place is distracting or even unintelligible.

Moreover, simplicity in writing does not condemn you to expressing only simple ideas. Rather, it helps you to express even complex and abstract ideas in such clear, concrete, and simple terms that your reader easily grasps your ideas on first reading.

You can best appreciate the virtues of simplicity by recognizing the ultimate purpose of your document. A legal memorandum should efficiently communicate ideas, and a brief should persuade. A document cannot perform either of these functions if the reader must pause at every sentence to ponder its meaning.

Unfortunately, unnecessary abstraction, complexity, and peculiarity found in some legal writing suggests that the writer's objective is to "sound like a lawyer" or to impress his supervising attorney or a judge with the breadth of his vocabulary. For example, one summer associate at a major law firm boasted to a fellow associate that his first office memorandum contained unusually sophisticated language that twice compelled his supervising attorney to resort to a dictionary. The law firm did not offer permanent employment to the boastful associate. He would have made a better impression if he had clearly and simply expressed ideas that reflected good, creative legal analysis.

As an advocate, you may be tempted someday to resort to peculiar legal jargon if the doubtful merit of your client's claims or defenses leaves you with little of value to say. You may consider using the jargon to distract the judge from the substantive emptiness of your arguments or to intimidate opposing parties when plain English would betray the emptiness of your threats. You should resist the temptation. If you fulfill your ethical duty to refrain from advancing frivolous claims and defenses, you can advance arguments that you are not ashamed to spell out in plain English.

Occasionally, a peculiar word or phrase earns its place in legal writing as a shorthand term for an unavoidably complex or unfamiliar concept. For example, Chapter 2 uses the term "stare decisis" to refer to a complex set of principles that help to define American legal method. Although this Latin term is unfamiliar to most students entering law school, it qualifies as a useful term of art because it is widely accepted among trained lawyers as convenient shorthand for a set of ideas that the more familiar term "precedent" does not fully convey. Surprisingly few forms of peculiar legal language, however, are justified as necessary terms of art. Therefore, you should critically evaluate any unusual language in your writing to ensure that it informs more than distracts.[1]

---

1. See R. Wydick, Plain English for Lawyers 53-55 (2d ed. 1985).

Legal jargon is particularly inappropriate in a document that is addressed to a layperson, perhaps a client, who may be unfamiliar with even rudimentary legal terminology. When addressing such an audience, not only should you exercise special care to avoid unnecessary jargon, you should explain in plain English the meanings of legal terms of art that other attorneys would easily recognize.

══════ E X E R C I S E 1 0 - 1 ══════

A simple contract should (1) introduce the parties to the contract, (2) recite any background facts that explain the motivations of the parties and thus help to explain their bargain, (3) define the parties' rights and obligations by setting forth their mutual promises, (4) and signify each party's agreement to the terms of the contract.

The following contract is written in antiquated jargon. Parts of the contract are taken from the contract interpreted in *McMichael v. Price*, 177 Okl. 186, 58 P.2d 549 (1936). Contract language from formbooks provided further inspiration.

Simplify all or part of the structure and language of the contract so that it expresses the terms of the parties' agreement in plain English. Feel free to use subject headings, section numbers, and paragraphing. Compare your revision with the sample contracts in Chapter 16.

Requirements Contract

This contract for the purchase and sale of sand entered into on this, the _____ day of _____, by and between Sooner Sand Co., a general partnership of which Harley T. Price and W. M. McMichael are partners, hereinafter known as the party of the first part, and Bassi Distributing Co., a joint venture of Bassi Trucking Co. and Hardcore Rock & Gravel, Inc., hereinafter known as the party of the second part, Witnesseth:

Whereas, the party of the first part is engaged in the business of selling and shipping sand from Phoenix to various customers in the State of Arizona but has not developed markets outside of Arizona and desires to supply sand wholesale to a distributor with customers outside the state; and

Whereas, the party of the second part has an established business in Phoenix selling and shipping sand to various customers in several states outside Arizona, including California, Nevada, Utah, and Colorado, and desires a stable source of supply of sand for that business;

Now, therefore, in consideration of the mutual covenants herein contained, and other good and valuable consideration the receipt of which is hereby acknowledged, the parties hereby represent, warrant, affirm, promise, covenant, and agree that the said party of the first part will, upon receipt of periodic written orders submitted by the said party of the second part, furnish all of the sand which the said party of the second part requires for shipment to various and sundry points outside of the State of Arizona, for a period of five (5) years from the date hereinabove, said sand to be of a grade and quality at least equal in quality and comparable with the sand of various grades sold by other sand companies in the City of Phoenix, Arizona; furthermore, the said party of the second part agrees to pay as payment and compensation for said sand so furnished a sum per ton which represents sixty percent (60%) of the current market price per ton of concrete at the place of destination of said shipment.

In witness whereof, the said parties have hereunto set their hands and seals the day and year first above written.

_____

Sooner Sand Co.—Authorized Agent

_____

Bassi Distributing Co.—Authorized Agent

B. SENTENCE STRUCTURE

1. Sentence Length and Complexity; Punctuation

Short, crisp sentences can be powerful:

‖ Jenkins lived to tell his side of the story. Roberts did not.

On the other hand, a succession of very short sentences may sound stilted or may require empty or repetitive transitional phrases to link the sentences together:

‖ It was 1:00 A.M. John left the party. He went home. He drove his BMW.

Moreover, long sentences that convey numerous thoughts in multiple clauses are not necessarily problematic; if punctuated and constructed sensibly, they may be clear and readable.

Unfortunately, however, legal writing often suffers from unnecessarily long and complex sentences that are poorly constructed. The reader of such a sentence is called upon to assimilate too much information at once and to guess at the proper relationships of the ideas.

Two characteristics of the process of legal writing may account for many excessively long and complex sentences. First, the writer has researched and pondered his analysis before verbalizing it, and he may have forgotten the difficulty that another lawyer encounters when exposed to the concepts for the first time. If so, he may attempt to convey a greater number of difficult concepts in a single sentence than the reader is prepared to digest. Second, many lawyers dictate their first drafts on a tape recorder and neglect to revise the transcribed draft adequately. Dictation tends to encourage long and complex sentences, because the speaker is deceived into believing that his inflection, dynamics in volume, and pauses provide adequate guides to sentence structure. In fact, transcripts of trials and presidential press conferences reveal that such oral guides to structure often do not transcribe adequately to the written page.

a. Closure and Visual Guides

You can use two devices to avoid or revise unmanageable sentences: closure and visual guides to structure.

Closure usually refers to punctuation that allows a reader to pause to assimilate one or more ideas before moving to the next. For example, the following passages illustrate three levels of closure. The first presents at least three distinct ideas in a single sentence punctuated only by commas:

> Although punitive damages are designed to punish the wrongdoer rather than compensate the victim for actual injury, many courts will not award punitive damages in the absence of proof of actual injury, and some courts will limit punitive damages to an amount that bears a reasonable relationship to the award of compensatory damages.

The sentence above is constructed reasonably well. However, the commas in the sentence invite only brief pauses between ideas, leaving the reader breathless if she is unfamiliar with the subject matter. Periods dividing the passage into three sentences encourage the reader to pause more substantially and to digest each idea before facing the next:

> Punitive damages are designed to punish the wrongdoer rather than compensate the victim for actual injury. Nonetheless, many courts will not award punitive damages in the absence of proof of actual injury. Moreover, some courts will limit punitive damages to an amount that bears a reasonable relationship to the award of compensatory damages.

If you desire to link the second and third ideas to one another more closely than to the first idea in the paragraph, you can replace the second period with a semicolon. The semicolon provides such a conceptual link with nearly the same level of closure as provided by a period:

> Punitive damages are designed to punish the wrongdoer rather than compensate the victim for actual losses. Nonetheless, many courts will not award punitive damages in the absence of proof of actual injury; moreover, some courts will limit punitive damages to an amount that bears a reasonable relationship to the award of compensatory damages.

In some passages, visual guides to the structure of a long sentence may effectively substitute for the closure provided by multiple short sentences. The following passages illustrate both techniques. The first sample passage takes advantage of closure by limiting each sentence to a single idea:

> The evidence supports three critical factual conclusions. First, the marijuana, cocaine, and heroin all belonged to Carson and Klein. Second, Rivers was unaware of the presence of those drugs in the house when he entered the living room. Third, when Klein offered to sell the marijuana to Rivers, Rivers declined and attempted to leave the house.

The closure is welcome in this example, because two of the factual conclusions set forth in separate sentences are sufficiently complex to require punctuation within those conclusions.

In the next sample passage, the series of conclusions in the first passage progresses through a single sentence without the disruption of substantial closure. It retains some of the qualities of closure by using numbers as the equivalent of road signs[2] to identify the end of one element of the series and the beginning of the next:

> The evidence supports three critical factual conclusions: (1) the marijuana, cocaine, and heroin all belonged to Carson and Klein; (2) Rivers was unaware of the presence of those drugs in the house when he entered the living room; and (3) when Klein offered to sell the marijuana to Rivers, Rivers declined and attempted to leave the house.

If the elements of the series are less complex, you can provide a subtler guide to sentence structure by repeating an introductory word or phrase, such as "that" in the following example:

> Top Notch Co. is not liable on this contract theory unless Jackson can prove that the personnel manual was part of Jackson's employment contract, that the manual contained a promise of job security, and that Top Notch breached such a promise when it discharged Jackson for refusing to shave his beard.

b. Toward a Flexible, Policy-Oriented Approach to Punctuation

Many routine conventions of punctuation provide similar guides to sentence structure and should be applied flexibly to achieve that goal. For example, the insertion of a comma to separate independent clauses joined by a conjunction[3] is not arbitrary; it often avoids temporary confusion in sentence structure, as illustrated by the following sentence:

Coastal Bank breached its loan commitment to the owner and the contractor threatened to terminate its performance.

Halfway through the sentence, many readers assume that the conjunction "and" joins "owner" to "the contractor." Thus, on encountering "the contractor," those readers conclude for a fraction of a second that the bank owed its loan commitment to the contractor as well as to the owner. By the time they reach the verb "threatened," they realize from context that "the contractor" is the subject of a new independent clause rather than the second in a series of two objects of the prepositional phrase "to the." By that time, however, the ambiguity in sentence structure has caused readers to hesitate for a moment and

---

2. Professor Richard Wydick calls this technique "tabulation." R. Wydick, Plain English for Lawyers 42 (2d ed. 1985).
3. See W. Strunk, Jr., and E. White, The Elements of Style 5 (3d ed. 1979).

perhaps even to regress by rereading the sentence. This momentary confusion may be even more pronounced in a more complicated compound sentence.

A comma inserted before the conjunction more quickly identifies "the contractor" as the beginning of a new independent clause:

Coastal Bank breached its loan commitment to the owner, and the contractor threatened to terminate its performance. ‖

This example illustrates two general principles of style. First, the reader of a brief or memorandum may be able to glean the meaning of each sentence from context, but this additional labor and the frequent instances of momentary confusion can leave the reader weary. Some conventions of punctuation or other matters of style may not be critical to the reader's ultimate comprehension, but they enhance the efficiency and ease with which the reader comprehends.

Second, you should apply rules or conventions of writing style the way that you apply rules of law: apply and extend them as far as necessary to vindicate their underlying purposes or policies, but no farther. For example, the following compound sentence is perfectly readable without a comma separating the independent clauses:

The robber ran and the police gave chase. ‖

Because this sentence is short and simple, the reader can recognize its structure at a glance, arguably making the comma unnecessary as a guide to structure.

You can avoid the comma question and raise others by placing a period after the first independent clause:

The robber ran. And the police gave chase. ‖

This punctuation gives special emphasis to the action in each clause, but many writers recoil at the idea of beginning a sentence with the simple conjunction "and" or "but." Such usage is not grammatically incorrect; it is simply stylistically questionable in many cases. If the clauses are simple and short, they will normally flow more smoothly if combined in a single sentence with a conjunction in the middle of the sentence. On the other hand, if you want to divide the clauses into two sentences to emphasize each clause or to provide your reader with closure after a long clause, you probably will prefer a stronger transition word than "and" or "but." Particularly in legal documents, most writers prefer to begin a sentence with a more substantial conjunctive adverb, such as "Moreover," "Furthermore, "In contrast," or "However":

Mr. Blumquist survived the initial explosion. However, he died a short time later of smoke inhalation. ‖

Thus, you will seldom need to begin a sentence with "and" or "but" to achieve important objectives in legal writing. But you should not reach the conclusion that this construction is universally incorrect. It will simply be a rare passage in legal writing that benefits from such construction. In this entire book, only a handful of sentences begin with "and" or "but." And the two in this paragraph are included primarily to underscore the theme of this subsection: many rules of composition should be viewed as general guides to style rather than absolute prohibitions on unconventional usage.

The history of the debate about the "serial" comma rule further illustrates these principles. According to the traditional rule, you should use a comma to separate each element of a series of three or more things, as in "meat, vegetables, and dairy products." During the "new English" and "new math" movements of the 1960s, grade school teachers began teaching a discretionary trend to omit the last comma of the series on the ground that the conjunction "and" or "or" adequately separates the last two elements of the series. The trend never permanently displaced the traditional rule: Strunk and White continued to advocate use of the final comma,[4] and many grade schools are now returning to the traditional teachings. Unfortunately, many students had in the meantime adopted an inflexible practice of always omitting the final comma.

In fact, omitting the final comma may hamper clarity in a series in which some elements have multiple subelements, such as "fish, fruits or vegetables and dairy products." Depending on the location of a final comma, this could mean either:

(1) {fish}, {fruits or vegetables}, and {dairy products}, or

(2) {fish}, {fruits}, or {vegetables and dairy products}.

Subtle, temporary ambiguities in structure sometimes arise even if the series uses only the conjunction "and" and not the disjunctive conjunction "or."

Armed with these insights, you can choose either of two approaches to the comma controversy, depending on the emphasis that you place on different policies of composition. If you value consistency as well as clarity, you could reasonably adopt the traditional convention of always using the final comma, because you know that it will sometimes be necessary for clarity. Alternatively, if you believe in restricting punctuation to the necessary minimum, you could exercise stylistic discretion to insert the final comma when it is necessary for clarity and to omit it otherwise.

When widely accepted, this flexible, policy-oriented approach to composition will end countless hours of office arguments over the proper "rule" governing the final comma in a series. Until then, you should be prepared to explain your reasoning to reviewers who dogmatically insist either that the final comma is incorrect or that it is mandatory.

EXERCISE 10-2

1. *Preposition Power*

A will provides: "I leave all my personal property in equal shares per capita to the issue of my brother, Steve Lee, and my daughter, Cathy Chin, then living at the time of my death." The testator is survived by Cathy Chin, by Cathy Chin's three daughters, and by Steve Lee's son, Kirby. You know from your research that "equal shares per capita" means that all the ultimate bene-

---

4. Id. at 1-2 (1st ed. 1959); id. at 2 (2d ed. 1972); id. at 2 (3d ed. 1979).

ficiaries will receive equal shares; however, the will is ambiguous in its identi-fication of the ultimate beneficiaries.

a. Which of the following distributions does the language most clearly support?

(i) Cathy Chin and Kirby Lee each take half of the property.

(ii) Cathy Chin's three daughters and Kirby Lee each take one fourth of the property.

b. Insert a single preposition in the will that would remove any doubt that the testator intended distribution (i). Achieve the same result through reorganization of the sentence.

c. Insert a single preposition in the will's provision that would remove any doubt that the testator intended distribution (ii).

2. *Care with Commas*

Which of the following sentences requires further punctuation? How would you correct it? Should you address these sentences with an inflexible rule of punctuation or with attention to principles of good writing underlying con-ventions of punctuation?

a. Two pieces of evidence link Jones to the crime: a witness observed Jones strike the victim with his fist and a glove recovered from the crime scene matches the one found in Jones's car.

b. The court dismissed the action and Romero appealed.

3. *Separating Prefaces to Main Clauses*

Compare the following sentences that commence with subordinate phrases and clauses. In which of the following sentences would you insert a comma to separate the subordinate word, phrase, or clause from the main clause? Where would you insert each comma? In which of the cases is the comma a discre-tionary matter of style, and in which cases is it more clearly necessary for clarity?

a. Later he mowed the lawn.

b. On January 1, 1987 he resolved to quit smoking.

c. After she examined the patient Dr. Ong requested a conference with the chief surgeon.

d. Based on Hart's conduct and oral representations and on the plain language of the policy manual it appears that the policy manual . . .

e. Although few courts have addressed the question whether a member of a city council enjoys the absolute immunity conferred on state legislators the policy of protecting the legislative process from . . .

4. *Calendar Commas*

In light of problem 2 above and other concerns of clarity, try to define a set of principles consistent with all the following examples of using commas to set off the parts of a date:

a. On June 10, 1986, the parties agreed to modify their contract.

b. The document dated June 10, 1986 represents a modification of an earlier agreement.

    c. Throughout the last week in June 1986, the parties negotiated a modification of their contract.

5. *Closure and Road Signs*

Redraft the following sentence to improve its readability. Break it into multiple sentences or clauses, or use any other device to lead the reader gracefully through the ideas it expresses.

> Plaintiff American Continental Can Co. brought this action against Defendants Conco Sheet Metal Co., Bassi Distributing Co., and Miller Trucking, Inc., alleging that Conco Sheet Metal Co. had sold it defective sheet metal, that Bassi Distributing Co. had fraudulently misrepresented the description and quality of Conco Sheet Metal Co.'s products, and that Miller Trucking Co. had negligently damaged sheet metal that it agreed to transport from the warehouse of Conco Sheet Metal Co. to the factory of American Continental Can Co., and requesting compensatory and punitive damages.

6. *The Ambiguous Series*

Identify the major elements of the series in the sentence set forth below. Where does the last element of the series begin? What different interpretations does the sentence permit? How would you use a comma to advance either interpretation over the other?

> In the event of default, the lessee must vacate the premises, forfeit the security deposit and pay Lessor's actual damages or pay liquidated damages under section 12 of this Lease.

2. *Concrete Verbs and Active Construction*

a. Concrete Verbs

Lawyers often sacrifice vigor and clarity in their legal writing by employing vague and abstract verbs such as "involve," "exist," or "occur":

|| A modification to the contract occurred on July 1.

Even more frequently, lawyers drain the strength from verbs by building sentences around a form of the phrase "there is":

|| There was a modification to the contract on July 1.

The author of the preceding sentence has converted the active verb "modify" into the noun "modification," creating a need for the verb "was," a form of the relatively abstract and passive infinitive "to be." Unless you really intend to focus attention on the mere existence or absence of modification, you could improve on this sentence by identifying the actors, abandoning the "be" verb, and focusing on the real action word in the sentence, "modify":

Nelson and Kubichek modified their contract on July 1.   ‖

In some cases, replacing abstract wording such as "there is" with a more concrete, active verb will enable you to add new meaning as well as vigor. For example, the following sentence abstractly comments on the absence of critical evidence:

There is no evidence in the record that Robert Emery intended to kill the   ‖
bank teller.

A more concrete verb can emphasize the absence not only of direct evidence of intent but also of circumstantial evidence from which a factfinder might infer intent:

No evidence in the record even suggests that Robert Emery intended to kill   ‖
the bank teller.

b. Active and Passive Construction

Avoidance of forms of "there is" in legal writing is simply a special branch of a more general preference for active voice in sentence structure. A clause in active voice presents its principal parts in the normal order of actor, verb, and object of the action, such as "curiosity killed the cat."

In contrast, the following sentence features three clauses in passive voice, each of which places the object before the verb and dispenses with the actor altogether:

The *Allen* doctrine has been criticized, but it continues to be applied because   ‖
it has been approved in dictum.

The following revision identifies the actors associated with each verb, but it still uses passive voice throughout, as revealed by the inverted order of object, verb, and actor:

The *Allen* doctrine has been criticized by dozens of commentators and a   ‖
handful of appellate judges, but it continues to be applied by trial judges
because it has been approved in dictum by the Supreme Court.   ‖

Active voice is more informative than the first example above, and it more directly and concisely conveys all the information presented in the second example:

Dozens of commentators and a handful of appellate judges have criticized   ‖
the *Allen* doctrine, but trial judges continue to apply it because the Supreme
Court has approved it in dictum.   ‖

The vigor of active construction can be especially useful in composing strong statements in persuasive writing. For example, the following sentence in passive voice fails to assign responsibility for the repair of the air conditioning:

‖ The air conditioning was not repaired until 60 days after the tenant gave
‖ written notice of the defect.

In contrast, the next sentence uses active voice to identify the landlord as the responsible party and to characterize the landlord's inaction as a culpable omission:

‖ The landlord neglected to repair the air conditioning until 60 days after the
‖ tenant gave written notice of the defect.

Although active voice generally is more direct, concise, or informative than passive voice, you may occasionally have reason to prefer passive voice. For example, you may use passive voice to deliberately omit reference to an actor or actors whose identities are unknown or unimportant:

‖ The bridge was erected in 1923.

Even in this case, some writers so strongly prefer active voice that they refer to the actor or actors generically simply to avoid passive construction:

‖ Workers built the bridge in 1923.

However, most writers would reasonably adopt the passive construction to avoid diverting the reader's attention to unimportant information.

In some cases, you may be aware of the identity of the actor but use passive construction to avoid drawing attention to that identity. For example, a defense attorney might desire to emphasize mitigating factors in a crime while avoiding any reminder to the jury that her client stands accused of the wrongdoing:

‖ The hostage was not harmed in any way.

Conversely, you may deliberately use passive voice to place unusual emphasis on the actor by placing the actor at the end of the sentence, as in the second of the following sentences:

‖ The defense wants you to believe that Mr. Cass committed suicide by
‖ injecting himself with a lethal dose of heroin. To the contrary, the evidence
‖ shows that the heroin was injected by the defendant, Ms. Borden.

In some sentences, if you place the actor or actors at the beginning of the sentence, you will unduly delay introducing the verb:

‖ Ms. Williams, the firm's top expert in tax law, and Mr. Scales, an eloquent
‖ oral advocate with 20 years of experience before the state appellate courts,
‖ argued the case.

With passive voice, you can introduce the simple object and verb early in the sentence:

The case was argued by Ms. Williams, the firm's top expert in tax law, and by Mr. Scales, an eloquent oral advocate with 20 years of experience before the state appellate courts.

In summary, you should prefer vigorous, concrete verbs in active construction unless you have a specific purpose for a vague, abstract, or passive verb.

═══════ E X E R C I S E   1 0 - 3 ═══════

1. *Benefits of Active, Concrete Verbs*

Replace the passive, abstract verbs in the following sentences with more active, concrete verbs.

a. There are only two Supreme Court decisions that address this issue.

b. It was argued by government counsel that the tax regulation was applicable to the land exchange.

c. The landlord was ordered by the court to achieve completion of the repairs within 30 days.

d. There was a conspiracy among four distributors to effect an immediate price increase.

2. *Benefits of Passive Construction*

By replacing the active verb with a passive verb, restructure the following sentence to minimize the number of words separating the subject, verb, and object and to emphasize the "clearly erroneous" standard.

Federal Rule of Civil Procedure 52(a), which provides that a federal trial court's findings of fact in a nonjury trial "shall not be set aside unless clearly erroneous," governs this appeal.

3. Effective Placement of Modifiers

For clarity, you should place a modifying word, phrase, or clause close to the part of the sentence that it modifies. On the other hand, to ensure a smooth flow in your writing, you should avoid interrupting important parts of a sentence with a lengthy modifier. The following sample sentences illustrate how these principles relate to one another.

The first sample sentence below attempts to describe the effects of cross-examination on a witness. Unfortunately, it subjects the reader to a classic dangling modifier:

Withering under relentless cross-examination, the prosecutor forced the witness to recant his earlier testimony.

The first five words of this sample sentence form a subordinate phrase. It is subordinate because, unlike the clause that follows it, it cannot stand alone as a full sentence; rather, it provides further information about an element of the clause. The subject of the independent clause, "the prosecutor," is positioned next to the modifying phrase and thus receives the impact of that phrase. But it is the witness, not the prosecutor, who withered under the cross-examination. You can remedy this defect in the sentence by changing the modifying phrase so that it addresses the action of the prosecutor:

> With relentless cross-examination, the prosecutor forced the witness to recant his earlier testimony.

But this alters the focus of the sentence. If you want to retain the focus on the witness, you can restructure the sentence so that the original modifying phrase is adjacent to the object that it modifies, "the witness":

> The witness, withering under the prosecutor's relentless cross-examination, recanted his earlier testimony.

That sentence structure leaves no doubt that the witness is the one who has withered. Unfortunately, it places the modifying phrase between the subject and the verb, separating important parts of the sentence. This separation would not be objectionable if the modifier were very short and simple, and it creates only a minor inconvenience in this sample sentence. However, a longer, more complex modifier in that position could be distracting:

> The witness, who had testified on direct examination that he was walking toward the intersection and therefore was in a position to see the signal, admitted on cross-examination that he had his back to the intersection at the time of the accident.

To eliminate the separation of subject and verb in the shorter sample sentence, you might consider gathering all the parts of the main clause and moving them to the beginning of the sentence:

> The witness recanted his earlier testimony, withering under the prosecutor's relentless cross-examination.

In other sentences, this structure is often quite successful. Unfortunately, in this sample sentence, it introduces the reader to the recantation before the withering, producing a sense of anticlimax. More important, it creates ambiguity about whether the witness or his earlier testimony was withering.

Perhaps the best revision of the sample sentence places the modifying phrase or clause at the beginning of the sentence, paving the way for an uninterrupted main clause:

> Withering under the prosecutor's relentless cross-examination, the witness recanted his earlier testimony.

Some might object to this structure on the ground that a long subordinate phrase or clause at the beginning of a sentence unduly delays introduction of the main clause. That objection is valid with the following qualification: a moderately long or complex subordinate phrase or clause ordinarily will be less distracting if it is placed at the beginning of the sentence than if it appears in the middle of the sentence and separates important parts of the main clause.

The following passages are sample revisions of a sentence with long and multiple subordinate clauses. When compared to the previous examples, these alternative revisions suggest that the best solutions to the problems discussed above sometimes differ with the circumstances of each sentence.

Unlike the more moderate introduction in the last sample revision above, the subordinate clauses in the following sentence inconveniently delay introduction of the main clause:

Because the consumer fraud statute applies to misrepresentations in either the "advertisement or sale" of merchandise, and because the "sale" of merchandise normally is associated with the passing of title from the seller to the buyer, *see* U.C.C. § 2-106(1), the statute appears to apply to a seller's misrepresentations made during the delivery of merchandise under a preexisting contract.

You would only increase the reader's frustration by moving the subordinate clauses to the middle of the sentence, between the subject and the verb:

The consumer fraud statute, because it applies to . . . , and because the "sale" of merchandise normally is . . . , appears to apply to a seller's misrepresentations . . .

You could reveal the information in the sentence more gracefully by starting with the main clause:

The consumer fraud statute appears to apply to a seller's misrepresentations made during the delivery of merchandise under a preexisting contract, because the statute applies to misrepresentations in either the "advertisement or sale," of merchandise, and because the "sale" of merchandise normally is associated with the passing of title from the seller to the buyer, *see* U.C.C. § 2-106(1).

In the context of this sample sentence, this structure does not produce the ambiguity or inappropriate sense of anticlimax that it produced in one of the revisions of first sample sentence above.

Of course, this revised sentence is nonetheless too long and complex. You can solve all the problems in this passage simply by breaking it into shorter sentences, as recommended in the discussion of closure in subsection 1 above:

The consumer fraud statute applies to misrepresentations in either the "advertisement or sale," of merchandise. The "sale" of merchandise normally is associated with the passing of title from the seller to the buyer. *See* U.C.C. § 2-106(1). Therefore, the statute appears to apply to . . .

E X E R C I S E   1 0 - 4

1. *Precise Placement of Modifiers*

Consider the different positions into which you could insert the word "only" in the following sentence:

Officer Jones fired his gun three times at the suspect.

Which of the positions is most consistent with the information in each of the following?

a. Officer Jones fired his gun three times, not five times as reported by a witness.

b. Officer Jones fired his gun three times, but no other officer fired his gun more than once.

2. *Modifying Clauses and Sentence Structure*

Revise the following sentences. Which of several possible revisions do you prefer, and why?

a. The trial judge, after reviewing the evidence and considering the arguments of the parties, ruled that the contraband was the product of an illegal search.

b. Protesting that he had not finished his testimony, the bailiff escorted the witness from the courtroom.

4. *Restrictive and Nonrestrictive Clauses*

Most writers confess to difficulty in identifying restrictive and nonrestrictive clauses and in choosing between the relative pronouns "that" and "which" once they have identified the clause. One noted scholar has offered the following introductory advice:

> A defining relative clause [a restrictive clause] is one that identifies the person or thing meant by limiting the denotation of the antecedent: *Each made a list of books that had influenced him;* not books generally, but books as defined by the *that*-clause. Contrast with this: *I always buy his books, which have influenced me greatly;* the [nonrestrictive] clause does not limit *his books,* which needs no limitation; it gives a reason . . . , or adds a new fact . . .
>
> (A) of *which* and *that, which* is appropriate to nondefining [nonrestrictive] and *that* to defining [restrictive] clauses; . . .[5]

---

5. H. Fowler, Modern English Usage 626, 699 (1965). Fowler also addresses the relationship between "who," "which," and "that":

> (B) of *which* and *who, which* belongs to things, and *who* to persons; (C) of *who* and *that, who* suits particular persons, and *that* generic persons.

Id. at 699.

a. The Role of the Comma

The following sample sentences illustrate that the distinction between a restrictive and nonrestrictive clause occasionally materially affects the content of a sentence in legal writing. The construction of the first sample sentence suggests that all reckless driving constitutes a felony and that a new statute therefore applies to all reckless driving:

The new statute mandates a jail term only for reckless driving, which constitutes a felony violation of the vehicle code.

This meaning is primarily conveyed by the comma, which suggests to the reader that the sentence would be perfectly sensible if it ended at "reckless driving" and that the clause following the comma simply adds additional, perhaps parenthetical, information. The clause following the comma is nonrestrictive, or nondefining, because it does not purport to identify a subset of the general category of things within the term "reckless driving."

Even without any changes in wording, the second sample sentence suggests by the absence of a comma that only some forms of reckless driving rise to the level of a felony and that the statute applies only to those forms of reckless driving:

The new statute mandates a jail term only for reckless driving which constitutes a felony violation of the vehicle code.

The absence of a comma invites the reader to rush to the end of the sentence to discover what kind of reckless driving is covered, suggesting that the sentence could not sensibly stop at the term "reckless driving." In this sentence, the clause following "reckless driving" is restrictive, or defining, because it identifies a subset of the things in the general category of reckless driving.

Both sentences, however, use the relative pronoun "which" to introduce the restrictive or nonrestrictive clauses, leaving the burden of conveying the restrictive or nonrestrictive nature of the clause to the presence or absence of a comma. To partially relieve the comma of that burden, purists or traditionalists use the relative pronoun "that" in a restrictive clause to emphasize the restrictive nature of the clause and to more clearly distinguish it from a nonrestrictive clause:

The new statute mandates a jail term only for reckless driving that constitutes a felony violation of the vehicle code.

b. The Choice Between "That" and "Which"

Because most writers do not have a natural ear for this traditional use of "that," they tend to use "which" in both restrictive and nonrestrictive clauses, as in the second sample sentence above. In fact, this practice is so widespread that it can be characterized as the popular approach. The few supervising attorneys who are purists on this matter will go "which hunting" when reviewing the work of associates, but they probably have limited effect on the writing habits of the general legal community:

> What grammarians say should be has perhaps less influence on what shall be than even the more modest of them realize; usage evolves itself little disturbed by their likes and dislikes.[6]

In many cases, any ambiguity or uncertainty resulting from using "which" in a restrictive clause will be insignificant. For example, the difference in meaning between the following two sentences is insignificant to the analysis that the writer intends to convey:

> (1) The court applied a fairness test, which inquires whether a transaction was consummated through fair dealing and at a fair price.
> (2) The court applied a fairness test that inquires whether a transaction was consummated through fair dealing and at a fair price.

Because the sentence refers to only one of many possible formulations of a test that incorporates considerations of fairness, the final clause probably should be restrictive, as in the second example. However, because emphasis of the restrictive nature of the clause is not necessary for analytic clarity, the following popular construction would be inoffensive:

> The court applied a fairness test which inquires whether a transaction was consummated through fair dealing and at a fair price.

Nonetheless, at least in those cases in which the choice of relative pronouns will affect clarity, you should follow the example of the Supreme Court, which clearly distinguished between restrictive and nonrestrictive clauses in the following excerpt from an opinion:

> Although the Court of Appeals' construction of the Act and of Regulation Z is shared by three of the four other Courts of Appeals *that* have ruled on the question, this view, *which* is essentially a claim that the plain language of the statute and the regulation requires the result reached by the court below, has recently been challenged on several fronts.[7]

c. Procedural Labels

You may also raise questions about restrictive and nonrestrictive clauses when you join procedural labels, such as "plaintiff," to the names of parties to litigation. In that context, you need not worry about a choice between "that" and "which," but you may pause before choosing between the insertion or omission of a comma.

For example, if Robert Jones is one of three plaintiffs in an action, then

---

6. Id. at 625.
7. Anderson Bros. Ford v. Valencia, 452 U.S. 205, 211-212 (1981) (emphasis added).

a phrase that uses his name to define "plaintiff" is restrictive and should omit any comma:

Plaintiff Robert Jones moves for summary judgment on the ground ‖ that . . .

In this example, "Robert Jones" restricts the universe of "plaintiffs" to one of the three plaintiffs in the litigation.

In contrast, if Jones is the only plaintiff, you could treat a similar reference as nonrestrictive and include commas:

Plaintiff, Robert Jones, moves for summary judgment on the ground ‖ that . . .

In this example, "Robert Jones" arguably supplies parenthetic information about a party who is already identified by the label "Plaintiff."

Alternatively, even if Jones is the only plaintiff, you could reasonably eliminate the commas by characterizing "Plaintiff" as a title that is joined with a name, as in "Dr. Long" or "Secretary-Treasurer Richard King":

Plaintiff Robert Jones . . . ‖

This is probably the least distracting stylistic option. However, you cannot adopt this usage of "plaintiff" as a title if you treat "plaintiff" as a common noun by preceding it with an article, such as "the." In that case, you must treat the party's name as a nonrestrictive modifier if he is the only plaintiff:

The plaintiff, Robert Jones, moves for summary judgment against the de- ‖ fendant, Cecelia Ynez . . .

═══════════ E X E R C I S E 1 0 - 5 ═══════════

Relative Pronouns and Wealthy Relatives

Compare the following alternative provisions of a will:

> I leave to my daughter my bank account that is in Western Savings.

or

> I leave to my daughter my bank account, which is in Western Savings.

After drafting the will, but before death, the testator closed the bank account at Western Savings and used the funds from that account to open a new one at First Interstate Bank.[8] Which provision would most likely bequeath the First Interstate bank account to the daughter?

---

8. The source of this problem is R. Berch, Words That/Which Cause Problems in Legal Writing, 25 Ariz. Bar Briefs No. 9 (1987).

C. PRECISION

1. An Analytical Approach

Once you clearly understand the idea that you want to communicate, you must select the words and phrases that precisely convey your intended meaning. For example, Chapter 1 discusses the judicial interpretation of the phrase "because of . . . sex" in Title VII of the Civil Rights Act of 1964. A careless writer might state the conclusion of that discussion in the following manner:

> Title VII does not prohibit an employer from discriminating against homosexuals.

This overstates the conclusion, because it suggests that Title VII would provide no remedy to a victim of race discrimination simply because he also happened to be homosexual. A more precise statement of the statutory interpretation focuses on the basis of the discrimination rather than on the status of the discriminatee:

> Title VII does not prohibit an employer from discriminating on the basis of homosexuality.

As suggested in Chapter 4, achieving precision in writing may require you to subordinate other potential goals, such as entertaining your reader. For example, many writers believe that they will bore their readers if they repeatedly use a single word or phrase to refer to the same idea throughout a passage. They often address this concern by engaging in "elegant variation": varying the word or phrase used to refer to the same idea. However, any entertainment value of the variation does not justify the confusion that typically results.

For example, perhaps to elegantly vary their phrasing, many legal writers intermittently use "while" as a synonym for "although" and "when" or "where" as a synonym for "if." The following construction is common:

> While the court declined to decide the issue of retroactivity in *Fleming,* its dictum in subsequent cases suggests that it has always assumed that the *Fleming* principle applies retroactively.

The primary meaning of "while" in this syntax is duration or simultaneity. But, of course, the writer does not mean that the court offered dictum in subsequent cases *at the same time* that it declined to decide the issue in a previous case. "Although" would more precisely convey the contrast or tension between the court's actions. In the context of the entire sentence, the less precise version does not cause serious confusion or inconvenience. By displaying care with details, however, the more precise wording strengthens the credibility of the writer on more substantive matters.

More substantial risks of confusion arise in the use of synonyms for "because." "Since" is particularly popular:

> Since the employer invited the applicant to read the policy manual at the initial interview, the manual became part of their bargain.

Although the multiple dictionary definitions of "since" typically include "because," the primary dictionary definition relates to time frame or sequence of events:

> From then till now; in the interval; before this; before now; ago; after that time.—*prep.* Continuously from the time of; as, *since* yesterday; subsequent to; after.—*conj.* In the interval after the time when, as: I have been ill twice *since* I saw you last. Without interruption, from the time when; as, *since* we saw you last; because; seeing that; inasmuch as.[9]

Therefore, most readers fail to recognize "since" as a signal for a causal relationship when they first encounter it in a sentence such as the example above. Although the reader undoubtedly later discovers the intended meaning of "since" from context, that process may produce momentary hesitation or even regression in reading. The ambiguity is more serious if the sentence otherwise refers to a time frame:

Since Rabin breached the contract on January 1, 1985, the three-year limitations period expired before Smith filed suit on January 10, 1988. ‖

This sentence will appear to some readers to make the marginally useful point that the limitations period expired after the breach of contract as well as before the filing of suit. The word "because" in place of "since" would more clearly convey the intended causal relationship: the breach of contract triggered the commencement of the running of the limitations period; therefore, the period expired before suit was filed.

You create an even greater risk of confusion if you replace "because" with "as," because causation is not a readily recognized connotation of "as":

Plaintiff is entitled to the equitable remedy of injunctive relief as his legal ‖ remedy is inadequate. ‖

One popular dictionary does not even clearly list "because" as a definition for "as;" the closest it comes is listing "since" as a definition of "as" in its conjunctive form.[10] As explained above, even this reference to "since" is ambiguous.

In each of these three examples, "because" would more precisely and unambiguously convey the writer's intended meaning of causal relationship, because it has no other meaning.[11] Moreover, "because" is self-descriptive: the root word "cause" within it suggests its meaning.

2. *Beyond Dogma*

Use of synonyms for "because" illustrates the range of considerations that often influence nuances in writing style. Despite the precision that "because" permits, many writers depart from it in the interests of elegant variation, or

---

9. New Webster's Dictionary 902 (encyclopedic ed. 1981).
10. Id. at 58.
11. See, e.g., id. at 86.

they reject it altogether because they think that it has an unsophisticated ring to it. However, few readers demand variation or stimulation from every word in a sentence. As with many other words, such as "the," "with," and "a," "because" precisely and unobtrusively performs its function without diverting the reader's attention from more substantively important parts of the sentence. Indeed, the text of this section has used each of those words repeatedly, presumably without offending the average reader.

The most interesting reason that writers give for substituting "since" or "as" for "because" is their recollection of an admonition in grade school never to begin a sentence with "because." Of course, if beginning a sentence with "because" were to offend some principle of syntax or other consideration of composition, replacing it at the beginning of the sentence with a synonym, and a poor one at that, would not cure the defect. In fact, some grade school teachers may have invented or repeated such a rule in reaction to students' early tendencies to write incomplete sentences, such as: "Because I missed the bus." Those teachers probably should have explained the requisite components of a complete sentence rather than place undeserved blame on the word "because."

One defense of "as" and "since" as expressions of causal relationship has potential merit. Some writers believe that "as" and "since" are not synonymous with "because" in that context but express slightly different shades of causation. Those writers use "because" to refer to a direct causal relationship and "since" or "as" to refer to a more attenuated relationship.[12] A style that carefully recognizes such a distinction arguably enhances precision. Unfortunately, few writers use "since" or "as" to connote a causal relationship in such a principled manner. More important, to a greater extent than in literary writing, legal writing tends to describe causal relationships that are sufficiently direct to justify use of "because" in place of the softer "since" or "as."

This discussion illustrates once again the importance of avoiding unthinking adherence to inflexible and arbitrary rules of composition. If you understand the reasoning supporting a convention of writing style, you will be better equipped to evaluate that convention. You may then opt to apply the convention universally, reject it completely, or apply it selectively to those situations in which application furthers the reasoning.

═══════════ E X E R C I S E 1 0 - 6 ═══════════

Precise Prose

Rewrite the following passage so it more precisely summarizes some of the ideas discussed toward the end of Chapter 1. Feel free to use helpful terms of art, but avoid using unnecessary jargon to create a false sense of precision.

> While lawmakers can throw out laws that judges have developed on their own by enacting a bill, the judicial offices retain an important role, as they will

---

12. See generally W. Strunk, Jr., & E. White, The Elements of Style 24 (3d ed. 1979) ("because" presented as concise replacement for the verbose phrase "the reason why is that," and "since" presented as primary replacement for "owing to the fact that"); E. White, The Second Tree from the Corner 17 (1984) ("Parnell was not a playmate of mine, as he was a few years older. . . .").

decide what the enacted bill means as it relates to a legal battle. Moreover, the judiciary will toss the new law out of court if it goes against the federal or applicable state constitution.

II. CONCISENESS

A legal document that effectively conveys its message in ten pages is more useful than one that rambles on for 20 pages to convey the same message. However, you must not achieve brevity in your writing at the cost of omitting important ideas or sacrificing clarity in expression. You should strive first to express all important ideas in sufficient detail to ensure reader comprehension. With that accomplished, you can trim the fat from your writing by omitting extraneous ideas and expressing the important ones efficiently.

Conciseness encompasses both limitations on content and attention to form and style. A legal writer can control content primarily through the scope and depth of analysis. Conciseness through form and style requires efficient organization, sentence structure, and phrasing.

A. CONTENT—SCOPE AND DEPTH OF ANALYSIS

"Scope of analysis" refers to the range of issues or topics that a writer addresses in a legal document. "Depth of analysis" refers to the level of detail with which the writer addresses a topic.

1. Scope of Analysis

The range of ideas addressed in a document obviously can dramatically affect the document's length. In analyzing a problem, you need not develop every theory that you have encountered in the library, regardless of the theory's relevance. Instead, you can (1) thoroughly discuss the most important and clearly relevant topics, (2) exclude distracting tangents that are highly unlikely to affect the outcome of the dispute, and (3) determine whether to discuss topics in between the two extremes, perhaps in less detail than would be appropriate for a mainstream theory.

As discussed more fully in Chapter 3, in applying these standards, you may find that you tend to apply different scopes of analysis to different kinds of documents. The scope of analysis ordinarily can be quite broad in your examination answers, because most of your professors will specifically test your ability to identify a wide range of issues. The scope of analysis should be much narrower in a brief, because briefs generally are most persuasive if they focus only on the strongest available arguments. The scope of analysis in a typical office memorandum often is somewhere in between that of an examination and a brief. An office memorandum should not fail to at least briefly discuss a theory or approach that may ultimately be helpful. On the other hand, to a greater extent than an examination answer, an office memorandum should focus on thorough development of the most helpful theories rather than on identification of every conceivable approach.

2. Depth of Analysis

By properly balancing varying depths of analysis in the discussion or argument section of your memorandum or brief, you can make the document more concise and readable. For convenience, this book will use the terms "light analysis" and "in-depth analysis" to refer to the opposite extremes on the spectrum. You engage in light analysis when you simply state a proposition of law and cite to supporting authority. You engage in in-depth analysis when you discuss the facts, holding, and reasoning of case law. You may also control the depth of analysis by choosing between (1) expressing a full deductive argument or (2) expressing an incomplete syllogism, leaving a premise of your deductive argument implicit.

a. Depth of Analysis of Legal Authority

The sample memorandum on pages 156-158 provides an example of balance between light analysis and in-depth analysis of authority from the fictitious state of Calzona. The second paragraph of the discussion section briefly outlines fundamental principles, which provide helpful background information and which almost certainly will not be disputed by the parties. For this purpose, the author of the memorandum has used light analysis by simply stating propositions of law and citing to supporting authority:

> An enforceable contract requires a bargained-for exchange in which a promisor exchanges his own promise for a return promise or performance. *Smith v. Newman,* 161 Calz. 443, 447, 667 P.2d 81, 84 (1984); *see also* Restatement (Second) of Contracts § 71 (1981). The requirement of an exchange is not satisfied if one party gives only an illusory promise, which does not commit the promisor to any future performance. *See Atco Corp. v. Johnson,* 155 Calz. 1211, 627 P.2d 781 (1980).

However, the memorandum also raises the more difficult question of whether a particular promise made by a lender was illusory, which the parties obviously dispute. An adequate discussion of that question requires more thorough analysis of case law to determine which precedent is more nearly analogous to the facts of the current dispute. Such in-depth analysis explores the facts, holding, and reasoning of each significant case:

In-depth analysis of *Atco*   In *Atco Corp.,* the manager of an automobile repair shop promised to forbear "until I want the money" from asserting a claim against the owner of an automobile for $900 in repairs; in exchange, a friend of the owner promised to act as guarantor of the owner's obligation. *Id.* at 1212, 627 P.2d at 782. The word "want" stated no legally recognizable commitment, because it permitted the manager at his own discretion to refuse to perform any forbearance at all. Because the manager incurred no obligation, the guarantor's promise was gratuitous and unenforceable. *Id.* at 1213-14, 627 P.2d at 782-84.

On the other hand, even if a promise leaves open the possibility that the promisor will escape obligation, the promise is valid if the promisor does not have complete control over the events on which the promisor's obligation is conditioned. *See Bonnie v. DeLaney,* 158 Calz. 212, 645 P.2d 887 (1982). In *Bonnie,* an agreement for the sale of a house provided that the Buyer could cancel the agreement if the buyer "cannot qualify for a 30-year mortgage loan for 90% of the sales price" with any of several banks listed in the agreement. *Id.* at 213, 645 P.2d at 888. In enforcing the agreement against the seller, the court distinguished *Atco Corp.* on the ground that the word "cannot" referred to the buyer's *ability* to obtain a loan rather than to his *desire.* Because his ability to obtain a loan was partly controlled by events and decisions outside his control, the promises in the sale agreement were nonillusory and binding. *Id.* at 214-15, 645 P.2d at 889-91.

> In-depth analysis of *Bonnie*

The light analysis in the paragraph first quoted in this subsection quickly establishes noncontroversial points without weighing the reader down with unnecessary detail. The more detailed analysis in the second and third paragraphs provides the reader with a fuller understanding of a specific legal doctrine, the illusory promise, thus creating a solid legal foundation for the fact analysis that will follow. In some discussions, the in-depth analysis may explore such things as the legislative history of a statute or general policy considerations.

You must strike an effective balance between light and in-depth analyses to achieve the dual goals of clarity and conciseness. Unless the issue is extremely simple, if you use only light analysis to discuss or argue a point, you may not define the applicable legal principles with sufficient clarity to permit thoughtful fact analysis. On the other hand, if you use in-depth analysis excessively, you may cause the reader to grow weary and to lose sight of the forest while wandering endlessly among individual trees.

To help strike this balance, you can use citations with explanatory parentheticals as a middle ground between light and in-depth analyses. For example, the following passage uses explanatory parentheticals to explain how the cited authorities support the proposition for which they are cited:

In other decisions, Arizona courts have assumed that the statute of frauds may be mitigated to protect a party's reliance on the promise to perform, but they have refused to apply the doctrine because the normal requirements of estoppel were not satisfied. *E.g., Trollope v. Koerner,* 106 Ariz. 10, 17, 18, 470 P.2d 91, 98-99 (1970) (insufficient reliance); *Mac Enterprises v. Del E. Webb Development Co.,* 132 Ariz. 331, 336, 645 P.2d 1245, 1250 (App. 1982) (no promise).

The brief reference to facts or holdings in the parentheses following the citations provides helpful information for the reader. A full paragraph of in-depth analysis of each case, on the other hand, would simply distract from the fuller discussion of the cases that are more nearly on point.

Another example uses an explanatory parenthetical to state the holding of nonbinding case law:

> The Arizona Statute of Frauds applies to ". . . an agreement which is not to be performed within one year from the making thereof." Ariz. Rev. Stat. Ann. § 44-101(5) (West 1967) (copy of full text attached). The statute probably applies to any employment contract with a fixed term that exceeds one year without qualification. *See, e.g., Waddell v. White,* 51 Ariz. 526, 539-40, 78 P.2d 490, 495-96 (1938). *But cf. Doyle v. Dixon,* 97 Mass. 208 (1867) (death of promisor could result in early full performance of promise not to compete for five years). Williams and Kramer agreed that their employment contract would remain in effect unconditionally for two years; therefore, it falls within the statute.

In this example, the author of the memorandum cited *Doyle* to help define the limits of the proposition for which *Waddell* is cited as affirmative support. *Doyle* does not warrant a full paragraph of in-depth analysis because it is a century-old case that interprets a different statute of frauds in a different factual context. The parenthetical, however, takes up little space and helpfully explains how the case provides a negative comparison to the main proposition.

b. Incomplete Syllogisms

So far, this section has discussed depth of analysis of legal principles. You may apply the same considerations to the complete deductive argument of major premise, minor premise, and conclusion. Normally, a memorandum or brief presents even a simple legal argument in a full syllogism with a discussion of the applicable legal rule, an application of the rule to the facts, and a conclusion:

> Under the Uniform Commercial Code (U.C.C.), the term "merchant" includes any person who "deals in goods of the kind." U.C.C. § 2-104(1). Wilson deals in used cars because he regularly buys and sells used cars as an adjunct to his car rental business. Therefore, he is a merchant of used cars under the U.C.C.

Alternatively, particularly if the argument is minor or tangential, you can present it in an incomplete syllogism:

Wilson is a "merchant" of used cars under the U.C.C. because he regularly buys and sells used cars as an adjunct to his car rental business. *See* U.C.C. § 2-104(1).

A more detailed statement could mention the statutory definition, still without tying it directly to the statutory term "merchant":

. . . because he regularly buys and sells used cars as an adjunct to his car rental business and thus "deals in goods of the kind." *See* U.C.C. § 2-104(1).

In each of these examples, the single textual sentence states a conclusion and the facts supporting it. The legal rule that forms the major premise is implicit or incomplete; the reader assumes that the cited authority supplies an abstract rule that permits the conclusion to follow from the facts. In some cases, a brief explanatory parenthetical after the citation helps to define the abstract legal rule and to show how the citation supports the fact analysis. With or without such a parenthetical, you can use this technique to make a minor point without disrupting the flow of the main analysis or distracting from more important discussions of authority.

B. FORM—EFFICIENT ORGANIZATION, SENTENCE STRUCTURE, AND PHRASING

1. Organization

By applying the principles of organization discussed in Chapter 9, you can write more concisely as well as more clearly. With good organization, you can eliminate unnecessary repetition and present ideas efficiently by building each subsection on the foundations laid in the previous ones.

You need not adopt an organizational framework that eliminates all repetition. Indeed, typical formats for office memoranda and briefs contemplate a form of repetition. Using an office memorandum format recommended in Chapter 8, for example, you can

(1) introduce your analysis in a statement of the issues and in brief answers at the beginning of the memorandum,

(2) explore your analysis fully in the discussion, and

(3) summarize your analysis and recommendations in a final conclusion.

In the same memorandum, you would

(1) state all the relevant facts near the beginning of the memorandum and

(2) analyze the facts relating to each issue in each corresponding section of the discussion.

This overlapping in the elements of a legal document is not wasteful, particularly if you recognize the distinct purposes of the elements.

Nonetheless, needless repetition within such a framework may add pages without adding clarity. Good organization on all levels should minimize this problem.

2. Sentence Structure and Phrasing

You can often trace verbosity within a sentence to unnecessary repetition, loose verb structure, and expression of implicit information. When one or more of these creatures invades your sentences, you will end up with wordy phrases. This results in sentences with a low ratio of words expressing useful ideas to words that convey marginally useful ideas or that simply connect substantive ideas to one another.[13] In editing surplus words from your writing, however, you must not shave your writing so close that you sacrifice clarity.

a. Repetition

As discussed in the previous section, some repetition is built into the general format of a legal document. Moreover, even at the level of words and phrases, carefully planned repetition may be justified on rare occasions as a guide to complex sentence structure or as a means of gaining unusual emphasis:

> Jack Bailey has declared his guilt with his own actions. He declared his guilt when he fled the murder scene on the arrival of neighbors; he declared his guilt when he later tried to conceal the murder weapon; and he declared his guilt today by offering incredible and inconsistent testimony.

However, needless repetition of words or phrases serves only to add words that contribute nothing to the substance of a sentence. Even worse, it may cause the reader to pause and wonder whether the repetitive words are intended to convey slightly different ideas:

> Section XXIV of the lease is null, void, invalid, completely unenforceable, and of no legal force or effect whatsoever.

With a much shorter, cleaner sentence employing only one of the adjectives, you can precisely convey the intended meaning:

> Section XXIV of the lease is void.

On the other hand, even closely related terms are not repetitive if they convey meanings that are different in a way that is significant to the analysis. For example, state and federal statutes prohibit various kinds of discrimination based on "race, color, or national origin." Although the classes encompassed by these terms may overlap, they are not identical. Thus, an employer who discriminates against a dark-skinned African-American in favor of a light-skinned African-American arguably discriminates on the basis of color, even though not necessarily on the basis of race or national origin.[14]

---

13. Richard Wydick recommends that writers maximize the ratio of "working words" to "glue words" in a sentence. R. Wydick, Plain English for Lawyers, ch. 2 (2d ed. 1985).

14. See generally Walker v. Secretary of Treasury, I.R.S., 713 F. Supp. 403 (N.D. Ga. 1989).

b. Verb Structure

You will often add extra words to your sentences when you transform verbs into nouns or use verbs in the passive voice. For example, the author of the following clause added unnecessary bulk to his writing by transforming the verb "objected" into the noun "objection," and introducing "presented" as a substitute verb:

Defense counsel presented an objection to the testimony on the ground that it was inadmissible[15] hearsay. ‖

You add further unnecessary bulk by using the passive voice, adding the words "was" and "by":

An objection to the testimony was presented by defense counsel on the ground that it was inadmissible hearsay. ‖

If you employ the verb "objected" to express the action in active voice, you can eliminate surplus words and lead the reader more directly to the main point:

Defense counsel objected to the testimony on the ground that it was inadmissible hearsay. ‖

c. Implicit Information

The clause following "objected" in the last sentence above reflects a different kind of verbosity: expression of implicit information. You can simply state the ground for objection; you need not expressly characterize it as a "ground":

Defense counsel objected that the testimony was inadmissible hearsay. ‖

Legal writers frequently express implicit information by referring to procedure when defining a substantive legal principle:

If a party proves that a contract requires a performance that would violate a criminal statute, the court will strike down the contract as illegal and unenforceable. ‖

Unless you really intend to emphasize burdens of proof and court procedures, you can convey all the necessary information in fewer words by focusing exclusively on substance:

---

15. "Inadmissible" is not a superfluous modifier of "hearsay" if one adopts the approach that some testimony to out-of-court statements, although hearsay, is admissible pursuant to exceptions to the general rule.

> A contract is illegal and unenforceable if performance of its obligations would violate a criminal statute.

d. Tension Between Clarity and Conciseness

In your quest to eliminate surplus words, you should remain sensitive to the tension between clarity and conciseness, taking care to retain words and phrases that communicate important information. For example, the following sentences reflect each kind of verbosity cited at the beginning of this section:

> Robert Jones, who is the plaintiff, brought this action against Mary Smith, the defendant. In this action, Jones filed a complaint that alleges that Smith committed a breach of the contract of employment between Smith and Jones.

You can combine these sentences into a single, much more concise sentence. At the margin, however, further revisions for conciseness may sacrifice important information, depending on your intended connotation and emphasis.

An initial revision reduces the number of words from 37 to 17, arguably without sacrificing clarity on any level:

> Plaintiff Robert Jones brought this action against Defendant Mary Smith, alleging that Smith breached their employment contract.

Among other things, this revision eliminates the repetition of "this action," recognizes that the filing of a complaint is implicit in other phrases, uses "breached" as a direct verb, and replaces wordy clauses and phrases such as "who is the plaintiff" and "between Smith and Jones" with single but equally precise words.

By treating "Plaintiff" and "Defendant" as implicit, and by replacing "brought this action" with "sued," you can trim another five words from the sentence:

> Robert Jones sued Mary Smith, alleging that Smith breached their employment contract.

This revision, however, may achieve conciseness at the expense of other considerations of style. To many readers, "sued" carries the negative connotation of a harassing litigant; therefore, counsel for Jones might prefer the softer, though less concise, phrase "brought this action." Also, if you wish to refer to the parties subsequently only as "Plaintiff" and "Defendant" or only as "Jones" and "Smith," you may prefer to emphasize the relationship of each party's name with his or her procedural title by initially using the full phrases "Plaintiff Robert Jones," and "Defendant Mary Smith,".

If you do not object to the last revision above, you could trim one more word from the sentence and achieve a more direct flow by eliminating the reference to "alleging":

> Robert Jones sued Mary Smith for breach of their employment contract.

Sticklers for precision, however, might argue that you should use the preposition "for" to introduce a description of the requested relief rather than the ground for liability.

To summarize, revisions for conciseness are matters of judgment that require sensitivity to considerations of emphasis, precision, connotation, and other elements of clarity.

=========== E X E R C I S E   1 0 - 7 ===========

1. *Verbosity*

Rewrite the following sentence to make it more direct and concise.

The Federal Rules of Civil Procedure, Rule 26(c), provides that the issuance of protective orders to the effect that certain matters ought not to be inquired into in the course of discovery is within the authorization of the court.

2. *Advanced Exercise*

Analyze the style problems in the following sentence, identify the nature of each problem, and rewrite the sentence to make it clearer and more concise.

With respect to time, the right to compensation for an injury, under the workmen's compensation acts is governed, in the absence of any provision to the contrary, by the law in force at the time of the occurrence of such injury.

81 Am. Jur. 2d Workmen's Compensation § 89, at 772 (1976).

III. PRESENTATION OF AUTHORITY, USE OF QUOTATIONS, AND CITATION FORM

A. PRESENTATION OF AUTHORITY

1. Subordination of Citations

Authors of law journal articles or treatises can gracefully insert case names at the beginning or in the middle of textual sentences, because they customarily drop the remainder of the citations to footnotes. With few exceptions, however, citations in briefs and in office memoranda remain in the text. Consequently, when drafting a brief or an office memorandum, you should avoid citing to authority in full at the beginning or in the middle of a textual sentence. Instead, unless you intend to emphasize a particularly significant case name and citation, you should subordinate the citation to a separate citation sentence, permitting you to reserve the main text for the ideas for which the authority is cited.

Unfortunately, many legal writers draw their readers' attention first to the authority, and only then to the proposition for which the authority is cited:

> In *Tucson Medical Center v. Zoslow,* 147 Ariz. 612, 614, 712 P.2d 459, 461 (App. 1985), the court held that, in the absence of an express restriction by contract or statute, a tenant generally has the unrestricted right to assign or sublet.

Because the case citation has no great independent significance in this example, you could improve this passage by moving the citation to a separate citation sentence. If you do not wish to emphasize the identity of the authoring court, you can make the strongest substantive statement by presenting the legal proposition as an unqualified statement of truth that one or more courts have incidentally discovered:

> In the absence of an express restriction by contract or statute, a tenant generally has the unrestricted right to assign or sublet. *E.g., Tucson Medical Center v. Zoslow,* 147 Ariz. 612, 614, 712 P.2d 459, 461 (App. 1985).

On the other hand, if the decisions of the authoring court are controlling on the court adjudicating the current dispute, you may want to identify the authoring court in the textual sentence, while continuing to subordinate the case name and the rest of the citation:

> The Arizona Court of Appeals has held that, in the absence of an express restriction by contract or statute, a tenant generally has the unrestricted right to assign or sublet. *Tucson Medical Center v. Zoslow,* 147 Ariz. 612, 614, 712 P.2d 459, 461 (App. 1985).

On rare occasions, you might appropriately retain a full citation to authority in a textual sentence if the citation itself has such great independent significance that it warrants such emphasis:

> In *Brown v. Board of Education,* 347 U.S. 483 (1954), the Supreme Court unanimously held that segregated public school systems violate the equal protection guarantee of the fourteenth amendment.

In this example, the case name, the identity of the authoring court, and even the date of the decision all trigger recognition in most readers. Alternatively, you could refer to the instantly recognizable case name in the textual sentence, saving the remainder of the citation for a separate citation sentence:

> In *Brown v. Board of Education,* the Supreme Court unanimously held that segregated public school systems violate the Equal Protection guarantee of the fourteenth amendment. 347 U.S. 483 (1954).

This form, however, is unconventional if it represents the initial citation to this authority in the memorandum or the brief.

Subordination of citations is even more important in the presentation of an in-depth case analysis. The following introduction to the analysis of a fictitious case not only inappropriately begins a textual sentence with a full cita-tion, it also begins exploring the details of the case without first explaining generally why the case warrants in-depth analysis:

> In *Bonnie v. DeLaney,* 158 Calz. 212, 645 P.2d 887 (1982), an agree-ment for the sale of a house provided that the Buyer could cancel the agree-ment if the buyer "cannot qualify for a 30-year mortgage loan for 90% of the sales price" with any of several banks listed in the agreement. *Id.* at 213, 645 P.2d at 888. In enforcing the agreement against the seller, the court distinguished . . .

The reader trudges through such a passage with little interest and at least moderate irritation, because he doesn't discover the point of the case until the end of the passage. A series of such paragraphs presenting a laundry list of cases can produce a rambling effect that causes the reader to lose track of the principles that the cases are meant to illustrate.

You can greatly improve the passage quoted above by introducing it with an overview of the point that the in-depth case analysis will illustrate:

> On the other hand, even if a promise leaves open the possibility that the promisor will escape obligation, the promise is valid if the promisor does not have complete control over the events upon which the promisor's obligation is conditioned. *See Bonnie v. DeLaney,* 158 Calz. 212, 645 P.2d 887 (1982). In *Bonnie,* an agreement for the sale of a house provided that the buyer could cancel the agreement if the buyer "cannot qualify for a 30-year mortgage loan for 90% of the sales price" with any of several banks listed in the agreement. *Id.* at 213, 645 P.2d at 888. In enforcing the agree-ment against the seller, the court distinguished . . .

The preceding passage uses a topic sentence to present an overview of the case analysis. In more complex analyses, you might precede the case analysis with a paragraph that provides the appropriate overview in two or more sentences.

This method of presenting authority enables you to introduce the case citation in a separate citation sentence and to begin the in-depth case analysis with an unobtrusive, short-form reference to the case name:

> . . . is conditioned. *See Bonnie v. DeLaney,* 158 Calz. 212, 645 P.2d 887 (1982). In *Bonnie,* . . .

Moreover, if you intend to analyze several cases on the same issue, you can use the topic sentence or overview paragraph to help you to express your synthesis of the case law. Synthesis of authority is a critical component of legal method, warranting further exploration of writing techniques that effectively display synthesis.

2. Synthesis of Case Law

Many legal rules are the products of synthesis of two or more legal au-thorities. In an office memorandum or a brief, you should present such legal rules with clear guides to your synthesis rather than with independent and unconnected analyses of the authorities.

For example, suppose that a section of an office memorandum analyzes the issue whether a federal civil rights act addresses employment discrimination against a person because he is French Canadian. The following sample passage presents a "laundry list" of case briefs. It is ineffective because it provides insufficient guidance to the author's synthesis, or perhaps because it betrays the author's failure to synthesize:

I. RACIAL CLASSIFICATIONS UNDER SECTION 1981

Section 1981 of title 42 of the United States Code provides in part as follows:

General statutory rules

> All persons within the jurisdiction of the United States shall have the same right in every State and Territory to make and enforce contracts . . . as is enjoyed by white citizens . . .

In-depth analysis without topic sentence to express an overview

In *Runyon v. McCrary*, 427 U.S. 160 (1976), African-American applicants to private, commercially operated, nonsectarian schools sued the schools through their parents. They alleged that the schools refused to admit them because of their race in violation of section 1981. A divided Supreme Court ruled that the school's discriminatory admissions policy violated the statute. It held that the statute applied to private contracts and that application of the statute to the school's admissions policy did not infringe upon the constitutional interests of the students or their parents in association, privacy, and parental control.

In-depth analysis without topic sentence to express overview or synthesis

In *McDonald v. Santa Fe Trail Transportation Co.*, 427 U.S. 273 (1976), white employees sued their employer and their union under section 1981 and Title VII of the Civil Rights Act of 1964. They alleged that their discharge for misappropriation of property was racially motivated because an African-American employee similarly charged was not dismissed. The Supreme Court acknowledged that the "immediate impetus" for the 1866 predecessor to section 1981 was "the necessity for further relief of the constitutionally emancipated former Negro slaves." *Id.* at 289. Nonetheless, on the strength of legislative history indicating that the bill would protect all races, the Supreme Court held that section 1981 imposes liability for discrimination aimed at any race, including whites. *Id.* at 289-96.

In *Saint Francis College v. Al-Khazraji*, 481 U.S. 604 (1987), a college professor of Arab ancestry sued his employer under section 1981 and other civil rights statutes. He alleged that the denial of his application for tenure was racially motivated because similarly situated Caucasians fared better in the tenure process. The trial court dismissed the section 1981 claim on the ground that it failed to state a claim of race discrimination because Arabs were not a race distinct from Caucasians. *Id.* at 606. The Court of Appeals reversed and remanded for further proceedings, and the Supreme Court affirmed the decision of the Court of Appeals.

The Supreme Court held that scientific knowledge and cultural attitudes at the time of enactment of the 1866 and 1870 predecessors to section 1981 shaped the racial classifications addressed by the statute. Legislative history and popular dictionary and encyclopedic sources of the era reflect the view that groups with relatively narrowly defined ancestral roots and ethnic characteristics, such as "Germans," "Greeks," "Jews," and "Gypsies," represent distinct races. The Supreme Court concluded that Arabs would be viewed as a separate race under those standards and that section 1981 therefore addresses discrimination based on Arab ancestry. *Id.* at 606-08.

In our case . . .

In-depth analysis without topic sentence to express overview or synthesis

The preceding passage does not give adequate notice of the points or issues that each case brief is intended to illustrate, nor does it explain how the authorities relate to one another. The following passage provides a better guide to the author's synthesis. It uses a transition sentence or paragraph to provide a preview of the point illustrated by each case brief and to explain how each authority relates to previously analyzed authorities. The passage below also flows more coherently because it limits its in-depth analysis to the announced topic of the section and refers only tersely to other potential problems in the scope of the statute.

I. RACIAL CLASSIFICATIONS UNDER SECTION 1981

Federal civil rights legislation prohibits certain kinds of racial discrimination in contractual relations:

> All persons within the jurisdiction of the United States shall have the same right in every State and Territory to make and enforce contracts . . . as is enjoyed by white citizens . . .

Statutory language

42 U.S.C. § 1981.

As suggested by the statutory reference to rights "enjoyed by white persons," the "immediate impetus" for the 1866 predecessor to section 1981 was "the necessity for further relief of the constitutionally emancipated former Negro slaves." *McDonald v. Santa Fe Trail Transportation Co.,* 427 U.S. 273, 289 (1976).

General guides from case law interpreting the statute

Topic sentence introducing in-depth analysis of *McDonald*

Transition paragraph expressing (1) relationship of *McDonald* to *Saint Francis* and (2) overview of *Saint Francis*

In-depth analysis of *Saint Francis*

Consequently, section 1981 applies most clearly to race discrimination against African-Americans. *See, e.g., Runyon v. McCrary,* 427 U.S. 160 (1976).

Section 1981's prohibition of discrimination, however, extends beyond discrimination against African-Americans and applies more generally to discrimination based on any racial classification. *McDonald v. Santa Fe Trail Transportation Co.,* 427 U.S. 273 (1976). In *McDonald,* white employees sued their employer and their union under section 1981 and Title VII of the Civil Rights Act of 1964. They alleged that their discharge for misappropriation of property was racially motivated because an African-American employee similarly charged was not dismissed. On the strength of legislative history indicating that the bill would protect all races, the Supreme Court held that section 1981 imposes liability for discrimination against members of any race, including whites. *Id.* at 289-96.

McDonald did not attempt to identify all the racial classifications protected under section 1981. More recently, the Supreme Court held that the applicable classifications are not those recognized by many contemporary scientific theories, but are the narrower and more numerous classifications generally recognized when Congress enacted the predecessors to section 1981. *Saint Francis College v. Al-Khazraji,* 481 U.S. 604 (1987).

In *Saint Francis,* a college professor of Arab ancestry sued his employer under section 1981 and other civil rights statutes. He alleged that the denial of his application for tenure was racially motivated because similarly situated Caucasians fared better in the tenure process. The trial court dismissed the section 1981 claim on the ground that it failed to state a claim of race discrimination because Arabs were not a race distinct from caucasians. *Id.* at 606. The Court of Appeals reversed and remanded for further proceedings, and the Supreme Court affirmed the decision the Court of Appeals.

The Supreme Court held that scientific knowledge and cultural attitudes at the time of enactment of the 1866 and 1870 predecessors to section 1981 shaped the racial classifications addressed by the statute. Legislative history and popular dictionary and encyclopedic sources of the era reflect the view that groups with relatively narrowly defined ancestral roots and ethnic characteristics, such as "Germans," "Greeks," "Jews," and "Gypsies," represent distinct races. The Supreme Court concluded that Arabs would be viewed as a separate race under those standards and that section 1981 therefore addresses discrimination based on Arab ancestry. *Id.* at 606-08.

In our case . . .

The two passages quoted above illustrate the parallels between effective law school study techniques and techniques for preparing documents in a law office. The first passage resembles one of a series of only loosely connected case briefs, such as those you might prepare for class discussion. The case briefs contain useful information, but you can more effectively apply that information to an examination problem if you synthesize the cases and then reorganize them in a course outline that emphasizes controlling principles and that subordinates the discussion of cases to the role of illustrating those principles.

In a law office, you will use a similar analytical process in presenting case law in a memorandum or brief. As illustrated in the second passage above, topic sentences or paragraphs introducing each case discussion emphasize principles and often act as transitions that convey case syntheses. The detailed discussion of each case simply illustrates a principle or qualification to a principle that you have already identified in a topic sentence. You should construct such a topic sentence or paragraph to introduce each in-depth case analysis. Your reader can then make her way through the series of individual case-brief trees without losing sight of the broader outlines of the forest.

In some analyses, you can state an overview of the complete synthesis in a single introductory sentence or paragraph rather than set it forth incrementally in the topic sentences of several paragraphs. For example, the third paragraph in the following passage from an office memorandum provides a synthesized overview of two cases that are subsequently discussed in detail:

Federal civil rights legislation imposes liability for deprivation of constitutional rights by agents of the state:

> Every person who, under color of [state law], subjects . . . any citizen of the United States . . . to the deprivation of any rights . . . secured by the Constitution and laws, shall be liable to the person injured. . . .

General statutory rules

42 U.S.C. § 1983.

Although section 1983 does not expressly limit its remedies, it implicitly incorporates a variety of common law immunity defenses. *City of Newport v. Fact Concerts, Inc.,* 453 U.S. 247, 258 (1981). A state judge, for example, is absolutely immune from liability for money damages even for allegedly unconstitutional judicial acts taken within the judge's subject matter jurisdiction. *Stump v. Sparkman,* 435 U.S. 349 (1978). This immunity defense protects the independence of the judiciary by encouraging judges to make

General immunity rules from interpretive case law

controversial decisions to the best of their abilities, uninhibited by the fear of suit. *See id.* at 355-56, 63.

Specific immunity rules from case law

Not all work-related tasks performed by a judge are judicial functions covered by absolute immunity. For example, a judge's hiring or firing a judicial employee may be a purely administrative act to which absolute immunity does not apply. *See, e.g., McMillan v. Svetanoff,* 793 F.2d 149 (7th Cir. 1986). In the Seventh Circuit, a judge's action relating to personnel is "judicial" rather than purely "administrative" only if the action implicates the judicial decisionmaking process that the immunity defense is designed to protect. *Compare id.* (firing court reporter was an administrative act unprotected by absolute immunity) *with Forrester v. White,* 792 F.2d 647 (7th Cir. 1986) (firing probation officer was judicial function protected by absolute immunity).

Synthesis of *McMillan* with *Forrester*

In-depth analysis of *McMillan*

In *McMillan,* a newly elected trial judge discharged his entire courtroom staff upon taking office and rehired only one of the dismissed employees. A discharged court reporter sued the judge under section 1983 and a related statute. She alleged that the judge had fired her because of her race and her political affiliation, in violation of her constitutional rights under the first and fourteenth amendments. The Seventh Circuit characterized the function of hiring and firing employees as "typically an administrative task." 793 F.2d at 155. It concluded that the act of firing a court reporter did not implicate the judicial decisionmaking process, because it did not involve judicial discretion requiring the exercise of the judge's "education, training, and experience in the law." *Id.* at 154-55. The act was therefore unprotected by the defense of absolute immunity.

In-depth analysis of *Forrester*

In contrast, in *Forrester,* the same court approved the defense of absolute immunity for a state appellate judge's allegedly discriminatory demotion and discharge of a juvenile and adult probation officer. 792 F.2d at 648. The probation officer's duties included preparing pre-sentencing reports, recommendations for disposition of juvenile cases, and recommendations for revocation of juvenile and adult probation and parole. *Id.* at 648-49. The information that the probation officer provided "directly implicated the exercise of the judge's discretionary judgment." *Id.* at 657. Thus, maintenance of judicial independence required absolute immunity to protect the judge's ability to demote and discharge the probation officer without fear of suit. *Id.* at 657-58.

In our case . . .

B. QUOTATIONS

1. *Selective Use of Quotations*

If the interpretation or application of a statute or contract is disputed by the parties, the starting point of your analysis is the actual language of the statute or contract. Accordingly, when presenting such an analysis in a memorandum or brief, you should quote the relevant statutory or contractual provisions.

You should generally quote more sparingly from case law. Supervising attorneys and judges are primarily interested in your original synthesis of case law and your analysis of the facts within the legal framework. They are not impressed by your demonstrated ability to cut and paste page-long passages written by others.

Occasionally, a passage from case law is so clear, concise, powerful, and narrowly tailored to your dispute that paraphrasing cannot improve on it. By quoting such a passage, you obviously will enhance the memorandum or brief. Often, however, a passage from case law will seem out of context if quoted, perhaps because it clashes with your writing style or because its relevant portions are unavoidably intermingled with distracting references to points not relevant to your dispute. In such a case, you can help focus the attention of your reader on important ideas, rather than on sudden shifts in style, by restating the rule or analysis of a case in your own words.

This general admonition against excessive quotation probably applies most strongly to appellate briefs. Most appellate judges or their law clerks have the luxury of sufficient time to study the important cases cited in appellate briefs. Moreover, appellate courts have the power to overrule at least some of the precedent likely to be cited in the briefs. Consequently, appellate judges in particular tend to look for original analysis, including policy analysis, rather than extensive quotation from authorities that a judge or a law clerk can easily secure from the library.

In contrast, busy trial judges preparing for hearings on motions may not have time to study carefully all the important cases cited in the briefs.[16] Additionally, they must follow, and cannot overrule, applicable appellate decisions within their jurisdiction. For both these reasons, some trial judges may appreciate passages in briefs that quote arguably controlling holdings from appellate case law. Similarly, some supervising attorneys ask their law clerks or associates to quote extensively from important case law in office memoranda, presumably because they want to second-guess the writer's analysis of the case law or because they want to determine whether portions of the quoted materials are suitable for quotation in their own briefs.

Still, when you do decide to quote authority in a brief or an office memorandum,

> you need not quote at epic length. Indeed, a sure way to induce skimming is the back-to-back employment of two quotes of more than ten lines each. . . . Select

---

16. See generally Fidel, Some Do's and Don'ts of Motion Writing, Ariz. Bar J., August 1983, at 9.

a short helpful quote, and show its application to your case. Give enough to make your point but not so much as to sink your brief from excess weight.[17]

If you believe that a trial judge or supervising attorney might want to read the full text of some statute or case law that is not readily available in her office or chambers, you need not clutter up the body of your document with lengthy quotation. You can simply attach photocopies of the authority as an appendix to your document.[18]

2. Presentation of Block Quotations

a. Basic Techniques

If you quote a substantial portion of any authority, you should set the quoted passage apart in a single-spaced, indented block, without quotation marks other than those that appear within the original quoted text. This blocking technique helps the reader to distinguish the lengthy quotation from the original text. The popular "Bluebook" citation manual requires block quotation only if the quoted passage exceeds 49 words.[19] The visual benefits of blocking, however, are evident in shorter passages. Therefore, you should consider blocking any quotation that runs for more than three lines of copy, even if it contains fewer than 50 words.

The principles stated in section A above about subordinating citations and introducing case analyses with topic sentences apply equally to block quotations. Unless the citation to a block quotation has independent significance, you should relegate it to the end of the quote. More important, you should introduce the quoted passage with a thesis statement, a substantive overview that summarizes the point that you intend the passage to convey to the reader.

The following passage inappropriately introduces a block quotation of a statutory provision with a citation that has little independent significance. Moreover, the absence of a substantive introduction induced the writer to convey the point of the quote with distracting underlining:

> Title 42 U.S.C. § 2000e-2(a)(1) provides:
>
> It shall be an <u>unlawful</u> employment practice for an employer—
> (1) to fail or refuse to hire or to discharge any individual, or otherwise <u>to discriminate against any individual</u> with respect to his compensation, terms, conditions, or privileges of employment, <u>because of such individual's</u> race, color, religion, <u>sex</u> or national origin . . .

Using a substantive introduction, you could revise this passage to subordinate the citation, provide the reader with helpful orientation, and minimize the need for underlining as a means of emphasis:

---

17. Id. at 10-11.
18. See id.
19. Harvard L. Rev. Ass'n, A Uniform System of Citation R. 5.1(a) (14th ed. 1986).

Federal law prohibits sex discrimination in employment:

> It shall be an unlawful employment practice for an employer—
> (1) to fail or refuse to hire or to discharge any individual, or otherwise
> to discriminate against any individual with respect to his compensation, terms,
> conditions, or privileges of employment, because of such individual's race,
> color, religion, sex or national origin . . .

42 U.S.C. § 2000e-2(a)(1) [Title VII § 703(a)(1)].

Alternatively, you may want to acknowledge that the name of the act in this example is familiar to most lawyers and therefore has independent significance. You can refer to the act in the introduction, while continuing to subordinate the code citation:

> Title VII of the Civil Rights Act of 1964 makes it unlawful for an employer to engage in sex discrimination:
>
> > It shall be an unlawful employment practice for an employer—
> > (1) to fail or refuse . . .

42 U.S.C. § 2000e-2(a)(1) [Title VII § 703(a)(1)].

Finally, if you want to refer repeatedly to this section of the statute throughout your brief or memorandum, you can emphasize the Act's section number, which is more familiar to most lawyers than the code number, by referring to it in the introduction:

> Section 703(a) of Title VII of the Civil Rights Act of 1964 makes it unlawful for an employer to engage in sex discrimination:
>
> > It shall be an unlawful employment practice for an employer—
> > (1) to fail or refuse . . .

42 U.S.C. § 2000e-2(a)(1). Section 703(a) identifies two principal elements of unlawful discrimination . . .

Even after judicious editing, you may find that a quoted passage is exceptionally long or complex. Particularly if the quotation addresses multiple themes, you can lead the reader through the such material by breaking the quotation into parts and preceding each part with a substantive introduction:

Under the Uniform Commercial Code, a response to an offer may be an acceptance even though it varies the terms of the offer:	**Introduction to U.C.C. § 2-207(1)**
> A definite and seasonable expression of acceptance or a written confirmation which is sent within a reasonable time operates as an acceptance even though it states terms additional to or different from those offered or agreed upon . . .	**Text of U.C.C. § 2-207(1)**

Introduction to proviso to U.C.C. § 2-207(1)

Text of proviso

U.C.C. § 2-207(1). However, a proviso to the same statute provides that the offeree may avoid acceptance and state a counteroffer if "acceptance is expressly made conditional on assent to the additional or different terms." *Id.*

Introduction to U.C.C. § 2-207(2)

If the original offeree's response is an acceptance, the statute provides that some of the new terms in the acceptance may be added to the contract without the express assent of the original offeror:

Text of U.C.C. § 2-207(2)

> The additional terms are to be construed as proposals for addition to the contract. Between merchants such terms become part of the contract unless:
> (a) The offer expressly limits acceptance to the terms of the offer;
> (b) they materially alter it; or
> (c) notification of objection to them has already been given or is given within a reasonable time after notice of them is received.

U.C.C. § 2-207(2).

b. Special Techniques for Advocacy

You can use a substantive introduction to a block quotation as effective preliminary advocacy in a brief. Your introduction will emphasize the point of the quote by presenting it in summary form. Indeed, because some judges tend to skim over block quotations, your substantive introduction may be the only statement of the point that the judge reads.

More important, quotations from contracts, statutes, or case law are often reasonably subject to varying interpretations, and a substantive introduction can encourage the reader to interpret the quoted passage in a favorable manner. For example, the following passage from an employment contract lists several grounds for discharging an employee, but it doesn't expressly state whether the list is exclusive:

> XI. Ajax Co. reserves the right to discharge any employee who
> (1) fails to perform satisfactorily,
> (2) commits gross insubordination, or
> (3) commits a criminal act on the work site.

Assuming that an employee hired under this contract is employed for an indefinite term, the traditional common law at-will rule would permit the employer to discharge the employee for any reason if the contractual list of grounds for discharge is not intended to be exclusive. On the other hand, if this section of the contract is interpreted to include an implicit promise by the employer to refrain from discharging an employee except for the listed reasons, then the contract would override the otherwise applicable common law rule.

When quoting this passage in the argument section of the brief for either the employer or a discharged employee, you will achieve the least impact with a stock introduction such as:

Section XI of the Employment Contract provides, in relevant part, as follows:

Instead, as counsel for the discharged employee, you should use an argumentative introductory sentence to characterize the provision as a restriction on the employer's freedom to terminate the employment contract:

The Employment Contract expressly identifies only three grounds for discharge, all relating to poor performance or serious misconduct:

XI. Ajax Co. reserves the right to discharge any employee who
    (1) fails to perform satisfactorily,
    (2) commits gross insubordination, or
    (3) commits a criminal act on the work site.

Employment Contract § XI. The parties obviously intended this list to be the exclusive . . .

Conversely, as counsel for the employer, you can use an argumentative introduction to characterize the provision as an affirmation of the employer's common law freedom to terminate:

No provision of the contract expressly limits Ajax Co.'s common law right to discharge any employee at Ajax's will. Indeed, the only provision addressing termination selects three particularly strong grounds for illustration and emphasis:

XI. Ajax Co. reserves the right to discharge any employee who
    (1) fails to perform satisfactorily,
    (2) commits gross insubordination, or
    (3) commits a criminal act on the work site.

Employment Contract § XI.
Vargas argues that the parties intended this list to be exclusive. On the contrary . . .

You can always begin arguing for a favorable interpretation after neutrally presenting the quoted passage. However, the reader is more likely to adopt your proposed interpretation if a substantive introduction biases him toward the interpretation before he reads the quoted passage.

═══════ E X E R C I S E 1 0 - 8 ═══════

Rewrite the following passage to subordinate citations and to introduce the block quotation with a brief substantive overview. You may assume that the case names are not sufficiently independently significant to warrant emphasis in textual sentences.

IV. DISCUSSION

    A. Liability for Discrimination under Section 1981

    • • • •

    1. First Amendment Defense

Lilly Prep School has asserted in a letter to our client that it has a first amendment right to teach and practice racial segregation in its classrooms. We expect it to raise this as a defense in any lawsuit that we file.

In *NAACP v. Alabama*, 357 U.S. 449 (1958), the Supreme Court recognized a first amendment right "to engage in association for the advancement of beliefs and ideas." *Id.* at 460. In *Runyon v. McCrary*, 427 U.S. 160 (1976), however, the Court stated:

> From this principle it may be assumed that parents have a First Amendment right to send their children to educational institutions that promote the belief that racial segregation is desirable, and that the children have an equal right to attend such institutions. But it does not follow that the *practice* of excluding racial minorities from such institutions is also protected by the same principle.

Id. at 176.

C. CITATION FORM

You must cite to authority in a manner that clearly and concisely identifies the source of the authority and that helps the reader find the authority in the library. A widely accepted citation form that meets these goals is presented in A Uniform System of Citation, commonly known as the "Bluebook," published by the Harvard Law Review Association. More flexible in its approach, and gaining in popularity, is the University of Chicago Manual of Legal Citation, prepared by the University of Chicago Law Review and the University of Chicago Law Forum.

For an immediate introduction to citation form, you need only refer to the numerous citations in the footnotes and example passages of this book. Below is a summary of the citation form, most of it taken from the Bluebook, reflected in many of those citations.

1. Constitutions and Codes

When citing to a specific constitutional provision, you should refer to the article or amendment number and, if appropriate, to a section number:

‖ U.S. Const. art. III § 1.
‖ U.S. Const. amend. XIV.
‖ Ariz. Const. art. VI § 1.

The first citation above refers to section 1 of article III of the United States Constitution. The second citation refers to the fourteenth amendment to that constitution. The third citation refers to section 1 of article VI of the Arizona Constitution.

You should cite to the title and section numbers of a codified statute:

42 U.S.C. § 1981.
Ariz. Rev. Stat. § 47-2207.

The first citation above refers to section 1981 in title 42 of the official United States Code. The second refers to section 2207 of Title 47 of the Arizona Revised Statutes, the title that encompasses Arizona's commercial code. Interestingly, almost all practicing attorneys in Arizona depart from the Bluebook by using the shortened abbreviation "A.R.S." when citing to the Arizona Revised Statutes.

If you believe that the information will be useful to your reader, you should also include the date of publication of a statute:

Iowa Code § 112 (Supp. 1988).

2. Case Law

a. Basic Citation Form

When citing to case law, you should specify the case name, the volume and page of the reporter, the court, and the year of decision:

Bell v. United States, 349 U.S. 81 (1955).
Bundy v. Jackson, 641 F.2d 934 (D.C. Cir. 1981).
Wagenseller v. Scottsdale Memorial Hospital, 147 Ariz. 370 (1985).
Schmidt v. American Leasco, 139 Ariz. 509 (App. 1983).

The first case cited above is a decision of the United States Supreme Court, found at page 81 of volume 349 of the official United States Reporter. The second is a decision of the District of Columbia Circuit of the United States Court of Appeals, found at page 934 of volume 641 of the federal reporter. The third is a decision of the Arizona Supreme Court, found at page 370 of volume 147 of the official Arizona Reports. The fourth citation includes the notation "App." within the parentheses to identify the source of the authority as the Arizona Court of Appeals. The corresponding notation, "S. Ct." was unnecessary in the third citation, because the Arizona Reports is primarily the reporter for the Arizona Supreme Court decisions, and a decision within is assumed to be one of the Arizona Supreme Court unless the citation specifies otherwise.

b. Parallel Citations

If a state court decision appears in more than one reporter system, you should cite to each reporter whenever possible:

‖ *Wagenseller v. Scottsdale Memorial Hospital,* 147 Ariz. 370, 710 P.2d
‖   1025 (1985).
‖ *City of San Francisco v. United Ass'n of Journeymen and Apprentices of the*
‖   *Plumbing and Pipefitting Indus., Local 38,* 42 Cal. 3d 810, 230 Cal.
‖   Rptr. 856, 726 P.2d 538 (1986).

The first decision cited above appears not only in the official Arizona Reports,
but also in volume 710 of West Publishing Company's unofficial, regional
Pacific Reporter, second series. The second decision appears in the official
California Reports, in the unofficial California Reporter, and in the Pacific
Reporter.

c. Specific Page Cites

When citing to a passage within a decision, you should cite to the specific
page or pages on which the passage appears:

‖ *Bundy v. Jackson,* 641 F.2d 934, 936-37 (D.C. Cir. 1981).
‖ *Wagenseller v. Scottsdale Memorial Hospital,* 147 Ariz. 370, 380 n.5, 710
‖   P.2d 1025, 1035 n.5 (1985).

In the first citation above, the cited passage appears on pages 936 to 937. In
the second citation, the cited passage appears in footnote 5, which is found on
page 380 of the Arizona Reports and on page 1035 of the Pacific Reporter.

d. Short-Form Citation

If you have fully cited to a case in a legal document, you may refer to it
within the subsequent few pages by a shortened case name, volume and reporter, and specific page cite:

‖ *Bundy,* 641 F.2d at 938.
‖ *Wagenseller,* 147 Ariz. at 381, 710 P.2d at 1036.

You may use "*Id.,*" along with new specific page cites if necessary, to refer to
the immediately preceding citation, whether to case law or other authority:

‖ *Wagenseller,* 147 Ariz. at 381, 710 P.2d at 1036.
‖ *Id.*
‖ *Id.* at 380, 710 P.2d at 1035.

3. Books and Articles

You should cite to books or treatises by the first initial and last name of
the author, title, page, and year of publication:

K. Llewellyn, The Bramble Bush 79 (1978).   ‖

You should cite to articles in law journals by the last name of the author, title, volume and page number of the journal, and year of publication:

Pound, Common Law and Legislation, 21 Harv. L. Rev. 383 (1908).   ‖

4. *Citation Signals*

Citation signals describe the relationship between the cited authority and either (1) the proposition for which it is cited or (2) other authority. An appropriate signal can take the place of a much longer phrase of equivalent prose. For example, the following sentence uses textual clauses after the first citation to describe the relationships among three cited authorities:

Under the "mailbox rule," an acceptance is effective when mailed if ‖ mailing is a means of communication authorized by the offer. *Reserve Insurance Co. v. Duckett*, 249 Md. 108, 238 A.2d 536 (1968). Another authority to the same effect is *Morrison v. Thoelke*, 155 So. 2d 889 (Fla. App. 1963). A contrary decision is found in *Rhode Island Tool Co. v. United States*, 128 F. Supp. 417 (Ct. Cl. 1955).

By replacing these clauses with the citation signals *"accord"* and *"contra,"* you can communicate the same information in a more concise fashion:

Under the "mailbox rule," an acceptance is effective when mailed if ‖ mailing is a means of communication authorized by the offer. *Reserve Insurance Co. v. Duckett*, 249 Md. 108, 238 A.2d 536 (1968); *accord Morrison v. Thoelke*, 155 So. 2d 889 (Fla. App. 1963). *Contra Rhode Island Tool Co. v. United States*, 128 F. Supp. 417 (Ct. Cl. 1955).

Of course, such citation signals can effectively replace ordinary prose only if legal readers and writers agree on the meanings that they convey. The following propositions and examples, most of them inspired by the Bluebook,[20] can serve as a basis for such agreement. Publishers of journals and treatises may adopt different conventions in their use of Roman typeface or italics in case citations; however, in a typewritten document, you should underline both the case name and the citation signal.

a. No Signal

You should use no signal if the proposition is a quotation or paraphrase from cited authority:

---

20. See Harvard L. Rev. Ass'n, A Uniform System of Citation R. 2.2 (14th ed. 1986).

> In Arizona, an employer is liable for wrongful discharge if it discharges an employee for a reason that violates an important public policy of the state. *Wagenseller v. Scottsdale Memorial Hospital,* 147 Ariz. 370, 378-79, 710 P.2d 1025, 1033-34 (1985).

b. *See; See Also; See Generally*

You should use the signal *"see"* if the proposition does not appear in the cited authority but logically follows directly from it, as when you tailor the holding of the cited authority to the facts of your own case:

> Johnson will be liable for wrongful discharge if he discharged Bailey for a reason that violates an important public policy of the state. *See Wagenseller v. Scottsdale Memorial Hospital,* 147 Ariz. 370, 378-79, 710 P.2d 1025, 1033-34 (1985).

You can use *"See also"* and *"see generally"* to signal a more attenuated relationship between the proposition and the supporting authority:

> . . . *See Wagenseller* . . . (1985); *see also Peterman* . . . (1959); *see generally* Annot., 12 A.L.R. 4th 544 (1982).

c. *E.g.; Accord*

You can use *"e.g."* to show that the cited authority is simply an example of numerous cases that could support the proposition:

> *E.g., Barnes v. Costle,* 561 F.2d 983 (D.C. Cir. 1977).

You may combine *"e.g."* with other signals:

> *See, e.g., Barnes v. Costle,* 561 F.2d 983 (D.C. Cir. 1977).

As an alternative to *"e.g.,"* you may cite to multiple authorities without the *"e.g."* signal, or you may cite first to the most important authority and then introduce other supporting authorities with the signal "accord":

> *Barnes v. Costle,* 561 F.2d 983 (D.C. Cir. 1977); *accord Bundy v. Jackson,* 641 F.2d 934 (D.C. Cir. 1981).

d. *Cf.; Contrast*

You should use *"cf.,"* along with an explanatory parenthetical, to introduce an authority that supports the stated proposition by analogy or distinction:

> The "Proposal to Purchase Real Estate" probably is not an offer to buy a lot within the subdivision, because it does not clearly identify which lot

would be purchased. *Cf. Craft v. Elder and Johnston Co.,* 38 N.E.2d 416 (1941) (newspaper ad for indefinite quantity of sewing machines was only an invitation to negotiate); *Lefkowitz v. Great Minneapolis Surplus Store,* 251 Minn. 188, 86 N.W.2d 689 (1957) (newspaper ad was an offer because it was unusually specific and definite).

The first citation above supports the proposition by showing how analogous facts in a different context supported the same result as the one proposed. The second citation indirectly supports the proposition by explaining that a different result from the one proposed was justified by materially different facts. To distinguish between these two different kinds of support, you might preface the second citation with a novel signal such as *"contrast."*

e. *Contra; But*

You should introduce an authority that opposes your proposition with *"Contra"* or with *"But"* combined with another signal, such as *"But see"* or *"But cf.":*

The "Proposal to Purchase Real Estate" probably is not an offer to buy a lot within the subdivision, because it does not clearly identify which lot would be purchased. *Cf. Craft v. Elder and Johnston Co.,* 38 N.E.2d 416 (1941) (newspaper ad for indefinite quantity of sewing machines was only an invitation to negotiate). *But cf. Buntz v. Great New Maine Surplus Store,* 251 N. Me. 188 (1957) (newspaper ad may be an offer even though it leaves quantity and description of goods uncertain).

f. *Compare . . . with*

You can use *"Compare . . . with,"* along with explanatory parentheticals, to directly compare different legal approaches or, as shown below, different results justified by fact distinctions:

A newspaper ad is an offer only if it is sufficiently complete and definite that it leaves no important terms open for further negotiation. *Compare Craft v. Elder and Johnston Co.,* 38 N.E.2d 416 (1941) (newspaper ad for indefinite quantity of sewing machines was only an invitation to negotiate) *with Lefkowitz v. Great Minneapolis Surplus Store,* 251 Minn. 188, 86 N.W.2d 689 (1957) (newspaper ad was an offer because it was unusually specific and definite).

IV. REVIEW AND REVISION

To polish your writing, you must critically review and revise early drafts. The need for revision is particularly evident in first drafts dictated into a tape recorder. Moreover, you may need to revise successive drafts several times to produce the best possible final document.

To critically review and revise your own writing, you must approach writing analytically rather than purely intuitively: you must become sufficiently familiar with style problems that you can spot them in your own writing, even when the familiarity of your own prose tends to make you comfortable. You can best develop these editing skills by studying writing style in books such as this one, by reviewing and critiquing your own work and that of others, and by asking others to review and critique your writing.

Unfortunately, time pressures and limits on the client's resources will sometimes compel you to produce a final draft after only one or two opportunities for revision. The minimally acceptable level of review and revision is easily stated: at the very least, you must proofread your first draft and make necessary changes, particularly if you have dictated the draft. Every judge has a horror story about an atrociously written brief, one that obviously was dictated and never proofread. No limitation on time or resources justifies such shoddy work.

The appropriate level of review and revision beyond the minimum is a matter of priorities and economics. A client with ample resources and with a great deal at stake in an important pretrial motion or appeal may expect its legal counsel to spare no expense in writing the best possible brief. You and your colleagues undoubtedly would begin work on the brief as early as possible, subject it to particularly critical review, and polish it through three, four, or more drafts.

In all but unusual cases, however, you would waste your client's money by spending as much time polishing a preliminary office memorandum or a letter to the client. Such a document should be clear, complete, and concise, but limits on resources may preclude more than one or two rewritings. Moreover, even if you ordinarily avoid procrastination, you will occasionally be stuck with an emergency "rush job" that leaves you little time for revision.

Consequently, you should strive to produce the best possible written product on the first draft. You can do this by learning to avoid style problems common to your writing and by devoting appropriate attention to the prewriting stage.

Ironically, to develop the ability to avoid common style problems on the first draft, you must identify and analyze your writing habits by initially devoting extra time and attention to multiple drafts. Perhaps with the aid of a colleague or a writing manual, you will gradually become sufficiently conscious of your writing problems and their solutions that you can begin to avoid those problems on first or second drafts, reducing the need for substantial editing.

For example, one summer associate in a major law firm learned from a writing consultant that he tended to overuse the passive, abstract verb form "there is." He resolved to use his word processing program to highlight this and related phrases in his first drafts, to revise the highlighted passages on second drafts, and eventually to become sufficiently sensitive to the problem to avoid it on first drafts.

You can further minimize the need for redrafting, and thus save time in the long run, by carefully formulating and organizing your analysis before beginning to write. You should prepare an outline of your document and consider discussing the outline with your supervising attorney or a peer. Because most people are less articulate when speaking than when writing, a careful outline is particularly important if you intend to dictate your first draft. Once satisfied with the broad outlines of your analysis, you can devote greater attention to the details when you begin writing or dictating.

V. SUMMARY

Your two most important goals in legal writing style are clarity and conciseness. These two goals ordinarily are consistent and complementary. When they conflict, you should give priority to clarity. More specifically:

(1) To write clearly, you should

(a) use simple, plain English unless a legal term of art will inform more than distract;

(b) flexibly use effective sentence structure and punctuation, with adequate closure and guides to structure;

(c) use concrete verbs in the active voice, unless passive construction serves a specific purpose;

(d) distinguish between restrictive and nonrestrictive clauses when necessary for clarity; and

(e) select the word or phrase that precisely conveys your meaning.

(2) To write concisely, you should

(a) maintain reasonable limitations on scope and depth of analysis; and

(b) avoid verbosity by adopting efficient organization, sentence structure, and phrasing.

(3) To present authority effectively, you should

(a) subordinate citations, emphasize ideas, and express your syntheses in topic sentences or paragraphs;

(b) use quotations selectively, subordinate the citations to quotations, and introduce quotations with substantive overviews; and

(c) use effective citation form and citation signals.

(4) To polish your writing, you should

(a) revise early drafts; and

(b) create the best possible product on first draft.

Finally, you should avoid applying conventions of composition mechanically. Instead, adopt an approach to writing that is analogous to legal method: strive to understand the purposes and policies of conventions of composition, and apply those conventions flexibly to satisfy the purposes and policies.

ADVOCACY

11

Introduction to Advocacy

Written advocacy is a special branch of legal method and writing that combines creative analysis, persuasive writing, and attention to local rules, special formats, and ethical considerations. This chapter provides an overview of advocacy at all stages of litigation.

The remaining chapters in Part IV examine written advocacy in the context of four kinds of documents: (1) a complaint and an answer, (2) briefs on a motion for summary judgment, (3) briefs on a motion to exclude evidence, and (4) appellate briefs. Each of those chapters includes at least one full sample pleading or brief. By studying this chapter and the documents in the following chapters, you will develop a general grasp of the methods and purposes of brief writing, enabling you to prepare a brief for any stage of litigation.

On the other hand, if most of the documents in the following chapters are outside the scope of your course of study, you can simply combine this chapter with any of the others. For example, if you intend to draft only an appellate brief, you should study this chapter to gain a general overview of techniques of advocacy, and you can turn to Chapter 15 to master concepts and techniques that are peculiar to appellate advocacy. Even then, you may want to glance through one or more of the other chapters in Part IV to better appreciate the stages of litigation through which your dispute proceeded before reaching the appellate court.

I. OVERVIEW—GENERAL FORMAT AND PROCEDURE

A. PROCEDURE

In a typical dispute, you will advocate your client's case in various written documents through several stages of litigation. If correspondence fails to resolve the dispute in its early stages, the parties may commence formal litigation by filing pleadings, typically a complaint and an answer. Before trial, you might file or respond to "motions" that request the judge to take certain actions, such as to make advance rulings on the admissibility of evidence at trial or to dispose of some or all of the claims and defenses without a trial. During a trial with a jury, you may submit or respond to briefs that request the judge to instruct the jury on the law in a certain way or even to decide the case "as a matter of law" without the jury. At the outset of a "bench" trial to the judge without a jury, you may submit a trial brief that invites the judge to find certain facts and to apply your interpretation of the law to the facts to reach certain conclusions. Finally, if either party appeals the judgment of the trial court, you will draft one or more briefs to one or more appellate courts, inviting each appellate court to either affirm or reverse the judgment of the court immediately below it.

Throughout these proceedings, the pleadings, motions, and appeals will follow similar briefing schedules:

(1) The party seeking relief or seeking reversal of the judgment of a lower court files a complaint, petition, or opening brief.

(2) The opposing party responds with an answer, response, or answering brief.

(3) Finally, the party who filed the petition or opening brief generally has the opportunity to file a reply brief that addresses points raised in the opposing party's answering brief or response. Under federal pleading rules, the drafter of a complaint will file a reply to the answer only if the defendant has asserted a counterclaim in the answer, in which case the reply is mandatory.[1]

B. BASIC FORMATS

The format of a pleading differs significantly from that of a brief. Various pretrial, trial, and appellate briefs, however, have much in common. Each will include some statement of the background of the case, followed by an argument and a conclusion.

In some ways, an appellate brief may be more detailed and formal than a pretrial brief. By the time a case reaches an appellate court, the litigants have developed some record of the facts or factual allegations, and they have advanced the dispute through significant procedural steps. Accordingly, an appellate brief's description of the background of a case typically includes a formal statement of facts and a summary of the procedural history. On the other hand, when the parties litigate a pretrial motion, the facts may be sketchy and the procedural history brief. Consequently, many pretrial briefs may combine the procedural history and statement of relevant facts in a brief "Introduction," "Background," or "Statement of Facts." As explored in Chapter 13, briefs on a motion for summary judgment are exceptional in their unusually formal pretrial presentation of facts.

An appellate brief may be more formal than a pretrial brief in other ways

---

1. Fed. R. Civ. P. 7(a).

as well. For example, rules of procedure and local court rules typically require an appellate brief to include a table of contents, table of authorities, and formal statement of issues. These are customarily omitted from all but the most complex pretrial briefs.[2] Depending on the complexity of the case and the nature of the immediate ruling sought, a trial brief may be as relatively informal as most pretrial briefs, or it may include one or more of the formalities usually reserved for appellate briefs.

These differences, however, are relatively superficial in light of the universality of the heart of any brief: the argument. Unlike an office memorandum, your brief will not explore the strengths and weaknesses of both sides of the dispute. Instead, you will use the brief to advocate the legal and factual analysis that best supports the claims or defenses of your client.

This orientation is reflected not only in the subtler facets of writing style but also in fundamental elements of format such as section headings. In the discussion section of an office memorandum, a section heading may be a neutral phrase that generally describes a topic of discussion and helps your reader recall an issue stated more formally at the beginning of the memorandum. In contrast, you will use a "point heading" in the argument section of a brief to state the conclusion that you want the judge to adopt on each issue. In each point heading, you will assert a point in a complete sentence as a prelude to your full deductive argument on that issue.

Sections III and IV of this chapter will address these and other techniques of written and oral advocacy in greater depth. First, however, section II will introduce you to a few of the many ethical obligations that you assume as an advocate.

II. GOOD FAITH, REASONABLENESS, AND FULL DISCLOSURE

A. ASSERTION OF CLAIMS AND DEFENSES

As an attorney, you owe a duty to your client to advocate her case vigorously.[3] In carrying out this duty, you will often argue for creative extension of existing law or for replacement of existing law with new rules.[4] Fundamental principles of professional responsibility, however, impose limits on your advocacy.[5] For example, as amended in 1983, Federal Rule of Civil Procedure 11 requires every attorney to certify that written advocacy is not advanced frivolously, in bad faith, or for other improper purpose:

---

2. Cf. Cal. R. Ct. 313(d) (motions brief exceeding ten pages must include a table of contents and table of authorities).

3. E.g., Model Code of Professional Responsibility AC 7-4 (1981); id. at Canon 7.

4. See generally Chapter 2.

5. See, e.g., Model Rules of Professional Conduct Rule 3.3(a)(1) (1983) (proscribing knowingly false statements of material fact or law).

254 II Part IV. Advocacy

Every pleading, motion, and other paper of a party represented by an attorney shall be signed by at least one attorney of record in the attorney's individual name, whose address shall be stated. . . . The signature of an attorney or party constitutes a certificate by the signer that the signer has read the pleading, motion, or other paper; that to the best of the signer's knowledge, information, and belief formed after reasonable inquiry it is well grounded in fact and is warranted by existing law or a good faith argument for the extension, modification, or reversal of existing law; and that it is not interposed for any improper purpose, such as to harass or to cause unnecessary delay or needless increase in the cost of litigation.[6]

Rule 11 requires federal courts to impose sanctions for violation of the rule. Such a sanction may include an order directing the certifying attorney, the represented party, or both to pay attorney's fees and other reasonable expenses incurred by the opposing party as a result of violation of the rule.[7]

The 1983 amendments to Rule 11 strengthened its provisions in at least two ways. First, the amended text supplements the original good-faith standard with a more stringent objective standard that requires reasonable prefiling inquiry into the facts and law supporting a pleading, motion, or other paper.[8] Second, the amended text rejects and replaces the original discretionary sanctions of striking the pleadings and bringing disciplinary proceedings. Those sanctions did not effectively deter abuses: striking unfounded pleadings imposed no significant penalty for a frivolous filing, and the drastic measure of disciplinary proceedings was rarely invoked. The monetary sanctions in the amended text are more effective precisely because they are both mandatory and flexible.[9]

The new standards and sanctions have prompted most attorneys to take Rule 11 seriously. In high-stakes litigation, a member of a law firm's litigation team may prepare an office memorandum specifically addressing the question of whether a proposed claim or defense might violate the firm's obligations under Rule 11.

Rule 11 "is not intended to chill an attorney's enthusiasm or creativity in pursuing factual or legal theories."[10] Indeed, "[t]he creativity and tenacity of attorneys must be lauded rather than chilled."[11] Nonetheless, Rule 11 appropriately discourages claims or defenses that are intended solely to harass the opponents or that reflect irresponsibly lax investigation.

---

6. Fed. R. Civ. P. 11 (as amended 480 U.S. 962 (1987)).
7. Id.
8. Fed. R. Civ. P. 11 advisory committee note (West 1985); Albright v. The Upjohn Co., 788 F.2d 1217 (6th Cir. 1986) (ordering sanctions against plaintiff's counsel for inadequate prefiling investigation of facts supporting claim against defendant); Annot., 95 A.L.R. Fed. 107 (1989).
9. See advisory committee note, supra note 8; Note, The Dynamics of Rule 11: Preventing Frivolous Litigation by Demanding Professional Responsibility, 61 N.Y.U.L. Rev. 300, 312-314 (1986).
10. Advisory committee note, supra note 8.
11. Note, The Dynamics of Rule 11, supra note 9, at 323.

B. DISCLOSURE OF ADVERSE AUTHORITY

As an advocate, you have no duty to argue your opponent's case or even to present a balanced analysis such as would be appropriate in an office memorandum. Nonetheless, every advocate is also an officer of the court[12] and has a general duty of candor and fairness to the court and to other lawyers.[13] Within this framework, the American Bar Association Model Rules of Professional Conduct specifically require every advocate to disclose significant authority adverse to the advocate's arguments:

A lawyer shall not knowingly: . . .
(3) fail to disclose to the tribunal legal authority in the controlling jurisdiction known to the lawyer to be directly adverse to the position of the client and not disclosed by opposing counsel.[14]

The scope of this duty depends in large part on the interpretation of the phrase "directly adverse." An early draft of the Model Rules would have required disclosure of any authority "that would probably have a substantial effect on the determination of a material issue."[15] Particularly in the absence of more clearly controlling authority, the proposed standard arguably would require you to disclose even clearly distinguishable adverse authority that nonetheless offered important guidance to the court through analogy, dictum, or general reasoning.

In contrast, if interpreted narrowly, the phrase "directly adverse" in the current rule might require you to disclose only authority that is more squarely on point. Of course, if you need disclose only adverse authority that is so clearly controlling that it is virtually certain to defeat your client's claim or defense, then the Rule would seldom have any practical application. You presumably would not bring such a claim or defense unless you intended to argue directly for an overruling of the adverse decision, in which case a rule requiring disclosure of the adverse authority is obviously superfluous.

In any event, the most sensible approach to disclosure is one that maintains your credibility as an advocate. If adverse authority within the forum jurisdiction is sufficiently analogous that the court would consider it in deciding a case, the judge or the judge's law clerk likely will discover the authority sometime before the end of the proceedings, even if it has escaped the notice of the opposing counsel. You can minimize the impact of such adverse authority by acknowledging it early in the proceedings and distinguishing or discrediting it.[16] Such an approach may be more nearly consistent with the proposed "sub-

---

12. E.g., Ex parte Garland, 71 U.S. (4 Wall) 333, 378 (1886) (cited in ABA Formal Opinion 146 (1935)).

13. See Model Rules of Professional Conduct Rule 3.3 (1983) (candor to court); ABA Formal Opinion 146 (1935).

14. Model Rules, Rule 3.3(a)(3) (1983) (taken from Model Code of Professional Responsibility DR 7-106(B)(1) (1969)).

15. Model Rules, Rule 3.1(c) (Discussion Draft, Jan. 30, 1980). An early interpretation of the general duty of candor and fairness described a duty of disclosure similar in scope. ABA Formal Opinion 280 (1949).

16. C. Wolfram, Modern Legal Ethics § 12.8, at 682 (1986).

stantial effect" standard for the disclosure rule than with the presumably narrower "directly adverse" standard adopted for the current rule. If so, effective
and vigorous advocacy may call for a higher level of disclosure than that minimally required by formal ethical rules.

The reference to "controlling jurisdiction" in the disclosure rule appears
to flatly exclude authority from other than the forum jurisdiction, even if it is
squarely on point. In some circumstances, however, broader disclosure than
required by a specific ethical rule may again be necessary to maintain your
credibility with the court. For example, if the question before the court is so
novel that no authority within the forum jurisdiction addresses it, and if adverse
authority from another jurisdiction would be particularly persuasive, then the
court might expect disclosure of the nonbinding adverse authority.

If an adverse authority does not meet these standards, you need not address it unless the other party relies on it or the court raises a question that
encompasses it. In an opening brief, for example, you should not waste time
by distinguishing marginally analogous adverse case law or by criticizing poorly
reasoned persuasive authority on which the opposing counsel is unlikely to
rely. Instead, you should concentrate on affirmatively presenting your own
arguments and supporting authority, and you should attack only the most
obvious adverse authority. Then, you can wait to see what authority the opposing counsel relies on in the answering brief, and you can attack that adverse
authority in your reply brief. Of course, if the court asks you broadly about
adverse precedent, you "should make such frank disclosure as the question
seems to warrant,"[17] regardless of the scope of ethical duties or strategic considerations that might otherwise apply.

C. MISLEADING LEGAL ARGUMENT

The ABA Model Rules of Professional Conduct prohibit a lawyer from
knowingly making "a false statement of . . . law to a tribunal."[18] However, a
legal analysis will not amount to a false statement about the law unless it clearly
falls outside the range of plausible interpretations of the legal authorities.

For example, defining the holding of a judicial opinion and determining
its effect as precedent is an exercise in legal realism that produces disagreement
among able jurists. Thus, as an advocate, you often have room to take an
aggressive stance in identifying facts that appear to have been material to a
decision and in characterizing the holding and reasoning of the decision.

As with other ethical questions, practical considerations of effective advocacy may provide the best guide to responsible conduct. Published precedent
on which you rely is readily accessible to the opposing counsel and to the
court. Careless or fraudulent analyses that cross the line separating creative
advocacy from misrepresentation almost certainly will be brought to the court's
attention. Few things can damage your credibility and effectiveness as an advocate more than a reputation for stretching legal authority beyond the limits
of plausible interpretation.

---

17. ABA Formal Opinion 280 (1949).
18. Model Rules, Rule 3.3(a)(1) (1983); see also id. at comment.

III. THE ARGUMENT

Your statements of issues, facts, and procedural history will vary greatly in style and content depending on the stage of the litigation at which you draft a legal document. Consequently, this book separately examines those elements of a pleading or a brief in Chapters 12-15. Many techniques of argumentation, however, apply broadly to all kinds of briefs and are appropriately introduced in this overview chapter. Specifically, this chapter will examine methods of (1) organizing arguments, (2) introducing arguments, (3) developing the elements of a deductive argument, and (4) writing persuasively.

A. ORGANIZING LEGAL ARGUMENTS

As discussed in Chapter 8, you ordinarily should discuss or argue discrete issues in separate sections of your office memorandum or brief. Moreover, your section and subsection headings should show the proper relationships among your topics and subtopics.

Beyond this, when drafting the argument section of your brief, you must decide the order in which to present your arguments. If your brief includes a formal statement of the issues, the organization of that statement will mirror the organization of your arguments. To determine the most appropriate order of arguments, you may need to balance neutral analytical considerations against strategic considerations. Moreover, in a responsive brief, you must decide whether to adopt or depart from the organizational structure of the opposing counsel's preceding brief.

As discussed in Chapter 9, neutral analytical considerations will lead you to argue threshold issues first and then to argue the issues that are dependent on the outcome of the threshold issues. Strategic considerations, however, may lead you to place your strongest argument first, even if that organization requires you to depart from a purely logical ordering of arguments.

The strategic considerations are based on the varying levels of emphasis associated with different parts of the argument section of the brief. At the level of a sentence, an idea generally will receive greater emphasis if placed at the beginning than if placed in the middle, but the place of greatest emphasis in a sentence is the end. The same might be true of a short brief submitted to a judge who has plenty of time to study it. The first argument in such a brief would receive the emphasis associated with any initial encounter that makes a first impression. Ideas in the middle of the brief might capture slightly less attention, but they could help lay the foundation for a forceful climax. Presumably, the climatic argument would leave a lasting impression on the judge because it is the last argument that the judge would read.

Unfortunately, briefs are seldom brief, and judges almost never have enough time to read them. Indeed, a trial judge with a full pretrial motions calendar may have enough time only to skim through your motions brief before oral argument. Far from being the place of greatest emphasis, the end of your brief may not be read at all, or at least it may not be read with the same care that the judge devoted to the beginning of the brief.

Consequently, advocates usually begin their briefs with their strongest arguments. In fact, aware of this practice, judges have come to expect that the first argument in a brief is the strongest argument, and they accordingly may be tempted to prejudge an entire brief on the basis of the merits of the first argument. This phenomenon, of course, simply reinforces the belief among advocates that they should lead with their strongest arguments. Accordingly, if one of your arguments is much stronger than the others, you can exercise discretion to present it before the others even though another issue is logically prior.

When you write a responsive brief, the organization selected by the opposing counsel for the preceding brief is yet another factor in your own deliberations about organization. In a complex case, you can conveniently respond to each point in a preceding brief by simply adopting the preceding brief's organizational structure and methodically knocking down each of your opponent's arguments. On the other hand, if you can more persuasively argue your case with a different organizational structure, you should not hesitate to depart from the structure adopted by your opponent.

For example, suppose that Maya Tortilla Co. has sued Bakeway Supermarkets, alleging that Bakeway (1) formed a contract with Maya; (2) breached its obligations, at least under Maya's interpretation of the contract; (3) and is liable to Maya for $20,000 in damages. Maya has filed a pretrial motion requesting the trial court to grant it summary judgment, which is judgment as a matter of law without a full trial on the facts. Maya has supported its motion with a preliminary showing of facts and with a brief that argues each of the issues in the order presented above. Bakeway can escape summary judgment on any issue by creating a genuine dispute of material fact on that issue, a dispute that must be resolved in a full trial.

As counsel for Bakeway, you could logically begin the argument of your answering brief with Maya's issue #1 because contract formation is a threshold issue: Bakeway did not assume any contractual obligations and consequent potential liability if it did not form a contract with Maya. Moreover, the opening brief begins with issue #1, and you could simplify your task by simply adopting the organizational structure of the opening brief.

However, suppose that you can most easily establish a genuine issue of fact on issue #2 because admissible evidence of contract negotiations creates a triable issue of fact about the meaning of the contract provision that states Bakeway's obligations. In those circumstances, you could reasonably begin your argument with issue #2, even though that organization departs from a purely logical ordering and from the structure of the opening brief. If you persuade the judge in your first argument that she should deny summary judgment on issue #2, she may then be more strongly disposed to order a trial on the other issues as well.

B. INTRODUCING LEGAL ARGUMENTS

1. Point Headings

In the argument section of your brief, you ordinarily will follow the pattern of deductive reasoning introduced in Chapter 3: for each issue or subissue, you will discuss the law and apply the law to the facts to reach a conclusion. Before you begin your full argument, however, you should introduce it in a "point heading." In each section or subsection that addresses a discrete issue, your argumentative point heading previews the conclusion.

Each point heading should be tailored to the facts of your case, much like the statement of an issue or a full statement of the holding of a decision in a student case brief. Indeed, you may view your point headings as statements of the holdings in your case that you want the court to adopt:

II. ARGUMENT

A. The UCC Requires the Alleged Agreement to Be in Writing, Because the Alleged Subject Matter Was Priced at More than $500.

• • •

B. The Undisputed Facts Show that Scott Paper Supply Did Not Adopt Sun Printing Co.'s Written Confirmation of the Alleged Agreement.

The advantages of point headings are obvious in multiple-issue briefs, in which you must divide the argument into sections and subsections. Even in a single-issue brief, however, you should begin your argument with a point heading. It will simply stand alone without any number or letter denoting division of the argument into sections:

II. ARGUMENT

The UCC Requires the Alleged Agreement to be in Writing, Because the Alleged Subject Matter Was Priced at More than $500.

Thus, your full argument should include four major elements, the first conveyed by the point heading: Conclusion, Rule, Application of the legal rule to facts, and Conclusion. The acronym "CRAC" may help you remember these elements. In contrast, "IRAC," introduced in Chapter 3, represents the elements of the more nearly neutral analysis of an office memorandum, the first represented in the section heading: Issue, Rule, Application of the legal rule to facts, and Conclusion. Thus, a section heading in an office memorandum can neutrally and cryptically refer to the issue addressed in that section. In contrast, the point heading of a brief advocates a position by asserting a point and inviting the judge to reach a particular conclusion. It thus sets the tone for the full argument.

2. *Introductory Paragraphs*

Immediately after the point heading, and before discussing the legal authority, you may want to use an introductory sentence or paragraph to illuminate the issue and to expand on the point heading:

> A. *The UCC Requires the Alleged Agreement to Be in Writing,*
> *Because the Alleged Subject Matter Was Priced at More than*
> *$500.*
>
> Scott Paper Supply alleges that Sun Printing Co. breached a contract
> to purchase a shipment of bond paper priced at $1,200. Sun Printing Co.
> denies that it ever agreed to such a purchase. This is precisely the kind of
> groundless contract claim that statutes of frauds are designed to bar.
> The Uniform Commercial Code statute of frauds generally bars . . .

Such an introductory paragraph can be particularly helpful in a responsive
brief. Rather than abstractly address the issues, an answering or reply brief
should respond directly to each of the preceding brief's arguments. In a responsive brief, the introductory paragraph following a point heading can set
up your full response by (1) summarizing the opposing party's argument and
(2) explaining generally why the opposing argument lacks merit:

> A. *Scott Paper Supply's Timely Confirmation of the Agreement*
> *Satisfied the UCC Statute of Frauds, Because Sun Printing Co.*
> *Failed to Object to It.*
>
> Scott Paper Supply argues that the Uniform Commercial Code statute
> of frauds bars enforcement of the purchase agreement because the agreement
> is not memorialized in a written document signed or expressly adopted by
> Scott. Scott's argument is meritless because the confirmation signed by Sun
> Printing Co. satisfied the requirements of the statute and because the UCC
> deems Scott to have implicitly adopted that confirmation by failing to object
> to it.
> The UCC provides that . . .

This technique is consistent with the techniques of organizing an argument in a responsive brief: first, affirmatively present your own arguments and
supporting authority, and only then discredit or distinguish the authority or
interpretation on which your opponent has relied. The introductory paragraph
in the preceding example does no more than emphasize and expand on the
point heading by briefly placing it in context. It still permits you to exercise
discretion to delay until the end of the section your full attack on the specific
authority relied on by the opposing party.

C. DEVELOPING THE DEDUCTIVE ARGUMENT

1. Arguing the Law

Chapters 3, 9, and 10 have provided you with the legal method and the
techniques of organization and writing with which you can construct an argument about the content of applicable law on a particular issue or subissue.
An outline of these principles will illustrate the range of considerations that
may enter into your strategic decisions when arguing the law within the argument portion of your brief.

a. Hierarchy of Authority

First, you must be sensitive to the hierarchy of authority. For example, suppose that (1) your client is not liable under common law standards for actions that he took as an employer, but (2) a federal statute will impose liability if it applies to your client's business. If applicable, the statutory law will supersede the common law. Therefore you must analyze the statute and argue either that it is unconstitutional or that it does not apply to your case. This statutory analysis might include arguments concerning the statutory language, the legislative history, the policy underlying the statute, or the limitations imposed by constitutional provisions.

b. Strength of Case Law as Precedent

Second, in analyzing case law, regardless of whether it interprets a statute or applies common law, you must appreciate the relative strength of different kinds of authorities. Case law from a higher court within the forum jurisdiction is potentially a source of binding law, and you must argue for a broader or narrower interpretation of its holding, depending on whether it supports or undermines your position. For example, in the following passage, the counsel for Beatty, a lender, encourages an expansive interpretation of favorable precedent and encourages narrower application of adverse precedent:

Weeks argues that Beatty's promise is illusory and therefore does not satisfy the consideration requirement. However, her position is inconsistent with Calzona Supreme Court authority. Applying the principles established in that authority, Beatty's promise is not illusory, and Week's promise is enforceable.	**Introduction to argument**
Even if a promise leaves open the possibility that the promisor will escape obligation, the promise is not illusory if the promisor does not have complete control over the events on which the promisor's obligation is conditioned. *See Bonnie v. DeLaney,* 158 Calz. 212, 645 P.2d 887 (1982). In *Bonnie,* an agreement for the sale of a house provided that the buyer could cancel the agreement if the buyer "cannot qualify for a 30-year mortgage loan for 90% of the sales price" with any of several banks listed in the agreement. *Id.* at 213, 645 P.2d at 888. In enforcing the agreement against the seller, the court emphasized that the word "cannot" referred to the buyer's ability to obtain a loan rather than to his desire. Because his ability to obtain a loan was partly controlled by events and decisions outside his control, the promises in the sale agreement were nonillusory and binding. *Id.* at 214-15, 645 P.2d at 889-91.	**In-depth analysis of favorable case law**

In-depth analysis of adverse case law

The *Bonnie* court distinguished its earlier decision, *Atco Corp. v. Johnson*, 155 Calz. 1211, 627 P.2d 781 (1980). In *Atco Corp.*, the manager of an automobile repair shop promised to forbear "until I want the money" from asserting a claim against the owner of an automobile for $900 in repairs. In exchange, a friend of the owner promised to act as guarantor of the owner's obligation. *Id.* at 1212, 627 P.2d at 782. The word "want" stated no legally recognizable commitment because it permitted the manager at his own discretion to refuse to perform any forbearance at all. Because the manager did not incur even a conditional obligation, the guarantor's promise was gratuitous and unenforceable. *Id.* at 1213-14, 627 P.2d at 782-84.

Synthesis that emphasizes favorable case law

Together, these cases show that any limitation on the promisor's freedom will validate his promise. A promise is illusory only if it leaves the promisor complete control over his actions.

In this example, counsel for the Beatty has synthesized the case law by applying a form of inductive reasoning in which he generalized from particular cases. The final paragraph represents this advocate's characterization of the legal rule. As illustrated on pages 109 and 158, the argument can now proceed with a fact analysis that either (1) directly applies this legal rule to the facts, or (2) employs another form of inductive reasoning to analogize the favorable precedent to Beatty's case and to distinguish the adverse precedent.

On the other hand, if the authority is from a lower court or from a court in another jurisdiction, it will have only persuasive influence. Even if you cannot distinguish persuasive adverse authority from the facts of your case, you can try to discredit its reasoning as unworthy of adoption as the rule of law in the forum jurisdiction. Conversely, if persuasive authority supports your position, you should argue that its reasoning is sound and is consistent with the policy of the forum jurisdiction.

For example, in the following passage, an advocate attempts to persuade a court in the imaginary state of New Maine to adopt the reasoning of California case law and to reject precedent from Washington and Florida:

Complimentary in-depth analysis of favorable case law

The Federal Gun Control Act (FGCA) preempts more stringent state gun control legislation. *California v. Biggs*, 123 Cal. 321, 567 P.2d 765 (1987). In *Biggs*, state officials sought to confiscate a private collection of automatic pistols under the authority of a California statute that bans private ownership of all automatic guns. The California Supreme Court found that the FCGA's registration requirements for most varieties of automatic guns implicitly authorizes private, registered ownership of such guns. It therefore held that the FCGA barred the state from prohibiting such ownership.

In reaching its decision, the California Supreme
Court exhaustively analyzed the legislative history of
the FCGA. It noted that . . .

Two courts had previously rejected the preemption argument adopted in *Biggs*, but each of them
overlooked the critical legislative history so carefully
analyzed in *Biggs*. *See Arzani v. Matlock*, 332 So. 2d
234 (Fla. 1986); *Washington v. Smedley*, 382 Wash.
283, 558 P.2d 777 (1986). For example, in *Arzani*,
the Court summarily held that . . .

> **Critical analysis
> of adverse case
> law**

The advocate obviously hopes that the preceding passage will persuade
the court to adopt the reasoning of *Biggs*. In the fact analysis, the advocate can
argue further that *Biggs* is analogous to the facts of her case and that the rule
of law it represents thus applies to those facts.

c. Depth of Analysis

Third, in presenting legal authority, you should exercise firm control over
depth of analysis. You may use
(1) "light analysis" to present fundamental and undisputed propositions
with direct statements of law and citation to authority,
(2) in-depth analysis of statutes or case law to explore policy and reasoning, and
(3) direct statements of law and citation to authority with explanatory
parentheticals for an intermediate level of analysis.

d. Presentation of Authority

Finally, you must lead your reader through your argument on a particular
issue or subissue. Three techniques explored in Chapter 10 are particularly
important: you should
(1) express your syntheses of authorities or other thesis statements in topic
sentences or paragraphs;
(2) unless the citations are independently significant, focus attention on
your ideas and relegate citations to subordinate citation sentences; and
(3) introduce quotations with substantive overviews that invite the judge
to adopt your interpretation of the quoted material.

2. Analyzing the Facts

As discussed in greater detail in Chapter 15 in the context of appellate
briefs, the opening statement of facts in a brief is most effective if it does not
prematurely argue the law or the application of the law to the facts. In contrast,
when you analyze the relevant facts in the argument section of a brief, you
should explicitly reach a conclusion by relating the facts to the previously dis-

cussed legal standards. You may accomplish this by (1) directly applying the law to the facts or (2) using a form of inductive reasoning to analogize or distinguish precedent by comparing the facts and reasoning of the precedent to your own case.

To illustrate the first technique, suppose that you have established in your discussion of the law that a state police officer can be liable for punitive damages for recklessly depriving a citizen of her right to be free from arrest without probable cause. In the fact analysis of your argument, you could directly apply that rule of law to the facts. In the following sample passage, the notations within brackets refer to pages of the trial court reporter's transcript on which critical testimony of witnesses is found.

> Substantial evidence in the record supports the jury's finding that Officer Mullins acted with at least reckless disregard for Wong's clearly established fourth amendment rights. Mullins's actions show that even he did not believe that Wong fit the dispatcher's description of the robbery suspect. According to his own testimony, when he initially spotted Wong moments after receiving the robbery report, he passed her by and continued looking for the suspect. [RT 324]. Only after failing to find a suspect who fit the dispatcher's description did he relocate Wong and summarily arrest her. [RT 326]. An experienced officer such as Mullins obviously knew that he didn't have probable cause to arrest Wong.
>
> The jury could infer from these facts that Officer Mullins felt compelled to arrest somebody for the robbery and that he recklessly gambled that Wong might have been involved simply because of her proximity to the robbery. This is precisely the kind of reckless disregard for constitutional rights that an award of punitive damages is designed to deter. . . .

Alternatively, your discussion of the law may include in-depth case analysis and synthesis of arguably controlling, analogous, or distinguishable authority. If so, you may want to use the second technique to compare those cases directly to your dispute in your fact analysis:

Analogizing favorable case law on the facts

> *Bonnie* is closely analogous to our case and thus supports the conclusion that Beatty's promise was not illusory. In both *Bonnie* and our case, the promised performance was conditioned on events not entirely within the control of the promisor. In *Bonnie,* the buyer could escape his obligations only if market conditions rendered him *unable* to obtain a satisfactory mortgage loan. Similarly, in our case, Beatty could terminate his obligation to refrain from collecting on the debt only if economic conditions affected his income and expenses so as to create a *need* for the money.

Distinguishing adverse case law on the facts

> Conversely, *Atco Corp.* is distinguishable from our case. The promisor in that case retained the freedom to escape all contractual obligations if, at his own discretion, he *wanted* to. In contrast, the Guarantee

Agreement in this case did not permit Beatty to demand his money whenever he *wanted* it. Instead, . . .

3. Conclusions

Immediately after your fact analysis in each argument of your brief, you should briefly repeat the conclusion that you previewed in the point heading for that section or subsection:

Scott Paper Supply timely objected to Sun Printing Co.'s written confirmation of the alleged agreement. Therefore, the confirmation does not satisfy the requirements of the statute of frauds.

Additionally, every brief should end with a formal conclusion section. Many attorneys squander this opportunity to summarize their analyses. The following boilerplate is typical:

CONCLUSION

For the foregoing reasons, appellant respectfully requests this court to reverse the judgment of the Superior Court.

Although this style is conventional, a more substantive conclusion ordinarily is more satisfying, particularly if the brief presents more than one argument.

A substantive conclusion need not take up much space. If your arguments are simple, your conclusion need only briefly and generally repeat the request for relief and the supporting grounds, as in this closing to a brief in support of a motion to exclude evidence before trial:

III. CONCLUSION

Under Rule 403, Powell is entitled to pretrial exclusion of all evidence of his membership in the Black Panther's organization. The prejudicial effect of the evidence substantially outweighs its probative value, and the prejudice can be avoided only through exclusion of the evidence before trial.

In a more complex case, the conclusion might briefly summarize multiple arguments:

III. CONCLUSION

Yazzi's statement to the police officer is inadmissible on three grounds. First, it is not relevant to any issue in this suit. Even if it were relevant, it would be excludable because its prejudicial value substantially outweighs its probative value. Finally, it is inadmissible hearsay not falling within the exception for statements for purposes of medical treatment. This evidence should be excluded before trial to avoid exposing it to the jury and causing irremediable prejudice.

D. PERSUASIVE WRITING STYLE

Supervising attorneys often complain that law students or recent graduates from law school do not use sufficiently strong language to write persuasively. Admittedly, advocacy calls for a different writing style from the more nearly neutral style appropriate for an office memorandum. Unfortunately, many supervising attorneys equate persuasive writing style with hyperbole, and they advise their writers to pepper every sentence of a brief with exaggerated modifiers. Such a style may grab a judge's attention, but it does not often persuade. Judges recognize overstatement and tend to take everything in such a brief with an extra pinch of salt. Even worse, a writing style that is too obvious in its advocacy tends to divert the judge's attention from the substance of the argument and to focus it on the style itself.

The most persuasive writing style may be one that the judge never notices, one that keeps her attention riveted on the substance of the arguments and that presents those arguments so clearly as to give her the impression that the brief merely confirms her own independent conclusions. The most important element of such writing is good substantive analysis; a few extra hours of research and reflection may lead to an argument that is easily written in a persuasive manner. Beyond that, persuasive legal writing is distinguished by (1) strong, but not exaggerated, language and (2) effective emphasis through sentence structure, specificity, and concreteness.

1. Persuasive Language

a. The Adversarial Approach

To clearly communicate your legal analysis to a supervising attorney in an office memorandum, you must candidly reveal uncertainties in the law and weaknesses in your client's case. In contrast, a brief in the same litigation generally should not explore the weaknesses of a client's case except as necessary to satisfy ethical duties or maintain credibility. The adversary system ensures that opposing counsel will test your arguments.

Thus, in an office memorandum, you might candidly admit the weakness of the support for a client's argument, as with the following fictitious analysis of a client's preemption argument:

> Only one state court has held that the Federal Gun Control Act preempts more stringent state gun control legislation. *See California v. Biggs,* 123 Cal. 321, 567 P.2d 765 (1987). Two other courts have interpreted the act to permit, or even encourage, more stringent state controls that are consistent with its policy. *See Arzani v. Matlock,* 332 So. 2d 234 (Fla. 1986); *Washington v. Smedley,* 382 Ariz. 283, 558 P.2d 777 (1986). To support our argument that the federal act preempts the New Maine gun registration legislation, we should emphasize the thorough reasoning of *Biggs* and try to discredit or distinguish *Arzani* and *Smedley.*
>
> In *Biggs,* . . .

In a brief to the court in the same case, you must state your client's argument more positively. Although you should acknowledge and attempt to distinguish or discredit the contrary authority, you can do so in a way that de-emphasizes its significance:

> The Federal Gun Control Act preempts more stringent state gun control legislation. *California v. Biggs,* 123 Cal. 321, 567 P.2d 765 (1987). In *Biggs,* state officials sought to confiscate . . .
>
> Two courts had previously rejected the preemption argument adopted in *Biggs,* but each of them overlooked the critical legislative history so carefully analyzed in *Biggs. See Arzani v. Matlock,* . . . ; *Washington v. Smedley.* . . . For example, in *Arzani,* . . .

The proposition for which *Biggs* is cited in the second example illustrates the power of the simple, unqualified statement. You should avoid unnecessary qualifiers that weaken arguments, such as the following introduction to the argument of your client, Mason:

> Mason contends that the Federal Gun Control Act preempts more stringent state gun control legislation.

Because the argument section of your brief obviously comprises a series of legal contentions, specific introductions to that effect are superfluous. You may set up a response to your opponent's propositions by referring to them as "arguments" or "contentions," but such a characterization of your own conclusions or statements of law tends to weaken them.

b. Cliches That Weaken or Offend

Ironically, modifiers that are designed to reinforce a proposition sometimes sap the strength from an otherwise powerful statement. For example, comments such as "It is abundantly clear that" have become such clichés that they have little effect on the judge except to make him wonder whether the words were added to shore up a shaky proposition that in fact is subject to great debate. Along with other forms of exaggeration, clichés such as these tend to make the advocacy in the writing too obvious and distracting. Most judges will accept your conclusions more readily if you offer them persuasive arguments than if you slap them with stock phrases that describe your arguments as persuasive.

The line between strong advocacy and overstatement is most delicate when referring directly to a matter within the court's discretionary power. For example, the word "should" in the following argument reflects lack of confidence in the argument:

> This court should exclude evidence of Jenkins' subjective intentions regarding the lease.

On the other hand, a stronger verb suggests a presumptuous challenge to the power of the court:

‖ This court must exclude evidence of Jenkins' subjective intentions regarding the lease.

On reading such an argument, the judge might be subconsciously inclined to demonstrate that she does indeed have the discretionary power to admit the evidence, the exercise of which would not likely be overturned on appeal. Restating the proposition in passive voice tends to soften and depersonalize the challenge:

‖ Evidence of Jenkins' subjective intentions regarding the lease must be excluded.

Nonetheless, the challenge to the judge's power remains implicit in this construction. Perhaps the best statement is one that focuses directly on the character of the evidence rather than on the power of the judge:

‖ Evidence of Jenkins' subjective intentions regarding the lease is inadmissible.

This proposition is strong and unqualified, yet it avoids expressing or directly implying a personal challenge to the judge.

c. Personal Attacks

Equally important to avoid are personal attacks on opposing counsel. Although you may become exasperated with apparently unreasonable or offensive conduct by your opponent, judges generally do not appreciate being caught in a crossfire of personal insults. Unless misconduct by a party or his attorney are properly the subject of a motion, judges are far more interested in your response to the opposing counsel's arguments than in your personal opinion of his intelligence, research skills, or personality. Thus, you may safely characterize the opposing counsel's argument as frivolous or internally inconsistent, but you should not comment that he is unable to write a coherent brief. If the opposing counsel's brief is poorly written or analyzed, it will speak for itself. Similarly, if your statement of facts or procedural history unemotionally records events that reflect the opposing counsel's intransigence or bad faith, the judge will undoubtedly draw negative conclusions about him without any further comment from you.

2. Sentence Structure

To preserve your credibility and to avoid ethical violations, you often must candidly acknowledge law that is adverse to your client's case and that you can neither discredit nor distinguish. You can minimize the resulting damage by using techniques of persuasive writing style to deemphasize the adverse law and to focus attention on more helpful points.

One such technique consists of placing helpful information in the main clause and relegating adverse information to a dependent subordinate clause, a clause that cannot stand by itself as a complete sentence. For example, as counsel for the plaintiff in a contract action, you can deemphasize the general rule against damages for emotional distress by disposing of it in an opening subordinate clause:

Although damages for emotional distress are not often awarded for breach of contract, Jones is entitled to such an award in this exceptional case because the central purpose of his contract with Runyon Pet Cemetery was to alleviate his grief over the loss of his dog.

You maintain credibility with this passage by facing, rather than evading, the general rule. Moreover, by placing the general rule in a subordinate clause, you invite the reader to give it only brief pause, as you might invite a guest at a restaurant to dine lightly on appetizers in anticipation of the main course.

Location of information within a sentence also affects emphasis. Generally, the end of a sentence conveys the greatest emphasis, the beginning of a sentence conveys secondary emphasis, and a parenthetical phrase or clause at a natural breaking point in the middle of the sentence conveys the least emphasis. For example, if you represent the defendant in the example above, you can emphasize the general rule by placing it at the end of the sentence:

On the strength of his assertion that the contract was intended to alleviate his grief over the loss of a dog, Jones demands an award of damages for emotional distress, despite the general rule that such damages are not awarded for breach of contract.

In this example, as in the first, the general rule is stated in a subordinate clause. Nonetheless, the order of clauses within the sentence emphasizes the general rule.

Generally, you will emphasize the general rule least by placing it in a parenthetical clause at a natural breaking point in the middle of the sentence:

Jones is entitled to an award of damages for emotional distress in this exceptional case, even though such awards are rare in contract actions, because the central purpose of his contract with Runyon Pet Cemetery was to alleviate his grief over the loss of his dog.

This passage may be the best of the three for the plaintiff because it places favorable information in the positions of greatest emphasis.

Of course, if you are willing to sacrifice other style objectives, you can create unusual emphasis in the middle of the sentence with an abrupt, dramatic, or unnatural interruption of the sentence:

Jones demands—and he admits that such awards are rare in contract actions—an award of damages for emotional distress.

IV. ORAL ARGUMENT TO THE COURT

In most appeals and in many pretrial and trial motions, you will argue your client's case orally to the court after submitting your written brief. Generally, your written brief will influence a judge more strongly than will your oral argument. Indeed, before oral argument, most judges read both parties' briefs and come to a tentative decision on the merits.

Nonetheless, oral argument is not yet a meaningless formality in our courts. It provides you with a final opportunity to emphasize critical points, respond to judges' questions, and perhaps change the mind of a judge who had tentatively decided to rule in favor of the opposing party.

A. GENERAL FORMAT

The typical oral argument follows a pattern similar to that of a briefing schedule: the advocate seeking relief or reversal of a judgment in a lower court argues first, the opposing advocate responds, and the first advocate has an opportunity for rebuttal. In some courts, the advocate arguing first must tell the court before she begins her argument whether she wishes to divide her time between opening argument and rebuttal.

Rebuttal is a powerful weapon. It provides the advocate who opens the oral argument with an opportunity to respond directly to the oral argument of the opponent. It also permits the advocate with the opening argument to have both the first and last word on the issues. Therefore, if you give the opening oral argument, you should always reserve a few minutes for rebuttal.

B. FORMALITY AND DEMEANOR

Appropriate courtroom attire is mandatory for any oral argument. Beyond that, the level of formality of the proceedings will vary among courts.

For pretrial and trial motions, some state trial court judges hold oral arguments in their chambers rather than in the courtroom. After friendly, informal introductions, all are seated. As the judge listens from behind his desk, you and the opposing counsel will deliver your arguments while seated in office chairs.

Other trial judges and virtually all appellate panels of judges, however, conduct oral arguments with greater formality. In those courts, you deliver your oral argument from a lectern in the courtroom.

If you are uncertain about the customs in a court or the expectations of a particular judge, you should not hesitate to seek advice from the staff of the clerk's office or from the judge's personal law clerk. To consult with them, you can use the telephone or simply arrive early on the day of the argument.

Your demeanor in oral argument should be as formal as your attire. You should be confident and relaxed but respectful of the judge. If you disagree with a judge during the argument, you need not make him defensive by being disagreeable. For example, if he asks you whether your formulation of a legal rule will have certain adverse policy ramifications, you should answer the question confidently but without arrogantly suggesting that the question is silly.

Thus, you should not respond to a judge's question or assertion with a challenge to his analytical skills, such as the following:

No, your Honor, that is incorrect. ‖

Instead, you should answer the question without casting doubt on the questioner:

Your Honor, the court should be able to avoid those potential problems of ‖ line-drawing by stating its holding in this appeal narrowly. I suggest the ‖ following formulation: . . . ‖

In some cases, you may even want to validate the question before answering it:

That question has occupied the attention of a number of courts and scholars, ‖ Your Honor. To answer it, I must review the rationale for the exclusionary ‖ rule. ‖

C. CONTENT OF THE ARGUMENT

1. *Introduction of the Argument*

In a formal courtroom argument, you should begin your presentation by introducing yourself and your representative capacity:

Good morning, Your Honors. I am Terry Malloy. I represent Bakeway ‖ Stores, the appellant on this appeal and the defendant in the trial court. ‖

Many advocates still begin their arguments with the traditional phrase

May it please the court, I am . . . ‖

Unless this language suits your personal style or that of the judges you are addressing, you can safely replace it with something more natural, like "Good morning . . ." or "Good afternoon . . .".

After the personal introduction, you can capture the judges' attention with a brief characterization of the motion or appeal. If the facts are compelling, you can describe the general nature of the case in a sentence or two. For example, suppose that a state is prosecuting prison inmates for possessing weapons materials in prison in violation of prison regulations and the state criminal code. The attorney for the defendant inmates has filed a motion to exclude from trial evidence obtained in an allegedly illegal search. He might introduce his oral argument at the suppression hearing with the following characterization of the case:

> Your Honor, the evidence in question is the product of a series of intrusive, physically brutal, and medically unsound body cavity searches of nearly a dozen unconsenting inmates, some of whom sustained permanent injuries as a result.

Alternatively, you can introduce your advocacy strongly by stating the issue in a way that invites a favorable response. In the criminal prosecution of the prison inmates, the prosecutor might begin her oral argument with the following:

> Your Honor, this motion presents the question of whether prison officials may constitutionally conduct emergency searches to maintain prison security against the threat of a planned, armed insurrection by inmates.

2. Body of the Argument

a. General Strategy

Many courts impose a time limit on each oral argument. Although the limits in some courts of last resort may be as long as 60 minutes for each side, 20 or 30 minutes is more typical. In most motions or appeals, you will not have time in 20 or 30 minutes to address every issue in the depth that the parties have examined in the briefs. Consequently, you should carefully study the arguments presented in both parties' briefs to determine the most effective strategy for oral argument.

Your strategy will differ depending on the circumstances of each case. In one appeal, for example, you may rely on multiple arguments that are both complex and interdependent. You may fear that, even with a well-organized brief to guide them, the judges may not fully appreciate how the arguments fit together to form the larger picture. You may thus decide to present an oral outline of all the arguments and their relationships, leaving the detail of each to your brief. More commonly, you can identify an argument in your brief that you wish to emphasize, perhaps because it addresses a critically important threshold issue, because it is your strongest theory, or even because it is the weakest link in your argumentative chain and needs extra support.

Whatever strategy you decide on, you should communicate your intentions immediately after the introduction to your argument. For example, at a hearing to suppress evidence obtained in an allegedly illegal search, the prosecutor may try to justify the search on several grounds. Although she will introduce evidence at the hearing supporting each of the grounds and will advocate each ground in her brief, she might use her oral argument to focus on the determinative issue of consent to search. If so, she should reveal her plans to the court:

> This hearing presents three major issues, all of which the briefs examine in detail. I will be happy to answer questions on any of the issues. However, I would like to focus my presentation on the issue of consent to search. If

the facts show that the inmates consented to the searches, this court need ‖ not address the more difficult questions related to expectations of privacy in ‖ prison and reasonableness of the search methods. ‖

b. Use of Facts

Many judges will advise oral advocates before argument that the judges are familiar with the facts of the case and that the advocates should proceed with their legal analyses. Even absent such an instruction, you ordinarily should not begin your argument with a recitation of the facts beyond a general characterization of the nature of the case. You might depart from this advice if the facts are particularly compelling and your legal arguments are not. In most cases, however, you will make better use of your limited time by arguing the law and applying the law to the facts without a separate introductory recitation of facts.

Whenever you rely on facts in an oral argument, be certain of the source of the facts. Be prepared to cite to the portion of the record that establishes the facts.

c. Responding to Questions

Questions from the bench constitute the most uncertain variable in oral argument. They ensure that oral advocacy in most cases is not a series of speeches but a dialogue, primarily between each advocate and the judges, and secondarily between the advocates as they respond to one another.

You should genuinely welcome the opportunity to respond to questions. A judge's questions may reveal areas in which she has confusion or doubts, permitting you to directly influence her thinking on those points.

Occasionally, a judge will press you for a concession on your weakest among several alternative arguments. Your waiving the argument might be the most effective way to turn the judge's attention to your stronger arguments. However, you should be reluctant to waive a point that you had earlier determined was sufficiently meritorious to warrant discussion in your brief. If you are arguing before a panel of judges, the other panel members may not share the doubts of the questioning judge; yet, if you waive the controversial point during oral argument, none of the judges will take up your cause on that theory. Thus, when pressed for a concession on an argument, you should first try to shift to a more productive topic of discussion without making the concession:

Your Honor, I prefer not to waive our argument that the prison offi- ‖ cials lacked probable cause to search, but I admit that our other arguments ‖ are stronger. Both in the trial court and on appeal, the defendant inmates ‖ have most strongly complained of the unreasonable method of the searches. ‖ On this issue the law is clear: . . .

Except when trying to avoid a waiver of an argument, you should not give the appearance of evading questions from the bench. Confront and answer the questions directly. To answer judges' questions effectively, you must come to the argument thoroughly prepared. In particular, you should be ready to

(1) discuss the facts, holding, and reasoning of any case that you seek to rely on or to distinguish;

(2) cite to the record to identify the source of facts on which you rely; and

(3) discuss the policy implications of alternative holdings among which the court must choose.

An excellent method of preparing for the oral argument is to hold practice sessions with colleagues acting as judges. Your colleagues can give you constructive criticism on your performance. Moreover, the questions they ask during the practice rounds will help you anticipate the questions likely to be asked by the judges in the actual oral argument.

Even with excellent preparation, you may not always anticipate every question that a judge may ask you. If you cannot formulate a satisfactory answer to a question, do not be afraid to say that you are unprepared to respond.

Because you cannot always predict the number of questions from the bench, you must build maximum flexibility into your argument. You should be prepared to do either of the following or anything in between:

(1) present your arguments uninterrupted until your time elapses or you otherwise finish your argument; or

(2) present a brief introduction, respond without break to a series of questions that takes up all your allotted time, and request that the court permit you to end with a prepared conclusion no longer than a few sentences.

3. The Conclusion

You should end your argument on a strong note, perhaps with a summary of your strongest points. A carefully planned conclusion will be particularly helpful if persistent questioning from the bench prevents you from covering all the points that you had planned to address in your oral argument. Faced with the impending expiration of your allotted time, you can fall back on the conclusion as a quick means of stating your points, if only in summary fashion.

D. NERVOUSNESS AND VERBAL STUMBLING

All but the most experienced oral advocates experience some anxiety at the prospect of facing an inquisitive panel of judges in a public setting. If you feel such anxiety, you may be concerned that your nervousness will interfere with your speech patterns, causing your voice to shake or causing you to stumble over your words or to pause to collect your thoughts. You need not worry excessively about such problems. First, as long as the judge can understand you, the substance of your arguments and of your responses to questions will be more important than your charisma and stage presence. Second, you can take some simple measures to control your nervousness.

Some law school moot court programs may exhalt form over substance: you may earn points if you can glibly respond to a judge's questions without pause, or lose points if you occasionally stumble over a difficult word. In actual oral arguments, however, judges will be more concerned with establishing a genuine dialogue with you. They will not be uncomfortable with a few moments of silence from you; indeed, most will expect you to pause to think deeply before answering a particularly difficult question. Moreover, if you speak sufficiently slowly, clearly, and loudly to make yourself understood, most judges will forgive you for the occasional verbal stumbling that nervousness may produce.

For example, a few months after the 1989 massacre of Chinese demonstrators near Tiananmen Square in Beijing, China, President Bush responded to a question in a news conference about the resulting tensions between the Chinese and American governments. President Bush rejected the Chinese government's suggestion that the United States should take the next step toward improving relations:

> The Chinese have a slogan: "He who ties the knot must untie it." They think we tied the knot. I don't see it that way.

President Bush's delivery was far from perfect: he stuttered and stumbled several times while groping for the word "slogan." Yet the substance of his response compensated for his lingual fumbling. He had deftly borrowed a rhetorical technique from another culture to concisely portray the two governments' disagreement about responsibility for the violent confrontations in and near Tiananmen Square. His response thus was infinitely more satisfying than the slickly articulated but evasive or vacuous responses often heard in political press conferences. The same will be true of your responses to a judge's questions.

Of course, your argument will be all the more effective if you can minimize distracting imperfections in your delivery caused by nervousness. Perhaps the best way to bring such nervousness under control is to approach your oral argument with the confidence that comes from thorough preparation. If you have carefully prepared your analysis and have rehearsed your argument, you can confidently assume that you will bring an expertise to the courtroom that the judge will appreciate.

To deal with nervousness at the beginning of your argument, you can prepare a carefully worded introduction that you can commit to memory, so that you will not find yourself groping for words at the outset. Then, after you have thus warmed up your speaking voice, you can speak more flexibly from a rough outline of your main argument before closing with a carefully planned conclusion.

V. SUMMARY

Effective advocacy requires sound analysis, sensible organization, and effective writing style. Specifically, you should:

(1) satisfy ethical duties in asserting claims and defenses, disclosing adverse authority, and representing the content of legal authority;

(2) organize your legal arguments in logical order, subject to overriding considerations of strategy;

(3) introduce each of your arguments with an effective point heading and introductory paragraph;

(4) present your analysis of the law, apply the law to the facts, and state the conclusion that you want the court to reach;

(5) apply principles of persuasive writing; and

(6) carefully prepare an oral argument that strategically supplements your brief.

The following chapters examine further techniques of persuasive writing in the context of particular legal documents.

12

Pleadings

I. THE COMPLAINT

"A civil action is commenced by filing a complaint with the court."[1] One might suppose that any lawyer would graduate from law school with a solid grasp of the mechanics of such a fundamental and significant document. However, few law students draft a complaint before leaving law school, and many graduate without having seen one. Not surprisingly, when faced with the task of preparing a complaint, you may be tempted to turn for guidance to the forms in form books or in your office files.

Forms may provide general guidance in some cases. In fact, many jurisdictions have officially authorized pleading forms for certain common kinds of suits. The California Judicial Council has even approved pleading forms that invite the user to choose among standard allegations by checking boxes.[2]

Nonetheless, you will more quickly and thoroughly master the skills of artful pleading if you understand the components of a complaint well enough to draft one "from scratch." Your primary tools in such a task are the results of your investigation of facts and your knowledge of the applicable law. Beyond that, rules of procedure and local court rules provide the necessary guidance.

A. FORMAT

Local court rules on pleading often specify a form for a caption that identifies the case and the nature of the document. For example, the Rules of

---

1. Fed. R. Civ. P. 3.
2. See B. Child, Drafting Legal Documents: Materials and Problems 12-21 (1988).

Practice for the United States District Court for the District of Arizona specify the precise location in the caption on the cover sheet for, among other things, the following information: (1) the name, address, state bar attorney number, and telephone number of the representing attorney; (2) the title of the court; (3) the names of the parties; and (4) a designation of the nature of the document.[3]

More substantively, the Federal Rules of Civil Procedure require a complaint, or any other pleading setting forth a claim for relief, to contain three elements:

1. A short and plain statement of the grounds upon which the court's jurisdiction depends . . .
2. A short and plain statement of the claim showing that the pleader is entitled to relief.
3. A demand for judgment for the relief the pleader seeks.[4]

Each of these elements warrants further examination.

1. Jurisdictional Statement

The jurisdictional statement is particularly important in a complaint filed in federal court, because the subject matter jurisdiction of federal courts is limited to that authorized by Article III of the United States Constitution and by federal statutes.[5] Therefore, in the initial paragraphs of a complaint in federal court, you should allege facts establishing subject matter jurisdiction based on a federal question,[6] diversity of citizenship,[7] or a special statutory grant of jurisdiction.[8] Although the jurisdictional statement is sufficient if it alleges facts that support the court's exercise of jurisdiction,[9] federal pleaders customarily cite to the specific statutes that grant jurisdiction:

> 3. This claim arises under Title VII of the Civil Rights Act of 1964; therefore, this court has subject matter jurisdiction under 42 U.S.C. § 2000e-5(f)(3) and 28 U.S.C. § 1331.[10]

Some jurisdictional statements in federal complaints also include allegations that establish that the court has personal jurisdiction over the defendant, if that is not apparent from the body of the complaint. Assuming that lack of personal jurisdiction is treated as an affirmative defense for pleading purposes,

---

3. D. Ariz. R. Prac. 10(a) (West 1988).
4. Fed. R. Civ. P. 8(a).
5. See, e.g., Mayor v. Cooper, 73 U.S. (6 Wall.) 247, 252 (1867).
6. 28 U.S.C. § 1331.
7. 28 U.S.C. § 1332.
8. E.g., 42 U.S.C. § 2000e-5(f)(3) (granting jurisdiction of actions brought under Title VII of the Civil Rights Act of 1964).
9. Aguirre v. Automotive Teamsters, 633 F.2d 168, 174 (9th Cir. 1980).
10. See also Fed. R. Civ. P., app., Form 2 ¶¶ (b), (c).

however, a complaint will not be insufficient for failure to affirmatively plead personal jurisdiction over the defendant.

Pleading subject matter jurisdiction is less important in state court than in federal court, because most state trial courts are courts of general jurisdiction. When state pleaders address subject matter jurisdiction at all, it is often with perfunctory introductory allegations that the amount in controversy exceeds that reserved for state courts of limited jurisdiction, perhaps coupled with a citation to the state constitutional or statutory provision that authorizes the court's exercise of general trial jurisdiction. Even this is usually unnecessary, because the request for relief ordinarily satisfies any jurisdictional amount in controversy.

Interestingly, perhaps without noting the difference between the subject matter jurisdictions of state and federal courts, some state legislatures have adopted all the elements of the governing federal rule of civil procedure, thus requiring a jurisdictional statement in state court complaints.[11] Pleaders in such states recognize that a special allegation of subject matter jurisdiction should be unnecessary in a state court complaint, but they appropriately feel compelled to satisfy the rule's express requirement by including some kind of jurisdictional statement. Consequently, even though the original federal rule almost certainly was not intended to impose on a plaintiff in federal court the burden of affirmatively pleading personal jurisdiction, state pleaders often begin their complaints with allegations of personal jurisdiction over the defendants. Such statements typically introduce the parties and allege in fairly conclusory fashion that the defendant has engaged in conduct in the state out of which the claim arises or has otherwise established the requisite contacts with the state.

2. Claim for Relief

Early state pleading codes that required allegations of "material facts" or "ultimate facts" supporting a cause of action generated considerable controversy over the intended meaning of the word "facts."[12] Perhaps to avoid that controversy, Federal Rule of Civil Procedure 8(a)(2) omits any reference to "facts" in its requirement of a statement of the claim for relief. Nonetheless, "Rule 8(a)(2) envisages the statement of circumstances, occurrences, and events in support of the claim presented."[13] Most people would use the word "fact" to describe allegations of that nature. Similarly, this book will use "fact" in this context while attempting to avoid the historical confusion surrounding the term.

Thus, in the main body of the complaint, you will allege facts and conclusions of liability that establish entitlement to relief. This may require prelimi-

---

11. See, e.g., Ariz. R. Civ. P. 8(a).

12. See, e.g., Cook, "Facts" and "Statements of Fact," 4 U. Chi. L. Rev. 233, 233-234, 235-239, 241-242, 246 (1936), reprinted in W. Bishkin and C. Stone, Law, Language, and Ethics 277-281 (1972).

13. Advisory Committee on Rules for Civil Procedure, Report of Proposed Amendments to the Rules of Civil Procedure for the United States District Courts 18-19 (1955), reprinted in R. Field & B. Kaplan, Materials for a Basic Course in Civil Procedure 439 (5th ed. 1984).

nary legal research as well as fact investigation. Your knowledge of the law enables you to identify legally significant facts, and your knowledge of the case helps you to determine what facts you can allege in good faith.

To draft your claim for relief artfully, you must decide on

(1) the extent, if any, to which you should supplement fact allegations with references to the law;

(2) the specific content of the fact allegations; and

(3) the appropriate level of specificity of the allegations.

a. Allegations of Fact and Citations to Law

Your complaint should allege facts and ultimate conclusions establishing a claim for relief; you need not cite to supporting legal authority.[14] This can be illustrated with the model of the syllogism of deductive reasoning:

> Major premise—Rule of Law
> Minor premise—Allegations of Fact
> Conclusion—Allegation of Liability or other Ultimate Conclusion

A complaint with the minimum necessary elements will explicitly set forth the minor premise and the conclusion, and it will leave the major premise implicit. Some complaints even omit an explicit statement of the ultimate conclusion of liability, on the theory that it is implicit in the request for relief.

For a simple example, a form complaint appended to the Federal Rules of Civil Procedure states a claim for debt that alleges subsidiary facts and the ultimate conclusion that the defendant "owes" money to the plaintiff:

> 2. Defendant on or about June 1, 1935, executed and delivered to Plaintiff a promissory note . . . whereby defendant promised to pay to plaintiff or order on June 1, 1936 the sum of _____ dollars with interest thereon at the rate of six percent. per annum.
> 3. Defendant owes to plaintiff the amount of said note and interest.[15]

These sample allegations do not explicitly state the major premise that a promise to pay money expressed in a written promissory note is enforceable under the common law of contracts or under some other legal authority. Whether the alleged facts state a claim for relief under applicable legal authority can be addressed in subsequent proceedings, such as on a motion to dismiss.[16]

Thus, in practice, citation to specific legal authority is much less common in the claim for relief than in the jurisdictional statement. The only references to legal authority commonly found in claims for relief are descriptive headings that introduce counts with general legal theories of relief, such as "Negligence," "Wrongful Discharge," "Employment Discrimination," or "Breach of Contract."

---

14. E.g., Doss v. South Central Bell Tel. Co., 834 F.2d 421 (5th Cir. 1987).

15. Fed. R. Civ. P., app. Form 3, 28 U.S.C. (1982).

16. See Fed. R. Civ. P. 12(b)(6).

Indeed, in a claim for relief, more specific citation to authority may restrict the claims properly pleaded. For example, in *London v. Coopers & Lybrand*,[17] the plaintiff's attorney alleged racial discrimination in employment, stating claims for relief under both Title VII of the Civil Rights Act of 1964 and 42 U.S.C. § 1981. Additionally, the initial complaint cited to both statutes as support for the claims. In an amended complaint, the pleader repeated the allegations of discrimination and the reference to § 1981. However, perhaps through an inadvertent typing error, the amended complaint omitted any citation or other reference to Title VII. The United States Court of Appeals for the Ninth Circuit held that the plaintiff had waived the Title VII claim by initially citing to Title VII and then by omitting the citation in the amended complaint.[18] If the pleader had never cited to specific authority, the fact allegations of the amended complaint presumably would have supported claims under Title VII, § 1981, and perhaps other state or federal laws, such as the emerging common law tort of wrongful discharge.

The overly technical approach in *London* is not clearly consistent with the objectives of federal pleading, and other courts have adopted a more forgiving attitude toward legal citation errors in pleadings. For example, in *Doss v. South Central Bell Telephone Co.*,[19] a federal civil rights complaint alleged facts and conclusions supporting a claim of age discrimination, but it incorrectly cited to Title VII rather than the applicable statute, the Age Discrimination in Employment Act of 1967. The procedural history showed that this error was not a "technical mistake" but reflected a "conscious decision made under an incorrect analysis of law."[20] Even in those circumstances, the court of appeals reversed the trial court's dismissal of the complaint, because the fact allegations adequately notified Bell of "the nature of [the plaintiff's] claim and the grounds on which she relied."[21]

Notwithstanding the risks created by unusual cases such as *London,* even in the Ninth Circuit a pleader will sometimes cite to authority in the claim for relief for a strategic purpose. For example, in cases in which the plaintiff wants a settlement at the outset of litigation, his attorney may briefly cite to authority to demonstrate to the defendant that the claim is substantial and that further litigation is unlikely to reduce the risk of liability. In most cases, however, the attorney could achieve the same result less subtly, and perhaps more effectively, with a demand letter that explains the merits of the claim. Such a letter could either precede or accompany the complaint.

In one exceptional case, the primary drafter of a state complaint preceded her first claim for relief with a special statutory section that included more than a page of quotations from, and citations to, state statutes that she alleged established a duty on the part of state officials to provide health care for the chronically mentally ill:

---

17. 644 F.2d 811 (9th Cir. 1981).
18. Id. at 814.
19. 834 F.2d 421 (5th Cir. 1987).
20. Id. at 424.
21. Id. at 425.

XIX
APPLICABLE STATE LAW

Pursuant to A.R.S. § 36-104.17, the Director of D.H.S. has the mandatory obligation to:

> Take appropriate steps to provide health care services to the medically dependent citizens of this state.

Furthermore, under A.R.S. § 36-204.A.1, the director has the responsibility to "[a]dopt rules and regulations for outpatient services" at Arizona State Hospital. . . .

XXIII

Pursuant to the foregoing statutes, D.H.S., Arizona State Hospital, and the Board have the duty to provide medical and health care to the needy sick, including the chronically mentally ill. . . .[22]

Because the theory of relief in this complaint was novel, the drafter of the complaint probably wanted to introduce the major premise of the claim into the complaint to minimize the risk that the judge or the opposing counsel would conclude at the outset that the claim was frivolous. In this case, the drafter's purpose was not to encourage an early settlement but to enhance the chances that the claim would survive pretrial challenges so that the theory of the claim could be developed on a full record at trial. The strategy worked: the claim survived to trial, the trial court granted extensive injunctive relief, and the state supreme court affirmed.[23]

The analysis of statutes in the *Arnold v. Sarn* complaint illustrates an exception to the general rule. Under the federal rules, citation to legal authority in a claim for relief is never mandatory, is only rarely strategically advantageous, and occasionally is detrimental to the pleading.

b. Substance of Allegations

One writer has recommended that pleaders pay heed to the journalist's five Ws when stating a claim for relief: who, what, where, when, and why.[24]

Who—In many complaints, you will introduce the parties in the jurisdictional allegations. Otherwise, your statement of the claim for relief should identify them and their relationship to one another. It should also identify any other significant actors.

---

22. Complaint in Arnold v. Sarn, No. C432355, ¶¶ XIX-XXIII (Ariz. Super. Ct. March 26, 1986) (filed by the Arizona Center for Law in the Public Interest).
23. Arnold v. Sarn, 160 Ariz. 593, 775 P.2d 521 (1989) (en banc).
24. D. Karlen, Procedure Before Trial in a Nutshell, 41-42 (West 1972).

What, Where, When—The statement of the claim should describe the events that give rise to the claim. You should take care to allege all facts or conclusions needed to support the request for relief. For example, you should support a request for specific performance with an allegation that the legal remedy is inadequate.

Why—You should allege any state of mind that is material to the claim or to the availability of special relief. For example, a request for punitive damages in a common law tort claim must be supported by an allegation of malice, willful misconduct, or at least recklessness, depending on the jurisdiction.

You need not allege all matters that may ultimately be in dispute; you need allege only the elements of your client's prima facie case. Affirmative defenses must be pleaded in the answer,[25] and the complaint need not anticipate them. The federal rules list 19 affirmative defenses;[26] statutes and case law may help you define the burdens of pleading on other matters. In case of doubt, you should plead a matter as part of the claim for relief.

For example, suppose that the jurisdiction in which the complaint is filed recognizes a cause of action for intentional infliction of emotional distress on proof of four elements: (1) the defendant engaged in extreme and outrageous conduct (2) with the intent to cause severe emotional distress or with reckless disregard for the possibility of those consequences, and (3) the conduct caused the plaintiff to suffer (4) severe emotional distress.[27] After introductory allegations establishing personal jurisdiction and identifying Jansen as the plaintiff and Bostich as one of the defendants, the count for this claim should allege facts supporting each of the four elements of the prima facie case:

COUNT I
Infliction of Emotional Distress

3. Jansen worked on an assembly line at the Zydeco Radio factory under the direct supervision of Bostich. As Jansen's supervisor, Bostich had the authority to impose production quotas on Jansen and to impose discipline, including termination, for failure to meet quotas.

Relationship of parties

4. From April 1 to June 10, 1984, Bostich engaged in the extreme and outrageous conduct of imposing impossible production quotas on Jansen and causing Jansen to believe that his job security depended on his meeting the quotas.[28]

Conduct

---

25. Fed. R. Civ. P. 8(c).
26. Id.
27. See, e.g., Watts v. Golden Age Nursing Home, 127 Ariz. 255, 258, 619 P.2d 1032, 1035 (1980) (citing Restatement (Second) of Torts § 46).
28. Whether the allegations of paragraphs 3 and 4 establish "extreme and outrageous conduct" will depend on the law of that jurisdiction and could be litigated on a motion to dismiss for failure to state a claim. See, e.g., Fed. R. Civ. P. 12(b)(6).

State of mind

Causation and
distress

Injuries

> 5. Bostich maliciously engaged in this conduct for the purpose of causing Jansen to suffer severe emotional distress.[29] Alternatively, Bostich recklessly disregarded the likelihood that Jansen would suffer such distress.
>
> 6. As a direct result of Bostich's conduct, on June 10, 1984, Jansen suffered a complete nervous breakdown requiring bed rest for three weeks and extensive medical care. Jansen continues to suffer from insomnia, headaches, inability to concentrate at work, general nervousness, and other emotional distress as a result of Bostich's conduct. The medical care to date has cost $1,647.
>
> Jansen therefore requests the following relief: . . .

In contrast, even if the allegations raise some question of whether the statute of limitations has expired, the complaint need not affirmatively allege that the statute of limitations has not expired or has been tolled. Instead, expiration of the statute of limitations is an affirmative defense that the defendant has the burden of pleading.[30]

c. Specificity of Fact Allegations

Modern rules of procedure abolish the rigid common law forms of action.[31] The federal rules and those of most states approve pleadings that give the court and opposing party only general notice of most claims and defenses.[32] Revelation of more specific evidentiary details is left to the discovery process, motions practice, and the pretrial conference.[33]

A bare allegation of liability without any supporting facts would be insufficient even under the federal rules:

> [Rule 8(a)(2)] requires the pleader to disclose adequate information as the basis of his claim for relief as distinguished from a bare averment that he wants relief and is entitled to it.[34]

Nonetheless, the rules permit fact allegations that are fairly general and conclusory.

The appropriate level of generality can be illustrated by a continuum that

---

29. This allegation of scienter should suffice not only to satisfy the second element of the tort but to support a request for punitive damages as well.

30. Fed. R. Civ. P. 8(c).

31. "There shall be one form of action to be known as "civil action." Fed. R. Civ. P. 2.

32. Cf. Fed. R. Civ. P. 9 (requiring specificity in allegations of certain matters).

33. See Fed. R. Civ. P. 12, 16, 26-37, 56.

34. Advisory Committee on Rules for Civil Procedure, Report of Proposed Amendments to the Rules of Civil Procedure for the United States District Courts 18-19 (1955), reprinted in R. Field and B. Kaplan, Materials for a Basic Course in Civil Procedure 439, 440 (5th ed. 1984).

represents varying degrees of specificity in fact allegations. The continuum begins with allegations of conclusions based on the analysis of implicit subsidiary facts. It gains steadily in specificity until it presents specific evidence that establishes subsidiary facts:

CONCLUSION	SPECIFIC EVIDENCE
negligence	eyewitness estimate of speed
	analysis of skid marks

As an example of extreme specificity, a complaint could state a claim for negligent operation of an automobile by alleging each bit of evidence with which the plaintiff hopes to prove negligence at trial:

3. . . . Jill Graham and Ben Cooper were standing at the corner of 7th Avenue and Washington Street at noon and observed the defendant driving his automobile at high speed west on Washington Street toward 9th Avenue. Each of them estimated that the defendant was traveling at approximately twice the posted speed limit of 35 miles per hour. An expert who examined skid marks at the accident scene estimated that the defendant's automobile was traveling at more than 60 miles per hour when it entered the intersection of Washington Street and 9th Avenue. . . .

Nearer to the other extreme, the complaint could allege the ultimate conclusion of negligence with only general supporting factual information:

2. On January 1, 1987, defendant negligently drove a motor vehicle in the intersection of Washington Street and 9th Avenue, striking plaintiff in the crosswalk.
3. As a result, . . .

This second example is adapted from a sample form in the Federal Rules of Civil Procedure,[35] illustrating the acceptability of general, conclusory allegations on most matters.

In those states that retain the more traditional "code pleading" requirements, the appropriate level of specificity probably would lie somewhere in the middle of the continuum. The complaint in such a state would allege the "ultimate facts" supporting the conclusions of liability, but it would not give a detailed account of all the evidence from which the facts and conclusions are derived. For example, the complaint might allege that the defendant operated the car negligently by exceeding the speed limit and by weaving between lanes, but it would not require allegations of the subsidiary evidence of speeding, such as the analysis of skid marks.[36]

Whether your complaint is governed by the federal standard of notice pleading or by more traditional rules, you may reap strategic advantages from alleging your claim for relief with the maximum generality allowable. Unneces-

---

35. Fed. R. Civ. P., app. Form 9 ¶¶ 2, 3.
36. See generally R. Field & B. Kaplan, Materials for a Basic Course in Civil Procedure 440-442 (5th ed. 1984).

sarily specific allegations might prematurely commit the plaintiff to a particular factual theory of the case or might reveal information helpful to the opposing party. For example, in one suit to recover a commission, an attorney specifically alleged that her client, the plaintiff, acted as agent for the defendant in a real estate transaction. That allegation was unnecessary to the client's claim for relief, which would have been supported by a more general allegation of contractual liability. Subsequent discovery revealed that the plaintiff probably did not act as the defendant's agent. The plaintiff's earlier allegations of agency, however, supported a defense and counterclaim for the defendant based on breaches of an agent's fiduciary duties. The plaintiff was forced to move to amend the complaint to delete the allegation of agency, an amendment necessary to avoid summary judgment for the defendant.

Despite the potential pitfalls of detailed allegations, few complaints are as conclusory as the passage above quoted from the sample federal negligence pleading. In some cases, greater specificity is required by applicable rules. For example, the Federal Rules of Civil Procedure provide that allegations of certain "special matters," such as fraud or mistake, shall state the circumstances with particularity.[37] Some courts have also required specific allegations in fields of high-volume litigation, such as civil rights.[38]

Even when particularity is not required, few pleaders achieve the generality reflected in the federal sample complaints. Some may include greater detail out of excessive caution; they may erroneously fear that less specific allegations would fail to state a proper claim. Many pleaders simply prefer to present a clearer, more sympathetic story than would be told with minimal notice pleading. In some cases, the pleader may hope that detailed allegations will more forcefully display the merits of the claim and will persuade the opposing party to settle quickly. In others, the pleader may hope to use the pleadings as a preliminary discovery device by eliciting specific answers to detailed allegations in the complaint.

In summary, the specificity of your allegations is partly a matter of style and strategy. As long as you take care to allege facts supporting every element of your prima facie case, you can tailor the specificity of your allegations to your strategic needs.

3. Request for Relief

Your complaint should end with a simple statement of the relief sought by your client. The main request for relief typically is for an injunction, an award of money damages, or both. Additionally, you should request an award of reasonable costs and attorney's fees if your client has a legal basis for such an award. Finally, you can retain flexibility by closing the request for relief with a catch-all request for "other appropriate relief":

---

37. E.g., Fed. R. Civ. P. 9(b); see Stern v. Leucadia Nat'l Corp., 844 F.2d 997 (2d Cir. 1988) (allegations of fraud based on information and belief must be accompanied by statement of facts on which belief is founded).

38. See, e.g., Whitacre v. Davey, 890 F.2d 1168 (D.C. Cir. 1989); Marcus, The Revival of Fact Pleading Under the Federal Rules of Civil Procedure, 86 Colo. L. Rev. 433, 451 (1986).

Jansen therefore requests judgment granting the following relief:

(1) an award of compensatory damages in an amount to be set at trial, but not less than $50,000;

(2) an award of punitive damages in an amount to be set at trial;

(3) an award of costs and attorney's fees; and

(4) such other relief as the court deems appropriate.

B. STYLE AND ORGANIZATION

1. *Writing Style*

Some of the lawyer's stuffiest jargon can be found in antiquated pleadings:

Comes now the plaintiff before this honorable court and, through his attorneys, Jenkins, Brown, and Little, alleges, pleads, and avers as follows: . . .

3. That the defendant did employ said plaintiff as a designer of clothes . . .;

4. That on July 6, 1927, said defendant did . . .

Wherefore, the plaintiff prays that this honorable court grant judgment for the plaintiff and award . . .

The Federal Rules reject jargon in favor of plain English: "Each averment of a pleading shall be simple, concise, and direct."[39] Stated in plain English, the allegations in the preceding example are unquestionably simpler and more concise:

Plaintiff alleges: . . .

3. The defendant employed the plaintiff as a designer of clothes . . .

4. On July 6, 1927, the defendant . . .

Plaintiff requests the following relief: . . .

Among other things, plain English avoids pretentious clichés. For example, one fairly recent complaint alleged that "Plaintiff and Defendant discussed their marriage agreement from time to time and on a great many occasions too numerous to mention herein." A more concise version achieves simplicity without loss of material substance: "Plaintiff and Defendant discussed their marriage agreement regularly and frequently."

2. *Organization*

To facilitate analysis of the claims by the court and the parties, you should set forth the allegations of your complaint in consecutively numbered para-

---

39. Fed. R. Civ. P. 8(e)(1). Ironically, the sample forms in the appendix to the Federal Rules contain their share of jargon.

graphs. Separation of the statements of different claims for relief into separate counts may be permissible or required, depending on the circumstances.

If you have joined separate claims for relief based on different transactions, federal rules require a statement of the claims in separate counts "whenever a separation facilitates the clear presentation of the matters set forth."[40] Otherwise, presentation of allegations in separate counts appears to be discretionary.

Even if your client's claims arise out of a single transaction, separate counts may be helpful if you rely on distinct legal theories that are based on different fact allegations. For example, a consumer injured by a faulty electrical appliance may have a cause of action against the retailer on two legal theories: products liability in tort, and breach of a contractual warranty. If you divide the allegations into separate counts, you can identify which fact allegations are material to each theory of relief. If some facts are common to both theories, one count can incorporate some of the allegations of the other:

COUNT I
Products Liability

4. On January 1, 1987, Green purchased a microwave oven from Retailer.

5. The microwave oven had an unreasonably dangerous defect . . .

COUNT II
Breach of Warranty

8. Green realleges the allegations in paragraphs 4-6.

9. Babcock Appliance Center warranted the microwave oven to be free of defects. . . .

You must also exercise discretion to determine whether to follow each count with a separate request for relief or to consolidate them in a single request after presentation of all counts. As with separation of theories into counts, separation of requests for relief to accompany different counts may be helpful if the available remedies vary with each count. For example, if punitive damages are available only on the products liability count and if attorney's fees are available only on the count for breach of warranty, separate requests for relief after each count may facilitate subsequent analysis of the claims. On the other hand, if the requests for relief on different counts are identical, consolidation in a single request obviously avoids pointless repetition.

II. THE ANSWER

To avoid judgment against him by default, the defendant must respond to a complaint by filing an answer or other appropriate response.[41] The answer

---

40. Fed. R. Civ. P. 10(b).

41. See Fed. R. Civ. P. 12(a). The defendant may move to dismiss the complaint on its face before filing an answer. Fed. R. Civ. P. 12(b).

must admit or deny each allegation of the complaint.[42] In addition, the answer may set forth affirmative defenses,[43] assert counterclaims against the plaintiff,[44] or both.[45] If the answer asserts a counterclaim, the original plaintiff must file a reply that admits or denies each allegation of the counterclaim and that may set forth affirmative defenses to the counterclaim.

A. ADMISSIONS AND DENIALS

If a defendant contests liability, he obviously is prepared to deny in good faith some of the material allegations of the complaint. On the other hand, nearly every complaint will contain some allegations that the defendant admits. Therefore, when drafting an answer, you should not generally deny all allegations of the complaint; instead, you should address each paragraph of the complaint and identify areas of dispute. For example, an answer to the complaint partially set forth earlier in this chapter might admit and deny allegations in the following manner:

ADMISSIONS AND DENIALS

1. Defendant Bostich admits the allegations in paragraphs 1-3 of Plaintiff Jansen's complaint.

2. Bostich denies the allegations in paragraph 4 of the complaint that he set impossible goals for Jansen and that he intimidated Jansen in his work. Bostich admits that he warned Jansen of the possibility of termination for failing to meet goals.

3. Bostich denies the allegations in paragraph 5 of the complaint.

4. Bostich has no information on which to form a belief in the truth of the allegations in paragraph 6 of the complaint, and he therefore denies them.[46]

B. AFFIRMATIVE DEFENSES

In a separate section of your answer, you should allege facts and conclusions supporting any affirmative defenses that your client, the defendant, may reasonably assert.[47] Even if the allegations of the complaint are true and are legally sufficient to state a claim for relief, a meritorious affirmative defense to the prima facie case will justify judgment for the defendant.

For example, in the litigation between Jansen and Bostich, suppose that the statute of limitations for tort actions in the jurisdiction is one year, that Jansen filed his complaint on June 10, 1985, and that Bostitch last communicated a supervisory ultimatum to Jansen on Friday, June 7, 1984. Bostitch may

---

42. Fed. R. Civ. P. 8(b).
43. Fed. R. Civ. P. 8(b), 8(c).
44. Fed. R. Civ. P. 7(a), 8(a).
45. An answer may also assert a cross-claim against an originally named codefendant or a third-party claim against a new "third-party defendant" that the defendant impleads. See id.
46. See generally Fed. R. Civ. P. 8(b) (form of denials).
47. See Fed. R. Civ. P. 8(b), 8(c).

be prepared to argue that the statute of limitations has expired on the ground that Jansen's cause of action accrued at the latest on June 7, 1984, the date of Bostitch's last act, rather than on Monday, June 10, 1984, the date of Jansen's nervous breakdown. If so, Bostich could assert this in fairly conclusory fashion as an affirmative defense:

AFFIRMATIVE DEFENSE

5. Bostitch last exercised any supervisory control over Jansen on June 7, 1984. Therefore, Jansen's cause of action accrued more than one year before the filing of his complaint, and the statute of limitations bars his action.

C. COUNTERCLAIMS

The defendant named in a complaint may himself wish to assert an independent claim for relief against the plaintiff. If so, the roles of the parties are reversed for purposes of the counterclaim, and the principles of pleading discussed in section I above apply to the counterclaim.[48]

For example, in the litigation between Jansen and Bostich, additional facts might support a claim against Jansen for battery:

COUNTERCLAIM
Battery

6. On the evening of Friday, July 12, 1984, Jansen struck Bostich over the head with a baseball bat as Bostich left the Zydeco Radio factory.

7. Jansen acted maliciously and for the specific purpose of causing serious injury to Bostich.

8. As a result of Jansen's malicious attack, Bostich lost consciousness, required treatment in a hospital emergency room, and suffered debilitating pain for 24 hours.

Therefore, Bostich requests the following relief: . . .

III. SUMMARY

When drafting pleadings, you should carefully follow the format prescribed by applicable rules. For example, federal rules require the drafter of a complaint to allege

(1) jurisdiction,

(2) a claim for relief, and

(3) a demand for judgment.

---

48. See Fed. R. Civ. P. 8(a).

In an answer, you
  (1) must admit or deny the allegations of the complaint, and
  (2) may also assert affirmative defenses or a counterclaim.

Generally, pleadings should allege ultimate conclusions and supporting facts but not legal standards. Although the claim for relief must allege all elements of the prima facie case, most allegations may be general and need not develop specific, evidentiary facts.

══════════ **E X E R C I S E   1 2 - 1** ══════════

Compare and critically evaluate the following three versions of a complaint in the same wrongful discharge action. Which level of specificity of allegations do you prefer? What other differences in style do the complaints reflect? Which styles do you prefer?

Thomas Sanchez
Simpson, Sanchez & Summers
303 North Central Avenue
Phoenix, Arizona 85002
(602) 229-1111
Bar No. 28371
Attorney for the plaintiff

IN THE SUPERIOR COURT
MARICOPA COUNTY, ARIZONA

GEORGE BRYANT, Plaintiff, v. MARIE JARDON, d.b.a. Chez Marie, Defendant.	No. _____ COMPLAINT

Plaintiff alleges:

COUNT 1

I

Plaintiff George Bryant is a resident of Phoenix, Arizona. Defendant Marie Jardon owns and operates Chez Marie, a restaurant located in Phoenix, Arizona.

II

Bryant worked for Jardon as a waiter at Chez Marie from August 16, 1984 to September 28, 1985.

III

At the time of his discharge on September 28, 1985, Bryant had an employment contract with Chez Marie that imposed substantive and procedural restrictions upon Jardon's right to terminate Bryant's employment.

IV

Acting through her agent, Mario Prieto, Jardon discharged Bryant September 28, 1985, in breach of her employment contract with Bryant.

V

As a result of Jardon's breach of contract, Bryant has suffered lost wages and other incidental and consequential losses.

COUNT 2

VI

Bryant realleges and incorporates paragraphs I-V above.

VII

Acting through her agent, Jardon maliciously and unlawfully discharged Bryant for reasons that violate public policy, causing Bryant lost wages and other injuries.

Bryant therefore requests judgment granting the following relief:

(1) an order reinstating Bryant to his position as waiter at Chez Marie;
(2) an award of compensatory and punitive damages;
(3) an award of costs and attorney's fees; and
(4) other appropriate relief.

Dated _____

by _____
Thomas Sanchez
Simpson, Sanchez & Summers
303 North Central Avenue
Phoenix, AZ 85002
Attorneys for Plaintiff

Thomas Sanchez
Simpson, Sanchez & Summers
303 North Central Avenue
Phoenix, Arizona 85002
(602) 229-1111
Bar No. 28371
Attorney for the plaintiff

ARIZONA SUPERIOR COURT
MARICOPA COUNTY

GEORGE BRYANT, Plaintiff, v. MARIE JARDON, d.b.a. Chez Marie, Defendant.	No. _____ COMPLAINT

Plaintiff alleges:

1. Plaintiff George Bryant is a resident of Phoenix, Arizona. Defendant Marie Jardon owns and operates Chez Marie, a restaurant located in Phoenix, Arizona.

I
BREACH OF PROMISE

2. Bryant worked for Jardon as a waiter at Chez Marie from August 16, 1984, to September 28, 1985. Mario Prieto acted as the maitre d' and supervisor of waiters at Chez Marie during Bryant's employment at Chez Marie. In all the events alleged below, Prieto acted on behalf of Jardon.

3. At the time of his discharge on September 28, 1985, Bryant had an employment contract with Chez Marie that included the terms of an "Employee Handbook." Bryant foreseeably relied to his detriment on promises contained in the Handbook.

4. The Employee Handbook contains promises of job security, including promises that (i) Jardon will not discharge any waiter except for inadequate performance and (ii) any waiter recommended for discharge has the right to meet with Jardon and Prieto to persuade them that the waiter should not be discharged. The Handbook also provides that Jardon will make the final determination in the event of disagreement between Prieto and Jardon on a discharge matter.

5. At all times during his employment at Chez Marie, Bryant performed his job in a manner that met the highest standards at Chez Marie. Despite the adequacy of Bryant's performance, Prieto discharged Bryant September 28, 1985. Although Bryant immediately requested a meeting with Prieto and Jar-

294

don to discuss the discharge, both Prieto and Jardon refused to convene such a meeting.

6. As a result of Jardon's breach of promises in the Handbook, Bryant has suffered lost wages and other incidental and consequential losses.

7. Jardon's breach of promises in the Handbook constitutes a breach of her employment contract with Bryant and has created an injustice that can be avoided only by enforcing the promises.

II
WRONGFUL DISCHARGE

8. Bryant realleges and incorporates paragraphs 1-7 above.

9. In discharging Bryant, Prieto was motivated by malice, by an invidiously discriminatory animus, and by concerns unrelated to the successful operation of Chez Marie. Jardon's termination of Bryant's employment therefore violated public policy.

Bryant therefore requests judgment granting the following relief:

(1) an order reinstating Bryant to his position as waiter at Chez Marie;
(2) an award of compensatory damages in an amount to be set at trial, but not less than $50,000.
(3) an award of punitive damages in an amount to be set at trial;
(4) an award of costs and attorney's fees; and
(5) such other relief as the court deems appropriate.

Dated _____

by _____,
Thomas Sanchez
Simpson, Sanchez & Summers
303 North Central Avenue
Phoenix, AZ 85002
Attorneys for Plaintiff

Thomas Sanchez
Simpson, Sanchez & Summers
303 North Central Avenue
Phoenix, Arizona 85002
(602) 229-1111
Bar No. 28371
Attorney for the plaintiff

IN THE SUPERIOR COURT OF THE STATE OF ARIZONA
IN AND FOR THE COUNTY OF MARICOPA

GEORGE BRYANT, 　　　　Plaintiff, 　　　v. MARIE JARDON, d.b.a. 　Chez Marie, and MARIO PRIETO, 　　　　Defendants.	No. _____ COMPLAINT

Plaintiff George Bryant, by and through his attorneys, Simpson, Sanchez and Summers, alleges the following:

1. This is an action for injunctive relief and for compensatory damages exceeding $10,000. This court has original jurisdiction pursuant to the Arizona Constitution, Article 6, § 14(3).

2. Plaintiff is a resident of Phoenix, Arizona. Defendant Marie Jardon owns and operates Chez Marie, a restaurant located in Phoenix, Arizona. Defendant Mario Prieto acted as the maitre d' and supervisor of waiters at Chez Marie during Bryant's employment at Chez Marie. All material events alleged below took place in Maricopa County.

I
FIRST CAUSE OF ACTION
(Breach of Contract)

3. Plaintiff worked for Defendants as a waiter at Chez Marie from August 16, 1984, to September 28, 1985. In all the events alleged below, Defendant Prieto acted on his own behalf as well as on behalf of Defendant Jardon.

4. On January 1, 1985, Defendants modified Plaintiff's employment contract to include promises of job security contained in the terms of an "Employee Handbook" and in oral assurances.

5. Among other things, the Employee Handbook contains the following promises of job security: (i) Defendants will not discharge any waiter except for inadequate performance and (ii) any waiter recommended for discharge has the right to meet with Defendants to persuade them that the waiter should not be discharged. The Handbook also provides that Defendant Jardon will make the final determination in the event of disagreement between Defendants on a

discharge matter. (Copy of text of excerpts of Handbook are attached and incorporated by this reference).

6. At all times during his employment at Chez Marie, Plaintiff performed his job in a manner that met the highest standards at Chez Marie. Despite the adequacy of Plaintiff's performance, Defendants discharged Plaintiff September 28, 1985. Although Plaintiff immediately requested a meeting with Defendants to discuss the discharge, Defendants refused to convene such a meeting.

7. As a result of Defendant's breach of contract, Plaintiff has suffered lost wages and other incidental and consequential losses.

WHEREFORE, Plaintiff demands judgment granting the following relief:

(1) an order reinstating Plaintiff to his former position at Chez Marie;
(2) an award of compensatory damages for all consequential and incidental losses;
(3) an award of costs and attorney's fees; and
(4) such other relief as the court deems appropriate.

II
SECOND CAUSE OF ACTION
(Promissory Estoppel)

8. Plaintiff realleges paragraphs 1-7 above and incorporates them by this reference.

9. On January 1, 1985, Defendants gave Plaintiff promises of job security by making oral assurances and by distributing the Employee Handbook. Plaintiff relied to his detriment on those promises by performing extraordinary services and by forbearing from taking other job opportunities. That reliance was reasonably foreseeable by Defendants.

10. Defendants' termination of Bryant's employment on September 28, 1985 constituted a breach of their promises of job security and has created an injustice that can be avoided only by enforcing the promises.

WHEREFORE, Plaintiff demands judgment granting the following relief:

(1) an order reinstating Plaintiff to his former position at Chez Marie;
(2) an award of compensatory damages for all consequential and incidental losses;
(3) an award of costs and attorney's fees; and
(4) such other relief as the court deems appropriate.

III
THIRD CAUSE OF ACTION
(Wrongful Discharge)

11. Plaintiff realleges paragraphs 1-10 above and incorporates them by this reference.

12. Defendants maliciously discharged Plaintiff because of his sexual ori-

entation and because Plaintiff's exemplary performance made Defendant Prieto jealous. Those reasons for discharge are arbitrary and unfair, reflect bad faith, and violate the public policy of state laws.

WHEREFORE Plaintiff demands judgment granting the following relief:

(1) an order reinstating Plaintiff to his position as waiter at Chez Marie;
(2) an award of compensatory damages in an amount to be set at trial;
(3) an award of punitive damages in an amount to be set at trial;
(4) an award of costs and attorney's fees; and
(5) such other relief as the court deems appropriate.

Dated _____

by _____
Thomas Sanchez
Simpson, Sanchez and Summers
303 North Central Avenue
Phoenix, AZ 85002
Attorneys for Plaintiff

13

Motion for Summary Judgment

I. PROCEDURAL CONTEXT

Summary judgment is a popular means of pretrial disposition. In most cases, you will have no difficulty alleging facts that state a claim for relief; therefore, your complaints will seldom be susceptible to attack for failure to state a claim. On the other hand, even if you allege a claim or defense in good faith, you may fail to gather substantial admissible evidence supporting the claim or defense. In such cases, the opposing party's motion for summary judgment exposes the absence of a triable issue of fact. It compels you to choose between making at least a preliminary showing of the evidence supporting your allegations or suffering adverse judgment before trial. In other cases, both parties concede the absence of any dispute of fact, stipulate to the facts, and use the motion for summary judgment to argue unsettled questions about the law and its application to the stipulated facts.

Summary judgment litigation often takes place only after each party has thoroughly investigated the case through the discovery process.[1] Indeed, the trial judge may delay resolution of a motion for summary judgment if further discovery is needed to permit the nonmoving party to support its opposition.[2] Nonetheless, if you successfully move for summary judgment, you will avoid the greater burdens of a full trial.

On the other hand, if the trial court denies your motion for summary

---

1. The procedures for discovery are set forth in Federal Rules of Civil Procedure 26-37.
2. Fed. R. Civ. P. 56(f). Under proposed amendments to the federal rules, however, a party could move for "summary establishment of the law," which would identify some facts as immaterial and thus limit the scope of discovery. See Agency Rulings, 58 U.S.L.W. 2313 (Nov. 28, 1989) (summarizing amendments to Fed. R. Civ. P. 56 proposed by the Committee on Rules of Practice and Procedure of the Judicial Conference of the United States).

judgment, your unsuccessful motion may hamper your ability to settle the case before trial. If the opposing counsel initially expected to settle the case, he may have only minimally prepared the case prior to summary judgment litigation. Your motion for summary judgment, however, will have forced your opponent to organize his facts and legal arguments. If the motion fails, he likely will be much more demanding in settlement negotiations for three reasons. First, the denial of the motion will strengthen his belief in the potential merits of his client's claims or defenses. Second, he will be more nearly prepared for trial after researching the law and gathering the facts to oppose your motion for summary judgment. Finally, his client will have invested significant resources in opposing the motion, expenditures that his client will likely incorporate into its new settlement position.[3] Consequently, you should not move for summary judgment unless you have a reasonable chance of success.

Summary judgment litigation provides you with a stimulating vehicle for developing brief-writing skills. You must remain constantly sensitive not only to the merits of the underlying claims or defenses but also to the standards for summary judgment. Moreover, the local rules of many courts prescribe a special format for summary judgment briefs, providing you a valuable opportunity to examine the role of procedural rules in written advocacy.

II. STANDARDS FOR SUMMARY JUDGMENT[4]

The federal rules authorize a court to grant summary judgment if the parties do not genuinely dispute any material facts and if the moving party is entitled to judgment as a matter of law.[5] In some cases, the court may use summary judgment proceedings to grant final judgment "as to one or more but fewer than all of the claims or parties,"[6] or to identify some uncontested material facts without granting any final judgment.[7]

When moving for summary judgment, you have the initial burden of showing that the pretrial record supports judgment in your favor. If you move for summary judgment on the strength of a claim or defense on which you would have the burden of proof at trial, you must support your motion for summary judgment with credible evidence tending to prove all the elements of

---

3. See, e.g., Ocampo, Jr., Moving Violations, California Lawyer, August 1984 at 47, 48.

4. This discussion does not incorporate amendments to Federal Rule of Civil Procedure 56 that were proposed, but not yet adopted, at the time of printing. See Agency Rulings, 58 U.S.L.W. 2313 (Nov. 28, 1989) (summarizing amendments proposed by the Committee on Rules of Practice and Procedure of the Judicial Conference of the United States). Also beyond the scope of this discussion are state standards for summary disposition that deviate from the federal rules. For example, motions for summary judgment are only rarely granted in California courts, perhaps because the moving party retains the burden of proof on all issues under California rules. See Karnow, Follow the Federal Lead on Summary Judgment, California Lawyer, December 1989, at 67.

5. Fed. R. Civ. P. 56(c), 56(e).

6. Fed. R. Civ. P. 54(b).

7. Fed. R. Civ. P. 56(d).

the claim or defense.[8] You could make such a showing with deposition testimony, answers to interrogatories, admissions, or other information and documents obtained during discovery, or with affidavits prepared specifically for the motion.[9]

As an alternative basis for summary judgment, you may demonstrate the absence of factual support for an element of a claim or defense relied on by the opposing party. If so, you need not affirmatively produce evidence tending to negate that element. Instead, you may satisfy your initial burden simply by reviewing the existing record and demonstrating that it contains no evidence supporting the critical element.[10]

Once you have satisfactorily supported your motion, the opposing party can avoid summary judgment by setting forth "specific facts" that establish a genuine issue of material fact for trial.[11] He may not rely on the allegations or denials in his own pleading but must point to facts in affidavits, deposition testimony, or other documentary evidence or fruits of discovery.[12]

Moreover, to warrant a trial, the factual issue must be both genuine and material.[13] For an illustration of the materiality requirement, suppose the record on summary judgment establishes without dispute that the defendant intentionally struck the plaintiff with a baseball bat. The defendant could not successfully respond to the plaintiff's motion for summary judgment by establishing even a genuine dispute of fact about the color of the shoes worn by the defendant on the day of the attack. Once the identity of the attacker and the nature of the attack have been established, a factual dispute about the attacker's footwear would not be material to the plaintiff's tort claim, because it would have no bearing on liability.

The court must not resolve genuine issues of material fact on summary judgment. To determine the genuineness of a factual issue, however, the court may undertake a limited evaluation of the strength of the facts presented by the nonmoving party. A factual issue is not genuine if the nonmoving party's factual support is so trivial that "the record taken as a whole could not lead a rational trier of fact to find for the non-moving party."[14] In short, the nonmoving party "must do more than simply show . . . some metaphysical doubt as to the material facts."[15]

These standards for summary judgment influence not only the nature of

---

8. See Celotex Corp. v. Catrett, 477 U.S. 317, 331 (1986) (Brennan, J., dissenting) (citing 10A C. Wright, A. Miller & M. Kane, Fed. Prac. & Proc. 2727 (12th ed. 1983)).

9. See Fed. R. Civ. P. 56(c).

10. Celotex Corp. v. Catrett, 477 U.S. 317, 322-324 (majority), 328-331 (Brennan, J., dissenting) (1986).

11. Fed. R. Civ. P. 56(e). Alternatively, the nonmoving party may concede the absence of any issue of material fact and simply argue that it, rather than the moving party, is entitled to judgment. In such a case, the parties typically file cross-motions for summary judgment, and each party asserts entitlement to judgment as a matter of law.

12. Fed. R. Civ. P. 56(e). See Southern Ramblers Sales, Inc. v. American Motors Corp., 375 F.2d 932, 937 (5th Cir.) ("Rule 56 [is] saying in effect, 'Meet these affidavit facts or judicially die.' "), cert. denied, 389 U.S. 832 (1967).

13. Fed. R. Civ. P. 56(c).

14. Matsushita Elec. Indus. Co. v. Zenith Radio Corp., 475 U.S. 574, 587 (1986).

15. Id. at 586.

the arguments in the supporting and opposing briefs, but also the requirements for the materials filed in support of the briefs.

III. FORMAT FOR SUMMARY JUDGMENT BRIEFS—OVERVIEW

Rules of procedure, local court rules, and custom suggest that materials supporting a motion for summary judgment should include the following:

(1) a motion requesting action by the court;

(2) a statement of facts;

(3) affidavits, or other materials not already in the record, that support the fact statement and the motion; and

(4) a supporting brief, sometimes referred to in court rules as a "memorandum of law" or "memorandum of points and authorities."

The requirements for the response are similar except that the nonmoving party need not file a formal motion opposing the motion for summary judgment. At most, the nonmoving party may wish to file a cover page that announces the response and briefly introduces the supporting brief and other materials. The moving party's reply, if any, consists solely of a brief that replies to the arguments raised in the nonmoving party's response.

Some local rules describe parts of the required format in surprising detail. For example, local rules for some United States District Courts specify the information required on designated lines of the caption of the title page of each document filed in support of the motion.[16] The most interesting of the local rules addressing summary judgment, however, are those specifying formats for the statements of facts.

IV. STATEMENTS OF FACTS

Before the advent of local rules governing motions for summary judgment, briefs and supporting materials often failed to pinpoint areas of factual dispute. Often, counsel for the moving party summarized the materials supporting the motion in a general narrative fact statement, and counsel for the nonmoving party summarized supporting materials in a general counterstatement of the facts. Worse yet, in some cases, one or both advocates omitted any consolidated statement of the facts and simply referred to the record in fact analyses dispersed throughout the argument section of the brief.

To help trial judges identify the potential areas of factual dispute, many courts have enacted local rules specifying special formats for briefs on motions for summary judgment. Among the best of these are the Uniform Rules of

---

16. E.g., D. Ariz. Local R. 10(a).

Practice of the Superior Court of Arizona, which require the moving party to state the facts in numbered paragraphs, similar to allegations in a complaint:

> Any party filing a motion for summary judgment shall set forth, separately from the memorandum of law, the specific facts relied upon in support of the motion. The facts shall be stated in concise numbered paragraphs.[17]

Unlike allegations in a complaint, this fact statement must include citations to supporting materials: "As to each fact, the statement shall refer to the specific portion of the record where the fact may be found."[18] If you represent the moving party, you might shrewdly entitle this section "Statement of Undisputed Material Facts," because you obviously hope that the opposing party cannot genuinely dispute them.

The local rules instruct the nonmoving party to identify areas of factual dispute in much the same way that an answer sets forth denials of allegations in a complaint:

> Any party opposing a motion for summary judgment shall file a statement in the form prescribed by this Rule, specifying those paragraphs in the moving party's statement of facts which are disputed, and also setting forth those facts which establish a genuine issue of material fact or otherwise preclude summary judgment in favor of the moving party.[19]

If you represent the nonmoving party, you might reasonably entitle this section "Statement of Undisputed and Disputed Material Facts," because you obviously hope that the court will rule that your documents establish a dispute with respect to at least some of the material facts.

Fact statements following this format provide the court with a clear guide to the opposing parties' positions on summary judgment. For example, the following represents excerpts from the plaintiff's statement of facts on his motion for summary judgment in a suit alleging race discrimination in violation of federal law:

1. Defendant, Irma Barnes, owns and operates "Irma's Diner," a restaurant and bar located in Mesa, Arizona. Barnes employs more than 15 employees in this business. (Exh. D, Deposition of Irma Barnes at 3-4).

2. Plaintiff, Michael Powell, is African-American. He worked as the night manager of the bar at Irma's Diner from January 1, 1986 to June 17, 1987. (Exh. B, Personnel Record for Michael Powell). . . .

3. • • •

4. On June 17, 1987, Barnes confronted Powell about Powell's selection of a soul band as musical entertainment for the bar. After using several racial slurs in the ensuing discussion, she fired Powell solely because of his race. (Exh. A, Affidavit of Michael Powell at 2). . . .

---

17. Ariz. Super. Ct. Unif. R. Prac. IV(f).
18. Id.
19. Id. The rules also permit the nonmoving party to join with the moving party in stipulating to facts not in dispute. Id.

Barnes's response to the motion for summary judgment should specifically identify which portions of Powell's statement of facts are disputed:

> 1. Barnes does not dispute paragraphs 1-3 of Powell's Statement of Facts.
> 2. Barnes does not dispute the assertions in paragraph 4 that Barnes fired Powell on June 17, 1987, after confronting Powell about his selection of musical entertainment. Barnes disputes that she used racial slurs or that race played any factor in her termination of Powell's employment. . . .

In addition, Barnes should set forth the specific facts that reflect a genuine factual dispute on the material issue of Barnes's racial animus. Barnes's counsel may accomplish this in either of two ways. First, she might state her version of the events in the same paragraph in which she rejects Powell's version:

> 2. Barnes does not dispute the assertions . . . musical entertainment. Barnes disputes . . . Powell's employment. In fact, Barnes never used racial slurs in Powell's presence, and she fired Powell solely because he displayed insubordination in the face of direct instructions by Powell to replace the band that Barnes had hired. (Plaintiff's Exh. D, Deposition of Irma Barnes at 24-25).

Alternatively, Barnes could assert her version of the events in a separate section that follows her identification of areas of dispute:

> STATEMENT OF UNDISPUTED AND DISPUTED FACTS
>
> 1. Barnes does not dispute . . .
> 2. Barnes does not dispute the assertions . . . musical entertainment. Barnes disputes . . . Powell's employment.
>
> ADDITIONAL FACTS
>
> 1. Barnes never used racial slurs in Powell's presence, and she fired Powell solely because he displayed insubordination in the face of direct instructions by Powell to replace the band Barnes had hired. (Plaintiff's Exh. D, Deposition of Irma Barnes at 24-25).

Some attorneys separately file supporting affidavits and other evidence. If those materials are not voluminous, however, you can more conveniently and appropriately attach them to the formal statement of facts.

The local rules quoted above probably permit you to attach the statement of facts under the same title sheet that states the motion and that covers the supporting brief, as long as you set forth the statement of facts separately from the brief itself. Nonetheless, attorneys operating under those and similar local rules customarily file the formal statement of facts under a caption as a separate document. This custom may have been inspired by local rules that restrict the length of motions briefs.[20] Because such rules usually exclude the formal statement of facts from the page limit,[21] litigants prefer to file the statement of facts separately to more easily demonstrate that the brief by itself does not exceed the page limit.

V. SUPPORTING EVIDENTIARY MATERIALS

Each assertion in your statement of facts should be supported by admitted alleged facts from the opposing party's pleading or by facts reflected in affidavits, materials generated through discovery, or other evidence. Rule 56 specifically provides that the affidavits must set forth "such facts as would be admissible in evidence."[22] More broadly, the determination of whether all the materials supporting and opposing summary judgment create a genuine issue of fact for trial should be based only on evidence that would be admissible at trial.[23] Therefore, even though your opponent may overlook this matter,[24] the materials supporting your fact statements in summary judgment litigation should establish the admissibility of the evidence in the materials.

For example, the following excerpt from an affidavit establishes the admissibility of other documents under the "business records" exception to the "hearsay rule" of evidence:[25]

5. The Payroll Action forms in Exhibits B and C are true copies of records that were prepared and kept by my personal secretary, Leslie West, in the course of her regularly conducted business activity, which includes maintaining such employment records as a uniform practice. Those forms include information within Ms. West's own knowledge and information that I transmitted to her on matters within my knowledge.

---

20. See, e.g., Ariz. Super. Ct. Local R. of Prac. for Maricopa County 3.2(f).

21. E.g., id.

22. Fed. R. Civ. P. 56(e). The Federal Rules of Evidence and their state counterparts govern the admissibility of evidence at trial.

23. See Tigg Corp. v. Dow Corning Corp., 822 F.2d 358 (3d Cir. 1987) (on review of partial summary judgment in contract dispute, discussing admissibility of extrinsic evidence of parties' intended meaning); see also Olympic Ins. Co. v. Harrison, Inc., 418 F.2d 669, 670 (5th Cir. 1969) (document produced in ordinary course of business was sufficiently reliable to form basis for summary judgment).

24. See, e.g., Catrett v. Johns-Manville Sales Corp., 826 F.2d 33, 37 (D.C. Cir. 1987) (regardless of whether letter qualified as a business records exception to the hearsay rule, trial court properly considered it on summary judgment because other party failed to object to its use), *cert. denied*, 108 S. Ct. 1028 (1988).

25. Fed. R. Evid. 803(6).

VI. THE MOTION

As with every document that you separately file with the trial court, you should begin your motion with a caption identifying the case and the nature of the document. In the motion itself, you should simply and clearly state your request for action and briefly introduce the grounds supporting the request.

Unfortunately, many lawyers have developed a tradition of loading motions with abstract boilerplate that says almost nothing about the motion or the dispute:

> Defendant, Sun Printing Co., by and through its undersigned attorneys, Jenkins, Powell, and Smith, P.C., hereby moves, pursuant to the Federal Rules of Civil Procedure, Rule 56, for an order granting summary judgment against Plaintiff, Scott Paper Supply, on the grounds that there exists no genuine issue of material fact and that Defendant is entitled to summary judgment as a matter of law. This motion is supported by the attached memorandum of law, the Statement of Material Facts separately filed with this court, and the documents and exhibits filed with this court.

A judge skims such boilerplate with glassy eyes. She does not need a superfluous reference to the legal representation; your identity as legal counsel is revealed at the top of the cover page and in your signature at the end of the motion. In addition, the judge is well aware of the basic abstract standards for summary judgment;[26] repeating those standards in the motion adds nothing to her knowledge about your case.

The judge will read your motion with greater interest if you clearly and concisely state what relief your client wants and why he is entitled to it. In particular, you should convey new information to the court by tailoring the abstract standards to the facts:

> Pursuant to Federal Rule of Civil Procedure 56, the defendant, Sun Printing Co., moves for summary judgment against the plaintiff, Scott Paper Supply. Sun Printing Co. is entitled to judgment under the U.C.C. Statute of Frauds because Scott Paper Supply cannot genuinely dispute that the agreement alleged by Scott was for paper priced at more than $500 and was never reduced to writing.
>
> This motion is supported by the attached memorandum of law, by the separately filed Statement of Undisputed Facts and accompanying exhibits, and by the record in this case.

An even crisper motion could state the first paragraph more concisely:

> Defendant, Sun Printing Co., moves for summary judgment against Plaintiff, Scott Paper Supply. See Fed. R. Civ. P. 56. Sun Printing Co. is

---

26. See Fidel, Some Do's and Don'ts of Motion Writing, Ariz. Bar J., August 1983, at 8, 9 (advising legal writers to omit "canned" recitations of basic summary judgment standards).

entitled to judgment because the oral agreement alleged by Scott Paper Supply is unenforceable under the U.C.C. Statute of Frauds as a matter of law.

As terse as this passage may sound, it contains more useful information than the longer string of boilerplate in the first example.

When opposing a motion, you should not state a formal counter-motion in the title page of your opposition materials. You may follow the caption immediately with your responsive brief. At the most, you might include in your title page a brief statement of opposition parallel to the motion:

Plaintiff, Scott Paper Supply, opposes Defendant's motion for summary judgment. Defendant, Sun Printing Co., is not entitled to judgment as a matter of law, because Scott Paper Supply has established a genuine factual dispute about the written documentation of the sale agreement.

This opposition is supported by the attached memorandum of law, by the . . .

VII. THE BRIEF

Your brief, or legal memorandum, is your tool of persuasion. With it, you argue for a favorable interpretation of the law and analysis of the facts. A motions brief typically includes three sections:
   (1) an introduction,
   (2) an argument, and
   (3) a conclusion.

A. THE INTRODUCTION

Because local rules of many courts require a separate, formal statement of facts in summary judgment materials, your brief need not begin with any introductory statements; you can launch immediately into your legal argument.[27] In most cases, however, you can enhance the persuasiveness of your brief by beginning with an introductory section, perhaps entitled "Introduction" or "Summary of Facts," which precedes the argument section. In this introductory section, you can summarize the facts in a more concise and less formal manner than is possible in the separate, formal statement. If you emphasize facts favorable to your client, you can make the judge more receptive to the argument that follows.

Alternatively, you may use an introductory section to present a summary of your argument or a combination of facts, procedural history, and summary of your argument. Chapter 15 advises against premature legal argument in a

---

27. But cf. Cal. R. Ct. 313(b) (state rule requiring statement of facts in every motions brief).

statement of facts in an appellate brief. However, this admonition applies with less force in the introduction to your summary judgment brief, because you will separately file a formal statement of facts for summary judgment.

Finally, you should consider preceding your argument with a formal statement of the issues, either in place of another form of introduction or in addition to it. Although motions briefs do not customarily state the issues, a formal statement would almost never detract from your brief and might be helpful in a complex case.

B. THE ARGUMENT

Chapters 3 and 11 discuss techniques of legal argument. Indeed, some of the examples in Chapter 11 are taken from sample summary judgment briefs. This section will address techniques of persuasion peculiar to summary judgment briefs.

Argument of nearly purely legal questions can be critical in some summary judgment litigation: if the court determines that material facts are not in dispute, or if the parties have stipulated to the absence of factual dispute, the court will decide whether a moving party is entitled to judgment as a matter of law.

Once you have established the law on an issue or subissue, you should thoroughly analyze the facts. Absent a stipulation to undisputed facts, careful fact analysis is important in summary judgment litigation because of the special significance of the presence or absence of genuine disputes of material fact. In arguing the facts, you should remember to cite to the record or to the formal, separately filed statement of facts. The samples in this chapter suggest several ways to cite to the record; any reasonable citation form is acceptable.

Also, you should incorporate the standards for summary judgment into your argument. For example, if you are moving for summary judgment, you should not argue that "the preponderance of the evidence shows that Sun Printing Co. objected to the contents of the confirmation within ten days after receipt." Such an argument gives the impression that you are inappropriately asking the judge to resolve a factual issue without a trial. Instead, your brief should refer to the "undisputed evidence" and the inferences that can be drawn from it, thus properly asserting the absence of a factual dispute.

Conversely, if you are opposing summary judgment, your brief should remind the judge periodically that nothing more than a genuine and material question of fact is needed to defeat summary judgment. In making this point, you should not simply reiterate the abstract standard; rather, you should identify issues of fact that make summary judgment inappropriate:

Opposition facts

> Scott Paper Supply's letter confirming the purchase agreement is dated September 1 [Exh. 2], and Scott's Distribution Manager personally mailed it that day [Exh. 3, Affidavit of Rosa Connor ¶ 3]. Scott Paper Supply never received any objection to the terms of the confirmation. [*Id.* at ¶ 4]. Moreover, Sun Printing Co. concedes that it has no record of making

any such objection. [Exh. 4, Sun's Answer to Scott's First Set of Interrogatories, No. 23].

In direct opposition to Sun Printing Co.'s assertions, this evidence shows that Sun Printing Co. received the confirmation and failed to object to it. At the very least, this evidence raises a genuine dispute of fact that must be resolved at trial.

Dispute of fact

C. THE CONCLUSION

You should end each section of the argument of your brief with a conclusion about the topic of that section, similar to the conclusion stated in the point heading that introduces the argument. Together, the point heading and the conclusion provide maximum emphasis in their positions as the first and last things the judge reads within a section. Finally, as illustrated in Chapter 11, the entire brief should end with a section entitled "Conclusion" that encompasses all the arguments of the brief.

VIII. SUMMARY

To prepare a motion for summary judgment, you should:

(1) draft a motion that requests summary judgment and briefly introduces the judge to the grounds for your motion;

(2) prepare evidentiary materials that will support your statement of facts, if they are not already in the record;

(3) draft a separate statement of facts with citation to the supporting materials; and

(4) draft a supporting brief that

(a) summarizes the facts and procedural history,

(b) argues the law and facts relating to the issues, with attention to the standards for summary judgment, and

(c) states your conclusions.

When opposing a motion for summary judgment, you should prepare a brief and a separate statement of facts with supporting materials. To oppose a motion or to reply to an opposition brief, you need not file a separate motion. Instead, you should submit a brief that responds to the arguments presented in the preceding brief.

Lisa Hall
Kendricks, Hall, & Oats, P.C.
3310 Alma School Rd., Suite 200
Mesa, Arizona 85283
(602) 839-0365
Bar No. 0076089

ARIZONA SUPERIOR COURT
MARICOPA COUNTY

CHARLOTTE REMBAR, Plaintiff, v. ALEXANDER HART d.b.a. COMCON, Defendant.	No. C732431 Defendant Hart's Motion for Summary Judgment (Oral Argument Requested) (Judge Wisdom)

Defendant Alexander Hart d.b.a. Comcon moves for summary judgment on all claims in this action. Under Arizona Rule of Civil Procedure 56, Hart is entitled to judgment as a matter of law because the undisputed facts show that Hart did not promise Rembar job security and did not discharge Rembar for an unlawful reason or in a wrongful manner.

This motion is supported by the attached Memorandum of Law, the separately filed Statement of Undisputed Facts, and the entire record before the court.

March 3, 1987

Lisa Hall for
Kendricks, Hall, & Oats, P.C.
3310 Alma School Rd., Suite 200
Mesa, Arizona 85283

MEMORANDUM OF LAW IN SUPPORT OF MOTION FOR SUMMARY JUDGMENT

I. INTRODUCTION

As set forth more fully in the Statement of Undisputed Facts, Alexander Hart employed Charlotte Rembar as a computer systems consultant for Hart's sole proprietorship, Comcon. Although Hart distributed an employment manual to Rembar, their employment contract permitted either party to terminate the contract at will.

On October 31, 1986, Hart discharged Rembar because of her "negative attitude." During her employment, Rembar often flirted with Hart, and Hart sometimes returned the flirtations; however, Hart and Rembar did not have a romantic relationship, and Hart never made any unwelcome advances toward Rembar.

Rembar has asserted three claims for relief in her complaint: breach of contract, wrongful discharge in violation of public policy, and intentional infliction of emotional distress. Because the record shows that Hart employed Rembar at will and that Hart discharged Rembar for a legitimate business reason, Hart is entitled to judgment as a matter of law on the contract claim. Hart is entitled to judgment on the tort claims because he discharged Rembar for a legitimate business reason and in a proper manner and because Arizona workers' compensation legislation provides the exclusive remedy for Rembar's alleged injuries.

II. ARGUMENT

A. Hart did not Breach his Employment Contract with Rembar by Discharging Rembar for her Negative Attitude.

Generally, "an employment contract of indefinite duration is terminable at will," permitting either party to "terminate the contract at any time for any reason or for no reason at all." *Leikvold v. Valley View Community Hospital,* 141 Ariz. 544, 546, 688 P.2d 170, 172 (1984). In some circumstances, an employee manual can become part of the employment contract, and promises of job security in the manual can restrict the employer's freedom to terminate the contract even though the term of the contract remains indefinite. *Id.* at 548, 688 P.2d at 174; *Wagenseller v. Scottsdale Memorial Hospital,* 147 Ariz. 370, 381, 710 P.2d 1025, 1036 (1985). Nonetheless, even assuming for purposes of summary judgment that Hart and Rembar's employment contract included the terms of the Comcon Policy Manual, Hart did not breach those terms for two reasons. First, neither the Policy Manual nor any other term of the contract imposed any restriction on Hart's freedom to terminate Hart's employment. Second, even if the employment contract permitted Hart to fire Rembar only for unsatisfactory performance, her negative attitude created such grounds for discharge.

Because the terms of the contract "are clear and unambiguous, the construction of the contract is a question of law for the court" and thus is appropriate for summary judgment. *Leikvold,* 141 Ariz. at 548, 688 P.2d at 174.

1. The Employment Contract Remained Terminable at Will.

Even assuming the Comcon Policy Manual was incorporated into the employment contract, it did not change the at-will nature of the contract because it contained no "provisions of job security." *Id.* at 547, 688 P.2d at 173 (quoting *Pine River State Bank v. Mettille,* 333 N.W.2d 622, 628 (Minn. 1983)).

The terms of Comcon's Policy Manual unambiguously left Hart free to terminate his contract with Rembar at his will. No provision of the Policy Manual purports to restrict the grounds for discharge of an employee. Instead, the only provisions relating to termination affirmatively reserve Hart's right to discharge employees. Policy Manual (Exh. A) § IV.

Because Rembar had worked at Comcon for more than 60 days, she was classified as a nonprobationary employee at the time of her discharge. *See id.* (Exh. A) § IV(A). Under the heading "Nonprobationary Employment," the Policy Manual especially emphasizes a particular ground for discharge: "Comcon reserves the right to terminate the employment of any employee who is not performing satisfactorily." *Id.* at § IV(B). However, it does not state or even suggest that unsatisfactory performance is the exclusive ground for discharge. Absent such a stated restriction, Hart remains free under the general rule to terminate the contract for any reason or for no reason at all.

Hart's employment contract with Rembar was terminable at will.

2. Hart Validly Fired Rembar for Unsatisfactory Performance.

Even if the Policy Manual had identified unsatisfactory performance as the sole ground for discharging nonprobationary employees, Hart would not have breached such a provision.

Hart discharged Rembar because of her "negative attitude." Nov. 3, 1986 Payroll Action (Exh. C); Affidavit of Alexander Hart ¶ 4 (Exh. D). Because Rembar's position required her to work closely with clients, a pleasant personality and a positive attitude were indispensable qualities for satisfactory job performance. *Id.* Therefore, even assuming that the employment contract provided for job security, Hart did not breach the contract because he discharged Rembar for unsatisfactory performance.

B. *Hart Did Not Wrongfully Discharge Rembar in Violation of Public Policy.*

1. Hart's Alleged Sexual Harassment Does Not Violate Arizona Public Policy, Because Employment Discrimination Laws Do Not Apply to Comcon.

The tort of wrongful discharge requires proof of a violation of an important public policy of the state reflected in the state's constitution, its statutes, or, in limited circumstances, its judicial decisions. *Wagenseller v. Scottsdale Memorial Hospital,* 147 Ariz. 370, 378-379, 710 P.2d 1025, 1033-1034 (1985). Rembar's allegations of sexual harassment suggest that she relies on the employment discrimination provisions of the Arizona Civil Rights Acts as her source of public policy.

However, those provisions apply only to employers with at least 15 employees. Ariz. Rev. Stat. Ann. § 41-1461(2) (West); *see also* 42 U.S.C. § 2000e(b) (identical limitation in Title VII of the Civil Rights Act of 1964).

Even if Hart is included in the total number of Comcon employees, Comcon has never employed more than nine employees. Affidavit of Alexander Hart ¶ 1 (Exh. D).

Therefore, the Arizona Civil Rights Act is not a source of public policy with respect to Rembar's employment and discharge.

    2. Even if the Arizona Civil Rights Act Were a Source of Public Policy in This Case, Hart Would Not Have Violated Its Policy, Because He Did Not Make Unwelcome Sexual Advances.

The state policy against sexual harassment is defined in the Arizona Civil Rights Act in its prohibition of sex discrimination in employment. Ariz. Rev. Stat. Ann. § 41-1463. An employer engages in sexual harassment by either (1) making submission to demands for sexual favors a condition of employment benefits, or (2) making unwelcome sexual advances that by their nature and frequency create a discriminatory work environment. *See, e.g., Meritor Savings Bank, FSB v. Vinson,* 477 U.S. 57 (1986) (applying identical provisions of Title VII); *see also Higdon v. Evergreen International Airlines, Inc.,* 138 Ariz. 163, 165 n.3, 673 P.2d 907, 909 n.3 (1983) (case law interpreting Title VII is persuasive authority for questions of interpreting the Arizona Civil Rights Act).

Even if Arizona's statutory policy against sexual harassment applied to Comcon, Hart would not have violated that policy, because he made no unwelcome sexual advances toward Rembar. Rembar's own frequent flirtations with Hart showed that she welcomed Hart's harmless flirtations and attentions. Hart never made advances that were not welcomed by Rembar, and he never conditioned benefits of employment on Rembar's acquiescing to his flirtations. Affidavit of Alexander Hart (Exh. D). Most important, Rembar's discharge had nothing to do with any flirtations between Hart and Rembar; Hart discharged Rembar solely because of her unsatisfactory job performance. *Id.* at ¶ 4.

In short, even if Hart were an employer covered by the Arizona Civil Rights Act, he would not have violated its prohibitions. Therefore, Hart did not contravene public policy.

C. Hart Did Not Engage in Extreme and Outrageous Conduct and Therefore Is Not Liable for Infliction of Emotional Distress.

An employer cannot be liable for infliction of emotional distress for an otherwise lawful termination of employment. *Daniel v. Magma Copper Co.,* 127 Ariz. 320, 324, 620 P.2d 699, 703 (App. 1980). The means by which an employer terminates might be independently tortious, but it would amount to intentional infliction of emotional distress only if the conduct was "extreme and outrageous." *Watts v. Golden Age Nursing Home,* 127 Ariz. 255, 258, 619 P.2d 1032, 1035 (1980). Conduct that is "extreme and outrageous" falls "within that quite narrow range" of conduct "at the very extreme edge of the spectrum." *Id.*

Hart is entitled to summary judgment on Rembar's claim for emotional distress for the same reasons that he is entitled to judgment on the claims for breach of contract and wrongful discharge. As discussed above, Hart's termination of Rembar's employment did not breach the contract or violate public policy. Therefore, the termination itself cannot be a basis for a claim of infliction of emotional distress.

Likewise, Hart did not accompany the termination with any extreme and outrageous conduct. Rembar's allegations of sexual harassment are simply not supported by the record. Hart discharged Rembar for a legitimate business reason and communicated his decision in a professional manner. Affidavit of Alexander Hart ¶¶ 3, 4 (Exh. D).

Because of its economic consequences, termination of employment is often an extremely distressing event for the discharged employee. However, discharge for business reasons is an economic fact of life and hardly amounts to the kind of extreme and outrageous conduct that results in tort liability.

D. *Even If Rembar's Allegations Were True, Her Tort Claims Would Be Superseded by the Arizona Worker's Compensation Statute.*

Arizona workers' compensation legislation applies to Hart because he employs "workmen . . . regularly . . . in the same business or establishment under contract of hire." Ariz. Rev. Stat. Ann. § 3-902. That legislation provides a special statutory remedy for injuries to an employee "arising out of and in the course of his employment." Ariz. Rev. Stat. Ann. § 3-1021. The worker's compensation remedy is exclusive, preempting other potential remedies under tort law. Ariz. Rev. Stat. Ann. § 3-1022(A).

Rembar's alleged injuries arose out of her employment: the alleged sexual harassment and discharge occurred at the workplace in the context of an employment relationship. Even if those allegations were true, Rembar's tort claims would be preempted as a matter of law by the workers' compensation statute.

III. CONCLUSION

Rembar cannot genuinely dispute Hart's showing on the facts that Hart promised Rembar no job security, that Hart discharged Rembar for unsatisfactory performance, and that Hart did not engage in sexual harassment. Therefore, Hart is entitled to summary judgment on all claims.

March 3, 1987

Lisa Hall for
Kendricks, Hall, & Oats, P.C.
3310 Alma School Rd., Suite 200
Mesa, Arizona 85283

COPY OF THE FOREGOING MAILED
March 3, 1986 to:

Roberts and Cray
101 E. Washington St.
Suite 600
Phoenix, Arizona 85001

Lisa Hall
Kendricks, Hall, & Oats, P.C.
3310 Alma School Rd., Suite 200
Mesa, Arizona 85283
(602) 839-0365
Bar No. 0076089

ARIZONA SUPERIOR COURT
MARICOPA COUNTY

CHARLOTTE REMBAR, Plaintiff, v. ALEXANDER HART d.b.a. COMCON, Defendant.	No. C732431 Defendant Hart's Statement of Undisputed Facts and Exhibits Supporting Motion for Summary Judgment (Judge Wisdom)

For purposes of summary judgment only, Defendant Alexander Hart d.b.a. Comcon presents the following undisputed facts:

1. Alexander Hart is the sole owner and manager of Comcon, a firm that provides expert consulting on computer systems to businesses in the Phoenix metropolitan area. From January to November 1986, Comcon employed eight employees other than Hart himself; Comcon has never employed a greater number of employees before or since. Affidavit of Alexander Hart ¶ 1 (Exh. D).

2. On January 1, 1986, Hart hired Charlotte Rembar for the position of Comcon consultant at a salary of $2,000/month. Jan. 1, 1986 Payroll Action (Exh. B). The only written record of Rembar's contract with Comcon is a Payroll Action form that states her date of hire and her salary. *Id.*; Affidavit of Alexander Hart ¶ 2 (Exh. D). The term of Rembar's employment was left indefinite. *Id.*

3. At or before the time of Rembar's hiring, Alexander Hart gave Rembar a Policy Manual that summarizes many of the personnel procedures at Comcon. Policy Manual (Exh. A). The Policy Manual contains no promises of job security; instead, it affirmatively reaffirms Hart's right to terminate both probationary and nonprobationary employees. *Id.* at § IV.

4. From the beginning of her employment at Comcon, Rembar sought to attract Hart's attentions with casual flirtations, such as references to his appearance and suggestive smiles. Hart returned the flirtations in a similar manner, but no sexual relationship developed between them. Any flirtations directed by Hart toward Rembar were welcomed, and even invited, by her. Hart never demanded sexual favors from Rembar, and he never conditioned any benefits of employment on Rembar's submitting to a sexual demand or otherwise reacting to a flirtation. Affidavit of Alexander Hart ¶ 3 (Exh. D).

5. In the fall of 1986, Hart became dissatisfied with Rembar's performance. Specifically, she displayed a negative attitude in her work. Because

Comcon consultants must work closely with their clients, a consultant with a negative attitude severely hampers Comcon's business relationships. Affidavit of Alexander Hart ¶ 4 (Exh. D).

6. Effective November 7, 1986, Hart terminated Rembar's employment because of her negative attitude. Nov. 3, 1986 Payroll Action (Exh. C). Hart communicated the discharge to Rembar in a normal, professional manner. Affidavit of Alexander Hart ¶ 4 (Exh. D).

March 3, 1987

Lisa Hall for
Kendricks, Hall, & Oats, P.C.
3310 Alma School Rd., Suite 200
Mesa, Arizona 85283

EXHIBIT A

I. INTRODUCTION

The success of Comcon lies in its ability to recruit and retain the best employees available nationally. To promote a stable and productive workforce, Comcon endeavors to provide attractive terms and conditions of employment, as reflected in the following policies.

II. SALARY

A. Initial Salary . . .

B. Change in Salary . . .

III. HOLIDAYS, VACATIONS, SICK LEAVE

A. Holidays . . .

B. Personal Leave . . .

IV. TERMINATION

A. Probationary Employment

Each employee will work on probationary status during his or her first 60 days of employment. During this probationary period, Comcon reserves the right to terminate the employee for any reason or for no reason at all.

B. Nonprobationary Employment

Comcon reserves the right to terminate the employment of any employee who is not performing satisfactorily.

E X H I B I T   B

PAYROLL ACTION

NATURE OF ACTION

___✓___ New Hire   _____ Change in Pay   _____ Termination

PREVIOUS PAY _____

NEW PAY $ 2,000/mo.

EFFECTIVE DATE 1-1-86

REASON FOR CHANGE OR TERMINATION

COMMENTS

Consultant

DATE 1-1-86

PROCESSED BY Leslie West

318

EXHIBIT C

PAYROLL ACTION

NATURE OF ACTION

_____ New Hire _____ Change in Pay ✓ Termination

PREVIOUS PAY ___$2,000/mo.___

NEW PAY _____

EFFECTIVE DATE ___11-7-86___

REASON FOR CHANGE OR TERMINATION

Negative attitude

COMMENTS

DATE ___11-3-86___

PROCESSED BY ___Leslie West___

EXHIBIT D

AFFIDAVIT OF ALEXANDER HART
IN SUPPORT OF MOTION FOR SUMMARY JUDGMENT

Maricopa County, Arizona

Alexander Hart, under oath, swears to the following information from personal knowledge:

1. I am the sole owner and manager of Comcon, a firm that provides consulting services to businesses on the development and use of computer systems. From January to November 1986, I employed eight employees, the largest workforce that I have employed since I formed Comcon in 1984. Specifically, during that period I employed a secretary, an accountant, and six consultants. Comcon participates in the Arizona Worker's Compensation program.

2. On January 1, 1986, I hired Charlotte Rembar for the position of consultant. The Payroll Action form identified in this motion as Exhibit B is the only written record of Rembar's hiring and her terms of employment. Rembar and I understood at the time of hiring that her term of employment was indefinite. On or before the time of her hiring, I gave her a Comcon Policy Manual, which reaffirms that Rembar had no definite term of employment.

3. From the beginning of her employment at Comcon, Rembar sought to attract my attentions with casual flirtations such as suggestive smiles and compliments on my grooming and appearance. She made it clear that she welcomed reciprocation, and I often returned her flirtations with similar smiles and comments. Our personal relationship never advanced beyond these casual flirtations. Specifically, we never had a sexual relationship, and I never made any unwelcome sexual advances toward Rembar, nor did I ever condition any benefits of employment on Rembar's submitting to any sexual demands or otherwise reacting in any way to my flirtations.

4. Sometime in the fall of 1986, I began to notice that Rembar displayed a negative attitude about me, about herself, and about her work. I find it extremely important to maintain a workforce with positive attitudes and pleasant personalities, because the consultants work closely with clients, and our business thus depends on maintaining good personal relationships with clients. To ensure that we maintained those relationships, I discharged Rembar effective November 7, 1986, to rid our workforce of her negativism. I communicated the discharge to Rembar in a normal, professional manner in an office meeting on November 3, 1986.

5. The Payroll Action forms in Exhibits B and C are true copies of records that were prepared and kept by my personal secretary, Leslie West, in the course of her regularly conducted business activity, which includes maintaining such employment records as a uniform practice. Those forms include information within Ms. West's own knowledge and information that I transmitted to her on matters within my knowledge. The Policy Manual in Exhibit A is a

true copy of a manual that I drafted and printed in June 1985 and have since distributed to all employees.

I swear under oath that the foregoing is true:

Alexander Hart   _3-1-87_
Alexander Hart   Date

14

Motion to Exclude Evidence Before Trial

To most law students or new associates, the term "motion in limine" is mysterious and a little intimidating. It will cease to be so once the legal profession replaces this Latin phrase with plain English. Black's Law Dictionary defines "in limine" as: "On or at the threshold; at the very beginning; preliminarily."[1] Simply put, the typical motion in limine is a motion to exclude evidence before trial. Conversely, but much more rarely, an advocate may use it to move for admission of evidence before trial if she anticipates an objection to the evidence.

Thus, in contrast to the typical motion for summary judgment, a motion to exclude evidence seeks to define the scope of the trial litigation rather than finally dispose of the case before trial. It generally is simpler than a motion for summary judgment. If you can strip the mystery away from the popular Latin phrase, you should have little trouble supporting or opposing the motion.

I. PRETRIAL EXCLUSION OF EVIDENCE

The Federal Rules of Civil Procedure expressly authorize "advance rulings from the court on the admissibility of evidence" in pretrial conferences.[2] Additionally, those Rules and the Federal Rules of Evidence implicitly authorize a trial court to rule on pretrial motions to exclude evidence other than in pretrial conference, or they at least leave undisturbed the court's inherent power to do so.[3]

---

1. Black's Law Dictionary 896 (5th ed. 1979).
2. Fed. R. Civ. P. 16(c)(3).
3. See generally Gamble, The Motion *In Limine:* A Pretrial Procedure That Has Come of Age, 33 Ala. L. Rev. 1, 2 & n.6 (1981).

Attorneys can and do object to evidence offered for admission during trial.[4] However, pretrial rulings on complex, potentially prejudicial, or particularly significant evidentiary matters tend to improve the efficiency and quality of the trial proceedings.[5]

For example, suppose a visitor to your client's factory sues your client for injuries sustained at the factory. At trial, the plaintiff's counsel asks a defense witness in front of the jury to confirm that your client offered to pay the plaintiff's medical expenses. You can immediately object that the question seeks a response that may lead the jury to find liability on an improper ground.[6] In most jurisdictions, the judge will sustain your objection and will order the witness not to provide the solicited testimony.[7] However, the damage to your client's case may be irreparable if the question alone improperly influences the jury's deliberations, despite the court's admonishments to the jury to ignore it. You could have protected your client more effectively had you earlier persuaded the judge to exclude the evidence before trial and to order the parties to refrain from referring to the evidence in any way at trial.

Additionally, pretrial litigation of complex evidentiary matters permits more thorough written and oral argument by the parties and more considered deliberation by the court, all without disrupting an ongoing trial.[8] Moreover, pretrial disposition of objections to particularly significant evidence gives the parties an opportunity before positions harden at trial to modify their trial strategies or to reassess their settlement positions.[9]

II. FORMAT—OVERVIEW

Local rules addressing motions typically provide for a motion and supporting brief, an opposing brief, and an optional reply brief.[10] However, unlike local rules that require a special format for some parts of a motion for summary judgment,[11] rules of procedure and local court rules of most jurisdictions specify no detailed format for a motion to exclude evidence. Instead, the common format is a product of custom and common sense. As with any legal document, you can best support or oppose a motion to exclude evidence if you understand the purposes of your document and draft it accordingly.

---

4. See generally Fed. R. Evid. 103.
5. See Fed. R. Civ. P. 16(a) (stating objectives of pretrial conference).
6. See Fed. R. Evid. 409 advisory committee note. Exclusion of such evidence also promotes a generally humanitarian policy of encouraging such assistance, regardless of liability. Id.
7. See Fed. R. Evid. 409.
8. Gamble, supra note 3, at 8.
9. See id. at 9-10.
10. See, e.g., U.S. Dist. Ct. Ariz. Local R. 11(a), (c), (d), (e), (h).
11. See supra Chapter 13.

III. THE MOTION

In a motion to exclude evidence, you should simply and clearly state the action requested and briefly summarize the grounds for the motion. In describing the relief requested, you probably should go beyond generally asking for exclusion of certain evidence. To ensure effective protection, you should describe the objectionable evidence as inclusively as possible and should request an order specifically prohibiting the opposing party from referring to the evidence:

> The defendant, Axxon Corp., moves for pretrial exclusion of all evidence that Axxon Corp. offered to provide medical care and pay the medical expenses of the plaintiff, Herb Taylor. The evidence is inadmissible under Federal Rule of Evidence 409.
>
> Specifically, Axxon Corp. requests an order directing Taylor and his counsel (1) to refrain from referring to such an offer in any way in the presence of the jury and (2) to take all necessary steps to ensure that their witnesses avoid such references.

To oppose a motion to exclude evidence, you need not file a separate motion; you can simply file a brief that opposes the original motion. At the most, you might want to draft a cover page for your brief that parallels the motion in summarizing the relief you seek and the supporting grounds:

> Plaintiff Herb Taylor opposes Defendant Axxon Corp.'s motion to exclude evidence of Axxon Corp.'s offer to provide and pay for medical care. The evidence is admissible to show the extent of Taylor's injuries. The court should not exclude the evidence for this purpose.

IV. THE BRIEF

Each brief on a motion to exclude evidence, or on any other motion, is sometimes referred to as a "memorandum of law" or a "memorandum of points and authorities." When preparing a brief supporting a motion to exclude evidence, you ordinarily should follow the familiar pattern of Introduction, Argument, and Conclusion. The party opposing your motion should file a responsive brief that directly answers the contentions of your supporting brief. Similarly, in your reply brief, if any, you should respond to the points made in the opposing brief.

On a motion for summary judgment, you will address at least some of the claims or defenses of the litigation on their merits. In contrast, on a motion to exclude evidence, you will typically focus more narrowly on the admissibility of certain evidence. Consequently, in your supporting or opposing briefs, you should address the merits of claims or defenses only to the extent necessary to address some element of admissibility, such as relevance. This narrow focus affects the scope of the introduction and argument sections of the briefs.

A. THE INTRODUCTION

In the introductory section of a brief supporting a motion to exclude evidence, you need not include a full statement of facts and procedural history. In light of the motion's focus on an evidentiary issue, your introduction need summarize only those portions of the facts and procedural history necessary to an understanding of that issue.

In addition, your introduction may include a statement explaining why you expect the nonmoving party to attempt to introduce the evidence at trial. It may also include a fairly conclusory statement of the need to resolve the matter before trial, although that point can be left to the argument section.

For example, the brief supporting the motion might begin with the following introductory points:

MEMORANDUM IN SUPPORT OF MOTION TO EXCLUDE EVIDENCE

I. INTRODUCTION

Nature of the case

Herb Taylor, a sales representative for Corbin Heavy Equipment Co., brought this tort action against Axxon Corp. He alleges negligence in the maintenance of the Axxon manufacturing plant in Albuquerque, New Mexico.

Facts

Specifically, Taylor alleges that, while touring the Axxon plant in January 1987 with Axxon General Manager Jerry Olshon, Taylor lost his footing, fell backwards, and struck his head against a forklift. [Complaint at ¶¶ 3, 4.] According to Olshon's deposition testimony, as a humanitarian gesture, Olshon immediately offered on behalf of Axxon to provide transportation to the nearest hospital and to pay for Taylor's medical expenses. [Deposition of Jerry Olshon at 18.] Taylor later developed difficulties with his eyesight, which he alleges are the result of his accident at the Axxon plant. [Complaint at ¶ 6.]

Belief that evidence will be introduced

The critical issue in this case is whether Axxon negligently maintained its plant, causing Taylor to fall. Taylor's counsel has examined Olshon extensively during deposition about Olshon's offer to pay medical expenses, leading Axxon to believe that Taylor's counsel will attempt to introduce that evidence at trial.

Evidence not admissible

Evidence of Olshon's offer to pay medical expenses is inadmissible to establish Axxon's liability, and Axxon will not introduce it for other purposes.

The evidence must be excluded before trial, because reference to it even in a question to a witness would indelibly and improperly influence the jury.

Need for pretrial exclusion

When opposing a motion, you should state any facts and procedural history that are material to your argument and that are not fairly stated in the opening brief:

I. INTRODUCTION

Plaintiff Taylor is prepared to prove that Defendant Axxon Corp.'s negligence proximately caused Taylor to lose nearly all sight in his right eye. Axxon apparently seeks to show that Taylor's injuries at the Axxon factory were slight and that Taylor's partial blindness must be unrelated. *See* Answer ¶ 6. Thus, the extent of Taylor's injuries at the factory are in issue.

Issues for trial

Taylor plans to introduce Axxon Corp.'s offer to provide and pay for medical care as evidence that Axxon's agent at the scene of the accident determined Taylor's injuries to be serious. The evidence is admissible for this purpose and should not be excluded.

Relevance of evidence on particular issue

B. THE ARGUMENT

1. Legal Rules

The argument section of a motion to exclude evidence follows the same general pattern discussed in Chapters 3 and 11. Each section or subsection within the argument should state a contention in a point heading, analyze the law and the facts, and restate or summarize the contention in a conclusion.

In the statement of legal standards in the opening brief supporting a motion to exclude evidence, you typically will focus on rules of evidence that restrict admissibility. If you prefer a thorough analysis, you may choose to develop the legal standards carefully:

Even relevant evidence is inadmissible "if its probative value is substantially outweighed by the danger that it will cause unfair prejudice." Fed. R. Evid. 403. Evidence presents such a danger if it has "an undue tendency to suggest a decision on an improper basis, commonly, though not necessarily, an emotional one." *Id.*, advisory committee note.

In this case, evidence of Powell's membership in the Black Panthers organization more than 20 years ago has little, if any, probative value . . .

On the other hand, the general standards for some of the more commonly invoked evidentiary rules are familiar to judges and attorneys. Therefore, you could exercise stylistic discretion to present those standards summarily, or even implicitly, and to move more quickly to the fact analysis:

Evidence of Powell's former membership in the Black Panthers organization should be excluded because it presents a danger of unfair prejudice that greatly outweighs its probative value. *See* Fed. R. Evid. 403.

The F.B.I. file report shows that Powell was a member of the Black Panthers nearly 20 years ago for the brief period of eight months. During that time, Powell participated in peaceful demonstrations and political rallies, and he met with other members in "strategy meetings." . . .

2. Application of Rules to Facts

As in any legal argument, the fact analysis should lead to a conclusion by relating the facts to the legal standard:

Little relevance

Purely political and social activities such as these have little or no probative value on the question of the likelihood that Powell provoked Beatty's assault. As a member of the Black Panthers organization, Powell did not espouse violence or engage in any violent activities.

Unfair prejudice

The primary effect of the evidence would be to inflame the passions of the jury. Despite the nonviolent role that Powell played as a member of the organization, many view the Black Panthers as a radical organization that actively sought violent confrontation with established institutions such as police agencies. Conservative jurors undoubtedly would react emotionally to the controversial image of the Black Panthers.

The evidence of Powell's membership in the Black Panthers organization therefore should be excluded on the ground that it presents a danger of unfair prejudice that substantially outweighs its probative value.

The argument section of an opposing brief or a reply brief will contain similar elements, except that each will be narrowly tailored to respond directly to contentions advanced in the brief that preceded it.

C. THE CONCLUSION

Chapter 11's discussion of conclusions uses examples from sample motions in limine. In summary, you should

(1) end each argument in a brief with a conclusion on that argument, and

(2) end the entire brief with a general summary of all the arguments and of your request for relief.

V. SUMMARY

To prepare a motion to exclude evidence before trial, you should

(1) draft a motion that simply and clearly requests the court to exclude specified evidence and to order the parties from referring to the evidence at trial;

(2) draft a supporting brief that

    (a) introduces the facts and procedural history relevant to the motion,

    (b) argues the law and facts relating to the evidentiary issues, and

    (c) states your conclusions; and

(3) attach any documentary evidence or affidavits necessary to support your motion, or refer to evidence already in the record.

To oppose a motion to exclude evidence, or to reply to an opposition brief, you need not file a separate motion. Instead, you should submit a brief that responds to the arguments presented in the preceding brief.

Deborah E. Driggs
State Bar No. 6081
David L. Keily
State Bar No. 12345
SACKS, TIERNEY, KASEN & KERRICK, P.A.
3300 North Central Avenue, Suite 2000
Phoenix, Arizona 85012-1576
Telephone: (602) 279-4900
Attorneys for Defendants Rayner

SUPERIOR COURT OF ARIZONA
MARICOPA COUNTY

AGUA FRIA SAND & ROCK, INC., an Arizona corporation, Plaintiff,	No. C-531100
v.	MOTION IN LIMINE TO EXCLUDE TESTIMONY AS TO TRANSACTIONS WITH OR STATEMENTS BY JACK M. RAYNER, SR. AND DALE FAY RAYNER
Estate of DALE FAY RAYNER, Deceased; JACK RAYNER, JR., Personal Representative of the Estate of DALE FAY RAYNER, Deceased; Estate of JACK RAYNER, JR., Personal Representative of the Estate of JACK RAYNER, SR., Deceased; JACK RAYNER, JR., Defendants.	(Oral Argument Requested) (Hon. Gloria G. Ybarra)

Defendants Rayner move for an order excluding testimony by the principals of Agua Fria, George R. Mutschler, Sr., and George R. Mutschler, Jr., about transactions with or statements by Jack M. Rayner, Sr., and Dale Fay Rayner. This motion is made pursuant to Arizona's Deadman's statute, A.R.S. § 12-2251, and is supported by the attached Memorandum of Points and Authorities.

DATED December 29, 1986.

By _____

Deborah E. Driggs
David L. Keily, for
SACKS, TIERNEY, KASEN & KERRICK, P.A.
Attorneys for Defendants

MEMORANDUM OF POINTS AND AUTHORITIES

I. FACTUAL BACKGROUND

Plaintiff Agua Fria Sand & Rock, Inc. (Agua Fria) brought this suit against defendants for fraud, breach of a duty of due care, and breach of a lease. Agua Fria was the assignee of a leasehold interest in certain real property owned by defendants. On this property, Agua Fria operated a sand and gravel mine. In February 1980, Agua Fria's plant and equipment were destroyed by a flood. After the flood, Agua Fria moved its operations to a new site on the property.

Agua Fria alleges that the defendants wrongfully evicted them from the new site. Although Agua Fria occupied the land as a tenant at will, it alleges that the defendants promised to execute and deliver a written lease for a term of twenty years.

The defendants deny that they had promised to execute and deliver a written lease for a term of twenty years to Agua Fria. They allege that Agua Fria was evicted because it had failed to make rental payments and to satisfy other lease obligations.

Jack M. Rayner, Sr., died on October 14, 1982. Dale Fay Rayner died on April 17, 1984. Jack M. Rayner, Jr., is the Personal Representative of the Estates of Jack M. Rayner, Sr., and Dale Fay Rayner. Agua Fria has sued Jack M. Rayner, Jr., in his capacity as Personal Representative of the estates of Jack M. Rayner, Sr., and Dale Fay Rayner.

II. ARGUMENT

The Arizona Deadman's Statute Bars Admission of Testimony of Transactions with, or Statements by, Jack M. Rayner, Sr., and Dale Fay Rayner.

To reduce the danger of fraudulent testimony, the Arizona Deadman's statute restricts the admission of testimony about transactions with, or about statements made by, the testator in certain suits:

> In an action by or against personal representatives, administrators, guardians or conservators in which judgment may be given for or against them as such, neither party shall be allowed to testify against the other as to any transaction with or statement by the testator, intestate or ward unless called to testify thereto by the opposite party, or required to testify thereto by the court. The provisions of this section shall extend to and include all actions by or against the heirs, devisees, legatees or legal representatives of a decedent arising out of any transaction with the decedent.

Ariz. Rev. Stat. Ann. § 12-2251 (Supp. 1985).

The statute clearly applies to this case. First, Agua Fria has filed suit against Jack M. Rayner, Jr., in his capacity as personal representative of the estates of Jack M. Rayner, Sr., and Dale Fay Rayner. Judgment may be granted for or against Jack M. Rayner, Jr., in his capacity as personal representative. Finally, Agua Fria plans to introduce evidence of an alleged oral agreement by the

331

deceased, Jack M. Rayner, Sr., and Dale Fay Rayner, to execute a written lease with a term of 20 years.

The statute authorizes admission of testimony of transactions with or statements by the deceased if "required . . . by the court." Therefore, such admission ultimately lies within the discretion of the trial court. *Mahan v. First National Bank,* 139 Ariz. 138, 140, 677 P.2d 301, 303 (App. 1984). The trial court's determination to admit testimony of transactions with or statements by the decedent will be upheld only if (1) independent evidence corroborates the transaction with the decedent, and (2) an injustice will result if the testimony is rejected. *Id.*

Agua Fria has no independent evidence to support its claims that the deceased promised to execute and deliver a written lease of the premises for a term of twenty years. Instead, Agua Fria rests on the bald assertion that the deceased made such promises. This type of uncorroborated testimony is exactly what the statute was intended to proscribe.

Second, no injustice will result from exclusion of testimony of transactions with or statements by Jack M. Rayner, Sr., and Dale Fay Rayner. The exclusion will apply equally to both parties. Moreover, exclusion of the testimony comports strongly with public policy to render incompetent as witnesses persons who will gain from inaccurate distortion of transactions with the decedent when death has rendered the decedent incapable of refuting these inaccuracies. *See Carrillo v. Taylor,* 81 Ariz. 14, 299 P.2d 188 (1956). The exclusion will simply preclude Plaintiff Agua Fria from evading the statute of frauds by making use of self-serving, uncorroborated declarations about what the deceased supposedly said. Agua Fria should not be able to manufacture lease obligations out of the alleged representations of those who are no longer able to refute them.

III. CONCLUSION

The objectionable testimony in this case is uncorroborated and will not result in an injustice if excluded. Therefore, this testimony should be excluded under the applicable Deadman's statute.

DATED December 29, 1986.

SACKS, TIERNEY & KASEN, P.A.

BY _____

Deborah E. Driggs
David L. Keily
3300 North Central Avenue
Phoenix, Arizona 85012-1576
Attorneys for Defendants

15

Appellate Briefs

Briefwriting on appeal differs from most pretrial briefwriting in three respects. First, if you have fully tried your case before appeal, you will analyze the appellate issues on a more complete factual record than was available during the litigation of pretrial motions. Second, in developing your arguments on appeal, you must consider standards of appellate review, which require varying levels of deference to trial court rulings and findings. Third, rules of procedure and local rules typically prescribe a more formal and detailed format for appellate briefs than for pretrial or trial briefs.

I. THE RECORD ON APPEAL

The proceedings in the trial court are recorded in two records: the trial court clerk's record and the reporter's transcript.[1] The trial history of a case can usually be most easily traced in the trial court clerk's record, which contains all the documents filed with the trial court, from the initial pleadings to the notice of appeal. It also includes the written judgment of the court, along with orders reflecting the court's rulings on procedural and other preliminary matters. A docket sheet attached to the clerk's record contains a brief entry for each document in the record. This provides a convenient index to the record and a summary of the history of the litigation. The reporter's transcript is a record of all the statements made in court during the litigation process. It includes oral arguments of the parties on motions, testimony of witnesses, rulings from the bench, and instructions to the jury.

---

1. See, e.g., U.S. Ct. App. 9th Cir. R. 10-2 (West 1988).

Shortly after a disappointed litigant has filed notice of appeal from the judgment of the trial court, the parties on appeal designate the portions of the clerk's record and reporter's transcript that are necessary for the appeal.[2] At least in some court systems, physical exhibits remain with the trial court clerk until requested by the appellate court.[3]

Before writing an appellate brief, you must master the record on appeal, because the evidence and arguments presented to the trial court help to define the scope of the appellate court's inquiry. Indeed, when referring in your brief to testimony, arguments, rulings, or other portions of the trial history, you should carefully cite to the pages of the clerk's record or reporter's transcript that reflect that information. Common abbreviations for citation to page 134 of the clerk's record are "CR 134," for "clerk's record" or "CT 134," for "clerk's transcript." The reporter's transcript is commonly cited as "RT 383." If either record is bound in multiple volumes, you must also cite to the volume number in some reasonable fashion. For example, you might cite to page 115 of the third volume of the reporter's transcript as "III RT 115" or "3 RT 115."

II. STANDARDS OF REVIEW

A. OVERVIEW

As introduced in the chapter on briefing cases, an appellate court will apply different standards of review to different kinds of trial court findings or rulings. For example, on a motion for summary judgment or a motion to dismiss an action for failure to state a claim, a trial court does not resolve any factual disputes; instead, it decides as a matter of law whether alleged or undisputed facts satisfy the applicable legal standards. When reviewing a trial court's granting of such a motion, the appellate court will place itself in the position of the trial court and decide, without deference to the trial court's analysis, whether the moving party satisfied its burden on the motion.[4]

In contrast, a jury's verdict or a trial judge's findings of fact rendered after trial represent the factfinder's resolution of factual disputes. When reviewing such findings, an appellate court will restrict its review, deferring to the factfinder's resolution of conflicting evidence.

Thus, to effectively argue your case on appeal, you must consider the standard of review, or the degree to which the appellate court will defer to a finding or ruling made in the trial court. Indeed, the outcome of some appeals will depend directly on the standard of review that the appellate court chooses to apply.[5]

---

2. E.g., id. at Rule 10-3. Indeed, the court reporter normally will not prepare a transcript of his or her shorthand trial notes until this designation. Id.; Fed. R. App. P. 10(b).

3. E.g., U.S. Ct. App. 9th Cir. R. 11-4.2 (West 1989).

4. Experimental Engg., Inc. v. United Technologies Corp., 614 F.2d 1244, 1246 (9th Cir. 1980) (reviewing dismissal of action for failure to state a claim); Heiniger v. City of Phoenix, 625 F.2d 842, 843-844 (9th Cir. 1980) (discussing standards of review for summary judgment).

5. See, e.g., Chaline v. KCOH, Inc., 693 F.2d 477, 480 n.3 (5th Cir. 1982); Walsh v. Centeio, 692 F.2d 1239, 1241 (9th Cir. 1982).

Appellate standards of review in the federal court system are typical of those in other court systems and will serve as general examples. Under the two most important standards, an appellate court restricts its review of questions of fact but not of questions of law.

B. RESTRICTED APPELLATE REVIEW OF FINDINGS OF FACT

The seventh amendment to the United States Constitution guarantees the right to a jury trial "in suits at common law," and it provides that "no fact tried by a jury shall be otherwise re-examined in any court of the United States, than according to the rules of the common law." Under the common law rules, an appellate court will not overturn the factual findings of a jury unless those findings are not supported by "any substantial evidence."[6] Federal statutes prescribe the same standard of review for the findings of some administrative agencies.[7]

For example, consider a jury's verdict that the defendant in a civil suit negligently caused the plaintiff to suffer injuries valued at $150,000. Assuming that the trial court properly instructed the jury on the law, the appellate court will affirm the jury's verdict if substantial evidence in the record supports the finding of negligence[8] and the calculation of damages, even if the appellate judges might have reached a different verdict had they evaluated the same evidence as jurors.

In civil suits in which the parties have no constitutional or statutory right to a jury, or in suits in which the parties have waived their right to a jury, the trial judge will both find the facts and rule on the law. Under Federal Rule of Civil Procedure 52(a), a federal court of appeals will not overturn the factual findings of a federal trial judge unless the findings are "clearly erroneous." Although Rule 52(a) applies only to civil proceedings and does not directly apply to a trial judge's factual findings on preliminary rulings in a criminal trial, some courts have adopted Rule 52(a)'s clearly-erroneous standard by analogy for that context.[9]

Under Rule 52(a), a trial judge trying a case without a jury will divide his findings into findings of fact and conclusions of law. For example, he may state as a conclusion of law that a federal antidiscrimination statute requires proof of intent to discriminate, and he may state as a finding of fact that the evidence shows no discriminatory intent. On appeal, the appellate court could review without restriction the trial judge's interpretation of the statute as requiring proof of intent to discriminate, and it would reverse the trial court's conclusion on that question if it interpreted the statute differently. In contrast, the appel-

---

6. E.g., Aetna Life Ins. Co. v. Kepler, 116 F.2d 1, 4 & n.1 (8th Cir. 1941).

7. E.g., 29 U.S.C. § 160(f) (appellate review of findings of the National Labor Relations Board).

8. Interestingly, a finding of negligence is not a pure finding of fact, because it requires the jury to define and apply a standard of care, resulting in a mixed conclusion of law and fact. For purposes of appellate review, however, such jury verdicts are treated as findings of fact. Appellate courts may distinguish more finely between a trial judge's findings of fact and conclusions of law.

9. E.g., United States v. Page, 302 F.2d 81, 85-86 (9th Cir. 1962) (en banc) (appellate review of trial judge's finding of consent to search). Of course, the defendant has a right to a jury determination of the ultimate facts regarding criminal liability. U.S. Const. amend. VI.

late court would not overturn the trial judge's factual finding of absence of discriminatory intent unless the record showed that finding to be clearly erroneous,[10] even if the appellate judges might have found discriminatory intent had they been the initial factfinders.

At least in theory, the clearly-erroneous standard of review of a trial judge's factual findings permits broader appellate review than does the substantial-evidence standard mandated by the seventh amendment for review of a jury's findings and mandated by statute for review of the findings of some administrative agencies:[11]

> Under the substantial-evidence standard, a reviewing court must uphold the findings of a jury or administrative agency if the record contains sufficient evidence to permit a reasonable person to make those findings. In contrast, the clearly-erroneous standard permits the reviewing court to review the entire record, and to overturn a finding of fact if it is convinced that the finding is clearly wrong, even though a reasonable person could have made the finding.[12]

An appellate court's deference to factual findings made in the trial court is supported by practical and policy considerations that recognize distinctions in the roles of trial and appellate courts. The factfinder in the trial court, either the judge or the jury, is generally in a better position than the appellate court to evaluate the evidence. This advantage is strongest when factual findings are based partly on the factfinder's evaluation of the credibility of witnesses: the mannerisms of the witness on the stand may be much more revealing than the cold print of the reporter's transcript. Accordingly, Rule 52(a) specifically directs appellate courts to give "due regard" to "the opportunity of the trial court to judge of the credibility of the witnesses."

Conversely, the trial court's advantage is weakest when factual findings are based largely on documentary evidence that is available in identical form to both the trial and appellate courts. Nonetheless, Rule 52(a) applies to "[f]indings of fact, whether based on oral or documentary evidence,"[13] suggesting that restrictions on appellate review must be at least partly based on policies other than a practical advantage enjoyed by the trial court.

In fact, restricted appellate review of findings of fact is independently justified by the importance of an appellate court's role in developing general principles of law relative to its role of correcting error in the judgment in a particular case. Admittedly, appellate courts should perform a limited "corrective" function by subjecting each trial judgment to some review for error and thus reducing the risk of injustice.[14] At least as important, however, is the appellate court's "institutional" function of "developing and declaring legal principles that will have application beyond the case that serves as the vehicle

---

10. See Pullman-Standard v. Swint, 456 U.S. 273, 287-288 (1982).

11. E.g., Loehr v. Offshore Logistics, Inc., 691 F.2d 758, 760-761 (5th Cir. 1982).

12. Calleros, Title VII and Rule 52(a): Standards of Appellate Review in Disparate Treatment Cases—Limiting the Reach of Pullman-Standard v. Swint, 58 Tul. L. Rev. 411 n.40 (1983) (citations omitted).

13. Fed. R. Civ. P. 52(a) (as amended 1983).

14. See Calleros, supra note 12, at 421-422.

for expression of the principles."[15] This institutional function is strongest in the highest appellate court in a jurisdiction.[16] It emphasizes the development of a cohesive body of legal standards rather than the review of evidence supporting findings of fact.

C. CONCLUSIONS OF LAW; MIXED CONCLUSIONS OF FACT AND LAW

In contrast to restricted appellate review of findings of fact, appellate review of a trial judge's conclusions of law is unrestricted. The appellate court may freely correct the trial court's formulation of legal standards.[17]

Often, however, classifying a finding as more nearly one of law than of fact in a nonjury trial is a difficult task.[18] Without doubt, Rule 52(a)'s clearly-erroneous standard applies to appellate review of a trial judge's findings of historical fact, such as findings about events and actions.[19] It also applies to review of "factual inferences" drawn by a trial court from "undisputed basic facts."[20] However, some trial court determinations fall between the two extremes of formulation of abstract legal standards and findings of historical fact or factual inference. For example, a trial judge's determination of whether the historical facts satisfy an abstract legal standard is a mixed finding of fact and law, which may contain elements of both factual inference and refinement of the legal standard.

Appellate review of a narrow class of such mixed findings is restricted under a special standard of review. Specifically, an appellate court will restrict its review of certain "discretionary" rulings of a trial judge, such as the determination to grant or deny an injunction.[21] Assuming that the trial judge formulated the correct legal rule before applying it to the facts, the appellate court will not overturn such a mixed finding of the trial judge unless she "abused" her discretion.

Most mixed findings, however, do not fall within this narrow class of discretionary rulings. Instead, for purposes of appellate standards of review, appellate courts must classify the findings under Rule 52(a) as findings of fact or conclusions of law. The proper means of accomplishing this classification is a matter of continuing debate.[22] However, the practical and policy considerations underlying restrictions on appellate review provide some guidance in the debate.

---

15. Id. at 420-421.

16. Indeed, under its "two-court rule," the United States Supreme Court will give particular deference to a finding of fact made by a trial judge and upheld on appeal in the intermediate court of appeals. See e.g., Rogers v. Lodge, 458 U.S. 613, 622-627 (1982).

17. Pullman-Standard v. Swint, 456 U.S. 273, 287 (1982).

18. Id. at 288.

19. E.g., Washington v. Watkins, 655 F.2d 1346, 1352 (5th Cir. 1981), *cert. denied*, 456 U.S. 949 (1982).

20. Commissioner v. Duberstein, 363 U.S. 278, 291 (1960) (citing United States v. United States Gypsum Co., 333 U.S. 364, 394 (1948)).

21. E.g., Calleros, supra note 12, at 431 n.143 (collecting examples); see also Mars Steel Corp. v. Continental Bank N.A., 880 F.2d 928 (7th Cir. 1989) (en banc) (review of decisions on Fed. R. Civ. P. 11 sanctions).

22. See Pullman-Standard v. Swint, supra note 17.

If a mixed question of fact and law requires the application of a simple, noncontroversial legal rule to complex historical facts, its resolution may primarily require the trial judge to refine her understanding of the facts rather than to engage in substantial legal reasoning. The trial judge is in the best position to make such a determination, and review of the resulting mixed finding requires exercise primarily of the appellate court's corrective function. Therefore, an appellate court should view the finding as more nearly a finding of factual inference than a conclusion of law.

Consider, for example, a dispute about whether numerous statements and actions by an employer cumulatively created a hostile working environment for female employees, in violation of Title VII. Although resolution of that question inevitably requires some refinement of the statutory language "conditions . . . of employment,"[23] it primarily requires an analysis of the facts. Thus, an appellate court undoubtedly would treat it as a question of fact for purposes of restricted appellate review.

Conversely, if a mixed question of fact and law requires the application of complex, uncertain, or highly controversial legal standards to simple historical facts, the trial judge's resolution of the question may primarily reflect refinement of her understanding of the content of the legal rules. The appellate court is at least equally capable of making such a determination, and it will primarily exercise its institutional function on review. Therefore, an appellate court should view the finding as more nearly a conclusion of law than one of factual inference.[24]

Consider, for example, the question in one United States Supreme Court case of whether the government presented "clear, unequivocal and convincing" proof that a naturalized citizen had fraudulently procured his certificate of naturalization during World War II by falsely renouncing his allegiance to Nazi Germany and falsely swearing allegiance to the United States. The technical nature of the special standard of proof and the uncertainty and political sensitivity of the legal concept of "allegience" made this question primarily one of law. Therefore, the appellate courts could review the trial court's determination without restriction.[25]

III. THE BRIEF—EFFECTIVE APPELLATE ADVOCACY

A. FORMAT—OVERVIEW

Rules of procedure and local court rules typically prescribe formats for appellate briefs that are more formal and detailed than those for motions memoranda and other briefs. When you represent the "appellant," the party bring-

---

23. 42 U.S.C. § 2000e-2(a)(1).

24. See generally United States v. McConney, 728 F.2d 1195, 1204 (9th Cir., *cert. denied*, 469 U.S. 824 (1984) (in a criminal case, adopting a "functional analysis that focuses on the nature of the inquiry required when we apply the relevant rule of law to the facts as established"); Calleros, Title VII and Rule 52(a): Standards of Appellate Review in Disparate Treatment Cases—Limiting the Reach of *Pullman-Standard v. Swint*, 58 Tul. L. Rev. 403, 425-432 (1983) (using different definitional framework to develop similar analysis).

25. Baumgartner v. United States, 322 U.S. 665 (1944).

ing the appeal, you must file the opening brief. Typical rules will require this brief to include the following substantive components:

(1) a statement of the issues raised on appeal;

(2) a statement of the procedural history of the case, usually entitled "Statement of the Case;"

(3) a statement of the facts relevant to issues raised on appeal;

(4) an argument; and

(5) a conclusion.

In addition, rules usually impose limitations on length and require formal components such as a table of contents and alphabetically arranged tables of authorities.[26]

Some rules may modify the organization of the components listed above, specify subcomponents of one or more of the components, or add other required components. For example, the Federal Rules of Appellate Procedure require the components listed above but combine the statements of procedural history and facts into a single section, referred to as "a statement of the case."[27] Supplementing those rules, the local rules for the United States Court of Appeals for the Ninth Circuit require the statement of the case to address jurisdictional matters, including the subject-matter jurisdiction of the trial court, the statutory basis for the appellate jurisdiction of the Court of Appeals, the appealability of the order appealed from, and the timeliness of the notice of appeal. The Ninth Circuit local rules also require separate sections that address such matters as the standard of appellate review and the identity of any related cases pending before the court.[28]

If you represent the "appellee," the party seeking affirmance of the judgment of the trial court, you must file an answering brief. This brief will contain the same components as that of the opening brief. However, to the extent that you do not contest the statement of the procedural history, facts, or issues, your answering brief need not repeat the substance of that portion of the opening brief; you may simply state that the appellee adopts all or part of the opening brief's statement.[29]

Finally, if you represent the appellant, you may file a reply brief. This brief should confine itself to rebutting points made in the appellee's answering brief.[30]

Rules of procedure or local court rules often specify a form for the cover sheets for appellate briefs, often even assigning different colors for the covers of opening, answering, and reply briefs.[31] The specified form for the information on the cover of an appellate brief varies in different jurisdictions. In some jurisdictions, the cover sheet includes the caption of the case in the same basic format as it appeared in trial pleadings and briefs.[32] In other jurisdictions, the caption and other critical identifying information is presented on several widely spaced lines that are centered on the cover page.

---

26. E.g., Ariz. R. of Civ. App. P. 13(a), 14(b).
27. Fed. R. App. P. 28(a)(3).
28. U.S. Ct. App. 9th Cir. Local R. 28-2 (West 1988).
29. See, e.g., Ariz. R. Civ. App. P. 13(b).
30. See, e.g., Ariz. R. Civ. App. P. 13(c).
31. E.g., Fed. R. App. P. 32(a).
32. For examples of this format, see the sample pleadings and briefs at the ends of Chapters 12-14 and this chapter.

B. STATEMENT OF ISSUES

The art of stating issues in a student case brief or an office memorandum is discussed in detail in Chapters 5 and 8. You should review those principles as a starting point for your drafting the statement of issues in your appellate brief. When drafting an issue statement in a brief, however, you should additionally strive to phrase the issue in a way that suggests a favorable response or otherwise serves to advocate your client's case.

1. Issue Statements as Preliminary Advocacy

Your statement of the issue can invite the court to apply an analytic framework or standard of review that best suits your client's arguments. Of course, you should develop that strategy primarily in the argument section of the brief. In addition, however, you can make the judge more receptive to your approach by initially exposing her to your strategy in your statement of the issues.

For example, suppose that you represent an appellant who appeals from a trial judge's decision to deny a preliminary injunction. You know that the appellate court will overturn that decision only if the trial judge abused her discretion, provided that the trial judge applied the proper legal standards to the facts.[33] However, you believe that her ruling leaves some room for question about the content of the legal rules governing injunctions that she applied to the facts. Accordingly, you might use the statement of the issue to invite the appellate court to find error in the trial judge's formulation of the legal rules, which formulation would be subject to unrestricted review:

I. In denying Surge Corp.'s request for a preliminary injunction, did the trial judge apply an incorrect legal rule by requiring a showing of likelihood of success on the merits, rather than using a "sliding scale" test that would justify a preliminary injunction upon a showing of especially great irreparable harm and at least substantial questions on the merits?

The opposing counsel may argue that the trial judge in fact applied a sliding-scale test and that the judge's balancing of the facts does not reflect an abuse of discretion under the most flexible of legal rules. Nonetheless, he might frame the issue so that it emphasizes the restricted standard of review of the ultimate ruling and refers only abstractly to potential questions about choices among legal rules:

---

33. See, e.g., Los Angeles Memorial Coliseum Comm'n v. National Football League, 634 F.2d 1197, 1200 (9th Cir. 1980).

I. Did the trial judge properly exercise her discretion to deny preliminary injunctive relief on the ground that Surge Corp. failed to make the requisite showing on the merits under applicable legal rules?

Of course, the nature of the opportunity to promote a favorable approach in the statement of the issue will vary with the circumstances of each appeal. For example, an appeal might raise a purely legal question about whether the court should recognize a special exception to the general common law contract requirement of consideration to suit the peculiar facts of an exceptional case. If so, the parties might use their statements of the issue, as well as their arguments, to appeal either to the appellate judges' senses of fairness and justice or to their beliefs in the virtue of certainty in the law.

In those circumstances, if you represent the party who would benefit from an exception to the principle, you might use the statement of the issue to vividly and concretely emphasize the peculiar facts of the case:

I. Does McGowin's moral obligation to perform his promise to pay Webb for past services give rise to a legal obligation in light of the serious physical injuries suffered by Webb and the immeasurable benefit he gave to McGowin in heroically saving McGowin's life?

This statement of the issue focuses the judges' attention on the appellate court's corrective function: reaching a just result on the unique facts of the particular case before it, even if that requires a departure from general principles.[34]

In contrast, if you represent the party who would benefit from application of the general principle, you might use the statement of the issue to promote the consideration rule in its abstract form or to emphasize the general policies supporting the rule:

I. Did the trial court correctly reject a "moral obligation" exception to the fundamental principle that a promise made in recognition of past services lacks consideration and therefore is unenforceable?

This issue focuses the judges' attention on factors related to the appellate court's institutional function: the wisdom of applying the rule in nearly every context, the importance of maintaining the vitality of a long-standing rule, and the need for certainty in the law.[35]

2. Credibility of the Advocate

In phrasing the statement of the issue to advocate an approach or a conclusion, you should not be so anxious to invite a favorable response that you

---

34. See generally Webb v. Mcgowin, 27 Ala. App. 82, 86, 168 So. 196, 199 (Samford, J., concurring) (departing from "strict letter of the rule" in the interests of justice), *cert. denied*, 232 Ala. 374, 168 So. 199 (1936).

35. See generally Mills v. Wyman, 3 Pick. 207 (Mass. 1825) (rejecting "moral obligation" exception in the interests of maintaining universal application of the consideration doctrine).

state a false issue. For example, assume that you represent a criminal defendant who appeals from a state conviction for illegal possession of cocaine. The applicable criminal statute defines "possession" as contemporaneous intent and ability to exercise physical control over the substance. If the trial judge correctly instructed the jury on the applicable legal rules and definitions, you might still argue that substantial evidence did not support the jury finding of ability to exercise control over the cocaine. If so, the following statement of the issue would not effectively advance your client's cause:

‖ I. Is proof of ability to control an illegal substance a requisite element of a
‖ conviction for illegal possession of that substance?

Under currently accepted legal definitions in the state, an appellate judge would readily agree that the question presented by this statement of the issue must be answered affirmatively. However, she would object that the question does not fairly characterize any nonfrivolous issue on appeal. Because the trial judge correctly instructed the jury on the applicable legal standards, your implicit attack on the completeness of the instructions would be futile. Instead, your issue statement must fairly address your client's true contention on appeal:

‖ I. Is the jury's finding of Wade's ability to control the cocaine unsupported
‖ by substantial evidence in light of undisputed testimony that the officers
‖ found Wade standing outside the locked automobile containing the cocaine
‖ without a key to the automobile?

Thus, you must recognize limits to your efforts to invite a favorable response to a statement of the issue. Specifically, you must maintain credibility and must fairly link the statement of the issue to your genuine argument on appeal.

C. STATEMENT OF PROCEDURAL HISTORY

Rules of procedure or local court rules will specify whether you must state the procedural history in a separate section or combine it with the historical facts. If the rules require you to state the procedural history in a separate section, they typically designate the section as the "Statement of the Case." If the rules instead require you to combine the facts and procedural history, they typically designate the combined section as either the "Statement of the Case" or the "Statement of Facts." With either format, the essential elements of a statement of procedural history are brief descriptions of "the nature of the case, the course of the proceedings, and its disposition in the court below."[36]

In the opening paragraph of the statement of procedural history, you should introduce the parties and generally describe the claims and defenses that they brought in the trial court. Next, you should chronologically recite the portions of the trial history and the rulings of the court that are relevant to the

---

36. Fed. R. App. P. 28(a)(3).

issues on appeal, including the trial court's final judgment and the appellant's filing notice of appeal. In a brief to a second-level court of appeal, you should also summarize the ruling of the intermediate appellate court. As described in section III above, court rules in some jurisdictions may require you to discuss additional matters.

D. STATEMENT OF FACTS

1. Format

Your statement of facts on appeal is subject to two limitations. First, except for matters within common knowledge or otherwise subject to judicial notice,[37] the appellate court and the litigants are constrained by the trial court record as the exclusive source for the facts of the dispute. In a fully tried case, those facts are reflected in testimony recorded in the reporter's transcript, in documentary evidence admitted at trial, and in any physical evidence admitted at trial and retained by the trial court clerk. If the trial court disposed of the case on the pleadings or on summary judgment, the facts are reflected in the allegations of the pleadings or in the preliminary showings of evidence on the motion for summary judgment.[38]

Second, if findings of fact are made by a jury or by the trial court, those findings take on greater significance than the underlying record of testimony and other evidence because of the restricted appellate review of such findings. If the appellant wishes to challenge the findings of fact as clearly erroneous or as unsupported by substantial evidence, then the appellant should refer to the underlying record of evidence to support the challenge. If the appellant instead chooses to limit the attack to a challenge of the trial judge's formulation of legal standards or the judge's application of those standards to facts, the appellant must rely on the findings of fact, perhaps with supplementary references to illuminating evidence that is consistent with the findings. The appellee, of course, should focus on either the findings or the underlying evidence supporting the findings, depending on which response most appropriately meets the appellant's challenge.

2. The Power of Facts

The opening statement of facts in a brief can play a surprisingly important role in persuasion. In many cases, applicable legal standards are sufficiently general, flexible, or unclear to support any of several conclusions on the application of the law to facts. Indeed, a judge's determination of whether the facts satisfy the applicable legal standard helps to further refine the legal standard.

In making this determination, a judge tries to reach a just result in the

---

37. See, e.g., Fed. R. Evid. 201 and advisory committee note on subdivision (f) (judicial notice of adjudicative facts in trial and on appeal); United States v. Pink, 315 U.S. 203, 216 (1942) (appellate judicial notice of record in other case).

38. See generally Ariz. S. Ct. R. 5(b)(5) (West 1988).

case before her while performing the separate institutional function of developing a coherent body of law that will satisfy general policy considerations and will provide useful precedent for the resolution of other disputes. Developing a coherent body of precedent is primarily the task of appellate courts, and is particularly important in the highest court in a jurisdiction. A trial judge will be most concerned about reaching a just result within the parameters of existing precedent.[39]

A persuasive statement of facts near the beginning of your brief may incline a judge to rule in favor of your client even before the judge has considered the legal analysis. If so, the judge may take advantage of the flexibility or uncertainty in the legal principles to reach the result that the facts have persuaded her to define as just, provided that she can do so without departing from clearly controlling precedent or otherwise upsetting the orderly development of a coherent body of law. A persuasive opening statement of facts will help make the judge receptive to the legal and factual analyses in the argument section of your brief.

3. Persuasive Presentation of Facts

To present the facts persuasively, you may be tempted to slant the record misleadingly in favor of your client's case or to introduce legal arguments and conclusions in the statement of facts. Neither technique is likely to succeed.

a. Advocacy with Credibility

If you riddle your statement of facts with exaggerations or misleading omissions, you will simply diminish your credibility. Instead, your statement of facts should display your client in a favorable light while reflecting a concern for completeness and accuracy. If the judge is convinced that your statement is accurate and complete, she may repeatedly refer to it as a fair summary of the record, resulting in maximum exposure of the subtle advocacy of your statement.

Rather than omit unfavorable facts, you should simply deemphasize them, while emphasizing favorable ones. In addition to the techniques of persuasive writing discussed in Chapter 11, you can use the organization of the entire fact statement to emphasize the favorable facts. Chronological order of facts may be the clearest and most logical. However, you can increase the impact of favorable events by describing them in the places of greatest emphasis: the beginning and end of the fact statement. If you can do so without unduly sacrificing clarity and continuity, you can justify departing from chronological order.

You can also emphasize favorable facts by using specific and concrete descriptions and strong verbs in active voice. Conversely, you can lessen the

---

39. See generally Calleros, Title VII and Rule 52(a): Standards of Appellate Review in Disparate Treatment Cases—Limiting the Reach of *Pullman-Standard v. Swint,* 58 Tul. L. Rev. 403, 420-422 (1983).

impact of unfavorable facts by describing them in general, abstract terms. For example, suppose that Samuel Hughes, the defendant in a prosecution for first-degree murder seeks to mitigate the offense by showing that he was intoxicated at the time of the crime and therefore could not have premeditated the killing. As the prosecutor, you can deemphasize his intoxication by referring to it generally, and you can emphasize his aggressive conduct by describing it in gruesome detail:

While under the influence of self-induced intoxication, the defendant mur- ‖
dered Grace Smith by bludgeoning her from behind with a baseball bat.   ‖

This statement relegates the defendant to anonymity by referring to him with a procedural label. In contrast, it names the victim, thus inviting the reader to recognize her as a person, rather than a statistic. Moreover, the description of the attack as one from behind tends to portray the victim as particularly sympathetic and defenseless. The statement not only refers to the defendant's impaired state of mind abstractly and in a subordinate phrase, it invites the reader to reject state of mind as a mitigating factor by characterizing it as self-induced. Finally, strong, vivid words such as "murdered" and "bludgeoning," convey the horror of the assault.

As counsel for the defendant, you might refer to the same incident with converse emphasis:

When the victim was killed by a blow to the head, Samuel Hughes was ‖
staggering from the effects of nearly three pints of whiskey.   ‖

In contrast to the prosecutor's statement, this one refers to the killing and the victim in abstract terms, in passive voice, and in a subordinate clause. Moreover, it humanizes the defendant by referring to him by name, and it describes his intoxication vividly.

b. Premature Legal Argument

If you prematurely introduce legal or factual argument into your statement of facts, you may undermine the effectiveness of your fact statement as a vehicle for making the judge receptive to your main argument. A judge knows that the legal argument of a brief will be one-sided, and he generally reserves judgment on legal conclusions until he has read both briefs. But he may be more willing to draw his own conclusions from an apparently complete and accurate statement of facts.

For example, if your statement of facts specifically characterizes a driver's operation of an automobile as negligent, it may produce a defensive reaction in the judge; he may warn himself that he should resist such a mixed conclusion of law and fact until he has thoroughly studied the arguments in both briefs. On the other hand, if your statement of facts vividly describes the automobile veering from lane to lane at an excessive speed it will implicitly invite the judge to draw his own conclusion that the driver acted negligently. Even if tentative or subconscious, that conclusion will predispose the judge toward accepting the advocate's explicit legal arguments and conclusions in the argument section of your brief.

Thus, when the judge reaches the argument section of the brief, he may resist arguments supporting conclusions that you had bluntly attempted to force on him in the statement of facts. He will be more comfortable with arguments that seem to confirm conclusions he had reached on his own after reading apparently nonargumentative facts.

4. Summary and Perspective

To ensure that your opening statement of facts makes the judge more receptive to your main argument, you should
  (1) state the facts completely and accurately;
  (2) emphasize favorable facts and deemphasize unfavorable ones through sentence structure, varying levels of specificity and concreteness, and general organization; and
  (3) avoid premature argument.

E. THE ARGUMENT

Earlier Chapters have provided you with the basic information and skills you need to formulate, organize, and express your arguments in any brief. In summary, for each issue you should
  (1) state your contention in an argumentative point heading,
  (2) argue for a favorable interpretation of legal authority,
  (3) apply the legal rules to the facts, and
  (4) state the conclusion that you want the appellate court to reach.
This section will supplement the earlier chapters by examining some characteristics of argumentation that are peculiar to appellate briefs.

1. Arguing the Law—The Role of Policy Analysis

Appellate briefs differ in style from pretrial and trial briefs in the greater extent to which they examine the underlying policies of legal standards. Depending on the procedural posture and other circumstances of a particular appeal, this difference in approach may reflect such factors as the restrictions on appellate review of factual findings, the appellate court's institutional function of developing a cohesive body of law, and the varying degrees to which stare decisis controls decisions at various levels of the court system.

For example, suppose that after the presentation of evidence to the jury in a contract dispute, a party requests the trial judge to rule on the merits as a matter of law on the ground that the jury could reasonably reach only one conclusion on the evidence. In considering such a motion for a "directed verdict," the trial judge has no authority to modify or overrule appellate precedents that establish the applicable contracts law or the standards for a directed verdict. Rather, the trial judge must seek to understand and to apply those rules to the evidence. Of course, the trial judge can engage in creative legal analysis to the extent that the content of the legal rules or their application to facts is uncertain, but that opportunity is relatively limited in many cases at the trial level. Accordingly, the briefs on such a motion likely will summarize the appellate precedent on the legal questions and will focus attention on the evidence and the inferences to be drawn from it.

On appeal from a final judgment, the emphasis often shifts from analysis of the factual record to the content of the legal rules, particularly if the trial judge or jury has made findings of fact after a full trial. Unless the appellant assumes the difficult burden of challenging such factual findings, the appellate briefs likely will explore questions about the content of legal rules, either in the abstract or in the process of determining whether the accepted facts satisfy the rules. Because the appellate court has at least limited power to overrule its own precedents, it will consider policy arguments favoring or opposing extension, modification, or overruling of those precedents.

The institutional function of the appellate courts further encourages policy analysis in appellate briefwriting. For two reasons, this effect is greatest in the highest court of a jurisdiction. First, unlike an intermediate court of appeals, the highest court is not bound by the precedent of any court within that jurisdiction.[40] Second, the highest courts in many jurisdictions will accept review of some kinds of lower court decisions only after a discretionary determination that the decision raises important questions about the development of a cohesive body of law or that it otherwise would significantly affect the outcome of many cases other than the one that serves as the vehicle for addressing the questions.

These qualities of courts of last resort are illustrated by the hearings in 1987 of the Senate Judiciary Committee on Judge Robert Bork's unsuccessful bid for confirmation to the United States Supreme Court. Some who actively opposed Judge Bork's confirmation to the Court had not opposed his earlier appointment to the United States Court of Appeals for the District of Columbia Circuit. They explained that Judge Bork's reportedly extremist views on constitutional law could work little mischief on the Court of Appeals because that court is constrained by Supreme Court precedent. However, they feared that his presence on the Supreme Court, which is not absolutely bound by even its own precedent, might hasten that court's retreat from hard-won advances in civil rights.[41]

Thus, more often than in trial briefs, appellate advocates will allocate substantial portions of their arguments to the policies underlying legal rules and to the social and jurisprudential consequences of retaining or abandoning those rules. Moreover, these characteristics typically will be even more pronounced in a court of last resort than in an intermediate court of appeals.

---

40. Of course, decisions of a state court of last resort on a question of federal law could be reviewed by the United States Supreme Court, and the state court would be bound by United States Supreme Court precedent on such questions.

41. See, e.g., The United States Senate Judiciary Committee Chairman's Consultants, Response Prepared to White House Analysis of Judge Bork's Record § VI(D) (Sept. 2, 1987), reprinted in 9 Cardozo L. Rev. 219, 293 (1987).

For example, the following two passages are excerpts of arguments about the proper application of precedent of the state supreme court, the highest court in the state. The first argument could be addressed to the trial court or even to the intermediate court of appeals. Because neither court can overrule the state supreme court precedent, the argument focuses on the applicability of the law of the precedent to the facts of the dispute:

> ### B. The trial judge erred in instructing the jury that Bramwell could be liable for the tort of wrongful discharge if he discharged Kirkeide in "bad faith" rather than in violation of public policy.

Introduction to argument

The trial court's instruction on the tort of wrongful discharge fails to distinguish between conduct that violates a public policy and conduct that is simply unfair or retaliatory in the context of a particular employment relationship. This instruction permitted the jury to award damages against Bramwell for conduct that is not tortious in this state.

The New Maine Supreme Court has recently recognized a cause of action in tort for wrongful discharge. However, it carefully limited its holding to **General legal rule** discharges that violate public policy:

> Thus, an employer is liable in tort for wrongful discharge if it discharges an employee for a reason that violates an important public policy of the state. Pronouncements of public policy will most often be found in our state's constitution and its legislation.

Blass v. Arcon Co., 337 N. Me. 771, 776 (1988).

In-depth case analysis

In *Blass,* the employer discharged a truck driver in retaliation for the driver's refusal to transport toxic wastes in unsafe containers. The employer was liable in tort for wrongful discharge because its conduct violated the policy of state environmental and occupational safety statutes. *Id.* at 777.

Application to facts

In contrast to *Blass,* Bramwell's discharge of Kirkeide in this case did not violate any public policy. Yet, the trial court's instruction permitted the jury to impose liability. . . .

In the preceding illustration, the *Blass* decision did not need to address whether a discharge can be tortious for reasons other than a violation of public policy; therefore, it does not preclude future extensions of the new tort of wrongful discharge. Nonetheless, the briefwriter has reasonably assumed that a trial court or intermediate court of appeals would not readily extend a newly recognized tort beyond the terms of the Supreme Court's holding. Thus, the briefwriter concentrates on explaining the holding of the *Blass* decision and distinguishing it.

In contrast, the following passage is addressed to the New Maine Supreme Court, the mythical author of the *Blass* decision. Because that court can overrule, limit, or extend its own precedent, the argument spends more time on policy analysis. Specifically, it argues that, as a matter of policy, the court should not broaden the tort of wrongful discharge beyond the holding of the *Blass* decision.

B. The trial judge erred in instructing the jury that Bramwell could be liable. . . .

The trial court's instruction on the tort of wrongful discharge fails to distinguish between conduct that violates a public policy and conduct that . . .

Introduction to argument

Although this court has recently recognized a cause of action in tort for wrongful discharge, it carefully limited its holding to discharges that violate public policy:

General legal rule

Thus, an employer is liable . . .
Blass v. Arcon Co., 337 N. Me. 771, 776 (1988).

In *Blass,* the employer discharged a truck driver in retaliation for the driver's refusal to transport toxic wastes in unsafe containers. . . .

In-depth case analysis

This court should reject Kirkeide's invitation to extend the tort of wrongful discharge beyond the holding of *Blass.* This state has long promoted the policy of freedom of contract, permitting contracting parties to shape their own rights and obligations. *E.g., Snell v. Abundes,* 128 N. Me. 217, 221 (1970). Even if limited to violations of public policy, the tort of wrongful discharge effectively limits the parties' freedom to create a contract that is terminable at will. This court should not restrict the freedom to contract any further. Therefore, this court should narrowly tailor the tort of wrongful discharge to impose liability only for discharges that offend the values of society as a whole, and not for discharges that merely reflect ill will between two private parties.

Policy analysis

If tort liability can be based on simple "bad faith," courts and juries will be forced to second-guess every discharge to determine whether it was motivated by legitimate business considerations or personal spite. . . .

Policy analysis

Application to facts

In our case, the trial court's instruction, approved by the court of appeals, extended the tort of wrongful discharge beyond the holding of *Blass.* By permitting an award of damages for a bad-faith discharge, . . .

2. Arguing the Law and the Facts

a. Strategic Choices

The appellant will seek to overturn unfavorable findings or conclusions of the trial court. Thus, as explained in section II above, the appellant will benefit from unrestricted appellate review of such findings or conclusions. Accordingly, if you represent the appellant, you should try to characterize unfavorable mixed findings of fact and law in a nonjury trial as conclusions of law, which are reviewable on appeal without restriction. On this matter, neither party is bound by the trial court's characterization of a finding as one of fact or law. In a jury trial, on the other hand, a jury's mixed finding of fact and law will always be treated as a finding of fact for purposes of restricted appellate review.

If an unfavorable finding is undeniably one of fact, you must make some strategic choices among alternative approaches on appeal. As counsel for the appellant you must decide whether to challenge the unfavorable finding of fact under a restricted standard of review, argue that the trial court applied the wrong legal rule to the facts, or both.

For example, suppose the plaintiff in a federal civil rights suit successfully sought compensatory and punitive damages against your client, a police officer, for false arrest in violation of the fourth amendment. At trial, the trial judge gave the following instructions to the jury over your objection:

> If you find that Officer Mullins arrested Ms. Wong without probable cause, you must find that Officer Mullins violated Ms. Wong's constitutional rights, and you must award Ms. Wong compensatory damages in the amount of her actual injuries. Furthermore, if you find that Officer Mullins was grossly and inexcusably careless with regard to Ms. Wong's constitutional rights, you may exercise discretion to award Ms. Wong punitive damages in an amount that will punish Officer Mullins and discourage him and others from similar violations.

Applying these instructions to the facts, the jury found Officer Mullins liable and awarded Ms. Wong $5,000 in compensatory damages and $25,000 in punitive damages. The trial court also awarded Ms. Wong her reasonable attorney's fees.

Your client, Officer Mullins, has appealed. As one of your arguments on appeal, you wish to challenge the award of punitive damages, which is necessarily premised on a jury finding that Officer Mullins was "grossly and inexcusably careless." You can attack the award in either or both of two ways.

First, to take advantage of unrestricted appellate review of matters of law, you can try to persuade the appellate court that the trial judge incorrectly instructed the jury on the law:

C. Officer Mullins is entitled to a new trial, because the trial judge erroneously instructed the jury that it could award punitive damages for conduct less culpable than reckless disregard for constitutional rights.	
The United States Supreme Court has established a recklessness standard for punitive damages in federal civil rights actions:	**General legal rule**
We hold that a jury may be permitted to assess punitive damages in an action under § 1983 when the defendant's conduct is shown to be motivated by evil motive or intent, or when it involves reckless or callous indifference to the federally protected rights of others.	
Smith v. Wade, 461 U.S. 30, 56 (1983).	
A standard based on reckless misconduct requires a greater showing of culpability than simple negligence. See *Johnson v. Lundell* . . . . In *Johnson,* . . .	**Related legal rules**
The extraordinary nature of punitive damages justifies close scrutiny of the trial judge's instructions to ensure that they recognize even fine distinctions in culpability. Otherwise, . . .	**Policy analysis**
In this case, the trial court instructed the jury that it could award punitive damages if it found that Officer Mullins was "grossly and inexcusably careless." This instruction did not adequately convey the requisite standard: reckless or callous disregard of constitutional rights.	**Application to facts; the instruction**
Even when coupled with the adjective "grossly," the word "careless" connotes only a breach of duty rising to the level of negligence. . . .	**Further analysis of instruction**
The trial court improperly instructed the jury on the standard for punitive damages. Officer Mullins is entitled to a new trial so that the jury may apply the proper legal standard to the facts.	**Conclusion**

Alternatively, if you are prepared to labor against a very restricted standard of review, you can try to persuade the appellate court to overturn the jury's implicit finding that Officer Mullins was "grossly and inexcusably careless." Under that approach, you must review the underlying evidence, such as the testimony at trial, and explain why the jury's finding is not supported by substantial evidence:

D. This court should vacate the award of punitive damages, because substantial evidence does not support the jury's finding that Officer Mullins acted with the requisite culpability to justify punitive damages.

Even if the trial court's instructions adequately conveyed the culpability required for an award of punitive damages, the jury did not properly find such culpability on the part of Officer Mullins. At most, the evidence supports the conclusion that Officer Mullins made a reasonable mistake in judgment in chaotic circumstances. Therefore, the trial judge erred in denying Mullins's Motion for Judgment Notwithstanding the Verdict on the issue of punitive damages, and this court should overturn the jury's award of punitive damages.

This court may overturn a finding of the jury if the finding is unsupported by substantial evidence in the record so that no reasonable juror could have made the finding on the evidence. _See_ . . . This substantial-evidence standard permits appellate courts to review jury findings to guard against verdicts based on bias, passion, or incompetence. _See_ . . . To satisfy the purposes of such review, this court should scrutinize the record for. . . .

Officer Mullins's uncontradicted testimony establishes the reasonableness of his actions. He testified that the report over his squad car radio identified the robbery suspect only as a young man of slight build with dark, shoulder-length hair. II RT 335-36. About one block from robbery site, Officer Mullins spotted Ms. Wong walking at a very brisk pace away from the robbery site. _Id._ at 336. He initially passed her by because he was looking for a male suspect. _Id._ at 337. However, when he found no other suspects in the vicinity, he realized that Ms. Wong fit the description of the robbery suspect except for her gender. _Id._ at 339. He remembered that Ms. Wong was wearing jeans and a sweatshirt, and he realized that an agitated witness might have been mistaken about her gender. _Id._ at 339-440. Consequently, he turned his squad car around, found Ms. Wong again, and stopped her for questioning. _Id._ at 440.

Other testimony supports Officer Mullins's version of the events. Ms. Wong herself testified that she had been walking at an unusually brisk pace. I RT 327. She also admitted that she had trouble answering Officer Mullins's questions. *Id.* at 331. Although in her testimony Ms. Wong offered innocent explanations for her hurried pace and her inability to communicate effectively with Officer Mullins, nothing in the record shows that these explanations were apparent to Officer Mullins at the time of the arrest. . . .

In sum, the evidence leads inescapably to one conclusion: in his eagerness to fulfill his duties as a police officer, Officer Mullins mistakenly arrested the wrong person, but he did not recklessly disregard anyone's constitutional rights in doing so. Quite the contrary, he took steps at several stages to safeguard Ms. Wong's rights.

Analysis of testimony: permissible inferences

The record simply does not contain substantial evidence supporting the jury's finding of sufficient culpability to justify an award of punitive damages. Apparently, the jurors misunderstood or ignored the trial court's instructions and based their verdict on irrelevant factors.

Conclusion

For these reasons, even if this court affirms the jury's finding of lack of probable cause, it must overturn the jury's award of punitive damages. The evidence does not support this extraordinary award.

Counsel for the appellee can respond to either of these arguments directly. In response to the first sample argument, page 351, she can argue either that (1) the law permits an award of punitive damages for culpability less than recklessness, or (2) the trial judge's instructions adequately conveyed the requisite standard of recklessness. In response to the second sample argument, pages 351-353, she can (1) emphasize the restricted standard of appellate review, (2) describe evidence in the record that supports a jury finding of recklessness, and (3) explain why that evidence should be viewed as "substantial."

b. Varieties of Fact Analysis

As illustrated in subsection a above, the appropriate nature and depth of fact analysis on appeal will depend in part on two factors: (1) the nature of the appellant's challenge to the trial court's judgment, and (2) the procedural posture of the case when the trial court disposed of it.

(1) Nature of Appellant's Challenge. For an example of the first factor, suppose that you represent the appellant and that you choose to challenge not the jury's findings of fact but only the trial judge's instructions on the law, as in the first sample passage on page 351. Your arguments on such a challenge will often focus on the law and include only modest fact analysis. Specifically, even if

"fact" is expansively defined to include the trial judge's actual instructions, your application of the law to the facts could include no more than a comparison of the correct legal rule to the actual instruction and a statement about the need for a new trial with proper instructions to the jury:

> In this case, the trial court instructed the jury that . . . This instruction did not adequately convey . . .
> . . . Officer Mullins is entitled to a new trial so that the jury may apply the proper legal standard to the facts.

Even when asking for a new trial, you could analyze the facts in much greater detail if you or the opposing counsel further invited the appellate court to examine the record and reach its own conclusion about the application of the proper rule to the facts. Ordinarily, however, the factfinder in the trial court should have the first opportunity to evaluate new, material evidence or to apply new, materially different instructions to the facts. Therefore, a more detailed fact analysis would contemplate an appellate procedure that is not mandatory and is not even clearly appropriate.

In contrast, detailed fact analysis will be mandatory if the appellant challenges the fact findings of the trial judge or jury. As illustrated in the second sample passage on pages 352-353 the parties then must review the record and argue whether the evidence supports the finding of fact under the applicable standard of review:

> Officer Mullins's uncontradicted testimony establishes the reasonableness of his actions. He testified that . . .
> Other testimony supports Officer Mullins's version of the events. Ms. Wong herself testified that . . .
> In sum, the evidence leads inescapably to one conclusion: . . .
> The record simply does not contain substantial evidence supporting the jury's finding. . . .

(2) Procedural Posture. Your fact analysis may also vary with the second factor: the procedural posture of the case at the time of trial disposition. Specifically, dispositions at different pretrial and trial stages will lead to appellate analyses of different kinds of facts.

For example, suppose that the trial court dismissed the action for failure of the complaint to state a claim for relief. On appeal, you can argue the law, but you will have no findings of fact or even underlying evidence in the record to which to apply the law. Instead, you must argue whether the factual allegations of the complaint state a claim for relief under the correct interpretation of the law.

In summary-judgment litigation, on the other hand, you ordinarily will develop a record of preliminary showings of fact with documents, affidavits, and discovery materials. Therefore, on appeal, you can argue whether the evidentiary materials submitted by both parties create a genuine issue of fact for trial under the applicable law.

Finally, the record will include formally introduced evidence if either party has appealed from the trial judge's denial of a motion for a directed verdict or for a judgment notwithstanding the verdict after presentation of the evidence in a jury trial. Moreover, on appeal from judgment after a full trial, the record will include both the evidence and the findings of the judge or jury. As explored above, the record in either case provides a fertile source for fact analysis if the appellant chooses to challenge the role of the factfinder under a restricted standard of review. On the other hand, if the appellant chooses to accept the findings of fact, his arguments will focus on analysis of the law.

F. THE CONCLUSION

Chapter 11's discussion about the conclusion section of a brief applies with full force to appellate briefs. At the least, your conclusion must briefly restate the action that your client requests the appellate court to take. In a complex case, your conclusion may also include a brief summary and synthesis of the arguments presented in your brief.

═══════ E X E R C I S E   1 5 - 1 ═══════

In addition to responding to the appellant's arguments on appeal, an appellee may file its own "cross-appeal" to affirmatively challenge aspects of a lower court's decision. The following appellate briefs are the Opening Brief, Answering Brief, and Reply Brief on a cross-appeal filed by the appellee of the main appeal. As noted by the editorial footnotes, the briefs on cross-appeal incorporate parts of the briefs filed on the main appeal. The briefs reproduced below appear in their original form, with the exception of corrections of minor typographical errors and the deletion of some references to the main appeal.

The briefs depart in many ways from the techniques suggested in Chapter 10 of this book, perhaps illustrating that a variety of styles can be effective forms of communication or persuasion. As you read these briefs, consider what changes you would make to conform the writing to your own style, and consider the following questions.

1. *Statements of the Case*

Study the procedural history traced in the statements of the case in the opening brief and the answering brief. Identify the trial court rulings challenged by each party. Is it clear why both Koepnick and Sears were dissatisfied, resulting in cross appeals? What standard did the trial court apply in reaching its decision on the point appealed from on the cross appeal? What standard of review should the appellate court apply?

2. *Statements of Fact*

Study the statements of fact in the opening and answering briefs. Could you identify the author of each statement if you read no other parts of the briefs? Does each fact statement successfully present an apparently complete and neutral summary of the facts while placing the advocate's client in the best possible light?

Consider the points of conflict between the two fact statements. In what instances is the apparent conflict simply a reflection of each advocate using techniques of writing style to emphasize some facts and deemphasize others? In what instances is the conflict rooted in genuine disagreement about the factual conclusions that find support in the record? What is the legal significance on appeal of conflicting evidence in the record on a material point, given the procedural posture of this case?

3. *Statements of Issues*

Study the statements of the issues in the opening and answering briefs. Does each advocate successfully phrase each issue in a way that invites a favorable response for his client? Does either state a false issue that easily invites a favorable response but that does not fairly pinpoint the real issue on appeal?

4. *Arguments*

Study the arguments in all three briefs. How important is fact analysis to the arguments in each brief? Would the allocation of resources between fact analysis and discussion of legal rules be different if the appellant were appealing from the trial court's rejection of a novel legal theory of recovery?

5. *Responsive Arguments*

Does the answering brief effectively respond to the opening brief? Does the reply brief effectively respond to the answering brief? Note how an unexpected argument in the answering brief sparked extended discussion of a procedural matter in the reply brief.

6. *Writing Style*

How would you change the writing style or presentation of authority in any of the briefs? Explain the reasons for your editing.

7. *Format*

How well do the briefs conform to the following formats for appellate briefs prescribed by the Arizona Rules of Civil Appellate Procedure?

Rule 13. Briefs
13(a) Brief of the Appellant. The brief of the appellant shall concisely and clearly set forth under appropriate headings and in the order here indicated:

1. A table of contents with page references.
2. A table of citations, which shall alphabetically arrange and index the cases, statutes and other authorities cited, with references to the pages of the brief on which they are cited.
3. A statement of the case, indicating briefly the basis of the appellate court's jurisdiction, the nature of the case, the course of the proceedings and the disposition in the court below.

4. A statement of facts relevant to the issues presented for review, with appropriate references to the record. . . .

5. A statement of the issues presented for review. . . .

6. An argument, which shall contain the contentions of the appellant with respect to the issues presented, and the reasons therefor, with citations to the authorities, statutes and parts of the record relied on. The argument may include a summary. . . .

7. A short conclusion stating the precise relief sought.

8. An appendix if desired.

13(b) Brief of the Appellee. The brief of the appellee shall conform to the requirements of the preceding subdivision, except that a statement of the case, a statement of the facts or a statement of the issues need not be included unless the appellee finds the statements of the appellant to be insufficient or incorrect.

13(c) Reply Brief. The appellant may file a reply brief, but it shall be confined strictly to rebuttal of points urged in the appellee's brief. No further briefs may be filed except as provided in Rule 13(e) or by leave of court. . . .

13(e) Briefs in Cases Involving Cross-Appeals. A party who files a cross-appeal may combine in one brief his brief as appellee and his brief as cross-appellant. If the appellant wishes to file a further brief, he may combine in one brief his reply brief as appellant and his brief as cross-appellee. The cross-appellant may file a reply brief on the issues of the cross-appeal.

Ariz. R. Civ. App. P. 13.

Fred Cole
Roger W. Perry
Gust, Rosenfeld, Divelbess & Henderson
3300 Valley Bank Center
Phoenix, Arizona 85073
Attorneys for Defendant-Appellee/Cross-Appellant

IN THE
COURT OF APPEALS
STATE OF ARIZONA
Division One

MAX KOEPNICK,
     Plaintiff-Appellant
     Cross-Appellee,

v.

SEARS, ROEBUCK & COMPANY,
     Defendant-Appellee
     Cross-Appellant.

1 CA-CIV 9147

MARICOPA County
Superior Court
No. C 502081

OPENING BRIEF ON CROSS APPEAL

358

TABLE OF CONTENTS

TABLE OF AUTHORITIES

APPELLEE'S OPENING BRIEF ON CROSS-APPEAL

STATEMENT OF THE CASE[42]

Plaintiff-appellant Max Koepnick ("Koepnick") commenced this action by filing a complaint on December 5, 1983 (C.T. 1). The defendants named in the complaint were defendant-appellee Sears, Roebuck & Company ("Sears") and the City of Mesa ("Mesa"). The complaint set forth claims in six counts, which were all alleged to have arisen out of an incident that occurred at the Sears store at Fiesta Mall in Mesa, Arizona on December 6, 1982. Sears was named as defendant in only four of the counts. These were Count One for false arrest, Count Four for trespass to chattel, Count Five for invasion of privacy and Count Six for malicious prosecution. Mesa was named as defendant in Count Two for false arrest and Count Three for assault and battery. Mesa was also named as a co-defendant with Sears in Counts Five and Six.

Prior to trial, Mesa moved for summary judgment on Count Two for false arrest (C.T. 55). The court granted Mesa's motion on that count based on the court's determination that probable cause existed for Mesa to detain Koepnick (Minute entry dated January 9, 1986).

Trial to a jury on the other counts of Koepnick's complaint commenced on January 10, 1986. At the close of Koepnick's case-in-brief, Sears moved for a directed verdict on all counts asserted against it (7R.T. 13). Plaintiff stipulated to the dismissal of Count Six for malicious prosecution against Sears, and the court granted Sears a directed verdict on Count Four for invasion of privacy (Minute entry dated January 21, 1986). Mesa made a similar motion and was granted directed verdicts on Count Two for false arrest, Count Five for invasion of privacy, Count Six for malicious prosecution and all plaintiff's claims for punitive damages (Minute entry dated January 21, 1986).

At the close of evidence, Sears and Mesa again moved for directed verdicts on all the remaining claims against them. These motions were denied (8R.T. 84-92). The remaining claims were submitted to the jury. The jury returned verdicts against Sears for $25,000.00 in compensatory damages and $500,000.00 in punitive damages on Count One for false arrest and $100.00 in compensatory damages and $25,000.00 punitive damages on Count Four for trespass to chattel (9R.T. 101-03). The jury also returned verdicts against Mesa for $50,000.00 on Count Three for assault and battery and $100.00 on Count Four for trespass to chattel (9R.T. 101-03). Judgment was entered on the verdicts on February 25, 1986 (C.T. 97; Appendix A).

Sears filed motions for judgment notwithstanding the verdicts and for a new trial on Counts One and Four on March 11, 1986 (C.T. 100). Mesa filed a motion for a new trial on March 11, 1986 (C.T. 101) and a motion for judgment notwithstanding the verdict or, in the alternative, for a new trial and for remittitur on March 12, 1986 (C.T. 104). An amended motion for judg-

---

42. The actual Opening Brief on cross-appeal incorporated by reference this party's Statement of the Case and Statement of the Facts from its Answering Brief (Response Brief) on the main appeal, which this party filed in the same document with the Opening Brief on cross-appeal. Those statements are reproduced in full here.

ment notwithstanding the verdicts and for new trial was filed by Sears on April 16, 1986 (C.T. 113).

A hearing on the post-trial motions was held on April 17, 1986. Upon consideration of the motions, the court granted Sears' and Mesa's motions for judgment N.O.V. on Count Four for trespass to chattel and granted Sears' motion for new trial on Count One for false arrest. The court granted judgment N.O.V. for defendants on the trespass to chattel claim as Koepnick failed to present evidence that the alleged trespass caused any damage or injury, which is an essential element of an actionable claim. The court granted a new trial on the false arrest claim as the court determined that reasonable cause to detain Koepnick existed as a matter of law and that, therefore, it had erred in instructing the jury on the issue of reasonable cause (Minute entry dated May 14, 1986; Appendix B).

A second hearing occurred on June 24, 1986 pertaining to further post-trial motions, and the court clarified its minute entry of May 14, 1986 (Minute entry dated June 27, 1986; Appendix C). (The trial court's attempt at clarification did not completely succeed in that the minute entry repeatedly refers to the "assault" claim when the court actually means to refer to the false arrest claim). The final order setting forth the court's disposition of the post-trial motions, including the granting of judgment on Count Four for trespass to chattel and the granting of Sears' motion for new trial on Count One for false arrest, was entered July 23, 1986 (C.T. 125; Appendix D).

Koepnick filed a notice of appeal on July 24, 1986, with respect to the trial court's order granting Sears' motion for judgment notwithstanding the verdict on Count Four for trespass to chattel and for a new trial on Count One for false arrest (C.T. 124). Sears filed a notice of cross-appeal with respect to the portions of the judgment dated February 24, 1986, granting judgment in favor of Koepnick and the portions of the order dated July 18, 1986, denying Sears' motion for judgment notwithstanding the verdict on Count One for false arrest and conditionally denying defendant Sears' motion for new trial on the Count Four for trespass to chattel (C.T. 128). No appeal was taken by either Koepnick or Mesa with respect to the adjudications of the claims asserted by Koepnick against Mesa. Accordingly, Mesa is not a party to this appeal.

The parties stipulated to waiving the posting of cost bonds on the appeals. This court has jurisdiction of the appeal and cross-appeal pursuant to A.R.S. §§ 12-1201 B and F.

STATEMENT OF FACTS

On December 6, 1982, Koepnick drove to the Sears store located at Fiesta Mall to get some screwdrivers (4R.T. 145-47). He arrived at approximately 5 P.M. (4R.T. 145). Once in the store, he was assisted by Mara Thomas, a sales clerk in the hardware department (4R.T. 147; 8R.T. 36). After Koepnick selected the tools he wanted, Thomas carried them to the cash register (4R.T. 148). Koepnick was waited on at the cash register by Bruce Rosenhan, another sales clerk, who rang up the tools for Koepnick (4R.T. 150-51; 7R.T. 88). These tools consisted of a set of screwdrivers, a wrench set, a nut-driver set, an open end wrench set and a set of pliers (7R.T. 88-89; Ex. 11). Koepnick asked Rosenhan for an itemized receipt (4R.T. 151; 7R.T. 88). Rosenhan bagged Koepnick's purchases, stapling the bag closed with the receipts on the outside (4R.T. 151; 7R.T. 89). Koepnick left the cash register area (4R.T. 171; 7R.T. 89).

After waiting on Koepnick, Rosenhan went out to work on the sales floor (7R.T. 90). Rosenhan saw Koepnick again in the hardware department approximately 15 minutes after he had waited on him (7R.T. 90-91). Koepnick came over to where he and Thomas were in the back of the department (7R.T. 90). Rosenhan saw Koepnick speak to Thomas and pull a large wrench out of the shopping bag Rosenhan had earlier stapled closed (7R.T. 91). At that time, Koepnick's bag was open and there were no receipts in view on it (7R.T. 91). Rosenhan realized that the wrench Koepnick pulled out of the bag was not one of the wrenches from the sets that he sold to Koepnick (7R.T. 91). When Rosenhan finished with the customer he was helping, he asked Thomas if Koepnick put the wrench back in his bag and whether she had sold it to him (7R.T. 92). Thomas told him that Koepnick put it back in his bag and that she had not sold that wrench to him or had anything to do with it (7R.T. 92). Rosenhan asked all the other employees present in the department whether they had sold that particular wrench to Koepnick and learned that none of them had either (7R.T. 92).

Rosenhan went to the front register and used the phone to call security (7R.T. 92). He spoke with Steve Lessard, one of the security agents on duty at that time in the store (4R.T. 77). It was approximately 5:35 to 5:40 when Lessard received the call from Rosenhan. (4R.T. 83). He informed Lessard that he believed that there was a customer in the store who was a shoplifter (4R.T. 77). Lessard told him to meet in the sewing machine department, which is located next to hardware (4R.T. 77-78). When Rosenhan and Lessard met, Rosenhan explained what had occurred with the purchase of the tools and the subsequent incident of the large wrench being observed in the bag (7R.T. 93; 4R.T. 78-79). Lessard radioed to Dave Pollock, another security agent on duty at Sears, and requested that he come and assist him (4R.T. 79).

When Pollock arrived, Lessard explained what he had learned from Rosenhan and asked him to watch Koepnick while he spoke with the other employees (4R.T. 79-80). Lessard went around the hardware department and spoke with each of the employees present there (4R.T. 80). Among the employees he spoke with was Mara Thomas, who informed Lessard of her contacts with Koepnick and confirmed the fact that she did not sell or help Koepnick with the large wrench he had in his bag (4R.T. 80-81; 8R.T. 41).

After Lessard had spoken with all of the employees in the hardware department and confirmed that none of them sold the wrench in question, he observed Koepnick in the socket aisle (4R.T. 82). Koepnick picked out some sockets and then put the bag he was carrying down at the cash register (4R.T. 82). Koepnick went back to the socket aisle and picked up another socket (4R.T. 82). While Koepnick was away from the cash register area, Lessard instructed Pollock to go by the shopping bag and confirm that the large wrench in question was still in it (4R.T. 82). When Pollock went over to the bag, he observed that the bag was pulled open and the wrench was inside (7R.T. 41). No receipts were seen in or on the bag by Pollock (7R.T. 41, 84). Pollock reported back to Lessard and told him what he saw (7R.T. 41).

Lessard and Pollock observed as Koepnick returned to the cash register and purchased some sockets (7R.T. 42; 4R.T. 82-83). As Koepnick began to leave the store, Lessard went to the clerk at the cash register and asked what items had been purchased, verifying that Koepnick had not paid for the crescent wrench in question at that time (7R.T. 83-84). Lessard and Pollock followed Koepnick out of the store (4R.T. 84). At no time did either observe Koepnick take any receipts off the shopping bag he was carrying (4R.T. 84). As they followed Koepnick out of the store, they discussed the information they had and decided to stop Koepnick with respect to the large wrench in question (4R.T. 84).

Koepnick estimated that it was approximately 6:15 P.M. when he exited the east door of the store (5R.T. 72). Lessard approached Koepnick as he walked into the parking lot area approximately 20 to 25 feet from the door of the store (4R.T. 87). Koepnick refused to stop when Lessard first spoke to him (5R.T. 178; 4R.T. 87-88). Koepnick testified that Lessard then came around in front of him, pulled the wrench in question out of the bag and told him that he did not have a receipt for it (4R.T. 178). Koepnick was also told he was under arrest for shoplifting (4R.T. 178). Both Koepnick and Lessard testified that Koepnick was shown identification by Lessard, although Koepnick testified that he did not see it clearly (4R.T. 179-80; 4R.T. 87-88). Koepnick did not show a receipt for the wrench when Lessard stopped him (4R.T. 91; 5R.T. 63).

Koepnick initially refused to return to the store with Lessard and Pollock (4R.T. 179). Koepnick was informed that he had to return to the store with them (4R.T. 180). After some further discussion, Koepnick was escorted up to the security office in the Sears store (4R.T. 179-81; 5R.T. 70-72). He was not handcuffed or physically injured in any way by the Sears employees (5R.T. 70, 72). Once in the security office, Koepnick was instructed to sit down to wait for the police to arrive (4R.T. 183).

In the security office, Lessard examined the shopping bag Koepnick had been carrying and found receipts for the purchase of the sockets (4R.T. 94; 5R.T. 72-73). No other receipts were found in or on the bag (4R.T. 95). Although Koepnick had the receipts for his other purchases in his front shirt pocket, he never attempted to show them to the Sears employees (5R.T. 63, 66). While waiting for the police to arrive, Koepnick asked if he could get a drink of water or go down to his truck, but those requests were refused (4R.T. 183).

While Pollock watched Koepnick, Lessard continued his investigation and began to prepare his report of the incident (4R.T. 97-98). Lessard telephoned the hardware department and spoke to Kim Miller, the hardware department manager. Lessard called the hardware department as he needed the stock number for the wrench in question (8R.T. 72). He also wanted to have the audit tape on the cash register checked as there were no receipts in the shopping bag for the tool sets that Rosenhan had told him he had rung up for Koepnick (8R.T. 72).

Officer Michael Campbell of the Mesa Police Department arrived at 6:30 P.M., approximately 15 minutes after Koepnick had been brought to the security office (6R.T. 67; 4R.T. 186). Campbell and Lessard stepped across the hall to permit Lessard to inform the officer as to what he had observed (4R.T.

186; 4R.T. 101-02). As Lessard was talking with Officer Campbell, Koepnick attempted to walk out of the security office (4R.T. 187; 4R.T. 58). Officer Campbell came out into the hallway and met Koepnick at the door to the security office (4R.T. 187; 4R.T. 59). Koepnick and Officer Campbell became involved in an altercation, resulting in Koepnick striking his head against the back wall of the security office (4R.T. 187-88; 4R.T. 60-64). After that occurred, Officer Campbell was able to handcuff Koepnick (6R.T. 96-98).

Officer Campbell had made the decision to arrest Koepnick when the altercation started (6R.T. 93). While he was being handcuffed by Officer Campbell, Koepnick took the receipts that had been in his shirt pocket and stuffed them inside his shirt (4R.T. 189; 6R.T. 96-97). Once Koepnick was handcuffed, Officer Campbell removed the receipts he had observed Koepnick stuffing inside his shirt (4R.T. 66; 6R.T. 100). The receipts that were found on Koepnick were examined and matched to the various tools Koepnick had in his shopping bag (4R.T. 191; 4R.T. 68).

During the altercation, Officer Campbell had instructed Pollock to use his radio to call for assistance (6T. 981). Sergeant Reynolds and Officer Gates came to the Sears security office in response to the request (6R.T. 108).

Lessard learned after the altercation that another sales clerk, Jeff Ward, had also been working in the hardware department that day (4R.T. 103-04). Ward, however, had left the sales floor before Rosenhan observed Koepnick with the wrench in the shopping bag and called Lessard down to investigate the situation (8R.T. 9-10). When Ward later returned to the hardware department, Miller informed him of the call from Lessard and that security had some questions about whether a customer paid for a certain wrench (8R.T. 110). Ward told Miller that he had rung up such a wrench for a customer (8R.T. 11). Miller took Ward up to the security office (8R.T. 11). They arrived about the time the altercation occurred between Koepnick and Officer Campbell (4R.T. 103; 8R.T. 12).

Once Lessard became aware of Ward's contact with Koepnick, he interviewed Ward (4R.T. 104). Ward stated that he had first observed Koepnick as Koepnick walked up to the cash register and pulled the receipt off a shopping bag that was lying on the counter (4R.T. 104; 8R.T. 6). Ward asked him if that was his package and Koepnick said it was (4R.T. 104; 8R.T. 6). Koepnick had a large combination wrench and a smaller set of wrenches with him to purchase (4T. 104; 8T. 6). Ward rang these items up, and Koepnick paid for them (4R.T. 104). Ward then bagged these wrenches in a smaller brown bag, which Koepnick placed inside the larger shopping bag he already had (4R.T. 104; 8R.T. 104; 8R.T. 8). Koepnick then placed the receipts Ward had prepared for the wrenches in his shirt pocket and left (8R.T. 8).

Ward did not see Koepnick again on the sales floor that night (8R.T. 9). After Ward finished ringing up the other customers at the cash register, he left the sales floor (8R.T. 9, 24). Ward told Lessard he had been on a break (4R.T. 72). Ward could not recall at trial exactly where he went when he left the sales floor (8R.T. 9).

After questioning Ward, Lessard discussed with the police officers the possibility that Koepnick had taken the wrench he purchased from Ward out to his truck and brought the shopping bag back in and put another wrench in it (4R.T. 69-70). Lessard was familiar with this method of shoplifting through his work as a security agent (4R.T. 105). The information Lessard had that caused him to believe that this was a possibility was (1) Ward's statement that he had bagged the large wrench in a separate brown bag that was not present in the large shopping bag Koepnick had when he was stopped, (2) Rosenhan's statement that there was a period of 15 minutes from the time he last saw Koepnick after his first purchase until he saw him again in the hardware department with the wrench, and (3) Koepnick's actions in not exhibiting the receipts for his purchases when he was detained (4R.T. 105-06, 111).

The police officers made the decision to search Koepnick's truck (6R.T. 101-02; 6R.T. 128). Officer Campbell testified that he asked Koepnick for permission to search the truck and Koepnick consented (6R.T. 130). Koepnick testified that he consented to the search only on the condition that he be allowed to go with them (4R.T. 194). Lessard accompanied Officer Gates down to Koepnick's truck (4R.T. 107). Officer Gates opened the vehicle and Lessard assisted him in looking in the truck (4R.T. 107). No Sears merchandise was found (4R.T. 107). The search of the truck lasted about two minutes (4R.T. 72-73). Nothing was taken or damaged in the search (4R.T. 110-11, 197).

Once Officer Gates and Lessard returned to the security office, the police officers discussed what action they would take (4R.T. 197-98). Sergeant Reynolds made the decision to cite Koepnick for disorderly conduct for his actions in striking Officer Campbell (6R.T. 130). After Koepnick received the citation, he was released by the Mesa Police Department (4R.T. 198).

ISSUES PRESENTED

1. Did the trial court err in denying Sears' motion for judgment notwithstanding the verdict on the claim for false arrest when the evidence is insufficient to support a finding by the jury that plaintiff was detained by Sears in an unreasonable manner or for an unreasonable length of time?

2. Did the trial err in denying Sears' motion for judgment notwithstanding the verdict on the punitive damage claims where the evidence fails to establish a prima facie case for such damages?

ARGUMENT

I. SEARS' MOTION FOR JUDGMENT NOTWITHSTANDING THE VERDICT ON THE CLAIM FOR FALSE ARREST SHOULD HAVE BEEN GRANTED BY THE TRIAL COURT.

A. *Applicable Standard of Review.*

The standard of review for determining the appropriateness of the granting of a judgment N.O.V. is whether the evidence is sufficient that reasonable men could discern facts to support the verdict. *Rancho Pescado, Inc. v. Northwestern Mutual Life Insurance Co.,* 140 Ariz. 174, 680 P.2d 1235 (App. 1984).

In reviewing a judgment N.O.V., the appellate court views the evidence most favorably to sustaining the verdict. *Lerner v. Brettschneider,* 123 Ariz. 152, 598 P.2d 515 (App. 1979). When the evidence is insufficient to meet the burden of proof to establish the claim, entry of judgment N.O.V. is proper. *Rancho Pescado, Inc. v. Northwestern Mutual Life Insurance Co.,* 140 Ariz. at 186, 680 P.2d at 1247; *Lerner v. Brettschneider,* 123 Ariz. at 155, 598 P.2d at 518.

B. There Was Insufficient Evidence to Justify Any Finding of Liability on the Claim of False Arrest.

A.R.S. § 13-1805C sets forth the statutory shopkeeper's privilege for detaining a suspected shoplifter. A detention is deemed privilege under this statute if it is made with reasonable cause for a proper purpose and done in a reasonable manner and for reasonable time. *Gortarez v. Smitty's Super Valu, Inc.,* 140 Ariz. 97, 680 P.2d 807 (1984). The undisputed evidence established the existence of all the elements necessary for this privilege. Therefore, Sears' motion for judgment notwithstanding the verdict on plaintiff's claim of false arrest should have been granted by the trial court.

1. Reasonable Cause.

The existence of reasonable cause and the reasonableness of the detention, both as to time and manner, are for the court to decide as a matter of law where there is no conflict in the evidence. *Id.* at 104. The trial court determined as a matter of law that reasonable cause did exist for plaintiff's detainment in granting of the motion for new trial. The propriety of that decision is discussed in Section I.E. of Sears' response brief, which is incorporated herein by reference to avoid duplication.

The remaining elements of A.R.S. § 13-1805C that must be established for the privilege to exist are (1) a proper purpose for the detention, (2) the reasonableness of the time of the detention, and (3) the reasonableness of the manner of the detention. Id. *Gortarez,* 140 Ariz. at 104.

2. Proper Purpose.

A.R.S. § 13-1805C sets forth two purposes for which a privileged detention may be made under the statute. They are (1) questioning the subject, or (2) summoning a law enforcement officer. Given Koepnick's testimony at trial, which must be accepted for the purposes of deciding a motion for judgment N.O.V., there is plainly a dispute in the evidence as to what questioning, if any, occurred during Sears' detention of him. Koepnick's testimony was that he was not questioned at all (4R.T. 184-85). There is, however, no question about the existence of the alternative purpose authorized by the statute for Koepnick's detention—summoning a law enforcement officer. It is undisputed that the Mesa Police Department was contacted by Sears and requested to respond to where plaintiff was being detained (Opening brief, p. 8). Thus, this element of the privilege is unquestionably present in this case.

3. The Length of Detention.

The reasonableness of the length of Koepnick's detention is also undisputedly established by the evidence. There is no evidence in the record that creates any issue of fact as to the reasonableness of the length of Sears' detention of Koepnick. The undisputed evidence is that plaintiff was taken to the Sears' security office and the police called without any undue delay on the part of Sears. No evidence of anything to the contrary is present in the record. Upon Officer Campbell's arrival, Lessard immediately began to explain the situation to him. Even before he could even finish, the altercation between Koepnick and Officer Campbell occurred. At that time, Koepnick was placed under arrest by Officer Campbell independently of any shoplifting and taken into the custody of the Mesa Police. From that point on plaintiff was no longer in Sears' custody.

These facts are undisputed. There is nothing in the evidence which would permit the jury to conclude that the length of Koepnick's detention by Sears for the express statutory purpose of summoning a law enforcement officer was unreasonable. Indeed, there was no way Sears could make Koepnick's detention for that purpose any shorter. The length of that detention was determined by the amount of time it took the Mesa Police to respond to the Sears store. This is something that Sears had no control over; in any event, there is no evidence to permit a jury to find that the actual amount of time it took the officer to respond was in any way unreasonable. Accordingly, the trial court should have determined that the length of Koepnick's detention by Sears was reasonable as a matter of law.

4. The Manner of Detention.

Neither is there any evidence in the record that creates any issue of fact as to the reasonableness of the manner of Koepnick's detention by Sears. The evidence is again undisputed that Koepnick was stopped by Lessard, escorted up to the Sears' security office and detained there until the police arrived. The Arizona Supreme Court in *Gortarez* stated that reasonable force may be used to detain a suspected shoplifter. 140 Ariz. at 104, 680 P.2d at 814. There is no evidence that any unreasonable force was ever used on plaintiff by Sears' employees. Sears' employees never struck or fought with Koepnick (5R.T. 70-72). They did not even handcuff or search him (4R.T. 96; 5R.T. 70). Koepnick confirmed in his testimony that he was not physically injured in any manner by Sears' employees (5R.T. 72). In short, there is absolutely no evidence to indicate that the manner of plaintiff's detention by Sears was unreasonable.

As indicated above, the reasonableness of the detention, both as to time and manner, is one for the court to decide as a matter of law where there is no conflict of the evidence. *Id.* As there was no conflicting evidence presented at trial as to these elements that would support a finding that the manner and length of Sears' detention of Koepnick was unreasonable, the trial court should have determined that the detention was reasonable as a matter of law and not submitted any issue of this claim to the jury. Accordingly, Sears' motion for judgment notwithstanding the verdict on the claim of false arrest should have been granted by the trial court.

II. SEARS' MOTION FOR JUDGMENT NOTWITHSTANDING THE VERDICT ON THE CLAIMS OF PUNITIVE DAMAGES SHOULD HAVE BEEN GRANTED BY THE TRIAL COURT.

A. *The Applicable Standard.*

The Arizona Supreme Court has recently modified the standard for determining whether there has been a *prima facie* showing permitting the assessment of punitive damages. The decisions discussing and applying this new standard include *Filasky v. Preferred Risk Mutual Insurance Co.,* No. CV-86-0237-T (filed March 2, 1987); *Gurule v. Illinois Mutual Life and Casualty Co.,* No. CV-86-0488-PR (filed March 2, 1987); *Rawlings v. Apodaca,* 151 Ariz. 149, 726 P.2d 565 (1986); and *Linthicum v. National Life Insurance Co.,* 150 Ariz. 326, 723 P.2d 675 (1986). The portion of the *Linthicum* Decision setting forth the new standard is quoted at length in Section IV.B. of Appellee's response brief, which is incorporated herein by reference to avoid duplication.[43]

Although the trial court denied Sears' motion for judgment N.O.V. with respect to punitive damages before the Supreme Court announced the more stringent standard in *Linthicum v. National Life Insurance Co.,* that standard applies to cases upon appellate review. See, e.g., *Hawkins v. Allstate Insurance Co.,* No. CV-86-0010-PR (filed February 26, 1987) (applying standard announced in *Linthicum* to trial court's pre-*Linthicum* ruling on motion for judgment notwithstanding the verdict).

Under the new standard, plaintiffs are not automatically entitled to an instruction on punitive damages upon the showing of a *prima facie* intentional tort. To recover punitive damages, something more is required over and above the "mere commission of a tort." *Rawlings v. Apodaca,* 151 Ariz. at 162, 726 P.2d at 587. There must be a showing of either an intent to injure the plaintiff or a conscious pursuit of a course of conduct knowing that it creates a substantial risk of significant harm to others. *Linthicum v. Nationwide Life Insurance Co.,* 150 Ariz. at 330, 723 P.2d at 679. The requirement of this "something more" or "evil mind" is to assure that punitive damages are awarded only where the purposes of deterrence are furthered. *Gurule v. Illinois Mutual Life and Casualty Co.,* slip op. at 3. The punishment resulting from punitive damage is appropriate only where there is "some element of outrage similar to that usually found in crime." *Rawlings v. Apodaca,* 151 Ariz. at 161, 726 P.2d at 578, *quoting* Restatement (Second) of Torts, § 908, comment b. (1979).

B. *The Evidence Fails to Show a* Prima Facie *Case for Punitive Damages with Respect to the Claim of False Arrest.*

As discussed in Section I.B. of this cross appeal brief, the evidence in the record is insufficient to make out a *prima facie* case of false arrest, let alone rise to the level necessary to permit the assessment of punitive damages. There is absolutely no evidence that suggests that Sears intended to injure Koepnick or

---

43. In its Answering Brief ("Response Brief") on the main appeal, this party quoted passages from *Linthicum* that required proof of conscious awareness of the evil of one's actions.

that it consciously pursued a course of conduct knowing that it created a substantial risk of tremendous harm to him. As the trial court determined, the facts are uncontradicted that Lessard actually and reasonably believed that when Koepnick left the store he had merchandise for which he had not paid. Acting on that reasonable belief, Lessard stopped Koepnick, had him return to the Sears security office and detained him there until the police arrived. As discussed above, Koepnick was not physically injured by Sears in any manner. Sears' detention of Koepnick ended when Koepnick was arrested by Officer Campbell at the time of the altercation in the security office. While Koepnick was injured in that altercation, there is nothing in the record that would permit a jury to find that the Sears employees could even foresee, let alone intend, that Koepnick would become involved in a fight with the police and be injured. In the absence of evidence that Sears acted with an "evil mind" as required under the new standard, Sears is entitled to judgment notwithstanding the verdict on the issue of punitive damages on the false arrest claim.

C. The Evidence Fails to Establish a Prima Facie Case for Punitive Damages with Respect to the Claim of Trespass to Chattel.

Steve Lessard's conduct with respect to the claim of trespass consists of accompanying a police officer out to plaintiff's truck in the parking lot and assisting him in searching the vehicle. No inference of "evil mind" can be reasonably drawn from these actions. The evidence fails to suggest any risk of significant harm or an intent to injure. The *police officers* made the decision to search the truck. Lessard's conduct in assisting the police officers in their investigation only evidences his intent to aid the police officers in their investigation. No other *reasonable* inference is to be drawn from such conduct.

How are the purposes of punishment and deterrence served by an award of punitive damages in this case? The evidence, even when viewed in a light most favorable to Koepnick, indicates that the Sears employees simply stopped someone whom they had reasonable cause to believe had shoplifted, detained him without injury until the police arrived and arrested him, and then accompanied the police in the search of his vehicle. As the record is devoid of any evidence that the Sears employees acted with an "evil mind," the issue of punitive damages on both the false arrest and trespass claim should never have been submitted to the jury. Sears is entitled to judgment notwithstanding the verdicts on the claims for punitive damages.

CONCLUSION

The trial court was correct in finding that reasonable cause existed as matter of law for Sears' detention of Koepnick. The court erred, however, in ruling that there was sufficient evidence to submit to the jury the issues of the reasonableness of the time and manner of the detention. Accordingly, the trial court's order of July 23, 1986 should be reversed to the extent that it provides for a new trial on these issues. The trial court should be instructed to enter judgment notwithstanding the verdict in favor of Sears on the false arrest claim.

The evidence was also insufficient to submit the issue of punitive damages to the jury on either the claims of false arrest or trespass to chattel. Accordingly, Sears is entitled to judgment notwithstanding the verdict on the issue of punitive damages as well.

Respectfully submitted this 13th day of April, 1987.

GUST, ROSENFELD, DIVELBESS & HENDERSON

By _____
    Fred Cole
    Roger W. Perry
    Attorneys for Defendant-Appellee/Cross-Appellant

Thomas J. Quarelli, Esq.
1832 E. Thomas
Phoenix, Arizona 85016

William J. Monahan, P.C.
340 E. Palm Lane, Suite 130
Phoenix, Arizona 85004

Paul G. Ulrich, P.C.
3030 N. Central, Suite 310
Phoenix, Arizona 85012

Attorneys for Plaintiff-Appellant/Cross-Appellee

IN THE COURT OF APPEALS
STATE OF ARIZONA
DIVISION ONE

MAX KOEPNICK,
    Plaintiff-Appellant,
    Cross-Appellee,

    v.

SEARS ROEBUCK & COMPANY,
    Defendant-Appellee,
    Cross-Appellant.

No. CA-CIV 9147

MARICOPA County
Superior Court
No. C-502081

APPELLANT'S CROSS-APPEAL ANSWERING BRIEF

TABLE OF CONTENTS

TABLE OF AUTHORITIES

1986 (C.T. 128). The parties have stipulated that the cost bonds for their respective appeals are waived. This Court has jurisdiction concerning this appeal pursuant to A.R.S. § 12-2101(F)(1).

APPELLANT'S CROSS-APPEAL ANSWERING BRIEF

STATEMENT OF THE CASE[44]

On December 5, 1983, Plaintiff/cross-appellee Max Koepnick sued Defendant/cross-appellant Sears, Roebuck & Co. ("Sears") and the City of Mesa ("Mesa") for false arrest, assault, trespass to chattel (by further detaining him while searching his truck), invasion of his right of privacy and malicious prosecution. These claims all arose out of Koepnick's arrest for alleged shoplifting on December 6, 1982 (Appendix A, C.T. 1). The counts in Koepnick's complaint alleging invasion of privacy against both defendants and malicious prosecution, false arrest and punitive damages against Mesa were all disposed of by directed verdicts (Appendix B, C.T. 97). Those issues are not involved in this appeal.

The remaining portions of Koepnick's complaint were tried to a jury on January 13-22, 1986. The jury awarded Koepnick $25,000 in compensatory damages and $500,000 in punitive damages against Sears for false arrest. It awarded him $100 in compensatory damages against both Sears and Mesa and $25,000 in punitive damages against Sears for trespass to Koepnick's personal property. The jury also awarded Koepnick $50,000 in compensatory damages against Mesa for assault (9R.T. 101-03). Judgment was entered against both defendants pursuant to those jury verdicts on February 25, 1986 (Appendix B, C.T. 97).

On March 11, 1986, Sears filed motions for judgment notwithstanding the verdicts and for new trial (C.T. No. 100). Mesa also filed a motion for a new trial on March 11, 1986 (C.T. 101). Mesa then also moved for judgment notwithstanding the verdict and, in the alternative, for new trial and for remittitur on March 12, 1986 (C.T. 104). Sears thereafter filed an amended motion for judgment notwithstanding the verdicts and for new trial on April 16, 1986 (C.T. 113). Koepnick filed responses to Mesa's and Sears' motions on March 20 and 25, 1986, respectively (C.T. 107, 108, 109). Both Sears and Mesa filed reply memoranda in support of their respective motions on April 16, 1986 (C.T. 114, 115).

On May 14, 1986, the trial court entered the following minute orders: (1) granting Sears' motion for new trial on Koepnick's false arrest claim; (2) granting Sears' and Mesa's motions for judgment N.O.V. with respect to Koepnick's claim of trespass to personal property; and (3) denying Mesa's motion for new trial or for judgment N.O.V. with respect to Koepnick's assault claim. On June 27, 1986, the trial court clarified its May 14, 1986 minute order by denying Sears' motion for judgment N.O.V. on Koepnick's false arrest claim to the extent it granted Sears' motion for new trial concerning that issue. Having granted a new trial on Koepnick's false arrest claim, the trial court also vacated his judgment against Sears for punitive damages. A formal written

---

44. The actual Answering Brief on cross-appeal incorporated by reference this party's Statement of the Case and Statement of Facts from its Opening Brief on the main appeal. Those statements are reproduced here, but this version of the brief omits an additional description of procedural history that appeared in the Opening Brief in the main appeal.

order incorporating all those rulings and directing that it be entered as a final judgment was filed on July 23, 1986 (C.T. 124).

On July 24, 1986, Koepnick filed a notice of appeal only from the portions of the trial court's order granting Sears' motion for new trial on his false arrest claim and for judgment N.O.V. on his claim of trespass to chattel (C.T. 124). The portion of the litigation involving Mesa has been settled. Mesa is therefore not a party to this appeal and has not filed a cross-appeal. Sears filed a notice of cross-appeal with respect to other portions of the judgment on August 5, 1986 (C.T. 128). The parties have stipulated that the cost bonds for their respective appeals are waived. This Court has jurisdiction concerning this appeal pursuant to A.R.S. §12-2101(F)(1).

STATEMENT OF FACTS

I. KOEPNICK AND HIS PURCHASES.

Max Koepnick was a manager, foreman, and mechanic for a large Queen Creek farming operation whose assets exceed $2,500,000 (4R.T. 145, 6R.T. 21). His lawsuit resulted from his detention and arrest for shoplifting while he was purchasing tools for the farm at the Sears store in Fiesta Mall, Mesa, Arizona, on December 6, 1982 (4R.T. 145-47). Koepnick paid cash for those tools and had the receipts for all of them in his possession when he was arrested, including the receipt for a 1-5/16″ open-end crescent wrench. That wrench was the precipitating cause of his arrest.

Koepnick drove to Sears in the farm pickup truck he used for business purposes (4R.T. 145-46). He entered the store at approximately 5:00 P.M. (4R.T. 145, 5T 68). Business in the Sears store happened to be slow at that particular time (3R.T. 13). Koepnick proceeded to the hardware department. He first purchased a five-wrench set, a nut-driver, an open-end wrench set, a plier set, and a set of screw drivers (Ex. 11). Bruce Rosenhan, Sears' hardware department manager, rang up those purchases on a cash register and stapled portions of the Sears seven-part handwritten receipt used at customers' requests for cash purchases to the outside of the bag (4R.T. 149, 173). Sears' policy was to staple the register receipt and the original of the seven-part receipt to the outside of the bag (3R.T. 22, 4R.T. 45). The customer's purchases were also recorded automatically on the cash register tape (3R.T. 18-19). The other six copies of the handwritten receipt may have been placed in a trash can on one of the shelves below the cash register (3R.T. 21).

Koepnick then left his purchases at the cash register counter to look for a wrench (4R.T. 151). During this time he flirted with a sales person, Mara Thomas, who showed him various tools. Ms. Thomas then escorted him to the register where he purchased a 1-5/16″ open-end crescent wrench. Sales clerk Jeff Ward made this sale. At that time, Ward prepared another handwritten seven-part form, since this sale was also for cash (8R.T. 8-9, Ex. 12). As had occurred with Koepnick's first purchases, the crescent wrench was bagged and stapled together with the receipt. This bag was placed inside the first, with the wrench handle sticking out (4R.T. 173). At trial, Koepnick denied the wrench was ever put into a separate brown bag (4R.T. 173, 74). He also testified all the receipts were stapled onto the original bag (4R.T. 17). Jeff Ward then left the hardware department to take a break (3R.T. 12, 8R.T. 9).

Koepnick picked up the bag from the register counter and started to leave. However, he then remembered he needed some spark plug sockets (4R.T. 174). He therefore went back to the register, set the bag down and proceeded to look for the sockets (4R.T. 175).

During this time, manager Rosenhan contacted Sears security guards Steve Lessard and Dave Pollack, who began observing Koepnick. Lessard spoke with all four hardware department employees then on the floor about whether there was a receipt for the open-end crescent wrench (3R.T. 9). None could remember ringing it up. However, Lessard failed to ask those employees if anyone else was then on a break *(id.)*. He simply assumed those four employees were the only ones on duty (3R.T. 10-11). Moreover, no one checked either the register tape or the receipts tray behind the counter (3R.T. 34). Doing so would have confirmed that Koepnick had in fact paid for the crescent wrench, since the cash register tape could have been checked against the wrench's stock number (3R.T. 19-20). Lessard also admitted at trial that he also could have searched for the six discarded copies of Koepnick's three sets of receipts that were probably in the trash container below the cash register (3R.T. 21-22).

Meanwhile, Lessard had Pollack walk past the bag on the counter to confirm visually that the wrench in the bag was a Sears product (3R.T. 28). Pollack could see a price tag sticker on the end of the wrench. However, although the stapled receipts on the bag were also in plain view, they were not checked against the merchandise (4R.T. 175). Lessard himself admitted that Pollack had an "easy view" of the receipts (3R.T. 29-30).

Lessard himself also saw the bag on the counter. However, he did not notice the handwritten receipts and cash register tape stapled to the top of the bag (3R.T. 27). He also testified at trial he could not dispute testimony that the register receipts and handwritten receipts were stapled to the top of the bag *(id.)*. He "didn't recall" whether anyone bothered to look for those receipts on the bag before Koepnick was stopped, although he conceded that it would have been a "fairly reasonable thing to do" (3R.T. 30).

While this "investigation" was occurring, Koepnick located and purchased the sockets, returned to the register counter, picked up his bag from the counter, tore off all the receipts, placed them in his shirt pocket and left the store. Lessard and Pollack followed him (4R.T. 177). Lessard estimated that he had between 20 and 25 minutes to make his investigation before he stopped Koepnick outside the store (3R.T. 14). He even had time to discuss with Pollack that they had "done a thorough investigation." (3R.T. 34).

II. KOEPNICK'S DETENTION, ARREST, ASSAULT AND EVENTUAL RELEASE.

Koepnick placed the time and location of his stop and arrest by Lessard and Pollack at 6:15 P.M., in a dark, dimly lighted area of the Sears parking lot (5R.T. 72). Koepnick's version of the facts was that in that dimly lighted area two punks accosted him, yelled "Hey," and positioned themselves on each side of him (4R.T. 178). They then jerked the wrench out of the bag stating, "You don't have a receipt, do you?" (4R.T. 180-81).

Koepnick thought he was being hustled. He asked who his captors were. Their response was, "We're security guards." (4R.T. 179). Koepnick asked them to "prove it." In response, one of the guards flashed his badge *(id.)*. However, Koepnick could not see it clearly (4R.T. 179-80). Koepnick was then told that he was going with the guards and that he was under arrest for shoplifting (4R.T. 180).

Koepnick was escorted to an upstairs security room, denied a drink of water, and seated, with no inquiry as to whether he had a receipt for the wrench (4R.T. 180). The Mesa police were called. When Koepnick attempted to enter the hallway to obtain a drink of water, he and Officer Campbell (who was wearing a bulletproof vest) got into a pushing match. As a result, Koepnick fell or was thrown head first through the wall of the security room, causing him to incur neck and other injuries (4R.T. 60-64).

Koepnick was then handcuffed. While he was recovering from the blow to his head, the Mesa police and the Sears security staff verified every item he had purchased against every receipt on the table of the security room (4R.T. 68). Lessard had also verified with Jeff Ward that Koepnick had in fact purchased the crescent wrench. The bag which supposedly contained the wrench had already been accounted for in the security office. However, despite all of Koepnick's purchases being fully accounted for, the Mesa police continued to detain him at Sears' insistence while Lessard conducted a non-consensual, unescorted search of his truck, looking for an alleged "brown bag." (4R.T. 71). Koepnick had approximately $1,200-1,400 in cash and all of his business records in the truck (4R.T. 197). The search, which required approximately 15 to 20 minutes, proved fruitless (4R.T. 197-98). During this time, Koepnick remained under detention. Had Lessard not decided to search Koepnick's truck, Koepnick would simply have been cited immediately for disorderly conduct and then released (6R.T. 115). Instead, after the search, Koepnick was then freed of his handcuffs and cited for disorderly conduct (4R.T. 198). He was finally permitted to leave the Sears security room at about 7:00 P.M. (4R.T. 199).

ISSUES PRESENTED

1. Did the trial court properly deny Sears' motion for judgment notwithstanding the verdict on Koepnick's false arrest claim where the evidence, viewed most favorably to him, was disputed as to each element of the statutory shopkeeper's privilege, A.R.S. § 13-1805(C)?

2. Did the trial court properly deny Sears' motion for judgment notwithstanding the verdict on Koepnick's false arrest punitive damage claim where the evidence presented reasonably established a *prima facie* case for such damages?

3. Koepnick submits that Sears' issue relating to the evidence supporting Koepnick's punitive damages judgment based on his trespass to chattel claim

is not properly before the Court in Sears' cross-appeal because the trial court granted its motion for judgment notwithstanding the verdict on other grounds and did not rule on this issue at that time. See Part II of the Argument portion of this Brief. Sears is therefore not a "party aggrieved" by any trial court ruling concerning that issue. Alternatively, the evidence supporting punitive damages as to Koepnick's trespass to chattel claim was sufficient to submit that issue to the jury as well.

ARGUMENT

I. THE TRIAL COURT PROPERLY DENIED SEARS' MOTION FOR JUDGMENT NOTWITHSTANDING THE VERDICT WITH RESPECT TO KOEPNICK'S FALSE ARREST CLAIM.

A. Applicable Standards of Review.

In reviewing the trial court's denial of a motion for judgment notwithstanding the verdict, the appellate court will review the evidence to determine whether it was of sufficient character that reasonable minds could differ as to inferences to be drawn from the facts. *Adroit Supply Co. v. Electric Mutual Liability Insurance Co.,* 112 Ariz. 385, 542 P.2d 810 (1975); *Marcal Limited Partnership v. Title Insurance Co. of Minnesota,* 150 Ariz. 191, 722 P.2d 359 (App. 1986). In doing so, this Court will view the evidence in the light most favorable to sustaining the verdict. It then must review the evidence to determine whether the evidence would permit a reasonable person to reach the challenged verdict. *Maxwell v. Aetna Life Insurance Co.,* 143 Ariz. 205, 693 P.2d 348 (App. 1984).

When the sufficiency of evidence to sustain the jury's verdicts is questioned on appeal, every conflict in the evidence and every reasonable inference therefrom will be resolved in favor of sustaining the verdict and judgment. See *McNelis v. Bruce,* 90 Ariz. 261, 367 P.2d 615 (1962). On appeal, a reviewing court must take the evidence in the light most favorable to upholding the jury's verdict. *Miller v. Schaffer,* 102 Ariz. 457, 432 P.2d 585 (1967). Applying these standards to the evidence in this record, Koepnick submits the trial court properly denied Sears' motion for directed verdict with respect to his false arrest claim.

B. Requirements to Sustain the Statutory Shopkeeper's Privilege.

A.R.S. § 13-1805(C) provides that a merchant "with reasonable cause may detain on the premises in a reasonable manner and for a reasonable time any person suspected of shoplifting . . . for questioning or summoning a law enforcement officer." The statute thus states four elements, all of which must be established to sustain the shopkeeper's privilege: (1) reasonable cause for detention; (2) reasonable manner for detention; (3) reasonable time; and

(4) proper purpose (for questioning or summoning a law enforcement officer). Koepnick submits that a directed verdict in Sears' favor with respect to his false arrest claim would not be justified unless the evidence satisfied the applicable standard of review previously stated with respect to all four elements required to establish the statutory privilege. Viewing the evidence most favorably to Koepnick, this record simply does not permit that conclusion.

Each of the elements of Sears' defense also required Sears to prove the affirmative of the issue. *E.g., Black, Robertshaw, Frederick, Copple & Wright, P.C. v. United States,* 130 Ariz. 110, 634 P.2d 298 (App. 1981); *Yeazell v. Copins,* 98 Ariz. 109, 402 P.2d 541 (App. 1965). Unless Sears could persuade a jury by a preponderance of the evidence and reasonable inferences therefrom that each statutory element had been satisfied, Sears thus could not prevail.

1. Reasonable Cause.

Given the facts and reasonable inferences therefrom most favorable to Koepnick, he was clearly entitled to have the reasonable cause issue submitted to the jury. In the first place, Lessard testified he had 20 to 25 minutes to make an investigation before Koepnick left the Sears store and stated that he had made a thorough investigation. He therefore did not have to make a "snap" decision based on incomplete evidence to detain someone who might be hurriedly leaving. Koepnick testified that all of the handwritten receipts for the tools he bought were stapled to the outside of his shopping bag in plain view. However, neither Lessard nor Pollack ever attempted to read them to determine whether the open-end crescent wrench was listed. Lessard was also unable to dispute Koepnick's testimony in this regard, and admitted that looking at the receipts would have been a reasonable thing to do.

Lessard also failed to make the basic inquiry whether there were other hardware department employees then on duty other than the four he interviewed. The possibility that another employee might have been on a break was certainly a reasonable one to be explored. The security guards also never looked for the extra copies of the seven-part receipt, although they might well have been found either in the receipts tray behind the counter or in a trash container on one of the shelves below the cash register. No one ever checked the register tape which would have shown the stock number for the open-end wrench Koepnick had paid for. Given all these deficiencies in the security guards' investigation, there was certainly a reasonable basis for disputing Sears' position that it had reasonable cause to detain Koepnick. Moreover, pursuant to A.R.S. § 13-1805(d), "reasonable cause" is a defense to a false arrest claim. Sears therefore had the burden of proving the affirmative of this issue. *E.g., Black, Robertshaw, Frederick, Copple & Wright, P.C. v. United States,* 130 Ariz. 110, 634 P.2d 298 (App. 1981); *Yeazell v. Copins,* 98 Ariz. 109, 402 P.2d 541 (1965). Unless it could persuade a jury by a preponderance of the evidence and reasonable inferences therefrom that the nature and extent of its investigation was appropriate under the circumstances, Sears could not prevail. Given all the deficiencies in the security guard's investigation and in view of the relatively lengthy time available for them to pursue the simple additional inquiries that could have been made, the trial court could not properly remove the "reasonable cause" issue from the jury in Sears' favor.

2. Proper Purpose.

Sears' Cross-Appeal Opening Brief at p. 3 concedes there was a factual dispute concerning what questioning, if any, occurred during Sears' detention of Koepnick. The statutory purpose of "questioning the subject" was thus admittedly not satisfied for purposes of obtaining a directed verdict.

The other possible proper purpose permitted by A.R.S. 13-1805(C) for privileged detention is "summoning a law enforcement officer." Koepnick acknowledges that Sears did contact the Mesa Police Department, but only after he was detained by Sears' employees. He was not necessarily detained for that purpose. Moreover, after Officer Campbell's investigation, the officer testified he would simply have cited Koepnick immediately for disorderly conduct and then let him go (6R.T. 115). Instead, Lessard, Sears' employee, insisted that Sears search Koepnick's truck even after all the receipts for his purchases had been accounted for (6R.T. 101, 102). Koepnick remained in detention for at least 15 to 20 minutes more while Lessard and Officer Gates searched his truck (4R.T. 197). His handcuffs were not removed until this search had been completed (4R.T. 197). Koepnick submits that this continuation of his detention was improper because it was motivated by Lessard's desire to search his truck, not for any legitimate reasons connected with the police officers' investigation. There was therefore an issue presented as to whether a proper purpose existed throughout the entire period of time in which Koepnick was detained.

3. Length of Detention.

Koepnick contends that the length of his detention was reasonable only until the Sears employees and Mesa police officers had completed their investigation. Once that occurred, Koepnick should have been released immediately. Instead, he was then detained for an additional 15 to 20 minutes at Lessard's request so Lessard could search his truck. Although Koepnick technically may have been in the police officers' custody during that additional period of time, the evidence clearly established that this additional period of detention would not have occurred but for Lessard's request. Under these circumstances, there is also a factual issue as to the propriety of the length of time Koepnick was detained so far as Sears is concerned.

4. Manner of Detention.

Factual disputes were also presented as to the manner in which Koepnick was detained by Sears. To begin with, he was accosted by Lessard and Pollack in an accusatory manner. Koepnick testified they stated, "You don't have a receipt, do you?" (4R.T. 180-181) rather than asking to see a receipt. Then, although Koepnick responded that he had a receipt, he was nevertheless detained for shoplifting without further questioning on that subject. Koepnick submits the manner of his initial detention was thus improper for that reason.

Koepnick was then escorted to an upstairs security room where he was denied a drink of water and seated with no inquiry as to whether he had a receipt for the wrench (4R.T. 180). When Koepnick entered the hallway to obtain a drink of water, he and Officer Campbell got into a pushing match which resulted in Koepnick falling or being thrown head first through the wall of the security room, causing him to incur neck and other injuries (4R.T. 60-64). Koepnick was then handcuffed. However, had Koepnick been offered a drink of water and had the proper inquiries been made by Sears employees initially, his injuries arguably would not have occurred.

Koepnick submits these facts all raise factual issues as to whether the manner of his detention was reasonable. Based on these facts, a jury could reasonably have found that Sears' security guards did not handle his detention in a reasonable manner.

II. THE TRIAL COURT PROPERLY DENIED SEARS' MOTION FOR JUDGMENT NOTWITHSTANDING THE VERDICT AS TO KOEPNICK'S PUNITIVE DAMAGES BASED ON HIS FALSE ARREST CLAIMS.

A. The Applicable Standards of Review.

The recent Arizona appellate decisions modifying the standard for determining whether there has been a *prima facie* showing permitting the assessment of punitive damages do not necessarily require that all prior jury verdicts awarding such damages be reversed. For example, *Filasky v. Preferred Risk Mutual Insurance Co.,* 152 Ariz. 591, 734 P.2d 76 (1987), instead recognizes that "a jury's decision to award punitive damages should be affirmed if any reasonable evidence exists to support it." *Gurule v. Illinois Mutual Life and Casualty Insurance Co.,* 152 Ariz. 600, 734 P.2d 85 (1987), also states that the appellate court must review the facts in a light most favorable to the party obtaining a punitive damage award and affirm the jury's verdict if a reasonable juror could conclude that the defendant either intended to violate his rights or consciously pursued a course of conduct knowing that it created a substantial risk of doing so. 734 P.2d at 88.

Of the various recent decisions, both *Hawkins v. Allstate Insurance Co.,* 152 Ariz. 490, 733 P.2d 1072 (1987), and this Court's Opinion in *Carter-Glogau Laboratories, Inc. v. Construction, Production & Maintenance Labors Local 383,* (1 CA-CIV 8107, 8128 filed October 30, 1986, review denied, May 12, 1987), have affirmed punitive damages awards where the evidence presented met the standards stated in *Linthicum v. Nationwide Life Insurance Co.,* 150 Ariz. 326, 723 P.2d 675 (1986). *Rawlings v. Apodaca,* 151 Ariz. 149, 726 P.2d 565 (1986), also remanded for further proceedings as to punitive damages where it was uncertain whether the trial judge had applied the appropriate standards.

According to *Gurule, supra,* the "evil mind" required for punitive damages may be satisfied by "defendant's conscious and deliberate disregard of the interests and rights of others." 152 Ariz. at 602, 734 P.2d at 87. It may also be established by defendant's expressed statements or inferred from his expressions, conduct or objectives. *Id.* If a defendant conducts himself in an outrageous or egregiously improper manner, the inference is permitted that he intended to injure or consciously disregarded the substantial risk that his conduct would cause significant harm. The "evil mind" may also be inferred if a defendant "deliberately continued his actions despite the inevitable or highly probable harm that would follow." *Id.*

B. *Applying These Standards, the Evidence Demonstrated a Prima Facie Case for Punitive Damages with Respect to Koepnick's False Arrest Claim.*

Numerous deficiencies in Sears' investigation support a jury's finding that its employees acted with conscious and deliberate disregard of Koepnick's rights and interests. The "bottom line" of Lessard's investigation at the time Koepnick left the Sears store was that he and Pollack "felt we had done a thorough enough investigation for us to ask [Koepnick] if he had a receipt for the wrench." (3R.T. 35). Significantly, Lessard himself apparently did not then believe he had sufficient cause to detain Koepnick for shoplifting at that time without further questioning. Yet Lessard and Pollack accosted Koepnick in a hostile and threatening manner in a dark corner of the parking lot and accused him of not having a receipt, instead of asking in a more normal manner whether he had a receipt. Then, even though Koepnick told Lessard and Pollack in response to their accusations that he *did* have a receipt, he was ordered under arrest for shoplifting without further discussion or inquiry (4R.T. 178-181). These facts clearly could support a reasonable conclusion that Sears' employees had the required "evil mind" in making their initial decision to detain Koepnick without adequate investigation or proper inquiry concerning whether he in fact had the receipts they should be seeking.

Further evidence supporting a *prima facie* case for punitive damages existed with reference to Sears' decision to continue to detain Koepnick even though the Mesa police officers were then willing to release him. By that time, all of the receipts in Koepnick's possession had been checked against his purchases and found to be satisfactory (4R.T. 68). Lessard had also verified with Jeff Ward that Koepnick had in fact purchased the crescent wrench, and the bag which supposedly contained the wrench had been accounted for in the security office. However, despite all these facts, the Mesa police officers continued to detain Koepnick at Sears' request while Lessard conducted a nonconsensual search of his truck, looking for an alleged "brown bag." (4R.T. 71). This search, which required approximately 15 to 20 minutes, predictably proved fruitless (4R.T. 197-98). During this time, Koepnick remained under detention and in handcuffs (4R.T. 197). Lessard's conduct is thus arguably precisely the sort of continuing wrongful conduct by Sears' employees that would support a jury verdict for punitive damages under the new "evil mind guiding an evil hand" standard.

C. *Sears' Argument Concerning the Evidence Supporting Koepnick's Punitive Damages with Respect to His Trespass to Chattel Claim Is Not Properly Before the Court in This Cross-Appeal. Alternatively, the Evidence Supporting Punitive Damages Was Sufficient to Submit That Issue to the Jury As Well.*

Sears' argument concerning the sufficiency of the evidence supporting Koepnick's punitive damages as to his trespass to chattel claim does not have the same legal basis as does its argument concerning punitive damages with respect to Koepnick's false arrest claim. The trial court instead granted Sears' motion for a judgment notwithstanding the verdict as to the trespass to chattel issue because "there was no showing by the plaintiff of any damage to the chattel or injury to the plaintiff arising from the alleged trespass by the defendants." (Order dated on July 18, 1986, C.T. No. 125, attached as Appendix D to Sears' Response Brief.)

There is no indication in the record that the trial court ruled on the issue of the sufficiency of evidence to support punitive damages as to Koepnick's trespass to chattel claim as an independent matter. Sears also prevailed as to this issue on another ground. Sears is thus not a "party aggrieved by the judgment" within the meaning of ARCAP 1 and cannot properly appeal from the trial court's ruling in its favor. *See e.g., McGough v. Insurance Co. of North America,* 143 Ariz. 26, 691 P.2d 738 (App. 1984); *Wolkin v. Civil Service Commission of Tucson,* 21 Ariz. App. 341, 519 P.2d 194 (1974). A party aggrieved by only part of a judgment can appeal only the part adversely affecting him. *Chambers v. United Farm Workers Organizing Committee,* AFL-CIO, 25 Ariz. App. 104, 541 P.2d 567 (1975). To preserve this issue for this Court's consideration, Sears should have listed it as a "cross-issue" presented in its Response Brief, since it is attempting to uphold the judgment for reasons allegedly supported by the record but different from those relied upon by the trial court. *E.g., Santanello v. Cooper,* 106 Ariz. 262, 475 P.2d 246 (1970); *Maricopa County v. Corporation Commission of Arizona,* 79 Ariz. 307, 289 P.2d 183 (1955). However, it has not done so. The issue has thus not properly been presented for this Court's consideration. See generally 1 Arizona Appellate Handbook §§ 3.2.2.1, 3.2.2.2 (2d ed. 1983).

In any event, the evidence previously stated with respect to Lessard's insistence that Koepnick continue to be detained further while his truck was searched, even though by then there was absolutely no objective basis to do so, also supports the reasonable conclusion that Lessard continued in his wrongful conduct, despite the continuing harm to Koepnick's liberty interests resulting from his continued detention: Koepnick remained in handcuffs while the search of his truck was occurring, and there had by then been demonstrated to be no objective basis whatsoever for any belief that Koepnick had been shoplifting. The facts discussed in the preceding section of this argument are here repeated and incorporated by reference. In short, on the merits, the jury here could reasonably find that Lessard had the requisite "evil mind" to meet the *Linthicum* standard for a *prima facie* case of punitive damages as to the trespass to chattel issue based on that conduct as well.

CONCLUSION

For all the foregoing reasons, the trial court properly denied Sears' motions for judgment notwithstanding the verdict as to Koepnick's false arrest claim for punitive damages with respect to the false arrest. Since the trial court did not decide the issue of punitive damages with respect to Koepnick's trespass to chattels claim, but instead granted Sears' motion for judgment notwithstanding the verdict as to that claim on other grounds, there is no proper basis for Sears' cross-appeal from that ruling. However, if the Court chooses to reach the merits of that issue, there was also sufficient evidence to support a punitive damages award concerning it as well. The trial court's rulings concerning the issues properly before this Court should therefore be affirmed.

DATED this _____ day of May, 1987.

Respectfully submitted,

THOMAS J. QUARELLI, ESQ.
WILLIAM J. MONAHAN, P.C.

By _____
    William J. Monahan

                    and

    PAUL G. ULRICH, P.C.

By _____
    Paul G. Ulrich
    Attorneys for Appellant
    Cross-Appellee

Fred Cole
Roger W. Perry
Gust, Rosenfeld, Divelbess & Henderson
3300 Valley Bank Center
Phoenix, Arizona 85073
Attorneys for Defendant-Appellee/Cross-Appellant

IN THE COURT OF APPEALS
STATE OF ARIZONA
DIVISION ONE

MAX KOEPNICK,
    Plaintiff-Appellant
    Cross-Appellee,

   v.

SEARS, ROEBUCK & COMPANY,
    Defendant-Appellee
    Cross-Appellant.

1 CA-CIV 9147

MARICOPA County
Superior Court
No. C 502081

APPELLEE'S REPLY BRIEF ON CROSS-APPEAL

TABLE OF CONTENTS

TABLE OF AUTHORITIES

ARGUMENT

I. ALL ISSUES RAISED BY SEARS IN THIS APPEAL ARE PROPERLY BEFORE THE COURT.

Koepnick's perceived need to argue about the technical appropriateness of the issues raised by Sears on appeal only serves to demonstrate his lack of confidence in the few substantive arguments he attempts to make. Koepnick's lack of confidence is understandable. Both his arguments to avoid addressing the issues raised by Sears, and his substantive arguments with respect to those issues, are devoid of merit.

In response to Sears' cross-appeal, Koepnick asserts that Sears has incorrectly raised the issue of the insufficiency of evidence to support an award of punitive damages on the claim of trespass to chattel. Koepnick argues that Sears does not have standing to raise this issue on the cross-appeal. He premises this argument on his contention that the trial court did not rule on Sears' motion for judgment N.O.V. with respect to this punitive damage claim so Sears cannot be considered a "party aggrieved by the judgment" (Cross-appeal answering brief, p. 11). Koepnick, however, is wrong in his assertion that there is no indication in the record of the trial court's ruling against Sears on this issue. The trial court, in its minute entry dated June 27, 1986, stated specifically in the second to last paragraph that "The motions for judgment notwithstanding the verdict and for new trial, for all other reasons, are denied." Thus the trial court did explicitly rule against Sears with respect to the motion for judgment N.O.V. on that punitive damage claim.

Koepnick is likewise mistaken on the appropriateness of the placement of the issues raised on the appeal in Sears' briefs. First, it must be noted that Sears did file a notice of cross-appeal in this action. The notice of cross-appeal indicates that Sears has appealed from all portions of *both* the judgment dated February 24, 1986, and the final order on the post-trial motions dated July 18, 1986, entered in the action adverse to it. The only items not appealed by Sears were the portions of the order dated July 18, 1986 setting forth the trial courts rulings in its favor. Thus, there is no question of the appellate court's jurisdiction to entertain each of the issues Sears raises on appeal. Sears is therefore entitled to have each of the errors of which it complains considered by the court.

Koepnick's contention that Sears must somehow set forth each specific issue in its notice of appeal to properly raise the issues has no support in the rules of civil appellate procedure. The form of the notice of appeal utilized by Sears was adopted directly from the forms set forth in the appendix to the rules of civil appellate procedure. As Rule 8(c), Ariz. R. Civ. App. P., and these forms indicate, a party properly appeals from the adverse portions of *judgments and final orders,* not from individual rulings of a trial court on instructions and the like. In short, the scope of Sears' and Koepnick's combined notices of appeal encompass any and all possible claims of error Sears may wish to assert on rulings and verdicts adverse to it in the trial court.

Second, the various issues raised by Sears both in response to Koepnick's appeal and in support of its cross-appeal are appropriately situated in its briefs.

Issues 4 through 6 of the issues presented in Sears' response brief are properly considered cross-issues to Koepnick's appeal. Sears presents each of these issues as alternative grounds for upholding the trial court's rulings in its favor on the post-trial motions that have been appealed by Koepnick. In fact, Koepnick's argument that such issues should be raised on a cross-appeal directly contradicts his position in attacking the propriety of Sears' cross-appeal of the trial court's failure to grant judgment N.O.V. on the claims for punitive damages.

In his response to the cross-appeal, Koepnick correctly cites *Santanello v. Cooper,* 106 Ariz. 262, 475 P.2d 246 (1970) and *Maricopa County v. Corporation Commission of Arizona,* 79 Ariz. 307, 289 P.2d 183 (1955) for the proposition that when an issue is presented by an appellee to simply support a trial court's ruling that is attacked on appeal, that issue can be raised without the need of a cross-appeal. That is precisely the situation with issues 4 through 6 presented by Sears as cross-issues in response to Koepnick's appeal. These issues simply offer alternative grounds, supported by the record, for upholding the trial court's rulings granting judgment N.O.V. on the trespass to chattel count and a new trial on the false arrest count. Thus, each of these issues is properly before the court for its consideration of Koepnick's appeal. To the extent that any of these issues should have been raised as a cross-appeal, the court has jurisdiction to consider them as such pursuant to Sears' notice of cross-appeal.

Sears' claim of error regarding the trial court's denial of the motion for judgment N.O.V. on the trespass to chattel punitive damage claim is slightly different from the cross-issues raised in response to Koepnick's appeal. As discussed above, the trial court did not grant judgment N.O.V in favor of Sears on this punitive damage claim. The punitive damage award was merely vacated as a result of the trial court's ruling on the underlying trespass to chattel claim. Sears, on the cross-appeal, is not merely defending the vacating of the punitive damage award by the trial court; it also seeks to obtain *additional relief* in the form of judgment entered in its favor on this claim. It is this type of situation that *Walters v. First Federal Savings and Loan Association of Phoenix,* 131 Ariz. 321, 641 P.2d 235 (1982) dealt with when it determined that a cross-appeal was necessary for the court to consider the alternative argument of collateral estoppel offered by the defendant in the plaintiff's appeal.

The rules governing whether an issue should be brought as a cross-issue or cross-appeal are succinctly summarized as follows:

> In other words, the appellee may not attack the decree with a view either to enlarging his own rights thereunder or of lessening the rights of his adversary, whether what he seeks is to correct an error or to supplement the decree with respect to a matter not dealt with below. But it is likewise settled that the appellee may, without taking a cross-appeal, urge in support of a decree any matter appearing in the record, although his argument may involve an attack upon the reasoning of the lower court or an insistence upon matter overlooked or ignored by it.

Maricopa County v. Corporation Commission of Arizona, 79 Ariz. 307, 311, 289 P.2d 183, 185 (1955) (quoting *United States v. American Ry. Express Co.,* 265 U.S. 425 (1924)). The issues raised by Sears on appeal have been presented in complete conformity with these rules of law. Koepnick's arguments to the contrary should be ignored.

Moreover, even if Koepnick were correct that Sears' cross-appeal on the punitive damage issue should have been brought as a cross-issue, the court may still entertain this issue as if it were raised as such. *See e.g., Kalil Bottling Co. v. Burroughs Corp.,* 127 Ariz. 278, 619 P.2d 1055 (1980) (appellate court treats issues raised in improper cross-appeal as cross-issues for consideration on the appeal). Given the fact that Sears did file a notice of cross-appeal, Koepnick's arguments on this aspect of the appeal are not jurisdictional. The court should consider all the issues raised by the parties on their merits, and not decide the case on briefing technicalities.

II. SEARS IS ENTITLED TO JUDGMENT NOTWITHSTANDING THE VERDICT ON THE FALSE ARREST CLAIM.

Koepnick fails to demonstrate any valid issue of fact that would preclude the granting of judgment in favor of Sears on the false arrest count. All four of the necessary elements for a privileged detention under A.R.S. § 13-1805 C are undisputedly established in the record. On the element of reasonable cause, the trial court, after hearing all the evidence, determined that reasonable cause existed for Koepnick's detention. This ruling was a proper exercise of the trial court's discretion and is fully justified by the evidence. There is no basis for this court to reverse the trial court's determination on this issue. To avoid duplication, Sears incorporates all its proper arguments on this issue by this reference.

The evidence also undisputedly establishes a proper purpose for Koepnick's detention pursuant to the statute. It is uncontroverted that Sears detained Koepnick to summon the Mesa police concerning the suspected shoplifting. Indeed, Koepnick never made any claim or offered any jury instruction with respect to some other purpose for his detention by Sears. For Koepnick to now make the bald, totally unsupported statement in his response brief that "He was not necessarily detained for that purpose" is ridiculous (Cross-appeal answering brief, p. 5). Koepnick does not even suggest any other purpose in support of this statement. As for the period of time after the police arrived, the evidence is also undisputed that Koepnick was ·legitimately in the Mesa police department's custody, not Sears. Probable cause existed for the police to detain Koepnick during this period, and Sears had no control over whether or how Koepnick was kept in detention by the police.

There is also no dispute concerning the reasonableness of the length of time Sears detained Koepnick. Koepnick concedes that the length of his detention in Sears' custody until the police arrived and investigated was reasonable (Cross-appeal answering brief, p. 6). As stated above, from that point on, Koepnick was in the Mesa police department's custody, not Sears. Koepnick was under arrest for his altercation with Officer Campbell. Prior to trial, the trial court ruled that probable cause existed for the Mesa police department's detention of Koepnick during that period for the alleged assault on Officer

Campbell. (See Minute Entry dated January 9, 1986). Koepnick has never raised any issue or objection with respect to that ruling.

Although Koepnick repeatedly states that Steve Lessard "requested" his continued detention by the Mesa police department during this period, such statements have no support in the record. Koepnick fails even to cite to the record when making such assertions of "fact" (See, e.g., cross-appeal answering brief, p. 6). The uncontroverted evidence is that Lessard simply told the police the information and knowledge he had in his possession (4R.T. 105-06). This information included the fact that the bag Jeff Ward stated he had wrapped the wrench in before placing it in the larger shopping bag was missing (4R.T. 104-05). Contrary to Koepnick's statements in his briefs, that bag was never accounted for in the security office (4R.T. 104-05). It was the police officers who made the decision to search Koepnick's truck (6R.T. 128). Lessard had no control over whether Koepnick was detained or released by the police during that period (8R.T. 59-60).

Finally, the element of the reasonableness of the manner of Sears' detention of Koepnick is also undisputedly established by the record. Koepnick's arguments in trying to explain why Sears' detention of him should be viewed as unreasonable are nothing less than frivolous. Koepnick's first argument revolves around the fact that, according to Koepnick's testimony, Lessard approached him and said, "You don't have a receipt, do you?" rather than asking to see his receipt. Even accepting all of Koepnick's testimony as true, as we must on this appeal, there is still no evidence of any abusive conduct that would rise to the level of a tortiously unreasonable specific manner of detention. If the court were to accept Koepnick's argument, potential liability would exist any time a subject stopped pursuant to A.R.S. § 13-1805 did not like the manner in which he was addressed. It is inconceivable that the legislature intended such a result when referring to a "reasonable manner" of detention in A.R.S. § 13-1805 C. Much more substantial conduct is required for liability to exist for false arrest.

Koepnick further argues that the manner of his detention was unreasonable in that he should have been questioned by Sears. A.R.S. § 13-1805 C, however, indicates that store personnel are not required to question a subject; they can simply detain for the purpose of summoning a law enforcement officer to handle the investigation.

Finally, Koepnick stretches so far as to attempt to attribute the injuries he received in his altercation with Officer Campbell in the hallway to the fact that the Sears employees declined to give him a drink of water. Koepnick's need for such a nonsensical argument makes readily apparent the total lack of any factual basis for any claim that Sears detained Koepnick unreasonably. The undisputed facts show that Koepnick was simply stopped outside the store and then taken to the security office to await the arrival of the police. According to even Koepnick's testimony, he was not physically or verbally abused by the Sears employees. As such, there is no evidence that would warrant submitting this issue to the jury.

As all the elements for a privileged detention under A.R.S. § 13-1805 C are undisputedly established in the record, Sears is entitled to have judgment entered in its favor on the false arrest claim.

III. SEARS IS ENTITLED TO JUDGMENT NOTWITHSTANDING THE VERDICTS ON THE PUNITIVE DAMAGE CLAIMS.

As Koepnick acknowledges in citing *Filasky v. Preferred Risk Mutual Insurance Co.*, 152 Ariz. 591, 734 P.2d 76 (1987) and *Gurule v. Illinois Mutual Life and Casualty Co.*, 152 Ariz. 600, 734 P.2d 85 (1987) (en banc), a punitive damage award will only be sustained on appeal when there is reasonable evidence to support it. In discussing the nature of an act necessary to permit punitive damages, the Arizona Supreme Court observed that "[p]unishment is an appropriate objective in a civil case only if the defendant's conduct or motive involves 'some element of outrage similar to that usually found in a crime'." *Gurule*, 434 P.2d at 86 (quoting *Rawlings v. Apodaca*, 151 Ariz. 149, 162, 726 P.2d 565, 578 (1986). Where a trial court submits the issue of punitive damages to the jury on slight and inconclusive evidence of such conduct, an appellate court may correct the error. *Filasky*, 734 P.2d at 84. In both *Filasky* and *Gurule*, the Supreme Court found that the evidence did not measure up to the requisite standard and reversed the awards of punitive damages. The same conclusion should be reached in this appeal.

A. The False Arrest Claim.

Koepnick attempts to support the punitive damage award on the false arrest claim based on alleged "deficiencies" in the initial investigation and Lessard's alleged "request" that the Mesa police officers continue to detain Koepnick while his truck was searched. Both of these arguments ignore the uncontroverted facts in the record and fail to demonstrate a level of conduct sufficient to justify an award of punitive damages. First, Koepnick's assertion that the investigation by Lessard was inadequate and unreasonable is belied by the trial court's ultimate determination that reasonable cause existed for Sears' detention of Koepnick. Inherent in the trial court's ruling that reasonable cause existed for Koepnick's detention is the determination that the pre-stop investigation conducted by Lessard was reasonable. If the facts and investigation relied on by Sears were unreasonable, reasonable cause could not exist for the detention. It would be completely illogical for the same evidence that the trial court found to establish reasonable cause for the detention to also be deemed sufficient to support an award of punitive damages for the same detention.

Koepnick's second argument for supporting the punitive damage award also fails to find justification in the record. There is no evidence to support Koepnick's contention that it was "Sears decision to continue to detain Koepnick even though the Mesa police officers were then willing to release him" (Cross-appeal answering brief, p. 10). Koepnick repeatedly asserts in his brief that Lessard "requested" that the police officers continue to detain Koepnick while his truck was searched. Koepnick, however, fails to cite any portion of the record for that proposition. He cannot; none exists.

Steve Lessard's role in the decision to search Mr. Koepnick's truck was simply that of providing information to the police concerning the possibility of merchandise being in the truck (4R.T. 105-06). It was the police who made the decision to search the truck (6R.T. 128). There is nothing in the record to permit a finding that Lessard requested or suggested that Koepnick continue to be detained by the police during this period. At that time, Koepnick was under arrest for his role in the altercation with Officer Campbell. The Mesa police department had reasonable cause for Koepnick's detention. Sears is not responsible for the manner or the length of time that a person is legitimately detained in police custody. Indeed, Lessard could not have required the Mesa police to release Koepnick even if he had thought the detention was improper (8R.T. 59-60).

Moreover, even if Lessard's actions could be considered as the cause of Koepnick's continued detention, his conduct was not the reprehensible, outrageous sort that would warrant punitive damages. Again, all he did was inform the police of certain facts and knowledge in his possession. The police made the final decision on what action would be taken with respect to such information. Such conduct by Lessard does not evidence an evil mind; it is not even tortious conduct. Sears is entitled to have judgment entered in its favor on the claim for punitive damages on the false arrest count.

B. Trespass to Chattel Claim.

Koepnick's argument for punitive damages on the trespass to chattel claim is identical to his second argument presented on the false arrest claim. The same comments made in response to Koepnick's position on the false arrest claim are applicable here. Koepnick's argument that Steve Lessard's conduct is responsible for the Mesa police officers' continued detention of Koepnick is just as meritless on this claim as it is on the false arrest claim. Moreover, Koepnick is again confusing his trespass to chattel claim with the false arrest claim. Koepnick's detention does not constitute an element of the tort of trespass to chattel. In essence, Koepnick is attempting to assert some kind of claim for double punitive damages for the same conduct on which he bases his claim for false arrest. Koepnick offers no authority to support his position, and it should be rejected accordingly.

CONCLUSION

The trial court properly granted Sears' judgment notwithstanding the verdict on the claim of trespass to chattel. The trial court erred, however, in not doing the same on the claim of false arrest. There are no issues of fact present to justify submitting this claim to the jury. This court should therefore reverse the trial court's ruling that denied Sears' motion for judgment N.O.V. on this count.

Furthermore, there was no evidence to justify the submission of the claims for punitive damages on either of the two counts submitted to the jury. Thus, regardless of the ultimate decisions on the trespass to chattel and false arrest counts, Sears is entitled to have the trial court instructed to grant it judgment N.O.V. on the punitive damage claims.

Respectfully submitted this 8th day of June, 1987.

GUST, ROSENFELD, DIVELBESS & HENDERSON

By _____
 Fred Cole
 Roger W. Perry
 Attorneys for Defendant-Appellee/Cross-Appellant

WRITING to PARTIES: CONTRACTS and CORRESPONDENCE

Parts III and IV examined advocacy to a court and written communication between members of a law firm. As a practicing attorney, however, you will communicate not only with judges and other attorneys but also with your clients and other parties.

For example, you may draft a written contract that the parties adopt as the final and complete expression of their negotiated agreement. If your client later complains that the other party has breached the contract, you may draft an "advice letter" to your client, advising her of her legal rights and recommending certain action. Depending on your client's assessment of her options, you might then send a "demand letter" to the opposing party, demanding that he take certain action to satisfy your client's claims.

Part V examines contracts and letters as examples of drafting directed to parties. It does not proceed on the premise that your immediate audience will invariably be the parties themselves. On the contrary, if you know that the opposing party is represented by counsel, you will ordinarily address your contract proposal or your demand letter to the opposing counsel. Similarly, if you or your law firm is the outside counsel for a corporation, you may address your advice letter to the corporation's in-house counsel. Nonetheless, more so than with office memoranda and briefs, contracts and letters are directed ultimately to the parties themselves.

Contracts and letters may also be useful at various stages of litigation. For example, a contract may precede a dispute, or it may express the parties' agreement to settle a dispute that has already proceeded through pretrial, trial, or even appellate litigation. Similarly, although you will often draft advice and demand letters at the earliest stages of litigation, you may use them at any stage of the litigation that raises new questions or that creates a new opportunity to state your demands.

CHAPTER 16

Contracts

I. BASIC APPROACHES

With some limits, parties can privately shape their legal rights and obligations by exchanging enforceable promises in a contract. Each party's promises impose contractual duties on that party and create contractual rights in the other.

The authors of one contracts casebook believe that the contractual promise is the greatest human invention, even greater than the wheel, the lever, and the pulley:

> . . . for it is the promise that breaks the ultimate physical restraint. It permits us to live a bit of the future today. When two or more employ the tool of promise in concert, they create a unique social engine—the *bargain*.[1]

Although this claim may provoke some debate between lawyers and engineers about the relative merits of the promise and the pulley, none will dispute that enforceable contracts are indispensable to modern commerce.

As with pleadings, you can readily find forms for contracts in a formbook or in a dusty file cabinet of a law office. However, many such forms are as antiquated as the parody of a contract presented in Exercise 10-1, page 199. You will produce a much better contract if you throw away the outdated forms, understand the purposes of each section of a contract, and express the agreement of the parties in plain, simple, clear English.

On the other hand, you need not reinvent the wheel with every contract. Some law firms produce high-quality form contracts for common transactions

---

1. D. Fessler & P. Loiseaux, Contracts, Morality, Economics and the Marketplace (Cases and Materials) 1 (1982).

that require similar provisions. For example, some firms have created and maintain a series of provisions for real estate contracts on computer disk. An attorney assigned to a real estate transaction can (1) leaf through a hard copy of the available provisions, (2) select the paragraphs that are best suited to the current transaction, (3) use a word processor to create a document with the selected paragraphs, and (4) tailor the document to the particular facts and requirements of the current transaction. Such a system can be highly successful if its users ensure that the forms are well written, and if they avoid complacency in tailoring the forms to particular transactions.

For contracts that do not lend themselves to a computerized form system, you should feel comfortable drafting "from scratch" without reliance on an antiquated form. You can draft with confidence if you understand the fundamental components of a contract.

II. FUNDAMENTAL COMPONENTS

A. GENERAL FORMAT

A contract should always contain the following provisions:
(1) an introduction identifying the parties to the transaction,
(2) a section describing the rights and obligations of the parties, and
(3) signature lines showing the parties' agreement to the terms of the contract.

A contract may also include:
(1) a statement of "recitals," which describes the background of the transaction and the parties' reasons for entering into the contract,
(2) a glossary of defined terms, or
(3) a section of miscellaneous provisions addressing such topics as termination or modification of the contract and the relationship of the contract to other transactions.

B. INTRODUCTION TO THE CONTRACT

In the first lines after the title of a contract, you should identify the parties as simply and clearly as possible. If more than two parties join in the transaction, or if at least one of the parties is a complex entity, you should set the parties' names apart from each other on the page.

For example, you can start with a descriptive section heading and use paragraphing to separate the parties' names:

I. PARTIES

The parties to this contract for the purchase and sale of sand are:
1. SOONER SAND CO., a general partnership consisting of Harley T. Price and W. M. McMichael, general partners, and

2. BASSI DISTRIBUTING CO., a joint venture of Bassi Trucking ‖
Co. and Hardcore Rock & Gravel, Inc.

If you use this format for the introduction, you can refer to the parties throughout the contract by the formal names of their business entities: SOONER SAND CO. and BASSI DISTRIBUTING CO. Alternatively, you can assign descriptive labels to the parties, such as Seller and Buyer:

1. Sooner Sand Co. (Seller), a general . . . ‖
2. Bassi Distributing Co. (Buyer), . . . ‖

Many drafters also like to assign a label to the contract itself and to include the date of the agreement in the introductory sentence:

This contract for the purchase and sale of sand (the "Agreement") is ‖
entered into on _____ by the following parties: ‖
1. Sooner Sand Co. (Seller), a general . . . ‖

C. RECITALS

Although not essential to an enforceable contract, a statement of the factual background of the transaction can help a neutral party interpret the contract if the parties dispute its meaning. Such recitals can even help establish consideration for the contract by showing the parties' reciprocal inducements or by providing a basis for implying obligations. For example, in the celebrated contracts case *Wood v. Lucy, Lady Duff-Gordon,*[2] Justice Cardozo of the New York Court of Appeals relied partly on the recitals of a written contract to imply an obligation by an exclusive agent to use reasonable efforts, thus satisfying the consideration requirement.

You should not confuse the recitals with the contract's statement of mutual promises. In the recitals, you should state only the background of the transaction and the motivations of the parties, not the actual obligations that the parties have assumed by their agreement.

Recitals in an outdated contract are easy enough to spot. Each recital of a background fact appears in a clause beginning with the word "Whereas" and is strung together with other recitals in a single, unmanageably long run-on sentence. To provide better guidance to your reader, you should (1) introduce the recitals with a section heading, such as "Recitals," "Background," or "Preamble," and (2) state your recitals in conventional sentences within numbered paragraphs:

II. RECITALS

1. SELLER is engaged in the business of selling and shipping sand from ‖
Phoenix to various customers in the State of Arizona but has not developed ‖

---

2. 222 N.Y. 88, 118 N.E. 214 (1917).

markets outside of Arizona. SELLER desires to supply sand wholesale to a distributor with customers outside the state.

    2. BUYER has an established business . . .

D. STATEMENT OF RECIPROCAL PROMISES

The heart of any contract is the parties' statement of their reciprocal promises. Those promises define the parties' mutual rights and obligations, which form the consideration for the agreement.

1. Introductory Clause; Recital of Consideration

Perhaps in an excess of caution, many drafters still begin their statements of reciprocal promises with outdated recitals of consideration such as the following:

> NOW, THEREFORE, in consideration of the mutual covenants herein contained, and other good and valuable consideration the receipt of which is hereby acknowledged, the parties hereby agree . . .

Aside from displaying an antiquated writing style, such passages fail to establish consideration in many jurisdictions. In some states, stating a promise in a signed writing raises a presumption of consideration,[3] but a recital of consideration has no additional legal effect.[4] In most transactions, moreover, the reference to "other . . . consideration" is simply false. Instead, the consideration consists of the mutual promises stated in the written contract. Rather than pompously recite the existence of consideration, you should simply state the mutual promises under a descriptive section heading and a simple introductory clause:

> III. MUTUAL RIGHTS AND OBLIGATIONS
>
> SELLER and BUYER agree to the following exchange:
>
> 1. *Supply.* For a period of five years from the date of formation of this contract, SELLER will supply BUYER with all the sand that BUYER requires . . .
>
>   2. *Delivery* . . .
>
>   3. *Quality* . . .
>
>   4. *Price.* For each ton of sand delivered, BUYER will pay SELLER a sum equal to . . .

---

3. See E. Farnsworth & W. Young, Cases and Materials on Contracts 117 (4th ed. 1988) (citing to Cal. Civ. Code § 1614 (West 1954) as typical statute).
4. See J. Calamari & J. Perillo, The Law of Contracts § 4-6 at 198 n.85 and accompanying text (3d ed. 1987).

Some drafters are tempted to begin each statement of an obligation with a phrase such as "SELLER promises to supply" or "SELLER agrees to supply." The reference to "promises" or "agrees," however, is unnecessary. If you begin your statement of mutual promises with an umbrella statement such as "SELLER and BUYER agree to the following exchange:", you need not repeatedly invoke the word "agree" in each statement of a promise. Moreover, to state a promise, you need not use the word "promise." Words such as "will" and "shall" appropriately convey a party's intent to commit herself to a future performance.

2. Precision in Drafting

a. Simplicity; Terms of Art

The terms of the exchange are a matter of negotiation between the parties. If you represent your client in the negotiations, you can participate in shaping the substance of the bargain. As part of that process, you may draft proposed contract provisions to serve as offers or counteroffers to the other party. In other cases, your client may ask you to prepare a formal written document expressing a bargain that the parties have previously negotiated. In either case, one of your primary tasks as drafter of the final document is to express the parties' negotiated rights and obligations as precisely as possible to reduce the risk of misunderstanding and costly disputes during performance of the contract.

To draft precisely, you should take advantage of helpful terms of art but avoid unnecessary jargon. For example, the provisions below refer to the buyer's "requirements," a legal term of art that has special meaning and legal consequences under the Uniform Commercial Code.[5] Otherwise, however, the provisions contain plain, simple English:

1. *Supply.* For a period of five years from the date of formation of this contract, SELLER will supply BUYER with all the sand that BUYER **requires** for BUYER's business of selling and shipping sand to customers outside the State of Arizona.

2. *Delivery.* BUYER may order sand as BUYER's **requirements** arise by sending a written purchase order to SELLER. . . .

Some legal terms are not necessarily terms of art but may be generally helpful and inoffensive. In the following passage, for example, the seller makes a special kind of promise by "warranting" the quality of the goods:

3. *Quality.* SELLER **warrants** that the quality of the sand that is delivered to BUYER will be at least equal to that of sand of corresponding grades sold by other sand companies in the City of Phoenix, Arizona.

---

5. U.C.C. § 2-306(1).

The word "warrants" in this passage is not a necessary term of art under the Uniform Commercial Code. The seller would assume the same legal obligation by simply promising that

|| SELLER will deliver to BUYER sand of a quality that is at least equal . . .[6]

Nonetheless, drafters typically and reasonably use the term "warrants" or "warranty" to draw attention to the special nature of a promise that goods or services will meet certain standards.

Similarly, many drafters use special phrases to draw attention to statements of "conditions," which qualify or limit contractual duties. For example, in a standard insurance contract, the insured will assume an absolute obligation to pay premiums to the insurer, but the insurer will pay money to the insured only if the insured suffers a loss of the type covered by the insurance contract. You could introduce the insured's conditional promise with the simple word "if":

|| If the insured suffers a covered loss as defined in section VI above, the
|| insurer will reimburse the insured for . . .

Many insurers, however, like to emphasize the conditional nature of their promises with special phrases, such as "on the condition that" or "in the event that":

|| In the event that the insured suffers a covered loss as defined in section V
|| above, the insurer . . .

Such language may catch the eye, but it is no more precise than "if." Therefore, if special emphasis is not your aim, you need not use the special phrase.

An even less defensible example of legal terminology in contracts is the use of "such" or "said" to refer to a particular thing that the contract has previously specifically identified:

|| On execution of this Employment Agreement, the Company will trans-
|| fer to Executive an option to purchase 100 shares of preferred stock at the
|| price of $100/share on or before June 1, 1991. . . . Executive may not
|| transfer the rights to *such* stock option at any time before January 1, 1991.

Before attending law school, you probably never considered using "such" or "said" in this way. In traditional nonlegal usage, the word "said" is not an adjective at all. In its primary nonlegal usage, "such" acts as an adjective, but it refers to a general class of persons or things with common characteristics:

|| Teresa is kind, gentle, and generous to everyone she meets. Such people
|| make the world a better place.

---

6. U.C.C. § 2-313(1)(a), (2).

"Such" is only secondarily recognized as a means of referring to a specific, previously identified thing.

Nonetheless, many legal drafters contend that "such" and "said" have taken on a special meaning in the legal community and that they therefore qualify as useful terms of art in contracts. However, if this special meaning is simply "previously mentioned," then "such" or "said" is really no more precise than the simpler and less distracting "the," "this," or "that":[7]

> . . . the Company will transfer to Executive an option to purchase 100 shares . . . Executive may not transfer the rights to **this** stock option at any time before January 1, 1991.

Of course, this level of precision would be inadequate to identify a particular stock option if the document had previously referred to several. In those circumstances, you can identify a particular stock option most precisely by giving it a special label:

> . . . the Company will transfer to Executive two stock options: (1) an option to purchase 500 shares of common stock at $50/share on or before June 1, 1992 (the Common Option), and (2) an option to purchase 100 shares of preferred stock at the price of $100/share on or before June 1, 1991 **(the Preferred Option).** . . . Executive may not transfer the rights to the **Preferred Option** at any time before January 1, 1991.

Some legal drafters tenaciously insist that "such" and "said" have become legal terms of art that satisfy even this higher standard of precision. They ascribe to "such" and "said" the special meaning "the one last referred to in this document." Thus, they interpret "said stock option" or "such stock option" to mean "the stock option last referred to above." But this argument strains the capacity of these simple words. In particular, the word "such" does not gracefully convey this level of precision, because this peculiar legal usage of "such" conflicts with its primary nonlegal usage as an adjective that refers to a general class of things.

For example, in the following excerpt from an employment contract, it is not clear whether an employer may discharge an employee for any violent acts on the premises or only for the particular violent acts of fighting and of damaging property:

> Employer may discipline Employee for any violent acts on the factory premises, such as fighting with other employees or maliciously damaging Employer's property. **Such** conduct constitutes grounds for immediate discharge.

If the reader ascribes the primary nonlegal meaning to the word "such" in the second sentence, that sentence could refer to a class of conduct describing any violent acts, of which fighting and damaging property are only two examples. If the reader ascribes some special legal meaning to the word "such" in the

---

7. See R. Wydick, Plain English for Lawyers 54 (2d ed. 1985) (analyzing "said").

second sentence, that sentence arguably refers only to the particular violent acts of fighting and damaging property; under that interpretation, the employer could discipline an employee for other violent acts, but not by discharging the employee. Thus, unless the reader knows precisely what meaning to ascribe to "such," the provision does not clearly state whether the employer may discharge an employee for violently destroying the employee's own property on the factory premises in a fit of anger.

Unfortunately, along with trusts and wills, contracts seem to be among the last refuges for marginally useful or even counterproductive legal jargon. You will serve your client and the profession well if you have the courage to use plain English and only truly helpful terms of art, even at the cost of ruffling some feathers within your law firm or the legal community.

b. Deliberate Imprecision

Occasionally, precision is neither feasible nor desirable. In some cases, for example, the parties may have failed to reach precise agreement on some point. If so, you may be forced to express their general agreement on that point in terms that are sufficiently imprecise to encompass the range of interpretations that describe their divergent positions.

For example, the buyer of factory equipment may demand during negotiations that the seller agree to repair or replace defective parts within ten days after receiving notice of the defect. The seller might counteroffer to repair or replace defective parts within 45 days after receiving notice of the defect. If the parties cannot agree on a time period measured by a specific number of days, they may instead agree on the vague language "within a reasonable time in light of all the circumstances," realizing that they might not share the same interpretation of that language in particular applications.

Language such as this may save the deal if negotiations are stalled on the sticky point. Moreover, if performance of the contract proceeds smoothly, the parties may never test their divergent interpretations of the language. On the other hand, if adverse circumstances place a strain on performance, the lack of perfect agreement on the precise meaning of the provision may erupt into a serious dispute. Thus, during the negotiation of such a deal, you must help your client weigh the benefits of reaching general agreement against the risks of subsequent disputes over the meaning of vague language.

3. Termination, Modification, and Merger Clauses

Substantive rules of contract law create special challenges for you when you draft either of two kinds of miscellaneous provisions: (1) restrictions on the parties' powers to orally terminate or modify a written contract, and (2) "merger clauses" designed to identify the signed contract as the complete and exclusive statement of the parties' agreement. These are certainly not the only kinds of provisions that present drafting challenges, but they serve to illustrate some interesting problems and helpful principles.

a. Restrictions on Termination or Modification

In many cases, parties to a written contract will seek to prevent their agents from casually entering into a subsequent oral agreement to modify or terminate the original written contract. A typical clause in the written contract states:

This agreement cannot be terminated or modified except in a signed, written ‖ agreement executed by the authorized agent of each party. ‖

Unfortunately, such a clause may not have the intended effect. Many courts hold that parties can orally agree to modify or terminate a written contract and that one of the parties can orally waive a specific contract right. Many of those courts will apply these principles to a specific provision requiring a writing for modification or termination. Under that approach, the parties can orally agree to "rescind," or eliminate, the clause that prohibits them from modifying the contract without a writing. Once they orally rescind that provision, the parties are free to orally modify or terminate the remainder of the agreement. A court can reach the same result by holding that a party effectively orally waived rights under a provision prohibiting oral modification or termination. Under that approach, the waiving party may be precluded from challenging a subsequent oral agreement to modify or terminate the substantive provisions of the contract.[8]

In a jurisdiction that is friendly to oral modifications or waivers, you may find it impossible to draft a restriction that absolutely precludes oral modification or waiver. You can start by adding an extra layer of prohibition in the clause:

The parties cannot terminate or modify this contract except in a signed, ‖ written agreement executed by the authorized agent of each party. More- ‖ over, this section's requirement of a writing is not subject to oral waiver or ‖ modification.

Of course, even this careful language may not successfully curb persistent attempts to orally modify or terminate the agreement. The parties presumably can orally rescind or waive the second sentence of the provision, paving the way for oral rescission or waiver of the main restriction, which in turn paves the way for oral termination or modification of the substantive terms of the agreement. Indeed, some courts might not even require the multiple layers of waivers or rescissions to take place in separate steps.[9]

Thus, in some jurisdictions, careful drafting may not be enough. If your client is troubled by the prospect of unauthorized oral modifications or terminations, you should research your state's law on this point. If you conclude

---

8. See generally C.I.T. Corp. v. Jonnet, 419 Pa. 435, 214 A.2d 620 (1965); Wagner v. Graziano Construction Co., 390 Pa. 445, 136 A.2d 82 (1957); 6 A. Corbin, Corbin on Contracts § 1295 (1962).

9. See generally Universal Builders, Inc. v. Moon Motor Lodge, Inc., 430 Pa. 550, 244 A.2d 10 (1968).

that you cannot contractually avoid the risk of unauthorized changes, you should candidly explain the limits of your drafting powers. So informed, your client can take other steps to avoid the risk, such as by increasing its administrative control over its agents.

b. Merger Clauses and Parole Evidence

When drafting a written contract, you will often want to include a "merger clause," which states that the written contract is the exclusive statement of the parties' agreement. If the other party subsequently asserts that the total agreement includes rights and obligations not expressed in the written contract, you can refer to the merger clause and seek to exclude evidence of the alleged unwritten obligations under the "parol evidence rule."

A typical merger clause refers only generally to the subject matter of the agreement:

> XXV. Prior Agreements Superseded—This written contract constitutes the parties' complete and exclusive statement of their agreement on the subject matter covered by this contract, and it supersedes all previous agreements, promises, or representations regarding that subject matter.

Unfortunately, such a clause does not eliminate the risk of litigation of a common question under the parol evidence rule: does the alleged additional agreement address topics within the subject matter of the main written contract so that the main contract supersedes it, or does the additional agreement address unrelated topics so that it can stand separately as an independent, enforceable contract?[10]

For example, suppose that on July 1, 1990 the parties signed a written contract for the lease of empty restaurant space. The lessee later asserted that the lessor also orally agreed on June 28, 1990 to sell dining tables and chairs to the lessee at a discounted rate. The lessor denies the oral agreement. He also points to the merger clause and argues that, assuming he did tentatively agree on June 28 to sell the dining furniture, the agreement was simply part of continuing negotiations that the parties abandoned and superseded in their July 1 agreement.

However, to successfully invoke the merger clause to exclude evidence of the oral agreement, the lessor must demonstrate that the alleged agreement to sell dining furniture falls within the subject matter of the July 1 contract; otherwise, the alleged June 28 agreement can stand outside the field occupied exclusively by the July 1 contract. Unfortunately, the merger clause cannot help the lessor much, because it fails to define the subject matter of the contract.

If you intend a written contract to broadly supersede prior agreements or promises on related transactions, you must describe the subject matter of your contract expansively so that the merger clause can have the intended effect. If you anticipate particular problems stemming from failed negotiations on collateral matters, you can address those matters explicitly:

---

10. See, e.g., Gianni v. R. Russell & Co., Inc., 281 Pa. 320, 126 A. 791 (1924).

XXV. Prior Agreements Superseded—This written contract constitutes the ‖ parties' complete and exclusive statement of their agreement on all matters relating to the lease of the Scottsdale premises, the operation of a restaurant on those premises, and the equipment needed for the operation. This contract supersedes all previous or contemporaneous agreements, promises, or representations regarding that subject matter. ‖

This merger clause expresses the parties' intent to abandon any prior agreement for the sale of restaurant equipment and to replace it with the terms of the lease agreement.

E. SIGNATURE LINES

You may end your contract with any reasonable means of presenting the parties' signatures as evidence of their agreement to the terms of the contract. You do not need to invoke formalistic jargon such as:

In witness whereof, the said parties have hereunto set their hands and ‖ seals the day and year first above written. ‖

Instead, you may simply precede the signature lines with the single word "Signed." At most, you might introduce the signatures with a clause such as "The undersigned parties agree to these terms."

If you have not already dated the contract at the beginning, you can include a space for the date next to each party's signature. The latest date on a signature line will represent one party's acceptance of the other party's offer and will mark the date of contract formation.

III. SUMMARY

To draft a simple contract, you should
(1) identify the parties in an introductory provision;
(2) recite the background facts, if helpful;
(3) state the reciprocal promises of the parties as precisely as possible; and
(4) provide signature lines as a means for the parties to express their assent to the terms of the contract.

EXERCISE 16-1

1. *Sample Requirements Contract*

Study the following contract. Compare it with the antiquated version presented in Exercise 10-1, page 199, and with your revision of that contract.

REQUIREMENTS CONTRACT

I. PARTIES

The parties to this contract for the purchase and sale of sand are:

1. Sooner Sand Co. (SELLER), a general partnership consisting of the general partners Harley T. Price and W. M. McMichael, and

2. Bassi Distributing Co. (BUYER), a joint venture of Bassi Trucking Co. and Hardcore Rock & Gravel, Inc.

II. RECITALS

1. SELLER is engaged in the business of selling and shipping sand from Phoenix to various customers in the State of Arizona but has not developed markets outside of Arizona. SELLER desires to supply sand wholesale to a distributor with customers outside the state.

2. BUYER has an established business in Phoenix selling and shipping sand to various customers in several states outside Arizona, including California, Nevada, Utah, and Colorado. BUYER desires a stable source of supply of sand for that business.

III. MUTUAL RIGHTS AND OBLIGATIONS

SELLER and BUYER agree to the following bargained-for exchange:

1. *Supply*. For a period of five years from the date of formation of this contract, SELLER will supply BUYER with all the sand that BUYER requires for BUYER's business of selling and shipping sand to customers outside the State of Arizona.

2. *Delivery*. BUYER will order sand as BUYER's requirements arise by sending a written purchase order to SELLER. On receipt of such a purchase order, SELLER will deliver the ordered sand within a reasonable time to BUYER's facility at 1531 Range Road in Glendale, Arizona.

3. *Quality*. SELLER warrants that the quality of the sand that is delivered to BUYER will be at least equal to that of sand of corresponding grades sold by other sand companies in the City of Phoenix, Arizona.

4. *Price*. For each ton of sand delivered, BUYER will pay SELLER a sum equal to sixty percent (60%) of the market price per ton of concrete in the City of Phoenix at the time of SELLER's delivery to BUYER.

5. *Term of Payment*. SELLER may give an invoice to BUYER for sand on or after SELLER delivers the sand to BUYER. BUYER will pay the full amount of such an invoice within thirty (30) days of its receipt of the invoice.

Signed:

_____   _____

SELLER—Authorized Agent for Sooner Sand Co.   Date

_____   _____

BUYER—Authorized Agent for Bassi Distributing Co.   Date

2. *Format for More Complex Agreement*

a. Compare the following outline of a sample contract with the sample contract in Exercise 16-1. The sample below displays an alternative introductory section, and it contemplates more complex provisions that must be subdivided into more numerous subsections.

b. In § 4.2 of the contract, draft a merger clause that identifies your document as the complete and exclusive statement of the parties' agreement. In particular, be certain to supersede prior failed negotiations in which SELLER proposed to lease trucks to BUYER for the transportation of the sand to other states.

REQUIREMENTS CONTRACT

This contract for the purchase and sale of sand (the Agreement) is entered into on _____ by the following parties:

1. SELLER—Sooner Sand Co., a general partnership consisting of Harley T. Price and W. M. McMichael, general partners, and

2. BUYER—Bassi Distributing Co., a joint venture of Bassi Trucking Co. and Hardcore Rock & Gravel, Inc.

RECITALS

1. SELLER is engaged . . .
2. BUYER has an established . . .

MUTUAL RIGHTS AND OBLIGATIONS

SELLER and BUYER agree to the following bargained-for exchange:

ARTICLE I
Definitions

1.1 *Grades of sand—* . . .

1.2 *Market price—* . . .

ARTICLE II
Supply of Sand

2.1 *Quantity—* . . .

2.2 *Quality—* . . .

2.3 *Delivery—* . . .

ARTICLE III
Payment

3.1 *Price—* . . .

3.2 *Terms of Payment—* . . .

• • • •

ARTICLE IV
Miscellaneous Provisions

4.1 *No Oral Modification—* . . .

4.2 *Prior Negotiations Superseded—* . . .

• • • •

SIGNED

_____

_____

Advice and Demand Letters[1]

As counselor and advocate, you will draft many kinds of letters to your client or to others on your client's behalf. Two of the most important are advice letters and demand letters. These letters are closely related to two kinds of documents examined in previous chapters: office memoranda and briefs. Like an office memorandum, an advice letter communicates a balanced legal analysis of a dispute or proposed action. In contrast, like a brief, a demand letter advocates a position, and it usually requests the addressee to take specific action.

I. ADVICE LETTERS

A. ADVICE LETTERS DISTINGUISHED FROM OPINION LETTERS

Many attorneys and commentators use the term "opinion letter" to refer to any letter addressed to a client that offers a legal analysis, opinion, or recommendation. Within this general class of letters, however, are two important subcategories, each of which warrants a narrowly descriptive label. The term "opinion letter" best describes only a small subcategory of letters in which you will provide your clients with formal opinions on certain kinds of legal questions. The term "advice letter" accurately describes the far more common kind of letter in which you will more generally analyze a legal problem and advise your client about the relative merits of alternative courses of action.

---

1. Many of the ideas in this chapter are taken with permission from lecture materials prepared by Frank M. Placenti and Mark Hileman, partners in the Phoenix law firm Streich, Lang, Weeks & Cardon, P.A.

More specifically, an opinion letter is a highly specialized and formal document that expresses your opinion or that of your law firm that a specified act is legally valid. For example, you might issue to a corporate client your formal opinion that the corporation has validly issued certain stock under applicable laws and under the articles and bylaws of the corporation. Because the client will significantly rely on such an opinion, the standards for an opinion letter are high, and its format is fairly rigid. Indeed, if you have any doubts about the legal validity of the action in question, you ordinarily will issue no opinion letter at all.

In contrast, in an advice letter, you will communicate your analysis of a legal problem to a client in much the same way that you would use an office memorandum to communicate the analysis to a supervising attorney. Even if you cannot definitively resolve the legal issues in the analysis, you can evaluate the relative merits of the parties' claims and defenses and estimate the probability of success on the merits. You can thus provide your client with valuable advice short of giving a definite opinion of the legality of certain actions.

In many law firms, only designated attorneys are authorized to issue formal opinion letters on behalf of the firm. Moreover, those attorneys tend to follow carefully developed forms when drafting their opinion letters, leaving little room for flexibility in format or creativity in analysis. Further examination of opinion letters is beyond the scope of this book. Instead, this chapter will explore the more common advice letter before addressing demand letters.

B. PURPOSE, AUDIENCE, AND WRITING STYLE

The writing style that you adopt for a document is in part a function of your intended audience and the purpose of your document. When you draft an office memorandum, you can easily identify your audience and purpose: you will communicate a balanced legal analysis to an experienced attorney. When you draft an advice letter, however, your audience and purpose may be less clear.

For example, the legal experience and general sophistication of your audience may vary greatly from one letter to the next. One client may be new to his business, have no legal training, and have learned English only after recently emigrating from a foreign country. Another client may be a sophisticated, experienced businessperson with at least a rudimentary knowledge of the laws that affect her business. Still another client may be a corporation with an in-house counsel to whom you will direct your advice letter. Obviously, you should adapt your writing style to suit the experience and sophistication of your audience. In a letter to the inexperienced client described above, you should take particular care to use plain, simple English and to avoid or explain even rudimentary legal terms. In letters to other, more experienced and legally knowledgeable clients, you can safely use more sophisticated language and legal terminology. In each case, however, your goal is the same: to communicate, not to impress.

One advice letter drafted by an associate in a major law firm provides a humorous example of the unintended effect you may have on your client if you fail to adapt your writing style to the client's needs. In the early 1980s, this law firm represented a man who had emigrated from Iran shortly after the Islamic revolution and the rise to power of the Ayatollah Khomeini. This client had violated a federal regulation in his business dealings in the United States, and he asked the law firm to advise him about the nature of the penalties and the possibility of avoiding them. In a letter, an associate of the law firm advised the client that he might avoid a fine if he "executed" a certain document. Unfortunately, the client had only a limited command of English, was painfully conscious of the executions by firing squad occurring daily in his homeland, and was anxious to skim the advice letter to determine what kinds of penalties an agency of the United States imposed for violation of its regulations. In these circumstances, the associate probably should have avoided the term "executed," which has a relatively innocuous legal meaning but which might have caused this client's heart to skip a beat or two when the client first glanced at the letter.

In some cases, you may have multiple audiences, thus complicating your task of choosing a suitable writing style. In one case, for example, an attorney anticipated that a federal regulatory agency would ultimately seek a copy of his advice letter to a client. Accordingly, rather than present a neutral, balanced analysis, the attorney advocated his client's position in a manner designed to persuade the regulatory agency to approve his client's actions. In essence, he wrote a brief that was packaged as an advice letter.

In other cases, your client may wish to share your advice letter with customers, partners, or other attorneys. If so, you should draft the letter with the needs of the secondary audience in mind. For example, if your law firm's client is a corporate manager, she may intend to discuss your advice letter with the corporation's separate, in-house counsel. If so, you may want to provide a full explanation of your underlying legal analysis or even to attach a copy of the formal office memorandum on which the advice letter is based.

C. FORMAT

You should flexibly adopt any format that suits your audience and the purpose of your advice letter. As a starting point, you can follow the basic elements of a reasonable format for an office memorandum:

Issues
Brief Answers
Facts
Discussion
Conclusion

With this format, your advice letter would
(1) restate the questions that your client posed to you,
(2) briefly summarize your conclusions,
(3) state the facts on which your analysis is based,
(4) summarize your analysis of the law and the facts, and
(5) state your conclusions and your strategic recommendations.
If your advice letter is simple and brief, you need not use formal section

headings to display the transitions between elements of your format. Instead, you can simply use sensible paragraphing to lead the reader from one element to the next. On the other hand, if your letter is long and complex, you should use section headings, just as you would in an office memorandum or a brief. You need not use precisely the same format headings as you would for an office memorandum. One attorney used the following primary headings in an advice letter to introduce the issues, brief answers, facts, discussion, and conclusion:

> Issues Addressed
> Executive Summary of Conclusions
> Background
> Analysis [divided into subsections]
> Recommendations

D. INTRODUCTION AND STATEMENT OF ISSUES

Immediately after the address and before the salutation of your advice letter, you should cryptically state the general subject matter of the letter:

Clay Franks
Vice-President, Construction
GRT Developers
1212 Central Ave, Suite 2201
Boomtown, Calzona 81717

RE: TRI Corp.'s possible breach of contract on the Westcourt project.

Dear Mr. Franks,

Then, in the first paragraph after the salutation, you should refer to your client's inquiry on this subject matter and state the issues that your letter addresses.

In some cases, your client will pose a general question that asks not for narrow legal conclusions but for strategic advice: "Should we fire TRI and sue it for breach of contract?" If so, you may want to inform your client of the legal issues on which your strategic advice will depend:

Dear Mr. Franks,

You have asked us to advise you whether you should fire TRI from the Westcourt project and sue it for breach of contract. In formulating our advice on this matter, we have analyzed the following questions:

(1) Did TRI breach the construction contract by using Cohoes pipe rather than the Reading pipe called for in the architect's plans?

(2) If so, was TRI's breach "material," thus permitting you cancel the construction contract and fire TRI from the project?

(3) If TRI has breached the contract, to what remedies is GRT entitled?

If you decide to introduce the primary parts of your letter with formal section headings, you could begin with *"Issues"*:

Dear Mr. Franks,

You have asked us to advise you whether you should fire TRI from the Westcourt project and sue it for breach of contract.

I. Issues

In formulating our advice on this matter, we have analyzed the following questions:

A. Did TRI breach the construction contract by using Cohoes pipe rather than the Reading pipe called for in the architect's plans?
B. If so, was TRI's breach "material," thus . . .

E. BRIEF ANSWERS

Some attorneys will discourage you from summarizing your conclusions in brief answers near the beginning of your advice letter. They fear that your client will fail to appreciate or will even misinterpret your conclusions if he has not read your full analysis first. However, like a supervising attorney reading an office memorandum, a client reading an advice letter is anxious to reach the "bottom line." You should not lightly withhold it from him out of some misplaced concern that he is not ready to face it. Moreover, mindful that he has paid for the entire letter, the client is nearly certain to read beyond the brief answers and to appreciate your full analysis. Thus, unless the letter is very short, or unless exceptional circumstances compel you to lay unusual groundwork before revealing an unfavorable conclusion,[2] you should satisfy your client's curiosity early in the letter.

If you use a simple format without section headings, you may briefly summarize your conclusions in a sentence or two immediately following your statement of the issues in the opening paragraph:

Dear Ms. Price,

You have asked us whether you would be liable for damages if you discharged your head chef in retaliation for his testifying against you in a hearing of the state Food and Beverage Commission. As discussed more fully below, we conclude that such a discharge would not constitute a breach of your employment contract, but it would render you liable under the state tort law of "wrongful discharge."

In a more complex letter, you could state your brief answers under some appropriate heading, such as "Brief Answers" or "Summary of Conclusions":

---

2. *See* H. Weihofen, Legal Writing Style 178, 199 (2d ed. 1980).

Dear Mr. Franks,

You have asked us to advise you whether you should fire TRI from the Westcourt project and sue it for breach of contract.

I. Issues

In formulating our advice on this matter, we have analyzed the following questions:

A. Did TRI breach the construction contract by using Cohoes pipe rather than the Reading pipe called for in the architect's plans?

B. If so, was TRI's breach "material," thus permitting you cancel the construction contract and fire TRI from the project?

C. If TRI has breached the contract, to what remedies is GRT entitled?

II. Summary of Conclusions

A. TRI breached the construction contract, because the architect's plans clearly call for Reading pipe and do not permit substitutes.

B. TRI's breach almost certainly is not material, because Cohoes pipe is nearly identical to Reading pipe in all important specifications. Therefore, you cannot cancel the contract.

C. GRT is entitled to the difference between the value of the Reading pipe and that of the Cohoes pipe, a difference that may be insubstantial.

In addition to providing these answers to the specific legal issues that you have formulated, you might add a sentence to your overview paragraph that summarizes your response to the client's general strategic question:

Dear Mr. Franks,

You have asked us to advise you whether you should fire TRI from the Westcourt project and sue it for breach of contract. In this letter, we summarize our legal analysis and advise you not to fire TRI or withhold its payments.

F. FACTS

In every advice letter, you should state the facts on which your analysis is based. By making a record of the factual premises of your analysis, you can protect yourself against criticism or liability if subsequently discovered facts render your legal analysis obsolete. Indeed, if your client has supplied you with the facts, you may want to disclaim responsibility for any fact investigation:

III. Facts

The advice in this letter is premised on the following facts, which you have supplied and which we have not independently investigated. If the following facts prove to be incomplete or incorrect, you should not rely on the advice in this letter without first consulting us.

G. LEGAL ANALYSIS

In the body of your letter, you should reach a conclusion on each issue by applying the relevant law to the facts. In a letter to a corporate client's in-house counsel or to a sophisticated client who has some legal knowledge, you can develop your legal analysis and cite to authority in much the same way that you would in an office memorandum. Other clients, however, will have little use for your in-depth analysis of authority. They would rather read a simplified summary of your legal analysis, and they are willing to assume that your underlying research and analysis has been thorough.

Thus, even if you have more fully expressed your analysis in another document, you may want to simplify the discussion in your advice letter. For example, as an initial reaction to a client's inquiry, you often will draft a full office memorandum addressed to a supervising attorney. The memorandum will then serve as a basis for formulating advice to the client. In the advice letter, however, you need not analyze the legal authority with the same depth and formality that you found useful in the memorandum. Instead, you can more simply and briefly convey your analysis of each issue by (1) abstractly summarizing the law with little or no citation to authority, (2) identifying the relevant facts, and (3) stating your conclusion:

> Under state tort law, you are liable for damages if you discharge an employee for a reason that violates public policy. Legislation of this state establishes public policies of maintaining health standards in restaurants and encouraging witnesses to testify at state administrative hearings. Therefore, if you discharge Chef Boyardi in retaliation for his testifying about violations of hygiene standards in your restaurant, you will be liable for violation of public policy.

In some cases, you can even leave the legal rule implicit by simply stating a conclusion, after identifying the facts on which it is based:

> Your contract with Chef Boyardi does not commit the parties to a definite term of employment, and it does not restrict your right to terminate the contract. Therefore, under state contract law, you can discharge Chef Boyardi at any time and for any reason without breaching the contract.

If your client has some legal training or expects to share your letter with another attorney, you may want to analyze authority to an extent that approaches the depth of analysis in your office memorandum. Alternatively, you can summarize your analysis in the letter and simply attach the office memorandum on which the advice in your letter is based. The client will rely primarily on the more accessible information in the letter, but he has access to your more thorough and formal memorandum if the need for it arises.

H. CONCLUSION; STRATEGIC RECOMMENDATIONS

In a final paragraph or section of your advice letter, you should summarize your subsidiary conclusions and offer your ultimate advice. If your client's legal rights and obligations are unclear, do not hesitate to convey the uncertainty with words and phrases that permit you to hedge. Even so, you should reach a conclusion, even if only a qualified one:

‖   Although the question is a close one, TRI's breach probably is not
‖ material. . . .

Your ultimate advice likely will be strategic, such as a recommendation to file a lawsuit, communicate a settlement offer, or refrain from discharging an employee. If the ultimate decision for the client is essentially a business decision, such as whether to purchase property for development, you should outline the legal consequences of the purchase but leave the actual business decision up to the client. On the other hand, if the ultimate decision is more clearly tied to the legal merits of a claim or defense, such as whether to settle a legal dispute, you can more strongly recommend a particular course of action.

Nonetheless, in all cases, you should invite the client to make the final decision. For example, when advising a client to settle, you should recommend a range of settlement offers within which your client can exercise some judgment to choose a particular position or to reject settlement altogether.

═══════ E X E R C I S E   1 7 - 1 ═══════

1. *Advice Letter Without Section Headings*

The following advice letter is addressed to a restaurant owner with no legal training. The author has used only paragraphing to signal the transition from one element of the letter to the next, and he has not cited to authority.

    a. Identify the purpose or purposes of each paragraph in the letter.

    b. Research the problem and rewrite the letter so that it conveys additional information to a client with legal training. Specifically, cite to authority and briefly analyze the authority. If appropriate, divide the expanded letter into sections with section headings.

August 1, 1990

Leona Price
Hep Crepe Restaurant
123 Washington St.
Spinach Village, New Maine 10307

Dear Ms. Price,

    You have asked us whether you would be liable for damages if you discharged your head chef in retaliation for his testifying against you in a hearing of the state Food and Beverage Commission. As discussed more fully below, we conclude that such a discharge would not constitute a breach of your employment contract, but it would render you liable under the state tort law of "wrongful discharge."

Our analysis is premised on the following facts, as you have supplied them. The state Food and Beverage Commission has recently held hearings on violations of state health and hygiene regulations at various restaurants within the Village. The Commission requested your head chef, Anthony Boyardi, to testify at the hearings. Under examination by Commissioners, Chef Boyardi testified that employees have failed to control rat and insect infestations, resulting in continuing violations of state regulations. Because you view Chef Boyardi's act of testifying as disloyal conduct, you wish to fire him.

Your contract with Chef Boyardi does not commit the parties to a definite term of employment, and it does not restrict your right to terminate the contract. Therefore, under state contract law, you can discharge Chef Boyardi at any time and for any reason without breaching the contract.

However, under state tort law, you will be liable for damages if you discharge an employee for a reason that violates public policy, regardless of whether the discharge would constitute a breach of contract. Legislation of this state establishes public policies of maintaining health standards in restaurants and encouraging witnesses to testify at state administrative hearings. Therefore, if you discharge Chef Boyardi in retaliation for his testifying at the administrative hearings, you will be liable for violation of public policy. Your liability may extend to damages designed to compensate Chef Boyardi for his losses and to additional damages designed to punish you for your intentional misconduct.

In conclusion, if you discharge Chef Boyardi in retaliation for his testimony, he will have a valid claim against you for damages. We advise you not to discharge him unless you are prepared to justify the discharge on other grounds.

If you have any questions on this matter, please call me at 123-4567.

Sincerely,

Robert Linzer
for Avila and Celaya, P.C.
222 N. 3d St.
Spinach Village, New Maine 10307

2. *Advice Letter with Section Headings*

a. Compare the following letter with the one in Exercise 1 above. Describe each way in which the letters differ in style and format.

b. Assume in the letter below that your client, Clay Franks, is an Anglo-American with racist tendencies and that the opposing party's representative, Cal Dunlap, is African-American. Do those facts affect your analysis of the problem? Does the letter below adequately address the problems potentially caused by your client's racism without unduly offending him? Should you be worried about offending him?

c. The letter below is addressed to a client who has at least a rudimentary knowledge of the law relating to performance and breach of construction contracts. Rewrite the letter so that it is appropriate for a client who has no legal training or knowledge. Specifically, summarize your analysis without citing to specific authority. If appropriate, eliminate the section headings and guide your reader through the simpler letter with good paragraphing and transition sentences.

> Marcia Todd
> Todd, Brown & King
> 1212 Central Ave., Suite 401
> Boomtown, Calzona 81717
> July 5, 1990

Clay Franks
Vice-President, Construction
GRT Developers
1212 Central Ave, Suite 2201
Boomtown, Calzona 81717

> RE: TRI Corp.'s possible breach of contract on the Westcourt project.

Dear Mr. Franks,

You have asked us to advise you whether you should fire TRI from the Westcourt project and sue it for breach of contract. In this letter, we summarize our legal analysis and advise you not to fire TRI or withhold its payments.

I. Issues

In formulating our advice on this matter, we have analyzed the following questions:

A. Did TRI breach the construction contract by using Cohoes pipe rather than the Reading pipe called for in the architect's plans?

B. If so, was TRI's breach "material," thus permitting you cancel the construction contract and fire TRI from the project?

C. If TRI has breached the contract, to what remedies is GRT entitled?

II. Summary of Conclusions

A. TRI breached the construction contract, because the architect's plans clearly call for Reading pipe and do not permit substitutes.

B. TRI's breach almost certainly is not material, because Cohoes pipe is nearly identical to Reading pipe in all important specifications. Therefore, you cannot cancel the contract.

C. GRT is entitled to the difference between the value of the Reading pipe and that of the Cohoes pipe, a difference that may be insubstantial.

III. Facts

The advice in this letter is premised on the following facts, which you have supplied. We have not independently investigated the facts. If the following facts prove to be incomplete or incorrect, you should not rely on the advice in this letter without first consulting us.

GRT Developers is constructing a shopping center at the southwest corner of 27th Ave. and Marconi Way in Boomtown. As Vice-President of the Construction Division, you have hired TRI to install the plumbing system. GRT's contract with TRI incorporates the architect's plans, which you first transmitted to TRI in a letter soliciting its bid on the project. Those plans clearly call for the plumbing subcontractor to use Reading brand pipe for all plumbing:

> All pipes in the plumbing system must be Reading pipe, in the sizes and grades specified in these plans, and no other brand pipe.

From the beginning, you have had difficulty working with TRI's foreman, Cal Dunlap. When TRI had completed about half the plumbing on the project, you discovered that TRI had installed Cohoes-brand pipe rather than Reading pipe. In a heated conversation with Dunlap, you demanded that TRI remove the Cohoes pipe, install Reading pipe, and compensate GRT for the resulting delay in construction. Dunlap agreed to install Reading pipe in the remainder of the plumbing, but he refused to replace the previously installed pipe. You now want to know whether you can fire TRI if Dunlap does not meet your demands.

Your own engineers have concluded that Cohoes pipe is equal to Reading pipe in durability and other relevant specifications. You do not know why the architect required Reading pipe, but you know that his brother-in-law is a sales manager for Reading Manufacturing Co.

IV. Analysis

If TRI has breached the construction contract, GRT may sue it for all foreseeable damages caused by the breach, provided that GRT can prove the damages with reasonable certainty. *See Johnson v. Coombs Construction Co.*, 345 Calz. 2d 331, 334 (1979). However, you may not fire TRI from the project unless TRI's breach is so substantial that a court would characterize it as "material," rather than "minor." *See Lehman Brothers, Inc. v. Steenhook Enterprises*, 401 Calz. 2d 112, 115 (1985). If a breach is only minor, you may not terminate the contract; instead, you must permit TRI to complete its performance, while reserving GRT's claim for damages resulting from its minor breach. *See id*. If you terminate the construction contract for only a minor breach, GRT will itself be guilty of the first material breach and will be liable to TRI for damages. *See id*.

A. Breach of Contract

The construction contract plainly requires TRI to use Reading pipe and no other. TRI has admitted that it used Cohoes pipe in approximately half of the plumbing. Therefore, TRI has breached the contract, and it is liable to GRT for foreseeable damages that GRT can prove with reasonable certainty.

B. Materiality of Breach

TRI's breach is material if it is so substantial that it either (1) robs GRT of the primary benefit that it expected from the contract, or (2) demonstrates that the TRI is not competent to perform the work and therefore should not be allowed to continue. *See id.* at 116. Stated conversely, the breach is minor if TRI is competent to complete the contract and GRT can be fully compensated for its losses by an award of money damages that is small in proportion to the value of the entire contract. *See id.*

In this case, TRI's breach probably is not material under either branch of the test of materiality. First, GRT's primary benefit from the plumbing contract presumably is high-quality durable plumbing. Cohoes pipe is equal to Reading pipe in durability and other relevant specifications. The architect apparently required Reading pipe for personal reasons and not because it is superior to Cohoes pipe. Therefore, unless GRT has some special need for Reading pipe, it will get its primary benefit from the contract even though half of the plumbing consists of Cohoes pipe.

Second, although TRI's use of Cohoes pipe shows that Dunlap departed from the architect's plans, we have no evidence that he has failed to follow more important specifications of the plans or that his crews have performed poorly in the actual installation. Dunlap probably knows that Cohoes pipe is equal to Reading pipe, and he may have simply not taken the architect's requirement seriously. Therefore, the events do not suggest that TRI is incompetent to perform Dunlap's promise to complete the installation of plumbing with Reading pipe.

In summary, a court likely would infer that your unhappiness with TRI stems more from your personal dislike for Dunlap than from problems caused by TRI's use of Cohoes pipe. Therefore, a court almost certainly will find that TRI's breach is not material.

C. Remedies

Assuming TRI's breach was only minor, you have no right to fire TRI from the project. Instead, you must permit TRI to complete its performance, and you may demand that it compensate GRT for any damages that result from its minor breach. If you are reasonably certain about the breach and the extent of damages, you may collect the damages yourself by withholding an appropriate amount of payments that GRT otherwise would owe to TRI. *See Johnson,* 345 Calz. 2d at 335. On the other hand, if you wrongfully withhold a substantial portion of TRI's payments above any amount that it owes GRT for breach, GRT may itself be liable for breach. *See id.*

Unfortunately, without further evidence that the choice between Reading pipe and Cohoes pipe will affect the value of your project in any way, you will have difficulty proving any damages. Therefore, we advise you not to withhold any payments owed to TRI.

V. Conclusion

Although TRI has breached its contract with GRT, the breach almost certainly is not material, and it may not have caused any damages. In these circumstances, if you fire TRI from the project, GRT will be liable to TRI for breach of contract. Indeed, even withholding TRI's payments to cover damages caused by its breach is risky, because we have difficulty identifying any such damages.

We recommend that you cooperate with Dunlap to ensure the best possible performance of TRI's remaining duties under the contract. In the meantime, you may want GRT's engineers to determine what damages, if any, the installation of Cohoes pipe has caused. If you find any damages, we will be happy to advise you about the best possible means of demanding compensation from TRI.

Please do not hesitate to call me if you have any questions about this matter. My direct line is 232-3232.

Sincerely,

Marcia Todd
for Todd, Brown & King

II. DEMAND LETTERS

A. PURPOSE, AUDIENCE, TONE, AND WRITING STYLE

With a demand letter, you may seek to achieve any one or more of three purposes. First, you may seek to persuade another party to take or cease some action. For example, you may send a demand letter to your client's tenant in an office building, demanding that it stop entering into unauthorized subleases and that it pay past rent due.

Second, you may seek to revoke a waiver of rights to permit your client to assert those rights in the future. For example, even though your client's lease agreement clearly requires payment of rent on the first of each month, your client may have implicitly waived his right to demand timely payment by frequently accepting late rent payments over the previous year without complaint. If so, you can help your client reassert his rights by sending a demand letter that (1) revokes any implied consent, (2) demands prompt payment of rent strictly according to the contract for the remainder of the lease, and (3) warns of your client's resolve to pursue legal remedies for future breaches of the lease.

Third, you may seek to "set up" the opposing party to help your client assert rights in the future. In such a letter, you do not really expect the opposing party to accede to your client's demand; rather, you hope to provoke a reaction that you can use to your client's advantage. For example, suppose that your client orally agreed to purchase goods from a supplier for a total price of $10,000, but the supplier has balked at performing. You know that your client will have trouble enforcing the oral agreement, because the Uniform Commercial Code generally requires such agreements to be evidenced in a writing signed by the party against whom enforcement is sought.[3] You might nonetheless send a letter to the supplier setting forth the terms of the oral agreement and demanding performance pursuant to those terms. In so doing, you may hold out little hope that the supplier will immediately perform as promised; instead, you hope that the supplier will either (1) respond by repeating its decision not to perform but admitting that it entered into the oral agreement or (2) fail to respond within ten days of receiving the letter, thus implicitly adopting your letter's description of the agreement.[4] Either reaction to the demand letter will satisfy the Uniform Commercial Code's requirement that the oral agreement be evidenced by a signed writing, thus enabling your client to assert a contract claim.[5]

The audience for your demand letter is the opposing party, her attorney, or both. Because your purpose is to persuade the other party to take or cease some action or to otherwise modify his relationship to your client, you will advocate your client's position in a demand letter in much the same way that you would advocate her position in a brief to a court. Indeed, you will often adopt an even stronger tone of advocacy in a demand letter than in a brief, because a self-interested adversary may be more difficult to persuade than a disinterested judge.

Of course, you should adopt a tone that will most likely achieve your goals. Your task is complicated, however, by the multiplicity of audiences and goals. For example, although your primary audience is the opposing party, her attorney, or both, your own client is an important secondary audience. Even if you think that a conciliatory tone will achieve the best results with the opposing party, your client may make it clear that she has hired you to take the strongest possible stance and to intimidate the opposing party. On the other hand, the community as a whole is a possible tertiary audience, because the opposing party may seek to gain public support by airing the dispute in the news media. If your demand letter is excessively strident, adverse public reaction may hinder your client's ability or willingness to assert her claims.

Thus, you should adopt a tone that is firm and precise, but not nasty. One partner in a law firm illustrates the proper tone by comparing the styles of three male public figures. During the 1988 Presidential campaign, George Bush projected an image that some characterized as "wimpy." A similar tone in a demand letter would not persuade the opposing party to do anything other than file your letter in the nearest waste basket. On the other hand,

---

3. U.C.C. § 2-201(1).
4. See U.C.C. § 2-201(2).
5. U.C.C. § 2-201(1, 2).

television personality "Mr. T" projects an image that many regard as menacing and unreasonable. A similar tone in a demand letter might intimidate or antagonize, but it would not necessarily persuade the opposing party to accede to your demands. A better image to project in a demand letter is that of a Clint Eastwood movie character: your words are spare and straightforward, and your demands are reasonable and are backed up with a big gun that everyone hopes you will not need to use.

Aside from tone, your style should be straightforward, businesslike, and professional. As is true in a brief, the most persuasive style in a demand letter is one that the reader does not notice, one that focuses the reader's attention on your demands, justifications, and threats. Thus, you should write in plain English and avoid legal jargon or florid, distracting prose.

B. FORMAT

You may flexibly adopt any reasonable format that will achieve the goals of your demand letter. At a minimum, your demand letter should include
(1) an introductory sentence or overview paragraph,
(2) a statement of the legal and factual support for your demands, and
(3) a specific statement of the demands and the consequences of the opposing party's failure to satisfy the demands.
You need not divide a simple demand letter into sections; good paragraphing will suffice. If you divide a long or complex demand letter into sections, you should use whatever section headings suit the purposes of your letter.

C. OVERVIEW

Immediately below the address and before the salutation of your demand letter, you should identify the general subject matter of the letter:

Arnold G. Hooper
Maxine C. Hooper
4094 East Laurel Lane
Fairbanks, New Maine 10713

RE: Eastern Savings and Loan Association Loan No. 082168

Dear Mr. and Mrs. Hooper,

In the first paragraph of your demand letter, you should provide any introductory information necessary to orient your reader. If this is your initial correspondence to the addressee, your opening paragraph should identify your representative capacity. Beyond that, the opening paragraph can provide such information as a general description of the relationships of the parties and an overview of your client's demands.

For example, the following, unusually direct opening sentence states the author's representative capacity and captures the reader's attention with a threat:

Dear Mr. and Mrs. Hooper,

Our client, Eastern Savings and Loan Association, has directed us to prepare to foreclose your interest in the above loan. . . .

In contrast, the following opening paragraph in a settlement proposal develops the background and purpose of the letter more deliberately, and it introduces the demand for payment in a more conciliatory fashion:

RE: *Araiza v. Udave*

Mr. Phillips,

I met last Wednesday night with my clients, the plaintiffs in the suit against Max and Josephine Udave. All the plaintiffs are keen to press their claims. Nonetheless, they have agreed to make the following settlement offer: they will withdraw their suit if Max and Josephine Udave pay them a total of $4,500, conditioned on actual payment by noon on October 31, 1988. In light of my following evaluation of the case, I think you will find this offer to be quite reasonable.

D. FACTUAL AND LEGAL BASIS FOR THE DEMANDS

Your explanation of the factual and legal justification for your client's demands may take many forms. In a routine collection letter, you can simply state the amount that is past due under an identified loan agreement or installment contract. In such a demand letter, the opposing party ordinarily will not dispute the general enforceability of such contracts, and you need not discuss the legal principles that make contractual obligations enforceable:

You are now delinquent in the installments due for the months of January and February, 1989. The total amount that you must pay Eastern Savings to bring your loan payments current is $1,103.72. Also, your next payment of $501 will be due on March 5, 1989. Therefore, after March 5, the amount necessary to bring your loan payments current will be $1,604.72.

In other cases, the fact or amount of the opposing party's liability may be more doubtful, prompting you to more thoroughly explain the legal basis for your client's demands. Such an explanation may look very much like the legal analysis and application to facts in a brief. For example, the following passage justifies a demand for consequential damages stemming from a breach of contract:

In addition, the plaintiffs will be entitled to foreseeable consequential damages stemming from the breach. *Southern Arizona School for Boys, Inc. v. Chery,* 119 Ariz. 277, 280, 580 P.2d 738, 741 (1978). Those will include the plaintiffs' expenditures on specialized accessories that were suitable only for the wedding and that some plaintiffs were unable to use. *See A.R.A.*

Manufacturing Co. v. Pierce, 86 Ariz. 136, 341 P.2d 928, 932 (1959) (victim of breach entitled to award of damages for wasted promotional expenditures). Those members of the wedding party who could not fully participate in the wedding, the sole event for which the specialized gowns were ordered, can also recover damages for that lost opportunity. *See, e.g., Mieske v. Bartell Drug Co.,* 91 Wash. 2d 682, 593 P.2d 1308 (1979) (in UCC case, upholding award of $7,500 for emotional value associated with contracting parties' loss of home movies of significant events). Indeed, the opportunity to participate in the wedding formed the basis for the contracts for the gowns.

All of these losses are itemized in Count I of the complaint. They total approximately $9,000. Because the plaintiffs will certainly prove a breach of contract and will establish at least some of their alleged damages, they will also be entitled to an award of attorney's fees, which could add thousands more to the total recovery.

The appropriate level of formality of your legal analysis will depend on the sophistication of your audience. If you address your demand letter to the opposing party's attorney, or if you are certain that the opposing party will consult an attorney, you can reasonably cite to legal authority, as in the immediately preceding example. On the other hand, if the opposing party does not have legal training, and if you can appropriately address your letter directly to that party, then you should express your arguments in terms that the party can understand. If you try to intimidate the opposing party with formal citations to authority, you might simply confuse or antagonize rather than persuade.

For example, the following excerpt of a demand letter to an insurance company's subrogation analyst assumes that the analyst has a sophisticated knowledge of business practices but has no formal legal training. The excerpt refers to three legal concepts: waiver, offer, and the "mailbox rule" governing the timing of acceptance. The author of the letter has tried to use these concepts in a persuasive manner without diverting the reader's attention to distracting citations:

> Even if Mr. Upton's premium had arrived after expiration of the grace period, his rights were preserved in the conversation between him and Diane Campbell, assistant to Dee Boston, on March 12. In that conversation, Ms. Campbell notified Mr. Upton that his claim would be covered but that she would delay processing his claim until he paid his late premium. Mr. Upton stated over the phone that he would mail his premium. In effect, Ms. Campbell waived any condition to coverage that would require Mr. Upton to deliver the premium to her within the grace period. She thus made the date of her receipt of the premium relevant only to the matter of processing his claim. At worst, Ms. Campbell may have communicated a new offer of coverage that invited Mr. Upton's return promise to pay the premium. If so, Mr. Upton accepted the offer either over the phone or under the "mailbox rule" when he placed his premium in the mailbox.

A demand letter is not the proper place to make concessions or admissions that may come back to haunt you later. Therefore, if you choose to adopt a conciliatory tone, do so in a way that does not preclude you from taking a stronger position in the future. For example, suppose that your client demands compensation on the basis of a strong contract claim and a weak tort claim. To maintain credibility and to avoid antagonizing the opposing party, you might invoke only the contract claim to justify your client's demands in a demand letter. If so, you should remain silent about the weaker tort claim or refer to it only vaguely. If you affirmatively concede the weakness of that claim in writing, you may hinder your ability to pursue it later if newly discovered facts enhance its potential merit.

You should also avoid ambiguous conciliatory language that might grant unintended rights to the opposing party. For example, in a letter demanding payment of amounts past due on a loan agreement, you should exercise caution before inviting the opposing party to apply to your client for an extension of the loan. If you state the invitation in a way that raises reasonable expectations in the opposing party of receiving the extension, you may obligate your client to grant such an extension.

E. DEMANDS AND THREATS

You should not send a demand letter unless your client has a well-defined goal that you can formulate into a straightforward demand to the opposing party. Moreover, to maximize the chances of achieving that goal, you must provide the opposing party with an incentive to satisfy your client's demand. If the opposing party is fair-minded and your demand is just, your persuasive presentation of the legal and factual bases for the demand may help induce him to accede to the demand. In most cases, however, you can provide the greatest incentive to the opposing party by threatening to take actions that would be less pleasant for the opposing party than acceding to the demand.

Thus, you must clearly state both your client's demand and the actions your client will take if the opposing party rejects the demand. To ensure prompt action, you should set a specific date by which the opposing party must satisfy your client's demand or suffer the adverse consequences of the threatened action. For example, if your client is demanding the payment of amounts past due on a loan or an installment contract, you should

(1) state the precise payment that your client demands;

(2) set a date by which the opposing party must deliver the payment to a particular address; and

(3) depending on the circumstances, threaten to foreclose on secured property, to sue on the contract, or to take other appropriate legal action if the demand is not satisfied.

The following excerpt from a loan collection letter illustrates the clarity, specificity, and directness for which you should strive:

> . . . Therefore, after March 5, the amount necessary to bring your loan payments current will be $1,604.72.
>
> If you desire to avoid legal proceedings, you must submit the above sum on or before March 17, 1989, in cash, cashier's check, or certified funds made payable to Eastern Savings and Loan Association. You must mail or deliver the payment directly to:

Eastern Savings and Loan Association
Suite 11000, Financial Plaza
1901 South Alma School Road
Fairbanks, New Maine 10701
Attention: Kathy Growl

Take notice that time is of the essence . . .

If Eastern Savings has not received the above amount on or before March 17, 1989, it will accelerate the principal balance of the loan and will immediately commence foreclosure proceedings. These proceedings could result in a sale of the property securing the loan. . . .

You should ensure that your letter satisfies any applicable statutory prerequisites to making the demand, such as requirements that the demand be made in a certain form or that it contain certain information:

Pursuant to the terms of the deed of trust, you have the right to challenge any such acceleration or to assert the absence of a default or any other defense in court. Under the laws of New Maine, however, a court will presume the debt to be valid unless you dispute the validity of the indebtedness, or any portion of it, within 30 days of your receipt of this notice.

Also, to avoid any dispute about the opposing party's receipt of your demand letter, you should always send the demand letter by registered mail. Finally, to preserve your credibility in future correspondence, you must confirm that your client is willing and able to back up its threats with action.

═══════ E X E R C I S E 1 7 - 2 ═══════

1. *Collection Letter*

Study the following collection letter and explain the purpose or purposes of each paragraph.

> Scott L. Short
> Stanley, Leeds & Cardon
> 100 W. Central Ave., Suite 2100
> Fairbanks, New Maine 10701
> February 15, 1989

CERTIFIED MAIL
RETURN RECEIPT REQUESTED

Arnold G. Hooper
Maxine C. Hooper
4094 East Laurel Lane
Fairbanks, New Maine 10713

RE: Eastern Savings and Loan Association Loan No. 082168.

Dear Mr. and Mrs. Hooper,

Our client, Eastern Savings and Loan Association, has directed us to prepare to foreclose your interest in the above loan. You are now delinquent in the installments due for the months of January and February 1989. The total amount that you must pay Eastern Savings to bring your loan payments current is $1,103.72. Also, your next payment of $501 will be due on March 5, 1989. Therefore, after March 5, the amount necessary to bring your loan payments current will be $1,604.72.

If you desire to avoid legal proceedings, you must submit the above sum on or before March 17, 1989, in cash, cashier's check, or certified funds made payable to Eastern Savings and Loan Association. You must mail or deliver the payment directly to:

> Eastern Savings and Loan Association
> Suite 11000, Financial Plaza
> 1901 South Alma School Road
> Fairbanks, New Maine 10701
> Attention: Kathy Growl

Take notice that time is of the essence on this matter. Eastern Savings will strictly adhere to the above deadline and future due dates despite any past acceptance of late or partial installment payments, any prior reinstatement, any prior negotiations, or any other actual or implied forbearance of any nature by Eastern Savings.

If Eastern Savings has not received the above amount on or before March 17, 1989, it will accelerate the principal balance of the loan and will immediately commence foreclosure proceedings. These proceedings could result in a sale of the property securing the loan.

Pursuant to the terms of the deed of trust, you have the right to challenge any such acceleration or to assert the absence of a default or any other defense in court. Under the laws of New Maine, however, a court will presume the debt to be valid unless you dispute the validity of the indebtedness, or any portion of it, within 30 days of your receipt of this notice.

> Very truly yours,
>
>
> Scott L. Short
> Stanley, Leeds & Cardon

2. *The Bad Example*

Study the following collection letter and explain why it is less effective than the letter in Exercise 1 above. Identify and describe each defect.

Green and Gain
120 West Washington
Phoenix, AZ 85003
April 4, 1989

Mr. and Mrs. Joe Smith
5555 North 55th Street
Phoenix, AZ 85055

Re: Delinquent Loan #9-1403726-841

Dear Borrower:

We are counsel of record for the Bank of Phoenix (hereinafter referred to as the Bank). Our client has informed us that you are behind in your loan payments, and has asked that we write you on its behalf to request that you take some action to bring your loans current. We understand that you presently are approximately $2,500.00 behind in your payments.

Over the past several months, the few loan payments you have actually made have been consistently late. While the Bank was happy to take whatever it could get from you, it would prefer that you try to make payments on time. If you are having difficulty making your payments, the Bank would be happy to consider and, if reasonable, would agree to an extension of your loan, a modification of its terms, or the extension of additional monies to see you through whatever difficulties you may be experiencing. If you desire to pursue this offer, please call your loan officer or some other authorized representative of the Bank.

Please be advised, however, that the Bank has no intention of waiting forever for you to make good on your commitments. Frankly, in our experience the Bank has very little patience with deadbeat borrowers such as you appear to be. The Bank has ruined the credit of thousands of borrowers who, like you, did not take their obligations seriously. Hundreds more have been forced into bankruptcy. Moreover, the Bank is a large, powerful institution which can afford to hire big law firms such as this one, against which the average debtor has little chance of prevailing. We sincerely hope that you will take the hint and pay up.

The Bank therefore suggests that you make arrangements to bring the aforementioned loan current by paying the amount hereinbefore stated or making such other arrangements as you and said Bank may subsequently agree upon.

Sincerely,

Bob Jenkins
Green & Gain

3. *Settlement Letter*

a. Study the settlement letter below and explain the purpose or purposes of each paragraph. Precisely what does the letter demand? What action does the author of the letter threaten to take if the demand is not met?

b. The letter below is addressed to the opposing party's attorney. Rewrite the letter so that it is appropriate for a client who has no legal training or knowledge. Specifically, summarize your analysis without citing to specific authority. If appropriate, eliminate the section headings and guide your reader through the simpler letter with good paragraphing and transition sentences.

> Charles Rehnquist, Esq.
> 333 S. Central Ave.
> Phoenix, Arizona 85001
> (602) 849-0101
> September 6, 1988

Robert M. Phillips Esq.
Kim, Phillips, Burley & Stewart
3301 E. Bethany Home Road, Suite B-111
Phoenix, Arizona 85012

RE: Araiza v. Udave

Mr. Phillips,

I met last Wednesday night with my clients, the plaintiffs in the suit against Max and Josephine Udave. All the plaintiffs are anxious to press their claims. Nonetheless, they have agreed to make the following settlement offer: they will withdraw their suit if Max and Josephine Udave pay them a total of $4,500, conditioned upon actual payment by noon on October 31, 1988. In light of my following evaluation of the case, I think you will find this offer to be quite reasonable.

I have no doubts about our ability to prove the claim for breach of contract. Indeed, your early correspondence and the defendants' answers to the complaint and interrogatories admit that Josephine failed to perform as promised. Even if she had acted in good faith and with best efforts, that would be no excuse for breach of the contract. Therefore, the defendants have essentially admitted to their breach of contract. The direct loss in value is easily computed: the difference between the value of each gown as promised ($550-$600 by your own correspondence) minus the value of the dress as delivered (we can prove that some are total losses).

In addition, the plaintiffs will be entitled to foreseeable consequential damages stemming from the breach. *Southern Arizona School for Boys, Inc. v. Chery,* 119 Ariz. 277, 280, 580 P.2d 738, 741 (1978). Those will include the plaintiffs' expenditures on specialized accessories that were suitable only for the wedding and that some plaintiffs were unable to use. *See A.R.A. Manufacturing Co. v. Pierce,* 86 Ariz. 136, 341 P.2d 928, 932 (1959) (victim of breach entitled to award of damages for wasted promotional expenditures). Those members of the wedding party who could not fully participate in the wedding, the sole event for which the specialized gowns were ordered, can also recover damages for that lost opportunity. *See, e.g., Mieske v. Bartell Drug Co.,* 91 Wash. 2d 682, 593 P.2d 1308 (1979) (in UCC case, upholding award of $7,500 for emotional value associated with contracting parties' loss of home movies of significant events). Indeed, the opportunity to participate in the wedding formed the basis for the contracts for the gowns.

All of these losses are itemized in Count I of the complaint. They total approximately $9,000. Because the plaintiffs will certainly prove a breach of contract and will establish at least some of their alleged damages, they will also be entitled to an award of attorney's fees, which could add thousands more to the total recovery.

Josephine's own theory of the case is that she breached the contract because she lost the ruffles. Coupled with her failure to warn the plaintiffs to obtain gowns from an alternative source, those facts should easily support the negligence claim in Count II. That claim provides even stronger support than Count I for an award of general compensatory damages, including damages for emotional distress.

Also solid are the claims for promissory fraud and consumer fraud in Counts III and VI. The consumer fraud statute prohibits use of deception, fraud, false promises, or suppression of material fact with intent that others rely, in connection with the sale of any merchandise. A.R.S. § 44-1522. "Merchandise" includes services. A.R.S. § 44-1521(5). Like the common law tort of promissory fraud, a claim under the consumer fraud statute will support an award of punitive damages. *Schmidt v. American Leasco,* 139 Ariz. 509, 512, 679 P.2d 532, 535 (App. 1983). We should have little trouble proving a claim under either theory: the plaintiffs will offer abundant and vivid testimony describing the way in which Max and Josephine deliberately misrepresented that many of the gowns would be ready on time, thus inducing many of the plaintiffs to wait until the last minute and beyond, when in fact Max and Josephine knew that the gowns could not possibly be completed on time. In light of the "evil minds" associated with such actions, these claims potentially could add thousands of dollars in punitive damages to the compensatory damages detailed in Count I.

In sum, the plaintiffs are angry and confident. They are anxious to go to an arbitration hearing, and they are ready to enforce their judgment by attaching the Udaves' property. Indeed, I experienced some difficulty getting them to agree to propose this settlement offer. I can assure you that it is not a bargaining posture; it represents their current bottom line. Despite their passionate views on this matter, however, they have compromised their full claims substantially. The $4,500 figure represents 50% of the compensatory damages for Count I, without costs or attorney's fees, and without any punitive damages.

This offer remains open until noon, September 22. Please call or write to me before then if your clients wish to settle.

Sincerely,

Charles Rehnquist, Esq.

4. *Response to Demand Letter: Demand for Withdrawal of Claim*

The following letter responds to a demand letter from an attorney for Framer Insurance Co. addressed to Michael Upton. Mr. Upton caused an automobile accident, resulting in injuries to Eileen Bradley, who was insured by Framer. Framer paid Ms. Bradley's claim for $10,000 in losses and medical expenses arising out of the accident. Framer then demanded that Mr. Upton reimburse Framer for Framer's payment to Ms. Bradley. Mr. Upton, however, claimed that he had liability insurance from Framer and that Framer thus was obligated to assume the cost of his liability to Ms. Bradley. The primary matter of dispute between Framer and Mr. Upton was whether Mr. Upton had validly renewed his insurance contract with Framer despite Framer's assertion that it received his late premium payment only after expiration of the policy's grace period.

a. Although it responds to a demand letter, the letter below is itself a demand letter, albeit a subtle one. What does it demand? What action does it implicitly threaten if the demand is not met? Should the author have stated the demand and threat more strongly?

b. Who is the audience for this letter? Assuming that Marilyn Brauscomb is not a lawyer, would she likely consult with Framer's attorney, Jon Drake, before deciding whether to drop Framer's claim against Mr. Upton? If so, should the author have advanced a more formal legal analysis with citation to authority?

Charles Rehnquist, Esq.
333 S. Central Ave.
Phoenix, Arizona 85001
(602) 849-0101
December 1, 1987

Marilyn Branscomb
Subrogation Analyst for Framer Insurance
P.O. Box 3108
Mesa, Calzona 89211

Policy No. 881347 94

Dear Ms. Brauscomb,

I represent Michael Upton in his claim for coverage under the above policy. I write in response to Jon C. Drake's letter dated October 30 to Michael Upton, in which Mr. Drake requests Mr. Upton to indemnify Framer for Framer's payment of claims to Eileen Bradley. I address this letter to you because Mr. Drake directed Mr. Upton to contact you. I'm sure that everyone hopes to resolve this matter before either party must incur the enormous legal expenses associated with litigation.

Mr. Upton is unwilling to pay the claim for two reasons. First, he claims liability coverage under his policy and thus expects Framer to satisfy Ms. Bradley's claims. Second, he challenges the damages claimed by Ms. Bradley.

The confusion about the possible lapse of Mr. Upton's insurance coverage stems from his not receiving Framer's bill or notice of grace period, apparently because of his change of address. Although I haven't seen a copy of the policy, I assume that it requires actual receipt of a late premium before expiration of the grace period. Even so, Mr. Upton suspects that the post office in fact delivered his premium within the three days remaining in the grace period, and he doubts Framer's claim that it received the premium a full week after it was posted two miles away. A jury would have the same doubts. Once Mr. Upton proves to a jury with his testimony and that of a witness that he posted the letter three days before expiration of the grace period, Framer would be hard pressed to prove that the letter took longer than the standard 1-3 days for delivery.

Although Ms. Campbell now denies the March 12 conversation, Mr. Upton is confident of his ability to prove his version of events before a jury, particularly in light of his previously communicated willingness to submit to a lie detector test. Of course, if litigation or other inquiry reveals that anyone within the Framer organization sought in bad faith to deny Mr. Upton coverage by covering up the facts, the resulting issues would transcend the relatively small dispute now before us. Thus, you should consider the possibility of a counterclaim to any claim that Framer might consider pursuing against Mr. Upton.

Even if Mr. Upton were not covered under this policy, it is highly unlikely that he would be liable for the full amount of Ms. Bradley's claim. Initially complaining of an injury to her finger, Ms. Bradley used the occasion of the accident to take advantage of chiropractic treatment, including vibratory massage, that required time away from work. As a matter of common knowledge, the chiropractic profession holds that countless persons suffer routinely from physical stresses that can be alleviated through chiropractic therapy as a supplement to other medical care. Mr. Upton thus suspects that Ms. Bradley's medical bills and time off from work represent an extravagant reaction to the accident. The medical bills and report do not conclusively resolve the question whether the chiropractic therapy was used to treat conditions suffered by Ms. Bradley that preexisted the accident. Nor do they resolve doubts about how much, if any, of the chiropractic care and resulting lost wages were reasonably necessary to treat any injuries that did stem from the March 12 accident. Thus, Framer acted unreasonably in paying Ms. Bradley's claim in full. Mr. Upton should not have to reimburse Framer for anything more than Ms. Bradley's actual damages.

In sum, even if Mr. Upton were not covered, he would not be inclined to indemnify Framer for anything but a small fraction of Ms. Bradley's extravagant bills. More than that, Mr. Upton is prepared to prove that he owes Framer nothing because Framer had a contractual duty to provide him insurance coverage for his liability to Ms. Bradley stemming from the March 12 accident.

If Framer drops its claim, Mr. Upton will be happy to cease any further inquiry into possible claims he might have against Framer based on bad faith or other misconduct that Framer may have engaged in. Please contact me by January 15, 1988, with your response.

Sincerely,

Charles Rehnquist, Esq.

cc Jon C. Drake

III. SUMMARY

In an advice or demand letter, you should

(1) use plain English whenever possible, and

(2) adapt your format and depth of legal analysis to your audience and your purpose.

In an advice letter, you should

(1) restate the questions that your client has posed to you and identify the legal issues that they encompass,

(2) briefly answer the issues,

(3) state the facts on which your analysis and advice are premised,

(4) discuss the law and apply the law to the facts to reach a conclusion for each issue, and

(5) summarize your subsidiary conclusions and state your advice.

In a demand letter, you should

(1) use an introductory sentence or paragraph to identify your representative capacity, provide an overview of the purpose of your letter, or orient the reader in some other fashion;

(2) state the legal and factual bases for your demand; and

(3) state your demands, including the time and place for satisfaction of the demands, and threaten to take action if the demands are not met.

‖ INDEX ‖

Watership Down

Watership Down

Richard Adams

AVON
PUBLISHERS OF BARD, CAMELOT AND DISCUS BOOKS

AVON BOOKS
A division of
The Hearst Corporation
959 Eighth Avenue
New York, New York 10019

First Avon Printing, September, 1975.
Fourth Printing

AVON TRADEMARK REG. U.S. PAT. OFF. AND
FOREIGN COUNTRIES, REGISTERED TRADEMARK—
MARCA REGISTRADA, HECHO EN U.S.A.

Printed in the U.S.A.

To JULIET *and* ROSAMOND,
remembering
the road to Stratford-on-Avon

Note

Nuthanger Farm is a real place, like all the other places in the book. But Mr. and Mrs. Cane, their little girl Lucy and their farmhands are fictitious and bear no intentional resemblance to any persons known to me, living or dead.

Acknowledgments

I acknowledge with gratitude the help I have received not only from my family but also from my friends Reg Sones and Hal Summers, who read the book before publication and made valuable suggestions.

I also wish to thank warmly Mrs. Margaret Apps and Miss Miriam Hobbs, who took pains with the typing and helped me very much.

I am indebted, for a knowledge of rabbits and their ways, to Mr. R. M. Lockley's remarkable book, *The Private Life of the Rabbit*. Anyone who wishes to know more about the migrations of yearlings, about pressing chin glands, chewing pellets, the effects of overcrowding in warrens, the phenomenon of re-absorption of fertilized embryos, the capacity of buck rabbits to fight stoats, or any other features of Lapine life, should refer to that definitive work.

Contents

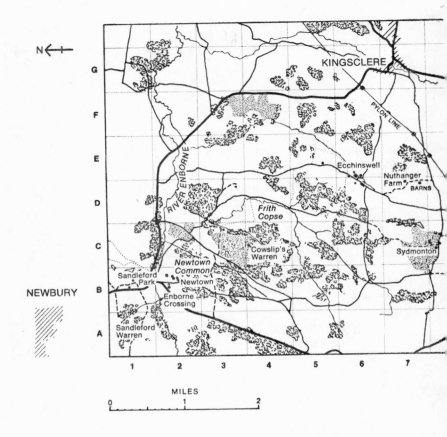

N

KINGSCLERE

PYLON LINE

G

F

E

Ecchinswell

Nuthanger
Farm
BARNS

D

RIVER ENBORNE

Frith
Copse

C

Cowslip's
Warren

Sydmonton

Newtown
Common

Sandleford
Park

Newtown

B

Enborne
Crossing

NEWBURY

A

Sandleford
Warren

1   2   3   4   5   6   7

MILES

0   1   2

LEGEND

Main road ▬▬▬▬▬

Minor road ▬▬▬▬▬

Footpath ·················

Bridle track

Railroad ┝┼┼┼┼┼┼┼┼┼┼┼┼┼┤

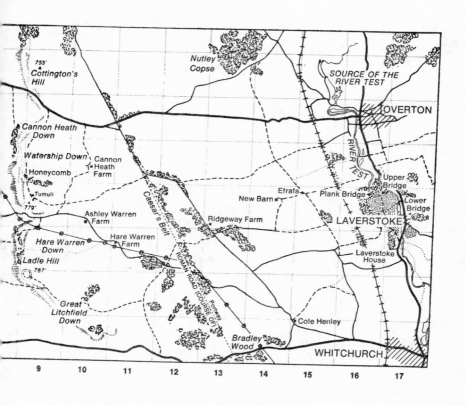

9 10 11 12 13 14 15 16 17

MAP REFERENCES

PART I

The story opens   **A 1**
The Enborne crossing   **B 2**
The Heather   SQUARE   **C 3**
Cowslip's Warren   **C 4**

PART II

The N.E. corner
of the Beech Hanger
on Watership Down   **D 9**
Nuthanger Farm   **D 7**

PART III

The combe where Bigwig met the fox   **D 12**
Where they crossed the railway line   **D 16**
The upper bridge on the Test   **D 16**
Where the punt was lying   **D 16**
Efrafa. The Crixa   **D 15**
The roadless railway arch   **D 15**

PART IV

The lower bridge and the weed pool   **D 17**
The copse where the fox struck   **C 13**

The map is adapted from one drawn by Marilyn Hemmett

Watership Down

PART I

The Journey

1

The Notice Board

> CHORUS : Why do you cry out thus, unless at some vision of horror?
> CASSANDRA : The house reeks of death and dripping blood.
> CHORUS : How so? 'Tis but the odor of the altar sacrifice.
> CASSANDRA : The stench is like a breath from the tomb.
>
> Aeschylus, *Agamemnon*

The primroses were over. Toward the edge of the wood, where the ground became open and sloped down to an old fence and a brambly ditch beyond, only a few fading patches of pale yellow still showed among the dog's mercury and oak-tree roots. On the other side of the fence, the upper part of the field was full of rabbit holes. In places the grass was gone altogether and everywhere there were clusters of dry droppings, through which nothing but the ragwort would grow. A hundred yards away, at the bottom of the slope, ran the brook, no more than three feet wide, half choked with kingcups, watercress and blue brooklime. The cart track crossed by a brick culvert and climbed the opposite slope to a five-barred gate in the thorn hedge. The gate led into the lane.

The May sunset was red in clouds, and there was still half an hour to twilight. The dry slope was dotted with rabbits—some nibbling at the thin grass near their holes, others pushing further down to look for dandelions or perhaps a cowslip that the rest had missed. Here and there one sat upright on an ant heap and looked about, with ears erect and nose in the wind. But a blackbird, singing undisturbed on the outskirts of the wood, showed that there was nothing alarming there, and in the other direction, along the brook, all was plain to be seen, empty and quiet. The warren was at peace.

At the top of the bank, close to the wild cherry where the blackbird sang, was a little group of holes almost hidden by brambles. In the green half-light, at the mouth of one of these holes, two rabbits were sitting together side by side. At length, the larger of the two came out, slipped along the bank under cover of the brambles and so down into the ditch and up into the field. A few moments later the other followed.

The first rabbit stopped in a sunny patch and scratched his ear with rapid movements of his hind leg. Although he was a yearling and still below full weight, he had not the harassed look of most "outskirters"—that is, the rank and file of ordinary rabbits in their first year who, lacking either aristocratic parentage or unusual size and strength, get sat on by their elders and live as best they can—often in the open—on the edge of their warren. He looked as though he knew how to take care of himself. There was a shrewd, buoyant air about him as he sat up, looked round and rubbed both front paws over his nose. As soon as he was satisfied that all was well, he laid back his ears and set to work on the grass.

His companion seemed less at ease. He was small, with wide, staring eyes and a way of raising and turning his head which suggested not so much caution as a kind of ceaseless, nervous tension. His nose moved continually, and when a bumblebee flew humming to a thistle bloom behind him, he jumped and spun round with a start that sent two nearby rabbits scurrying for holes before the nearest, a buck with black-tipped ears, recognized him and returned to feeding.

"Oh, it's only Fiver," said the black-tipped rabbit, "jumping at bluebottles again. Come on, Buckthorn, what were you telling me?"

"Fiver?" said the other rabbit. "Why's he called that?"

"Five in the litter, you know: he was the last—and the smallest. You'd wonder nothing had got him by now. I always say a man couldn't see him and a fox wouldn't want him. Still, I admit he seems to be able to keep out of harm's way." *

---

* Rabbits can count up to four. Any number above four is *hrair*—"a lot," or "a thousand." Thus they say *U Hrair*—"The Thousand"—to mean, collectively, all the enemies (or *elil,* as they call them) of rabbits—fox, stoat, weasel, cat, owl, man, etc.

The small rabbit came closer to his companion, lolloping on long hind legs.

"Let's go a bit further, Hazel," he said. "You know, there's something queer about the warren this evening, although I can't tell exactly what it is. Shall we go down to the brook?"

"All right," answered Hazel, "and you can find me a cowslip. If you can't find one, no one can."

He led the way down the slope, his shadow stretching behind him on the grass. They reached the brook and began nibbling and searching close beside the wheel ruts of the track.

It was not long before Fiver found what they were looking for. Cowslips are a delicacy among rabbits, and as a rule there are very few left by late May in the neighborhood of even a small warren. This one had not bloomed and its flat spread of leaves was almost hidden under the long grass. They were just starting on it when two larger rabbits came running across from the other side of the nearby cattle wade.

"Cowslip?" said one. "All right—just leave it to us. Come on, hurry up," he added, as Fiver hesitated. "You heard me, didn't you?"

"Fiver found it, Toadflax," said Hazel.

"And we'll eat it," replied Toadflax. "Cowslips are for Owsla*— don't you know that? If you don't, we can easily teach you."

Fiver had already turned away. Hazel caught him up by the culvert.

"I'm sick and tired of it," he said. "It's the same all the time. 'These are my claws, so this is my cowslip.' 'These are my teeth, so this is my burrow.' I'll tell you, if ever I get into the Owsla, I'll treat outskirters with a bit of decency."

There were probably more than five rabbits in the litter when Fiver was born, but his name, *Hrairoo,* means "Little Thousand"—i.e., the little one of a lot or, as they say of pigs, "the runt."

* Nearly all warrens have an *Owsla,* or group of strong or clever rabbits—second-year or older—surrounding the Chief Rabbit and his doe and exercising authority. Owslas vary. In one warren, the Owsla may be the band of a warlord: in another, it may consist largely of clever patrollers or garden-raiders. Sometimes a good storyteller may find a place; or a seer, or intuitive rabbit. In the Sandleford warren at this time, the Owsla was rather military in character (though, as will be seen later, not so military as some).

"Well, you can at least expect to be in the Owsla one day," answered Fiver. "You've got some weight coming and that's more than I shall ever have."

"You don't suppose I'll leave you to look after yourself, do you?" said Hazel. "But to tell you the truth, I sometimes feel like clearing out of this warren altogether. Still, let's forget it now and try to enjoy the evening. I tell you what—shall we go across the brook? There'll be fewer rabbits and we can have a bit of peace. Unless you feel it isn't safe?" he added.

The way in which he asked suggested that he did in fact think that Fiver was likely to know better than himself, and it was clear from Fiver's reply that this was accepted between them.

"No, it's safe enough," he answered. "If I start feeling there's anything dangerous I'll tell you. But it's not exactly danger that I seem to feel about the place. It's—oh, I don't know—something oppressive, like thunder: I can't tell what; but it worries me. All the same, I'll come across with you."

They ran over the culvert. The grass was wet and thick near the stream and they made their way up the opposite slope, looking for drier ground. Part of the slope was in shadow, for the sun was sinking ahead of them, and Hazel, who wanted a warm, sunny spot, went on until they were quite near the lane. As they approached the gate he stopped, staring.

"Fiver, what's that? Look!"

A little way in front of them, the ground had been freshly disturbed. Two piles of earth lay on the grass. Heavy posts, reeking of creosote and paint, towered up as high as the holly trees in the hedge, and the board they carried threw a long shadow across the top of the field. Near one of the posts, a hammer and a few nails had been left behind.

The two rabbits went up to the board at a hopping run and crouched in a patch of nettles on the far side, wrinkling their noses at the smell of a dead cigarette end somewhere in the grass. Suddenly Fiver shivered and cowered down.

"Oh, Hazel! This is where it comes from! I know now—something very bad! Some terrible thing—coming closer and closer."

He began to whimper with fear.

"What sort of thing—what do you mean? I thought you said there was no danger?"

"I don't know what it is," answered Fiver wretchedly. "There isn't any danger here, at this moment. But it's coming—it's coming. Oh, Hazel, look! The field! It's covered with blood!"

"Don't be silly, it's only the light of the sunset. Fiver, come on, don't talk like this, you're frightening me!"

Fiver sat trembling and crying among the nettles as Hazel tried to reassure him and to find out what it could be that had suddenly driven him beside himself. If he was terrified, why did he not run for safety, as any sensible rabbit would? But Fiver could not explain and only grew more and more distressed. At last Hazel said,

"Fiver, you can't sit crying here. Anyway, it's getting dark. We'd better go back to the burrow."

"Back to the burrow?" whimpered Fiver. "It'll come there— don't think it won't! I tell you, the field's full of blood—"

"Now stop it," said Hazel firmly. "Just let me look after you for a bit. Whatever the trouble is, it's time we got back."

He ran down the field and over the brook to the cattle wade. Here there was a delay, for Fiver—surrounded on all sides by the quiet summer evening—became helpless and almost paralyzed with fear. When at last Hazel had got him back to the ditch, he refused at first to go underground and Hazel had almost to push him down the hole.

The sun set behind the opposite slope. The wind turned colder, with a scatter of rain, and in less than an hour it was dark. All color had faded from the sky: and although the big board by the gate creaked slightly in the night wind (as though to insist that it had not disappeared in the darkness, but was still firmly where it had been put), there was no passer-by to read the sharp, hard letters that cut straight as black knives across its white surface. They said:

THIS IDEALLY SITUATED ESTATE, COMPRISING SIX ACRES OF EXCELLENT BUILDING LAND, IS TO BE DEVELOPED WITH HIGH CLASS MODERN RESIDENCES BY SUTCH AND MARTIN, LIMITED, OF NEWBURY, BERKS.

2

The Chief Rabbit

The darksome statesman, hung with weights and woe,
Like a thick midnight-fog, moved there so slow,
He did not stay, nor go.

Henry Vaughan, *The World*

In the darkness and warmth of the burrow Hazel suddenly
woke, struggling and kicking with his back legs. Something was
attacking him. There was no smell of ferret or weasel. No instinct
told him to run. His head cleared and he realized that he was alone
except for Fiver. It was Fiver who was clambering over him,
clawing and grabbing like a rabbit trying to climb a wire fence in a
panic.

"Fiver! Fiver, wake up, you silly fellow! It's Hazel. You'll hurt
me in a moment. Wake up!"

He held him down. Fiver struggled and woke.

"Oh, Hazel! I was dreaming. It was dreadful. You were there.
We were sitting on water, going down a great, deep stream, and
then I realized we were on a board—like that board in the field—all
white and covered with black lines. There were other rabbits
there—bucks and does. But when I looked down, I saw the board
was all made of bones and wire; and I screamed and you said,
'Swim—everybody swim'; and then I was looking for you everywhere and trying to drag you out of a hole in the bank. I found
you, but you said, 'The Chief Rabbit must go alone,' and you
floated away down a dark tunnel of water."

"Well, you've hurt my ribs, anyway. Tunnel of water indeed!
What rubbish! Can we go back to sleep now?"

"Hazel—the danger, the bad thing. It hasn't gone away. It's
here—all round us. Don't tell me to forget about it and go to sleep.
We've got to go away before it's too late."

"Go away? From here, you mean? From the warren?"

"Yes. Very soon. It doesn't matter where."

"Just you and I?"

"No, everyone."

"The whole warren? Don't be silly. They won't come. They'll say you're out of your wits."

"Then they'll be here when the bad thing comes. You must listen to me, Hazel. Believe me, something very bad is close upon us and we ought to go away."

"Well, I suppose we'd better go and see the Chief Rabbit and you can tell *him* about it. Or I'll try to. But I don't expect he'll like the idea at all."

Hazel led the way down the slope of the run and up toward the bramble curtain. He did not want to believe Fiver, and he was afraid not to.

It was a little after ni-Frith, or noon. The whole warren were underground, mostly asleep. Hazel and Fiver went a short way above ground and then into a wide, open hole in a sand patch and so down, by various runs, until they were thirty feet into the wood, among the roots of an oak. Here they were stopped by a large, heavily built rabbit—one of the Owsla. He had a curious, heavy growth of fur on the crown of his head, which gave him an odd appearance, as though he were wearing a kind of cap. This had given him his name, Thlayli, which means, literally, "Furhead" or, as we might say, "Bigwig."

"Hazel?" said Bigwig, sniffing at him in the deep twilight among the tree roots. "It is Hazel, isn't it? What are you doing here? And at this time of day?" He ignored Fiver, who was waiting further down the run.

"We want to see the Chief Rabbit," said Hazel. "It's important, Bigwig. Can you help us?"

"We?" said Bigwig. "Is *he* going to see him, too?"

"Yes, he must. Do trust me, Bigwig. I don't usually come and talk like this, do I? When did I ever ask to see the Chief Rabbit before?"

"Well, I'll do it for you, Hazel, although I'll probably get my head bitten off. I'll tell him I know you're a sensible fellow. He ought to know you himself, of course, but he's getting old. Wait here, will you?"

Bigwig went a little way down the run and stopped at the entrance to a large burrow. After speaking a few words that Hazel could not catch, he was evidently called inside. The two rabbits waited in silence, broken only by the continual nervous fidgeting of Fiver.

The Chief Rabbit's name and style was Threarah, meaning "Lord Rowan Tree." For some reason he was always referred to as "*The* Threarah"—perhaps because there happened to be only one threar, or rowan, near the warren, from which he took his name. He had won his position not only by strength in his prime, but also by level-headedness and a certain self-contained detachment, quite unlike the impulsive behavior of most rabbits. It was well known that he never let himself become excited by rumor or danger. He had coolly—some even said coldly—stood firm during the terrible onslaught of the myxomatosis, ruthlessly driving out every rabbit who seemed to be sickening. He had resisted all ideas of mass emigration and enforced complete isolation on the warren, thereby almost certainly saving it from extinction. It was he, too, who had once dealt with a particularly troublesome stoat by leading it down among the pheasant coops and so (at the risk of his own life) onto a keeper's gun. He was now, as Bigwig said, getting old, but his wits were still clear enough. When Hazel and Fiver were brought in, he greeted them politely. Owsla like Toadflax might threaten and bully. The Threarah had no need.

"Ah, Walnut. It is Walnut, isn't it?"

"Hazel," said Hazel.

"Hazel, of course. How very nice of you to come and see me. I knew your mother well. And your friend—"

"My brother."

"Your brother," said the Threarah, with the faintest suggestion of "Don't correct me any more, will you?" in his voice. "Do make yourselves comfortable. Have some lettuce?"

The Chief Rabbit's lettuce was stolen by the Owsla from a garden half a mile away across the fields. Outskirters seldom or never saw lettuce. Hazel took a small leaf and nibbled politely. Fiver refused, and sat blinking and twitching miserably.

"Now, how are things with you?" said the Chief Rabbit. "Do tell me how I can help you."

"Well, sir," said Hazel rather hesitantly, "it's because of my brother—Fiver here. He can often tell when there's anything bad about, and I've found him right again and again. He knew the flood was coming last autumn and sometimes he can tell where a wire's been set. And now he says he can sense a bad danger coming upon the warren."

"A bad danger. Yes, I see. How very upsetting," said the Chief Rabbit, looking anything but upset. "Now, what sort of danger, I wonder?" He looked at Fiver.

"I don't know," said Fiver. "B-but it's bad. It's so b-bad that—it's very bad," he concluded miserably.

The Threarah waited politely for a few moments and then he said, "Well, now, and what ought we to do about it, I wonder?"

"Go away," said Fiver instantly. "Go away. All of us. Now. Threarah, sir, we must all go away."

The Threarah waited again. Then, in an extremely understanding voice, he said, "Well, I never did! That's rather a tall order, isn't it? What do you think yourself?"

"Well, sir," said Hazel, "my brother doesn't really think about these feelings he gets. He just has the feelings, if you see what I mean. I'm sure you're the right person to decide what we ought to do."

"Well, that's very nice of you to say that. I hope I am. But now, my dear fellows, let's just think about this a moment, shall we? It's May, isn't it? Everyone's busy and most of the rabbits are enjoying themselves. No elil for miles, or so they tell me. No illness, good weather. And you want me to tell the warren that young—er—young—er—your brother here has got a hunch and we must all go traipsing across country to goodness knows where and risk the consequences, eh? What do you think they'll say? All delighted, eh?"

"They'd take it from you," said Fiver suddenly.

"That's very nice of you," said the Threarah again. "Well, perhaps they would, perhaps they would. But I should have to consider it very carefully indeed. A most serious step, of course. And then—"

"But there's no time, Threarah, sir," blurted out Fiver. "I can feel the danger like a wire round my neck—like a wire— Hazel, help!" He squealed and rolled over in the sand, kicking frantically, as a rabbit does in a snare. Hazel held him down with both forepaws and he grew quieter.

"I'm awfully sorry, Chief Rabbit," said Hazel. "He gets like this sometimes. He'll be all right in a minute."

"What a shame! What a shame! Poor fellow, perhaps he ought to go home and rest. Yes, you'd better take him along now. Well, it's really been extremely good of you to come and see me, Walnut. I appreciate it very much indeed. And I shall think over all you've said most carefully, you can be quite sure of that. Bigwig, just wait a moment, will you?"

As Hazel and Fiver made their way dejectedly down the run outside the Threarah's burrow, they could just hear, from inside, the Chief Rabbit's voice assuming a rather sharper note, interspersed with an occasional "Yes, sir," "No, sir."

Bigwig, as he had predicted, was getting his head bitten off.

3

Hazel's Decision

What am I lying here for? . . . We are lying here as though we had a chance of enjoying a quiet time. . . . Am I waiting until I become a little older?

Xenophon, *The Anabasis*

"But, Hazel, you didn't really think the Chief Rabbit would act on your advice, did you? What were you expecting?"

It was evening once more and Hazel and Fiver were feeding outside the wood with two friends. Blackberry, the rabbit with tipped ears who had been startled by Fiver the night before, had listened carefully to Hazel's description of the notice board, remarking that he had always felt sure that men left these things about to act as signs or messages of some kind, in the same way that rabbits left marks on runs and gaps. It was another neighbor, Dandelion, who had now brought the talk back to the Threarah and his indifference to Fiver's fear.

"I don't know what I expected," said Hazel. "I'd never been near the Chief Rabbit before. But I thought, 'Well, even if he won't listen, at least no one can say afterward that we didn't do our best to warn him.' "

"You're sure, then, that there's really something to be afraid of?"

"I'm quite certain. I've always known Fiver, you see."

Blackberry was about to reply when another rabbit came noisily through the thick dog's mercury in the wood, blundered down into the brambles and pushed his way up from the ditch. It was Bigwig.

"Hello, Bigwig," said Hazel. "You're off duty?"

"Off duty," said Bigwig, "and likely to remain off duty."

"How do you mean?"

"I've left the Owsla, that's what I mean."

"Not on our account?"

"You could say that. The Threarah's rather good at making himself unpleasant when he's been woken up at ni-Frith for what he considers a piece of trivial nonsense. He certainly knows how to get under your skin. I dare say a good many rabbits would have kept quiet and thought about keeping on the right side of the Chief, but I'm afraid I'm not much good at that. I told him that the Owsla's privileges didn't mean all that much to me in any case and that a strong rabbit could always do just as well by leaving the warren. He told me not to be impulsive and think it over, but I shan't stay. Lettuce-stealing isn't my idea of a jolly life, nor sentry duty in the burrow. I'm in a fine temper, I can tell you."

"No one will steal lettuces soon," said Fiver quietly.

"Oh, that's you, Fiver, is it?" said Bigwig, noticing him for the first time. "Good, I was coming to look for you. I've been thinking about what you said to the Chief Rabbit. Tell me, is it a sort of tremendous hoax to make yourself important, or is it true?"

"It *is* true," said Fiver. "I wish it weren't."

"Then you'll be leaving the warren?"

They were all startled by the bluntness with which Bigwig went to the point. Dandelion muttered, "Leave the warren, Frithrah!" while Blackberry twitched his ears and looked very intently, first at Bigwig and then at Hazel.

It was Hazel who replied. "Fiver and I will be leaving the warren tonight," he said deliberately. "I don't know exactly where we shall go, but we'll take anyone who's ready to come with us."

"Right," said Bigwig, "then you can take me."

The last thing Hazel had expected was the immediate support of a member of the Owsla. It crossed his mind that although Bigwig would certainly be a useful rabbit in a tight corner, he would also be a difficult one to get on with. He certainly would not want to do what he was told—or even asked—by an outskirter. "I don't care if he is in the Owsla," thought Hazel. "If we get away from the warren, I'm not going to let Bigwig run everything, or why bother to go?" But he answered only, "Good. We shall be glad to have you."

He looked round at the other rabbits, who were all staring either at Bigwig or at himself. It was Blackberry who spoke next.

"I think I'll come," he said. "I don't quite know whether it's you who've persuaded me, Fiver. But anyway, there are too many bucks in this warren, and it's pretty poor fun for any rabbit that's not in the Owsla. The funny thing is that you feel terrified to stay and I feel terrified to go. Foxes here, weasels there, Fiver in the middle, begone dull care!"

He pulled out a burnet leaf and ate it slowly, concealing his fear as best he could; for all his instincts were warning him of the dangers in the unknown country beyond the warren.

"If we believe Fiver," said Hazel, "it means that we think no rabbits at all ought to stay here. So between now and the time when we go, we ought to persuade as many as we can to join us."

"I think there are one or two in the Owsla who might be worth sounding," said Bigwig. "If I can talk them over, they'll be with me when I join you tonight. But they won't come because of Fiver. They'll be juniors, discontented fellows like me. You need to have heard Fiver yourself to be convinced by him. He's convinced me. It's obvious that he's been sent some kind of message, and I believe in these things. I can't think why he didn't convince the Threarah."

"Because the Threarah doesn't like anything he hasn't thought of for himself," answered Hazel. "But we can't bother with him any more now. We've got to try to collect some more rabbits and meet again here, fu Inlé. And we'll start fu Inlé, too: we can't wait longer. The danger's coming closer all the time—whatever it is—and, besides, the Threarah isn't going to like it if he finds out that you've been trying to get at rabbits in the Owsla, Bigwig. Neither is Captain Holly, I dare say. They won't mind odds and ends like us clearing off, but they won't want to lose you. If I were in your place, I'd be careful whom I picked to talk to."

4

The Departure

Fu Inlé means "after moonrise." Rabbits, of course, have no idea of precise time or of punctuality. In this respect they are much the same as primitive people, who often take several days over assembling for some purpose and then several more to get started. Before such people can act together, a kind of telepathic feeling has to flow through them and ripen to the point when they all know that they are ready to begin. Anyone who has seen the martins and swallows in September, assembling on the telephone wires, twittering, making short flights singly and in groups over the open, stubbly fields, returning to form longer and even longer lines above the yellowing verges of the lanes—the hundreds of individual birds merging and blending, in a mounting excitement, into swarms, and these swarms coming loosely and untidily together to create a great, unorganized flock, thick at the center and ragged at the edges, which breaks and re-forms continually like clouds or waves—until that moment when the greater part (but not all) of them know that the time has come: they are off, and have begun once more that great southward flight which many will not survive; anyone seeing this has seen at work the current that flows (among creatures who think of themselves primarily as part of a group and only secondarily, if at all, as individuals) to fuse them together and impel them into action without conscious thought or will: has seen at work the angel which drove the First Crusade into Antioch and drives the lemmings into the sea.

It was actually about an hour after moonrise and a good while before midnight when Hazel and Fiver once more came out of their burrow behind the brambles and slipped quietly along the bottom of the ditch. With them was a third rabbit, Hlao—Pipkin—a friend of Fiver. (Hlao means any small concavity in the grass where moisture may collect—e.g., the dimple formed by a dandelion or thistle cup.) He too was small, and inclined to be timid, and Hazel and Fiver had spent the greater part of their last evening in the warren in persuading him to join them. Pipkin had agreed rather hesitantly. He still felt extremely nervous about what might happen once they left the warren, and had decided that the best way to avoid trouble would be to keep close to Hazel and do exactly what he said.

The three were still in the ditch when Hazel heard a movement above. He looked up quickly.

"Who's there?" he said. "Dandelion?"

"No, I'm Hawkbit," said the rabbit who was peering over the edge. He jumped down among them, landing rather heavily. "Do you remember me, Hazel? We were in the same burrow during the snow last winter. Dandelion told me you were going to leave the warren tonight. If you are, I'll come with you."

Hazel could recall Hawkbit—a rather slow, stupid rabbit whose company for five snowbound days underground had been distinctly tedious. Still, he thought, this was no time to pick and choose. Although Bigwig might succeed in talking over one or two, most of the rabbits they could expect to join them would not come from the Owsla. They would be outskirters who were getting a thin time and wondering what to do about it. He was running over some of these in his mind when Dandelion appeared.

"The sooner we're off the better, I reckon," said Dandelion. "I don't much like the look of things. After I'd persuaded Hawkbit here to join us, I was just starting to talk to a few more, when I found that Toadflax fellow had followed me down the run. 'I want to know what you're up to,' he said, and I don't think he believed me when I told him I was only trying to find out whether there were any rabbits who wanted to leave the warren. He asked me if I was sure I wasn't working up some kind of plot against the Threarah and he got awfully angry and suspicious. It put the wind up me, to tell you the truth, so I've just brought Hawkbit along and left it at that."

"I don't blame you," said Hazel. "Knowing Toadflax, I'm

surprised he didn't knock you over first and ask questions afterward. All the same, let's wait a little longer. Blackberry ought to be here soon."

Time passed. They crouched in silence while the moon shadows moved northward in the grass. At last, just as Hazel was about to run down the slope to Blackberry's burrow, he saw him come out of his hole, followed by no less than three rabbits. One of these, Buckthorn, Hazel knew well. He was glad to see him, for he knew him for a tough, sturdy fellow who was considered certain to get into the Owsla as soon as he reached full weight.

"But I dare say he's impatient," thought Hazel, "or he may have come off worst in some scuffle over a doe and taken it hard. Well, with him and Bigwig, at least we shan't be too badly off if we run into any fighting."

He did not recognize the other two rabbits and when Blackberry told him their names—Speedwell and Acorn—he was none the wiser. But this was not surprising, for they were typical outskirters —thin-looking six-monthers, with the strained, wary look of those who are only too well used to the thin end of the stick. They looked curiously at Fiver. From what Blackberry had told them, they had been almost expecting to find Fiver foretelling doom in a poetic torrent. Instead, he seemed more calm and normal than the rest. The certainty of going had lifted a weight from Fiver.

More time went slowly by. Blackberry scrambled up into the fern and then returned to the top of the bank, fidgeting nervously and half inclined to bolt at nothing. Hazel and Fiver remained in the ditch, nibbling half-heartedly at the dark grass. At last Hazel heard what he was listening for; a rabbit—or was it two?—approaching from the wood.

A few moments later Bigwig was in the ditch. Behind him came a hefty, brisk-looking rabbit something over twelve months old. He was well known by sight to all the warren, for his fur was entirely gray, with patches of near-white that now caught the moonlight as he sat scratching himself without speaking. This was Silver, a nephew of the Threarah, who was serving his first month in the Owsla.

Hazel could not help feeling relieved that Bigwig had brought only Silver—a quiet, straightforward fellow who had not yet really found his feet among the veterans. When Bigwig had spoken earlier of sounding out the Owsla, Hazel had been in two minds. It was only too likely that they would encounter dangers beyond the warren and that they would stand in need of some good fighters. Again, if Fiver was right and the whole warren was in imminent peril, then of course they ought to welcome any rabbit who was ready to join them. On the other hand, there seemed no point in taking particular pains to get hold of rabbits who were going to behave like Toadflax.

"Wherever we settle down in the end," thought Hazel, "I'm determined to see that Pipkin and Fiver aren't sat on and cuffed around until they're ready to run any risk just to get away. But is Bigwig going to see it like that?"

"You know Silver, don't you?" asked Bigwig, breaking in on his thoughts. "Apparently some of the younger fellows in the Owsla have been giving him a thin time—teasing him about his fur, you know, and saying he only got his place because of the Threarah. I thought I was going to get some more, but I suppose nearly all the Owsla feel they're very well off as they are."

He looked about him. "I say, there aren't many here, are there? Do you think it's really worth going on with this idea?"

Silver seemed about to speak when suddenly there was a pattering in the undergrowth above and three more rabbits came over the bank from the wood. Their movement was direct and purposeful, quite unlike the earlier, haphazard approach of those who were now gathered in the ditch. The largest of the three newcomers was in front and the other two followed him, as though under orders. Hazel, sensing at once that they had nothing in common with himself and his companions, started and sat up tensely. Fiver muttered in his ear, "Oh, Hazel, they've come to—" but broke off short. Bigwig turned toward them and stared, his nose working rapidly. The three came straight up to him.

"Thlayli?" said the leader.

"You know me perfectly well," replied Bigwig, "and I know you, Holly. What do you want?"

"You're under arrest."

"Under arrest? What do you mean? What for?"

"Spreading dissension and inciting to mutiny. Silver, you're under arrest too, for failing to report to Toadflax this evening and causing your duty to devolve on a comrade. You're both to come with me."

Immediately Bigwig fell upon him, scratching and kicking. Holly fought back. His followers closed in, looking for an opening to join the fight and pin Bigwig down. Suddenly, from the top of the bank, Buckthorn flung himself headlong into the scuffle, knocked one of the guards flying with a kick from his back legs and then closed with the other. He was followed a moment later by Dandelion, who landed full on the rabbit whom Buckthorn had kicked. Both guards broke clear, looked round for a moment and then leaped up the bank into the wood. Holly struggled free of Bigwig and crouched on his haunches, scuffling his front paws and growling, as rabbits will when angry. He was about to speak when Hazel faced him.

"Go," said Hazel, firmly and quietly, "or we'll kill you."

"Do you know what this means?" replied Holly. "I am Captain of Owsla. You know that, don't you?"

"Go," repeated Hazel, "or you will be killed."

"It is you who will be killed," replied Holly. Without another word he, too, went back up the bank and vanished into the wood.

Dandelion was bleeding from the shoulder. He licked the wound for a few moments and then turned to Hazel.

"They won't be long coming back, you know, Hazel," he said. "They've gone to turn out the Owsla, and then we'll be for it right enough."

"We ought to go at once," said Fiver.

"Yes, the time's come now, all right," replied Hazel. "Come on, down to the stream. Then we'll follow the bank—that'll help us to keep together."

"If you'll take my advice—" began Bigwig.

"If we stay here any longer I shan't be able to," answered Hazel.

With Fiver beside him, he led the way out of the ditch and down the slope. In less than a minute the little band of rabbits had disappeared into the dim, moonlit night.

In the Woods

These young rabbits . . . must move out if they are to survive. In a wild
and free state they . . . stray sometimes for miles . . . wandering until
they find a suitable environment.
                    R. M. Lockley, *The Private Life of the Rabbit*

It was getting on toward moonset when they left the fields
and entered the wood. Straggling, catching up with one another,
keeping more or less together, they had wandered over half a mile
down the fields, always following the course of the brook. Although
Hazel guessed that they must now have gone further from the
warren than any rabbit he had ever talked to, he was not sure
whether they were yet safely away: and it was while he was
wondering—not for the first time—whether he could hear sounds
of pursuit that he first noticed the dark masses of the trees and the
brook disappearing among them.

Rabbits avoid close woodland, where the ground is shady, damp
and grassless and they feel menaced by the undergrowth. Hazel did
not care for the look of the trees. Still, he thought, Holly would no
doubt think twice before following them into a place like that, and
to keep beside the brook might well prove safer than wandering
about the fields in one direction and another, with the risk of
finding themselves, in the end, back at the warren. He decided to
go straight into the wood without consulting Bigwig, and to trust
that the rest would follow.

"If we don't run into any trouble and the brook takes us through
the wood," he thought, "we really shall be clear of the warren and
then we can look for somewhere to rest for a bit. Most of them still
seem to be more or less all right, but Fiver and Pipkin will have had
as much as they can stand before long."

From the moment he entered it, the wood seemed full of noises.
There was a smell of damp leaves and moss, and everywhere the
splash of water went whispering about. Just inside, the brook made
a little fall into a pool, and the sound, enclosed among the trees,

echoed as though in a cave. Roosting birds rustled overhead; the night breeze stirred the leaves; here and there a dead twig fell. And there were more sinister, unidentified sounds from further away; sounds of movement.

To rabbits, everything unknown is dangerous. The first reaction is to startle, the second to bolt. Again and again they startled, until they were close to exhaustion. But what did these sounds mean and where, in this wilderness, could they bolt to?

The rabbits crept closer together. Their progress grew slower. Before long they lost the course of the brook, slipping across the moonlit patches as fugitives and halting in the bushes with raised ears and staring eyes. The moon was low now and the light, wherever it slanted through the trees, seemed thicker, older and more yellow.

From a thick pile of dead leaves beneath a holly tree, Hazel looked down a narrow path lined on either side with fern and sprouting fireweed. The fern moved slightly in the breeze, but along the path there was nothing to be seen except a scatter of last year's fallen acorns under an oak. What was in the bracken? What lay round the further bend? And what would happen to a rabbit who left the shelter of the holly tree and ran down the path? He turned to Dandelion beside him.

"You'd better wait here," he said. "When I get to the bend I'll stamp. But if I run into trouble, get the others away."

Without waiting for an answer, he ran into the open and down the path. A few seconds brought him to the oak. He paused a moment, staring about him, and then ran on to the bend. Beyond, the path was the same—empty in the darkening moonlight and leading gently downhill into the deep shadow of a grove of ilex trees. Hazel stamped, and a few moments later Dandelion was beside him in the bracken. Even in the midst of his fear and strain it occurred to him that Dandelion must be very fast: he had covered the distance in a flash.

"Well done," whispered Dandelion. "Running our risks for us, are you—like El-ahrairah?" *

Hazel gave him a quick, friendly glance. It was warm praise and cheered him. What Robin Hood is to the English and John Henry

---

* The stresses are the same as in the phrase "Never say die."

to the American Negroes, Elil-Hrair-Rah, or El-ahrairah—The Prince with a Thousand Enemies—is to rabbits. Uncle Remus might well have heard of him, for some of El-ahrairah's adventures are those of Brer Rabbit. For that matter, Odysseus himself might have borrowed a trick or two from the rabbit hero, for he is very old and was never at a loss for a trick to deceive his enemies. Once, so they say, he had to get home by swimming across a river in which there was a large and hungry pike. El-ahrairah combed himself until he had enough fur to cover a clay rabbit, which he pushed into the water. The pike rushed at it, bit it and left it in disgust. After a little, it drifted to the bank and El-ahrairah dragged it out and waited a while before pushing it in again. After an hour of this, the pike left it alone, and when it had done so for the fifth time, El-ahrairah swam across himself and went home. Some rabbits say he controls the weather, because the wind, the damp and the dew are friends and instruments to rabbits against their enemies.

"Hazel, we'll have to stop here," said Bigwig, coming up between the panting, crouching bodies of the others. "I know it's not a good place, but Fiver and this other half-sized fellow you've got here—they're pretty well all in. They won't be able to go on if we don't rest."

The truth was that every one of them was tired. Many rabbits spend all their lives in the same place and never run more than a hundred yards at a stretch. Even though they may live and sleep above ground for months at a time, they prefer not to be out of distance of some sort of refuge that will serve for a hole. They have two natural gaits—the gentle, lolloping forward movement of the warren on a summer evening and the lightning dash for cover that every human has seen at some time or other. It is difficult to imagine a rabbit plodding steadily on: they are not built for it. It is true that young rabbits are great migrants and capable of journeying for miles, but they do not take to it readily.

Hazel and his companions had spent the night doing everything that came unnaturally to them, and this for the first time. They had been moving in a group, or trying to: actually, they had straggled widely at times. They had been trying to maintain a steady pace, between hopping and running, and it had come hard. Since entering the wood they had been in severe anxiety. Several were almost tharn—that is, in that state of staring, glazed paralysis that comes over terrified or exhausted rabbits, so that they sit and watch their enemies—weasels or humans—approach to take their lives. Pipkin sat trembling under a fern, his ears drooping on either side of his head. He held one paw forward in an awkward, unnatural way and kept licking it miserably. Fiver was little better off. He still looked cheerful, but very weary. Hazel realized that until they were rested they would all be safer where they were than stumbling along in the open with no strength left to run from an enemy. But if they lay brooding, unable to feed or go underground, all their troubles would come crowding into their hearts, their fears would mount and they might very likely scatter, or even try to return to the warren. He had an idea.

"Yes, all right, we'll rest here," he said. "Let's go in among this fern. Come on, Dandelion, tell us a story. I know you're handy that way. Pipkin here can't wait to hear it."

Dandelion looked at Pipkin and realized what it was that Hazel was asking him to do. Choking back his own fear of the desolate, grassless woodland, the before-dawn-returning owls that they could hear some way off, and the extraordinary, rank animal smell that seemed to come from somewhere rather nearer, he began.

6

The Story of the Blessing of El-ahrairah

Why should he think me cruel
  Or that he is betrayed?
I'd have him love the thing that was
  Before the world was made.
                    W. B. Yeats, *A Woman Young and Old*

"Long ago, Frith made the world. He made all the stars, too, and the world is one of the stars. He made them by scattering his droppings over the sky and this is why the grass and the trees grow so thick on the world. Frith makes the rivers flow. They follow him as he goes through the sky, and when he leaves the sky they look for him all night. Frith made all the animals and birds, but when he first made them they were all the same. The sparrow and the kestrel were friends and they both ate seeds and flies. And the fox and the rabbit were friends and they both ate grass. And there was plenty of grass and plenty of flies, because the world was new and Frith shone down bright and warm all day.

"Now, El-ahrairah was among the animals in those days and he had many wives. He had so many wives that there was no counting them, and the wives had so many young that even Frith could not count them, and they ate the grass and the dandelions and the lettuces and the clover, and El-ahrairah was the father of them all." (Bigwig growled appreciatively.) "And after a time," went on Dandelion, "after a time the grass began to grow thin and the rabbits wandered everywhere, multiplying and eating as they went.

"Then Frith said to El-ahrairah, 'Prince Rabbit, if you cannot control your people, I shall find ways to control them. So mark what I say.' But El-ahrairah would not listen and he said to Frith, 'My people are the strongest in the world, for they breed faster and eat more than any of the other people. And this shows how much they love Lord Frith, for of all the animals they are the most responsive to his warmth and brightness. You must realize, my lord, how important they are and not hinder them in their beautiful lives.'

"Frith could have killed El-ahrairah at once, but he had a mind to keep him in the world, because he needed him to sport and jest and play tricks. So he determined to get the better of him, not by means of his own great power but by means of a trick. He gave out that he would hold a great meeting and that at that meeting he would give a present to every animal and bird, to make each one different from the rest. And all the creatures set out to go to the meeting place. But they all arrived at different times, because Frith made sure that it would happen so. And when the blackbird came, he gave him his beautiful song, and when the cow came, he gave her sharp horns and the strength to be afraid of no other creature. And so in their turn came the fox and the stoat and the weasel. And to each of them Frith gave the cunning and the fierceness and the desire to hunt and slay and eat the children of El-ahrairah. And so they went away from Frith full of nothing but hunger to kill the rabbits.

"Now, all this time El-ahrairah was dancing and mating and boasting that he was going to Frith's meeting to receive a great gift. And at last he set out for the meeting place. But as he was going there, he stopped to rest on a soft, sandy hillside. And while he was resting, over the hill came flying the dark swift, screaming as he went, 'News! News! News!' For you know, this is what he has said ever since that day. So El-ahrairah called up to him and said, 'What news?' 'Why,' said the swift, 'I would not be you, El-ahrairah. For Frith has given the fox and the weasel cunning hearts and sharp teeth, and to the cat he has given silent feet and eyes that can see in the dark, and they are gone away from Frith's place to kill and devour all that belongs to El-ahrairah." And he dashed on over the hills. And at that moment El-ahrairah heard the voice of Frith calling, 'Where is El-ahrairah? For all the others have taken their gifts and gone and I have come to look for him.'

"Then El-ahrairah knew that Frith was too clever for him and he was frightened. He thought that the fox and the weasel were coming with Frith and he turned to the face of the hill and began to dig. He dug a hole, but he had dug only a little of it when Frith came over the hill alone. And he saw El-ahrairah's bottom sticking out of the hole and the sand flying out in showers as the digging went on. When he saw that, he called out, 'My friend, have you seen El-ahrairah, for I am looking for him to give him my gift?' 'No,' answered El-ahrairah, without coming out, 'I have not seen him. He is far away. He could not come.' So Frith said, 'Then come out of that hole and I will bless you instead of him.' 'No, I cannot,' said El-ahrairah, 'I am busy. The fox and the weasel are coming. If you want to bless me you can bless my bottom, for it is sticking out of the hole.' "

All the rabbits had heard the story before: on winter nights, when the cold draft moved down the warren passages and the icy wet lay in the pits of the runs below their burrows; and on summer evenings, in the grass under the red may and the sweet, carrion-scented elder bloom. Dandelion was telling it well, and even Pipkin forgot his weariness and danger and remembered instead the great indestructibility of the rabbits. Each one of them saw himself as

El-ahrairah, who could be impudent to Frith and get away with it.

"Then," said Dandelion, "Frith felt himself in friendship with El-ahrairah, because of his resourcefulness, and because he would not give up even when he thought the fox and the weasel were coming. And he said, 'Very well, I will bless your bottom as it sticks out of the hole. Bottom, be strength and warning and speed forever and save the life of your master. Be it so!' And as he spoke, El-ahrairah's tail grew shining white and flashed like a star: and his back legs grew long and powerful and he thumped the hillside until the very beetles fell off the grass stems. He came out of the hole and tore across the hill faster than any creature in the world. And Frith called after him, 'El-ahrairah, your people cannot rule the world, for I will not have it so. All the world will be your enemy, Prince with a Thousand Enemies, and whenever they catch you, they will kill you. But first they must catch you, digger, listener, runner, prince with the swift warning. Be cunning and full of tricks and your people shall never be destroyed.' And El-ahrairah knew then that although he would not be mocked, yet Frith was his friend. And every evening, when Frith has done his day's work and lies calm and easy in the red sky, El-ahrairah and his children and his children's children come out of their holes and feed and play in his sight, for they are his friends and he has promised them that they can never be destroyed."

7

The Lendri and the River

Quant au courage moral, il avait trouvé fort rare, disait-il, celui de deux heures après minuit; c'est-à-dire le courage de l'improviste.
                                                    Napoleon Bonaparte

As Dandelion ended, Acorn, who was on the windward side of the little group, suddenly started and sat back, with ears up and nostrils twitching. The strange, rank smell was stronger than ever and after a few moments they all heard a heavy movement close by. Suddenly, on the other side of the path, the fern parted and there looked out a long, dog-like head, striped black and white. It was pointed downward, the jaws grinning, the muzzle close to the ground. Behind, they could just discern great, powerful paws and a shaggy black body. The eyes were peering at them, full of savage cunning. The head moved slowly, taking in the dusky lengths of the wood ride in both directions, and then fixed them once more with its fierce, terrible stare. The jaws opened wider and they could see the teeth, glimmering white as the stripes along the head. For long moments it gazed and the rabbits remained motionless, staring back without a sound. Then Bigwig, who was nearest to the path, turned and slipped back among the others.

"A lendri," he muttered as he passed through them. "It may be dangerous and it may not, but I'm taking no chances with it. Let's get away."

They followed him through the fern and very soon came upon another, parallel path. Bigwig turned into it and broke into a run. Dandelion overtook him and the two disappeared among the ilex trees. Hazel and the others followed as best they could, with Pipkin limping and staggering behind, his fear driving him on in spite of the pain in his paw.

Hazel came out on the further side of the ilexes and followed the path round a bend. Then he stopped dead and sat back on his haunches. Immediately in front of him, Bigwig and Dandelion were staring out from the sheer edge of a high bank, and below the bank ran a stream. It was in fact the little river Enborne, twelve to fifteen feet wide and at this time of year two or three feet deep with spring rain, but to the rabbits it seemed immense, such a river as they had never imagined. The moon had almost set and the night was now dark, but they could see the water faintly shining as it flowed and could just make out, on the further side, a thin belt of nut trees and alders. Somewhere beyond, a plover called three or four times and was silent.

One by one, most of the others came up, stopped at the bank and looked at the water without speaking. A chilly breeze was moving and several of them trembled where they sat.

"Well, this is a nice surprise, Hazel," said Bigwig at length. "Or were you expecting this when you took us into the wood?"

Hazel realized wearily that Bigwig was probably going to be troublesome. He was certainly no coward, but he was likely to remain steady only as long as he could see his way clear and be sure of what to do. To him, perplexity was worse than danger; and when he was perplexed he usually grew angry. The day before, Fiver's warning had troubled him, and he had spoken in anger to the Threarah and left the Owsla. Then, while he was in an uncertain mood about the idea of leaving the warren, Captain Holly had appeared in capital time to be attacked and to provide a perfect reason for their departure. Now, at the sight of the river, Bigwig's assurance was leaking again and unless he, Hazel, could restore it in some way, they were likely to be in for trouble. He thought of the Threarah and his wily courtesy.

"I don't know what we should have done without you just now, Bigwig," he said. "What was that animal? Would it have killed us?"

"A lendri," said Bigwig. "I've heard about them in the Owsla. They're not really dangerous. They can't catch a rabbit that runs, and nearly always you can smell them coming. They're funny things: I've heard of rabbits living almost on top of them and coming to no harm. But they're best avoided, all the same. They'll dig out rabbit kittens and they'll kill an injured rabbit if they find one. They're one of the Thousand, all right. I ought to have guessed from the smell, but it was new to me."

"It had killed before it met us," said Blackberry with a shudder. "I saw the blood on its lips."

"A rat, perhaps, or pheasant chicks. Lucky for us it *had* killed, otherwise it might have been quicker. Still, fortunately we did the right thing. We really came out of it very well," said Bigwig.

Fiver came limping down the path with Pipkin. They, too, checked and stared at the sight of the river.

"What do you think we ought to do now, Fiver?" asked Hazel.

Fiver looked down at the water and twitched his ears.

"We shall have to cross it," he said. "But I don't think I can swim, Hazel. I'm worn out, and Pipkin's a good deal worse than I am."

"Cross it?" cried Bigwig. "Cross it? Who's going to cross it? What do you want to cross it for? I never heard such nonsense."

Like all wild animals, rabbits can swim if they have to: and some even swim when it suits them. Rabbits have been known to live on the edge of a wood and regularly swim a brook to feed in the fields beyond. But most rabbits avoid swimming, and certainly an exhausted rabbit could not swim the Enborne.

"I don't want to jump in there," said Speedwell.

"Why not just go along the bank?" asked Hawkbit.

Hazel suspected that if Fiver felt they ought to cross the river, it might be dangerous not to. But how were the others to be persuaded? At this moment, as he was still wondering what to say to them, he suddenly realized that something had lightened his spirits. What could it be? A smell? A sound? Then he knew. Nearby, across the river, a lark had begun to twitter and climb. It was morning. A blackbird called one or two deep, slow notes and was followed by a wood pigeon. Soon they were in a gray twilight and could see that the stream bordered the further edge of the wood. On the other side lay open fields.

8

The Crossing

The centurion . . . commanded that they which could swim should cast themselves first into the sea and get to land. And the rest, some on boards and some on broken pieces of the ship. And so it came to pass, that they escaped all safe to land.

The Acts of the Apostles, Chapter 27

The top of the sandy bank was a good six feet above the water. From where they sat, the rabbits could look straight ahead upstream, and downstream to their left. Evidently there were nesting holes in the sheer face below them, for as the light grew they saw three or four martins dart out over the stream and away into the fields beyond. In a short time one returned with his beak full, and they could hear the nestlings squeaking as he flew out of sight beneath their feet. The bank did not extend far in either direction. Upstream, it sloped down to a grassy path between the trees and the water. This followed the line of the river, which ran straight from almost as far away as they could see, flowing smoothly without fords, gravel shallows or plank bridges. Immediately below them lay a wide pool and here the water was almost still. Away to their left, the bank sloped down again into clumps of alder, among which the stream could be heard chattering over gravel. There was a glimpse of barbed wire stretched across the water and they guessed that this must surround a cattle wade, like the one in the little brook near the home warren.

Hazel looked at the path upstream. "There's grass down there," he said. "Let's go and feed."

They scrambled down the bank and set to nibbling beside the water. Between them and the stream itself stood half-grown clumps of purple loosestrife and fleabane, which would not flower for nearly two months yet. The only blooms were a few early meadowsweet and a patch of pink butterbur. Looking back at the face of the bank, they could see that it was in fact dotted thickly with martins' holes. There was a narrow foreshore at the foot of the little cliff and this was littered with the rubbish of the colony— sticks, droppings, feathers, a broken egg and a dead nestling or two. The martins were now coming and going in numbers over the water.

Hazel moved close to Fiver and quietly edged him away from the others, feeding as he went. When they were a little way off, and half concealed by a patch of reeds, he said, "Are you sure we've got to cross the river, Fiver? What about going along the bank one way or the other?"

"No, we need to cross the river, Hazel, so that we can get into those fields—and on beyond them too. I know what we ought to be looking for—a high, lonely place with dry soil, where rabbits can see and hear all round and men hardly ever come. Wouldn't that be worth a journey?"

"Yes, of course it would. But is there such a place?"

"Not near a river—I needn't tell you that. But if you cross a river you start going up again, don't you? We ought to be on the top—on the top and in the open."

"But, Fiver, I think they may refuse to go much further. And then again, you say all this and yet you say you're too tired to swim?"

"I can rest, Hazel, but Pipkin's in a pretty bad way. I think he's injured. We may have to stay here half the day."

"Well, let's go and talk to the others. They may not mind staying. It's crossing they're not going to fancy, unless something frightens them into it."

As soon as they had made their way back, Bigwig came across to them from the bushes at the edge of the path.

"I was wondering where you'd got to," he said to Hazel. "Are you ready to move on?"

"No, I'm not," answered Hazel firmly. "I think we ought to stay here until ni-Frith. That'll give everyone a chance to rest and then we can swim across to those fields."

Bigwig was about to reply, but Blackberry spoke first.

"Bigwig," he said, "why don't you swim over now, and then go out into the field and have a look round? The wood may not stretch very far one way or the other. You could see from there; and then we might know which would be the best way to go."

"Oh, well," said Bigwig rather grudgingly, "I suppose there's some sense in that. I'll swim the embleer* river as many times as you like. Always glad to oblige."

Without the slightest hesitation, he took two hops to the water, waded in and swam across the deep, still pool. They watched him pull himself out beside a flowering clump of figwort, gripping one of the tough stems in his teeth, shake a shower of drops out of his fur and scutter into the alder bushes. A moment later, between the nut trees, they saw him running off into the field.

"I'm glad he's with us," said Hazel to Silver. Again he thought wryly of the Threarah. "He's the fellow to find out all we need to know. Oh, I say, look, he's coming back already."

Bigwig was racing back across the field, looking more agitated than he had at any time since the encounter with Captain Holly. He ran into the water almost headlong and paddled over fast, leaving an arrowhead ripple on the calm brown surface. He was speaking as he jerked himself out on the sandy foreshore.

"Well, Hazel, if I were you I shouldn't wait until ni-Frith. I should go now. In fact, I think you'll have to."

* Stinking—the word for the smell of a fox.

"Why?" asked Hazel.

"There's a large dog loose in the wood."

Hazel started. "What?" he said. "How do you know?"

"When you get into the field you can see the wood sloping down to the river. Parts of it are open. I saw the dog crossing a clearing. It was trailing a chain, so it must have broken loose. It may be on the lendri's scent, but the lendri will be underground by now. What do you think will happen when it picks up our scent, running from one side of the wood to the other, with dew on it? Come on, let's get over quickly."

Hazel felt at a loss. In front of him stood Bigwig, sodden wet, undaunted, single-minded—the very picture of decision. At his shoulder was Fiver, silent and twitching. He saw Blackberry watching him intently, waiting for his lead and disregarding Bigwig's. Then he looked at Pipkin, huddled into a fold of sand, more panic-stricken and helpless than any rabbit he had ever seen. At this moment, up in the wood, there broke out an excited yelping and a jay began to scold.

Hazel spoke through a kind of light-headed trance. "Well, you'd better get on, then," he said, "and anyone else who wants to. Personally, I'm going to wait until Fiver and Pipkin are fit to tackle it."

"You silly blockhead!" cried Bigwig. "We'll all be finished! We'll—"

"Don't stamp about," said Hazel. "You may be heard. What do you suggest, then?"

"Suggest? There's no suggesting to be done. Those who can swim, swim. The others will have to stay here and hope for the best. The dog may not come."

"I'm afraid that won't do for me. I got Pipkin into this and I'm going to get him out."

"Well, you didn't get Fiver into it, did you? He got you into it."

Hazel could not help noticing, with reluctant admiration, that although Bigwig had lost his temper, he was apparently in no hurry on his own account and seemed less frightened than any of them. Looking round for Blackberry, he saw that he had left them and was up at the top of the pool, where the narrow beach tailed away into a gravel spit. His paws were half buried in the wet gravel and he was nosing at something large and flat on the waterline. It looked like a piece of wood.

"Blackberry," he said, "can you come back here a moment?"

Blackberry looked up, tugged out his paws and ran back.

"Hazel," he said quickly, "that's a piece of flat wood—like that piece that closed the gap by the Green Loose above the warren—you remember? It must have drifted down the river. So it floats. We could put Fiver and Pipkin on it and make it float again. It might go across the river. Can you understand?"

Hazel had no idea what he meant. Blackberry's flood of apparent nonsense only seemed to draw tighter the mesh of danger and bewilderment. As though Bigwig's angry impatience, Pipkin's terror and the approaching dog were not enough to contend with, the cleverest rabbit among them had evidently gone out of his mind. He felt close to despair.

"Frithrah, yes, I see!" said an excited voice at his ear. It was Fiver. "Quick, Hazel, don't wait! Come on, and bring Pipkin!"

It was Blackberry who bullied the stupefied Pipkin to his feet and forced him to limp the few yards to the gravel spit. The piece of wood, hardly bigger than a large rhubarb leaf, was lightly aground. Blackberry almost drove Pipkin onto it with his claws. Pipkin crouched shivering and Fiver followed him aboard.

"Who's strong?" said Blackberry. "Bigwig! Silver! Push it out!"

No one obeyed him. All squatted, puzzled and uncertain. Blackberry buried his nose in the gravel under the landward edge of the board and raised it, pushing. The board tipped. Pipkin squealed and Fiver lowered his head and splayed his claws. Then the board righted itself and drifted out a few feet into the pool with the two rabbits hunched upon it, rigid and motionless. It rotated slowly and they found themselves staring back at their comrades.

"Frith and Inlé!" said Dandelion. "They're sitting on the water! Why don't they sink?"

"They're sitting on the wood and the wood floats, can't you see?" said Blackberry. "Now we swim over ourselves. Can we start, Hazel?"

During the last few minutes Hazel had been as near to losing his head as he was ever to come. He had been at his wits' end, with no reply to Bigwig's scornful impatience except his readiness to risk his own life in company with Fiver and Pipkin. He still could not understand what had happened, but at least he realized that Blackberry wanted him to show authority. His head cleared.

"Swim," he said. "Everybody swim."

He watched them as they went in. Dandelion swam as well as he ran, swiftly and easily. Silver, too, was strong. The others paddled and scrambled over somehow, and as they began to reach the other side, Hazel plunged. The cold water penetrated his fur almost at once. His breath came short and as his head went under he could hear a faint grating of gravel along the bottom. He paddled across awkwardly, his head tilted high out of the water, and made for the figwort. As he pulled himself out, he looked round among the sopping rabbits in the alders.

"Where's Bigwig?" he asked.

"Behind you," answered Blackberry, his teeth chattering.

Bigwig was still in the water, on the other side of the pool. He had swum to the raft, put his head against it and was pushing it forward with heavy thrusts of his back legs. "Keep still," Hazel heard him say in a quick, gulping voice. Then he sank. But a moment later he was up again and had thrust his head over the back of the board. As he kicked and struggled, it tilted and then, while the rabbits watched from the bank, moved slowly across the pool and grounded on the opposite side. Fiver pushed Pipkin onto the stones and Bigwig waded out beside them, shivering and breathless.

"I got the idea once Blackberry had shown us," he said. "But it's hard to push it when you're in the water. I hope it's not long to sunrise. I'm cold. Let's get on."

There was no sign of the dog as they made haste through the alders and up the field to the first hedgerow. Most of them had not understood Blackberry's discovery of the raft and at once forgot it. Fiver, however, came over to where Blackberry was lying against the stem of a blackthorn in the hedge.

"You saved Pipkin and me, didn't you?" he said. "I don't think Pipkin's got any idea what really happened; but I have."

"I admit it was a good idea," replied Blackberry. "Let's remember it. It might come in handy again sometime."

9

The Crow and the Beanfield

With the beanflower's boon,
And the blackbird's tune,
And May, and June!

                                        Robert Browning, *De Gustibus*

The sun rose while they were still lying in the thorn. Already several of the rabbits were asleep, crouched uneasily between the thick stems, aware of the chance of danger but too tired to do more than trust to luck. Hazel, looking at them, felt almost as insecure as he had on the riverbank. A hedgerow in open fields was no place to remain all day. But where could they go? He needed to know more about their surroundings. He moved along the hedge, feeling the breeze from the south and looking for some spot where he could sit and scent it without too much risk. The smells that came down from the higher ground might tell him something.

He came to a wide gap which had been trodden into mud by cattle. He could see them grazing in the next field, further up the slope. He went cautiously out into the field, squatted down against a clump of thistles and began to smell the wind. Now that he was clear of the hawthorn scent of the hedge and the reek of cattle dung, he became fully aware of what had already been drifting into his nostrils while he was lying among the thorn. There was only one smell on the wind and it was new to him: a strong, fresh, sweet fragrance that filled the air. It was healthy enough. There was no harm in it. But what was it and why was it so strong? How could it exclude every other smell, in open country on a south wind? The source must be close by. Hazel wondered whether to send one of the rabbits to find out. Dandelion would be over the top and back almost as fast as a hare. Then his sense of adventure and mischief prompted him. He would go himself and bring back some news before they even knew that he had gone. That would give Bigwig something to bite on.

He ran easily up the meadow toward the cows. As he came they raised their heads and gazed at him, all together, for a moment, before returning to their feeding. A great black bird was flapping and hopping a little way behind the herd. It looked rather like a large rook, but, unlike a rook, it was alone. He watched its greenish, powerful beak stabbing the ground, but could not make out what it was doing. It so happened that Hazel had never seen a crow. It did not occur to him that it was following the track of a mole, in the hope of killing it with a blow of its beak and then pulling it out of its shallow run. If he had realized this, he might not have classed it light-heartedly as a "Not-hawk"—that is, anything from a wren to a pheasant—and continued on his way up the slope.

The strange fragrance was stronger now, coming over the top of the rise in a wave of scent that struck him powerfully—as the scent of orange blossom in the Mediterranean strikes a traveler who smells it for the first time. Fascinated, he ran to the crest. Nearby was another hedgerow and beyond, moving gently in the breeze, stood a field of broad beans in full flower.

Hazel squatted on his haunches and stared at the orderly forest of small, glaucous trees with their columns of black-and-white bloom. He had never seen anything like this. Wheat and barley he knew, and once he had been in a field of turnips. But this was entirely different from any of those and seemed, somehow, attractive, wholesome, propitious. True, rabbits could not eat these plants: he could smell that. But they could lie safely among them for as long as they liked, and they could move through them easily and unseen. Hazel determined then and there to bring the rabbits up to the beanfield to shelter and rest until the evening. He ran back and found the others where he had left them. Bigwig and Silver were awake, but all the rest were still napping uneasily.

"Not asleep, Silver?" he said.

"It's too dangerous, Hazel," replied Silver. "I'd like to sleep as much as anyone, but if we all sleep and something comes, who's going to spot it?"

"I know. I've found a place where we can sleep safely for as long as we like."

"A burrow?"

"No, not a burrow. A great field of scented plants that will cover us, sight and smell, until we're rested. Come out here and smell it, if you like."

Both rabbits did so. "You say you've seen these plants?" said Bigwig, turning his ears to catch the distant rustling of the beans.

"Yes, they're only just over the top. Come on, let's get the others moving before a man comes with a hrududu* or they'll scatter all over the place."

Silver roused the others and began to coax them into the field. They stumbled out drowsily, responding with reluctance to his repeated assurance that it was "only a little way."

They became widely separated as they straggled up the slope. Silver and Bigwig led the way, with Hazel and Buckthorn a short distance behind. The rest idled along, hopping a few yards and then pausing to nibble or to pass droppings on the warm, sunny grass. Silver was almost at the crest when suddenly, from halfway up, there came a high screaming—the sound a rabbit makes, not to call for help or to frighten an enemy, but simply out of terror. Fiver and Pipkin, limping behind the others, and conspicuously under-sized and tired, were being attacked by the crow. It had flown low along the ground. Then, pouncing, it had aimed a blow of its great bill at Fiver, who just managed to dodge in time. Now it was leaping and hopping among the grass tussocks, striking at the two rabbits with terrible darts of its head. Crows aim at the eyes and Pipkin, sensing this, had buried his head in a clump of rank grass and was trying to burrow further in. It was he who was screaming.

Hazel covered the distance down the slope in a few seconds. He had no idea what he was going to do, and if the crow had ignored him he would probably have been at a loss. But by dashing up he distracted its attention and it turned on him. He swerved past it, stopped and, looking back, saw Bigwig come racing in from the opposite side. The crow turned again, struck at Bigwig and missed. Hazel heard its beak hit a pebble in the grass with a sound like a snail shell when a thrush beats it on a stone. As Silver followed Bigwig, it recovered itself and faced him squarely. Silver stopped short in fear and the crow seemed to dance before him, its great black wings flapping in a horrible commotion. It was just about to stab when Bigwig ran straight into it from behind and knocked it

* Tractor—or any motor.

sideways, so that it staggered across the turf with a harsh, raucous cawing of rage.

"Keep at it!" cried Bigwig. "Come in behind it! They're cowards! They only attack helpless rabbits."

But already the crow was making off, flying low with slow, heavy wing beats. They watched it clear the further hedge and disappear into the wood beyond the river. In the silence there was a gentle, tearing sound as a grazing cow moved nearer.

Bigwig strolled over to Pipkin, muttering a ribald Owsla lampoon.

> "Hoi, hoi u embleer Hrair,
> M'saion ulé hraka vair." *

"Come on, Hlao-roo," he said. "You can get your head out now. Having quite a day, aren't we?"

He turned away and Pipkin tried to follow him. Hazel remembered that Fiver had said he thought he was injured. Now, as he watched him limping and staggering up the slope, it occurred to him that he might actually be wounded in some way. He kept trying to put his near-side front paw to the ground and then drawing it up again, hopping on three legs.

"I'll have a look at him as soon as they're settled under cover," he thought. "Poor little chap, he won't be able to get much further like that."

At the top of the slope Buckthorn was already leading the way into the beanfield. Hazel reached the hedge, crossed a narrow turf verge on the other side and found himself looking straight down a long, shadowy aisle between two rows of beans. The earth was soft and crumbling, with a scattering of the weeds that are found in cultivated fields—fumitory, charlock, pimpernel and mayweed, all growing in the green gloom under the bean leaves. As the plants moved in the breeze, the sunlight dappled and speckled back and forth over the brown soil, the white pebbles and weeds. Yet in this ubiquitous restlessness there was nothing alarming, for the whole forest took part in it and the only sound was the soft, steady movement of the leaves. Far along the bean row Hazel glimpsed Buckthorn's back and followed him into the depths of the field.

---

* "Hoi, hoi, the stinking Thousand, We meet them even when we stop to pass our droppings."

Soon after, all the rabbits had come together in a kind of hollow. Far around, on all sides, stood the orderly rows of beans, securing them against hostile approach, roofing them over and covering their scent. They could hardly have been safer underground. Even a little food could be had at a pinch, for here and there were a few pale twists of grass and here and there a dandelion.

"We can sleep here all day," said Hazel. "But I suppose one of us ought to stay awake; and if I take the first turn it'll give me a chance to have a look at your paw, Hlao-roo. I think you've got something in it."

Pipkin, who was lying on his left side, breathing quickly and heavily, rolled over and stretched out his front paw, underside turned upward. Hazel peered closely into the thick, coarse hair (a rabbit's foot has no pads) and after a few moments saw what he had expected—the oval shank of a snapped-off thorn sticking out through the skin. There was a little blood and the flesh was torn.

"You've got a big thorn in there, Hlao," he said. "No wonder you couldn't run. We'll have to get it out."

Getting the thorn out was not easy, for the foot had become so tender that Pipkin winced and pulled away even from Hazel's tongue. But after a good deal of patient effort Hazel succeeded in working out enough of the stump to get a grip with his teeth. The thorn came out smoothly and the wound bled. The spine was so long and thick that Hawkbit, who happened to be close by, woke Speedwell to have a look at it.

"Frith above, Pipkin!" said Speedwell, sniffing at the thorn where it lay on a pebble. "You'd better collect a few more like that: then you can make a notice board and frighten Fiver. You might have poked the lendri's eye out for us, if you'd only known."

"Lick the place, Hlao," said Hazel. "Lick it until it feels better and then go to sleep."

The Road and the Common

Timorous answered, that they . . . had got up that difficult place: but,
said he, the further we go, the more danger we meet with; wherefore we
turned, and are going back again.

John Bunyan, *The Pilgrim's Progress*

After some time, Hazel woke Buckthorn. Then he
scratched a shallow nest in the earth and slept. One watch
succeeded another through the day, though how the rabbits judged
the passing of the time is something that civilized human beings
have lost the power to feel. Creatures that have neither clocks nor
books are alive to all manner of knowledge about time and the
weather; and about direction, too, as we know from their extraordinary migratory and homing journeys. The changes in the warmth
and dampness of the soil, the falling of the sunlight patches, the
altering movement of the beans in the light wind, the direction and
strength of the air currents along the ground—all these were
perceived by the rabbit awake.

The sun was beginning to set when Hazel woke to see Acorn
listening and sniffing in the silence, between two white-skinned
flints. The light was thicker, the breeze had dropped and the beans
were still. Pipkin was stretched out a little way away. A yellow-and-
black burying beetle, crawling across the white fur of his belly,
stopped, waved its short, curved antennae and then moved on
again. Hazel grew tense with sudden misgiving. He knew that these
beetles come to dead bodies, on which they feed and lay their eggs.
They will dig away the earth from under the bodies of small
creatures, such as shrew mice and fallen fledglings, and then lay
their eggs on them before covering them with soil. Surely Pipkin
could not have died in his sleep? Hazel sat up quickly. Acorn
started and turned toward him and the beetle scurried away over
the pebbles as Pipkin moved and woke.

"How's the paw?" said Hazel.

Pipkin put it to the ground. Then he stood on it.

"It feels much better," he said. "I think I shall be able to go as well as the others now. They won't leave me behind, will they?"

Hazel rubbed his nose behind Pipkin's ear. "No one's going to leave anyone else behind," he said. "If you had to stay, I'd stay with you. But don't pick up any more thorns, Hlao-roo, because we may have to go a long way."

The next moment all the rabbits leaped up in panic. From close at hand the sound of a shot tore across the fields. A peewit rose screaming. The echoes came back in waves, like a pebble rolling round a box, and from the wood across the river came the clattering of wood pigeons' wings among the branches. In an instant the rabbits were running in all directions through the bean rows, each one tearing by instinct toward holes that were not there.

Hazel stopped short on the edge of the beans. Looking about him, he could see none of the others. He waited, trembling, for the next shot: but there was silence. Then he felt, vibrating along the ground, the steady tread of a man going away beyond the crest over which they had come that morning. At that moment Silver appeared, pushing his way through the plants close by.

"I hope it's the crow, don't you?" said Silver.

"I hope no one's been silly enough to bolt out of this field," answered Hazel. "They're all scattered. How can we find them?"

"I don't think we can," said Silver. "We'd better go back to where we were. They'll come in time."

It was in fact a long time before all the rabbits had come back to the hollow in the middle of the field. As he waited, Hazel realized more fully than ever how dangerous was their position, without holes, wandering in country they did not know. The lendri, the dog, the crow, the marksman—they had been lucky to escape them. How long would their luck hold? Would they really be able to travel on as far as Fiver's high place—wherever it might be?

"I'd settle for any decent, dry bank, myself," he thought, "as long as there was some grass and no men with guns. And the sooner we can find one the better."

Hawkbit was the last to return and as he came up Hazel set off at once. He looked cautiously out from among the beans and then darted into the hedgerow. The wind, as he stopped to sniff it, was reassuring, carrying only the scents of evening dew, may and cow dung. He led the way into the next field, a pasture: and here they all fell to feeding, nibbling their way over the grass as easily as though their warren were close by.

When he was halfway across the field, Hazel became aware of a hrududu approaching very fast on the other side of the further hedge. It was small and less noisy than the farm tractor which he had sometimes watched from the edge of the primrose wood at home. It passed in a flash of man-made, unnatural color, glittering here and there and brighter than a winter holly tree. A few moments later came the smells of petrol and exhaust. Hazel stared, twitching his nose. He could not understand how the hrududu could move so quickly and smoothly through the fields. Would it return? Would it come through the fields faster than they could run, and hunt them down?

As he paused, wondering what was best to be done, Bigwig came up.

"There's a road there, then," he said. "That'll give some of them a surprise, won't it?"

"A road?" said Hazel, thinking of the lane by the notice board. "How do you know?"

"Well, how do you suppose a hrududu can go that fast? Besides, can't you smell it?"

The smell of warm tar was now plain on the evening air.

"I've never smelled that in my life," said Hazel with a touch of irritation.

"Ah," said Bigwig, "but then you were never sent out stealing lettuces for the Threarah, were you? If you had been, you'd have learned about roads. There's nothing to them, really, as long as you let them alone by night. They're elil then, all right."

"You'd better teach me, I think," said Hazel. "I'll go up with you and we'll let the others follow."

They ran on and crept through the hedge. Hazel looked down at the road in astonishment. For a moment he thought that he was looking at another river—black, smooth and straight between its banks. Then he saw the gravel embedded in the tar and watched a spider running over the surface.

"But that's not natural," he said, sniffing the strange, strong smells of tar and oil. "What is it? How did it come there?"

"It's a man thing," said Bigwig. "They put that stuff there and then the hrududil run on it—faster than we can; and what else can run faster than we?"

"It's dangerous, then? They can catch us?"

"No, that's what's so odd. They don't take any notice of us at all. I'll show you, if you like."

The other rabbits were beginning to reach the hedge as Bigwig hopped down the bank and crouched on the verge of the road. From beyond the bend came the sound of another approaching car. Hazel and Silver watched tensely. The car appeared, flashing green and white, and raced down toward Bigwig. For an instant it filled the whole world with noise and fear. Then it was gone and Bigwig's fur was blowing in the whack of wind that followed it down the hedges. He jumped back up the bank among the staring rabbits.

"See? They don't hurt you," said Bigwig. "As a matter of fact, I don't think they're alive at all. But I must admit I can't altogether make it out."

As on the riverbank, Blackberry had moved away and was already down on the road on his own account, sniffing out toward the middle, halfway between Hazel and the bend. They saw him start and jump back to the shelter of the bank.

"What is it?" said Hazel.

Blackberry did not answer, and Hazel and Bigwig hopped toward him along the verge. He was opening and shutting his mouth and licking his lips, much as a cat does when something disgusts it.

"You say they're not dangerous, Bigwig," he said quietly. "But I think they must be, for all that."

In the middle of the road was a flattened, bloody mass of brown prickles and white fur, with small black feet and snout crushed round the edges. The flies crawled upon it, and here and there the sharp points of gravel pressed up through the flesh.

"A yona," said Blackberry. "What harm does a yona do to anything but slugs and beetles? And what can eat a yona?"

"It must have come at night," said Bigwig.

"Yes, of course. The yonil always hunt by night. If you see them by day, they're dying."

"I know. But what I'm trying to explain is that at night the hrududil have great lights, brighter than Frith himself. They draw creatures toward them, and if they shine on you, you can't see or think which way to go. Then the hrududu is quite likely to crush you. At least, that's what we were taught in the Owsla. I don't intend to try it."

"Well, it *will* be dark soon," said Hazel. "Come on, let's get across. As far as I can see, this road's no good to us at all. Now that I've learned about it, I want to get away from it as soon as I can."

By moonrise they had made their way through Newtown churchyard, where a little brook runs between the lawns and under the path. Wandering on, they climbed a hill and came to Newtown Common—a country of peat, gorse and silver birch. After the meadows they had left, this was a strange, forbidding land. Trees, herbage, even the soil—all were unfamiliar. They hesitated among the thick heather, unable to see more than a few feet ahead. Their fur became soaked with the dew. The ground was broken by rifts and pits of naked black peat, where water lay and sharp white stones, some as big as a pigeon's, some as a rabbit's skull, glimmered in the moonlight. Whenever they reached one of these rifts the rabbits huddled together, waiting for Hazel or Bigwig to climb the further side and find a way forward. Everywhere they came upon beetles, spiders and small lizards which scurried away as they pushed through the fibrous, resistant heather. Once Buckthorn disturbed a snake, and leaped into the air as it whipped between his paws to vanish down a hole at the foot of a birch.

The very plants were unknown to them—pink lousewort with its sprays of hooked flowers, bog asphodel and the thin-stemmed blooms of the sundews, rising above their hairy, fly-catching mouths, all shut fast by night. In this close jungle all was silence. They went more and more slowly, and made long halts in the peat cuts. But if the heather itself was silent, the breeze brought distant night sounds across the open common. A cock crowed. A dog ran barking and a man shouted at it. A little owl called "Kee-wik, kee-wik" and something—a vole or a shrew—gave a sudden squeal. There was not a noise but seemed to tell of danger.

Late in the night, toward moonset, Hazel was looking up from a cut where they were crouching to a little bank above. As he was wondering whether to climb up to it, to see whether he could get a clear view ahead, he heard a movement behind him and turned to find Hawkbit at his shoulder. There was something furtive and hesitant about him and Hazel glanced at him sharply, wondering for a moment whether he could have sickness or poison on him.

"Er—Hazel," said Hawkbit, looking past him into the face of the dreary black cliff. "I—er—that is to say we—er—feel that we— well, that we can't go on like this. We've had enough of it."

He stopped. Hazel now saw that Speedwell and Acorn were behind him, listening expectantly. There was a pause.

"Go on, Hawkbit," said Speedwell, "or shall I?"

"More than enough," said Hawkbit, with a kind of foolish importance.

"Well, so have I," answered Hazel, "and I hope there won't be much more. Then we can all have a rest."

"We want to stop now," said Speedwell. "We think it was stupid to come so far."

"It gets worse and worse the further we go," said Acorn. "Where are we going and how long will it be before some of us stop running for good and all?"

"It's the place that worries you," said Hazel. "I don't like it myself, but it won't go on forever."

Hawkbit looked sly and shifty. "We don't believe you know where we *are* going," he said. "You didn't know about the road, did you? And you don't know what there is in front of us."

"Look here," said Hazel, "suppose you tell me what you want to do and I'll tell you what I think about it."

"We want to go back," said Acorn. "We think Fiver was wrong."

"How can you go back through all we've come through?" replied Hazel. "And probably get killed for wounding an Owsla officer, if you ever do get back? Talk sense, for Frith's sake."

"It wasn't we who wounded Holly," said Speedwell.

"You were there and Blackberry brought you there. Do you think they won't remember that? Besides—"

Hazel stopped as Fiver approached, followed by Bigwig.

"Hazel," said Fiver, "could you come up on the bank with me for a few moments? It's important."

"And while you're there," said Bigwig, scowling round at the others from under the great sheaf of fur on his head, "I'll just have a few words with these three. Why don't you get washed, Hawkbit? You look like the end of a rat's tail left in a trap. And as for you, Speedwell—"

Hazel did not wait to hear what Speedwell looked like. Following Fiver, he scrambled up the lumps and shelves of peat to the overhang of gravelly earth and thin grass that topped them. As soon as Fiver had found a place to clamber out, he led the way along the edge to the bank which Hazel had been looking at before Hawkbit spoke to him. It stood a few feet above the nodding, windy heather and was open and grassy at the top. They climbed it and squatted down. To their right the moon, smoky and yellow in thin night cloud, stood over a clump of distant pine trees. They looked southward across the dismal waste. Hazel waited for Fiver to speak, but he remained silent.

"What was it you wanted to say to me?" asked Hazel at last.

Fiver made no reply and Hazel paused in perplexity. From below, Bigwig was just audible.

"And you, Acorn, you dog-eared, dung-faced disgrace to a gamekeeper's gibbet, if I only had time to tell you—"

The moon sailed free of the cloud and lit the heather more brightly, but neither Hazel nor Fiver moved from the top of the bank. Fiver was looking far out beyond the edge of the common. Four miles away, along the southern skyline, rose the seven-hundred-and-fifty-foot ridge of the downs. On the highest point, the beech trees of Cottington's Clump were moving in a stronger wind than that which blew across the heather.

"Look!" said Fiver suddenly. "That's the place for us, Hazel. High, lonely hills, where the wind and the sound carry and the ground's as dry as straw in a barn. That's where we ought to be. That's where we have to get to."

Hazel looked at the dim, far-off hills. Obviously, the idea of trying to reach them was out of the question. It might well prove to be all they could do to find their way across the heather to some quiet field or copse bank like those they had been used to. It was lucky that Fiver had not come out with this foolish notion in front of any of the others, especially as there was trouble enough already. If only he could be persuaded to drop it here and now, there would be no harm done—unless, indeed, he had already said anything to Pipkin.

"I don't think we could get the others to go as far as that, Fiver," he said. "They're frightened and tired as it is, you know. What we need is to find a safe place soon, and I'd rather succeed in doing what we can than fail to do what we can't."

Fiver gave no sign of having heard him. He seemed to be lost in his own thoughts. When he spoke again, it was as though he were talking to himself. "There's a thick mist between the hills and us. I can't see through it, but through it we shall have to go. Or into it, anyway."

"A mist?" said Hazel. "What do you mean?"

"We're in for some mysterious trouble," whispered Fiver, "and it's not elil. It feels more like—like mist. Like being deceived and losing our way."

There was no mist around them. The May night was clear and fresh. Hazel waited in silence and after a time Fiver said, slowly and expressionlessly, "But we must go on, until we reach the hills." His voice sank and became that of a sleep-talker. "Until we reach the hills. The rabbit that goes back through the gap will run his head into trouble. That running—not wise. That running—not safe. Running—not—" He trembled violently, kicked once or twice and became quiet.

In the hollow below, Bigwig seemed to be drawing to a close. "And now, you bunch of mole-snouted, muck-raking, hutch-hearted sheep ticks, get out of my sight sharp. Otherwise I'll—" He became inaudible again.

Hazel looked once more at the faint line of the hills. Then, as Fiver stirred and muttered beside him, he pushed him gently with one forepaw and nuzzled his shoulder.

Fiver started. "What was I saying, Hazel?" he asked. "I'm afraid I can't remember. I meant to tell you—"

"Never mind," answered Hazel. "We'll go down now. It's time we were getting them on again. If you have any more queer feelings like that, keep close to me. I'll look after you."

11

Hard Going

Then Sir Beaumains . . . rode all that ever he might ride through marshes and fields and great dales, that many times . . . he plunged over the head in deep mires, for he knew not the way, but took the gainest way in that wooness. . . . And at the last him happened to come to a fair green way.

Malory, *Le Morte d'Arthur*

When Hazel and Fiver reached the floor of the hollow they found Blackberry waiting for them, crouching on the peat and nibbling at a few brown stalks of sedge grass.

"Hello," said Hazel. "What's happened? Where are the others?"

"Over there," answered Blackberry. "There's been a fearful row. Bigwig told Hawkbit and Speedwell that he'd scratch them to pieces if they didn't obey him. And when Hawkbit said he wanted to know who was Chief Rabbit, Bigwig bit him. It seems a nasty business. Who *is* Chief Rabbit, anyway—you or Bigwig?"

"I don't know," answered Hazel, "but Bigwig's certainly the strongest. There was no need to go biting Hawkbit: he couldn't have gone back if he'd tried. He and his friends would have seen that if they'd been allowed to talk for a bit. Now Bigwig's put their backs up, and they'll think they've got to go on because he makes them. I want them to go on because they can see it's the only thing to do. There are too few of us for giving orders and biting people. Frith in a fog! Isn't there enough trouble and danger already?"

They went over to the far end of the pit. Bigwig and Silver were talking with Buckthorn under an overhanging broom. Nearby, Pipkin and Dandelion were pretending to feed on a patch of scrub. Some way away, Acorn was making a great business of licking Hawkbit's throat, while Speedwell watched.

"Keep still if you can, poor old chap," said Acorn, who obviously wanted to be overheard. "Just let me clean the blood out. Steady, now!" Hawkbit winced in an exaggerated manner and backed away. As Hazel came up, all the rabbits turned and stared at him expectantly.

"Look," said Hazel, "I know there's been some trouble, but the best thing will be to try to forget it. This is a bad place, but we'll soon get out of it."

"Do you really think we will?" asked Dandelion.

"If you'll follow me now," replied Hazel desperately, "I'll have you out of it by sunrise."

"If I don't," he thought, "they'll very likely tear me to bits: and much good may it do them."

For the second time he made his way out of the pit, and the others followed. The weary, frightening journey began again, broken only by alarms. Once a white owl swept silently overhead, so low that Hazel saw its dark, searching eyes looking into his own. But either it was not hunting or he was too big to tackle, for it disappeared over the heather; and although he waited motionless for some time, it did not return. Once Dandelion struck the smell of a stoat and they all joined him, whispering and sniffing over the ground. But the scent was old and after a time they went on again. In this low undergrowth their disorganized progress and uneven, differing rhythms of movement delayed them still more than in the wood. There were continual stampings of alarm, pausing, freezing to the spot at the sound of movement real or imagined. It was so dark that Hazel seldom knew for certain whether he was leading or whether Bigwig or Silver might not be ahead. Once, hearing an unaccountable noise in front of him, which ceased on the instant, he kept still for a long time; and when at last he moved cautiously forward, found Silver crouching behind a tussock of cocksfoot for fear of the sound of his own approach. All was confusion, ignorance, clambering and exhaustion. Throughout the bad dream of the night's journey, Pipkin seemed to be always close beside him. Though each of the others vanished and reappeared like fragments floating round a pool, Pipkin never left him; and his need for encouragement became at last Hazel's only support against his own weariness.

"Not far now, Hlao-roo, not far now," he kept muttering, until he realized that what he said had become meaningless, a mere refrain. He was not speaking to Pipkin or even to himself. He was talking in his sleep, or something very near it.

At last he saw the first of the dawn, like light faintly perceived round a corner at the far end of an unknown burrow; and in the same moment a yellowhammer sang. Hazel's feelings were like those which might pass through the mind of a defeated general. Where were his followers exactly? He hoped, not far away. But were they? All of them? Where had he led them? What was he going to do now? What if an enemy appeared at this moment? He had answers to none of these questions and no spirit left to force himself to think about them. Behind him, Pipkin shivered in the damp, and he turned and nuzzled him—much as the general, with nothing left to do, might fall to considering the welfare of his servant, simply because the servant happened to be there.

The light grew stronger and soon he could see that a little way ahead there was an open track of bare gravel. He limped out of the heather, sat on the stones and shook the wet from his fur. He could see Fiver's hills plainly now, greenish-gray and seeming close in the rain-laden air. He could even pick out the dots of furze bushes and stunted yew trees on the steep slopes. As he gazed at them, he heard an excited voice further down the track.

"He's done it! Didn't I tell you he'd do it?"

Hazel turned his head and saw Blackberry on the path. He was bedraggled and exhausted, but it was he who was speaking. Out of the heather behind him came Acorn, Speedwell and Buckthorn. All four rabbits were now staring straight at him. He wondered why. Then, as they approached, he realized that they were looking not at him, but past him at something further off. He turned round. The gravel track led downhill into a narrow belt of silver birch and rowan. Beyond was a thin hedge; and beyond that, a green field between two copses. They had reached the other side of the common.

"Oh, Hazel," said Blackberry, coming up to him round a puddle in the gravel. "I was so tired and confused, I actually began to wonder whether you knew where you were going. I could hear you in the heather, saying 'Not far now' and it was annoying me. I thought you were making it up. I should have known better. Frithrah, you're what I call a Chief Rabbit!"

"Well done, Hazel!" said Buckthorn. "Well done!"

Hazel did not know what to reply. He looked at them in silence and it was Acorn who spoke next.

"Come on!" he said. "Who's going to be first into that field? I can still run." He was off, slowly enough, down the slope, but when Hazel stamped for him to stop he did so at once.

"Where are the others?" said Hazel. "Dandelion? Bigwig?"

At that moment Dandelion appeared out of the heather and sat on the path, looking at the field. He was followed first by Hawkbit and then by Fiver. Hazel was watching Fiver as he took in the sight of the field, when Buckthorn drew his attention back to the foot of the slope.

"Look, Hazel," he said, "Silver and Bigwig are down there. They're waiting for us."

Silver's light-gray fur showed up plainly against a low spray of gorse, but Hazel could not see Bigwig until he sat up and ran toward them.

"Splendid, Hazel," he said. "Everybody's here. Let's get them into that field."

A few moments later they were under the silver birches and as the sun rose, striking flashes of red and green from the drops on ferns and twigs, they scrambled through the hedge, across a shallow ditch and into the thick grass of the meadow.

1 2

The Stranger in the Field

Nevertheless, even in a crowded warren, visitors in the form of young rabbits seeking desirable dry quarters may be tolerated . . . and if powerful enough they may obtain and hold a place.

R. M. Lockley, *The Private Life of the Rabbit*

To come to the end of a time of anxiety and fear! To feel the cloud that hung over us lift and disperse—the cloud that dulled the heart and made happiness no more than a memory! This at least is one joy that must have been known by almost every living creature.

Here is a boy who was waiting to be punished. But then, unexpectedly, he finds that his fault has been overlooked or forgiven and at once the world reappears in brilliant colors, full of delightful prospects. Here is a soldier who was waiting, with a heavy heart, to suffer and die in battle. But suddenly the luck has changed. There is news! The war is over and everyone bursts out singing! He will go home after all! The sparrows in the plowland were crouching in terror of the kestrel. But she has gone; and they fly pell-mell up the hedgerow, frisking, chattering and perching where they will. The bitter winter had all the country in its grip. The hares on the down, stupid and torpid with cold, were resigned to sinking further and further into the freezing heart of snow and silence. But now—who would have dreamed it?—the thaw is trickling, the great tit is ringing his bell from the top of a bare lime tree, the earth is scented; and the hares bound and skip in the warm wind. Hopelessness and reluctance are blown away like a fog and the dumb solitude where they crept, a place desolate as a crack in the ground, opens like a rose and stretches to the hills and the sky.

The tired rabbits fed and basked in the sunny meadow as though they had come no further than from the bank at the edge of the nearby copse. The heather and the stumbling darkness were forgotten as though the sunrise had melted them. Bigwig and Hawkbit chased each other through the long grass. Speedwell jumped over the little brook that ran down the middle of the field and when Acorn tried to follow him and fell short, Silver joked with him as he scrambled out and rolled him in a patch of dead oak leaves until he was dry. As the sun rose higher, shortening the shadows and drawing the dew from the grass, most of the rabbits came wandering back to the sun-flecked shade among the cow parsley along the edge of the ditch. Here, Hazel and Fiver were sitting with Dandelion under a flowering wild cherry. The white petals spun down around them, covering the grass and speckling their fur, while thirty feet above a thrush sang, "Cherry dew, cherry dew. Knee deep, knee deep, knee deep."

"Well, this is the place all right, isn't it, Hazel?" said Dandelion lazily. "I suppose we'd better start having a look along the banks soon, although I must say I'm in no particular hurry. But I've got an idea it may be going to rain before much longer."

Fiver looked as though he were about to speak, but then shook his ears and turned to nibbling at a dandelion.

"That looks a good bank, along the edge of the trees up there," answered Hazel. "What do you say, Fiver? Shall we go up there now or shall we wait a bit longer?"

Fiver hesitated and then replied, "Just as you think, Hazel."

"Well, there's no need to do any serious digging, is there?" said Bigwig. "That sort of thing's all right for does, but not for us."

"Still, we'd better make one or two scrapes, don't you think?" said Hazel. "Something to give us shelter at a pinch. Let's go up to the copse and look round. We might as well take our time and make quite sure where we'd like to have them. We don't want to have to do the work twice."

"Yes, that's the style," said Bigwig. "And while you're doing that, I'll take Silver and Buckthorn here and have a run down the fields beyond, just to get the lie of the land and make sure there isn't anything dangerous."

The three explorers set off beside the brook, while Hazel led the other rabbits across the field and up to the edge of the woodland. They went slowly along the foot of the bank, pushing in and out of the clumps of red campion and ragged robin. From time to time one or another would begin to scrape in the gravelly bank, or venture a little way in among the trees and nut bushes to scuffle in the leaf mold. After they had been searching and moving on quietly for some time, they reached a place from which they could see that the field below them broadened out. Both on their own side and opposite, the wood edges curved outward, away from the brook. They also noticed the roofs of a farm, but some distance off. Hazel stopped and they gathered round him.

"I don't think it makes much difference where we do a bit of scratching," he said. "It's all good, so far as I can see. Not the slightest trace of elil—no scent or tracks or droppings. That seems unusual, but it may be just that the home warren attracted more elil than other places. Anyway, we ought to do well here. Now I'll tell you what seems the right thing to me. Let's go back a little way, between the woods, and have a scratch near that oak tree there—just by that white patch of stitchwort. I know the farm's a long way off, but there's no point in being nearer to it than we need. And if we're fairly close to the wood opposite, the trees will help to break the wind a bit in winter."

"Splendid," said Blackberry. "It's going to cloud over, do you see? Rain before sunset and we'll be in shelter. Well, let's make a start. Oh, look! There's Bigwig coming back along the bottom, and the other two with him."

The three rabbits were returning down the bank of the stream and had not yet seen Hazel and the others. They passed below them, into the narrower part of the field between the two copses, and it was not until Acorn had been sent halfway down the slope to attract their attention that they turned and came up to the ditch.

"I don't think there's going to be much to trouble us here, Hazel," said Bigwig. "The farm's a good way away and the fields between don't show any signs of elil at all. There's a man track—in fact, there are several—and they look as though they were used a good deal. Scent's fresh and there are the ends of those little white sticks that they burn in their mouths. But that's all for the best, I reckon. We keep away from the men and the men frighten the elil away."

"Why do the men come, do you suppose?" asked Fiver.

"Who knows why men do anything? They may drive cows or sheep in the fields, or cut wood in the copses. What does it matter? I'd rather dodge a man than a stoat or a fox."

"Well, that's fine," said Hazel. "You've found out a lot, Bigwig, and all to the good. We were just going to make some scrapes along the bank there. We'd better start. The rain won't be long now, if I know anything about it."

Buck rabbits on their own seldom or never go in for serious digging. This is the natural job of a doe making a home for her litter before they are born, and then her buck helps her. All the same, solitary bucks—if they can find no existing holes to make use of—will sometimes scratch out short tunnels for shelter, although it is not work that they tackle at all seriously. During the morning the digging proceeded in a light-hearted and intermittent way. The bank on each side of the oak tree was bare and consisted of a light, gravelly soil. There were several false starts and fresh choices, but by ni-Frith they had three scrapes of a sort. Hazel, watching, lent help here and there and encouraged the others. Every so often he slipped back to look out over the field and make sure that all was safe. Only Fiver remained solitary. He took no part in the digging but squatted on the edge of the ditch, fidgeting backward and forward, sometimes nibbling and then starting up suddenly as though he could hear some sound in the wood. After speaking to him once or twice and receiving no reply, Hazel thought it best to let him alone. The next time he left the digging he kept away from Fiver and sat looking at the bank, as though entirely concerned with the work.

A little while after ni-Frith the sky clouded over thickly. The light grew dull and they could smell rain approaching from the west. The blue tit that had been swinging on a bramble, singing "Heigh ho, go-and-get-another-bit-of-moss," stopped his acrobatics and flew into the wood. Hazel was just wondering whether it would be worthwhile starting a side passage to link Bigwig's hole to Dandelion's, when he felt a stamp of warning from somewhere close by. He turned quickly. It was Fiver who had stamped and he was now staring intently across the field.

Beside a tussock of grass a little way outside the opposite copse, a rabbit was sitting and gazing at them. Its ears were erect and it was evidently giving them the full attention of sight, smell and hearing. Hazel rose on his hind legs, paused, and then sat back on his haunches, in full view. The other rabbit remained motionless. Hazel, never taking his eyes off it, heard three or four of the others coming up behind him. After a moment he said,

"Blackberry?"

"He's down the hole," replied Pipkin.

"Go and get him."

Still the strange rabbit made no move. The wind rose and the long grass began to flutter and ripple in the dip between them. From behind, Blackberry said,

"You wanted me, Hazel?"

"I'm going over to speak to that rabbit," said Hazel. "I want you to come with me."

"Can I come?" asked Pipkin.

"No, Hlao-roo. We don't want to frighten him. Three's too many."

"Be careful," said Buckthorn, as Hazel and Blackberry set off down the slope. "He may not be the only one."

At several points the brook was narrow—not much wider than a rabbit run. They jumped it and went up the opposite slope.

"Just behave as if we were back at home," said Hazel. "I don't see how it can be a trap, and anyway we can always run."

As they approached, the other rabbit kept still and watched them intently. They could see now that he was a big fellow, sleek and handsome. His fur shone and his claws and teeth were in perfect condition. Nevertheless, he did not seem aggressive. On the contrary, there was a curious, rather unnatural gentleness about the way in which he waited for them to come nearer. They stopped and looked at him from a little distance.

"I don't think he's dangerous," whispered Blackberry. "I'll go up to him first if you like."

"We'll both go," replied Hazel. But at this moment the other rabbit came toward them of his own accord. He and Hazel touched their noses together, sniffing and questioning silently. The stranger had an unusual smell, but it was certainly not unpleasant. It gave Hazel an impression of good feeding, of health and of a certain indolence, as though the other came from some rich, prosperous country where he himself had never been. He had the air of an aristocrat and as he turned to gaze at Blackberry from his great brown eyes, Hazel began to see himself as a ragged wanderer, leader of a gang of vagabonds. He had not meant to be the first to speak, but something in the other's silence compelled him.

"We've come over the heather," he said.

The other rabbit made no reply, but his look was not that of an enemy. His demeanor had a kind of melancholy which was perplexing.

"Do you live here?" asked Hazel, after a pause.

"Yes," replied the other rabbit; and then added, "We saw you come."

"We mean to live here, too," said Hazel firmly.

The other rabbit showed no concern. He paused and then answered, "Why not? We supposed you would. But I don't think there are enough of you, are there, to live very comfortably on your own?"

Hazel felt puzzled. Apparently the stranger was not worried by the news that they meant to stay. How big was his warren? Where was it? How many rabbits were concealed in the copse and watching them now? Were they likely to be attacked? The stranger's manner told nothing. He seemed detached, almost bored, but perfectly friendly. His lassitude, his great size and beautiful, well-groomed appearance, his unhurried air of having all he wanted and of being unaffected by the newcomers one way or the other—all these presented Hazel with a problem unlike anything he had had to deal with before. If there was some kind of trick, he had no idea what it might be. He decided that he himself, at any rate, would be perfectly candid and plain.

"There are enough of us to protect ourselves," he said. "We don't want to make enemies, but if we meet with any kind of interference—"

The other interrupted smoothly. "Don't get upset—you're all very welcome. If you're going back now, I'll come over with you: that is, unless you have any objection."

He set off down the slope. Hazel and Blackberry, after looking at each other for a moment, caught him up and went beside him. He moved easily, without haste and showed less caution than they in crossing the field. Hazel felt more mystified than ever. The other rabbit evidently had no fear that they might set upon him, hrair to one, and kill him. He was ready to go alone among a crowd of suspicious strangers, but what he stood to gain from this risk it was impossible to guess. Perhaps, thought Hazel wryly, teeth and claws would make no impression on that great, firm body and shining pelt.

When they reached the ditch, all the other rabbits were squatting together, watching their approach. Hazel stopped in front of them but did not know what to say. If the stranger had not been there, he would have given them an account of what had happened. If Blackberry and he had driven the stranger across the field by force, he could have handed him over for safekeeping to Bigwig or Silver. But to have him sitting beside him, looking his followers over in silence and courteously waiting for someone else to speak first— this was a situation beyond Hazel's experience. It was Bigwig, straightforward and blunt as always, who broke the tension.

"Who is this, Hazel?" he said. "Why has he come back with you?"

"I don't know," answered Hazel, trying to look frank and feeling foolish. "He came of his own accord."

"Well, we'd better ask *him*, then," said Bigwig, with something like a sneer. He came close to the stranger and sniffed, as Hazel had done. He, too, was evidently affected by the peculiar smell of prosperity, for he paused as though in uncertainty. Then, with a rough, abrupt air, he said, "Who are you and what do you want?"

"My name is Cowslip," said the other. "I don't want anything. I hear you've come a long way."

"Perhaps we have," said Bigwig. "We know how to defend ourselves, too."

"I'm sure you do," said Cowslip, looking round at the mud-stained, bedraggled rabbits with an air of being too polite to comment. "But it can be hard to defend oneself against the weather. There's going to be rain and I don't think your scrapes are finished." He looked at Bigwig, as though waiting for him to ask another question. Bigwig seemed confused. Clearly, he could make no more of the situation than Hazel. There was silence except for the sound of the rising wind. Above them, the branches of the oak tree were beginning to creak and sway. Suddenly, Fiver came forward.

"We don't understand you," he said. "It's best to say so and try to get things clear. Can we trust you? Are there many other rabbits here? Those are the things we want to know."

Cowslip showed no more concern at Fiver's tense manner than he had at anything that had gone before. He drew a forepaw down the back of one ear and then replied,

"I think you're puzzling yourselves unnecessarily. But if you want the answers to your questions, then I'd say yes, you can trust us: we don't want to drive you away. And there is a warren here, but not as big a one as we should like. Why should we want to hurt you? There's plenty of grass, surely?"

In spite of his strange, clouded manner, he spoke so reasonably that Hazel felt rather ashamed.

"We've been through a lot of danger," he said. "Everything new seems like danger to us. After all, you might be afraid that we were coming to take your does or turn you out of your holes."

Cowslip listened gravely. Then he answered,

"Well, as to holes, that was something I thought I might mention. These scrapes aren't very deep or comfortable, are they? And although they're facing out of the wind now, you ought to know that this isn't the usual wind we get here. It's blowing up this rain from the south. We usually have a west wind and it'll go straight into these holes. There are plenty of empty burrows in our warren and if you want to come across you'll be welcome. And now if you'll excuse me, I won't stay any longer. I hate the rain. The warren is round the corner of the wood opposite."

He ran down the slope and over the brook. They watched him leap the bank of the further copse and disappear through the green bracken. The first scatters of rain were beginning to fall, pattering into the oak leaves and pricking the bare pink skin inside their ears.

"Fine, big fellow, isn't he?" said Buckthorn. "He doesn't look as though he had much to bother about, living here."

"What should we do, Hazel, do you think?" asked Silver. "It's true what he said, isn't it? These scrapes—well, we can crouch in them out of the weather, but no more than that. And as we can't all get into one, we shall have to split up."

"We'll join them together," said Hazel, "and while we're doing that I'd like to talk about what he said. Fiver, Bigwig and Blackberry, can you come with me? The rest of you split how you like."

The new hole was short, narrow and rough. There was no room for two rabbits to pass. Four were like beans in a pod. For the first time, Hazel began to realize how much they had left behind. The holes and tunnels of an old warren become smooth, reassuring and comfortable with use. There are no snags or rough corners. Every length smells of rabbit—of that great, indestructible flood of Rabbitry in which each one is carried along, sure-footed and safe. The heavy work has all been done by countless great-grandmothers and their mates. All the faults have been put right and everything in use is of proved value. The rain drains easily and even the wind of midwinter cannot penetrate the deeper burrows. Not one of Hazel's rabbits had ever played any part in real digging. The work they had done that morning was trifling and all they had to show for it was rough shelter and little comfort.

There is nothing like bad weather to reveal the shortcomings of a dwelling, particularly if it is too small. You are, as they say, stuck with it and have leisure to feel all its peculiar irritations and discomforts. Bigwig, with his usual brisk energy, set to work. Hazel, however, returned and sat pensive at the lip of the hole, looking out at the silent, rippling veils of rain that drifted across and across the little valley between the two copses. Closer, before his nose, every blade of grass, every bracken frond was bent, dripping and glistening. The smell of last year's oak leaves filled the air. It had turned chilly. Across the field the bloom of the cherry tree under which they had sat that morning hung sodden and spoiled. While Hazel gazed, the wind slowly veered round into the west, as Cowslip had said it would, and brought the rain driving into the mouth of the hole. He backed down and rejoined the others. The pattering and whispering of the rain sounded softly but distinctly outside. The fields and woods were shut in under it, emptied and subdued. The insect life of the leaves and grass was stilled. The thrush should have been singing, but Hazel could hear no thrush. He and his companions were a muddy handful of scratchers, crouching in a narrow, drafty pit in lonely country. They were not out of the weather. They were waiting, uncomfortably, for the weather to change.

"Blackberry," said Hazel, "what did you think of our visitor and how would you like to go to his warren?"

"Well," replied Blackberry, "what I think is this. There's no way of finding out whether he's to be trusted except to try it. He seemed friendly. But then, if a lot of rabbits were afraid of some newcomers and wanted to deceive them—get them down a hole and attack them—they'd start—wouldn't they?—by sending someone who was plausible. They might want to kill us. But then again, as he said, there's plenty of grass and as for turning them out or taking their does, if they're all up to his size and weight they've nothing to fear from a crowd like us. They must have seen us come. We were tired. Surely that was the time to attack us? Or while we were separated, before we began digging? But they didn't. I reckon they're more likely to be friendly than otherwise. There's only one thing beats me. What do they stand to get from asking us to join their warren?"

"Fools attract elil by being easy prey," said Bigwig, cleaning the mud out of his whiskers and blowing through his long front teeth. "And *we're* fools until we've learned to live here. Safer to teach us, perhaps. I don't know—give it up. But I'm not afraid to go and find out. If they *do* try any tricks, they'll find I know a few as well. I wouldn't mind taking a chance, to sleep somewhere more comfortable than this. We haven't slept since yesterday afternoon."

"Fiver?"

"I think we ought to have nothing to do with that rabbit or his warren. We ought to leave this place at once. But what's the good of talking?"

Cold and damp, Hazel felt impatient. He had always been accustomed to rely on Fiver and now, when he really needed him, he was letting them down. Blackberry's reasoning had been first-rate and Bigwig had at least shown which way any sound-hearted rabbit would be likely to lean. Apparently the only contribution Fiver could make was this beetle-spirited vaporing. He tried to remember that Fiver was undersized and that they had had an anxious time and were all weary. At this moment the soil at the far end of the burrow began to crumble inward: then it fell away and Silver's head and front paws appeared.

"Here we are," said Silver cheerfully. "We've done what you wanted, Hazel: and Buckthorn's through next door. But what I'd like to know is, how about What's-His-Name? Cowpat—no—Cowslip? Are we going to his warren or not? Surely we're not going to sit cowering in this place because we're frightened to go and see him. Whatever will he think of us?"

"I'll tell you," said Dandelion, from over his shoulder. "If he's not honest, he'll know we're afraid to come: and if he *is,* he'll think we're suspicious, cowardly skulkers. If we're going to live in these fields, we'll have to get on terms with his lot sooner or later, and it goes against the grain to hang about and admit we daren't visit them."

"I don't know how many of them there are," said Silver, "but *we're* quite a crowd. Anyhow, I hate the idea of just keeping away. How long have rabbits been elil? Old Cowslip wasn't afraid to come into the middle of us, was he?"

"Very well," said Hazel. "That's how I feel myself. I just wanted to know whether you did. Would you like Bigwig and me to go over there first, by ourselves, and report back?"

"No," said Silver. "Let's all go. If we're going at all, for Frith's sake let's do it as though we weren't afraid. What do you say, Dandelion?"

"I think you're right."

"Then we'll go now," said Hazel. "Get the others and follow me."

Outside, in the thickening light of the late afternoon, with the rain trickling into his eyes and under his scut, he watched them as they joined him. Blackberry, alert and intelligent, looking first up and then down the ditch before he crossed it. Bigwig, cheerful at the prospect of action. The steady, reliable Silver. Dandelion, the dashing storyteller, so eager to be off that he jumped the ditch and ran a little way into the field before stopping to wait for the rest. Buckthorn, perhaps the most sensible and staunch of them all. Pipkin, who looked round for Hazel and then came over to wait beside him. Acorn, Hawkbit and Speedwell, decent enough rank-and-filers as long as they were not pushed beyond their limits. Last of all came Fiver, dejected and reluctant as a sparrow in the frost. As Hazel turned from the hole, the clouds in the west broke slightly and there was a sudden dazzle of watery, pale gold light.

"O El-ahrairah!" thought Hazel. "These are rabbits we're going to meet. You know them as well as you know us. Let it be the right thing that I'm doing."

"Now, brace up, Fiver!" he said aloud. "We're waiting for you, and getting wetter every moment."

A soaking bumblebee crawled over a thistle bloom, vibrated its wings for a few seconds and then flew away down the field. Hazel followed, leaving a dark track behind him over the silvered grass.

Hospitality

In the afternoon they came unto a land
In which it seemed always afternoon.
All round the coast the languid air did swoon,
Breathing like one that hath a weary dream.

Tennyson, *The Lotus-Eaters*

The corner of the opposite wood turned out to be an acute point. Beyond it, the ditch and trees curved back again in a re-entrant, so that the field formed a bay with a bank running all the way round. It was evident now why Cowslip, when he left them, had gone among the trees. He had simply run in a direct line from their holes to his own, passing on his way through the narrow strip of woodland that lay between. Indeed, as Hazel turned the point and stopped to look about him, he could see the place where Cowslip must have come out. A clear rabbit track led from the bracken, under the fence and into the field. In the bank on the further side of the bay the rabbit holes were plain to see, showing dark and distinct in the bare ground. It was as conspicuous a warren as could well be imagined.

"Sky above us!" said Bigwig. "Every living creature for miles must know that's there! Look at all the tracks in the grass, too! Do you think they sing in the morning, like the thrushes?"

"Perhaps they're too secure to bother about concealing themselves," said Blackberry. "After all, the home warren was fairly plain to be seen."

"Yes, but not like that! A couple of hrududil could go down some of those holes."

"So could I," said Dandelion. "I'm getting dreadfully wet."

As they approached, a big rabbit appeared over the edge of the ditch, looked at them quickly and vanished into the bank. A few moments later two others came out and waited for them. They, too, were sleek and unusually large.

"A rabbit called Cowslip offered us shelter here," said Hazel. "Perhaps you know that he came to see us?"

Both rabbits together made a curious, dancing movement of the head and front paws. Apart from sniffing, as Hazel and Cowslip had done when they met, formal gestures—except between mating rabbits—were unknown to Hazel and his companions. They felt mystified and slightly ill at ease. The dancers paused, evidently waiting for some acknowledgment or reciprocal gesture, but there was none.

"Cowslip is in the great burrow," said one of them at length. "Would you like to follow us there?"

"How many of us?" asked Hazel.

"Why, all of you," answered the other, surprised. "You don't want to stay out in the rain, do you?"

Hazel had supposed that he and one or two of his comrades would be taken to see the Chief Rabbit—who would probably not be Cowslip, since Cowslip had come to see them unattended—in his burrow, after which they would all be given different places to go to. It was this separation of which he had been afraid. He now realized with astonishment that there was apparently a part of the warren underground which was big enough to contain them all together. He felt so curious to visit it that he did not stop to make any detailed arrangements about the order in which they should go down. However, he put Pipkin immediately behind him. "It'll warm his little heart for once," he thought, "and if the leaders *do* get attacked, I suppose we can spare him easier than some." Bigwig he asked to bring up the rear. "If there's any trouble, get out of it," he said, "and take as many as you can with you." Then he followed their guides into one of the holes in the bank.

The run was broad, smooth and dry. It was obviously a highway, for other runs branched off it in all directions. The rabbits in front went fast and Hazel had little time to sniff about as he followed. Suddenly he checked. He had come into an open place. His whiskers could feel no earth in front and none was near his sides. There was a good deal of air ahead of him—he could feel it moving—and there was a considerable space above his head. Also, there were several rabbits near him. It had not occurred to him that there would be a place underground where he would be exposed on three sides. He backed quickly and felt Pipkin at his tail. "What a fool I was!" he thought. "Why didn't I put Silver there?" At this moment he heard Cowslip speaking. He jumped, for he could tell that he was some way away. The size of the place must be immense.

"Is that you, Hazel?" said Cowslip. "You're welcome, and so are your friends. We're glad you've come."

No human beings, except the courageous and experienced blind, are able to sense much in a strange place where they cannot see, but with rabbits it is otherwise. They spend half their lives underground in darkness or near-darkness, and touch, smell and hearing convey as much or more to them than sight. Hazel now had the clearest knowledge of where he was. He would have recognized the place if he had left at once and come back six months later. He was at one end of the largest burrow he had ever been in; sandy, warm and dry, with a hard, bare floor. There were several tree roots running across the roof and it was these that supported the unusual span. There was a great number of rabbits in the place—many more than he was bringing. All had the same rich, opulent smell as Cowslip.

Cowslip himself was at the other end of the hall and Hazel realized that he was waiting for him to reply. His own companions were still coming out of the entrance burrow one by one and there was a good deal of scrabbling and shuffling. He wondered if he ought to be very formal. Whether or not he could call himself a Chief Rabbit, he had had no experience of this sort of thing. The Threarah would no doubt have risen to the occasion perfectly. He did not want to appear at a loss or to let his followers down. He decided that it would be best to be plain and friendly. After all, there would be plenty of time, as they settled down in the warren, to show these strangers that they were as good as themselves, without risking trouble by putting on airs at the start.

"We're glad to be out of the bad weather," he said. "We're like all rabbits—happiest in a crowd. When you came over to see us in the field, Cowslip, you said your warren wasn't large, but judging by the holes we saw along the bank, it must be what we'd reckon a fine, big one."

As he finished he sensed that Bigwig had just entered the hall, and knew that they were all together again. The stranger rabbits seemed slightly disconcerted by his little speech and he felt that for some reason or other he had not struck the right note in complimenting them on their numbers. Perhaps there were not very many of them after all? Had there been disease? There was no smell or sign of it. These were the biggest and healthiest rabbits he had ever met. Perhaps their fidgeting and silence had nothing to do with what he had said? Perhaps it was simply that he had not spoken very well, being new to it, and they felt that he was not up to their fine ways? "Never mind," he thought. "After last night I'm sure of my own lot. We wouldn't be here at all if we weren't handy in a pinch. These other fellows will just have to get to know us. They don't seem to dislike us, anyway."

There were no more speeches. Rabbits have their own conventions and formalities, but these are few and short by human standards. If Hazel had been a human being he would have been expected to introduce his companions one by one and no doubt each would have been taken in charge as a guest by one of their hosts. In the great burrow, however, things happened differently. The rabbits mingled naturally. They did not talk for talking's sake, in the artificial manner that human beings—and sometimes even their dogs and cats—do. But this did not mean that they were not communicating; merely that they were not communicating by talking. All over the burrow, both the newcomers and those who were at home were accustoming themselves to each other in their own way and their own time; getting to know what the strangers smelled like, how they moved, how they breathed, how they scratched, the feel of their rhythms and pulses. These were their topics and subjects of discussion, carried on without the need of speech. To a greater extent than a human in a similar gathering, each rabbit, as he pursued his own fragment, was sensitive to the trend of the whole. After a time, all knew that the concourse was not going to turn sour or break up in a fight. Just as a battle begins in a state of equilibrium between the two sides, which gradually alters one way or the other until it is clear that the balance has tilted so far that the issue can no longer be in doubt—so this gathering of rabbits in the dark, beginning with hesitant approaches, silences, pauses, movements, crouchings side by side and all manner of tentative appraisals, slowly moved, like a hemisphere of the world into summer, to a warmer, brighter region of mutual liking and approval, until all felt sure that they had nothing to fear. Pipkin, some way away from Hazel, crouched at his ease between two huge rabbits who could have broken his back in a second, while Buckthorn and Cowslip started a playful scuffle, nipping each other like kittens and then breaking off to comb their ears in a comical pretense of sudden gravity. Only Fiver sat alone and apart. He seemed either ill or very much depressed, and the strangers avoided him instinctively.

The knowledge that the gathering was safely round the corner came to Hazel in the form of a recollection of Silver's head and paws breaking through gravel. At once, he felt warm and relaxed. He had already crossed the whole length of the hall and was pressed close to two rabbits, a buck and a doe, each of whom was fully as large as Cowslip. When both together took a few slow hops down one of the runs nearby, Hazel followed and little by little they all three moved out of the hall. They came to a smaller burrow, deeper underground. Evidently this belonged to the couple, for they settled down as though at home and made no objection when Hazel did the same. Here, while the mood of the great hall slowly passed from them, all three were silent for a time.

"Is Cowslip the Chief Rabbit?" asked Hazel at length.

The other replied with a question. "Are you called Chief Rabbit?"

Hazel found this awkward to answer. If he replied that he was, his new friends might address him so for the future, and he could imagine what Bigwig and Silver would have to say about that. As usual, he fell back on plain honesty.

"We're only a few," he said. "We left our warren in a hurry to escape from bad things. Most stayed behind and the Chief Rabbit was one of them. I've been trying to lead my friends, but I don't know whether they'd care to hear me called Chief Rabbit."

"That'll make him ask a few questions," he thought. " 'Why did you leave? Why didn't the rest come? What were you afraid of?' And whatever am I going to say?"

When the other rabbit spoke, however, it was clear that either he had no interest in what Hazel had said, or else he had some other reason for not questioning him.

"We don't call anyone Chief Rabbit," he said. "It was Cowslip's idea to go and see you this afternoon, so he was the one who went."

"But who decides what to do about elil? And digging and sending out scouting parties and so on?"

"Oh, we never do anything like *that*. Elil keep away from here.

There was a homba last winter, but the man who comes through the fields, he shot it with his gun."

Hazel stared. "But men won't shoot a homba."

"Well, *he* killed *this* one, anyway. He kills owls too. We never need to dig. No one's dug in my lifetime. A lot of the burrows are lying empty, you know: rats live in one part, but the man kills them as well, when he can. We don't need expeditions. There's better food here than anywhere else. Your friends will be happy living here."

But he himself did not sound particularly happy and once again Hazel felt oddly perplexed. "Where does the man—" he began. But he was interrupted.

"I'm called Strawberry. This is my doe, Nildro-hain.* Some of the best empty burrows are quite close. I'll show you, in case your friends want to settle into them. The great burrow is a splendid place, don't you think? I'm sure there can't be many warrens where all the rabbits can meet together underground. The roof's all tree roots, you know, and of course the tree outside keeps the rain from coming through. It's a wonder the tree's alive, but it is."

Hazel suspected that Strawberry's talking had the real purpose of preventing his own questions. He was partly irritated and partly mystified.

"Never mind," he thought. "If we all get as big as these chaps, we shall do pretty well. There must be some good food round here somewhere. His doe's a beautiful creature, too. Perhaps there are some more like her in the warren."

Strawberry moved out of the burrow and Hazel followed him into another run, leading deeper down below the wood. It was certainly a warren to admire. Sometimes, when they crossed a run that led upward to a hole, he could hear the rain outside, still falling in the night. But although it had now been raining for several hours, there was not the least damp or cold either in the deep runs or in the many burrows that they passed. Both the drainage and the ventilation were better than he had been accustomed to. Here and there other rabbits were on the move. Once they came upon Acorn, who was evidently being taken on a tour of the same kind. "Very friendly, aren't they?" he said to

* "Song of the Blackbird."

Hazel as they passed one another. "I never dreamed we'd reach a place like this. You've got wonderful judgment, Hazel." Strawberry waited politely for him to finish speaking and Hazel could not help feeling pleased that he must have heard.

At last, after skirting carefully round some openings from which there was a distinct smell of rats, they halted in a kind of pit. A steep tunnel led up into the air. Rabbit runs tend to be bow-shaped; but this was straight, so that above them, through the mouth of the hole, Hazel could see leaves against the night sky. He realized that one wall of the pit was convex and made of some hard substance. He sniffed at it uncertainly.

"Don't you know what those are?" said Strawberry. "They're bricks; the stones that men make their houses and barns out of. There used to be a well here long ago, but it's filled up now—the men don't use it any more. That's the outer side of the well shaft. And this earth wall here is completely flat because of some man thing fixed behind it in the ground, but I'm not sure what."

"There's something stuck on it," said Hazel. "Why, they're stones, pushed into the surface! But what for?"

"Do you like it?" asked Strawberry.

Hazel puzzled over the stones. They were all the same size, and pushed at regular intervals into the soil. He could make nothing of them.

"What are they for?" he asked again.

"It's El-ahrairah," said Strawberry. "A rabbit called Laburnum did it, some time ago now. We have others, but this is the best. Worth a visit, don't you think?"

Hazel was more at a loss than ever. He had never seen a laburnum and was puzzled by the name, which in Lapine is "Poison Tree." How could a rabbit be called Poison? And how could stones be El-ahrairah? What, exactly, was it that Strawberry was saying was El-ahrairah? In confusion he said, "I don't understand."

"It's what we call a Shape," explained Strawberry. "Haven't you seen one before? The stones make the shape of El-ahrairah on the wall. Stealing the King's lettuce. *You* know?"

Hazel had not felt so much bewildered since Blackberry had talked about the raft beside the Enborne. Obviously, the stones could not possibly be anything to do with El-ahrairah. It seemed to him that Strawberry might as well have said that his tail was an oak tree. He sniffed again and then put a paw up to the wall.

"Steady, steady," said Strawberry. "You might damage it and that wouldn't do. Never mind. We'll come again some other time."

"But where are—" Hazel was beginning, when Strawberry once more interrupted him.

"I expect you'll be hungry now. I know I am. It's going on raining all night, I'm certain of that, but we can feed underground here, you know. And then you can sleep in the great burrow, or in my place if you prefer. We can go back more quickly than we came. There's a run that goes almost straight. Actually, it passes across—"

He chatted on relentlessly, as they made their way back. It suddenly occurred to Hazel that these desperate interruptions seemed to follow any question beginning "Where?" He thought he would put this to the proof. After a while Strawberry ended by saying, "We're nearly at the great burrow now, but we're coming in by a different way."

"And where—" said Hazel. Instantly Strawberry turned into a side run and called, "Kingcup? Are you coming down to the great burrow?" There was silence. "That's odd!" said Strawberry, returning and once more leading the way. "He's generally there about this time. I often call for him, you know."

Hazel, hanging back, made a quick search with nose and whiskers. The threshold of the burrow was covered with a day-old fall of soft soil from the roof above. Strawberry's prints had marked it plainly and there were no others whatsoever.

14

"Like Trees in November"

Courts and camps are the only places to learn the world in. . . . Take the tone of the company that you are in.
The Earl of Chesterfield, *Letters to His Son*

The great burrow was less crowded than when they had left it. Nildro-hain was the first rabbit they met. She was among a group of three or four fine does who were talking quietly together and seemed to be feeding as well. There was a smell of greenstuff. Evidently some kind of food was available underground, like the Threarah's lettuce. Hazel stopped to speak to Nildro-hain. She asked whether he had gone as far as the well pit and the El-ahrairah of Laburnum.

"Yes, we did," said Hazel. "It's something quite strange to me, I'm afraid. But I'd rather admire you and your friends than stones on a wall."

As he said this, he noticed that Cowslip had joined them and that Strawberry was talking to him quietly. He caught the words "never been near a Shape" and a moment later Cowslip replied, "Well, it makes no difference from our point of view."

Hazel suddenly felt tired and depressed. He heard Blackberry behind Cowslip's sleek, heavy shoulder and went across to him.

"Come out into the grass," he said quietly. "Bring anyone else who'll come."

At that moment Cowslip turned to him and said, "You'll be glad of something to eat now. I'll show you what we've got down here."

"One or two of us are just going to silflay," * said Hazel.

"Oh, it's still raining much too hard for that," said Cowslip, as though there could be no two ways about it. "We'll feed you here."

"I should be sorry to quarrel over it," said Hazel firmly, "but some of us need to silflay. We're used to it, and rain doesn't bother us."

---

* Go above ground to feed.

Cowslip seemed taken aback for a moment. Then he laughed. The phenomenon of laughter is unknown to animals; though it is possible that dogs and elephants may have some inkling of it. The effect on Hazel and Blackberry was overwhelming. Hazel's first idea was that Cowslip was showing the symptom of some kind of disease. Blackberry clearly thought that he might be going to attack them and backed away. Cowslip said nothing, but his eerie laughter continued. Hazel and Blackberry turned and scuttled up the nearest run as though he had been a ferret. Halfway up they met Pipkin, who was small enough first to let them pass and then to turn round and follow them.

The rain was still falling steadily. The night was dark and, for May, cold. They all three hunched themselves in the grass and nibbled while the rain ran off their fur in streams.

"My goodness, Hazel," said Blackberry, "did you really want to silflay? This is terrible! I was just going to eat whatever it is they have and then go to sleep. What's the idea?"

"I don't know," replied Hazel. "I suddenly felt I had to get out and I wanted your company. I can see what's troubling Fiver; though he'll get over it, I dare say. There *is* something strange about these rabbits. Do you know they push stones into the wall?"

"They do what?"

Hazel explained. Blackberry was as much at a loss as he had been himself. "But I'll tell you another thing," he said. "Bigwig wasn't so far wrong. They *do* sing like the birds. I was in a burrow belonging to a rabbit called Betony. His doe has a litter and she was making a noise over them rather like a robin in autumn. To send them to sleep, she said. It made me feel queer, I can tell you."

"And what do *you* think of them, Hlao-roo?" asked Hazel.

"They're very nice and kind," answered Pipkin, "but I'll tell you how they strike me. They all seem terribly sad. I can't think why, when they're so big and strong and have this beautiful warren. But they put me in mind of trees in November. I expect I'm being silly, though, Hazel. You brought us here and I'm sure it must be a fine, safe place."

"No, you're not being silly. I hadn't realized it, but you're perfectly right. They all seem to have something on their minds."

"But after all," said Blackberry, "we don't know why they're so few. They don't fill the warren, anything like. Perhaps they've had some sort of trouble that's left them sad."

"We don't know because they don't tell us. But if we're going to stay here we've got to learn to get on with them. We can't fight them: they're too big. And we don't want them fighting us."

"I don't believe they *can* fight, Hazel," said Pipkin. "Although they're so big, they don't seem like fighters to me. Not like Bigwig and Silver."

"You notice a lot, don't you, Hlao-roo?" said Hazel. "Do you notice it's raining harder than ever? I've got enough grass in my stomach for a bit. We'll go down again now, but let's keep to ourselves for a while."

"Why not sleep?" said Blackberry. "It's over a night and a day now and I'm dropping."

They returned down a different hole and soon found a dry, empty burrow, where they curled up together and slept in the warmth of their own tired bodies.

When Hazel woke he perceived at once that it was morning— some time after sunrise, by the smell of it. The scent of apple blossom was plain enough. Then he picked up the fainter smells of buttercups and horses. Mingled with these came another. Although it made him uneasy, he could not tell for some moments what it was. A dangerous smell, an unpleasant smell, a totally unnatural smell—quite close outside: a smoke smell—something was burning. Then he remembered how Bigwig, after his reconnaissance on the previous day, had spoken of the little white sticks in the grass. That was it. A man had been walking over the ground outside. That must have been what had awakened him.

Hazel lay in the warm, dark burrow with a delightful sense of security. He could smell the man. The man could not smell him. All the man could smell was the nasty smoke he was making. He fell to thinking of the Shape in the well pit, and then dropped into a drowsy half-dream, in which El-ahrairah said that it was all a trick of his to disguise himself as Poison Tree and put the stones in the wall, to engage Strawberry's attention while he himself was getting acquainted with Nildro-hain.

Pipkin stirred and turned in his sleep, murmuring, "Sayn lay narn, Marli?" ("Is groundsel nice, Mother?") and Hazel, touched to think that he must be dreaming of old days, rolled over on his side to give him room to settle again. At that moment, however, he heard a rabbit approaching down some run close by. Whoever it was, he was calling—and stamping as well, Hazel noticed—in an unnatural way. The sound, as Blackberry had said, was not unlike birdsong. As he came closer, Hazel could distinguish the word.

"Flayrah! Flayrah!"

The voice was Strawberry's. Pipkin and Blackberry were waking, more at the stamping than the voice, which was thin and novel, not striking through their sleep to any deep instinct. Hazel slipped out of the burrow into the run and at once came upon Strawberry busily thumping a hind leg on the hard earth floor.

"My mother used to say, 'If you were a horse the ceiling would fall down,' " said Hazel. "Why do you stamp underground?"

"To wake everyone," answered Strawberry. "The rain went on nearly all night, you know. We generally sleep right through the early morning if it's rough weather. But it's turned fine now."

"Why actually wake everybody, though?"

"Well, the man's gone by and Cowslip and I thought the flayrah ought not to lie about for long. If we don't go and get it the rats and rooks come and I don't like fighting rats. I expect it's all in the day's work to an adventurous lot like you."

"I don't understand."

"Well, come along with me. I'm just going back along this run for Nildro-hain. We haven't got a litter at present, you see, so she'll come out with the rest of us."

Other rabbits were making their way along the run and Strawberry spoke to several of them, more than once remarking that he would enjoy taking their new friends across the field. Hazel began to realize that he liked Strawberry. On the previous day he had been too tired and bewildered to size him up. But now that he had had a good sleep, he could see that Strawberry was really a harmless, decent sort of fellow. He was touchingly devoted to the beautiful Nildro-hain; and he evidently had moods of gaiety and a great capacity for enjoyment. As they came up into the May morning he hopped over the ditch and skipped into the long grass as blithe as a squirrel. He seemed quite to have lost the preoccupied air that had troubled Hazel the night before. Hazel himself paused in the mouth of the hole, as he always had behind the bramble curtain at home, and looked out across the valley.

The sun, risen behind the copse, threw long shadows from the trees southwestward across the field. The wet grass glittered and nearby a nut tree sparkled iridescent, winking and gleaming as its branches moved in the light wind. The brook was swollen and Hazel's ears could distinguish the deeper, smoother sound, changed since the day before. Between the copse and the brook, the slope was covered with pale lilac lady's-smocks, each standing separately in the grass, a frail stalk of bloom above a spread of cressy leaves. The breeze dropped and the little valley lay completely still, held in long beams of light and enclosed on either side by the lines of the woods. Upon this clear stillness, like feathers on the surface of a pool, fell the calling of a cuckoo.

"It's quite safe, Hazel," said Cowslip behind him in the hole. "I know you're used to taking a good look round when you silflay, but here we generally go straight out."

Hazel did not mean to alter his ways or take instructions from Cowslip. However, no one had pushed him and there was no point in bickering over trifles. He hopped across the ditch to the further bank and looked round him again. Several rabbits were already running down the field toward a distant hedge dappled white with great patches of maybloom. He saw Bigwig and Silver and went to join them, flicking the wet off his front paws step by step, like a cat.

"I hope your friends have been looking after you as well as these fellows have looked after us, Hazel," said Bigwig. "Silver and I really feel at home again. If you ask me, I reckon we've all made a big change for the better. Even if Fiver's wrong and nothing terrible *has* happened back at the old warren, I'd still say we're better off here. Are you coming along to feed?"

"What is this business about going to feed, do you know?" asked Hazel.

"Haven't they told you? Apparently there's flayrah to be had down the fields. Most of them go every day."

(Rabbits usually eat grass, as everyone knows. But more appetizing food—e.g., lettuce or carrots, for which they will make an expedition or rob a garden—is flayrah.)

"Flayrah? But isn't it rather late in the morning to raid a

garden?" said Hazel, glancing at the distant roofs of the farm behind the trees.

"No, no," said one of the warren rabbits, who had overheard him. "The flayrah's left in the field, usually near the place where the brook rises. We either eat it there or bring it back—or both. But we'll have to bring some back today. The rain was so bad last night that no one went out and we ate almost everything in the warren."

The brook ran through the hedgerow, and there was a cattle wade in the gap. After the rain the edges were a swamp, with water standing in every hoofprint. The rabbits gave them a wide berth and came through by another gap further up, close to the gnarled trunk of an old crab-apple tree. Beyond, surrounding a thicket of rushes, stood an enclosure of posts and rails half as high as a man. Inside it, the kingcups bloomed and the brook whelmed up from its source.

On the pasture nearby Hazel could see scattered, russet-and-orange-colored fragments, some with feathery light green foliage showing up against the darker grass. They gave off a pungent, horsy smell, as if freshly cut. It attracted him. He began to salivate and stopped to pass hraka. Cowslip, coming up nearby, turned toward him with his unnatural smile. But now Hazel, in his eagerness, paid no attention. Powerfully drawn, he ran out of the hedgerow toward the scattered ground. He came to one of the fragments, sniffed it and tasted it. It was carrot.

Hazel had eaten various roots in his life, but only once before had he tasted carrot, when a cart horse had spilled a nose bag near the home warren. These were old carrots, some half eaten already by mice or fly. But to the rabbits they were redolent with luxury, a feast to drive all other feelings out of mind. Hazel sat nibbling and biting, the rich, full taste of the cultivated roots filling him with a wave of pleasure. He hopped about the grass, gnawing one piece after another, eating the green tops along with the slices. No one interrupted him. There seemed to be plenty for all. From time to time, instinctively, he looked up and sniffed the wind, but his caution was half-hearted. "If elil come, let them," he thought. "I'll fight the lot. I couldn't run, anyway. What a country! What a warren! No wonder they're all as big as hares and smell like princes!" "Hello, Pipkin! Fill yourself up to the ears! No more shivering on the banks of streams for you, old chap!"

"He won't know how to shiver in a week or two," said Hawkbit, with his mouth full. "I feel so much better for this! I'd follow you anywhere, Hazel. I wasn't myself in the heather that night. It's bad when you know you can't get underground. I hope you understand."

"It's all forgotten," answered Hazel. "I'd better ask Cowslip what we're supposed to do about taking some of this stuff back to the warren."

He found Cowslip near the spring. He had evidently finished feeding and was washing his face with his front paws.

"Are there roots here every day?" asked Hazel. "Where—" He checked himself just in time. "I'm learning," he thought.

"Not always roots," replied Cowslip. "These are last year's, as you'll have noticed. I suppose the remains are being cleared out. It may be anything—roots, greenstuff, old apples: it all depends. Sometimes there's nothing at all, especially in good summer weather. But in hard weather, in winter, there's nearly always something. Big roots, usually, or kale, or sometimes corn. We eat that too, you know."

"Food's no problem, then. The whole place ought to be full of rabbits. I suppose—"

"If you really have finished," interrupted Cowslip, "—and there's no hurry; do take your time—you could try carrying. It's easy with these roots—easier than anything except lettuce. You simply bite onto one, take it back to the warren and put it in the great burrow. I generally take two at a time, but then I've had a lot of practice. Rabbits don't usually carry food, I know, but you'll learn. It's useful to have a store. The does need some for their young when they're getting bigger; and it's particularly convenient for all of us in bad weather. Come back with me and I'll help if you find the carrying difficult at first."

It took Hazel some trouble to learn to grip half a carrot in his mouth and carry it, like a dog, across the field and back to the warren. He had to put it down several times. But Cowslip was encouraging and he was determined to keep up his position as the resourceful leader of the newcomers. At his suggestion they both waited at the mouth of one of the larger holes to see how his companions were shaping. They all seemed to be making an effort and doing their best, although the smaller rabbits—especially Pipkin—clearly found the task an awkward one.

"Cheer up, Pipkin," said Hazel. "Think how much you'll enjoy eating it tonight. Anyway, I'm sure Fiver must find it as hard as you: he's just as small."

"I don't know where he is," said Pipkin. "Have you seen him?"

Now that Hazel thought about it, he had not. He became a little anxious and, as he returned across the field with Cowslip, did his best to explain something of Fiver's peculiar temperament. "I do hope he's all right," he said. "I think perhaps I'll go and look for him when we've carried this next lot. Have you any idea where he might be?"

He waited for Cowslip to reply, but he was disappointed. After a few moments Cowslip said, "Look, do you see those jackdaws hanging round the carrots? They've been a nuisance for several days now. I must get someone to try to keep them off until we've finished carrying. But they're really too big for a rabbit to tackle. Now, sparrows—"

"What's that got to do with Fiver?" asked Hazel sharply.

"In fact," said Cowslip, breaking into a run, "I'll go myself."

But he did not engage the jackdaws and Hazel saw him pick up another carrot and start back with it. Annoyed, he joined Buckthorn and Dandelion and the three of them returned together. As they came up to the warren bank he suddenly caught sight of Fiver. He was sitting half concealed under the low spread of a yew tree on the edge of the copse, some way from the holes of the warren. Putting down his carrot, Hazel ran across, scrambled up the bank and joined him on the bare ground under the low, close boughs. Fiver said nothing and continued to stare over the field.

"Aren't you coming to learn to carry, Fiver?" asked Hazel at length. "It's not too difficult once you get the hang of it."

"I'll have nothing to do with it," answered Fiver in a low voice. "Dogs—you're like dogs carrying sticks."

"Fiver! Are you trying to make me angry? I'm not going to get angry because you call me stupid names. But you're letting the others do all the work."

"I'm the one who ought to get angry," said Fiver. "But I'm no good at it, that's the trouble. Why should they listen to me? Half of them think I'm mad. You're to blame, Hazel, because you know I'm not and still you won't listen."

"So you don't like this warren any better even now? Well, I think you're wrong. Everyone makes mistakes sometimes. Why shouldn't you make a mistake, like everybody else? Hawkbit was wrong in the heather and you're wrong now."

"Those are rabbits down there, trotting along like a lot of squirrels with nuts. How can that be right?"

"Well, I'd say they've copied a good idea from the squirrels and that makes them better rabbits."

"Do you suppose the man, whoever he is, puts the roots out there because he has a kind heart? What's he up to?"

"He's just throwing away rubbish. How many rabbits have had a good meal off men's rubbish heaps? Shot lettuces, old turnips? You know we all do, when we can. It's not poisoned, Fiver, I can tell you that. And if he wanted to shoot rabbits he's had plenty of chances this morning. But he hasn't done it."

Fiver seemed to grow even smaller as he flattened himself on the hard earth. "I'm a fool to try to argue," he said miserably. "Hazel—dear old Hazel—it's simply that I *know* there's something unnatural and evil twisted all round this place. I don't know what it is, so no wonder I can't talk about it. I keep getting near it, though. You know how you poke your nose against wire netting and push it up against an apple tree, but you still can't bite the bark because of the wire. I'm close to this—whatever it is—but I can't grip it. If I sit here alone I may reach it yet."

"Fiver, why not do as I say? Have a meal on those roots and then go underground and sleep. You'll feel all the better for it."

"I tell you I'll have nothing to do with the place," said Fiver. "As for going underground, I'd rather go back over the heather. The roof of that hall is made of bones."

"No, no—tree roots. But, after all, you were underground all night."

"I wasn't," said Fiver.

"What? Where were you, then?"

"Here."

"All night?"

"Yes. A yew tree gives good shelter, you know."

Hazel was now seriously worried. If Fiver's horrors had kept him above ground all night in the rain, oblivious of cold and prowling elil, then clearly it was not going to be easy to talk him out of them. He was silent for some time. At last he said, "What a shame! I still think you'd do better to come and join us. But I'll let you alone now and come and see how you're feeling later. Don't go eating the yew tree, either."

Fiver made no reply and Hazel went back to the field.

The day was certainly not one to encourage foreboding. By ni-Frith it was so hot that the lower part of the field was humid. The air was heavy with thick, herbal smells, as though it were already late June; the water mint and marjoram, not yet flowering, gave off scent from their leaves and here and there an early meadowsweet stood in bloom. The chiffchaff was busy all morning, high in a silver birch near the abandoned holes across the dip; and from deep in the copse, somewhere by the disused well, came the beautiful song of the blackcap. By early afternoon there was a stillness of heat, and a herd of cows from the higher fields slowly grazed their way down into the shade. Only a few of the rabbits remained above ground. Almost all were asleep in the burrows. But still Fiver sat alone under the yew tree.

In the early evening Hazel sought out Bigwig and together they ventured into the copse behind the warren. At first they moved cautiously, but before long they grew confident at finding no trace of any creature larger than a mouse.

"There's nothing to smell," said Bigwig, "and no tracks. I think Cowslip's told us no more than the truth. There really aren't any elil here. Different from that wood where we crossed the river. I don't mind telling you, Hazel, I was scared stiff that night, but I wasn't going to show it."

"So was I," answered Hazel. "But I agree with you about this place. It seems completely clear. If we—"

"This is odd, though," interrupted Bigwig. He was in a clump of brambles, in the middle of which was a rabbit hole that led up from one of the warren passages below. The ground was soft and damp, with old leaves thick in the mold. Where Bigwig had stopped there were signs of commotion. The rotten leaves had been thrown up in showers. Some were hanging on the brambles and a few flat, wet clots were lying well out in open ground beyond the clump. In the center the earth had been laid bare and was scored with long scratches and furrows, and there was a narrow, regular hole, about the same size as one of the carrots they had carried that morning. The two rabbits sniffed and stared, but could make nothing of it.

"The funny thing is there's no smell," said Bigwig.

"No—only rabbit, and that's everywhere, of course. And man— that's everywhere, too. But that smell might very well have nothing to do with it. All it tells us is that a man walked through the wood and threw a white stick down. It wasn't a man that tore up this ground."

"Well, these mad rabbits probably dance in the moonlight or something."

"I wouldn't be surprised," said Hazel. "It would be just like them. Let's ask Cowslip."

"That's the only silly thing you've said so far. Tell me, since we came here has Cowslip answered any question you've asked him?"

"Well, no—not many."

"Try asking him where he dances in the moonlight. Say 'Cowslip, where—' "

"Oh, you've noticed that, too, have you? He won't answer 'Where' anything. Neither will Strawberry. I think they may be nervous of us. Pipkin was right when he said they weren't fighters. So they're keeping up a mystery to stay even with us. It's best just to put up with it. We don't want to upset them and it's bound to smooth itself out in time."

"There's more rain coming tonight," said Bigwig. "Soon, too, I think. Let's go underground and see if we can get them to talk a bit more freely."

"I think that's something we can only wait for. But I agree about going underground now. And for goodness' sake let's get Fiver to come with us. He troubles me. Do you know he was out all night in the rain?"

As they went back through the copse Hazel recounted his talk with Fiver that morning. They found him under the yew tree and after a rather stormy scene, during which Bigwig grew rough and impatient, he was bullied rather than persuaded into going down with them into the great burrow.

It was crowded, and as the rain began to fall more rabbits came down the runs. They pushed about, cheerful and chattering. The carrots which had been brought in were eaten between friends or carried away to does and families in burrows all over the warren. But when they were finished the hall remained full. It was pleasantly warm with the heat of so many bodies. Gradually the talkative groups settled into a contented silence, but no one seemed disposed to go to sleep. Rabbits are lively at nightfall, and when evening rain drives them underground they still feel gregarious. Hazel noticed that almost all his companions seemed to have become friendly with the warren rabbits. Also, he found that whenever he moved into one group or another, the warren rabbits evidently knew who he was and treated him as the leader of the newcomers. He could not find Strawberry, but after a time Cowslip came up to him from the other end of the hall.

"I'm glad you're here, Hazel," he said. "Some of our lot are suggesting a story from somebody. We're hoping one of your people would like to tell one, but we can begin ourselves, if you'd prefer."

There is a rabbit saying, "In the warren, more stories than passages"; and a rabbit can no more refuse to tell a story than an Irishman can refuse to fight. Hazel and his friends conferred. After a short time Blackberry announced, "We've asked Hazel to tell you about our adventures: how we made our journey here and had the good luck to join you."

There was an uncomfortable silence, broken only by shuffling and whispering. Blackberry, dismayed, turned back to Hazel and Bigwig.

"What's the matter?" he asked in a low voice. "Surely there's no harm in that?"

"Wait," replied Hazel quietly. "Let them tell us if they don't like it. They have their own ways here."

However, the silence continued for some time, as though the other rabbits did not care to mention what they thought was wrong.

"It's no good," said Blackberry at last. "You'll have to say something yourself, Hazel. No, why should you? I'll do it." He spoke up again. "On second thoughts, Hazel remembers that we have a good storyteller among us. Dandelion will tell you a story of El-ahrairah. That can't go wrong, anyway," he whispered.

"Which one, though?" said Dandelion.

Hazel remembered the stones by the well pit. "The King's Lettuce," he answered. "They think a lot of that, I believe."

Dandelion took up his cue with the same plucky readiness that he had shown in the wood. "I'll tell the story of the King's Lettuce," he said aloud.

"We shall enjoy that," replied Cowslip immediately.

"He'd better," muttered Bigwig.

Dandelion began.

15

The Story of the King's Lettuce

Don Alfonso: "Eccovi il medico, signore belle."
Ferrando and Guglielmo: "Despina in maschera, che triste pelle!"
Lorenzo da Ponte, Cosi fan Tutte

"They say that there was a time when El-ahrairah and his followers lost all their luck. Their enemies drove them out and they were forced to live down in the marshes of Kelfazin. Now, where the marshes of Kelfazin may be I do not know, but at the time when El-ahrairah and his followers were living there, of all the dreary places in the world they were the dreariest. There was no food but coarse grass and even the grass was mixed with bitter rushes and docks. The ground was too wet for digging: the water stood in any hole that was made. But all the other animals had grown so suspicious of El-ahrairah and his tricks that they would not let him out of that wretched country and every day Prince Rainbow used to come walking through the marshes to make sure that El-ahrairah was still there. Prince Rainbow had the power of the sky and the power of the hills and Frith had told him to order the world as he thought best.

"One day, when Prince Rainbow was coming through the marshes, El-ahrairah went up to him and said, 'Prince Rainbow, my people are cold and cannot get underground because of the wet. Their food is so dull and poor that they will be ill when the bad weather comes. Why do you keep us here against our will? We do no harm.'

" 'El-ahrairah,' replied Prince Rainbow, 'all the animals know that you are a thief and a trickster. Now your tricks have caught up with you and you have to live here until you can persuade us that you will be an honest rabbit.'

" 'Then we shall never get out,' said El-ahrairah, 'for I would be ashamed to tell my people to stop living on their wits. Will you let us out if I can swim across a lake full of pike?'

" 'No,' said Prince Rainbow, 'for I have heard of that trick of yours, El-ahrairah, and I know how it is done.'

" 'Will you let us go if I can steal the lettuces from King Darzin's garden?' asked El-ahrairah.

"Now, King Darzin ruled over the biggest and richest of the animal cities in the world at that time. His soldiers were very fierce and his lettuce garden was surrounded by a deep ditch and guarded by a thousand sentries day and night. It was near his palace, on the edge of the city where all his followers lived. So when El-ahrairah talked of stealing King Darzin's lettuces, Prince Rainbow laughed and said,

" 'You can try, El-ahrairah, and if you succeed I will multiply your people everywhere and no one will be able to keep them out of a vegetable garden from now till the end of the world. But what will really happen is that you will be killed by the soldiers and the world will be rid of a smooth, plausible rascal.'

" 'Very well,' said El-ahrairah. 'We shall see.'

"Now, Yona the hedgehog was nearby, looking for slugs and snails in the marshes, and he heard what passed between Prince Rainbow and El-ahrairah. He slipped away to the great palace of King Darzin and begged to be rewarded for warning him against his enemies.

" 'King Darzin,' he sniffled, 'that wicked thief El-ahrairah has said he will steal your lettuces and he is coming to trick you and get into the garden.'

"King Darzin hurried down to the lettuce garden and sent for the captain of the guard.

" 'You see these lettuces?' he said. 'Not one of them has been stolen since the seed was sown. Very soon now they will be ready and then I mean to hold a great feast for all my people. But I have heard that that scoundrel El-ahrairah means to come and steal them if he can. You are to double the guards: and all the gardeners and weeders are to be examined every day. Not one leaf is to go out of the garden until either I or my chief taster gives the order.'

"The captain of the guard did as he was told. That night El-ahrairah came out of the marshes of Kelfazin and went secretly up to the great ditch. With him was his trusty Captain of Owsla, Rabscuttle. They squatted in the bushes and watched the doubled guards patrolling up and down. When the morning came they saw all the gardeners and weeders coming up to the wall and every one was looked at by three guards. One was new and had come instead of his uncle who was ill, but the guards would not let him in because they did not know him by sight and they nearly threw him into the ditch before they would even let him go home. El-ahrairah and Rabscuttle came away in perplexity and that day, when Prince Rainbow came walking through the fields, he said, 'Well, well, Prince with the Thousand Enemies, where are the lettuces?'

" 'I am having them delivered,' answered El-ahrairah. 'There will be rather too many to carry.' Then he and Rabscuttle went secretly down one of their few holes where there was no water, put a sentry outside and thought and talked for a day and a night.

"On the top of the hill near King Darzin's palace there was a garden and here his many children and his chief followers' children used to be taken to play by their mothers and nursemaids. There was no wall round the garden. It was guarded only when the children were there: at night it was empty, because there was nothing to steal and no one to be hunted. The next night Rabscuttle, who had been told by El-ahrairah what he had to do, went to the garden and dug a scrape. He hid in the scrape all night; and the next morning, when the children were brought to play, he slipped out and joined them. There were so many children that each one of the mothers and nursemaids thought that he must belong to somebody else, but as he was about the same size as the children and not much different to look at, he was able to make friends with some of them. Rabscuttle was full of tricks and games and quite soon he was running and playing just as if he had been one of the children himself. When the time came for the children to go home, Rabscuttle went, too. They came up to the gate of the city and the guards saw Rabscuttle with King Darzin's son. They stopped him and asked which was his mother, but the King's son said, 'You let him alone. He's my friend,' and Rabscuttle went in with all the others.

"Now, as soon as Rabscuttle got inside the King's palace, he scurried off and went into one of the dark burrows; and here he hid all day. But in the evening he came out and made his way to the royal storerooms, where the food was being got ready for the King and his chief followers and wives. There were grasses and fruits and roots and even nuts and berries, for King Darzin's people went everywhere in those days, through the woods and fields. There were no soldiers in the storerooms and Rabscuttle hid there in the dark. And he did all he could to make the food bad, except what he ate himself.

"That evening King Darzin sent for the chief taster and asked him whether the lettuces were ready. The chief taster said that several of them were excellent and that he had already had some brought into the stores.

" 'Good,' said the King. 'We will have two or three tonight.'

"But the next morning the King and several of his people were taken ill with bad stomachs. Whatever they ate, they kept on getting ill, because Rabscuttle was hiding in the storerooms and spoiling the food as fast as it was brought in. The King ate several more lettuces, but he got no better. In fact, he got worse.

"After five days Rabscuttle slipped out again with the children and came back to El-ahrairah. When he heard that the King was ill and that Rabscuttle had done all he wanted, El-ahrairah set to work to disguise himself. He clipped his white tail and made Rabscuttle nibble his fur short and stain it with mud and blackberries. Then he covered himself all over with trailing strands of goose grass and big burdocks and he even found ways to alter his smell. At last even his own wives could not recognize him, and El-ahrairah told Rabscuttle to follow some way behind and off he went to King Darzin's palace. But Rabscuttle waited outside, on the top of the hill.

"When he got to the palace, El-ahrairah demanded to see the captain of the guard. 'You are to take me to the King,' he said.

'Prince Rainbow has sent me. He has heard that the King is ill and he has sent for me, from the distant land beyond Kelfazin, to find the cause of his sickness. Be quick! I am not accustomed to be kept waiting.'

" 'How do I know this is true?' asked the captain of the guard.

" 'It is all one to me,' replied El-ahrairah. 'What is the sickness of a little king to the chief physician of the land beyond the golden river of Frith? I will return and tell Prince Rainbow that the King's guard were foolish and gave me such treatment as one might expect from a crowd of flea-bitten louts.'

"He turned and began to go away, but the captain of the guard became frightened and called him back. El-ahrairah allowed himself to be persuaded and the soldiers took him to the King.

"After five days of bad food and bad stomach, the King was not inclined to be suspicious of someone who said that Prince Rainbow had sent him to make him better. He begged El-ahrairah to examine him and promised to do all he said.

"El-ahrairah made a great business of examining the King. He looked at his eyes and his ears and his teeth and his droppings and the ends of his claws and he inquired what he had been eating. Then he demanded to see the royal storerooms and the lettuce garden. When he came back he looked very grave and said, 'Great King, I know well what sorry news it will be to you, but the cause of your sickness is those very lettuces by which you set such store.'

" 'The lettuces?' cried King Darzin. 'Impossible! They are all grown from good, healthy seed and guarded day and night.'

" 'Alas!' said El-ahrairah. 'I know it well! But they have been infected by the dreaded Lousepedoodle, that flies in ever decreasing circles through the Gunpat of the Cludge—a deadly virus—dear me, yes!—isolated by the purple Avvago and maturing in the gray-green forests of the Okey Pokey. This, you understand, is to put the matter for you in simple terms, insofar as I can. Medically speaking, there are certain complexities with which I will not weary you.'

" 'I cannot believe it,' said the King.

" 'The simplest course,' said El-ahrairah, 'will be to prove it to you. But we need not make one of your subjects ill. Tell the soldiers to go out and take a prisoner.'

"The soldiers went out and the first creature they found was Rabscuttle, grazing on the hilltop. They dragged him through the gates and into the King's presence.

" 'Ah, a rabbit,' said El-ahrairah. 'Nasty creature! So much the better. Disgusting rabbit, eat that lettuce!'

"Rabscuttle did so and soon afterward he began to moan and thrash about. He kicked in convulsions and rolled his eyes. He gnawed at the floor and frothed at the mouth.

" 'He is very ill,' said El-ahrairah. 'He must have got an exceptionally bad one. Or else, which is more probable, the infection is particularly deadly to rabbits. But, in any event, let us be thankful it was not Your Majesty. Well, he has served our purpose. Throw him out! I would strongly advise Your Majesty,' went on El-ahrairah, 'not to leave the lettuces where they are, for they will shoot and flower and seed. The infection will spread. I know it is disappointing, but you must get rid of them.'

"At that moment, as luck would have it, in came the captain of the guard, with Yona the hedgehog.

" 'Your Majesty,' he cried, 'this creature returns from the marshes of Kelfazin. The people of El-ahrairah are mustering for war. They say they are coming to attack Your Majesty's garden and steal the royal lettuces. May I have Your Majesty's order to take out the soldiers and destroy them?'

" 'Aha!' said the King. 'I have thought of a trick worth two of that. "Particularly deadly to rabbits." Well! Well! Let them have all the lettuces they want. In fact, you are to take a thousand down to the marshes of Kelfazin and leave them there. Ho! Ho! What a joke! I feel all the better for it!'

" 'Ah, what deadly cunning!' said El-ahrairah. 'No wonder Your Majesty is ruler of a great people. I believe you are already recovering. As with many illnesses, the cure is simple, once perceived. No, no, I will accept no reward. In any case, there is nothing here that would be thought of value in the shining land beyond the golden river of Frith. I have done as Prince Rainbow required. It is sufficient. Perhaps you will be so good as to tell your guards to accompany me to the foot of the hill?' He bowed, and left the palace.

"Later that evening, as El-ahrairah was urging his rabbits to growl more fiercely and run up and down in the marshes of Kelfazin, Prince Rainbow came over the river.

" 'El-ahrairah,' he called, 'am I bewitched?'

" 'It is quite possible,' said El-ahrairah. 'The dreaded Lousepe-doodle—'

" 'There are a thousand lettuces in a pile at the top of the marsh. Who put them there?'

" 'I told you they were being delivered,' said El-ahrairah. 'You could hardly expect my people, weak and hungry as they are, to carry them all the way from King Darzin's garden. However, they will soon recover now, under the treatment that I shall prescribe. I am a physician, I may say, and if you have not heard as much, Prince Rainbow, you may take it that you soon will, from another quarter. Rabscuttle, go out and collect the lettuces.'

"Then Prince Rainbow saw that El-ahrairah had been as good as his word, and that he himself must keep his promise, too. He let the rabbits out of the marshes of Kelfazin and they multiplied everywhere. And from that day to this, no power on earth can keep a rabbit out of a vegetable garden, for El-ahrairah prompts them with a thousand tricks, the best in the world."

16

Silverweed

He said, "Dance for me" and he said,
"You are too beautiful for the wind
To pick at, or the sun to burn." He said,
"I'm a poor tattered thing, but not unkind
To the sad dancer and the dancing dead."

Sidney Keyes, *Four Postures of Death*

"Well done," said Hazel, as Dandelion ended.

"He's very good, isn't he?" said Silver. "We're lucky to have him with us. It raises your spirits just to hear him."

"That's put their ears flat for them," whispered Bigwig. "Let's just see them find a storyteller to beat him."

They were all in no doubt that Dandelion had done them credit. Ever since their arrival most of them had felt out of their depth among these magnificent, well-fed strangers, with their detached manners, their Shapes on the wall, their elegance, their adroit evasion of almost all questions—above all, their fits of un-rabbit-like melancholy. Now, their own storyteller had shown that they were no mere bunch of tramps. Certainly, no reasonable rabbit could withhold admiration. They waited to be told as much, but after a few moments realized with surprise that their hosts were evidently less enthusiastic.

"Very nice," said Cowslip. He seemed to be searching for something more to say, but then repeated, "Yes, very nice. An unusual tale."

"But he must know it, surely?" muttered Blackberry to Hazel.

"I always think these traditional stories retain a lot of charm," said another of the rabbits, "especially when they're told in the real, old-fashioned spirit."

"Yes," said Strawberry. "Conviction, that's what it needs. You really have to *believe* in El-ahrairah and Prince Rainbow, don't you? Then all the rest follows."

"Don't say anything, Bigwig," whispered Hazel: for Bigwig was scuffling his paws indignantly. "You can't force them to like it if they don't. Let's wait and see what they can do themselves." Aloud, he said, "Our stories haven't changed in generations, you know. After all, we haven't changed ourselves. Our lives have been the same as our fathers' and their fathers' before them. Things are different here. We realize that, and we think your new ideas and ways are very exciting. We're all wondering what kind of things *you* tell stories about."

"Well, we don't tell the old stories very much," said Cowslip. "Our stories and poems are mostly about our own lives here. Of course, that Shape of Laburnum that you saw—that's old-fashioned now. El-ahrairah doesn't really mean much to us. Not that your friend's story wasn't very charming," he added hastily.

"El-ahrairah is a trickster," said Buckthorn, "and rabbits will always need tricks."

"No," said a new voice from the further end of the hall, beyond

Cowslip. "Rabbits need dignity and, above all, the will to accept their fate."

"We think Silverweed is one of the best poets we've had for many months," said Cowslip. "His ideas have a great following. Would you like to hear him now?"

"Yes, yes," said voices from all sides. "Silverweed!"

"Hazel," said Fiver suddenly, "I want to get a clear idea of this Silverweed, but I daren't go closer by myself. Will you come with me?"

"Why, Fiver, whatever do you mean? What is there to be afraid of?"

"Oh, Frith help me!" said Fiver, trembling. "I can smell him from here. He terrifies me."

"Oh, Fiver, don't be absurd! He just smells the same as the rest of them."

"He smells like barley rained down and left to rot in the fields. He smells like a wounded mole that can't get underground."

"He smells like a big, fat rabbit to me, with a lot of carrots inside. But I'll come with you."

When they had edged their way through the crowd to the far end of the burrow, Hazel was surprised to realize that Silverweed was a mere youngster. In the Sandleford warren no rabbit of his age would have been asked to tell a story, except perhaps to a few friends alone. He had a wild, desperate air and his ears twitched continually. As he began to speak, he seemed to grow less and less aware of his audience and continually turned his head, as though listening to some sound, audible only to himself, from the entrance tunnel behind him. But there was an arresting fascination in his voice, like the movement of wind and light on a meadow, and as its rhythm entered into his hearers the whole burrow became silent.

The wind is blowing, blowing over the grass.
It shakes the willow catkins; the leaves shine silver.
Where are you going, wind? Far, far away
Over the hills, over the edge of the world.
Take me with you, wind, high over the sky.
I will go with you, I will be rabbit-of-the-wind,
Into the sky, the feathery sky and the rabbit.

The stream is running, running over the gravel,
Through the brooklime, the kingcups, the blue and gold
    of spring.
Where are you going, stream? Far, far away
Beyond the heather, sliding away all night.
Take me with you, stream, away in the starlight.
I will go with you, I will be rabbit-of-the-stream,
Down through the water, the green water and the rabbit.

In autumn the leaves come blowing, yellow and brown.
They rustle in the ditches, they tug and hang on the hedge.
Where are you going, leaves? Far, far away
Into the earth we go, with the rain and the berries.
Take me, leaves, O take me on your dark journey.
I will go with you, I will be rabbit-of-the-leaves,
In the deep places of the earth, the earth and the rabbit.

Frith lies in the evening sky. The clouds are red about him.
I am here, Lord Frith, I am running through the long grass.
O take me with you, dropping behind the woods,
Far away, to the heart of light, the silence.
For I am ready to give you my breath, my life,
The shining circle of the sun, the sun and the rabbit.

Fiver, as he listened, had shown a mixture of intense absorption and incredulous horror. At one and the same time he seemed to accept every word and yet to be stricken with fear. Once he drew in his breath, as though startled to recognize his own half-known thoughts: and when the poem was ended he seemed to be struggling to come to himself. He bared his teeth and licked his lips, as Blackberry had done before the dead hedgehog on the road.

A rabbit in fear of an enemy will sometimes crouch stock still, either fascinated or else trusting to its natural inconspicuousness to remain unnoticed. But then, unless the fascination is too powerful, there comes the point when keeping still is discarded and the rabbit, as though breaking a spell, turns in an instant to its other resource—flight. So it seemed to be with Fiver now. Suddenly he leaped up and began to push his way violently across the great burrow. Several rabbits were jostled and turned angrily on him, but he took no notice. Then he came to a place where he could not push between two heavy warren bucks. He became hysterical, kicking and scuffling, and Hazel, who was behind him, had difficulty in preventing a fight.

"My brother's a sort of poet, too, you know," he said to the bristling strangers. "Things affect him very strongly sometimes and he doesn't always know why."

One of the rabbits seemed to accept what Hazel had said, but the other replied, "Oh, another poet? Let's hear him, then. That'll be . some return for my shoulder, anyway. He's scratched a great tuft of fur out."

Fiver was already beyond them and thrusting toward the further entrance tunnel. Hazel felt that he must follow him. But after all the trouble that he himself had taken to be friendly, he felt so cross at the way in which Fiver had antagonized their new friends that as he passed Bigwig, he said, "Come and help me to get some sense into him. The last thing we want is a fight now." He felt that Fiver really deserved a short touch of Bigwig.

They followed Fiver up the run and overtook him at the entrance. Before either of them could say a word, he turned and began to speak as though they had asked him a question.

"You felt it, then? And you want to know whether I did? Of course I did. That's the worst part of it. There isn't any trick. He speaks the truth. So as long as he speaks the truth it can't be folly—that's what you're going to say, isn't it? I'm not blaming you, Hazel. I felt myself moving toward him like one cloud drifting into another. But then at the last moment I drifted wide. Who knows why? It wasn't my own will; it was an accident. There was just some little part of me that carried me wide of him. Did I say the roof of that hall was made of bones? No! It's like a great mist of folly that covers the whole sky: and we shall never see to go by Frith's light any more. Oh, what will become of us? A thing can be true and still be desperate folly, Hazel."

"What on earth's all this?" said Hazel to Bigwig in perplexity.

"He's talking about that lop-eared nitwit of a poet down there," answered Bigwig. "I know that much. But why he seems to think we should want to have anything to do with him and his fancy talk—that's more than I can imagine. You can save your breath, Fiver. The only thing that's bothering us is the row you've started. As for Silverweed, all I can say is, I'll keep Silver and he can be just plain Weed."

Fiver gazed back at him with eyes that, like a fly's, seemed larger than his head. "You think that," he said. "You believe that. But each of you, in his own way, is thick in that mist. Where is the—"

Hazel interrupted him and as he did so Fiver started. "Fiver, I won't pretend that I didn't follow you up here to speak angrily. You've endangered our good start in this warren—"

"Endangered?" cried Fiver. "Endangered? Why, the whole place—"

"Be quiet. I was going to be angry, but you're obviously so much upset that it would be pointless. But what you *are* going to do now is to come underground with the two of us and sleep. Come on! And don't say any more for the moment."

One respect in which rabbits' lives are less complicated than those of humans is that they are not ashamed to use force. Having no alternative, Fiver accompanied Hazel and Bigwig to the burrow where Hazel had spent the previous night. There was no one there and they lay down and slept.

The Shining Wire

When the green field comes off like a lid
Revealing what was much better hid,
   Unpleasant;
And look! Behind, without a sound
The woods have come up and are standing round
   In deadly crescent.
And the bolt is sliding in its groove,
Outside the window is the black remover's van,
And now with sudden, swift emergence
Come the women in dark glasses, the hump-backed surgeons
   And the scissor-man.

W. H. Auden, *The Witnesses*

It was cold, it was cold and the roof was made of bones. The roof was made of the interlaced sprays of the yew tree, stiff twigs twisted in and out, over and under, hard as ice and set with dull red berries. "Come on, Hazel," said Cowslip. "We're going to carry the yew berries home in our mouths and eat them in the great burrow. Your friends must learn to do that if they want to go our way." "No! No!" cried Fiver. "Hazel, no!" But then came Bigwig, twisting in and out of the branches, his mouth full of berries. "Look," said Bigwig, "I can do it. I'm running another way. Ask me where, Hazel! Ask me where! Ask me where!" Then they were running another way, running, not to the warren but over the fields in the cold, and Bigwig dropped the berries—blood-red drops, red droppings hard as wire. "It's no good," he said. "No good biting them. They're cold."

Hazel woke. He was in the burrow. He shivered. Why was there no warmth of rabbit bodies lying close together? Where was Fiver? He sat up. Nearby, Bigwig was stirring and twitching in his sleep, searching for warmth, trying to press against another rabbit's body no longer there. The shallow hollow in the sandy floor where Fiver had lain was not quite cold: but Fiver was gone.

"Fiver!" said Hazel in the dark.

As soon as he had spoken he knew there would be no reply. He pushed Bigwig with his nose, butting urgently. "Bigwig! Fiver's gone! Bigwig!"

Bigwig was wide awake on the instant and Hazel had never felt so glad of his sturdy readiness.

"What did you say? What's wrong?"

"Fiver's gone."

"Where's he gone?"

"Silf—outside. It can only be silf. You know he wouldn't go wandering about in the warren. He hates it."

"He's a nuisance, isn't he? He's left this burrow cold, too. You think he's in danger, don't you? You want to go and look for him?"

"Yes, I must. He's upset and overwrought and it's not light yet. There may be elil, whatever Strawberry says."

Bigwig listened and sniffed for a few moments.

"It's very nearly light," he said. "There'll be light enough to find him by. Well, I'd better come with you, I suppose. Don't worry—he can't have gone far. But by the King's Lettuce! I won't half give him a piece of my mind when we catch him."

"I'll hold him down while you kick him, if only we can find him. Come on!"

They went up the run to the mouth of the hole and paused together. "Since our friends aren't here to push us," said Bigwig, "we may as well make sure the place isn't crawling with stoats and owls before we go out."

At that moment a brown owl's call sounded from the opposite wood. It was the first call, and by instinct they both crouched motionless, counting four heartbeats until the second followed.

"It's moving away," said Hazel.

"How many field mice say that every night, I wonder? You know the call's deceptive. It's meant to be."

"Well, I can't help it," said Hazel. "Fiver's somewhere out there and I'm going after him. You were right, anyway. It *is* light—just."

"Shall we look under the yew tree first?"

But Fiver was not under the yew tree. The light, as it grew, began to show the upper field, while the distant hedge and brook remained dark, linear shapes below. Bigwig jumped down from the bank into the field and ran in a long curve across the wet grass. He stopped almost opposite the hole by which they had come up, and Hazel joined him.

"Here's his line, all right," said Bigwig. "Fresh, too. From the hole straight down toward the brook. He won't be far away."

When raindrops are lying it is easy to see where grass has recently been crossed. They followed the line down the field and reached the hedge beside the carrot ground and the source of the brook. Bigwig had been right when he said the line was fresh. As soon as they had come through the hedge they saw Fiver. He was feeding, alone. A few fragments of carrot were still lying about near the spring, but he had left these untouched and was eating the grass not far from the gnarled crab-apple tree. They approached and he looked up.

Hazel said nothing and began to feed beside him. He was now regretting that he had brought Bigwig. In the darkness before morning and the first shock of discovering that Fiver was gone, Bigwig had been a comfort and a stand-by. But now, as he saw Fiver, small and familiar, incapable of hurting anyone or of concealing what he felt, trembling in the wet grass, either from fear or from cold, his anger melted away. He felt only sorry for him and sure that, if they could stay alone together for a while, Fiver would come round to an easier state of mind. But it was probably too late to persuade Bigwig to be gentle: he could only hope for the best.

Contrary to his fears, however, Bigwig remained as silent as himself. Evidently he had been expecting Hazel to speak first and was somewhat at a loss. For some time all three moved on quietly over the grass, while the shadows grew stronger and the wood pigeons clattered among the distant trees. Hazel was beginning to feel that all would be well and that Bigwig had more sense than he had given him credit for, when Fiver sat up on his hind legs, cleaned his face with his paws and then, for the first time, looked directly at him.

"I'm going now," he said. "I feel very sad. I'd like to wish you well, Hazel, but there's no good to wish you in this place. So just goodbye."

"But where are you going, Fiver?"

"Away. To the hills, if I can get there."

"By yourself, alone? You can't. You'd die."

"You wouldn't have a hope, old chap," said Bigwig. "Something would get you before ni-Frith."

"No," said Fiver very quietly. "You are closer to death than I."

"Are you trying to frighten me, you miserable little lump of chattering chickweed?" cried Bigwig. "I've a good mind—"

"Wait, Bigwig," said Hazel. "Don't speak roughly to him."

"Why, you said yourself—" began Bigwig.

"I know. But I feel differently now. I'm sorry, Bigwig. I was going to ask you to help me to make him come back to the warren. But now—well, I've always found that there was something in what Fiver had to say. For the last two days I've refused to listen to him and I still think he's out of his senses. But I haven't the heart to drive him back to the warren. I really believe that for some reason or other the place is frightening him out of his wits. I'll go with him a little way and perhaps we can talk. I can't ask you to risk it, too. Anyway, the others ought to know what we're doing and they won't unless you go and tell them. I'll be back before ni-Frith. I hope we both shall."

Bigwig stared. Then he turned furiously on Fiver. "You wretched little black beetle," he said. "You've never learned to obey orders, have you? It's me, me, me all the time. 'Oh, I've got a funny feeling in my toe, so we must all go and stand on our heads!' And now we've found a fine warren and got into it without even having to fight, *you've* got to do your best to upset everyone! And then you risk the life of one of the best rabbits we've got, just to play nursey while you go wandering about like a moon-struck field mouse. Well, *I'm* finished with you, I'll tell you plain. And now I'm going back to the warren to make sure everyone else is finished with you as well. *And* they will be—don't make any mistake about that."

He turned and dashed back through the nearest gap in the hedge. On the instant, a fearful commotion began on the farther side. There were sounds of kicking and plunging. A stick flew into the air. Then a flat, wet clod of dead leaves shot clean through the gap and landed clear of the hedge, close to Hazel. The brambles thrashed up and down. Hazel and Fiver stared at each other, both fighting against the impulse to run. What enemy was at work on the other side of the hedge? There were no cries—no spitting of a cat, no squealing of a rabbit—only the crackling of twigs and the tearing of the grass in violence.

By an effort of courage against all instinct, Hazel forced himself forward into the gap, with Fiver following. A terrible sight lay before them. The rotten leaves had been thrown up in showers. The earth had been laid bare and was scored with long scratches and furrows. Bigwig was lying on his side, his back legs kicking and struggling. A length of twisted copper wire, gleaming dully in the first sunlight, was looped round his neck and ran taut across one forepaw to the head of a stout peg driven into the ground. The running knot had pulled tight and was buried in the fur behind his ear. The projecting point of one strand had lacerated his neck and drops of blood, dark and red as yew berries, welled one by one down his shoulder. For a few moments he lay panting, his side heaving in exhaustion. Then again began the struggling and fighting, backward and forward, jerking and falling, until he choked and lay quiet.

Frenzied with distress, Hazel leaped out of the gap and squatted beside him. Bigwig's eyes were closed and his lips pulled back from the long front teeth in a fixed snarl. He had bitten his lower lip and from this, too, the blood was running. Froth covered his jaws and chest.

"Thlayli!" said Hazel, stamping. "Thlayli! Listen! You're in a snare—a snare! What did they say in the Owsla? Come on—think. How can we help you?"

There was a pause. Then Bigwig's back legs began to kick once more, but feebly. His ears drooped. His eyes opened unseeing and the whites showed bloodshot as the brown irises rolled one way and the other. After a moment his voice came thick and low, bubbling out of the bloody spume in his mouth.

"Owsla—no good—biting wire. Peg—got to—dig out."

A convulsion shook him and he scrabbled at the ground, covering himself in a mask of wet earth and blood. Then he was still again.

"Run, Fiver, run to the warren," cried Hazel. "Get the others—Blackberry, Silver. Be quick! He'll die."

Fiver was off up the field like a hare. Hazel, left alone, tried to understand what was needed. What was the peg? How was he to dig it out? He looked down at the foul mess before him. Bigwig was lying across the wire, which came out under his belly and seemed to disappear into the ground. Hazel struggled with his own incomprehension. Bigwig had said, "Dig." That at least he understood. He began to scratch into the soft earth beside the body, until after a time his claws scraped against something smooth and firm. As he paused, perplexed, he found Blackberry at his shoulder.

"Bigwig just spoke," he said to him, "but I don't think he can now. He said, 'Dig out the peg.' What does that mean? What have we got to do?"

"Wait a moment," said Blackberry. "Let me think, and try not to be impatient."

Hazel turned his head and looked down the course of the brook. Far away, between the two copses, he could see the cherry tree where two days before he had sat with Blackberry and Fiver in the sunrise. He remembered how Bigwig had chased Hawkbit through the long grass, forgetting the quarrel of the previous night in the joy of their arrival. He could see Hawkbit running toward him now and two or three of the others—Silver, Dandelion and Pipkin. Dandelion, well in front, dashed up to the gap and checked, twitching and staring.

"What is it, Hazel? What's happened? Fiver said—"

"Bigwig's in a wire. Let him alone till Blackberry tells us. Stop the others crowding round."

Dandelion turned and raced back as Pipkin came up.

"Is Cowslip coming?" said Hazel. "Perhaps *he* knows—"

"He wouldn't come," replied Pipkin. "He told Fiver to stop talking about it."

"Told him *what*?" asked Hazel incredulously. But at that moment Blackberry spoke and Hazel was beside him in a flash.

"This is it," said Blackberry. "The wire's on a peg and the peg's in the ground—there, look. We've got to dig it out. Come on—dig beside it."

Hazel dug once more, his forepaws throwing up the soft, wet soil and slipping against the hard sides of the peg. Dimly, he was aware of the others waiting nearby. After a time he was forced to stop, panting. Silver took his place, and was followed by Buckthorn. The nasty, smooth, clean, man-smelling peg was laid bare to the length of a rabbit's ear, but still it did not come loose. Bigwig had not moved. He lay across the wire, torn and bloody, with closed eyes. Buckthorn drew his head and paws out of the hole and rubbed the mud off his face.

"The peg's narrower down there," he said. "It tapers. I think it could be bitten through, but I can't get my teeth to it."

"Send Pipkin in," said Blackberry. "He's smaller."

Pipkin plunged into the hole. They could hear the wood splintering under his teeth—a sound like a mouse in a shed wainscot at midnight. He came out with his nose bleeding.

"The splinters prick you and it's hard to breathe, but the peg's nearly through."

"Fiver, go in," said Hazel.

Fiver was not long in the hole. He, too, came out bleeding.

"It's broken in two. It's free."

Blackberry pressed his nose against Bigwig's head. As he nuzzled him gently the head rolled sideways and back again.

"Bigwig," said Blackberry in his ear, "the peg's out."

There was no response. Bigwig lay still as before. A great fly settled on one of his ears. Blackberry thrust at it angrily and it flew up, buzzing, into the sunshine.

"I think he's gone," said Blackberry. "I can't feel his breathing."

Hazel crouched down by Blackberry and laid his nostrils close to Bigwig's, but a light breeze was blowing and he could not tell whether there was breath or not. The legs were loose, the belly flaccid and limp. He tried to think of what little he had heard of snares. A strong rabbit could break his neck in a snare. Or had the point of the sharp wire pierced the windpipe?

"Bigwig," he whispered, "we've got you out. You're free."

Bigwig did not stir. Suddenly it came to Hazel that if Bigwig was dead—and what else could hold *him* silent in the mud?—then he himself must get the others away before the dreadful loss could drain their courage and break their spirit—as it would if they stayed by the body. Besides, the man would come soon. Perhaps he was already coming, with his gun, to take poor Bigwig away. They must go; and he must do his best to see that all of them—even he himself—put what had happened out of mind, forever.

"My heart has joined the Thousand, for my friend stopped running today," he said to Blackberry, quoting a rabbit proverb.

"If only it were not Bigwig," said Blackberry. "What shall we do without him?"

"The others are waiting," said Hazel. "We have to stay alive. There has to be something for them to think about. Help me, or it will be more than I can do."

He turned away from the body and looked for Fiver among the

rabbits behind him. But Fiver was nowhere to be seen and Hazel was afraid to ask for him, in case to do so should seem like weakness and a need for comfort.

"Pipkin," he snapped, "why don't you clean up your face and stop the bleeding? The smell of blood attracts elil. You know that, don't you?"

"Yes, Hazel. I'm sorry. Will Bigwig—"

"And another thing," said Hazel desperately. "What was it you were telling me about Cowslip? Did you say he told Fiver to be quiet?"

"Yes, Hazel. Fiver came into the warren and told us about the snare, and that poor Bigwig—"

"Yes, all right. And then Cowslip—?"

"Cowslip and Strawberry and the others pretended not to hear. It was ridiculous, because Fiver was calling out to everybody. And then as we were running out Silver said to Cowslip, 'Surely you're coming?' And Cowslip simply turned his back. So then Fiver went up and spoke to him very quietly, but I heard what Cowslip answered. He said, 'Hills or Inlé, it's all one to me where you go. You hold your tongue.' And then he struck at Fiver and scratched his ear."

"I'll kill him," gasped a low, choking voice behind them. They all leaped round. Bigwig had raised his head and was supporting himself on his forepaws alone. His body was twisted and his hind parts and back legs still lay along the ground. His eyes were open, but his face was such a fearful mask of blood, foam, vomit and earth that he looked more like some demon creature than a rabbit. The immediate sight of him, which should have filled them with relief and joy, brought only terror. They cringed away and none said a word.

"I'll kill him," repeated Bigwig, spluttering through his fouled whiskers and clotted fur. "Help me, rot you! Can't anyone get this stinking wire off me?" He struggled, dragging his hind legs. Then he fell again and crawled forward, trailing the wire through the grass with the broken peg snickering behind it.

"Let him alone!" cried Hazel, for now they were all pressing forward to help him. "Do you want to kill him? Let him rest! Let him breathe!"

"No, not rest," panted Bigwig. "I'm all right." As he spoke he fell again and immediately struggled up on his forepaws as before. "It's my back legs. Won't move. That Cowslip! I'll kill him!"

"Why do we let them stay in that warren?" cried Silver. "What sort of rabbits are they? They left Bigwig to die. You all heard Cowslip in the burrow. They're cowards. Let's drive them out—kill them! Take the warren and live there ourselves!"

"Yes! Yes!" they all answered. "Come on! Back to the warren! Down with Cowslip! Down with Silverweed! Kill them!"

"O embleer Frith!" cried a squealing voice in the long grass.

At this shocking impiety, the tumult died away. They looked about them, wondering who could have spoken. There was silence. Then, from between two great tussocks of hair grass came Fiver, his eyes blazing with a frantic urgency. He growled and gibbered at them like a witch hare and those nearest to him fell back in fear. Even Hazel could not have said a word for his life. They realized that he was speaking.

"The warren? You're going to the warren? You fools! That warren's nothing but a death hole! The whole place is one foul elil's larder! It's snared—everywhere, every day! That explains everything: everything that's happened since we came here."

He sat still and his words seemed to come crawling up the sunlight, over the grass.

"Listen, Dandelion. You're fond of stories, aren't you? I'll tell you one—yes, one for El-ahrairah to cry at. Once there was a fine warren on the edge of a wood, overlooking the meadows of a farm. It was big, full of rabbits. Then one day the white blindness came and the rabbits fell sick and died. But a few survived, as they always do. The warren became almost empty. One day the farmer thought, 'I could increase those rabbits: make them part of my farm—their meat, their skins. Why should I bother to keep rabbits in hutches? They'll do very well where they are.' He began to shoot all elil—lendri, homba, stoat, owl. He put out food for the rabbits, but not too near the warren. For his purpose they had to become accustomed to going about in the fields and the wood. And then he snared them—not too many: as many as he wanted and not as many as would frighten them all away or destroy the warren. They grew big and strong and healthy, for he saw to it that they had all of the best, particularly in winter, and nothing to fear—except the running knot in the hedge gap and the wood path. So they lived as he wanted them to live and all the time there were a few who disappeared. The rabbits became strange in many ways, different from other rabbits. They knew well enough what was happening. But even to themselves they pretended that all was well, for the food was good, they were protected, they had nothing to fear but the one fear; and that struck here and there, never enough at a time to drive them away. They forgot the ways of wild rabbits. They forgot El-ahrairah, for what use had they for tricks and cunning, living in the enemy's warren and paying his price? They found out other marvelous arts to take the place of tricks and old stories. They danced in ceremonious greeting. They sang songs like the birds and made Shapes on the walls; and though these could help them not at all, yet they passed the time and enabled them to tell themselves that they were splendid fellows, the very flower of Rabbitry, cleverer than magpies. They had no Chief Rabbit—no, how could they?—for a Chief Rabbit must be El-ahrairah to his warren and keep them from death: and here there was no death but one, and what Chief Rabbit could have an answer to that? Instead, Frith sent them strange singers, beautiful and sick like oak apples, like robins' pincushions on the wild rose. And since they could not bear the truth, these singers, who might in some other place have been wise, were squeezed under the terrible weight of the warren's secret until they gulped out fine folly—about dignity and acquiescence, and anything else that could make believe that the rabbit loved the shining wire. But one strict rule they had; oh yes, the strictest. No one must ever ask where another rabbit was and anyone who asked 'Where?'—except in a song or a poem—must be silenced. To say 'Where?' was bad enough, but to speak openly of the wires—that was intolerable. For that they would scratch and kill."

He stopped. No one moved. Then, in the silence, Bigwig lurched to his feet, swayed a moment, tottered a few steps toward Fiver and fell again. Fiver paid him no heed, but looked from one to another among the rabbits. Then he began speaking again.

"And then *we* came, over the heather in the night. Wild rabbits, making scrapes across the valley. The warren rabbits didn't show themselves at once. They needed to think what was best to be done. But they hit on it quite soon. To bring us into the warren and tell us nothing. Don't you see? The farmer only sets so many snares at a time, and if one rabbit dies, the others will live that much longer. You suggested that Hazel should tell them our adventures, Blackberry, but it didn't go down well, did it? Who wants to hear about brave deeds when he's ashamed of his own, and who likes an open, honest tale from someone he's deceiving? Do you want me to go on? I tell you, every single thing that's happened fits like a bee in a foxglove. And kill them, you say, and help ourselves to the great burrow? We shall help ourselves to a roof of bones, hung with shining wires! Help ourselves to misery and death!"

Fiver sank down into the grass. Bigwig, still trailing his horrible, smooth peg, staggered up to him and touched his nose with his own.

"I'm still alive, Fiver," he said. "So are all of us. You've bitten through a bigger peg than this one I'm dragging. Tell us what to do."

"Do?" replied Fiver. "Why, go—now. I told Cowslip we were going before I left the burrow."

"Where?" said Bigwig. But it was Hazel who answered.

"To the hills," he said.

South of them, the ground rose gently away from the brook. Along the crest was the line of a cart track and beyond, a copse. Hazel turned toward it and the rest began to follow him up the slope in ones and twos.

"What about the wire, Bigwig?" said Silver. "The peg will catch and tighten it again."

"No, it's loose now," said Bigwig. "I could shake it off if I hadn't hurt my neck."

"Try," said Silver. "You won't get far otherwise."

"Hazel," said Speedwell suddenly, "there's a rabbit coming down from the warren. Look!"

"Only one?" said Bigwig. "What a pity! You take him, Silver. I won't deprive you. Make a good job of it while you're at it."

They stopped and waited, dotted here and there about the slope. The rabbit who was coming was running in a curious, headlong manner. Once he ran straight into a thick-stemmed thistle, knocking himself sideways and rolling over and over. But he got up and came blundering on toward them.

"Is it the white blindness?" said Buckthorn. "He's not looking where he's going."

"Frith forbid!" said Blackberry. "Shall we run away?"

"No, he couldn't run like that with the white blindness," said Hazel. "Whatever ails him, it isn't that."

"It's Strawberry!" cried Dandelion.

Strawberry came through the hedge by the crab-apple tree, looked about him and made his way to Hazel. All his urbane self-possession had vanished. He was staring and trembling and his great size seemed only to add to his air of stricken misery. He cringed before them in the grass as Hazel waited, stern and motionless, with Silver at his side.

"Hazel," said Strawberry, "are you going away?"

Hazel made no answer, but Silver said sharply, "What's that to you?"

"Take me with you." There was no reply and he repeated, "Take me with you."

"We don't care for creatures who deceive us," said Silver. "Better go back to Nildro-hain. No doubt she's less particular."

Strawberry gave a kind of choking squeal, as though he had been wounded. He looked from Silver to Hazel and then to Fiver. At last, in a pitiful whisper, he said,

"The wires."

Silver was about to answer, but Hazel spoke first.

"You can come with us," he said. "Don't say any more. Poor fellow."

A few minutes later the rabbits had crossed the cart track and vanished into the copse beyond. A magpie, seeing some light-colored object conspicuous on the empty slope, flew closer to look. But all that lay there was a splintered peg and a twisted length of wire.

PART II

On Watership Down

Watership Down

What is now proved was once only imagin'd.
William Blake, *The Marriage of Heaven and Hell*

It was evening of the following day. The north-facing escarpment of Watership Down, in shadow since early morning, now caught the western sun for an hour before twilight. Three hundred feet the down rose vertically in a stretch of no more than six hundred—a precipitous wall, from the thin belt of trees at the foot to the ridge where the steep flattened out. The light, full and smooth, lay like a gold rind over the turf, the furze and yew bushes, the few wind-stunted thorn trees. From the ridge, the light seemed to cover all the slope below, drowsy and still. But down in the grass itself, between the bushes, in that thick forest trodden by the beetle, the spider and the hunting shrew, the moving light was like a wind that danced among them to set them scurrying and weaving. The red rays flickered in and out of the grass stems, flashing minutely on membranous wings, casting long shadows behind the thinnest of filamentary legs, breaking each patch of bare soil into a myriad individual grains. The insects buzzed, whined, hummed, stridulated and droned as the air grew warmer in the sunset. Louder yet calmer than they, among the trees, sounded the yellowhammer, the linnet and greenfinch. The larks went up, twittering in the scented air above the down. From the summit, the apparent immobility of the vast blue distance was broken, here and there, by wisps of smoke and tiny, momentary flashes of glass. Far below lay the fields green with wheat, the flat pastures grazed by horses, the darker greens of the woods. They, too, like the hillside jungle, were tumultuous with evening, but from the remote height turned to stillness, their fierceness tempered by the air that lay between.

At the foot of the turf cliff, Hazel and his companions were crouching under the low branches of two or three spindle trees. Since the previous morning they had journeyed nearly three miles. Their luck had been good, for everyone who had left the warren was still alive. They had splashed through two brooks and wandered fearfully in the deep woodlands west of Ecchinswell. They had rested in the straw of a starveall, or lonely barn, and woken to find themselves attacked by rats. Silver and Buckthorn, with Bigwig helping them, had covered the retreat until, once all were together outside, they had taken to flight. Buckthorn had been bitten in the foreleg, and the wound, in the manner of a rat bite, was irritant and painful. Skirting a small lake, they had stared to see a great gray fisher bird that stabbed and paddled in the sedge, until a flight of wild duck had frightened them away with their clamor. They had crossed more than half a mile of open pasture without a trace of cover, expecting every moment some attack that did not come. They had heard the unnatural humming of a pylon in the summer air; and had actually gone beneath it, on Fiver's assurance that it could do them no harm. Now they lay under the spindle trees and sniffed in weariness and doubt at the strange, bare country round them.

Since leaving the warren of the snares they had become warier, shrewder, a tenacious band who understood each other and worked together. There was no more quarreling. The truth about the warren had been a grim shock. They had come closer together, relying on and valuing each other's capacities. They knew now that it was on these and on nothing else that their lives depended, and they were not going to waste anything they possessed between them. In spite of Hazel's efforts beside the snare, there was not one of them who had not turned sick at heart to think that Bigwig was dead and wondered, like Blackberry, what would become of them now. Without Hazel, without Blackberry, Buckthorn and Pipkin— Bigwig would have died. Without himself he would have died, for which else, of them all, would not have stopped running after such punishment? There was no more questioning of Bigwig's strength, Fiver's insight, Blackberry's wits or Hazel's authority. When the rats came, Buckthorn and Silver had obeyed Bigwig and stood their ground. The rest had followed Hazel when he roused them and, without explanation, told them to go quickly outside the barn. Later, Hazel had said that there was nothing for it but to cross the open pasture and under Silver's direction they had crossed it, with Dandelion running ahead to reconnoiter. When Fiver said the iron tree was harmless they believed him.

Strawberry had had a bad time. His misery made him slow-witted and careless and he was ashamed of the part he had played at the warren. He was soft and more used than he dared admit to indolence and good food. But he made no complaint and it was plain that he was determined to show what he could do and not to be left behind. He had proved useful in the woodland, being better accustomed to thick woods than any of the others. "He'll be all right, you know, if we give him a chance," said Hazel to Bigwig by the lake. "So he darned well ought to be," replied Bigwig, "the great dandy"—for by their standards Strawberry was scrupulously clean and fastidious. "Well, I won't have him brow-beaten, Bigwig, mind. That won't help him." This Bigwig had accepted, though rather sulkily. Yet he himself had become less overbearing. The snare had left him weak and overwrought. It was he who had given the alarm in the barn, for he could not sleep and at the sound of scratching had started up at once. He would not let Silver and Buckthorn fight alone, but he had felt obliged to leave the worst of it to them. For the first time in his life, Bigwig had found himself driven to moderation and prudence.

As the sun sank lower and touched the edge of the cloud belt on the horizon, Hazel came out from under the branches and looked carefully round the lower slope. Then he stared upward over the anthills, to the open down rising above. Fiver and Acorn followed him out and fell to nibbling at a patch of sainfoin. It was new to them, but they did not need to be told that it was good and it raised their spirits. Hazel turned back and joined them among the big, rosy-veined, magenta flower spikes.

"Fiver," he said, "let me get this right. You want us to climb up this place, however far it is, and find shelter on the top. Is that it?"

"Yes, Hazel."

"But the top must be very high. I can't even see it from here. It'll be open and cold."

"Not in the ground: and the soil's so light that we shall be able to scratch some shelter easily when we find the right place."

Hazel considered again. "It's getting started that bothers me. Here we are, all tired out. I'm sure it's dangerous to stay here. We've nowhere to run to. We don't know the country and we can't get underground. But it seems out of the question for everybody to climb up there tonight. We should be even less safe."

"We shall be forced to dig, shan't we?" said Acorn. "This place is almost as open as that heather we crossed, and the trees won't hide us from anything hunting on four feet."

"It would have been the same any time we came," said Fiver.

"I'm not saying anything against it, Fiver," replied Acorn, "but we need holes. It's a bad place not to be able to get underground."

"Before everyone goes up to the top," said Hazel, "we ought to find out what it's like. I'm going up myself to have a look round. I'll be as quick as I can and you'll have to hope for the best until I get back. You can rest and feed, anyway."

"You're not going alone," said Fiver firmly.

Since each one of them was ready to go with him in spite of their fatigue, Hazel gave in and chose Dandelion and Hawkbit, who seemed less weary than the others. They set out up the hillside, going slowly, picking their way from one bush and tussock to another and pausing continually to sniff and stare along the great expanse of grass, which stretched on either side as far as they could see.

A man walks upright. For him it is strenuous to climb a steep hill, because he has to keep pushing his own vertical mass upward and cannot gain any momentum. The rabbit is better off. His forelegs support his horizontal body and the great back legs do the work. They are more than equal to thrusting uphill the light mass in front of them. Rabbits can go fast uphill. In fact, they have so much power behind that they find going downhill awkward, and sometimes, in flight down a steep place, they may actually go head over heels. On the other hand, the man is five or six feet above the hillside and can see all round. To him the ground may be steep and rough but on the whole it is even, and he can pick his direction easily from the top of his moving, six-foot tower. The rabbits' anxieties and strain in climbing the down were different, therefore, from those which you, reader, will experience if you go there. Their main trouble was not bodily fatigue. When Hazel had said that they were all tired out, he had meant that they were feeling the strain of prolonged insecurity and fear.

Rabbits above ground, unless they are in proved, familiar surroundings close to their holes, live in continual fear. If it grows intense enough they can become glazed and paralyzed by it— "tharn," to use their own word. Hazel and his companions had been on the jump for nearly two days. Indeed, ever since they had left their home warren, five days before, they had faced one danger after another. They were all on edge, sometimes starting at nothing and, again, lying down in any patch of long grass that offered. Bigwig and Buckthorn smelled of blood and everyone else knew they did. What bothered Hazel, Dandelion and Hawkbit was the openness and strangeness of the down and their inability to see very far ahead. They climbed not over but through the sun-red grass, among the awakened insect movement and the light ablaze. The grass undulated about them. They peered over anthills and looked cautiously round clumps of teazle. They could not tell how far away the ridge might be. They topped each short slope only to find another above it. To Hazel, it seemed a likely place for a weasel: or the white owl, perhaps, might fly along the escarpment at twilight, looking inward with its stony eyes, ready to turn a few feet sideways and pick off the shelf anything that moved. Some elil wait for their prey, but the white owl is a seeker and he comes in silence.

As Hazel still went up, the south wind began to blow and the June sunset reddened the sky to the zenith. Hazel, like nearly all wild animals, was unaccustomed to look up at the sky. What he thought of as the sky was the horizon, usually broken by trees and hedges. Now, with his head pointing upward, he found himself gazing at the ridge, as over the skyline came the silent, moving, red-tinged cumuli. Their movement was disturbing, unlike that of trees or grass or rabbits. These great masses moved steadily, noiselessly and always in the same direction. They were not of his world.

"O Frith," thought Hazel, turning his head for a moment to the bright glow in the west, "are you sending us to live among the clouds? If you spoke truly to Fiver, help me to trust him." At this moment he saw Dandelion, who had run well ahead, squatting on an anthill clear against the sky. Alarmed, he dashed forward.

"Dandelion, get down!" he said. "Why are you sitting up there?"

"Because I can see," replied Dandelion, with a kind of excited joy. "Come and look! You can see the whole world."

Hazel came up to him. There was another anthill nearby and he copied Dandelion, sitting upright on his hind legs and looking about him. He realized now that they were almost on level ground. Indeed, the slope was no more than gentle for some way back along the line by which they had come; but he had been preoccupied with the idea of danger in the open and had not noticed the change. They were on top of the down. Perched above the grass, they could see far in every direction. Their surroundings were empty. If anything had been moving they would have seen it immediately: and where the turf ended, the sky began. A man, a fox—even a rabbit—coming over the down would be conspicuous. Fiver had been right. Up here, they would have clear warning of any approach.

The wind ruffled their fur and tugged at the grass, which smelled of thyme and self-heal. The solitude seemed like a release and a blessing. The height, the sky and the distance went to their heads and they skipped in the sunset. "O Frith on the hills!" cried Dandelion. "He must have made it for us!"

"He may have made it, but Fiver thought of it for us," answered Hazel. "Wait till we get him up here! Fiver-rah!"

"Where's Hawkbit?" said Dandelion suddenly.

Although the light was still clear, Hawkbit was not to be seen anywhere on the upland. After staring about for some time, they ran across to a little mound some way away and looked again. But they saw nothing except a field mouse, which came out of its hole and began furricking in a patch of seeded grasses.

"He must have gone down," said Dandelion.

"Well, whether he has or not," said Hazel, "we can't go on looking for him. The others are waiting and they may be in danger. We must go down ourselves."

"What a shame to lose him, though," said Dandelion, "just when we'd reached Fiver's hills without losing anyone. He's such a duffer; we shouldn't have brought him up. But how could anything have got hold of him here, without our seeing?"

"No, he's gone back, for sure," said Hazel. "I wonder what Bigwig will say to him? I hope he won't bite him again. We'd better get on."

"Are you going to bring them up tonight?" asked Dandelion.

"I don't know," said Hazel. "It's a problem. Where's the shelter to be found?"

They made for the steep edge. The light was beginning to fail. They picked their direction by a clump of stunted trees which they had passed on their way up. These formed a kind of dry oasis—a little feature common on the downs. Half a dozen thorns and two or three elders grew together above and below a bank. Between them the ground was bare and the naked chalk showed a pallid, dirty white under the cream-colored elder bloom. As they approached, they suddenly saw Hawkbit sitting among the thorn trunks, cleaning his face with his paws.

"We've been looking for you," said Hazel. "Where in the world have you been?"

"I'm sorry, Hazel," replied Hawkbit meekly. "I've been looking at these holes. I thought they might be some good to us."

In the low bank behind him were three rabbit holes. There were two more flat on the ground, between the thick, gnarled roots. They could see no footmarks and no droppings. The holes were clearly deserted.

"Have you been down?" asked Hazel, sniffing round.

"Yes, I have," said Hawkbit. "Three of them, anyway. They're shallow and rather rough, but there's no smell of death or disease and they're perfectly sound. I thought they might do for us—just for the moment, anyway."

In the twilight a swift flew screaming overhead and Hazel turned to Dandelion.

"News! News!" he said. "Go and get them up here."

Thus it fell to one of the rank and file to make a lucky find that brought them at last to the downs: and probably saved a life or two, for they could hardly have spent the night in the open, either on or under the hill, without being attacked by some enemy or other.

19

Fear in the Dark

"Who's in the next room?—who?
  A figure wan
With a message to one in there of something due?
  Shall I know him anon?"
"Yea, he; and he brought such; and you'll know him anon."
                    Thomas Hardy, *Who's in the Next Room?*

The holes certainly were rough—"Just right for a lot of vagabonds* like us," said Bigwig—but the exhausted and those who wander in strange country are not particular about their quarters. At least there was room for twelve rabbits and the burrows were dry. Two of the runs—the ones among the thorn trees—led straight down to burrows scooped out of the top of the chalk subsoil. Rabbits do not line their sleeping places and a hard, almost rocky floor is uncomfortable for those not accustomed to it. The holes in the bank, however, had runs of the usual bow shape, leading down to the chalk and then curving up again to burrows with floors of trampled earth. There were no connecting passages, but the rabbits were too weary to care. They slept four to a burrow, snug and secure. Hazel remained awake for some time, licking Buckthorn's leg, which was stiff and tender. He was reassured to find no smell of infection, but all that he had ever heard about rats decided him to see that Buckthorn got a good deal of rest and was kept out of the dirt until the wound was better. "That's the third one of us to get hurt: still, all in all, things could have been far worse," he thought, as he fell asleep.

The short June darkness slipped by in a few hours. The light returned early to the high down, but the rabbits did not stir. Well

---

* Bigwig's word was *hlessil,* which I have rendered in various places in the story as wanderers, scratchers, vagabonds. A *hlessi* is a rabbit living in the open, without a hole. Solitary bucks and unmated rabbits who are wandering do this for quite long periods, especially in summer. Bucks do not usually dig much in any case, although they will scratch shallow shelters or make use of existing holes where these are available. Real digging is done for the most part by does preparing for litters.

after dawn they were still sleeping, undisturbed in a silence deeper than they had ever known. Nowadays, among fields and woods, the noise level by day is high—too high for some kinds of animal to tolerate. Few places are far from human noise—cars, buses, motorcycles, tractors, lorries. The sound of a housing estate in the morning is audible a long way off. People who record birdsong generally do it very early—before six o'clock—if they can. Soon after that, the invasion of distant noise in most woodland becomes too constant and too loud. During the last fifty years the silence of much of the country has been destroyed. But here, on Watership Down, there floated up only faint traces of the daylight noise below.

The sun was well up, though not yet as high as the down, when Hazel woke. With him in the burrow were Buckthorn, Fiver and Pipkin. He was nearest to the mouth of the hole and did not wake them as he slipped up the run. Outside, he stopped to pass hraka and then hopped through the thorn patch to the open grass. Below, the country was covered with early-morning mist which was beginning to clear. Here and there, far off, were the shapes of trees and roofs, from which streamers of mist trailed down like broken waves pouring from rocks. The sky was cloudless and deep blue, darkening to mauve along the whole rim of the horizon. The wind had dropped and the spiders had already gone well down into the grass. It was going to be a hot day.

Hazel rambled about in the usual way of a rabbit feeding—five or six slow, rocking hops through the grass; a pause to look round, sitting up with ears erect; then busy nibbling for a short time, followed by another move of a few yards. For the first time for many days he felt relaxed and safe. He began to wonder whether they had much to learn about their new home.

"Fiver was right," he thought. "This is the place for us. But we shall need to get used to it and the fewer mistakes we make the better. I wonder what became of the rabbits who made these holes? Did they stop running or did they just move away? If we could only find them they could tell us a lot."

At this moment he saw a rabbit come rather hesitantly out of the hole furthest from himself. It was Blackberry. He, too, passed hraka, scratched himself and then hopped into the full sunlight and combed his ears. As he began to feed, Hazel came up and fell in with him, nibbling among the grass tussocks and wandering on wherever his friend pleased. They came to a patch of milkwort—a blue as deep as that of the sky—with long stems creeping through the grass and each minute flower spreading its two upper petals like wings. Blackberry sniffed at it, but the leaves were tough and unappetizing.

"What is this stuff, do you know?" he asked.

"No, I don't," said Hazel. "I've never seen it before."

"There's a lot we don't know," said Blackberry. "About this place, I mean. The plants are new, the smells are new. We're going to need some new ideas ourselves."

"Well, you're the fellow for ideas," said Hazel. "I never know anything until you tell me."

"But you go in front and take the risks first," answered Blackberry. "We've all seen that. And now our journey's over, isn't it? This place is as safe as Fiver said it would be. Nothing can get near us without our knowing: that is, as long as we can smell and see and hear."

"We can all do that."

"Not when we're asleep: and we can't see in the dark."

"It's bound to be dark at night," said Hazel, "and rabbits have got to sleep."

"In the open?"

"Well, we can go on using these holes if we want to, but I expect a good many will lie out. After all, you can't expect a bunch of bucks to dig. They might make a scrape or two—like that day after we came over the heather—but they won't do more than that."

"That's what I've been thinking about," said Blackberry. "Those rabbits we left—Cowslip and the rest—a lot of the things they did weren't natural to rabbits—pushing stones into the earth and carrying food underground and Frith knows what."

"The Threarah's lettuce was carried underground, if it comes to that."

"Exactly. Don't you see, they'd altered what rabbits do naturally because they thought they could do better? And if they altered their ways, so can we if we like. You say buck rabbits don't dig. Nor they do. But they could, if they wanted to. Suppose we had deep, comfortable burrows to sleep in? To be out of bad weather and underground at night? Then we *would* be safe. And there's nothing to stop us having them, except that buck rabbits won't dig. Not can't—won't."

"What's your idea, then?" asked Hazel, half interested and half reluctant. "Do you want us to try to turn these holes into a regular warren?"

"No, these holes won't do. It's easy to see why they've been deserted. Only a little way down and you come to this hard white stuff that no one can dig. They must be bitterly cold in winter. But there's a wood just over the top of the hill. I got a glimpse of it last night when we came. Suppose we go up higher now, just you and I, and have a look at it?"

They ran uphill to the summit. The beech hanger lay some little way off to the southeast, on the far side of a grassy track that ran along the ridge.

"There are some big trees there," said Blackberry. "The roots must have broken up the ground pretty deep. We could dig holes and be as well off as ever we were in the old warren. But if Bigwig and the others won't dig or say they can't—well, it's bare and bleak here. That's why it's lonely and safe, of course; but when bad weather comes we shall be driven off the hills for sure."

"It never entered my head to try to make a lot of bucks dig regular holes," said Hazel doubtfully, as they returned down the slope. "Rabbit kittens need holes, of course; but do we?"

"We were all born in a warren that was dug before our mothers were born," said Blackberry. "We're used to holes and not one of us has ever helped to dig one. And if ever there was a new one, who dug it? A doe. I'm quite sure, myself, that if we don't change our natural ways we shan't be able to stay here very long. Somewhere else, perhaps; but not here."

"It'll mean a lot of work."

"Look, there's Bigwig come up now and some of the others with him. Why not put it to them and see what they say?"

During silflay, however, Hazel mentioned Blackberry's idea to no one but Fiver. Later on, when most of the rabbits had finished feeding and were either playing in the grass or lying in the sunshine, he suggested that they might go across to the hanger— "Just to see what sort of a wood it is." Bigwig and Silver agreed at once and in the end no one stayed behind.

It was different from the meadow copses they had left: a narrow belt of trees, four or five hundred yards long but barely fifty wide; a kind of windbreak common on the downs. It consisted almost entirely of well-grown beeches. The great, smooth trunks stood motionless in their green shade, the branches spreading flat, one above another in crisp, light-dappled tiers. Between the trees the ground was open and offered hardly any cover. The rabbits were perplexed. They could not make out why the wood was so light and still and why they could see so far between the trees. The continuous, gentle rustling of the beech leaves was unlike the sounds to be heard in a copse of nut bushes, oak and silver birch.

Moving uncertainly in and out along the edge of the hanger, they came to the northeast corner. Here there was a bank from which they looked out over the empty stretches of grass beyond. Fiver, absurdly small beside the hulking Bigwig, turned to Hazel with an air of happy confidence.

"I'm sure Blackberry's right, Hazel," he said. "We ought to do our best to make some holes here. I'm ready to try, anyway."

The others were taken aback. Pipkin, however, readily joined Hazel at the foot of the bank and soon two or three more began scratching at the light soil. The digging was easy and although they often broke off to feed or merely to sit in the sun, before midday Hazel was out of sight and tunneling between the tree roots.

The hanger might have little or no undergrowth but at least the branches gave cover from the sky: and kestrels, they soon realized, were common in this solitude. Although kestrels seldom prey on anything bigger than a rat, they will sometimes attack young rabbits. No doubt this is why most grown rabbits will not remain under a hovering kestrel. Before long, Acorn spotted one as it flew up from the south. He stamped and bolted into the trees, followed by the other rabbits who were in the open. They had not long come out and resumed digging when they saw another—or perhaps the same one—hovering some way off, high over the very fields that they had crossed the previous morning. Hazel placed Buckthorn as a sentry while the day's haphazard work went on, and twice more during the afternoon the alarm was given. In the early evening they were disturbed by a horseman cantering along the ridge track that passed the north end of the wood. Otherwise they saw nothing larger than a pigeon all day.

After the horseman had turned south near the summit of

Watership and disappeared in the distance, Hazel returned to the edge of the wood and looked out northward toward the bright, still fields and the dim pylon line stalking away into the distance north of Kingsclere. The air was cooler and the sun was beginning once more to reach the north escarpment.

"I think we've done enough," he said, "for today, anyway. I should like to go down to the bottom of the hill and find some really good grass. This stuff's all right in its way but it's rather thin and dry. Does anyone feel like coming with me?"

Bigwig, Dandelion and Speedwell were ready, but the others preferred to graze their way back to the thorn trees and go underground with the sun. Bigwig and Hazel picked the line that offered most cover and, with the others following, set out on the four or five hundred yards to the foot of the hill. They met no trouble and were soon feeding in the grass at the edge of the wheatfield, the very picture of rabbits in an evening landscape. Hazel, tired though he was, did not forget to look for somewhere to bolt if there should be an alarm. He was lucky enough to come upon a short length of old, overgrown ditch, partly fallen in and so heavily overhung with cow parsley and nettles that it was almost as sheltered as a tunnel; and all four of them made sure that they could reach it quickly from the open.

"That'll be good enough at a pinch," said Bigwig, munching clover and sniffing at the fallen bloom from a wayfaring tree. "My goodness, we've learned a few things since we left the old warren, haven't we? More than we'd have learned in a lifetime back there. And digging! It'll be flying next, I suppose. Have you noticed that this soil's quite different from the soil in the old warren? It smells differently and it slides and falls quite differently, too."

"That reminds me," said Hazel. "I meant to ask you. There was one thing at that terrible warren of Cowslip's that I admired very much—the great burrow. I'd like to copy it. It's a wonderful idea to have a place underground where everybody can be together—talk and tell stories and so on. What do you think? Could it be done?"

Bigwig considered. "I know this," he said. "If you make a burrow too big the roof starts falling in. So if you want a place like that you'll need something to hold the roof up. What did Cowslip have?"

"Tree roots."

"Well, there are those where we're digging. But are they the right sort?"

"We'd better get Strawberry to tell us what he knows about the great burrow; but it may not be much. I'm sure he wasn't alive when it was dug."

"He may not be dead when it falls in either. That warren's tharn as an owl in daylight. He was wise to leave when he did."

Twilight had fallen over the cornfield, for although long red rays still lit the upper down, the sun had set below. The uneven shadow of the hedge had faded and disappeared. There was a cool smell of moisture and approaching darkness. A cockchafer droned past. The grasshoppers had fallen silent.

"Owls'll be out," said Bigwig. "Let's go up again."

At this moment, from out in the darkening field, there came the sound of a stamp on the ground. It was followed by another, closer to them, and they caught a glimpse of a white tail. They both immediately ran to the ditch. Now that they had to use it in earnest, they found it even narrower than they had thought. There was just room to turn round at the far end and as they did so Speedwell and Dandelion tumbled in behind them.

"What is it?" asked Hazel. "What did you hear?"

"There's something coming up the line of the hedge," replied Speedwell. "An animal. Making a lot of noise, too."

"Did you see it?"

"No, and I couldn't smell it either. It's downwind. But I heard it plainly enough."

"I heard it, too," said Dandelion. "Something fairly big—as big as a rabbit, anyway—moving clumsily but trying to keep concealed, or so it seemed to me."

"Homba?"

"No, that we *should* have smelled," said Bigwig, "wind or no wind. From what you say, it sounds like a cat. I hope it's not a stoat. *Hoi, hoi, u embleer hrair!* What a nuisance! We'd better sit tight for a bit. But get ready to bolt if it spots us."

They waited. Soon it grew dark. Only the faintest light came through the tangled summer growth above them. The far end of the ditch was so much overgrown that they could not see out of it, but the place where they had come in showed as a patch of sky—an arc of very dark blue. As the time passed, a star crept out from among the overhanging grasses. It seemed to pulsate in a rhythm as faint and uneven as that of the wind. At length Hazel turned his eyes away from watching it.

"Well, we can snatch some sleep here," he said. "The night's not cold. Whatever it was you heard, we'd better not risk going out."

"Listen," said Dandelion. "What's that?"

For a moment Hazel could hear nothing. Then he caught a distant but clear sound—a kind of wailing or crying, wavering and intermittent. Although it did not sound like any sort of hunting call, it was so unnatural that it filled him with fear. As he listened, it ceased.

"What in Frith's name makes a noise like that?" said Bigwig, his great fur cap hackling between his ears.

"A cat?" said Speedwell, wide-eyed.

"That's no cat!" said Bigwig, his lips drawn back in a stiffened, unnatural grimace. "That's no cat! Don't you know what it is? Your mother—" He broke off. Then he said, very low, "Your mother told you, didn't she?"

"No!" cried Dandelion. "No! It's some bird—some rat—wounded—"

Bigwig stood up. His back was arched and his head nodded on his stiffened neck.

"The Black Rabbit of Inlé," he whispered. "What else—in a place like this?"

"Don't talk like that!" said Hazel. He could feel himself trembling, and braced his legs against the sides of the narrow cut.

Suddenly the noise sounded again, nearer: and now there could be no mistake. What they heard was the voice of a rabbit, but changed out of all recognition. It might have come from the cold spaces of the dark sky outside, so unearthly and desolate was the sound. At first there was only a wailing. Then, distinct and beyond mistaking, they heard—they all heard—words.

"Zorn! Zorn!" * cried the dreadful, squealing voice. "All dead! O zorn!"

Dandelion whimpered. Bigwig was scuffling into the ground.

"Be quiet!" said Hazel. "And stop kicking that earth over me! I want to listen."

* *Zorn* means "finished" or "destroyed," in the sense of some terrible catastrophe.

At that moment, quite distinctly, the voice cried, "Thlayli! O Thlayli!"

At this, all four rabbits felt the trance of utter panic. They grew rigid. Then Bigwig, his eyes set in a fixed, glazed stare, began to jerk his way up the ditch toward the opening. "You have to go," he muttered, so thickly that Hazel could hardly catch the words. "You have to go when he calls you."

Hazel felt so much frightened that he could no longer collect his wits. As on the riverbank, his surroundings became unreal and dream-like. Who—or what—was calling Bigwig by name? How could any living creature in this place know his name? Only one idea remained to him—Bigwig must be prevented from going out, for he was helpless. He scrambled past him, pressing him against the side of the ditch.

"Stay where you are," he said, panting. "Whatever sort of rabbit it is, I'm going to see for myself." Then, his legs almost giving way beneath him, he pulled himself out into the open.

For a few moments he could see little or nothing; but the smells of dew and elder bloom were unchanged and his nose brushed against cool grass blades. He sat up and looked about him. There was no creature nearby.

"Who's there?" he said.

There was silence, and he was about to speak again when the voice replied, "Zorn! O zorn!"

It came from the hedge along the side of the field. Hazel turned toward the sound and in a few moments made out, under a clump of hemlock, the hunched shape of a rabbit. He approached it and said, "Who are you?" but there was no reply. As he hesitated, he heard a movement behind him.

"I'm here, Hazel," said Dandelion, in a kind of choking gasp.

Together they went closer. The figure did not move as they came up. In the faint starlight they both saw a rabbit as real as themselves: a rabbit in the last stages of exhaustion, its back legs trailing behind its flattened rump as though paralyzed: a rabbit that stared, white-eyed, from one side to the other, seeing nothing, yet finding no respite from its fear, and then fell to licking wretchedly at one ripped and bloody ear that drooped across its face: a rabbit that suddenly cried and wailed as though entreating the Thousand to come from every quarter to rid it of a misery too terrible to be borne.

It was Captain Holly of the Sandleford Owsla.

20

A Honeycomb and a Mouse

His face was that of one who has undergone a long journey.
                                          The Epic of Gilgamesh

In the Sandleford warren, Holly had been a rabbit of consequence. He was greatly relied upon by the Threarah and had more than once carried out difficult orders with a good deal of courage. During the early spring, when a fox had moved into a neighboring copse, Holly, with two or three volunteers, had kept it steadily under observation for several days and reported all its movements, until one evening it left as suddenly as it had come. Although he had decided on his own initiative to arrest Bigwig, he had not the reputation of being vindictive. He was, rather, a stander of no nonsense who knew when duty was done and did it himself. Sound, unassuming, conscientious, a bit lacking in the rabbit sense of mischief, he was something of the born second-in-command. There could have been no question of trying to persuade him to leave the warren with Hazel and Fiver. To find him under Watership Down at all, therefore, was astonishing enough. But to find him in such a condition was all but incredible.

In the first moments after they had recognized the poor creature under the hemlock, Hazel and Dandelion felt completely stupefied, as though they had come upon a squirrel underground or a stream that flowed uphill. They could not trust their senses. The voice in the dark had proved not to be supernatural, but the reality was frightening enough. How could Captain Holly be here, at the foot of the down? And what could have reduced him—of all rabbits—to this state?

Hazel pulled himself together. Whatever the explanation might be, the immediate need was to take first things first. They were in open country, at night, away from any refuge but an overgrown ditch, with a rabbit who smelled of blood, was crying uncontrollably and looked as though he could not move. There might very well be a stoat on his trail at this moment. If they were going to help him they had better be quick.

"Go and tell Bigwig who it is," he said to Dandelion, "and come back with him. Send Speedwell up the hill to the others and tell him to make it clear that no one is to come down. They couldn't help and it would only add to the risk."

Dandelion had no sooner gone than Hazel became aware that something else was moving in the hedge. But he had no time to wonder what it might be, for almost immediately another rabbit appeared and limped to where Holly was lying.

"You must help us if you can," he said to Hazel. "We've had a very bad time and my master's ill. Can we get underground here?"

Hazel recognized him as one of the rabbits who had come to arrest Bigwig, but he did not know his name.

"Why did you stay in the hedge and leave him to crawl about in the open?" he asked.

"I ran away when I heard you coming," replied the other rabbit. "I couldn't get the captain to move. I thought you were elil and there was no point in staying to be killed. I don't think I could fight a field mouse."

"Do you know me?" said Hazel. But before the other could answer, Dandelion and Bigwig came out of the darkness. Bigwig stared at Holly for a moment and then crouched before him and touched noses.

"Holly, this is Thlayli," he said. "You were calling me."

Holly did not answer, but only stared fixedly back at him. Bigwig looked up. "Who's that who came with him?" he said. "Oh, it's you, Bluebell. How many more of you?"

"No more," said Bluebell. He was about to go on when Holly spoke.

"Thlayli," he said. "So we *have* found you."

He sat up with difficulty and looked round at them.

"You're Hazel, aren't you?" he asked. "And that's—oh, I should know, but I'm in very poor shape, I'm afraid."

"It's Dandelion," said Hazel. "Listen—I can see that you're exhausted, but we can't stay here. We're in danger. Can you come with us to our holes?"

"Captain," said Bluebell, "do you know what the first blade of grass said to the second blade of grass?"

Hazel looked at him sharply, but Holly replied, "Well?"

"It said, 'Look, there's a rabbit! We're in danger!' "

"This is no time—" began Hazel.

"Don't silence him," said Holly. "We wouldn't be here at all without his blue tit's chatter. Yes, I can go now. Is it far?"

"Not too far," said Hazel, thinking it all too likely that Holly would never get there.

It took a long time to climb the hill. Hazel made them separate, himself remaining with Holly and Bluebell while Bigwig and Dandelion went out to either side. Holly was forced to stop several times and Hazel, full of fear, had hard work to suppress his impatience. Only when the moon began to rise—the edge of its great disc growing brighter and brighter on the skyline below and behind them—did he at last beg Holly to hurry. As he spoke he saw, in the white light, Pipkin coming down to meet them.

"What are you doing?" he said sternly. "I told Speedwell no one was to come down."

"It isn't Speedwell's fault," said Pipkin. "You stood by me at the river, so I thought I'd come and look for you, Hazel. Anyway, the holes are just here. Is it really Captain Holly you've found?"

Bigwig and Dandelion approached.

"I'll tell you what," said Bigwig. "These two will need to rest for a good long time. Suppose Pipkin here and Dandelion take them to an empty burrow and stay with them as long as they want? The rest of us had better keep away until they feel better."

"Yes, that's best," said Hazel. "I'll go up with you now."

They ran the short distance to the thorn trees. All the other rabbits were above ground, waiting and whispering together.

"Shut up," said Bigwig, before anyone had asked a question. "Yes, it is Holly, and Bluebell is with him—no one else. They're in a bad way and they're not to be troubled. We'll leave this hole empty for them. Now I'm going underground myself and so will you if you've got any sense."

But before he went, Bigwig turned to Hazel and said, "You got yourself out of that ditch down there instead of me, didn't you, Hazel? I shan't forget that."

Hazel remembered Buckthorn's leg and took him down with him. Speedwell and Silver followed them.

"I say, what's happened, Hazel?" asked Silver. "It must be something very bad. Holly would never leave the Threarah."

"I don't know," replied Hazel, "and neither does anyone else yet. We'll have to wait until tomorrow. Holly may stop running, but I don't think Bluebell will. Now let me alone to do this leg of Buckthorn's."

The wound was a great deal better and soon Hazel fell asleep.

The next day was as hot and cloudless as the last. Neither Pipkin nor Dandelion was at morning silflay; and Hazel relentlessly took the others up to the beech hanger to go on with the digging. He questioned Strawberry about the great burrow and learned that its ceiling, as well as being vaulted with a tangle of fibers, was strengthened by roots going vertically down into the floor. He remarked that he had not noticed these.

"There aren't many, but they're important," said Strawberry. "They take a lot of the load. If it weren't for those roots the ceiling would fall after heavy rain. On stormy nights you could sense the extra weight in the earth above, but there was no danger."

Hazel and Bigwig went underground with him. The beginnings of the new warren had been hollowed out among the roots of one of the beech trees. It was still no more than a small, irregular cave with one entrance. They set to work to enlarge it, digging between the roots and tunneling upward to make a second run that would emerge inside the wood. After a time Strawberry stopped digging and began moving about between the roots, sniffing, biting and scuffling in the soil with his front paws. Hazel supposed that he was tired and pretending to be busy while he had a rest, but at length he came back to them and said that he had some suggestions.

"It's this way," he explained. "There isn't a big spread of fine roots above here. That was a lucky chance in the great burrow and I don't think you can expect to find it again. But, all the same, we can do pretty well with what we've got."

"And what *have* we got?" asked Blackberry, who had come down the run while he was talking.

"Well, we've got several thick roots that go straight down—more than there were in the great burrow. The best thing will be to dig round them and leave them. They shouldn't be gnawed through and taken out. We shall need them if we're going to have a hall of any size."

"Then our hall will be full of these thick, vertical roots?" asked Hazel. He felt disappointed.

"Yes, it will," said Strawberry, "but I can't see that it's going to be any the worse for that. We can go in and out among them and they won't hinder anyone who's talking or telling a story. They'll make the place warmer and they'll help to conduct sound from above, which might be useful some time or other."

The excavation of the hall (which came to be known among them as the Honeycomb) turned out to be something of a triumph for Strawberry. Hazel contented himself with organizing the diggers and left it to Strawberry to say what was actually to be done. The work went on in shifts and the rabbits took it in turns to feed, play and lie in the sun above ground. Throughout the day the solitude remained unbroken by noise, men, tractors or even cattle, and they began to feel still more deeply what they owed to Fiver's insight. By the late afternoon the big burrow was beginning to take shape. At the north end, the beech roots formed a kind of irregular colonnade. This gave way to a more open central space: and beyond, where there were no supporting roots, Strawberry left blocks of the earth untouched, so that the south end consisted of three or four separate bays. These narrowed into low-roofed runs that led away into sleeping burrows.

Hazel, much better pleased now that he could see for himself how the business was going to turn out, was sitting with Silver in the mouth of the run when suddenly there was a stamping of "Hawk! Hawk!" and a dash for cover by the rabbits outside. Hazel, safe where he was, remained looking out past the shadow of the wood to the open, sunlit grass beyond. The kestrel sailed into view and took up station, the black-edged flange of its tail bent down and its pointed wings beating rapidly as it searched the down below.

"But do you think it *would* attack us?" asked Hazel, watching it drop lower and recommence its poised fluttering. "Surely it's too small?"

"You're probably right," replied Silver. "All the same, would you care to go out there and start feeding?"

"I'd like to try standing up to some of these elil," said Bigwig, who had come up the run behind them. "We're afraid of too many. But a bird from the air would be awkward, especially if it came fast. It might get the better of even a big rabbit if it took him by surprise."

"See the mouse?" said Silver suddenly. "There, look. Poor little beast."

They could all see the field mouse, which was exposed in a patch of smooth grass. It had evidently strayed too far from its hole and now could not tell what to do. The kestrel's shadow had not passed over it, but the rabbits' sudden disappearance had made it uneasy and it was pressed to the ground, looking uncertainly this way and that. The kestrel had not yet seen it, but could hardly fail to do so as soon as it moved.

"Any moment now," said Bigwig callously.

On an impulse, Hazel hopped down the bank and went a little way into the open grass. Mice do not speak Lapine, but there is a very simple, limited *lingua franca* of the hedgerow and woodland. Hazel used it now.

"Run," he said. "Here; quick."

The mouse looked at him, but did not move. Hazel spoke again and the mouse began suddenly to run toward him as the kestrel turned and slid sideways and downward. Hazel hastened back to the hole. Looking out, he saw the mouse following him. When it had almost reached the foot of the bank it scuttered over a fallen twig with two or three green leaves. The twig turned, one of the leaves caught the sunlight slanting through the trees and Hazel saw it flash for an instant. Immediately the kestrel came lower in an oblique glide, closed its wings and dropped.

Before Hazel could spring back from the mouth of the hole, the mouse had dashed between his front paws and was pressed to the ground between his back legs. At the same moment the kestrel, all beak and talons, hit the loose earth immediately outside like a missile thrown from the tree above. It scuffled savagely and for an instant the three rabbits saw its round, dark eyes looking straight down the run. Then it was gone. The speed and force of the pounce, not a length away, were terrifying and Hazel leaped backward, knocking Silver off his balance. They picked themselves up in silence.

"Like to try standing up to that one?" said Silver, looking round at Bigwig. "Let me know when. I'll come and watch."

"Hazel," said Bigwig, "I know you're not stupid, but what did we get out of that? Are you going in for protecting every mole and shrew that can't get underground?"

The mouse had not moved. It was still crouching a little inside the run, on a level with their heads and outlined against the light. Hazel could see it watching him.

"Perhaps hawk not gone," he said. "You stay now. Go later."

Bigwig was about to speak again when Dandelion appeared in the mouth of the hole. He looked at the mouse, pushed it gently aside and came down the run.

"Hazel," he said, "I thought I ought to come and tell you about Holly. He's much better this evening, but he had a very bad night and so did we. Every time he seemed to be going to sleep, he kept starting up and crying. I thought he was going out of his mind. Pipkin kept talking to him—he was first-rate—and he seems to set a lot of store by Bluebell. Bluebell kept on making jokes. He was worn out before the morning and so were the lot of us—we've been sleeping all day. Holly's been more or less himself since he woke up this afternoon, and he's been up to silflay. He asked where you and the others would be tonight and, as I didn't know, I came to ask."

"Is he fit to talk to us, then?" asked Bigwig.

"I think so. It would be the best thing for him, if I'm any judge: and if he was with all of us together he'd be less likely to have another bad night."

"Well, where *are* we going to sleep?" said Silver.

Hazel considered. The Honeycomb was still rough-dug and half finished, but it would probably be as comfortable as the holes under the thorn trees. Besides, if it proved otherwise, they would have all the more inducement to improve it. To know that they were actually making use of their day's hard work would please everybody and they were likely to prefer this to a third night in the chalk holes.

"I should think here," he said. "But we'll see how the others feel."

"What's this mouse doing in here?" asked Dandelion.

Hazel explained. Dandelion was as puzzled as Bigwig had been.

"Well, I'll admit I hadn't any particular idea when I went out to help it," said Hazel. "I have now, though, and I'll explain later what it is. But, first of all, Bigwig and I ought to go and talk to Holly. And, Dandelion, you go and tell the rest what you told me, will you, and see what they want to do tonight?"

They found Holly with Bluebell and Pipkin, on the turf by the anthill where Dandelion had first looked over the down. Holly was sniffing at a purple orchis. The head of mauve blooms rocked gently on its stem as he pushed his nose against it.

"Don't frighten it, master," said Bluebell. "It might fly away. After all, it's got a lot of spots to choose from. Look at them all over the leaves."

"Oh, get along with you, Bluebell," answered Holly good-humoredly. "We need to learn about the ground here. Half the plants are strange to me. This isn't one to eat, but at least there's plenty of burnet and that's always good." A fly settled on his wounded ear and he winced and shook his head.

Hazel was glad to see that Holly was evidently in better spirits. He began to say that he hoped he felt well enough to join the others, but Holly soon interrupted him with questions.

"Are there many of you?" he asked.

"Hrair," said Bigwig.

"All that left the warren with you?"

"Every one," replied Hazel proudly.

"No one hurt?"

"Oh, several have been hurt, one way and another."

"Never a dull moment, really," said Bigwig.

"Who's this coming? I don't know him."

Strawberry came running down from the hanger and as he joined them began to make the same curious dancing gesture of head and forepaws which they had first seen in the rainy meadow before they entered the great burrow. He checked himself in some confusion and, to forestall Bigwig's rebuke, spoke to Hazel at once.

"Hazel-rah," he said (Holly looked startled, but said nothing), "everyone wants to stay in the new warren tonight: and they're all hoping that Captain Holly will feel able to tell them what's happened and how he came here."

"Well, naturally, we all want to know," said Hazel to Holly.

"This is Strawberry. He joined us on our journey and we've been glad to have him. But do you think you can manage it?"

"I can manage it," said Holly. "But I must warn you that it will strike the frost into the heart of every rabbit that hears it."

He himself looked so sad and dark as he spoke that no one made any reply, and after a few moments all six rabbits made their way up the slope in silence. When they reached the corner of the wood, they found the others feeding or basking in the evening sun on the north side of the beech trees. After a glance round among them Holly went up to Silver, who was feeding with Fiver in a patch of yellow trefoil.

"I'm glad to see you here, Silver," he said. "I hear you've had a rough time."

"It hasn't been easy," answered Silver. "Hazel's done wonders and we owe a lot to Fiver here as well."

"I've heard of you," said Holly, turning to Fiver. "You're the rabbit who saw it all coming. You talked to the Threarah, didn't you?"

"He talked to me," said Fiver.

"If only he'd listened to you! Well, it can't be changed now, till acorns grow on thistles. Silver, there's something I want to say and I can say it more easily to you than to Hazel or Bigwig. I'm not out to make any trouble here—trouble for Hazel, I mean. He's your Chief Rabbit now, that's plain. I hardly know him, but he must be good or you'd all be dead; and this is no time to be squabbling. If any of the other rabbits are wondering whether I might want to alter things, will you let them know that I shan't?"

"Yes, I will," said Silver.

Bigwig came up. "I know it's not owl time yet," he said, "but everyone's so eager to hear you, Holly, that they want to go underground at once. Will that suit you?"

"Underground?" replied Holly. "But how can you all hear me underground? I was expecting to talk here."

"Come and see," said Bigwig.

Holly and Bluebell were impressed by the Honeycomb.

"This is something quite new," said Holly. "What keeps the roof up?"

"It doesn't need to be kept up," said Bluebell. "It's right up the hill already."

"An idea we found on the way," said Bigwig.

"Lying in a field," said Bluebell. "It's all right, master, I'll be quiet while you're speaking."

"Yes, you must," said Holly. "Soon no one will want jokes."

Almost all the rabbits had followed them down. The Honeycomb, though big enough for everybody, was not so airy as the great burrow and on this June evening it seemed somewhat close.

"We can easily make it cooler, you know," said Strawberry to Hazel. "In the great burrow they used to open tunnels for the summer and close them for the winter. We can dig another run on the evening side tomorrow and pick up the breeze."

Hazel was just going to ask Holly to begin when Speedwell came down the eastern run. "Hazel," he said, "your—er—visitor—your mouse. He wants to speak to you."

"Oh, I'd forgotten him," said Hazel. "Where is he?"

"Up the run."

Hazel went up. The mouse was waiting at the top.

"You go now?" said Hazel. "You think safe?"

"Go now," said the mouse. "No wait owl. But a what I like a say. You 'elp a mouse. One time a mouse 'elp a you. You want 'im 'e come."

"Frith in a pond!" muttered Bigwig, further down the run. "And so will all his brothers and sisters. I dare say the place'll be crawling. Why don't you ask them to dig us a burrow or two, Hazel?"

Hazel watched the mouse make off into the long grass. Then he returned to the Honeycomb and settled down near Holly, who had just begun to speak.

"For El-ahrairah to Cry"

Love the animals. God has given them the rudiments of thought and joy untroubled. Don't trouble it, don't harass them, don't deprive them of their happiness, don't work against God's intent.

Dostoevsky, *The Brothers Karamazov*

Acts of injustice done
Between the setting and the rising sun
In history lie like bones, each one.

W. H. Auden, *The Ascent of F.6*

"The night you left the warren, the Owsla were turned out to look for you. How long ago it seems now! We followed your scent down to the brook, but when we told the Threarah that you appeared to have set off downstream, he said there was no point in risking lives by following you. If you were gone, you were gone. But anyone who came back was to be arrested. So then I called off the search.

"Nothing unusual happened the next day. There was a certain amount of talk about Fiver and the rabbits who'd gone with him. Everyone knew that Fiver had said that something bad was going to happen and all sorts of rumors started. A lot of rabbits said there was nothing in it, but some thought that Fiver might have foreseen men with guns and ferrets. That was the worst thing anyone could think of—that or the white blindness.

"Willow and I talked things over with the Threarah. 'These rabbits,' he said, 'who claim to have the second sight—I've known one or two in my time. But it's not usually advisable to take much notice of them. For one thing, many are just plain mischievous. A weak rabbit who can't hope to get far by fighting sometimes tries to make himself important by other means and prophecy is a favorite. The curious thing is that when he turns out to be wrong, his friends seldom seem to notice, as long as he puts on a good act and keeps talking. But then again, you may get a rabbit who really has this odd power, for it does exist. He foretells a flood perhaps, or ferrets and guns. All right; so a certain number of rabbits will stop running. What's the alternative? To evacuate a warren is a tremendous business. Some refuse to go. The Chief Rabbit leaves with as many as will come. His authority is likely to be put to the most severe test and if he loses it he won't get it back in a hurry. At the best, you've got a big bunch of hlessil trailing round in the open, probably with does and kittens tacked on. Elil appear in hordes. The remedy's worse than the disease. Almost always, it's better for the warren as a whole if rabbits sit tight and do their best to dodge their dangers underground.' "

"Of course, I never sat down and thought," said Fiver. "It would take the Threarah to think all that out. I simply had the screaming horrors. Great golden Frith, I hope I never have them like that again! I shall never forget it—that and the night I spent under the yew tree. There's terrible evil in the world."

"It comes from men," said Holly. "All other elil do what they have to do and Frith moves them as he moves us. They live on the earth and they need food. Men will never rest till they've spoiled the earth and destroyed the animals. But I'd better go on with this tale of mine.

"The next day in the afternoon, it began to rain.

("Those scrapes we dug in the bank," whispered Buckthorn to Dandelion.)

"Everyone was underground, just chewing pellets or sleeping. I'd gone up for a few minutes to pass hraka. I was on the edge of the wood, quite near the ditch, when I saw some men come through the gate at the top of the opposite slope, up by that board thing. I don't know how many there were—three or four, I suppose. They had long black legs and they were burning white sticks in their mouths. They didn't seem to be going anywhere. They began walking slowly about in the rain, looking at the hedges and the brook. After a time they crossed the brook and came clumping up toward the warren. Whenever they came to a rabbit hole, one of them would prod at it; and they kept talking all the time. I remember the smell of the elder bloom in the rain and the smell of the white sticks. Later, when they came closer, I slipped underground again. I could hear them for some time, thumping about and talking. I kept thinking, 'Well, they've got no guns and no ferrets.' But somehow I didn't like it."

"What did the Threarah say?" asked Silver.

"I've no idea. I didn't ask him and neither did anyone else, as far as I know. I went to sleep and when I woke there was no sound up above. It was evening and I decided to silflay. The rain had settled in, but I pottered round and fed for a while all the same. I couldn't see that anything was altered, except that here and there the mouth of a hole had been poked in.

"The next morning was clear and fine. Everyone was out for silflay as usual. I remember Nightshade told the Threarah that he ought to be careful not to tire himself now that he was getting on in years: and the Threarah said he'd show him who was getting on in years and cuffed him and pushed him down the bank. It was all quite good-humored, you know, but he did it just to show Nightshade that the Chief Rabbit was still a match for him. I was going out for lettuces that morning and for some reason or other I'd decided to go alone."

"Three's the usual number for a lettuce party," said Bigwig.

"Yes, I know three used to be the usual number, but there was some special reason why I went alone that day. Oh, yes, I remember—I wanted to see if there were any early carrots. I thought they might just be ready, and I reckoned that if I was going hunting about in a strange part of the garden I'd be better off by myself. I was out most of the morning and it can't have been long before ni-Frith when I came back through the wood. I was coming down Silent Bank—I know most rabbits preferred the Green Loose, but I nearly always went by Silent Bank. I'd got into the open part of the wood, where it comes down toward the old fence, when I noticed a hrududu in the lane at the top of the opposite slope. It was standing at the gate by the board and a lot of men were getting out. There was a boy with them and he had a gun. They took down some big, long things—I don't know how to describe them to you—they were made of the same sort of stuff as a hrududu and they must have been heavy, because it took two men to carry one of them. The men carried these things into the field and the few rabbits who were above ground went down. I didn't. I'd seen the gun and I thought they were probably going to use ferrets and perhaps nets. So I stayed where I was and watched. I thought, 'As soon as I'm sure what they're up to, I'll go and warn the Threarah.'

"There was more talking and more white sticks. Men never hurry, do they? Then one of them got a spade and began filling in the mouths of all the holes he could find. Every hole he came to, he cut out the turf above and pushed it into the hole. That puzzled me, because with ferrets they want to drive the rabbits out. But I was expecting that they'd leave a few holes open and net them: although that would have been a foolish way to ferret, because a rabbit that went up a blocked run would be killed underground and then the man wouldn't get his ferret back very easily, you know."

"Don't make it too grim, Holly," said Hazel, for Pipkin was shuddering at the thought of the blocked run and the pursuing ferret.

"Too grim?" replied Holly bitterly. "I've hardly started yet. Would anyone like to go away?" No one moved and after a few moments he continued.

"Then another of the men fetched some long, thin, bending things. I haven't got words for all these men things, but they were something like lengths of very thick bramble. Each of the men took one and put it on one of the heavy things. There was a kind of hissing noise and—and—well, I know you must find this difficult to understand, but the air began to turn bad. For some reason I got a strong scent of this stuff that came out of the bramble things, even though I was some way off: and I couldn't see or think. I seemed to be falling. I tried to jump up and run, but I didn't know where I was and I found I'd run down to the edge of the wood, toward the men. I stopped just in time. I was bewildered and I'd lost all idea of warning the Threarah. After that I just sat where I was.

"The men put a bramble into each hole they'd left open and after that nothing happened for a little while. And then I saw Scabious— you remember Scabious? He came out of a hole along the hedge—one they hadn't noticed. I could see at once that he'd smelled this stuff. He didn't know what he was doing. The men didn't see him for a few moments and then one of them stuck out his arm to show where he was and the boy shot him. He didn't kill him—Scabious began to scream—and one of the men went over and picked him up and hit him. I really believe he may not have suffered very much, because the bad air had turned him silly: but I wish I hadn't seen it. After that, the man stopped up the hole that Scabious had come out of.

"By this time the poisoned air must have been spreading through the runs and burrows underground. I can imagine what it must have been like—"

"You can't," said Bluebell. Holly stopped and after a pause Bluebell went on.

"I heard the commotion beginning before I smelled the stuff myself. The does seemed to get it first and some of them began trying to get out. But the ones who had litters wouldn't leave the kittens and they were attacking any rabbit who came near them. They wanted to fight—to protect the kittens, you know. Very soon the runs were crammed with rabbits clawing and clambering over each other. They went up the runs they were accustomed to use and found them blocked. Some managed to turn round, but they couldn't get back because of the rabbits coming up. And then the runs began to be blocked lower down with dead rabbits and the live rabbits tore them to pieces.

"I shall never know how I got away with what I did. It was a chance in a thousand. I was in a burrow near one of the holes that the men were using. They made a lot of noise putting the bramble thing in and I've got an idea it wasn't working properly. As soon as I picked up the smell of the stuff I jumped out of the burrow, but I was still fairly clear-headed. I came up the run just as the men were taking the bramble out again. They were all looking at it and talking and they didn't see me. I turned round, actually in the mouth of the hole, and went down again.

"Do you remember the Slack Run? I suppose hardly a rabbit went down there in our lifetime—it was so very deep and it didn't lead anywhere in particular. No one knows even who made it. Frith must have guided me, for I went straight down into the Slack Run and began creeping along it. I was actually digging at times. It was all loose earth and fallen stones. There were all sorts of forgotten shafts and drops that led in from above, and down those were coming the most terrible sounds—cries for help, kittens squealing for their mothers, Owsla trying to give orders, rabbits cursing and fighting each other. Once a rabbit came tumbling down one of the shafts and his claws just scratched me, like a horse-chestnut bur falling in autumn. It was Celandine and he was dead. I had to tear at him before I could get over him—the place was so low and narrow—and then I went on. I could smell the bad air, but I was so deep down that I must have been beyond the worst of it.

"Suddenly I found there was another rabbit with me. He was the only one I met in the whole length of the Slack Run. It was Pimpernel and I could tell at once that he was in a bad way. He was spluttering and gasping, but he was able to keep going. He asked if I was all right, but all I said was, 'Where do we get out?' 'I can show you that,' he said, 'if you can help me along.' So I followed him and every time he stopped—he kept forgetting where we were—I shoved him hard. I even bit him once. I was terrified that he was going to die and block the run. At last we began to come up and I could smell fresh air. We found we'd got into one of those runs that led out into the wood."

"The men had done their work badly," resumed Holly. "Either they didn't know about the wood holes or they couldn't be bothered to come and block them. Almost every rabbit that came up in the field was shot, but I saw two get away. One was Nose-in-the-Air, but I don't remember who the other was. The noise was very frightening and I would have run myself, but I kept waiting to see whether the Threarah would come. After a while I began to realize that there were a few other rabbits in the wood. Pine Needles was there, I remember, and Butterbur and Ash. I got hold of all I could and told them to sit tight under cover.

"After a long time the men finished. They took the bramble things out of the holes and the boy put the bodies on a stick—"

Holly stopped and pressed his nose under Bigwig's flank.

"Well, never mind about that bit," said Hazel in a steady voice. "Tell us how you came away."

"Before that happened," said Holly, "a great hrududu came into the field from the lane. It wasn't the one the men came in. It was very noisy and it was yellow—as yellow as charlock: and in front there was a great silver, shining thing that it held in its huge front paws. I don't know how to describe it to you. It looked like Inlé, but it was broad and not so bright. And this thing—how can I tell you—it tore the field to bits. It destroyed the field."

He stopped again.

"Captain," said Silver, "we all know you've seen things bad beyond telling. But surely that's not quite what you mean?"

"Upon my life," said Holly, trembling, "it buried itself in the ground and pushed great masses of earth in front of it until the field was destroyed. The whole place became like a cattle wade in winter and you could no longer tell where any part of the field had been, between the wood and the brook. Earth and roots and grass and bushes it pushed before it and—and other things as well, from underground.

"After a long time I went back through the wood. I'd forgotten any idea of collecting other rabbits, but there were three who joined me all the same—Bluebell here and Pimpernel and young Toadflax. Toadflax was the only member of the Owsla I'd seen and I asked him about the Threarah, but he couldn't talk any kind of sense. I never found out what happened to the Threarah. I hope he died quickly.

"Pimpernel was light-headed—chattering nonsense—and Bluebell and I weren't much better. For some reason all I could think of was Bigwig. I remembered how I'd gone to arrest him—to kill him, really—and I felt I had to find him and tell him I'd been wrong: and this idea was all the sense I had left. The four of us went wandering away and we must have gone almost in a half-circle, because after a long time we came to the brook, below what had been our field. We followed it down into a big wood; and that night, while we were still in the wood, Toadflax died. He was clear-headed for a short time before and I remember something he said. Bluebell had been saying that he knew the men hated us for raiding their crops and gardens, and Toadflax answered, 'That wasn't why they destroyed the warren. It was just because we were in their way. They killed us to suit themselves.' Soon after that he went to sleep, and a little later, when we were alarmed by some noise or other, we tried to wake him and realized he was dead.

"We left him lying where he was and went on until we reached the river. I needn't describe it because I know you were all there. It was morning by this time. We thought you might be somewhere near and we began to go along the bank, upstream, looking for you. It wasn't long before we found the place where you must have crossed. There were tracks—a great many—in the sand under a steep bank, and hraka about three days old. The tracks didn't go upstream or downstream, so I knew you must have gone over. I swam across and found more tracks on the other side: so then the others came over, too. The river was high. I suppose you must have had it easier, before all the rain.

"I didn't like the fields on the other side of the river. There was a man with a gun who kept walking everywhere. I took the other two on, across a road, and soon we came to a bad place—all heather and soft black earth. We had a hard time there, but again I came upon hraka about three days old and no sign of holes or rabbits, so I thought there was a chance that they were yours. Bluebell was all right, but Pimpernel was feverish and I was afraid he was going to die, too.

"Then we had a bit of luck—or so we thought at the time. That night we fell in with a hlessi on the edge of the heather—an old, tough rabbit with his nose all scratched and scarred—and he told us that there was a warren not far off and showed us which way to go. We came to woods and fields again, but we were so much exhausted that we couldn't start looking for the warren. We crept into a ditch and I hadn't the heart to tell one of the others to keep awake. I tried to keep awake myself, but I couldn't."

"When was this?" asked Hazel.

"The day before yesterday," said Holly, "early in the morning. When I woke it was still some time before ni-Frith. Everything was quiet and all I could smell was rabbit, but I felt at once that something was wrong. I woke Bluebell and I was just going to wake Pimpernel when I realized that there was a whole bunch of rabbits all round us. They were great, big fellows and they had a very odd smell. It was like—well, like—"

"We know what it was like," said Fiver.

"I thought you probably did. Then one of them said, 'My name's Cowslip. Who are you and what are you doing here?' I didn't like the way he spoke, but I couldn't see that they had any reason to wish us harm, so I told him that we'd had a bad time and come a long way and that we were looking for some rabbits from our warren—Hazel, Fiver and Bigwig. As soon as I said those names this rabbit turned to the others and cried, 'I knew it! Tear them to pieces!' And they all set on us. One of them got me by the ear and ripped it up before Bluebell could pull him off. We were fighting the lot of them. I was so much taken by surprise that I couldn't do a great deal at first. But the funny thing was that although they were so big and yelling for our blood, they couldn't fight at all: they obviously didn't know the first thing about fighting. Bluebell knocked down a couple twice his size, and although my ear was pouring with blood I was never really in danger. All the same, they were too many for us, and we had to run. Bluebell and I had just got clear of the ditch when we realized that Pimpernel was still there. He was ill, as I told you, and he didn't wake in time. So after all he'd been through, poor Pimpernel was killed by rabbits. What do you think of that?"

"I think it was a damned shame," said Strawberry, before anyone else could speak.

"We were running down the fields, beside a little stream," Holly went on. "Some of these rabbits were still chasing us and suddenly I thought, 'Well, I'll have one of them anyway.' I didn't care for the idea of doing nothing more than just run away to save our skins—not after Pimpernel. I saw that this Cowslip was ahead of the others and out on his own, so I let him catch me up and then I suddenly turned and went for him. I had him down and I was just going to rip him up when he squealed out, 'I can tell you where your friends have gone.' 'Hurry up, then,' I said, with my back legs braced in his stomach. 'They've gone to the hills,' he panted. 'The high hills you can see away over there. They went yesterday morning.' I pretended not to believe him and acted as though I was going to kill him. But he didn't alter his story, so I scratched him and let him go and away we came. It was clear weather and we could see the hills plainly enough.

"After that we had the worst time of all. If it hadn't been for Bluebell's jokes and chatter we'd have stopped running for certain."

"Hraka one end, jokes the other," said Bluebell. "I used to roll a joke along the ground and we both followed it. That was how we kept going."

"I can't really tell you much about the rest of it," said Holly. "My ear was terribly painful and all the time I kept thinking that Pimpernel's death was my fault. If I hadn't gone to sleep he wouldn't have died. Once we tried to sleep again, but my dreams were more than I could bear. I was out of my mind, really. I had only this one idea—to find Bigwig and tell him that he'd been right to leave the warren.

"At last we reached the hills, just at nightfall of the next day. We were past caring—we came over the flat, open land at owl time. I don't know what I'd been expecting. You know how you let yourself think that everything will be all right if you can only get to a certain place or do a certain thing. But when you get there you find it's not that simple. I suppose I'd had some sort of foolish notion that Bigwig would be waiting to meet us. We found the hills were enormous—bigger than anything we'd ever seen. No woods, no cover, no rabbits: and night setting in. And then everything seemed to go to pieces. I saw Scabious, as plain as grass—and heard him crying, too: and I saw the Threarah and Toadflax and Pimpernel. I tried to talk to them. I was calling Bigwig, but I didn't really expect him to hear because I was sure he wasn't there. I can remember coming out from a hedge into the open and I know I was really hoping that the elil would come and make an end of me. But when I came to my senses, there was Bigwig. My first thought was that I must be dead, but then I began to wonder whether he was real or not. Well, you know the rest. It's a pity I frightened you so much. But if I wasn't the—the Black Rabbit, there's hardly a living creature that can ever have been closer to him than we have."

After a silence, he added, "You can imagine what it means to Bluebell and me to find ourselves underground, among friends. It wasn't I who tried to arrest you, Bigwig—that was another rabbit, long, long ago."

22

The Story of the Trial of El-ahrairah

Has he not a rogue's face? . . . Has a damn'd Tyburn-face, without the benefit of the clergy.

Congreve, *Love for Love*

Rabbits (says Mr. Lockley) are like human beings in many ways. One of these is certainly their staunch ability to withstand disaster and to let the stream of their life carry them along, past reaches of terror and loss. They have a certain quality which it would not be accurate to describe as callousness or indifference. It is, rather, a blessedly circumscribed imagination and an intuitive feeling that Life is Now. A foraging wild creature, intent above all upon survival, is as strong as the grass. Collectively, rabbits rest secure upon Frith's promise to El-ahrairah. Hardly a full day had elapsed since Holly had come crawling in delirium to the foot of Watership Down. Yet already he was near recovery, while the more light-hearted Bluebell seemed even less the worse for the dreadful catastrophe that he had survived. Hazel and his companions had suffered extremes of grief and horror during the telling of Holly's tale. Pipkin had cried and trembled piteously at the death of Scabious, and Acorn and Speedwell had been seized with convulsive choking as Bluebell told of the poisonous gas that murdered underground. Yet, as with primitive humans, the very strength and vividness of their sympathy brought with it a true release. Their feelings were not false or assumed. While the story was being told, they heard it without any of the reserve or detachment that the kindest of civilized humans retains as he reads his newspaper. To themselves, they seemed to struggle in the poisoned runs and to blaze with rage for poor Pimpernel in the ditch. This was their way of honoring the dead. The story over, the demands of their own hard, rough lives began to re-assert themselves in their hearts, in their nerves, their blood and appetites. Would that the dead were not dead! But there is grass that must be eaten, pellets that must be chewed, hraka that must be passed, holes that must be dug, sleep that must be slept. Odysseus brings not one man to shore with him. Yet he sleeps sound beside Calypso and when he wakes thinks only of Penelope.

Even before Holly had finished his story, Hazel had fallen to sniffing at his wounded ear. He had not previously been able to get a good look at it, but now that he did, he realized that terror and fatigue had probably not been the principal causes of Holly's collapse. He was badly wounded—worse than Buckthorn. He must have lost a lot of blood. His ear was in ribbons and there was any amount of dirt in it. Hazel felt annoyed with Dandelion. As several of the rabbits began to silflay, attracted by the mild June night and the full moon, he asked Blackberry to wait. Silver, who had been about to leave by the other run, returned and joined them.

"Dandelion and the other two seem to have cheered you up, all right," said Hazel to Holly. "It's a pity they didn't *clean* you up as well. That dirt's dangerous."

"Well, you see—" began Bluebell, who had remained beside Holly.

"Don't make a joke," said Hazel. "You seem to think—"

"I wasn't going to," said Bluebell. "I was only going to say that I wanted to clean the captain's ear, but it's too tender to be touched."

"He's quite right," said Holly. "I'm afraid I made them neglect it, but do as you think best, Hazel. I'm feeling much better now."

Hazel began on the ear himself. The blood had caked black and the task needed patience. After a while the long, jagged wounds bled again as they slowly became clean. Silver took over. Holly, bearing it as well as he could, growled and scuffled, and Silver cast about for something to occupy his attention.

"Hazel," he asked, "what was this idea you had—about the mouse? You said you'd explain it later. How about trying it out on us now?"

"Well," said Hazel, "the idea is simply that in our situation we can't afford to waste anything that might do us good. We're in a strange place we don't know much about and we need friends. Now, elil can't do us good, obviously, but there are many creatures that aren't elil—birds, mice, yonil and so on. Rabbits don't usually have much to do with them, but their enemies are our enemies, for the most part. I think we ought to do all we can to make these creatures friendly. It might turn out to be well worth the trouble."

"I can't say I fancy the idea myself," said Silver, wiping Holly's blood out of his nose. "These small animals are more to be despised than relied upon, I reckon. What good can they do us? They can't dig for us, they can't get food for us, they can't fight for us. They'd *say* they were friendly, no doubt, as long as we were helping them; but that's where it would stop. I heard that mouse tonight—'You want 'im, 'e come.' You bet he will, as long as there's any grub or warmth going, but surely we're not going to have the warren overrun with mice and—and stag beetles, are we?"

"No, I didn't mean quite that," said Hazel. "I'm not suggesting we should go about looking for field mice and inviting them to join us. They wouldn't thank us for that, anyway. But that mouse tonight—we saved his life—"

"*You* saved his life," said Blackberry.

"Well, his life was saved. He'll remember that."

"But how's it going to help us?" asked Bluebell.

"To start with, he can tell us what he knows about the place—"

"What mice know. Not what rabbits need to know."

"Well, I admit a mouse might or might not come in handy," said Hazel. "But I'm sure a bird would, if we could only do enough for it. We can't fly, but some of them know the country for a long way round. They know a lot about the weather, too. All I'm saying is this. If anyone finds an animal or bird, that isn't an enemy, in need of help, for goodness' sake don't miss the opportunity. That would be like leaving carrots to rot in the ground."

"What do you think?" said Silver to Blackberry.

"I think it's a good idea, but real opportunities of the kind Hazel has in mind aren't likely to come very often."

"I think that's about right," said Holly, wincing as Silver resumed licking. "The idea's all right as far as it goes, but it won't come to a great deal in practice."

"I'm ready to give it a try," said Silver. "I reckon it'll be worth it, just to see Bigwig telling bedtime stories to a mole."

"El-ahrairah did it once," said Bluebell, "*and* it worked. Do you remember?"

"No," said Hazel, "I don't know that story. Let's have it."

"Let's silflay first," said Holly. "This ear's had all I can stand for the time being."

"Well, at least it's clean now," said Hazel. "But I'm afraid it'll never be as good as the other, you know. You'll have a ragged ear."

"Never mind," said Holly. "I'm still one of the lucky ones."

The full moon, well risen in a cloudless eastern sky, covered the high solitude with its light. We are not conscious of daylight as that which displaces darkness. Daylight, even when the sun is clear of clouds, seems to us simply the natural condition of the earth and air. When we think of the downs, we think of the downs in daylight, as we think of a rabbit with its fur on. Stubbs may have envisaged the skeleton inside the horse, but most of us do not: and we do not usually envisage the downs without daylight, even though the light is not a part of the down itself as the hide is part of the horse itself. We take daylight for granted. But moonlight is another matter. It is inconstant. The full moon wanes and returns again. Clouds may obscure it to an extent to which they cannot obscure daylight. Water is necessary to us, but a waterfall is not. Where it is to be found it is something extra, a beautiful ornament. We need daylight and to that extent it is utilitarian, but moonlight we do not need. When it comes, it serves no necessity. It transforms. It falls upon the banks and the grass, separating one long blade from another; turning a drift of brown, frosted leaves from a single heap to innumerable flashing fragments; or glimmering lengthways along wet twigs as though light itself were ductile. Its long beams pour, white and sharp, between the trunks of trees, their clarity fading as they recede into the powdery, misty distance of beech woods at night. In moonlight, two acres of coarse bent grass, undulant and ankle deep, tumbled and rough as a horse's mane, appear like a bay of waves, all shadowy troughs and hollows. The growth is so thick and matted that even the wind does not move it, but it is the moonlight that seems to confer stillness upon it. We do not take moonlight for granted. It is like snow, or like the dew on a July morning. It does not reveal but changes what it covers. And its low intensity—so much lower than that of daylight—makes us conscious that it is something added to the down, to give it, for only a little time, a singular and marvelous quality that we should admire while we can, for soon it will be gone again.

As the rabbits came up by the hole inside the beech wood, a swift gust of wind passed through the leaves, checkering and dappling the ground beneath, stealing and giving light under the branches. They listened, but beyond the rustle of the leaves there came from the open down outside no sound except the monotonous tremolo of a grasshopper warbler, far off in the grass.

"What a moon!" said Silver. "Let's enjoy it while it's here."

As they went over the bank they met Speedwell and Hawkbit returning.

"Oh, Hazel," said Hawkbit, "we've been talking to another mouse. He'd heard about the kestrel this evening and was very friendly. He told us about a place just the other side of the wood where the grass has been cut short—something to do with horses, he said. 'You like a nice a grass? 'E very fine grass.' So we went there. It's first-rate."

The gallop turned out to be a good forty yards wide, mown to less than six inches. Hazel, with a delightful sense of having been proved right by events, set to work on a patch of clover. They all munched for some time in silence.

"You're a clever chap, Hazel," said Holly at last. "You and your mouse. Mind you, we'd have found the place ourselves sooner or later, but not as soon as this."

Hazel could have pressed his chin glands for satisfaction, but he replied merely, "We shan't need to go down the hill so much, after all." Then he added, "But, Holly, you smell of blood, you know. It may be dangerous, even here. Let's go back to the wood. It's such a beautiful night that we can sit near the holes to chew pellets and Bluebell can tell us his story."

They found Strawberry and Buckthorn on the bank; and when everyone was comfortably chewing, with ears laid flat, Bluebell began.

* * *

"Dandelion was telling me last night about Cowslip's warren and how he told the story of the King's Lettuce. That's what put me in mind of this tale, even before Hazel explained his idea. I used to hear it from my grandfather and he always said that it happened after El-ahrairah had got his people out of the marshes of Kelfazin. They went to the meadows of Fenlo and there they dug their holes. But Prince Rainbow had his eye on El-ahrairah; and he was determined to see that he didn't get up to any more of his tricks.

"Now one evening, when El-ahrairah and Rabscuttle were sitting on a sunny bank, Prince Rainbow came through the meadows and with him was a rabbit that El-ahrairah had never seen before.

" 'Good evening, El-ahrairah,' said Prince Rainbow. 'This is a great improvement on the marshes of Kelfazin. I see all your does are busy digging holes along the bank. Have they dug a hole for you?'

" 'Yes,' said El-ahrairah. 'This hole here belongs to Rabscuttle and myself. We liked the look of this bank as soon as we saw it.'

" 'A very nice bank,' said Prince Rainbow. 'But I am afraid I have to tell you, El-ahrairah, that I have strict orders from Lord Frith himself not to allow you to share a hole with Rabscuttle.'

" 'Not share a hole with Rabscuttle?' said El-ahrairah. 'Why ever not?'

" 'El-ahrairah,' said Prince Rainbow, 'we know you and your tricks: and Rabscuttle is nearly as slippery as you are. Both of you in one hole would be altogether too much of a good thing. You would be stealing the clouds out of the sky before the moon had changed twice. No—Rabscuttle must go and look after the holes at the other end of the warren. Let me introduce you. This is Hufsa. I want you to be his friend and look after him.'

" 'Where does he come from?' asked El-ahrairah. 'I certainly haven't seen him before.'

" 'He comes from another country,' said Prince Rainbow, 'but he is no different from any other rabbit. I hope you will help him to settle down here. And while he is getting to know the place, I'm sure you will be glad to let him share your hole.'

"El-ahrairah and Rabscuttle felt desperately annoyed that they were not to be allowed to live together in their hole. But it was one of El-ahrairah's rules never to let anyone see when he was angry and, besides, he felt sorry for Hufsa because he supposed that he was feeling lonely and awkward, being far away from his own people. So he welcomed him and promised to help him settle down. Hufsa was perfectly friendly and seemed anxious to please everyone; and Rabscuttle moved down to the other end of the warren.

"After a time, however, El-ahrairah began to find that something was always going wrong with his plans. One night, in the spring, when he had taken some of his people to a cornfield to eat the green shoots, they found a man with a gun walking about in the moonlight and were lucky to get away without trouble. Another time, after El-ahrairah had reconnoitered the way to a cabbage garden and scratched a hole under the fence, he arrived the next morning to find it blocked with wire, and he began to suspect that his plans were leaking out to people who were not intended to learn them.

"One day he determined to set a trap for Hufsa, to find out whether it was he who was at the bottom of the trouble. He showed him a path across the fields and told him that it led to a lonely barn full of swedes and turnips: and he went on to say that he and Rabscuttle meant to go there the next morning. In fact El-ahrairah had no such plans and took care not to say anything about the path or the barn to anyone else. But next day, when he went cautiously along the path, he found a wire set in the grass.

"This made El-ahrairah really angry, for any of his people might have been snared and killed. Of course he did not suppose that Hufsa was setting wires himself, or even that he had known that a wire was going to be set. But evidently Hufsa was in touch with somebody who did not stick at setting a wire. In the end, El-ahrairah decided that probably Prince Rainbow was passing on Hufsa's information to a farmer or a gamekeeper and not bothering himself about what happened as a result. His rabbits' lives were in danger because of Hufsa—to say nothing of all the lettuces and cabbages they were missing. After this, El-ahrairah tried not to tell Hufsa anything at all. But it was difficult to prevent him from hearing things because, as you all know, rabbits are very good at keeping secrets from other animals, but no good at keeping secrets from each other. Warren life doesn't make for secrecy. He considered killing Hufsa. But he knew that if he did, Prince Rainbow would come and they would end in more trouble. He felt decidedly uneasy even about keeping things from Hufsa, because he thought that if Hufsa realized that they knew he was a spy, he would tell Prince Rainbow and Prince Rainbow would probably take him away and think of something worse.

"El-ahrairah thought and thought. He was still thinking the next evening, when Prince Rainbow paid one of his visits to the warren.

"'You are quite a reformed character these days, El-ahrairah,' said Prince Rainbow. 'If you are not careful, people will begin to trust you. Since I was passing by, I thought I would just stop to thank you for your kindness in looking after Hufsa. He seems quite at home with you.'

" 'Yes, he does, doesn't he?' said El-ahrairah. 'We grow in beauty side by side; we fill one hole with glee. But I always say to my people, "Put not your trust in princes, nor in any—" '

" 'Well, El-ahrairah,' said Prince Rainbow, interrupting him, 'I am sure I can trust *you*. And to prove it, I have decided that I will grow a nice crop of carrots in the field behind the hill. It is an excellent bit of ground and I am sure they will do well. Especially as no one would dream of stealing them. In fact, you can come and watch me plant them, if you like.'

" 'I will,' said El-ahrairah. 'That will be delightful.'

"El-ahrairah, Rabscuttle, Hufsa and several other rabbits accompanied Prince Rainbow to the field behind the hill; and they helped him to sow it with long rows of carrot seed. It was a light, dry sort of soil—just the thing for carrots—and the whole business infuriated El-ahrairah, because he was certain that Prince Rainbow was doing it to tease him and to show that he felt sure that he had clipped his claws at last.

" 'That will do splendidly,' said Prince Rainbow when they had finished. 'Of course, I know that no one would dream of stealing my carrots. But if they did—if they *did* steal them, El-ahrairah—I should be very angry indeed. If King Darzin stole them, for instance, I feel sure that Lord Frith would take away his kingdom and give it to someone else.'

"El-ahrairah knew that Prince Rainbow meant that if he caught him stealing the carrots he would either kill him or else banish him and put some other rabbit over his people: and the thought that the other rabbit would probably be Hufsa made him grind his teeth. But he said, 'Of course, of course. Very right and proper.' And Prince Rainbow went away.

"One night, in the second moon after the planting, El-ahrairah and Rabscuttle went to look at the carrots. No one had thinned them out and the tops were thick and green. El-ahrairah judged that most of the roots would be a little thinner than a forepaw. And it was while he was looking at them in the moonlight that his plan came to him. He had become so cautious about Hufsa—and indeed no one ever knew where Hufsa would be next—that on the way back he and Rabscuttle made for a hole in a lonely bank and went down it to talk together. And there El-ahrairah promised Rabscuttle not only that he would steal Prince Rainbow's carrots, but also that between them they would see the back of Hufsa into the bargain. They came out of the hole and Rabscuttle went to the farm to steal some seed corn. El-ahrairah spent the rest of the night gathering slugs; and a nasty business it was.

"The next evening El-ahrairah went out early and after a little while found Yona the hedgehog pottering along the hedge.

" 'Yona,' he said, 'would you like a whole lot of nice, fat slugs?'

" 'Yes, I would, El-ahrairah,' said Yona, 'but they're not so easily found. You'd know that if you were a hedgehog.'

" 'Well, here are some nice ones,' said El-ahrairah, 'and you can have them all. But I can give you a great many more if you will do what I say and ask no questions. Can you sing?'

" 'Sing, El-ahrairah? No hedgehog can sing.'

" 'Good,' said El-ahrairah. 'Excellent. But you will have to try if you want those slugs. Ah! There is an old, empty box, I see, that the farmer has left in the ditch. Better and better. Now you listen to me.'

"Meanwhile, in the wood, Rabscuttle was talking to Hawock the pheasant.

" 'Hawock,' he said, 'can you swim?'

" 'I never go near water if I can avoid it, Rabscuttle,' said Hawock. 'I dislike it very much. But I suppose if I had to, I could make shift to keep afloat for a little while.'

" 'Splendid,' said Rabscuttle. 'Now attend. I have a whole lot of corn—and you know how scarce it is at this time of year—and you can have it all, if only you will do a little swimming in the pond on the edge of the wood. Just let me explain as we go down there.' And off they went through the wood.

"Fu Inlé, El-ahrairah strolled into his hole and found Hufsa chewing pellets. 'Ah, Hufsa, you're here,' he said. 'That's fine. I can't trust anyone else, but you'll come with me, won't you? Just you and I—no one else must know.'

" 'Why, what's to be done, El-ahrairah?' asked Hufsa.

" 'I've been looking at those carrots of Prince Rainbow's,' replied El-ahrairah. 'I can't stand it any longer. They're the best I've ever seen. I'm determined to steal them—or most of them, anyway. Of course, if I took a lot of rabbits on an expedition of this kind we'd soon be in trouble. Things would leak out and Prince Rainbow would be sure to get to hear. But if you and I go alone, no one will ever know who did it.'

" 'I'll come,' said Hufsa. 'Let's go tomorrow night.' For he thought that that would give him time to tell Prince Rainbow.

" 'No,' said El-ahrairah, 'I'm going now. At once.'

"He wondered whether Hufsa would try to turn him against this idea, but when he looked at him he could see that Hufsa was thinking that this would be the end of El-ahrairah and that he himself would be made king of the rabbits.

"They set out together in the moonlight.

"They had gone a good way along the hedge when they came upon an old box lying in the ditch. Sitting on top of the box was Yona the hedgehog. His prickles were stuck all over with dog-rose petals and he was making an extraordinary squeaking, grunting noise and waving his black paws. They stopped and looked at him.

" 'Whatever are you doing, Yona?' asked Hufsa in astonishment.

" 'Singing to the moon,' answered Yona. 'All hedgehogs have to sing to the moon to make the slugs come. Surely you know that?

" 'O Slug-a-Moon, O Slug-a-Moon,
O grant thy faithful hedgehog's boon!'

" 'What a frightful noise!' said El-ahrairah and indeed it was. 'Let's get on quickly before he brings all the elil round us.' And on they went.

"After a time they drew near the pond on the edge of the wood. As they approached it they heard a squawking and splashing and then they saw Hawock the pheasant scuttering about in the water, with his long tail feathers floating out behind him.

" 'Whatever has happened?' said Hufsa. 'Hawock, have you been shot?'

" 'No, no,' replied Hawock. 'I always go swimming in the full moon. It makes my tail grow longer and, besides, my head wouldn't stay red, white and green without swimming. But you must know that, Hufsa, surely? Everyone knows that.'

" 'The truth is, he doesn't like other animals to catch him at it,' whispered El-ahrairah. 'Let's go on.'

"A little further on they came to an old well by a big oak tree.

The farmer had filled it up long ago, but the mouth looked very deep and black in the moonlight.

" 'Let's have a rest,' said El-ahrairah, 'just for a short time.'

"As he spoke, a most curious-looking creature came out of the grass. It looked something like a rabbit, but even in the moonlight they could see that it had a red tail and long green ears. In its mouth it was carrying the end of one of the white sticks that men burn. It was Rabscuttle, but not even Hufsa could recognize him. He had found some sheep-dip powder at the farm and sat in it to make his tail red. His ears were festooned with trails of bryony and the white stick was making him feel ill.

" 'Frith preserve us!' said El-ahrairah. 'What can it be? Let's only hope it isn't one of the Thousand!' He leaped up, ready to run. 'Who are you?' he asked, trembling.

"Rabscuttle spat out the white stick.

" 'So!' he said commandingly. 'So you have seen me, El-ahrairah! Many rabbits live out their lives and die, but few see me. Few or none! I am one of the rabbit messengers of Lord Frith, who go about the earth secretly by day and return nightly to his golden palace! He is even now awaiting me on the other side of the world and I must go to him swiftly, through the heart of the earth! Farewell, El-ahrairah!'

"The strange rabbit leaped over the edge of the well and disappeared into the darkness below.

" 'We have seen what we should not!' said El-ahrairah in an awe-stricken voice. 'How dreadful is this place! Let us go quickly!'

"They hurried on and presently they came to Prince Rainbow's field of carrots. How many they stole I cannot say; but of course, as you know, El-ahrairah is a great prince and no doubt he used powers unknown to you and me. But my grandfather always said that before morning the field was stripped bare. The carrots were hidden down a deep hole in the bank beside the wood and El-ahrairah and Hufsa made their way home. El-ahrairah collected two or three followers and stayed underground with them all day, but Hufsa went out in the afternoon without saying where he was going.

"That evening, as El-ahrairah and his people began to silflay under a fine red sky, Prince Rainbow came over the fields. Behind him were two great black dogs.

" 'El-ahrairah,' he said, 'you are under arrest.'

" 'What for?' asked El-ahrairah.

" 'You know very well what for,' said Prince Rainbow. 'Let me have no more of your tricks and insolence, El-ahrairah. Where are the carrots?'

" 'If I am under arrest,' said El-ahrairah, 'may I be told what for? It is not fair to tell me I am under arrest and then to ask me questions.'

" 'Come, come, El-ahrairah,' said Prince Rainbow, 'you are merely wasting time. Tell me where the carrots are and I will only send you to the great North and not kill you.'

" 'Prince Rainbow,' said El-ahrairah, 'for the third time, may I know for what I am under arrest?'

" 'Very well,' said Prince Rainbow, 'if this is the way you want to die, El-ahrairah, you shall have the full process of law. You are under arrest for stealing my carrots. Are you seriously asking for a trial? I warn you that I have direct evidence and it will go ill with you.'

"By this time all El-ahrairah's people were crowding round, as near as they dared for the dogs. Only Rabscuttle was nowhere to be seen. He had spent the whole day moving the carrots to another secret hole and he was now hiding because he could not get his tail white again.

" 'Yes, I would like a trial,' said El-ahrairah, 'and I would like to be judged by a jury of animals. For it is not right, Prince Rainbow, that you should both accuse me and be the judge as well.'

" 'A jury of animals you shall have,' said Prince Rainbow. 'A jury of elil, El-ahrairah. For a jury of rabbits would refuse to convict you, in spite of the evidence.'

"To everyone's surprise, El-ahrairah immediately replied that he would be content with a jury of elil: and Prince Rainbow said that he would bring them that night. El-ahrairah was sent down his hole and the dogs were put on guard outside. None of his people was allowed to see him, although many tried.

"Up and down the hedges and copses the news spread that El-ahrairah was on trial for his life and that Prince Rainbow was going to bring him before a jury of elil. Animals came crowding in. Fu Inlé, Prince Rainbow returned with the elil—two badgers, two foxes, two stoats, an owl and a cat. El-ahrairah was brought up and placed between the dogs. The elil sat staring at him and their eyes glittered in the moon. They licked their lips: and the dogs muttered that they had been promised the task of carrying out the sentence. There were a great many animals—rabbits and others—and every one of them felt sure that this time it was all up with El-ahrairah.

" 'Now,' said Prince Rainbow, 'let us begin. It will not take long. Where is Hufsa?'

"Then Hufsa came out, bowing and bobbing his head, and he told the elil that El-ahrairah had come the night before, when he was quietly chewing pellets, and terrified him into going with him to steal Prince Rainbow's carrots. He had wanted to refuse, but he had been too much frightened. The carrots were hidden in a hole that he could show them. He had been forced to do what he did, but the next day he had gone as quickly as possible to tell Prince Rainbow, whose loyal servant he was.

" 'We will recover the carrots later,' said Prince Rainbow. 'Now, El-ahrairah, have you any evidence to call or anything to say? Make haste.'

" 'I would like to ask the witness some questions,' said El-ahrairah; and the elil agreed that this was only fair.

" 'Now, Hufsa,' said El-ahrairah, 'can we hear a little more about this journey that you and I are supposed to have made? For really I can remember nothing about it at all. You say we went out of the hole and set off in the night. What happened then?'

" 'Why, El-ahrairah,' said Hufsa, 'you can't possibly have forgotten. We came along by the ditch, and don't you remember that we saw a hedgehog sitting on a box singing a song to the moon?'

" 'A hedgehog doing *what?*' said one of the badgers.

" 'Singing a song to the moon,' said Hufsa eagerly. 'They do that, you know, to make the slugs come. He had rose petals stuck all over him and he was waving his paws and—'

" 'Now, steady, steady,' said El-ahrairah kindly, 'I wouldn't like you to say anything you don't mean. Poor fellow,' he added to the jury, 'he really believes these things he says, you know. He doesn't mean any harm, but—'

" 'But he *was*,' shouted Hufsa. 'He was singing, "O Slug-a-Moon! O Slug-a-Moon! O grant—" '

" 'What the hedgehog sang is not evidence,' said El-ahrairah.

'Really, one is inclined to wonder what is. Well, all right. We saw a hedgehog covered with roses, singing a song on a box. What happened then?'

" 'Well,' said Hufsa, 'then we went on and came to the pond, where we saw a pheasant.'

" 'Pheasant, eh?' said one of the foxes. 'I wish I'd seen it. What was it doing?'

" 'It was swimming round and round in the water,' said Hufsa.

" 'Wounded, eh?' said the fox.

" 'No, no,' said Hufsa. 'They all do that, to make their tails grow longer. I'm surprised you don't know.'

" 'To make *what?*' said the fox.

" 'To make their tails grow longer,' said Hufsa sulkily. 'He said so himself.'

" 'You've only had this stuff for a very short time,' said El-ahrairah to the elil. 'It takes a bit of getting used to. Look at me. I've been forced to live with it for the last two months, day in and day out. I've been as kind and understanding as I can, but apparently just to my own harm.'

"A silence fell. El-ahrairah, with an air of fatherly patience, turned back to the witness.

" 'My memory is so bad,' he said. 'Do go on.'

" 'Well, El-ahrairah,' said Hufsa, 'you're pretending very cleverly, but even you won't be able to say you've forgotten what happened next. A huge, terrifying rabbit, with a red tail and green ears, came out of the grass. He had a white stick in his mouth and he plunged into the ground down a great hole. He told us he was going through the middle of the earth to see Lord Frith on the other side.'

"This time not one of the elil said a word. They were staring at Hufsa and shaking their heads.

" 'They're all mad, you know,' whispered one of the stoats, 'nasty little beasts. They'll say anything when they're cornered. But this one is the worst I've ever heard. How much longer have we got to stay here? I'm hungry.'

"Now El-ahrairah had known beforehand that while elil detest all rabbits, they would dislike most the one who looked the biggest fool. That was why he had agreed to a jury of elil. A jury of rabbits might have tried to get to the bottom of Hufsa's story; but not the

elil, for they hated and despised the witness and wanted to be off
hunting as soon as they could.

" 'So it comes to this,' said El-ahrairah. 'We saw a hedgehog
covered with roses, singing a song: and then we saw a perfectly
healthy pheasant swimming round and round the pond: and then
we saw a rabbit with a red tail, green ears and a white stick, and he
jumped straight down a deep well. Is that right?'

" 'Yes,' said Hufsa.

" 'And then we stole the carrots?'

" 'Yes.'

" 'Were they purple with green spots?'

" 'Were what purple with green spots?'

" 'The carrots.'

" 'Well, you know they weren't, El-ahrairah. They were the
ordinary color. They're down the hole!' shouted Hufsa desperately.
'Down the hole! Go and look!'

"The court adjourned while Hufsa led Prince Rainbow to the
hole. They found no carrots and returned.

" 'I've been underground all day,' said El-ahrairah, 'and I can
prove it. I ought to have been asleep, but it's very difficult when
m'learned friend—well, never mind. I simply mean that obviously I
couldn't have been out moving carrots or anything else. If there
ever *were* any carrots,' he added. 'But I've nothing more to say.'

" 'Prince Rainbow,' said the cat, 'I hate all rabbits. But I don't
see how we can possibly say that it's been proved that that rabbit
took your carrots. The witness is obviously out of his mind—mad
as the mist and snow—and the prisoner will have to be released.'
They all agreed.

" 'You had better go quickly,' said Prince Rainbow to El-ahrairah. 'Go down your hole, El-ahrairah, before I hurt you myself.'

" 'I will, my lord,' said El-ahrairah. 'But may I beg you to
remove that rabbit you sent among us, for he troubles us with his
foolishness?'

"So Hufsa went away with Prince Rainbow and El-ahrairah's
people were left in peace, apart from indigestion brought on by
eating too many carrots. But it was a long time before Rabscuttle
could get his tail white again, so my grandfather always said."

23

Kehaar

> The wing trails like a banner in defeat,
> No more to use the sky for ever but live with
>   famine and pain a few days.
> He is strong and pain is worse to the strong
>   incapacity is worse.
> No one but death the redeemer will humble that head,
> The intrepid readiness, the terrible eyes.
>
> Robinson Jeffers, *Hurt Hawks*

Human beings say, "It never rains but it pours." This is not very apt, for it frequently does rain without pouring. The rabbits' proverb is better expressed. They say, "One cloud feels lonely": and indeed it is true that the appearance of a single cloud often means that the sky will soon be overcast. However that may be, the very next day provided a dramatic second opportunity to put Hazel's idea into practice.

It was early morning and the rabbits were beginning to silflay, coming up into clear gray silence. The air was still chilly. There was a good deal of dew and no wind. Five or six wild duck flew overhead in a swiftly moving V, intent on some far-off destination. The sound made by their wings came down distinctly, diminishing as they went away southward. The silence returned. With the melting of the last of the twilight there grew a kind of expectancy and tension, as though it were thawing snow about to slide from a sloping roof. Then the whole down and all below it, earth and air, gave way to the sunrise. As a bull, with a slight but irresistible movement, tosses its head from the grasp of a man who is leaning over the stall and idly holding its horn, so the sun entered the world in smooth, gigantic power. Nothing interrupted or obscured its coming. Without a sound, the leaves shone and the grass coruscated along the miles of the escarpment.

Outside the wood, Bigwig and Silver combed their ears, sniffed the air and hopped away, following their own long shadows to the grass of the gallop. As they moved over the short turf—nibbling, sitting up and looking round them—they approached a little hollow, no more than three feet across. Before they reached the edge Bigwig, who was ahead of Silver, checked and crouched, staring. Although he could not see into the hollow, he knew that there was some creature in it—something fairly big. Peering through the blades of grass round his head, he could see the curve of a white back. Whatever the creature was, it was nearly as big as himself. He waited, stock still, for some little time, but it did not move.

"What has a white back, Silver?" whispered Bigwig.

Silver considered. "A cat?"

"No cats here."

"How do you know?"

At that moment they both heard a low, breathy hissing from the hollow. It lasted for a few moments. Then there was silence once more.

Bigwig and Silver had a good opinion of themselves. Apart from Holly, they were the only survivors of the Sandleford Owsla and they knew that their comrades looked up to them. The encounter with the rats in the barn had been no joke and had proved their worth. Bigwig, who was generous and honest, had never for a moment resented Hazel's courage on the night when his own superstitious fear had got the better of him. But the idea of going back to the Honeycomb and reporting that he had glimpsed an unknown creature in the grass and left it alone was more than he could swallow. He turned his head and looked at Silver. Seeing that he was game, he took a final look at the strange white back and then went straight up to the edge of the hollow. Silver followed.

It was no cat. The creature in the hollow was a bird—a big bird, nearly a foot long. Neither of them had ever seen a bird like it before. The white part of its back, which they had glimpsed through the grass, was in fact only the shoulders and neck. The lower back was light gray and so were the wings, which tapered to long, black-tipped primaries folded together over the tail. The head was very dark brown—almost black—in such sharp contrast to the white neck that the bird looked as though it were wearing a kind of hood. The one dark red leg that they could see ended in a webbed foot and three powerful, taloned toes. The beak, hooked slightly downward at the end, was strong and sharp. As they stared, it opened, disclosing a red mouth and throat. The bird hissed savagely and tried to strike, but still it did not move.

"It's hurt," said Bigwig.

"Yes, you can tell that," replied Silver. "But it's not wounded anywhere that I can see. I'll go round—"

"Look out!" said Bigwig. "He'll have you!"

Silver, as he started to move round the hollow, had come closer to the bird's head. He jumped back just in time to avoid a quick, darting blow of the beak.

"That would have broken your foot," said Bigwig.

As they squatted, looking at the bird—for they both sensed intuitively that it would not rise—it suddenly burst into loud, raucous cries—"Yark! Yark! Yark!"—a tremendous sound at close quarters—that split the morning and carried far across the down. Bigwig and Silver turned and ran.

They collected themselves sufficiently to pull up short of the wood and make a more dignified approach to the bank. Hazel came to meet them in the grass. There was no mistaking their wide eyes and dilated nostrils.

"Elil?" asked Hazel.

"Well, I'm blessed if I know, to tell you the truth," replied Bigwig. "There's a great bird out there, like nothing I've ever seen."

"How big? As big as a pheasant?"

"Not quite so big," admitted Bigwig, "but bigger than a wood pigeon: and a lot fiercer."

"Is that what cried?"

"Yes. It startled me, all right. We were actually beside it. But for some reason or other it can't move."

"Dying?"

"I don't think so."

"I'll go and have a look at it," said Hazel.

"It's savage. For goodness' sake be careful."

Bigwig and Silver returned with Hazel. The three of them squatted outside the bird's reach as it looked sharply and desperately from one to the other. Hazel spoke in the hedgerow patois.

"You hurt? You no fly?"

The answer was a harsh gabbling which they all felt immediately to be exotic. Wherever the bird came from, it was somewhere far away. The accent was strange and guttural, the speech distorted. They could catch only a word here and there.

"Come keel—kah! kah!—you come keel—yark!—t'ink me finish—me no finish—'urt you damn plenty—" The dark brown head flickered from side to side. Then, unexpectedly, the bird began to drive its beak into the ground. They noticed for the first time that the grass in front of it was torn and scored with lines. For some moments it stabbed here and there, then gave up, lifted its head and watched them again.

"I believe it's starving," said Hazel. "We'd better feed it. Bigwig, go and get some worms or something, there's a good fellow."

"Er—what did you say, Hazel?"

"Worms."

"Me dig for worms?"

"Didn't the Owsla teach—oh, all right, I'll do it," said Hazel. "You and Silver wait here."

After a few moments, however, Bigwig followed Hazel back to the ditch and began to join him in scratching at the dry ground. Worms are not plentiful on the downs and there had been no rain for days. After a time Bigwig looked up.

"What about beetles? Wood lice? Something like that?"

They found some rotten sticks and carried them back. Hazel pushed one forward cautiously.

"Insects."

The bird split the stick three ways in as many seconds and snapped up the few insects inside. Soon there was a small pile of debris in the hollow as the rabbits brought anything from which it could get food. Bigwig found some horse dung along the track, dug the worms out of it, overcame his disgust and carried them one by one. When Hazel praised him, he muttered something about "the first time any rabbit's done this and don't tell the blackbirds." At last, long after they had all grown weary, the bird stopped feeding and looked at Hazel.

"Finish eat." It paused. "Vat for you do?"

"You hurt?" said Hazel.

The bird looked crafty. "No hurt. Plenty fight. Stay small time, den go."

"You stay there you finish," said Hazel. "Bad place. Come homba, come kestrel."

"Damn de lot. Fight plenty."

"I bet it would, too," said Bigwig, looking with admiration at the two-inch beak and thick neck.

"We no want you finish," said Hazel. "You stay here you finish. We help you maybe."

"Piss off!"

"Come on," said Hazel immediately to the others. "Let it alone." He began to lollop back to the wood. "Let it try keeping the kestrels off for a bit."

"What's the idea, Hazel?" said Silver. "That's a savage brute. You can't make a friend out of that."

"You may be right," said Hazel. "But what's the good of a blue tit or a robin to us? They don't fly any distance. We need a big bird."

"But why do you want a bird so particularly?"

"I'll explain later," said Hazel. "I'd like Blackberry and Fiver to hear as well. But let's go underground now. If you don't want to chew pellets, I do."

During the afternoon Hazel organized more work on the warren. The Honeycomb was as good as finished—though rabbits are not methodical and are never really certain when anything is finished—and the surrounding burrows and runs were taking shape. Quite early in the evening, however, he made his way once more to the hollow. The bird was still there. It looked weaker and less alert, but snapped feebly as Hazel came up.

"Still here?" said Hazel. "You fight hawk?"

"No fight," answered the bird. "No fight, but vatch, vatch, alvays vatch. Ees no good."

"Hungry?"

The bird made no reply.

"Listen," said Hazel. "Rabbits not eat birds. Rabbits eat grass. We help you."

"Vat for 'elp me?"

"Never mind. We make you safe. Big hole. Food too."

The bird considered. "Legs fine. Ving no good. 'E bad."

"Well, walk, then."

"You 'urt me, I 'urt you like damn."

Hazel turned away. The bird spoke again.

"Ees long vay?"

"No, not far."

"Come, den."

It got up with a good deal of difficulty, staggering on its strong blood-red legs. Then it opened its wings high above its body and Hazel jumped back, startled by the great, arching span. But at once it closed them again, grimacing with pain.

"Ving no good. I come."

It followed Hazel docilely enough across the grass, but he was careful to keep out of its reach. Their arrival outside the wood caused something of a sensation, which Hazel cut short with a peremptory sharpness quite unlike his usual manner.

"Come on, get busy," he said to Dandelion and Buckthorn. "This bird's hurt and we're going to shelter it until it's better. Ask Bigwig to show you how to get it some food. It eats worms and insects. Try grasshoppers, spiders—anything. Hawkbit! Acorn! Yes, and you too, Fiver—come out of that rapt trance, or whatever you're in. We need an open, wide hole, broader than it's deep, with a flat floor a little below the level of the entrance: by nightfall."

"We've been digging all the afternoon, Hazel—"

"I know. I'll come and help you," said Hazel, "in just a little while. Only get started. The night's coming."

The astonished rabbits obeyed him, grumbling. Hazel's authority was put to something of a test, but held firm with the support of Bigwig. Although he had no idea what Hazel had in mind, Bigwig was fascinated by the strength and courage of the bird and had already accepted the idea of taking it in, without troubling himself about the reason. He led the digging while Hazel explained to the bird, as well as he could, how they lived, their ways of protecting themselves from their enemies and the kind of shelter they could provide. The amount of food the rabbits produced was not very large, but once inside the wood the bird clearly felt safer and was able to hobble about and do some foraging for itself.

By owl time Bigwig and his helpers had scratched out a kind of lobby inside the entrance to one of the runs leading down from the wood. They lined the floor with beech twigs and leaves. As darkness began to fall, the bird was installed. It was still suspicious, but seemed to be in a good deal of pain. Evidently, since it could not think of any better plan for itself, it was ready to try a rabbit hole to save its life. From outside, they could see its dark head alert in the gloom, the black eyes still watchful. It was not asleep when they themselves finished a late silflay and went underground.

Black-headed gulls are gregarious. They live in colonies where they forage and feed, chatter and fight all day long. Solitude and reticence are unnatural to them. They move southward in the breeding season and at such times a wounded one is only too likely to find itself deserted. The gull's savagery and suspicion had been due partly to pain and partly to the unnerving knowledge that it had no companions and could not fly. By the following morning its natural instincts to mix with a flock and to talk were beginning to return. Bigwig made himself its companion. He would not hear of the gull going out to forage. Before ni-Frith the rabbits had managed to produce as much as it could eat—for a time, at all events—and were able to sleep through the heat of the day. Bigwig, however, remained with the gull, making no secret of his admiration, talking and listening to it for several hours. At the evening feed he joined Hazel and Holly near the bank where Bluebell had told his story of El-ahrairah.

"How's the bird now?" asked Hazel.

"A good deal better, I think," replied Bigwig. "He's very tough, you know. My goodness, what a life he's had! You don't know what you're missing! I could sit and listen to him all day."

"How was it hurt?"

"A cat jumped on him in a farmyard. He never heard it until the last moment. It tore the muscle of one of his wings, but apparently he gave it something to remember before he made off. Then he got himself up here somehow or other and just collapsed. Think of standing up to a cat! I can see now that I haven't really started yet. Why shouldn't a rabbit stand up to a cat? Let's just suppose that—"

"But what is this bird?" interrupted Holly.

"Well, I can't quite make out," answered Bigwig. "But if I understand him properly—and I'm not at all sure that I do—he says that where he comes from there are thousands of his kind—more than we can possibly imagine. Their flocks make the whole air white and in the breeding season their nests are like leaves in a wood—so he says."

"But where? I've never seen *one*, even."

"He says," said Bigwig, looking very straight at Holly, "he says that a long way from here the earth stops and there isn't any more."

"Well, obviously it stops somewhere. What is there beyond?"

"Water."

"A river, you mean?"

"No," said Bigwig, "not a river. He says there's a vast place of water, going on and on. You can't see to the other side. There isn't another side. At least there is, because he's been there. Oh, I don't know—I must admit I can't altogether understand it."

"Was it telling you that it's been outside the world and come back again? That must be untrue."

"I don't know," said Bigwig, "but I'm sure he's not lying. This water, apparently, moves all the time and keeps breaking against the earth: and when he can't hear that, he misses it. That's his name—Kehaar. It's the noise the water makes."

The others were impressed in spite of themselves.

"Well, why's it here?" asked Hazel.

"He shouldn't be He ought to have been off to this Big Water place a long time ago, to breed. Apparently a lot of them come away in winter, because it gets so cold and wild. Then they go back in summer. But he's been hurt once already this spring. It was nothing much, but it held him up. He rested and hung around a rookery for a bit. Then he got stronger and left them, and he was coming along when he stopped in the farmyard and met this foul cat."

"So when it's better it'll go on again?" said Hazel.

"Yes."

"We've been wasting our time, then."

"Why, Hazel, what is it you have in mind?"

"Go and get Blackberry and Fiver: we'd better have Silver, too. Then I'll explain."

The quiet of the evening silflay, when the western sun shone straight along the ridge, the grass tussocks threw shadows twice as long as themselves and the cool air smelled of thyme and dog roses, was something which they had all come to enjoy even more than former evenings in the meadows of Sandleford. Although they could not know it, the down was more lonely than it had been for hundreds of years. There were no sheep, and villagers from Kingsclere and Sydmonton no longer had any occasion to walk over the hills, either for business or for pleasure. In the fields of

Sandleford the rabbits had seen men almost every day. Here, since their arrival, they had seen one, and him on a horse. Looking round the little group that gathered on the grass, Hazel saw that all of them—even Holly—were looking stronger, sleeker and in better shape than when they had first come to the down. Whatever might lie ahead, at least he could feel that he had not failed them so far.

"We're doing well here," he began, "or so it seems to me. We're certainly not a bunch of hlessil any more. But all the same, there's something on my mind. I'm surprised, as a matter of fact, that I should be the first one of us to start thinking about it. Unless we can find the answer, then this warren's as good as finished, in spite of all we've done."

"Why, how can that be, Hazel?" said Bigwig.

"Do you remember Nildro-hain?" asked Hazel.

"She stopped running. Poor Strawberry."

"I know. And we have no does—not one—and no does means no kittens and in a few years no warren."

It may seem incredible that the rabbits had given no thought to so vital a matter. But men have made the same mistake more than once—left the whole business out of account, or been content to trust to luck and the fortune of war. Rabbits live close to death and when death comes closer than usual, thinking about survival leaves little room for anything else. But now, in the evening sunshine on the friendly, empty down, with a good burrow at his back and the grass turning to pellets in his belly, Hazel knew that he was lonely for a doe. The others were silent and he could tell that his words had sunk in.

The rabbits grazed or lay basking in the sun. A lark went twittering up into the brighter sunshine above, soared and sang and came slowly down, ending with a sideways, spread-wing glide and a wagtail's run through the grass. The sun dipped lower. At last Blackberry said, "What's to be done? Set out again?"

"I hope not," said Hazel. "It all depends. What I'd like to do is get hold of some does and bring them here."

"Where from?"

"Another warren."

"But are there any on these hills? How do we find out? The wind never brings the least smell of rabbits."

"I'll tell you how," said Hazel. "The bird. The bird will go and search for us."

"Hazel-rah," cried Blackberry, "what a marvelous idea! That bird could find out in a day what we couldn't discover for ourselves in a thousand! But are you certain it can be persuaded to do it? Surely as soon as it gets better it'll simply fly away and leave us?"

"I can't tell," answered Hazel. "All we can do is feed it and hope for the best. But, Bigwig, since you seem to be getting on with it so well, perhaps you can explain to it how much this means to us. It has only to fly over the downs and let us know what it sees."

"You leave him to me," said Bigwig. "I think I know how to do it."

Hazel's anxiety and the reason for it were soon known to all the rabbits and there was not one who did not realize what they were up against. There was nothing very startling in what he had said. He was simply the one—as a Chief Rabbit ought to be—through whom a strong feeling, latent throughout the warren, had come to the surface. But his plan to make use of the gull excited everyone and was seen as something that not even Blackberry could have hit upon. Reconnaissance is familiar to all rabbits—indeed, it is second nature—but the idea of making use of a bird, and one so strange and savage, convinced them that Hazel, if he could really do it, must be as clever as El-ahrairah himself.

For the next few days a lot of hard work went into feeding Kehaar. Acorn and Pipkin, boasting that they were the best insect-catchers in the warren, brought in great numbers of beetles and grasshoppers. At first the gull's principal hardship was lack of water. He suffered a good deal and was reduced to tearing at the stems of the long grasses for moisture. However, during his third night in the warren it rained for three or four hours and puddles formed on the track. A cluttery spell set in, as it often does in Hampshire when haytime approaches. High winds from the south laid the grass flat all day, turning it to a dull, damascene silver. The great branches of the beeches moved little, but spoke loudly. There were squalls of rain on the wind. The weather made Kehaar restless. He walked about a good deal, watched the flying clouds and snapped up everything the foragers brought. Searching became harder, for in the wet the insects burrowed into the deep grass and had to be scratched out.

One afternoon Hazel, who now shared a burrow with Fiver as in the old days, was woken by Bigwig to be told that Kehaar had something to say to him. He made his way to Kehaar's lobby without coming above ground. The first thing he noticed was that the gull's head was molting and turning white, though a dark brown patch remained behind each eye. Hazel greeted him and was surprised to be answered in a few words of halting, broken Lapine. Evidently Kehaar had prepared a short speech.

"Meester 'Azel, ees rabbits vork 'ard," said Kehaar. "I no finish now. Soon I go fine."

"That's good news," said Hazel. "I'm glad."

Kahaar relapsed into hedgerow vernacular.

"Meester Pigvig, 'e plenty good fella."

"Yes, he is."

" 'E say you no getting mudders. Ees finish mudders. Plenty trouble for you."

"Yes, that's true. We don't know what to do. No mothers anywhere."

"Listen. I get peeg, fine plan. I go fine now. Ving, 'e better. Vind finish, den I fly. Fly for you. Find plenty mudders, tell you vere dey are, ya?"

"Why, what a splendid idea, Kehaar! How clever of you to think of it! You very fine bird."

"Ees finish mudders for me dis year. Ees too late. All mudders sitting on nest now. Eggs come."

"I'm sorry."

"Nudder time I get mudder. Now I fly for you."

"We'll do everything we possibly can to help you."

The next day the wind dropped and Kehaar made one or two short flights. However, it was not until three days later that he felt able to set out on his search. It was a perfect June morning. He was snapping up numbers of the little white-shelled downland snails from the wet grass and cracking them in his great beak, when he suddenly turned to Bigwig and said,

"Now I fly for you."

He opened his wings. The two-foot span arched above Bigwig, who sat perfectly still while the white feathers beat the air round his head in a kind of ceremonious farewell. Laying his ears flat in the fanned draft, he stared up at Kehaar as the gull rose, rather heavily, into the air. When he flew, his body, so long and graceful on the ground, took on the appearance of a thick, stumpy cylinder, from the front of which his red beak projected between his round black eyes. For a few moments he hovered, his body rising and falling between his wings. Then he began to climb, sailed sideways over the grass and disappeared northward below the edge of the escarpment. Bigwig returned to the hanger with the news that Kehaar had set out.

The gull was away several days—longer than the rabbits had expected. Hazel could not help wondering whether he really would return, for he knew that Kehaar, like themselves, felt the mating urge and he thought it quite likely that after all he would be off to the Big Water and the raucous, teeming gull colonies of which he had spoken with such feeling to Bigwig. As far as he was able, he kept his anxiety to himself, but one day when they were alone, he asked Fiver whether he thought Kehaar would return.

"He will return," said Fiver unhesitatingly.

"And what will he bring with him?"

"How can I tell?" replied Fiver. But later, when they were underground, silent and drowsy, he said suddenly, "The gifts of El-ahrairah. Trickery; great danger; and blessing for the warren." When Hazel questioned him again, he seemed to be unaware that he had spoken and could add nothing more.

Bigwig spent most of the hours of daylight watching for Kehaar's return. He was inclined to be surly and short, and once, when Bluebell remarked that he thought Meester Pigvig's fur cap was molting in sympathy for absent friends, he showed a flash of his old sergeant-major spirit and cuffed and abused him twice round the Honeycomb, until Holly intervened to save his faithful jester from further trouble.

It was late one afternoon, with a light north wind blowing and the smell of hay drifting up from the fields of Sydmonton, when Bigwig came hurtling down into the Honeycomb to announce that Kehaar was back. Hazel suppressed his excitement and told everyone to keep out of the way while he went to see him alone. On second thoughts, however, he took Fiver and Bigwig with him.

The three of them found Kehaar back in his lobby. It was full of droppings, messy and malodorous. Rabbits will not excrete underground and Kehaar's habit of fouling his own nest had always disgusted Hazel. Now, in his eagerness to hear his news, the guano smell seemed almost welcome.

"Glad to see you back, Kehaar," he said. "Are you tired?"

"Ving 'e still go tired. Fly liddle bit, stop liddle bit, everyt'ing go fine."

"Are you hungry? Shall we get you some insects?"

"Fine. Fine. Good fellas. Plenty beetle." (All insects were "beetle" to Kehaar.)

Clearly, he had missed their attentions and was ready to enjoy being back. Although he no longer needed to have food brought to the lobby, he evidently felt that he deserved it. Bigwig went to get his foragers and Kehaar kept them busy until sunset. At last he looked shrewdly at Fiver and said,

"Eh, Meester Liddle Von, you know vat I pring, ya?"

"I've no idea," replied Fiver, rather shortly.

"Den I tell. All dis peeg 'ill, I go along 'im, dis vay, dat vay, vere sun come up, vere sun go down. Ees no rabbits. Ees nodings, nodings."

He stopped. Hazel looked at Fiver apprehensively.

"Den I go down, go down in bottom. Ees farm vid peeg trees all round, on liddle hill. You know?"

"No, we don't know it. But go on."

"I show you. 'E not far. You see 'im. Und here ees rabbits. Ees rabbits live in box; live vid men. You know?"

"Live with men? Did you say 'live with men'?"

"Ya, ya, live vid men. In shed; rabbits live in box in shed. Men pring food. You know?"

"I know this happens," said Hazel. "I've heard of it. That's fine, Kehaar. You've been very thorough. But it can't help us, can it?"

"I t'ink ees mudders. In peeg box. But else ees no rabbits; not in fields, not in voods. No rabbits. Anyvays I no see 'em."

"That sounds bad."

"Vait. I tell more. Now you 'ear. I go flying, oder vay, vere sun go middle of day. You know, dis vay ees Peeg Vater."

"Did you go to the Big Water, then?" asked Bigwig.

"Na, na, not near so far. But out dis vay ees river, you know?"

"No, we haven't been so far."

"Ees river," repeated Kehaar. "Und here ees town of rabbits."

"On the other side of the river?"

"Na, na. You go dat vay, ees peeg fields all de vay. Den after long vay ees come to town of rabbits, ver' big. Und after dat ees iron road und den river."

"Iron road?" asked Fiver.

"Ya, ya, iron road. You not seen heem—iron road? Men make heem."

Kehaar's speech was so outlandish and distorted at the best of times that it was only too common for the rabbits to be unsure what he meant. The vernacular words which he used now for "iron" and "road" (familiar enough to seagulls) his listeners had scarcely ever heard. Kehaar was quick to impatience and now, as often, they felt at a disadvantage in the face of his familiarity with a wider world than their own. Hazel thought quickly. Two things were clear. Kehaar had evidently found a big warren some way off to the south: and whatever the iron road was, the warren was on this side both of it and of a river. If he had understood rightly, it seemed to follow that the iron road and the river could be ignored for their purposes.

"Kehaar," he said, "I want to be certain. Can we get to the rabbits' town without bothering about the iron road and the river?"

"Ya, ya. Not go to iron road. Rabbits' town in bushes for peeg, lonely fields. Plenty mudders."

"How long would it take to go from here to the—to the town?"

"I t'ink two days. Ees long vay."

"Good for you, Kehaar. You've done everything we hoped. You rest now. We'll feed you as long as you want."

"Sleep now. Tomorrow plenty beetle, ya, ya."

The rabbits made their way back to the Honeycomb. Hazel told Kehaar's news and a long, disorderly, intermittent discussion began. This was their way of reaching a conclusion. The fact that there was a warren two or three days' journey to the south flickered and oscillated down among them as a penny wavers down through deep water, moving one way and the other, shifting, vanishing, reappearing, but always sinking toward the firm bottom. Hazel let the talk run on as long as it would, until at last they dispersed and slept.

The next morning they went about their lives as usual, feeding Kehaar and themselves, playing and digging. But all this time, just as a drop of water slowly swells until it is heavy enough to fall from a twig, the idea of what they meant to do was becoming clear and unanimous. By the following day Hazel saw it plain. It so happened that the time for speaking came when he was sitting on the bank at sunrise, with Fiver and three or four others. There was no need to summon a general gathering. The thing was settled. When it reached them, those who were not there would accept what he had said without having heard him at all.

"This warren that Kehaar found," said Hazel, "he said it was big."

"So we can't take it by force," said Bigwig.

"I don't think I want to go and join it," said Hazel. "Do you?"

"And leave here?" replied Dandelion. "After all our work? Besides, I reckon we'd have a thin time. No, I'm sure none of us wants to do that."

"What we want is to get some does and bring them back here," said Hazel. "Will that be difficult, do you think?"

"I should have thought not," said Holly. "Big warrens are often overcrowded and some of the rabbits can't get enough to eat. The young does get edgy and nervous and some of them don't have any kittens on that account. At least, the kittens begin to grow inside them and then they melt away again into their bodies. You know this?"

"I didn't know," said Strawberry.

"That's because you've never been overcrowded. But our warren—the Threarah's warren—was overcrowded a year or two back and a lot of the younger does were re-absorbing their litters before they were born. The Threarah told me that long ago El-ahrairah made a bargain with Frith. Frith promised him that rabbits were not to be born dead or unwanted. If there's little chance of a decent life for them, it's a doe's privilege to take them back into her body unborn."

"Yes, I remember the bargain story," said Hazel. "So you think there may be discontented does? That's hopeful. We're agreed, then, that we ought to send an expedition to this warren and that there's a good chance of being successful without fighting. Do you want everyone to go?"

"I'd say not," said Blackberry. "Two or three days' journey; and we're all in danger, both going and coming. It would be less dangerous for three or four rabbits than for hrair. Three or four can travel quickly and aren't conspicuous: and the Chief Rabbit of this warren would be less likely to object to a few strangers coming with a civil request."

"I'm sure that's right," said Hazel. "We'll send four rabbits: and they can explain how we come to be in this difficulty and ask to be allowed to persuade some does to come back with them. I don't see that any Chief Rabbit can object to that. I wonder which of us would be the best to send?"

"Hazel-rah, you mustn't go," said Dandelion. "You're needed here and we don't want to risk you. Everyone's agreed on that."

Hazel had known already that they would not let him lead the embassy. It was a disappointment, but nevertheless he felt that they were right. The other warren would have little opinion of a Chief Rabbit who ran his own errands. Besides, he was not particularly impressive in appearance or as a speaker. This was a job for someone else.

"All right," he said. "I knew you wouldn't let me go. I'm not the right fellow anyway—Holly is. He knows everything about moving in the open and he'll be able to talk well when he gets there."

No one contradicted this. Holly was the obvious choice, but to select his companions was less easy. Everyone was ready to go, but the business was so important that at last they considered each rabbit in turn, discussing who would be the most likely to survive the long journey, to arrive in good shape and to go down well in a strange warren. Bigwig, rejected on the grounds that he might quarrel in strange company, was inclined to be sulky at first, but came round when he remembered that he could go on looking after Kehaar. Holly himself wanted to take Bluebell but, as Blackberry said, one funny joke at the expense of the Chief Rabbit might ruin everything. Finally they chose Silver, Buckthorn and Strawberry. Strawberry said little, but was obviously very much pleased. He had suffered a good deal to show that he was no coward and now he had the satisfaction of knowing that he was worth something to his new friends.

They started early in the morning, in the gray light. Kehaar had undertaken to fly out later in the day, to make sure they were going in the right direction and bring back news of their progress. Hazel and Bigwig went with them to the southern end of the hanger and watched as they slipped away, heading to the west of the distant farm. Holly seemed confident and the other three were in high spirits. Soon they were lost to sight in the grass and Hazel and Bigwig turned back into the wood.

"Well, we've done the best we can," said Hazel. "The rest's up to them and to El-ahrairah now. But surely it ought to be all right?"

"Not a doubt of it," said Bigwig. "Let's hope they're back soon. I'm looking forward to a nice doe and a litter of kittens in my burrow. Lots of little Bigwigs, Hazel! Think of that, and tremble!"

24

Nuthanger Farm

When Robyn came to Notyngham,
  Sertenly withouten layn,
He prayed to God and myld Mary
  To bryng hym out save agayn.

Beside him stod a gret-hedid munke,
  I pray to God woo he be!
Fful sone he knew gode Robyn,
  As sone as he hym se.

Robin Hood and the Monk (Child's *Ballads*, No. 119)

Hazel sat on the bank in the midsummer night. There had been no more than five hours' darkness and that of a pallid, twilit quality which kept him wakeful and restless. Everything was going well. Kehaar had found Holly during the afternoon and corrected his line a little to the west. He had left him in the shelter of a thick hedge, sure of his course for the big warren. It seemed certain now that two days would be enough for the journey. Bigwig and some of the other rabbits had already begun enlarging their burrows in preparation for Holly's return. Kehaar had had a violent quarrel with a kestrel, screaming insults in a voice fit to startle a Cornish harbor: and although it had ended inconclusively, the kestrel seemed likely to regard the neighborhood of the hanger with healthy respect for the future. Things had not looked better since they had first set out from Sandleford.

A spirit of happy mischief entered into Hazel. He felt as he had on the morning when they crossed the Enborne and he had set out alone and found the beanfield. He was confident and ready for adventure. But what adventure? Something worth telling to Holly and Silver on their return. Something to—well, not to diminish what they were going to do. No, of course not—but just to show them that their Chief Rabbit was up to anything that they were up to. He thought it over as he hopped down the bank and sniffed out a patch of salad burnet in the grass. What, now, would be likely to give them just a little, not unpleasant shock? Suddenly he thought, "Suppose, when they got back, that there were one or two does here already?" And in the same moment he remembered what Kehaar had said about a box full of rabbits at the farm. What sort of rabbits could they be? Did they ever come out of their box? Had they ever seen a wild rabbit? Kehaar had said that the farm was not far from the foot of the down, on a little hill. So it could easily be reached in the early morning, before its men were about. Any dogs would probably be chained, but the cats would be loose. A rabbit could outrun a cat as long as he kept in the open and saw it coming first. The important thing was not to be stalked unawares. He should be able to move along the hedgerows without attracting elil, unless he was very unlucky.

But what did he intend to do, exactly? Why was he going to the farm? Hazel finished the last of the burnet and answered himself in the starlight. "I'll just have a look round," he said, "and if I can find those box rabbits I'll try to talk to them; nothing more than that. I'm not going to take any risks—well, not real risks—not until I see whether it's worth it, anyway."

Should he go alone? It would be safer and more pleasant to take a companion; but not more than one. They must not attract attention. Who would be best? Bigwig? Dandelion? Hazel rejected them. He needed someone who would do as he was told and not start having ideas of his own. At once he thought of Pipkin. Pipkin would follow him without question and do anything he asked. At this moment he was probably asleep in the burrow which he shared with Bluebell and Acorn, down a short run leading off the Honeycomb.

Hazel was lucky. He found Pipkin close to the mouth of the burrow and already awake. He brought him out without disturbing the other two rabbits and led him up by the run that gave on the bank. Pipkin looked about him uncertainly, bewildered and half expecting some danger.

"It's all right, Hlao-roo," said Hazel. "There's nothing to be afraid of. I want you to come down the hill and help me to find a farm I've heard about. We're just going to have a look round it."

"Round a farm, Hazel-rah? What for? Won't it be dangerous? Cats and dogs and—"

"No, you'll be quite all right with me. Just you and me—I don't want anyone else. I've got a secret plan; you mustn't tell the others—for the time being, anyway. I particularly want you to come and no one else will do."

This had exactly the effect that Hazel intended. Pipkin needed no further persuasion and they set off together, over the grass track, across the turf beyond and down the escarpment. They went through the narrow belt of trees and came into the field where Holly had called Bigwig in the dark. Here Hazel paused, sniffing and listening. It was the time before dawn when owls return, usually hunting as they go. Although a full-grown rabbit is not really in danger from owls, there are few who take no account of them. Stoats and foxes might be abroad also, but the night was still and damp and Hazel, secure in his mood of gay confidence, felt sure that he would either smell or hear any hunter on four feet.

Wherever the farm might be, it must lie beyond the road that ran along the opposite edge of the field. He set off at an easy pace, with Pipkin close behind. Moving quietly in and out of the hedgerow up which Holly and Bluebell had come and passing, on their way, under the cables humming faintly in the darkness above, they took only a few minutes to reach the road.

There are times when we know for a certainty that all is well. A batsman who has played a fine innings will say afterward that he felt he could not miss the ball, and a speaker or an actor, on his lucky day, can sense his audience carrying him as though he were swimming in miraculous, buoyant water. Hazel had this feeling now. All round him was the quiet summer night, luminous with starlight but paling to dawn on one side. There was nothing to fear and he felt ready to skip through a thousand farmyards one after the other. As he sat with Pipkin on the bank above the tar-smelling road, it did not strike him as particularly lucky when he saw a young rat scuttle across from the opposite hedge and disappear into a clump of fading stitchwort below them. He had known that some guide or other would turn up. He scrambled quickly down the bank and found the rat nosing in the ditch.

"The farm," said Hazel, "where's the farm—near here, on a little hill?"

The rat stared at him with twitching whiskers. It had no particular reason to be friendly, but there was something in Hazel's look that made a civil answer natural.

"Over road. Up lane."

The sky was growing lighter each moment. Hazel crossed the road without waiting for Pipkin, who caught him up under the hedge bordering the near side of the little lane. From here, after another listening pause, they began to make their way up the slope toward the northern skyline.

Nuthanger is like a farm in an old tale. Between Ecchinswell and the foot of Watership Down and about half a mile from each, there is a broad knoll, steeper on the north side but falling gently on the south—like the down ridge itself. Narrow lanes climb both slopes and come together in a great ring of elm trees which encircles the flat summit. Any wind—even the lightest—draws from the height of the elms a rushing sound, multifoliate and powerful. Within this ring stands the farmhouse, with its barns and outbuildings. The house may be two hundred years old or it may be older, built of brick, with a stone-faced front looking south toward the down. On the east side, in front of the house, a barn stands clear of the ground on staddle stones; and opposite is the cow byre.

As Hazel and Pipkin reached the top of the slope, the first light showed clearly the farmyard and buildings. The birds singing all about them were those to which they had been accustomed in former days. A robin on a low branch twittered a phrase and listened for another that answered him from beyond the farm-house. A chaffinch gave its little falling song and further off, high in an elm, a chiffchaff began to call. Hazel stopped and then sat up, the better to scent the air. Powerful smells of straw and cow dung mingled with those of elm leaves, ashes and cattle feed. Fainter traces came to his nose as the overtones of a bell sound in a trained ear. Tobacco, naturally: a good deal of cat and rather less dog and then, suddenly and beyond doubt, rabbit. He looked at Pipkin and saw that he, too, had caught it.

While these scents reached them they were also listening. But beyond the light movements of birds and the first buzzing of the flies immediately around them, they could hear nothing but the continual susurration of the trees. Under the northern steep of the down the air had been still, but here the southerly breeze was magnified by the elms, with their myriads of small, fluttering leaves, just as the effect of sunlight on a garden is magnified by dew. The sound, coming from the topmost branches, disturbed Hazel because it suggested some huge approach—an approach that was never completed: and he and Pipkin remained still for some time, listening tensely to this loud yet meaningless vehemence high overhead.

They saw no cat, but near the house stood a flat-roofed dog kennel. They could just glimpse the dog asleep inside—a large, smooth-haired, black dog, with head on paws. Hazel could not see a chain; but then, after a moment, he noticed the line of a thin rope that came out through the kennel door and ended in some sort of fastening on the roof. "Why a rope?" he wondered and then thought, "Because a restless dog cannot rattle it in the night."

The two rabbits began to wander among the outbuildings. At first they took care to remain in cover and continually on the watch for cats. But they saw none and soon grew bolder, crossing open spaces and even stopping to nibble at dandelions in the patches of weeds and rough grass. Guided by scent, Hazel made his way to a low-roofed shed. The door was half open and he went through it with scarcely a pause at the brick threshold. Immediately opposite the door, on a broad wooden shelf—a kind of platform—stood a wire-fronted hutch. Through the mesh he could see a brown bowl, some greenstuff and the ears of two or three rabbits. As he stared, one of the rabbits came close to the wire, looked out and saw him.

Beside the platform, on the near side, was an up-ended bale of straw. Hazel jumped lightly on it and from there to the thick planks, which were old and soft-surfaced, dusty and covered with chaff. Then he turned back to Pipkin, waiting just inside the door.

"Hlao-roo," he said, "there's only one way out of this place.

You'll have to keep watching for cats or we may be trapped. Stay at the door and if you see a cat outside, tell me at once."

"Right, Hazel-rah," said Pipkin. "It's all clear at the moment."

Hazel went up to the side of the hutch. The wired front projected over the edge of the shelf so that he could neither reach it nor look in, but there was a knothole in one of the boards facing him and on the far side he could see a twitching nose.

"I am Hazel-rah," he said. "I have come to talk to you. Can you understand me?"

The answer was in slightly strange but perfectly intelligible Lapine.

"Yes, we understand you. My name is Boxwood. Where do you come from?"

"From the hills. My friends and I live as we please, without men. We eat the grass, lie in the sun and sleep underground. How many are you?"

"Four. Bucks and does."

"Do you ever come out?"

"Yes, sometimes. A child takes us out and puts us in a pen on the grass."

"I have come to tell you about my warren. We need more rabbits. We want you to run away from the farm and join us."

"There's a wire door at the back of this hutch," said Boxwood. "Come down there: we can talk more easily."

The door was made of wire netting on a wooden frame, with two leather hinges nailed to the uprights and a hasp and staple fastened with a twist of wire. Four rabbits were crowded against the wire, pressing their noses through the mesh. Two—Laurel and Clover—were short-haired black Angoras. The others, Boxwood and his doe Haystack, were black-and-white Himalayans.

Hazel began to speak about the life of the downs and the excitement and freedom enjoyed by wild rabbits. In his usual straightforward way he told about the predicament of his warren in having no does and how he had come to look for some. "But," he said, "we don't want to steal your does. All four of you are welcome to join us, bucks and does alike. There's plenty for everyone on the hills." He went on to talk of the evening feed in the sunset and of early morning in the long grass.

The hutch rabbits seemed at once bewildered and fascinated. Clover, the Angora doe—a strong, active rabbit—was clearly excited by Hazel's description and asked several questions about the warren and the downs. It became plain that they thought of their life in the hutch as dull but safe. They had learned a good deal about elil from some source or other and seemed sure that few wild rabbits survived for long. Hazel realized that although they were glad to talk to him and welcomed his visit because it brought a little excitement and change into their monotonous life, it was not within their capacity to take a decision and act on it. They did not know how to make up their minds. To him and his companions, sensing and acting was second nature; but these rabbits had never had to act to save their lives or even to find a meal. If he was going to get any of them as far as the down, they would have to be urged. He sat quiet for a little, nibbling a patch of bran spilled on the boards outside the hutch. Then he said,

"I must go back now to my friends in the hills: but we shall return. We shall come one night, and when we do, believe me, we shall open your hutch as easily as the farmer does: and then, any of you who wish will be free to come with us."

Boxwood was about to reply when suddenly Pipkin spoke from the floor. "Hazel, there's a cat in the yard outside!"

"We're not afraid of cats," said Hazel to Boxwood, "as long as we're in the open." Trying to appear unhurried, he went back to the floor by way of the straw bale and crossed over to the door. Pipkin was looking through the hinge. He was plainly frightened.

"I think it's smelled us, Hazel," he said. "I'm afraid it knows where we are."

"Don't stay there, then," said Hazel. "Follow me close and run when I do." Without waiting to look out through the hinge, he went round the half-open door of the shed and stopped on the threshold.

The cat, a tabby with white chest and paws, was at the further end of the little yard, walking slowly and deliberately along the side of a pile of logs. When Hazel appeared in the doorway it saw him at once and stood stock still, with staring eyes and twitching tail. Hazel hopped slowly across the threshold and stopped again. Already sunlight was slanting across the yard, and in the stillness the flies buzzed about a patch of dung a few feet away. There was a smell of straw and dust and hawthorn.

"You look hungry," said Hazel to the cat. "Rats getting too clever, I suppose?"

The cat made no reply. Hazel sat blinking in the sunshine. The cat crouched almost flat on the ground, thrusting its head forward between its front paws. Close behind, Pipkin fidgeted and Hazel, never taking his eyes from the cat, could sense that he was trembling.

"Don't be frightened, Hlao-roo," he whispered. "I'll get you away, but you must wait till it comes for us. Keep still."

The cat began to lash its tail. Its hindquarters lifted and wagged from side to side in mounting excitement.

"Can you run?" said Hazel. "I think not. Why, you pop-eyed, back-door saucer-scraper—"

The cat flung itself across the yard and the two rabbits leaped into flight with great thrusts of their hind legs. The cat came very fast indeed and although both of them had been braced ready to move on the instant, they were barely out of the yard in time. Racing up the side of the long barn, they heard the Labrador barking in excitement as it ran to the full extent of its rope. A man's voice shouted to it. From the cover of the hedge beside the lane they turned and looked back. The cat had stopped short and was licking one paw with a pretense of nonchalance.

"They hate to look silly," said Hazel. "It won't give us any more trouble. If it hadn't charged at us like that, it would have followed us much further and probably called up another as well. And somehow you can't make a dash unless they do it first. It's a good thing you saw it coming, Hlao-roo."

"I'm glad if I helped, Hazel. But what were we up to, and why did you talk to the rabbits in the box?"

"I'll tell you all about it later on. Let's go into the field now and feed; then we can make our way home as slowly as you like."

25

The Raid

He went consenting, or else he was no king. . . . It was no one's place to
say to him, "It is time to make the offering."

Mary Renault, *The King Must Die*

As things turned out, Hazel and Pipkin did not come back
to the Honeycomb until the evening. They were still feeding in the
field when it came on to rain, with a cold wind, and they took
shelter first in the nearby ditch and then—since the ditch was on a
slope and had a fair flow of rainwater in about ten minutes—
among some sheds halfway down the lane. They burrowed into a
thick pile of straw and for some time remained listening for rats.
But all was quiet and they grew drowsy and fell asleep, while
outside the rain settled in for the morning. When they woke it was
mid-afternoon and still drizzling. It seemed to Hazel that there was
no particular hurry. The going would be troublesome in the wet,
and anyway no self-respecting rabbit could leave without a forage
round the sheds. A pile of mangels and swedes occupied them for
some time and they set out only when the light was beginning to
fade. They took their time and reached the hanger a little before
dark, with nothing worse to trouble them than the discomfort of
soaking-wet fur. Only two or three of the rabbits were out to a
rather subdued silflay in the wet. No one remarked on their
absence and Hazel went underground at once, telling Pipkin to say
nothing about their adventure for the time being. He found his
burrow empty, lay down and fell asleep.

Waking, he found Fiver beside him as usual. It was some time
before dawn. The earth floor felt pleasantly dry and snug and he
was about to go back to sleep when Fiver spoke.

"You've been wet through, Hazel."

"Well, what about it? The grass is wet, you know."

"You didn't get so wet on silflay. You were soaked. You weren't
here at all yesterday, were you?"

"Oh, I went foraging down the hill."

"Eating swedes: and your feet smell of farmyard—hens' droppings and bran. But there's some other funny thing besides—something I *can't* smell. What happened?"

"Well, I had a bit of a brush with a cat, but why worry?"

"Because you're concealing something, Hazel. Something dangerous."

"It's Holly that's in danger, not I. Why bother about me?"

"Holly?" replied Fiver in surprise. "But Holly and the others reached the big warren early yesterday evening. Kehaar told us. Do you mean to say you didn't know?"

Hazel felt fairly caught out. "Well, I know now," he replied. "I'm glad to hear it."

"So it comes to this," said Fiver. "You went to a farm yesterday and escaped from a cat. And whatever you were up to, it was so much on your mind that you forgot to ask about Holly last night."

"Well, all right, Fiver—I'll tell you all about it. I took Pipkin and went to that farm that Kehaar told us about where there are rabbits in a hutch. I found the rabbits and talked to them and I've taken a notion to go back one night and get them out, to come and join us here."

"What for?"

"Well, two of them are does, that's what for."

"But if Holly's successful we shall soon have plenty of does: and from all I've ever heard of hutch rabbits, they don't take easily to wild life. The truth is, you're just a silly show-off."

"A silly show-off?" said Hazel. "Well, we'll just see whether Bigwig and Blackberry think so."

"Risking your life and other rabbits' lives for something that's of little or no value to us," said Fiver. "Oh, yes, of course the others will go with you. You're their Chief Rabbit. You're supposed to decide what's sensible and they trust you. Persuading them will prove nothing, but three or four dead rabbits will prove you're a fool, when it's too late."

"Oh, be quiet," answered Hazel. "I'm going to sleep."

During silflay next morning, with Pipkin for a respectful chorus, he told the others about his visit to the farm. As he had expected, Bigwig jumped at the idea of a raid to free the hutch rabbits.

"It can't go wrong," he said. "It's a splendid idea, Hazel! I don't know how you open a hutch, but Blackberry will see to that. What annoys me is to think you ran from that cat. A good rabbit's a match for a cat, any day. My mother went for one once and she fairly gave it something to remember, I can tell you: scratched its fur out like willow herb in autumn! Just leave the farm cats to me and one or two of the others!"

Blackberry took a little more convincing: but he, like Bigwig and Hazel himself, was secretly disappointed not to have gone on the expedition with Holly: and when the other two pointed out that they were relying on him to tell them how to get the hutch open, he agreed to come.

"Do we need to take everyone?" he asked. "You say the dog's tied up and I suppose there can't be more than three cats. Too many rabbits will only be a nuisance in the dark: someone will get lost and we shall have to spend time looking for him."

"Well, Dandelion, Speedwell and Hawkbit, then," said Bigwig, "and leave the others behind. Do you mean to go tonight, Hazel-rah?"

"Yes, the sooner the better," said Hazel. "Get hold of those three and tell them. Pity it's going to be dark—we could have taken Kehaar: he'd have enjoyed it."

However, their hopes for that night were disappointed, for the rain returned before dusk, settling in on a northwest wind and carrying up the hill the sweet-sour smell of flowering privet from cottage hedges below. Hazel sat on the bank until the light had quite faded. At last, when it was clear that the rain was going to stay for the night, he joined the others in the Honeycomb. They had persuaded Kehaar to come down out of the wind and wet, and one of Dandelion's tales of El-ahrairah was followed by an extraordinary story that left everyone mystified but fascinated, about a time when Frith had to go away on a journey, leaving the whole world to be covered with rain. But a man built a great floating hutch that held all the animals and birds until Frith returned and let them out.

"It won't happen tonight, will it, Hazel-rah?" asked Pipkin, listening to the rain in the beech leaves outside. "There's no hutch here."

"Kehaar'll fly you up to the moon, Hlao-roo," said Bluebell, "and you can come down on Bigwig's head like a birch branch in the frost. But there's time to go to sleep first."

Before Fiver slept, however, he talked again to Hazel about the raid.

"I suppose it's no good asking you not to go?" he said.

"Look here," answered Hazel, "have you got one of your bad turns about the farm? If you have, why not say so straight out? Then we'd all know where we were."

"I've no feelings about the farm one way or the other," said Fiver. "But that doesn't necessarily mean it's all right. The feelings come when they will—they don't always come. Not for the lendri, not for the crow. If it comes to that, I've no idea what's happening to Holly and the others. It might be good or bad. But there's something that frightens me about you yourself, Hazel: just you, not any of the others. You're all alone, sharp and clear, like a dead branch against the sky."

"Well, if you mean you can see trouble for me and not for any of the others, tell them and I'll leave it to them to decide whether I ought to keep out of it. But that's giving up a lot, Fiver, you know. Even with your word for it, someone's bound to think I'm afraid."

"Well, I say it's not worth the risk, Hazel. Why not wait for Holly to come back? That's all we have to do."

"I'll be snared if I wait for Holly. Can't you see that the very thing I want is to have these does here when he comes back? But look, Fiver, I'll tell you what. I've come to trust you so much that I'll take the greatest care. In fact, I won't even go into the farmyard myself. I'll stay outside, at the top of the lane: and if that's not meeting your fears halfway, then I don't know what is."

Fiver said no more and Hazel turned his thoughts to the raid and the difficulty he foresaw of getting the hutch rabbits to go the distance back to the warren.

The next day was bright and dry, with a fresh wind that cleared up what remained of the wet. The clouds came racing over the ridge from the south as they had on the May evening when Hazel first climbed the down. But now they were higher and smaller, settling at last into a mackerel sky like a beach at low tide. Hazel took Bigwig and Blackberry to the edge of the escarpment, whence they could look across to Nuthanger on its little hill. He described the approach and went on to explain how the rabbit hutch was to be found. Bigwig was in high spirits. The wind and the prospect of action excited him and he spent some time with Dandelion,

Hawkbit and Speedwell, pretending to be a cat and encouraging them to attack him as realistically as they could. Hazel, whose talk with Fiver had somewhat clouded him, recovered as he watched them tussling over the grass and ended by joining in himself, first as an attacker and then as the cat, staring and quivering for all the world like the Nuthanger tabby.

"I shall be disappointed if we don't meet a cat after all this," said Dandelion, as he waited for his turn to run at a fallen beech branch from one side, claw it twice and dash out again. "I feel a really dangerous animal."

"You vatch heem, Meester Dando," said Kehaar, who was hunting for snails in the grass nearby. "Meester Pigvig, 'e vant you t'ink all vun peeg yoke; make you prave. Cat 'e no yoke. You no see 'im, you no 'ear 'im. Den yomp! 'E come."

"But we're not going there to eat, Kehaar," said Bigwig. "That makes all the difference. We shan't stop watching for cats the whole time."

"Why not eat the cat?" said Bluebell. "Or bring one back here for breeding? That ought to improve the warren stock no end."

Hazel and Bigwig had decided that the raid should be carried out as soon after dark as the farm was quiet. This meant that they would cover the half mile to the outlying sheds at sunset, instead of risking the confusion of a night journey over ground that only Hazel knew. They could steal a meal among the swedes, halt till darkness and cover the short distance to the farm after a good rest. Then—provided they could cope with the cats—there would be plenty of time to tackle the hutch; whereas if they were to arrive at dawn they would be working against time before men came on the scene. Finally, the hutch rabbits would not be missed until the following morning.

"And remember," said Hazel, "it'll probably take these rabbits a long time to get to the down. We shall have to be patient with them. I'd rather do that in darkness, elil or no elil. We don't want to be messing about in broad daylight."

"If it comes to the worst," said Bigwig, "we can leave the hutch rabbits and bolt. Elil take the hindmost, don't they? I know it's tough, but if there's real trouble we ought to save our own rabbits first. Let's hope that doesn't happen, though."

When they came to set out, Fiver was nowhere to be seen. Hazel felt relieved, for he had been afraid that Fiver might say something that would lower their spirits. But there was nothing worse to contend with than Pipkin's disappointment at being left behind; and this was dispelled when Hazel assured him that the only reason was that he had already done his bit. Bluebell, Acorn and Pipkin came with them to the foot of the hill and watched them down the hedgerow.

They reached the sheds in the twilight after sunset. The summer nightfall was unbroken by owls and so quiet that they could plainly hear the intermittent, monotonous "Chug chug chug" of a nightingale in the distant woods. Two rats among the swedes showed their teeth, thought better of it and left them alone. When they had foraged, they rested comfortably in the straw until the western light was quite gone.

Rabbits do not name the stars, but nevertheless Hazel was familiar with the sight of Capella rising; and he watched it now until it stood gold and bright in the dark northeastern horizon to the right of the farm. When it reached a certain point which he had fixed, beside a bare branch, he roused the others and led them up the slope toward the elms. Near the top he slipped through the hedge and brought them down into the lane.

Hazel had already told Bigwig of his promise to Fiver to keep out of danger; and Bigwig, who had changed much since the early days, had no fault to find.

"If that's what Fiver says, you'd better do it, Hazel," he said. "Anyhow, it'll suit us. You stay outside the farm in a safe place and we'll bring the rabbits out to you: then you can take over and get us all away." What Hazel had not said was that the idea that he should remain in the lane was his own suggestion, and that Fiver had acquiesced only because he could not persuade him to give up the idea of the raid altogether.

Crouching under a fallen branch on the verge of the lane, Hazel watched the others as they followed Bigwig down toward the farmyard. They went slowly, rabbit fashion, hop, step and pause. The night was dark and they were soon out of sight, though he could hear them moving down the side of the long barn. He settled down to wait.

Bigwig's hopes of action were fulfilled almost at once. The cat that he met as he reached the far end of the barn was not Hazel's tabby, but another; ginger, black and white (and therefore a female); one of those slim, trotting, quick-moving, tail-twitching cats that sit on farm windowsills in the rain or keep watch from the tops of sacks on sunny afternoons. It came briskly round the corner of the barn, saw the rabbits and stopped dead.

Without an instant's hesitation Bigwig went straight for it, as though it had been the beech branch on the down. But quicker even than he Dandelion ran forward, scratched it and leaped clear. As it turned, Bigwig threw his full weight upon it from the other side. The cat closed with him, biting and scratching, and Bigwig rolled over on the ground. The others could hear him swearing like a cat himself and struggling for a hold. Then he sank one back leg into the cat's side and kicked backward rapidly, several times.

Anyone who is familiar with cats knows that they do not care for a determined assailant. A dog that tries to make itself pleasant to a cat may very well get scratched for its pains. But let that same dog rush in to the attack and many a cat will not wait to meet it. The farm cat was bewildered by the speed and fury of Bigwig's charge. It was no weakling and a good ratter, but it had the bad luck to be up against a dedicated fighter who was spoiling for action. As it scrabbled out of Bigwig's reach, Speedwell cuffed it across the face. This was the last blow struck, for the wounded cat made off across the yard and disappeared under the fence of the cow byre.

Bigwig was bleeding from three deep, parallel scratches on the inside of one hind leg. The others gathered round, praising him, but he cut them short, looking round the dark yard as he tried to get his bearings.

"Come on," he said. "Quickly, too, while the dog's still quiet. The shed: the hutch—where do we go?"

It was Hawkbit who found the little yard. Hazel had been anxious in case the shed door might be shut; but it stood just ajar and the five of them slipped in one after the other. In the thick gloom they could not make out the hutch, but they could both smell and hear the rabbits.

"Blackberry," said Bigwig quickly, "you come with me and get the hutch open. You other three, keep watching. If another cat comes, you'll have to take it on yourselves."

"Fine," said Dandelion. "Just leave it to us."

Bigwig and Blackberry found the straw bale and climbed on the planks. As they did so, Boxwood spoke from the hutch.

"Who's that? Hazel-rah, have you come back?"

"Hazel-rah has sent us," answered Blackberry. "We've come to let you out. Will you come with us?"

There was a pause and some movement in the hay and then Clover replied, "Yes, let us out."

Blackberry sniffed his way round to the wire door and sat up, nosing over the frame, the hasp and the staple. It took him some time to realize that the leather hinges were soft enough to bite. Then he found that they lay so smooth and flush with the frame that he could not get his teeth to them. Several times he tried to find a grip and at last sat back on his haunches, at a loss.

"I don't think this door's going to be any good," he said. "I wonder whether there's some other way?"

At that moment it happened that Boxwood stood on his hind legs and put his front paws high on the wire. Beneath his weight the top of the door was pressed slightly outward and the upper of the two leather hinges gave slightly where the outer nail held it to the body of the hutch itself. As Boxwood dropped back on all fours, Blackberry saw that the hinge had buckled and risen just clear of the wood.

"Try it now," he said to Bigwig.

Bigwig got his teeth to the hinge and pulled. It tore a very little.

"By Frith, that'll do," said Blackberry, for all the world like the Duke of Wellington at Salamanca. "We just need time, that's all."

The hinge had been well made and did not give way until they had put it to a great deal more tugging and biting. Dandelion grew nervous and twice gave a false alarm. Bigwig, realizing that the sentries were on the jump from watching and waiting with nothing to do, changed places with him and sent Speedwell up to take over from Blackberry. When at last Dandelion and Speedwell had pulled the leather strip off the nail, Bigwig came back to the hutch himself. But they did not seem much nearer to success. Whenever one of the rabbits inside stood up and rested its forepaws on the upper part of the wire, the door pivoted lightly on the axis of the staple and the lower hinge. But the lower hinge did not tear. Blowing through his whiskers with impatience, Bigwig brought

Blackberry back from the threshold. "What's to be done?" he said. "We need some magic, like that lump of wood you shoved into the river."

Blackberry looked at the door as Boxwood, inside, pushed it again. The upright of the frame pressed tight against the lower strip of leather, but it held smooth and firm, offering no purchase for teeth.

"Push it the other way—push from this side," he said. "You push, Bigwig. Tell that rabbit inside to get down."

When Bigwig stood up and pushed the top of the door inward, the frame immediately pivoted much further than before, because there was no sill along the bottom of the outer side to stop it. The leather hinge twisted and Bigwig nearly lost his balance. If it had not been for the metal staple arresting the pivoting, he might actually have fallen inside the hutch. Startled, he jumped back, growling.

"Well, you said magic, didn't you?" said Blackberry with satisfaction. "Do it again."

No strip of leather held by only one broad-headed nail at each end can stand up for long to repeated twisting. Soon one of the nailheads was almost out of sight under the frayed edges.

"Careful now," said Blackberry. "If it gives way suddenly, you'll go flying. Just pull it off with your teeth."

Two minutes later the door hung sagging on the staple alone. Clover pushed the hinge side open and came out, followed by Boxwood.

When several creatures—men or animals—have worked together to overcome something offering resistance and have at last succeeded, there follows often a pause—as though they felt the propriety of paying respect to the adversary who has put up so good a fight. The great tree falls, splitting, cracking, rushing down in leaves to the final, shuddering blow along the ground. Then the foresters are silent, and do not at once sit down. After hours, the deep snowdrift has been cleared and the lorry is ready to take the men home out of the cold. But they stand a while, leaning on their spades and only nodding unsmilingly as the car-drivers go through, waving their thanks. The cunning hutch door had become nothing but a piece of wire netting, tacked to a frame made from four strips of half-by-half; and the rabbits sat on the planks, sniffing and nosing it without talking. After a little while the other two occupants of the hutch, Laurel and Haystack, came hesitantly out and looked about them.

"Where is Hazel-rah?" asked Laurel.

"Not far away," said Blackberry. "He's waiting in the lane."

"What is the lane?"

"The lane?" said Blackberry in surprise. "Surely—"

He stopped as it came over him that these rabbits knew neither lane nor farmyard. They had not the least idea of their most immediate surroundings. He was reflecting on what this meant when Bigwig spoke.

"We mustn't wait about now," he said. "Follow me, all of you."

"But where?" said Boxwood.

"Well, out of here, of course," said Bigwig impatiently.

Boxwood looked about him. "I don't know—" he began.

"Well, I do," said Bigwig. "Just come with us. Never mind anything else."

The hutch rabbits looked at each other in bewilderment. It was plain that they were afraid of the great, bristling buck, with his strange shock of fur and his smell of fresh blood. They did not know what to do or understand what was expected of them. They remembered Hazel; they had been excited by the forcing of the door and curious to come through it once it was open. Otherwise, they had no purpose whatever and no means of forming one. They had no more idea of what was involved than a small child who says he will accompany the climbers up the fell.

Blackberry's heart sank. What was to be done with them? Left to themselves, they would hop slowly about the shed and the yard until the cats got them. Of their own accord they could no more run to the hills than fly to the moon. Was there no simple, plain idea that might get them—or some of them—on the move? He turned to Clover.

"I don't suppose you've ever eaten grass by night," he said. "It tastes much better than by day. Let's all go and have some, shall we?"

"Oh, yes," said Clover, "I'd like that. But will it be safe? We're all very much afraid of the cats, you know. They come and stare at us sometimes through the wire and it makes us shiver."

This showed at least the beginnings of sense, thought Blackberry.

"The big rabbit is a match for any cat," he replied. "He nearly killed one on the way here tonight."

"And he doesn't want to fight another if he can help it," said Bigwig briskly. "So if you *do* want to eat grass by moonlight, let's go to where Hazel-rah's waiting for us."

As Bigwig led the way into the yard, he could make out the shape of the cat that he had beaten, watching from the woodpile. Cat-like, it was fascinated by the rabbits and could not leave them alone, but it evidently had no stomach for another fight and as they crossed the yard it stayed where it was.

The pace was frighteningly slow. Boxwood and Clover seemed to have grasped that there was some sort of urgency and were clearly doing their best to keep up, but the other two rabbits, once they had hopped into the yard, sat up and looked about them in a foolish manner, completely at a loss. After a good deal of delay, during which the cat left the woodpile and began to move stealthily round toward the side of the shed, Blackberry managed to get them out into the farmyard. But here, finding themselves in an even more open place, they settled into a kind of static panic, like that which sometimes comes upon inexperienced climbers exposed on a sheer face. They could not move, but sat blinking and staring about them in the darkness, taking no notice of Blackberry's coaxing or Bigwig's orders. At this moment a second cat—Hazel's tabby— came round the further end of the farmhouse and made toward them. As it passed the kennel the Labrador woke and sat up, thrusting out its head and shoulders and looking first to one side and then the other. It saw the rabbits, ran to the length of its rope and began to bark.

"Come on!" said Bigwig. "We can't stay here. Up the lane, everybody, and quickly, too." Blackberry, Speedwell and Hawkbit ran at once, taking Boxwood and Clover with them into the darkness under the barn. Dandelion remained beside Haystack, begging her to move and expecting every moment to feel the cat's claws in his back. Bigwig leaped across to him.

"Dandelion," he said in his ear, "get out of it, unless you want to be killed!"

"But the—" began Dandelion.

"Do as I say!" said Bigwig. The noise of barking was fearful and he himself was close to panic. Dandelion hesitated a moment longer. Then he left Haystack and shot up the lane, with Bigwig beside him.

They found the others gathered round Hazel, under the bank. Boxwood and Clover were trembling and seemed exhausted. Hazel was talking to them reassuringly, but broke off as Bigwig appeared out of the dark. The dog stopped barking and there was quiet.

"We're all here," said Bigwig. "Shall we go, Hazel?"

"But there were four hutch rabbits," said Hazel. "Where are the other two?"

"In the farmyard," said Blackberry. "We couldn't do anything with them: and then the dog began to bark."

"Yes, I heard it. You mean they're loose?"

"They'll be a lot looser soon," said Bigwig angrily. "The cats are there."

"Why did you leave them, then?"

"Because they wouldn't move. It was bad enough before the dog started."

"Is the dog tied?" asked Hazel.

"Yes, it's tied. But do you expect any rabbit to stand his ground a few feet from an angry dog?"

"No, of course not," replied Hazel. "You've done wonders, Bigwig. They were just telling me, before you came, that you gave one of the cats such a beating that it was afraid to come back for more. Now look, do you think you and Blackberry, with Speedwell here and Hawkbit, can get these two rabbits back to the warren? I'm afraid you may need most of the night. They can't go very fast and you'll have to be patient with them. Dandelion, you come with me, will you?"

"Where, Hazel-rah?"

"To fetch the other two," said Hazel. "You're the fastest, so it won't be so dangerous for you, will it? Now, don't hang about, Bigwig, there's a good fellow. I'll see you tomorrow."

Before Bigwig could reply he had disappeared under the elms. Dandelion remained where he was, looking at Bigwig uncertainly.

"Are you going to do what he says?" asked Bigwig.

"Well, are *you?*" said Dandelion.

It took Bigwig no more than a moment to realize that if he said he was not, complete disorganization would follow. He could not take all the others back into the farm, and he could not leave them alone. He muttered something about Hazel being too embleer clever by half, cuffed Hawkbit off a sow thistle he was nibbling and led his five rabbits over the bank into the field. Dandelion, left alone, set off after Hazel into the farmyard.

As he went down the side of the barn, he could hear Hazel out in the open, near the doe Haystack. Neither of the hutch rabbits had moved from where he and Bigwig had left them. The dog had returned to its kennel; but although it was not to be seen, he felt that it was awake and watchful. He came cautiously out of the shadow and approached Hazel.

"I'm just having a chat with Haystack here," said Hazel. "I've been explaining that we've got a little way to go. Do you think you could hop across to Laurel and get him to join us?"

He spoke almost gaily, but Dandelion could see his dilated eyes and the slight trembling of his front paws. He himself was now sensing something peculiar—a kind of luminosity—in the air. There seemed to be a curious vibration somewhere in the distance. He looked round for the cats and saw that, as he feared, both were crouching in front of the farmhouse a little way off. Their reluctance to come closer could be attributed to Bigwig: but they would not go away. Looking across the yard at them, Dandelion felt a sudden clutch of horror.

"Hazel!" he whispered. "The cats! Dear Frith, why are their eyes glittering green like that? Look!"

Hazel sat up quickly and as he did so Dandelion leaped back in real terror, for Hazel's eyes were shining a deep, glowing red in the dark. At that moment the humming vibration grew louder, quenching the rushing of the night breeze in the elms. Then all four rabbits sat as though transfixed by the sudden, blinding light that poured over them like a cloudburst. Their very instinct was numbed in this terrible glare. The dog barked and then became silent once more. Dandelion tried to move, but could not. The awful brightness seemed to cut into his brain.

The car, which had driven up the lane and over the brow under the elms, came on a few more yards and stopped.

"Lucy's rabbits is out, look!"

"Ah! Best get 'un in quick. Leave loights on!"

The sound of men's voices, from somewhere beyond the fierce light, brought Hazel to his senses. He could not see, but nothing, he realized, had happened to his hearing or his nose. He shut his eyes and at once knew where he was.

"Dandelion! Haystack! Shut your eyes and run," he said. A moment later he smelled the lichen and cool moisture of one of the staddle stones. He was under the barn. Dandelion was near him and a little further away was Haystack. Outside, the men's boots scraped and grated over the stones.

"That's it! Get round be'ind 'un."

" 'E won't go far!"

"Pick 'n up, then!"

Hazel moved across to Haystack. "I'm afraid we'll have to leave Laurel," he said. "Just follow me."

Keeping under the raised floor of the barn, they all three scuttled back toward the elm trees. The men's voices were left behind. Coming out into the grass near the lane, they found the darkness behind the headlights full of the fumes of exhaust—a hostile, choking smell that added to their confusion. Haystack sat down once more and could not be persuaded to move.

"Shouldn't we leave her, Hazel-rah?" asked Dandelion. "After all, the men won't hurt her—they've caught Laurel and taken him back to the hutch."

"If it was a buck, I'd say yes," said Hazel. "But we need this doe. That's what we came for."

At this moment they caught the smell of burning white sticks and heard the men returning up the farmyard. There was a metallic bumping as they rummaged in the car. The sound seemed to rouse Haystack. She looked round at Dandelion.

"I don't want to go back to the hutch," she said.

"You're sure?" asked Dandelion.

"Yes. I'll go with you."

Dandelion immediately turned for the hedgerow. It was only when he had crossed it and reached the ditch beyond that he realized that he was on the opposite side of the lane from that on which they had first approached. He was in a strange ditch. However, there seemed to be nothing to worry about—the ditch led down the slope and that was the way home. He moved slowly along it, waiting for Hazel to join them.

Hazel had crossed the lane a few moments after Dandelion and Haystack. Behind him, he heard the men moving away from the hrududu. As he topped the bank, the beam of a torch shone up the lane and picked out his red eyes and white tail disappearing into the hedge.

"There's ol' woild rabbit, look!"

"Ah! Reckon rest of ours ain't s' far off. Got up there with 'un, see? Best go'n 'ave a look."

In the ditch, Hazel overtook Haystack and Dandelion under a clump of brambles.

"Get on quickly if you can," he said to Haystack. "The men are just behind."

"We can't get on, Hazel," said Dandelion, "without leaving the ditch. It's blocked."

Hazel sniffed ahead. Immediately beyond the brambles, the ditch was closed by a pile of earth, weeds and rubbish. They would have to come into the open. Already the men were over the bank and the torchlight was flickering up and down the hedgerow and through the brambles above their very heads. Then, only a few yards away, footfalls vibrated along the edge of the ditch. Hazel turned to Dandelion.

"Listen," he said, "I'm going to run across the corner of the field, from this ditch to the other one, so that they see me. They'll try to shine that light on me for sure. While they're doing that, you and Haystack climb the bank, get into the lane and run down to the swede shed. You can hide there and I'll join you. Ready?"

There was no time to argue. A moment later Hazel broke almost under the men's feet and ran across the field.

"There 'e goes!"

"Keep torch on 'un, then. Noice and steady!"

Dandelion and Haystack scrambled over the bank and dropped into the lane. Hazel, with the torch beam behind him, had almost reached the other ditch when he felt a sharp blow on one of his hind legs and a hot, stinging pain along his side. The report of the cartridge sounded an instant later. As he somersaulted into a clump of nettles in the ditch bottom, he remembered vividly the scent of beanflowers at sunset. He had not known that the men had a gun.

Hazel crawled through the nettles, dragging his injured leg. In a few moments the men would shine their torch on him and pick him up. He stumbled along the inner wall of the ditch, feeling the blood flowing over his foot. Suddenly he was aware of a draft against one side of his nose, a smell of damp, rotten matter and a hollow, echoing sound at his very ear. He was beside the mouth of a land drain which emptied into the ditch—a smooth, cold tunnel, narrower than a rabbit hole, but wide enough. With flattened ears and belly pressed to the wet floor he crawled up it, pushing a little pile of thin mud in front of him, and lay still as he felt the thud of boots coming nearer.

"I don' roightly know, John, whether you 'it 'e er not."

"Ah, I 'it 'un all roight. That's blood down there, see?"

"Ah, well, but that don't signify. 'E might be a long ways off by now. I reckon you've lost 'e."

"I reckon 'e's in them nettles."

" 'Ave a look, then."

"No, 'e ain't."

"Well, us can't go beggarin' up and down 'ere 'alf bloody night. We got to catch them as got out th'utch. Didn't ought 'ave fired be roights, John. Froightened they off, see? You c'n 'ave a look for 'im tomorrow, if 'e's 'ere."

The silence returned, but still Hazel lay motionless in the whispering chill of the tunnel. A cold lassitude came over him and he passed into a dreaming, inert stupor, full of cramp and pain. After a time, a thread of blood began to trickle over the lip of the drain into the trampled, deserted ditch.

*   *   *

Bigwig, crouched close to Blackberry in the straw of the cattle shed, leaped to flight at the sound of the shot two hundred yards up the lane. He checked himself and turned to the others.

"Don't run!" he said quickly. "Where do you want to run to, anyway? No holes here."

"Further away from the gun," replied Blackberry, white-eyed.

"Wait!" said Bigwig, listening. "They're running down the lane. Can't you hear them?"

"I can hear only two rabbits," answered Blackberry, after a pause, "and one of them sounds exhausted."

They looked at each other and waited. Then Bigwig got up again.

"Stay here, all of you," he said. "I'll go and bring them in."

Out on the verge he found Dandelion urging Haystack, who was lamed and spent.

"Come in here quickly," said Bigwig. "For Frith's sake, where's Hazel?"

"The men have shot him," replied Dandelion.

They reached the other five rabbits in the straw. Dandelion did not wait for their questions.

"They've shot Hazel," he said. "They'd caught that Laurel and put him back in the hutch. Then they came after us. The three of us were at the end of a blocked ditch. Hazel went out of his own accord, to distract their attention while we got away. But we didn't know they had a gun."

"Are you sure they killed him?" said Speedwell.

"I didn't actually see him hit, but they were very close to him."

"We'd better wait," said Bigwig.

They waited a long time. At last Dandelion and Bigwig went cautiously back up the lane. They found the bottom of the ditch trampled by boots and streaked with blood, and returned to tell the others.

The journey back, with the three limping hutch rabbits, lasted more than two weary hours. All were dejected and wretched. When at last they reached the foot of the down Bigwig told Blackberry, Speedwell and Hawkbit to leave them and go on to the warren. They approached the wood just at first light and a rabbit ran to meet them through the wet grass. It was Fiver. Blackberry stopped and waited beside him while the other two went on in silence.

"Fiver," he said, "there's bad news. Hazel—"

"I know," replied Fiver. "I know now."

"How do you know?" asked Blackberry, startled.

"As you came through the grass just now," said Fiver, very low, "there was a fourth rabbit behind you, limping and covered with blood. I ran to see who it was, and then there were only three of you, side by side."

He paused and looked across the down, as though still seeking the bleeding rabbit who had vanished in the half-light. Then, as Blackberry said nothing more, he asked, "Do you know what happened?"

When Blackberry had told his news, Fiver returned to the warren and went underground to his empty burrow. A little later Bigwig brought the hutch rabbits up the hill and at once called everyone to meet in the Honeycomb. Fiver did not appear.

It was a dismal welcome for the strangers. Not even Bluebell could find a cheerful word. Dandelion was inconsolable to think that he might have stopped Hazel breaking from the ditch. The meeting came to an end in a dreary silence and a half-hearted silflay.

Later that morning Holly came limping into the warren. Of his three companions, only Silver was alert and unharmed. Buckthorn was wounded in the face and Strawberry was shivering and evidently ill from exhaustion. There were no other rabbits with them.

26

Fiver Beyond

On his dreadful journey, after the shaman has wandered through dark forests and over great ranges of mountains, . . . he reaches an opening in the ground. The most difficult stage of the adventure now begins. The depths of the underworld open before him.

Uno Harva, quoted by Joseph Campbell
in *The Hero with a Thousand Faces*

Fiver lay on the earth floor of the burrow. Outside, the downs were still in the intense, bright heat of noon. The dew and gossamer had dried early from the grass and by midmorning the finches had fallen silent. Now, along the lonely expanses of wiry turf, the air wavered. On the footpath that led past the warren, bright threads of light—watery, a mirage—trickled and glittered across the shortest, smoothest grass. From a distance the trees along the edge of the beech hanger appeared full of great, dense shadows, impenetrable to the dazzled eye. The only sound was the "Zip, zip" of the grasshoppers, the only scent that of the warm thyme.

In the burrow, Fiver slept and woke uneasily through the heat of the day, fidgeting and scratching as the last traces of moisture dried out of the earth above him. Once, when a trickle of powdery soil fell from the roof, he leaped out of sleep and was in the mouth of the run before he came to himself and returned to where he had been lying. Each time he woke, he remembered the loss of Hazel and suffered once more the knowledge that had pierced him as the shadowy, limping rabbit disappeared in the first light of morning on the down. Where was that rabbit now? Where had it gone? He began to follow it among the tangled paths of his own thoughts, over the cold, dew-wet ridge and down into the dawn mist of the fields below.

The mist swirled round Fiver as he crept through thistles and nettles. Now he could no longer see the limping rabbit ahead. He was alone and afraid, yet perceiving old, familiar sounds and smells—those of the field where he was born. The thick weeds of summer were gone. He was under the bare ash boughs and the flowering blackthorn of March. He was crossing the brook, going up the slope toward the lane, toward the place where Hazel and he had come upon the notice board. Would the board still be there? He looked timidly up the slope. The view was blotted with mist, but as he neared the top he saw a man busy over a pile of tools—a spade, a rope and other, smaller implements, the use of which he did not know. The notice board lay flat on the ground. It was smaller than he remembered and fixed to a single, long, square post, sharpened at the further end to put into the earth. The surface of the board was white, just as he had seen it before, and covered with the sharp black lines like sticks. Fiver came hesitantly up the slope and stopped close to the man, who stood looking down into a deep, narrow hole sunk in the ground at his feet. The man turned to Fiver with the kind of amiability that an ogre might show to a victim whom they both know that he will kill and eat as soon as it suits him to do so.

"Ah! An' what am I doin', eh?" asked the man.

"What *are* you doing?" answered Fiver, staring and twitching with fear.

"I'm just putt'n up this 'ere ol' board," said the man. "And I s'pose you wants t' know what for, eh?"

"Yes," whispered Fiver.

"It's fer that there old 'Azel," said the man. "On'y where 't'is, see, we got t' put up a bit of a notice, like, on 'is account. And what d'you reckon it says, eh?"

"I don't know," said Fiver. "How—how can a board say anything?"

"Ah, but it do, see?" replied the man. "That's where we knows what you don't. That's why we kills you when we 'as a mind to. Now, you wants take a good look at that there board and then very likely you'll know more 'n what you knows now."

In the livid, foggy twilight, Fiver stared at the board. As he stared, the black sticks flickered on the white surface. They raised their sharp, wedge-shaped little heads and chattered together like a nestful of young weasels. The sound, mocking and cruel, came faintly to his ears, as though muffled by sand or sacking. "In memory of Hazel-rah! In memory of Hazel-rah! In memory of Hazel-rah! Ha ha ha ha ha ha!"

"Well, that's where 't'is, see?" said the man. "And I've got t'ang 'im up on this 'ere board. That's t' say, soon's I gets it stood up proper. Same as you'd 'ang up jay, like, or old stoat. Ah! Gon' 'ang 'im up."

"No!" cried Fiver. "No, you shan't!"

"On'y I ain't got 'im, see?" went on the man. "That's why I can't get done. I can't 'ang 'im up, 'cos 'e've gone down th' bloody 'ole, that's where 'e've gone. 'E've gone down th' bloody 'ole, just when I'd got 'n lined an' all, and I can't get 'n out."

Fiver crept up to the man's boots and peered into the hole. It was circular, a cylinder of baked earthenware that disappeared vertically into the ground. He called, "Hazel! Hazel!" Far down in the hole, something moved and he was about to call again. Then the man bent down and hit him between the ears.

Fiver was struggling in a thick cloud of earth, soft and powdery. Someone was saying, "Steady, Fiver, steady!" He sat up. There was soil in his eyes, his ears and nostrils. He could not smell. He shook himself and said, "Who is it?"

"It's Blackberry. I came to see how you were. It's all right; a bit of the roof's fallen, that's all. There've been falls all over the warren today—it's the heat. Anyway, it woke you from a nightmare, if I know anything. You were thrashing about and calling out for Hazel. You poor old chap! What a miserable thing it is to have happened! We must try to bear it as best we can. We've all got to stop running one day, you know. They say Frith knows all the rabbits, every one."

"Is it evening?" asked Fiver.

"Not yet, no. But it's a fair time after ni-Frith. Holly and the others have come back, you know. Strawberry's very ill and they haven't any does with them—not one. Everything's as bad as it could be. Holly's still asleep—he was completely exhausted. He said he'd tell us what happened this evening. When we told him about poor Hazel, he said— Fiver, you're not listening. I expect you'd rather I kept quiet."

"Blackberry," said Fiver, "do you know the place where Hazel was shot?"

"Yes, Bigwig and I went and looked at the ditch before we came away. But you mustn't—"

"Could you go there with me now?"

"Go back there? Oh, no. It's a long way, Fiver, and what would be the good? The risk, and this fearful heat, and you'd only make yourself wretched."

"Hazel isn't dead," said Fiver.

"Yes, the men took him away. Fiver, I saw the blood."

"Yes, but you didn't see Hazel, because he isn't dead. Blackberry, you must do what I ask."

"You're asking too much."

"Then I shall have to go alone. But what I'm asking you to do is to come and save Hazel's life."

When at last Blackberry had reluctantly given in and they had set out down the hill, Fiver went almost as fast as though he were running for cover. Again and again he urged Blackberry to make haste. The fields were empty in the glare. Every creature bigger than a bluebottle was sheltering from the heat. When they reached the outlying sheds beside the lane, Blackberry began to explain how he and Bigwig had gone back to search; but Fiver cut him short.

"We have to go up the slope, I know that: but you must show me the ditch."

The elms were still. There was not the least sound in the leaves. The ditch was thick with cow parsley, hemlock and long trails of green-flowering bryony. Blackberry led the way to the trampled patch of nettles and Fiver sat still among them, sniffing and looking about him in the silence. Blackberry watched him disconsolately. A faint breath of wind stole across the fields and a blackbird began to sing from somewhere beyond the elms. At last Fiver began to move along the bottom of the ditch. The insects buzzed round his ears and suddenly a little cloud of flies flew up, disturbed from a projecting stone. No, not a stone. It was smooth and regular—a circular lip of earthenware. The brown mouth of a drain, stained black at the lower edge by a thin, dried thread of blood: of rabbit's blood.

"The bloody hole!" whispered Fiver. "The bloody hole!"

He peered into the dark opening. It was blocked. Blocked by a rabbit. That was plain to be smelled. A rabbit whose faint pulse could just be heard, magnified in the confined tunnel.

"Hazel?" said Fiver.

Blackberry was beside him at once. "What is it, Fiver?"

"Hazel's in that hole," said Fiver, "and he's alive."

27

"You Can't Imagine It Unless You've Been There"

My Godda bless, never I see sucha people.
Signor Piozzi, quoted by Cecilia Thrale

In the Honeycomb, Bigwig and Holly were waiting to begin the second meeting since the loss of Hazel. As the air began to cool, the rabbits woke and first one and then another came down the runs that led from the smaller burrows. All were subdued and doubtful at heart. Like the pain of a bad wound, the effect of a deep shock takes some while to be felt. When a child is told, for the first time in his life, that a person he has known is dead, although he does not disbelieve it, he may well fail to comprehend it and later ask—perhaps more than once—where the dead person is and when he is coming back. When Pipkin had planted in himself, like some somber tree, the knowledge that Hazel would never return, his bewilderment exceeded his grief: and this bewilderment he saw on every side among his companions. Faced with no crisis of action and with nothing to prevent them from continuing their life in the warren as before, the rabbits were nevertheless overcome by the conviction that their luck was gone. Hazel was dead and Holly's expedition had totally failed. What would follow?

Holly, gaunt, his staring pelt full of goose grass and fragments of burdock, was talking with the three hutch rabbits and reassuring them as best he could. No one could say now that Hazel had thrown away his life in a foolhardy prank. The two does were the only gain that anyone had made—the warren's only asset. But they were plainly so ill at ease in their new surroundings that Holly was already contending against his own belief that there was little to be hoped for from them. Does who are upset and on edge tend to be infertile; and how were these does to make themselves at home in strange conditions and a place where everyone was lost so poorly in his thoughts? They would die, perhaps, or wander away. He buckled once more to the task of explaining that he was sure better times lay ahead—and as he did so, felt himself the least convinced of any.

Bigwig had sent Acorn to see whether there was anyone still to come. Acorn returned to say that Strawberry felt too ill and that he could find neither Blackberry nor Fiver.

"Well, leave Fiver," said Bigwig. "Poor fellow, he'll feel better by himself for a time, I dare say."

"He's not in his burrow, though," said Acorn.

"Never mind," said Bigwig. But the thought came to him, "Fiver and Blackberry? Could they have left the warren without telling anyone? If they have, what will happen when the others get to know?" Should he ask Kehaar to go and look for them while there was still light? But if Kehaar found them, what then? They could not be compelled to return. Or if they were, what good would that do, if they wanted to be gone? At that moment Holly began to speak and everyone became quiet.

"We all know we're in a mess," said Holly, "and I suppose

before long we shall have to talk about what's best to be done. But I thought that first of all I ought to tell you how it is that we four—Silver, Buckthorn, Strawberry and I—have come back without any does. You don't have to remind me that when we set out, everyone thought it was going to be straightforward. And here we are, one rabbit sick, one wounded and nothing to show for it. You're all wondering why."

"No one's blaming you, Holly," said Bigwig.

"I don't know whether I'm to blame or not," replied Holly. "But you'll tell me that when you've heard the story.

"That morning when we left, it was good weather for hlessil on the move and we all felt there was no hurry. It was cool, I remember, and looked as if it would be some time before the day got really bright and cloudless. There's a farm not far away from the other end of this wood, and although there were no men about so early, I didn't fancy going that way, so we kept up on high ground on the evening side. We were all expecting to come to the edge of the down, but there isn't any steep edge as there is on the north. The upland just goes on and on, open, dry and lonely. There's plenty of cover for rabbits—standing corn, hedges and banks—but no real woodland: just great, open fields of light soil with big white flintstones. I was hoping that we might find ourselves in the sort of country we used to know—meadows and woods—but we didn't. Anyhow, we found a track with a good, thick hedge along one side and we decided to follow that. We took it easy and stopped a good deal, because I was taking care to avoid running into elil. I'm sure it's bad country for stoats as well as foxes, and I hadn't much idea what we were going to do if we met one."

"I'm pretty certain we did pass close to a weasel," said Silver. "I could smell it. But you know how it is with elil—if they're not actually hunting, they often take no notice of you. We left very little scent, and buried our hraka as though we were cats."

"Well, before ni-Frith," went on Holly, "the track brought us to a long, thin wood running right across the way we were going. These downland woods are queer, aren't they? This was no thicker than the one above us now, but it stretched as far as we could see either way, in a dead straight line. I don't like straight lines: men make them. And sure enough, we found a road beside this wood. It was a very lonely, empty road, but all the same I didn't want to hang about there, so we went straight through the wood and out the other side. Kehaar spotted us in the fields beyond and told us to alter our direction. I asked him how we were getting on and he said we were about halfway, so I thought we might as well start looking for somewhere to lie up for the night. I didn't fancy the open, and in the end we made scrapes in the bottom of a kind of little pit we found. Then we had a good feed and passed the night very well.

"I don't think we need tell you everything about the journey. It came on to rain just after the morning feed and there was a nasty, cold wind with it, so we stayed where we were until after ni-Frith. It brightened up then and we went on. The going wasn't very nice because of the wet, but by early evening I reckoned we ought to be near the place. I was looking round when a hare came through the grass and I asked him whether he knew of a big warren close by.

" '*Efrafa?*' he asked. 'Are you going to Efrafa?' *

" 'If that's what it's called,' I answered.

" 'Do you know it?'

" 'No,' I said, 'we don't. We want to know where it is.'

" 'Well,' he said, 'my advice to you is to run, and quickly.'

"I was just wondering what to make of that, when suddenly three big rabbits came over the bank, just the way I did that night when I came to arrest you, Bigwig: and one of them said, 'Can I see your marks?'

" 'Marks?' I said. 'What marks? I don't understand.'

" 'You're not from Efrafa?'

" 'No,' I said, 'we're going there. We're strangers.'

" 'Will you come with me?' No 'Have you come far?' or 'Are you wet through?' or anything like that.

"So then these three rabbits took us off down the bank and that was how we came to Efrafa, as they call it. And I'd better try and tell you something about it, so that you'll know what a dirty little bunch of sniveling hedge-scrapers we are here.

"Efrafa is a big warren—a good deal bigger than the one we came from—the Threarah's, I mean. And the one fear of every rabbit in it is that men are going to find them and infect them with the white blindness. The whole warren is organized to conceal its

---

* The first syllable is stressed and not the second, as in the word "Majesty."

existence. The holes are all hidden and the Owsla have every rabbit in the place under orders. You can't call your life your own: and in return you have safety—if it's worth having at the price you pay.

"As well as the Owsla, they have what they call a Council, and each of the Council rabbits has some special thing he looks after. One looks after feeding; another's responsible for the ways in which they keep hidden; another looks after breeding, and so on. As far as the ordinary rabbits are concerned, only a certain number can be above ground at one time. Every rabbit is marked when he's a kitten: they bite them, deep, under the chin or in a haunch or forepaw. Then they can be told by the scar for the rest of their lives. You mustn't be found above ground unless it's the right time of day for your Mark."

"Who's to stop you?" growled Bigwig.

"That's the really frightening part. The Owsla—well, you can't imagine it unless you've been there. The Chief is a rabbit named Woundwort: General Woundwort, they call him. I'll tell you more about him in a minute. Then under him there are captains—each one in charge of a Mark—and each captain has his own officers and sentries. There's a Mark captain with his band on duty at every time of the day and night. If a man happens to come anywhere near, which isn't often, the sentries give warning long before he comes close enough to see anything. They give warning of elil, too. They prevent anyone dropping hraka except in special places in the ditches, where it's buried. And if they see any rabbit above ground whom they don't recognize as having the right to be there, they ask to see his mark. Frith knows what happens if he can't explain himself—but I can guess pretty well. Rabbits in Efrafa quite often go days at a time without the sight of Frith. If their Mark's on night silflay, then they feed by night, wet or fine, warm or cold. They're all used to talking, playing and mating in the burrows underground. If a Mark can't silflay at their appointed time for some reason or other—say there was a man working somewhere near—that's just too bad. They miss their turn till next day."

"But surely it alters them very much, living like that?" asked Dandelion.

"Very much indeed," replied Holly. "Most of them can't do anything but what they're told. They've never been out of Efrafa and never smelled an enemy. The one aim of every rabbit in Efrafa is to get into the Owsla, because of the privileges: and the one aim of everyone in the Owsla is to get into the Council. The Council have the best of everything. But the Owsla have to keep very strong and tough. They take it in turn to do what they call Wide Patrol. They go out over the country—all round the place—living in the open for days at a time. It's partly to find out anything they can, and partly to train them and make them tough and cunning. Any hlessil they find they pick up and bring back to Efrafa. If they won't come, they kill them. They reckon hlessil a danger, because they may attract the attention of men. The Wide Patrols report back to General Woundwort, and the Council decide what to do about anything new that they think may be dangerous."

"They missed you on the way in, then?" said Bluebell.

"Oh, no, they didn't! We learned later that some time after we'd been brought in by this rabbit—Captain Campion—a runner arrived from a Wide Patrol to say that they'd picked up the track of three or four rabbits coming toward Efrafa from the north, and were there any orders? He was sent back to say that we were safely under control.

"Anyway, this Captain Campion took us down to a hole in the ditch. The mouth of the hole was a bit of old earthenware pipe and if a man had pulled it out, the opening would have fallen in and showed no trace of the run inside. And there he handed us over to another captain—because he had to go back above ground for the rest of his spell of duty, you see. We were taken to a big burrow and told to make ourselves at home.

"There were other rabbits in the burrow and it was by listening to them and asking questions that I learned most of what I've been telling you. We got talking to some of the does and I made friends with one called Hyzenthlay.* I told her about our problem here and why we'd come, and then she told us about Efrafa. When she'd finished I said, 'It sounds terrible. Has it always been like this?' She said no, her mother had told her that in years gone by the warren had been elsewhere and much smaller, but when General Woundwort came, he had made them move to Efrafa and then he'd worked out this whole system of concealment and perfected it until rabbits in Efrafa were as safe as stars in the sky. 'Most rabbits here

---

* Hyzenthlay: "Shine-Dew-Fur"—fur-shining-like-dew.

die of old age, unless the Owsla kill them off,' she said. 'But the trouble is, there are more rabbits now than the warren can hold. Any fresh digging that's allowed has to be done under Owsla supervision and they do it terribly slowly and carefully. It all has to be hidden, you see. We're overcrowded and a lot of rabbits don't get above ground as much as they need to. And for some reason there are not enough bucks and too many does. A lot of us have found we can't produce litters, because of the overcrowding, but no one is ever allowed to leave. Only a few days ago, several of us does went to the Council and asked whether we could form an expedition to start a new warren somewhere else. We said we'd go far, far away—as far away as they liked. But they wouldn't hear of it—not on any account. Things can't go on like this—the system's breaking down. But it doesn't do to be heard talking about it.'

"Well, I thought, this sounds hopeful. Surely they won't object to our proposals? We only want to take a few does and no bucks. They've got more does than there's room for and we want to take them further away than anyone here can ever have been.

"A little later another captain came and said we were to come with him to the Council meeting.

"The Council meet in a kind of big burrow. It's long and rather narrow—not as good as this Honeycomb of ours, because they've got no tree roots to make a wide roof. We had to wait outside while they were talking about all sorts of other things. We were just one piece of daily Council business: 'Strangers apprehended.' There was another rabbit waiting and he was under special guard—Owslafa, they call them: the Council police. I've never been near anyone so frightened in my life—I thought he'd go mad with fear. I asked one of these Owslafa what was the matter and he said that this rabbit, Blackavar, had been caught trying to run away from the warren. Well, they took him inside and first of all we heard the poor fellow trying to explain himself, and then he was crying and begging for mercy: and when he came out they'd ripped both his ears to shreds, worse than this one of mine. We were all sniffing at him, absolutely horror-stricken; but one of the Owslafa said, 'You needn't make such a fuss. He's lucky to be alive.' So while we were chewing on that, someone came out and said the Council were ready for us.

"As soon as we got in, we were put up in front of this General

Woundwort, and he really is a grim customer. I don't think even you'd match up to him, Bigwig. He's almost as big as a hare and there's something about his mere presence that frightens you, as if blood and fighting and killing were all just part of the day's work to him. I thought he'd begin by asking us some questions about who we were and what we wanted, but he didn't do anything like that. He said, 'I'm going to explain the rules of the warren and the conditions on which you'll live here. You must listen carefully, because the rules are to be kept and any breaking of them will be punished.' So then I spoke up at once and said that there was a misunderstanding. We were an embassy, I said, come from another warren to ask for Efrafa's goodwill and help. And I went on to explain that all we wanted was their agreement to our persuading a few does to come back with us. When I'd finished, General Woundwort said that it was out of the question: there was nothing to discuss. I replied that we'd like to stay with them for a day or two and try to persuade them to change their mind.

" 'Oh, yes,' he said, 'you'll stay. But there'll be no further occasion for you to take up the Council's time—for the next few days at any rate.'

"I said that seemed very hard. Our request was surely a reasonable one. And I was just going to ask them to consider one or two things from our point of view, when another of the Councillors—a very old rabbit—said, 'You seem to think you're here to argue with us and drive a bargain. But we're the ones to say what you're going to do.'

"I said they should remember that we were representing another warren, even if it was smaller than theirs. We thought of ourselves as their guests. And it was only when I'd said that that I realized with a horrible shock that they thought of us as their prisoners: or as good as prisoners, whatever *they* might call it.

"Well, I'd rather say no more about the end of that meeting. Strawberry tried all he could to help me. He spoke very well about the decency and comradeship natural to animals. 'Animals don't behave like men,' he said. 'If they have to fight, they fight; and if they have to kill, they kill. But they don't sit down and set their wits to work to devise ways of spoiling other creatures' lives and hurting them. They have dignity and animality.'

"But it was all no use. At last we fell silent and General

Woundwort said, 'The Council can't spare any more time for you now, and I shall have to leave it to your Mark captain to tell you the rules. You'll join the Right Flank Mark under Captain Bugloss. Later, we shall see you again and you'll find us perfectly friendly and helpful to rabbits who understand what's expected of them.'

"So then the Owsla took us out to join the Right Flank Mark. Apparently Captain Bugloss was too busy to see us and I took care to keep out of his way, because I thought he might want to start marking us then and there. But soon I began to understand what Hyzenthlay had meant when she said the system wasn't working properly any more. The burrows were overcrowded—at least by our standards. It was easy to escape attention. Even in one Mark the rabbits don't all know each other. We found places in a burrow and tried to get some sleep, but early in the night we were woken and told to silflay. I thought there might be a chance to run for it in the moonlight, but there seemed to be sentries everywhere. And besides the sentries, the Captain kept two runners with him, whose job was to rush off at once in any direction from which an alarm might be given.

"When we'd fed we went underground again. Nearly all the rabbits were very subdued and docile. We avoided them, because we meant to escape if we could and we didn't want to get known. But try as I would, I couldn't think of a plan.

"We fed again some time before ni-Frith the next day, and then it was back underground. The time dragged terribly. At last—it must have been as evening was coming on—I joined a little group of rabbits listening to a story. And do you know, it was 'The King's Lettuce'? The rabbit who was telling it was nowhere near as good as Dandelion, but I listened all the same, just for something to do. And it was when he got to the bit where El-ahrairah dresses up and pretends to be the doctor at King Darzin's palace that I suddenly had an idea. It was a very risky one, but I thought there was a chance that it might work, simply because every rabbit in Efrafa usually does what he's told without question. I'd been watching Captain Bugloss and he struck me as a nice enough fellow, conscientious and a bit weak and rather harassed by having more to do than he could really cope with.

"That night, when we were called to silflay, it was pitch dark and raining; but you don't bother about a little thing like that in

Efrafa—you're only too glad to get out and get some food. All the rabbits trooped up; and we waited until the very last. Captain Bugloss was out on the bank, with two of his sentries. Silver and the others went out in front of me and then I came up to him panting as if I'd been running.

" 'Captain Bugloss?'

" 'Yes?' he said. 'What is it?'

" 'You're wanted by the Council, at once.'

" 'Why, what do you mean?' he asked. 'What for?'

" 'No doubt they'll tell you that when they see you,' I answered. 'I shouldn't keep them waiting if I were you.'

" 'Who are you?' he said. 'You're not one of the Council runners. I know them all. What Mark are you?'

" 'I'm not here to answer your questions,' I said. 'Shall I go back and tell them you won't come?'

"He looked doubtful at that and I made as if I were going. But then, all of a sudden, he said, 'Very well'—he looked awfully frightened, poor fellow—'but who's to take over here while I'm gone?'

" 'I am,' I said. 'General Woundwort's orders. But come back quickly. I don't want to hang about half the night doing your job.' He scuttled off. I turned to the other two and said, 'Stay here, and look alive, too. I'm going round the sentries.'

"Well, then the four of us ran off into the dark and, sure enough, after we'd gone a little way two sentries popped up and tried to stop us. We all piled straight into them. I thought they'd run, but they didn't. They fought like mad and one of them tore Buckthorn all down the nose. But of course there were four of us; and in the end we broke past them and simply tore across the field. We had no idea which way we were going, what with the rain and the night: we just ran. I think the reason why the pursuit was a bit slow off the mark was because poor old Bugloss wasn't there to give the orders. Anyway, we had a fair start. But presently we could hear that we were being followed—and, what was worse, we were being overtaken.

"The Efrafan Owsla are no joke, believe me. They're all picked for size and strength and there's nothing they don't know about moving in wet and darkness. They're all so much afraid of the Council that they're not afraid of anything else. It wasn't long before I knew we were in trouble. The patrol that was after us could actually follow us in the dark and rain faster than we could run away, and before long they were close behind. I was just going to tell the others that there was nothing for it but to turn and fight when we came to a great, steep bank that seemed to slope almost straight up into the air. It was steeper than this hillside below us here, and the slope seemed to be regular, as if men had made it.

"Well, there was no time to think about it, so up we went. It was covered with rough grass and bushes. I don't know how far it was to the top exactly, but I should guess it was as high as a well-grown rowan tree—perhaps a bit higher. When we got to the top we found ourselves on small, light stones that shifted as we ran on them. That gave us away completely. Then we came upon broad, flat pieces of wood and two great, fixed bars of metal that made a noise—a kind of low, humming noise in the dark. I was just saying to myself, 'This is men's work, all right,' when I fell over the other side. I hadn't realized that the whole top of the bank was only a very short distance across and the other side was just as steep. I went head over heels down the bank in the dark and fetched up against an elder bush—and there I lay."

Holly stopped and fell silent, as though pondering on what he remembered. At last he said,

"It's going to be very hard to describe to you what happened next. Although all four of us were there, we don't understand it ourselves. But what I'm going to say now is the cold truth. Lord Frith sent one of his great Messengers to save us from the Efrafan Owsla. Each one of us had fallen over the edge of the bank in one place or another. Buckthorn, who was half blinded with his own blood, went down almost to the bottom. I'd picked myself up and was looking back at the top. There was just enough light in the sky to see the Efrafans if they came over. And then—then an enormous thing—I can't give you any idea of it—as big as a thousand hrududil—bigger—came rushing out of the night. It was full of fire and smoke and light and it roared and beat on the metal lines until the ground shook beneath it. It drove in between us and the Efrafans like a thousand thunderstorms with lightning. I tell you, I was beyond being afraid. I couldn't move. The flashing and the noise—they split the whole night apart. I don't know what happened to the Efrafans: either they ran away or it cut them down. And then suddenly it was gone and we heard it disappearing, rattle and bang, rattle and bang, far away in the distance. We were completely alone.

"For a long time I couldn't move. At last I got up and found the others, one by one, in the dark. None of us said a word. At the bottom of the slope we discovered a kind of tunnel that went right through the bank from one side to the other. We crept into it and came out on the side where we'd gone up. Then we went a long way through the fields, until I reckoned we must be well clear of Efrafa. We crawled into a ditch and slept there, all four of us, until morning. There was no reason why anything shouldn't have come and killed us, and yet we knew we were safe. You may think it's a wonderful thing to be saved by Lord Frith in his power. How many rabbits has that happened to, I wonder? But I tell you, it was far more frightening than being chased by the Efrafans. Not one of us will forget lying on that bank in the rain while the fire creature went by above our heads. Why did it come on our account? That's more than we shall ever know.

"The next morning I cast around a bit and soon I knew which was the right direction. You know how you always do. The rain had stopped and we set out. But it was a very hard journey back. We were exhausted long before the end—all except Silver: I don't know what we'd have done without him. We went on for a day and a night without any real rest at all. We all felt that the only thing we wanted to do was to get back here as soon as we could. When I reached the wood this morning I was just limping along in a bad dream. I'm not really much better than poor old Strawberry, I'm afraid. He never complained, but he'll need a long rest and I rather think I shall, too. And Buckthorn—that's the second bad wound he's had. But that's not the worst now, is it? We've lost Hazel: the worst thing that could have happened. Some of you asked me earlier this evening if I would be Chief Rabbit. I'm glad to know you trust me, but I'm completely done in and I can't possibly take it on yet. I feel as dry and empty as an autumn puffball—I feel as though the wind could blow my fur away."

28

At the Foot of the Hill

Marvellous happy it was to be
Alone, and yet not solitary.
O out of terror and dark, to come
In sight of home.

Walter de la Mare, The Pilgrim

"You're not too tired to silflay, are you?" asked Dandelion. "And at the proper time of day, for a change? It's a lovely evening, if my nose says right. We ought to try not to be more miserable than we can help, you know."

"Just before we silflay," said Bigwig, "can I tell you, Holly, that I don't believe anyone else could have brought himself and three other rabbits safely back out of a place like that?"

"Frith meant us to get back," replied Holly. "That's the real reason why we're here."

As he turned to follow Speedwell up the run that led into the wood, he found Clover beside him. "You and your friends must find it strange to go outside and eat grass," he said. "You'll get used to it, you know. And I can promise you that Hazel-rah was right when he told you it's a better life here than in a hutch. Come with me and I'll show you a patch of nice, short tail-grass, if Bigwig hasn't had it all while I've been away."

Holly had taken to Clover. She seemed more robust and less timid than Boxwood and Haystack and was evidently doing her best to adapt herself to warren life. What her stock might be he could not tell, but she looked healthy.

"I like it underground all right," said Clover, as they came up into the fresh air. "The closed space is really very much like a hutch, except that it's darker. The difficult thing for us is going to be feeding in the open. We're not used to being free to go where we like and we don't know what to do. You all act so quickly and half the time I don't know why. I'd prefer not to feed very far from the hole, if you don't mind."

They moved slowly across the sunset grass, nibbling as they went: Clover was soon absorbed in feeding, but Holly stopped continually to sit up and sniff about him at the peaceful, empty down. When he noticed Bigwig, a little way off, staring fixedly to the north, he at once followed his gaze.

"What is it?" he asked.

"It's Blackberry," replied Bigwig. He sounded relieved.

Blackberry came hopping rather slowly down from the skyline. He looked tired out, but as soon as he saw the other rabbits he came on faster and made his way to Bigwig.

"Where have you been?" asked Bigwig. "And where's Fiver? Wasn't he with you?"

"Fiver's with Hazel," said Blackberry. "Hazel's alive. He's been wounded—it's hard to tell how badly—but he won't die."

The other three rabbits looked at him speechlessly. Blackberry waited, enjoying the effect.

"Hazel's *alive?*" said Bigwig. "Are you sure?"

"Quite sure," said Blackberry. "He's at the foot of the hill at this very moment, in that ditch where you were the night Holly and Bluebell arrived."

"I can hardly believe it," said Holly. "If it's true, it's the best news I've ever heard in my life. Blackberry, you really are sure? What happened? Tell us."

"Fiver found him," said Blackberry. "Fiver took me with him, nearly all the way back to the farm: then he went along the ditch and found Hazel gone to ground up a land drain. He was very weak from loss of blood and he couldn't get out of the drain by himself. We had to drag him by his good hind leg. He couldn't turn round, you see."

"But how on earth did Fiver know?"

"How does Fiver know what he knows? You'd better ask him. When we'd got Hazel into the ditch, Fiver looked to see how badly he was hurt. He's got a nasty wound in one hind leg, but the bone isn't broken: and he's torn all along one side. We cleaned up the places as well as we could and then we started out to bring him back. It's taken us the whole evening. Can you imagine it—daylight, dead silence and a lame rabbit reeking of fresh blood? Luckily, it's been the hottest day we've had this summer—not a mouse stirring. Time and again we had to take cover in the cow parsley and rest. I was all on the jump, but Fiver was like a butterfly on a stone. He sat in the grass and combed his ears. 'Don't get upset,' he kept saying. 'There's nothing to worry about. We can take our time.' After what I'd seen, I'd have believed him if he'd said we could hunt foxes. But when we got to the bottom of the hill Hazel was completely finished and he couldn't go any further. He and Fiver have taken shelter in the overgrown ditch and I came on to tell you. And here I am."

There was silence while Bigwig and Holly took in the news. At last Bigwig said, "Will they stay there tonight?"

"I think so," replied Blackberry. "I'm sure Hazel won't be able to manage the hill until he's a good deal stronger."

"I'll go down there," said Bigwig. "I can help to make the ditch a bit more comfortable, and probably Fiver will be able to do with someone else to help to look after Hazel."

"I should hurry, then, if I were you," said Blackberry. "The sun will be down soon."

"Hah!" said Bigwig. "If I meet a stoat, it'd better look out, that's all. I'll bring you one back tomorrow, shall I?" He raced off and disappeared over the edge.

"Let's go and get the others together," said Holly. "Come on, Blackberry, you'll have to tell the whole thing, from the beginning."

The three quarters of a mile in the blazing heat, from Nuthanger to the foot of the hill, had cost Hazel more pain and effort than anything in his life. If Fiver had not found him, he would have died in the drain. When Fiver's urging had penetrated his dark, ebbing stupor, he had at first actually tried not to respond. It was so much easier to remain where he was, on the far side of the suffering he had undergone. Later, when he found himself lying in the green gloom of the ditch, with Fiver searching his wounds and assuring him that he could stand and move, still he could not face the idea of setting out to return. His torn side throbbed and the pain in his leg seemed to have affected his senses. He felt dizzy and could not hear or smell properly. At last, when he understood that Fiver and Blackberry had risked a second journey to the farm, in the broadest of daylight, solely to find him and save his life, he forced himself to his feet and began to stumble down the slope to the road. His sight was swimming and he had to stop again and again. Without Fiver's encouragement he would have lain down once more and given up.

In the road, he could not climb the bank and had to limp along the verge until he could crawl under a gate. Much later, as they came under the pylon line, he remembered the overgrown ditch at the foot of the hill and set himself to reach it. Once there, he lay down and at once returned to the sleep of total exhaustion.

When Bigwig arrived, just before dark, he found Fiver snatching a quick feed in the long grass. It was out of the question to disturb Hazel by digging, and they spent the night crouched beside him on the narrow floor.

Coming out in the gray light before dawn, the first creature Bigwig saw was Kehaar, foraging between the elders. He stamped to attract his attention and Kehaar sailed across to him with one beat of his wings and a long glide.

"Meester Pigvig, you find Meester 'Azel?"

"Yes," said Bigwig, "he's in the ditch here."

"'E not dead?"

"No, but he's wounded and very weak. The farm man shot him with a gun, you know."

"You get black stones out?"

"How do you mean?"

"Alvays vid gun ees coming liddle black stones. You never see?"

"No, I don't know about guns."

"Take out black stones, 'e get better. 'E come now, ya?"

"I'll see," said Bigwig. He went down to Hazel and found him awake and talking to Fiver. When Bigwig told him that Kehaar was outside he dragged himself up the short run and into the grass.

"Dis damn gun," said Kehaar. "'E put liddle stones for 'urt you. I look, ya?"

"I suppose you'd better," said Hazel. "My leg's still very bad, I'm afraid."

He lay down and Kehaar's head flicked from side to side as though he were looking for snails in Hazel's brown fur. He peered closely up the length of the torn flank.

"Ees not stones 'ere," he said. "Go in, go out—no stop. Now I see you leg. Maybe 'urt you, not long."

Two shotgun pellets were buried in the muscle of the haunch. Kehaar detected them by smell and removed them exactly as he might have picked spiders out of a crack. Hazel had barely time to flinch before Bigwig was sniffing at the pellets in the grass.

"Now ees more bleed," said Kehaar. "You stay, vait maybe vun, two day. Den goot like before. Dose rabbits up dere, all vait, vait for Meester 'Azel. I tell dem 'e come." He flew off before they could reply.

As things turned out, Hazel stayed three days at the foot of the hill. The hot weather continued and for much of the time he sat under the elder branches, dozing above ground like some solitary hlessi and feeling his strength returning. Fiver stayed with him, keeping the wounds clean and watching his recovery. Often they would say nothing for hours together, lying in the rough, warm grass while the shadows moved to evening, until at last the local blackbird cocked its tail and tuck-tucked away to roost. Neither spoke of Nuthanger Farm, but Hazel showed plainly enough that for the future Fiver, when he gave advice, would have no hard task to get him to accept it.

"Hrairoo," said Hazel one evening, "what would we have done without you? We'd none of us be here, would we?"

"You're sure we *are* here, then?" asked Fiver.

"That's too mysterious for me," replied Hazel. "What do you mean?"

"Well, there's another place—another country, isn't there? We go there when we sleep; at other times, too; and when we die. El-ahrairah comes and goes between the two as he wants, I suppose, but I could never quite make that out, from the tales. Some rabbits will tell you it's all easy there, compared with the waking dangers that they understand. But I think that only shows they don't know much about it. It's a wild place, and very unsafe. And where are we really—there or here?"

"Our bodies stay here—that's good enough for me. You'd better go and talk to that Silverweed fellow—he might know more."

"Oh, you remember him? I felt that when we were listening to him, you know. He terrified me and yet I knew that I understood him better than anyone else in that place. He knew where he belonged, and it wasn't here. Poor fellow, I'm sure he's dead. They'd got him, all right—the ones in that country. They don't give their secrets away for nothing, you know. But look! Here come Holly and Blackberry, so we'd better feel sure we're here just for the moment, anyway."

Holly had already come down the hill on the previous day to see

Hazel and tell again the story of his escape from Efrafa. When he had spoken of his deliverance by the great apparition in the night, Fiver had listened attentively and asked one question, "Did it make a noise?" Later, when Holly had gone back, he told Hazel that he felt sure there was some natural explanation, though he had no idea what it could be. Hazel, however, had not been greatly interested. For him, the important thing was their disappointment and the reason for it. Holly had achieved nothing and this was entirely due to the unexpected unfriendliness of the Efrafan rabbits. This evening, as soon as they had begun to feed, Hazel returned to the matter.

"Holly," he said, "we're hardly any nearer to solving our problem, are we? You've done wonders and got nothing to show for it, and the Nuthanger raid was only a silly lark, I'm afraid—and an expensive one for me, at that. The real hole has still got to be dug."

"Well," said Holly, "you say it was only a lark, Hazel, but at least it gave us two does: and they're the only two we've got."

"Are they any good?"

The kind of ideas that have become natural to many male human beings in thinking of females—ideas of protection, fidelity, romantic love and so on—are, of course, unknown to rabbits, although rabbits certainly do form exclusive attachments much more frequently than most people realize. However, they are not romantic and it came naturally to Hazel and Holly to consider the two Nuthanger does simply as breeding stock for the warren. This was what they had risked their lives for.

"Well, it's hard to say, yet," replied Holly. "They're doing their best to settle down with us—Clover particularly. She seems very sensible. But they're extraordinarily helpless, you know—I've never seen anything like it—and I'm afraid they may turn out to be delicate in bad weather. They might survive next winter and then again they might not. But you weren't to know that when you got them out of the farm."

"With a bit of luck, they might each have a litter before the winter," said Hazel. "I know the breeding season's over, but everything's so topsy-turvy with us here that there's no saying."

"Well, you ask me what I think," said Holly. "I'll tell you. I think they're precious little to be the only thing between us and the end of everything we've managed to do so far. I think they may very well not have any kittens for some time, partly because this isn't the season and partly because the life's so strange to them. And when they do, the kittens will very likely have a lot of this man-bred hutch stock in them. But what else is there to hope for? We must do the best we can with what we've got."

"Has anyone mated with them yet?" asked Hazel.

"No, neither of them has been ready so far. But I can see some fine old fights breaking out when they are."

"That's another problem. We can't go on with nothing but these two does."

"But what else can we do?"

"I know *what* we've got to do," said Hazel, "but I still can't see *how*. We've got to go back and get some does out of Efrafa."

"You might as well say you were going to get them out of Inlé, Hazel-rah. I'm afraid I can't have given you a very clear description of Efrafa."

"Oh, yes, you have—the whole idea scares me stiff. But we're going to do it."

"It can't be done."

"It can't be done by fighting or fair words, no. So it will have to be done by means of a trick."

"There's no trick will get the better of that lot, believe me. There are far more of them than there are of us: they're very highly organized: and I'm only telling the truth when I say that they can fight, run and follow a trail every bit as well as we can, and a lot of them, much better."

"The trick," said Hazel, turning to Blackberry, who all this time had been nibbling and listening in silence, "the trick will have to do three things. First, it will have to get the does out of Efrafa and secondly it will have to put paid to the pursuit. For a pursuit there's bound to be and we can't expect another miracle. But that's not all. Once we're clear of the place, we've got to become impossible to find—beyond the reach of any Wide Patrol."

"Yes," said Blackberry doubtfully. "Yes, I agree. To succeed we should have to manage all those things."

"Yes. And this trick, Blackberry, is going to be devised by you."

The sweet, carrion scent of dogwood filled the air; in the evening sunshine, the insects hummed around the dense white cymes hanging low above the grass. A pair of brown-and-orange beetles, disturbed by the feeding rabbits, took off from a grass stem and flew away, still coupled together.

"They mate. We don't," said Hazel, watching them go. "A trick, Blackberry: a trick to put us right once and for all."

"I can see how to do the first thing," said Blackberry. "At least, I think I can. But it's dangerous. The other two I can't see at all yet and I'd like to talk it over with Fiver."

"The sooner Fiver and I get back to the warren the better," said Hazel. "My leg's good enough now, but all the same I think we'll leave it for tonight. Good old Holly, will you tell them that Fiver and I will come early tomorrow morning? It worries me to think that Bigwig and Silver may start fighting about Clover at any moment."

"Hazel," said Holly, "listen. I don't like this idea of yours at all. I've been in Efrafa and you haven't. You're making a bad mistake and you might very well get us all killed."

It was Fiver who replied. "It ought to feel like that, I know," he said, "but somehow it doesn't: not to me. I believe we can do it. Anyway, I'm sure Hazel's right when he says it's the only chance we've got. Suppose we go on talking about it for a bit?"

"Not now," said Hazel. "Time for underground down here— come on. But if you two race up the hill, you'll probably be in time for some more sunshine at the top. Good night."

29

Return and Departure

He which hath no stomach to this fight,
Let him depart, his passport shall be made
And crowns for convoy put into his purse.
We would not die in that man's company
That fears his fellowship, to die with us.

Shakespeare, *Henry V*

The following morning all the rabbits were out at silflay by
dawn and there was a good deal of excitement as they waited for
Hazel. During the previous few days Blackberry had had to repeat
several times the story of the journey to the farm and the finding of
Hazel in the drain. One or two had suggested that Kehaar must
have found Hazel and told Fiver secretly. But Kehaar denied this
and, when pressed, replied cryptically that Fiver was one who had
traveled a good deal further than he had himself. As for Hazel, he
had acquired, in everyone's eyes, a kind of magical quality. Of all
the warren, Dandelion was the last rabbit to fail to do justice to a
good story and he had made the most of Hazel's heroic dash out of
the ditch to save his friends from the farmers. No one had even
suggested that Hazel might have been reckless in going to the farm.
Against all odds he had got them two does: and now he was
bringing their luck back to the warren.

Just before sunrise Pipkin and Speedwell saw Fiver coming
through the wet grass near the summit of the down. They ran out to
meet him and waited with him until Hazel came up to them. Hazel
was limping and had evidently found the climb a strain, but after
resting and feeding for a short time he was able to run down to the
warren almost as fast as the others. The rabbits crowded round.
Everyone wanted to touch him. He was sniffed and tussled with
and rolled over in the grass until he felt almost as though he were
being attacked. Human beings, on occasions of this kind, are
usually full of questions, but the rabbits expressed their delight
simply by proving to themselves through their senses that this was
really Hazel-rah. It was all he could do to stand up to the rough

play. "I wonder what would happen if I lay down under it?" he thought. "They'd kick me out, I dare say. They wouldn't have a crippled Chief Rabbit. This is a test as well as a welcome, even though they don't know it themselves. I'll test them, the rascals, before I'm done."

He pushed Buckthorn and Speedwell off his back and broke away to the edge of the wood. Strawberry and Boxwood were on the bank and he joined them and sat washing and combing himself in the sunrise.

"We can do with a few well-behaved fellows like you," he said to Boxwood. "Look at that rough lot out there—they nearly finished me off! What on earth do you make of us and how are you settling down?"

"Well, of course we find it strange," said Boxwood, "but we're learning. Strawberry here has been helping me a great deal. We were just seeing how many smells I could tell on the wind, but that's something that'll only come slowly. The smells are awfully strong on a farm, you know, and they don't mean much when you live behind wire. As far as I can make out, you all live by smell."

"Don't take too many risks to begin with," said Hazel. "Keep near the burrows—don't go out alone—all that sort of thing. And how about you, Strawberry? Are you better?"

"More or less," answered Strawberry, "as long as I sleep a lot and sit in the sun, Hazel-rah. I've been terrified half out of my wits—that's the bottom of it. I've had the shivers and the horrors for days. I kept thinking I was back in Efrafa."

"What was it like in Efrafa?" asked Hazel.

"I'd rather die than go back to Efrafa," said Strawberry, "or risk going anywhere near it. I don't know which was worse, the boredom or the fear. All the same," he added after a few moments, "there are rabbits there who'd be the same as we are if they could only live naturally, like us. Several would be glad to leave the place if they only could."

Before they went underground Hazel talked to almost all the rabbits. As he expected, they were disappointed over the failure at Efrafa and full of indignation at the ill-treatment of Holly and his companions. More than one thought, like Holly, that the two does were likely to give rise to trouble.

"There should have been more, Hazel," said Bigwig. "We shall all be at each other's throats, you know—I don't see how it's to be helped."

Late in the afternoon Hazel called everyone into the Honeycomb.

"I've been thinking things over," he said. "I know you must all have been really disappointed not to have got rid of me at Nuthanger Farm the other day, so I've decided to go a bit further next time."

"Where?" asked Bluebell.

"To Efrafa," replied Hazel, "if I can get anyone to come with me: and we shall bring back as many does as the warren needs."

There were murmurs of astonishment, and then Speedwell asked, "How?"

"Blackberry and I have got a plan," said Hazel, "but I'm not going to explain it now, for this reason. You all know that this is going to be a dangerous business. If any of you get caught and taken into Efrafa, they'll make you talk, all right. But those who don't know a plan can't give it away. I'll explain it later on, at the proper time."

"Are you going to need many rabbits, Hazel-rah?" asked Dandelion. "From all I hear, the whole lot of us wouldn't be enough to fight the Efrafans."

"I hope we shan't have to fight at all," replied Hazel, "but there's always the possibility. Anyway, it'll be a long journey home with the does, and if by any chance we meet a Wide Patrol on the way, there have got to be enough of us to deal with them."

"Would we have to go into Efrafa?" asked Pipkin timidly.

"No," said Hazel, "we shall—"

"I never thought, Hazel," interrupted Holly, "I never thought that the time would come when I should feel obliged to speak against you. But I can only say again that this is likely to be a complete disaster. I know what you think—you're counting on General Woundwort not having anyone as clever as Blackberry and Fiver. You're quite right—I don't think he has. But the fact remains that no one can get a bunch of does away from that place. You all know that I've spent my life patrolling and tracking in the open. Well, there are rabbits in the Efrafan Owsla who are better at it than I am—I'm admitting it: and they'll hunt you down with your does and kill you. Great Frith! We all have to meet our match some time or other! I know you want only to help us all, but do be sensible and give this scheme up. Believe me, the best thing to do with a place like Efrafa is to stay as far away from it as possible."

Talk broke out all over the Honeycomb. "That must be right!" "Who wants to be torn to pieces?" "That rabbit with the mutilated ears—" "Well, but Hazel-rah must know what's doing." "It's too far." "I don't want to go."

Hazel waited patiently for quiet. At last he said, "It's like this. We can stay here and try to make the best of things as they are, or we can put them right once and for all. Of course there's a risk: anyone knows that who's heard what happened to Holly and the others. But haven't we faced one risk after another, all the way from the warren we left? What do you mean to do? Stay here and scratch each other's eyes out over two does, when there are plenty in Efrafa that you're afraid to go and get, even though they'd be only too glad to come and join us?"

Someone called out, "What does Fiver think?"

"I'm certainly going," said Fiver quietly. "Hazel's perfectly right and there's nothing the matter with his plan. But I promise you this, all of you. If I do come, later on, to feel any kind of misgiving, I shan't keep it to myself."

"And if that happens, I shan't ignore it," said Hazel.

There was silence. Then Bigwig spoke.

"You may as well all know that I'm going," he said, "and we shall have Kehaar with us, if that appeals to you at all."

There was a buzz of surprise.

"Of course, there are some of us who ought to stay here," said Hazel. "The farm rabbits can't be expected to go; and I'm not asking anyone who went the first time to go back again."

"I'll come, though," said Silver. "I hate General Woundwort and his Council with all my guts and if we're really going to make fools of them I want to be there, as long as I don't have to go back inside the place—that I couldn't face. But, after all, you're going to need someone who knows the way."

"I'll come," said Pipkin. "Hazel-rah saved my— I mean, I'm sure he knows what's—" He became confused. "Anyway, I'll come," he repeated, in a very nervous voice.

There was a scuffling in the run that led down from the wood and Hazel called, "Who's that?"

"It's I, Hazel-rah—Blackberry."

"Blackberry!" said Hazel. "Why, I thought you'd been here all the time. Where have you been?"

"Sorry not to have come before," said Blackberry. "I've been talking to Kehaar, as a matter of fact, about the plan. He's improved it a good deal. If I'm not mistaken, General Woundwort's going to look remarkably silly before we've finished. I thought at first that it couldn't be done, but now I feel sure it can."

"Come where the grass is greener," said Bluebell,

"And the lettuces grow in rows,

"And a rabbit of free demeanor

"Is known by his well-scratched nose.

"I think I shall have to come, just to satisfy my curiosity. I've been opening and shutting my mouth like a baby bird to know about this plan and no one puts anything in. I suppose Bigwig's going to dress up as a hrududu and drive all the does across the field."

Hazel turned on him sharply. Bluebell sat up on his hind legs and said, "Please, General Woundwort, sir, I'm only a little hrududu and I've left all my petrol on the grass, so if you wouldn't mind eating the grass, sir, while I just give this lady a ride—"

"Bluebell," said Hazel, "shut up!"

"I'm sorry, Hazel-rah," replied Bluebell in surprise. "I didn't mean any harm. I was only trying to cheer everyone up a bit. After all, most of us feel frightened at the idea of going to this place and you can't blame us, can you? It sounds horribly dangerous."

"Well, look here," said Hazel, "we'll finish this meeting now. Let's wait and see what we decide—that's the rabbits' way. No one has to go to Efrafa who doesn't want to, but it's clear enough that some of us mean to go. Now I'm off to talk to Kehaar myself."

He found Kehaar just inside the trees, snapping and tearing with his great beak at a foul-smelling piece of flaking brown flesh which seemed to be hanging from a tracery of bones. He wrinkled his nose in disgust at the odor, which filled the wood around and was already attracting ants and bluebottles.

"What on earth is that, Kehaar?" he asked. "It smells appalling!"

"You not know? Heem feesh, feesh, come from Peeg Vater. Ees goot."

"Come from Big Water? (Ugh!) Did you find it there?"

"Na, na. Men have heem. Down to farm ees plenty peeg rubbish place, all t'ings dere. I go for food, find heem, all smell like Peeg Vater, pick heem up, pring heem back: make me t'ink all about Peeg Vater." He began to tear again at the half-eaten kipper. Hazel sat choking with nausea and disgust as Kehaar lifted it entire and beat it against a beech root, so that small fragments flew round them. He collected himself and made an effort.

"Kehaar," he said, "Bigwig says you told him you'd come and help us to get the mothers out of the big warren."

"Ya, ya, I come for you. Meester Pigvig, 'e need me for 'elp 'im. Van 'e dere, 'e talk to me, I not rabbit. Ees goot, ya?"

"Yes, rather. It's the only possible way. You're a good friend to us, Kehaar."

"Ya, ya, 'elp you for get mudders. But now ees dis, Meester 'Azel. Always I vant Peeg Vater now—alvays, alvays. Ees hearing Peeg Vater, vant to fly to Peeg Vater. Now soon you go for get mudders, I 'elp you, 'ow you like. Den, ven you getting mudders, I leave you dere, fly avay, no come back. But I come back anudder time, ya? Come in autumn, in vinter I come live 'ere vid you, ya?"

"We shall miss you, Kehaar. But when you come back we'll have a fine warren here, with lots of mothers. You'll be able to feel proud of all you did to help us."

"Ya, vill be so. But Meester 'Azel, ven you go? I vant 'elp you, but I no vant vait for go Peeg Vater. Ees hard now for stay, you know? Dis vat you do, do heem queek, ya?"

Bigwig came up the run, put his head out of the hole and stopped in horror.

"Frith up a tree!" he said. "What a fearful smell! Did you kill it, Kehaar, or did it die under a stone?"

"You like, Meester Pigvig? I pring you nice liddle pit, ya?"

"Bigwig," said Hazel, "go and tell all the others that we're setting off at daybreak tomorrow. Holly will be Chief Rabbit here until we get back and Buckthorn, Strawberry and the farm rabbits are to stay with him. Anyone else who wants to stay will be perfectly free to do so."

"Don't worry," said Bigwig, from the hole. "I'll send them all up to silflay with Kehaar. They'll go anywhere you like before a duck can dive."

PART III

Efrafa

30

A New Journey

An undertaking of great advantage, but nobody to know what it is.
Company Prospectus of the South Sea Bubble

With the exception of Buckthorn and the addition of Bluebell, the rabbits who set off from the southern end of the beech hanger early the next morning were those who had left Sandleford with Hazel five weeks before. Hazel had said nothing more to persuade them, feeling that it would be better simply to leave things to set in his favor. He knew that they were afraid, for he was afraid himself. Indeed, he guessed that they, like himself, could not be free from the thought of Efrafa and its grim Owsla. But working against this fear was their longing and need to find more does and the knowledge that there were plenty of does in Efrafa. Then there was their sense of mischief. All rabbits love to trespass and steal and when it comes to the point very few will admit that they are afraid to do so; unless (like Buckthorn or Strawberry on this occasion) they know that they are not fit and that their bodies may let them down in the pinch. Again, in speaking about his secret plan, Hazel had aroused their curiosity. He had hoped that, with Fiver behind him, he could lure them with hints and promises: and he had been right. The rabbits trusted him and Fiver, who had gotten them out of Sandleford before it was too late, crossed the Enborne and the common, taken Bigwig out of the wire, founded the warren on the downs, made an ally of Kehaar and produced two does against all odds. There was no telling what they would do next. But they were evidently up to something; and since Bigwig and Blackberry seemed to be confidently in on it, no one was ready to say that he would rather stay out; especially since Hazel had made it clear that anyone who wished could remain at home and welcome—implying that if he was so poor-spirited as to choose to miss the exploit, they could do without him. Holly, in whom loyalty was second nature, had said no more to queer the pitch. He accompanied them as far as the end of the wood with all the cheerfulness he could muster; only begging Hazel, out of hearing of the rest, not to underrate the danger. "Send news by Kehaar when he reaches you," he said, "and come back soon."

Nevertheless, as Silver guided them southward along higher ground to the west of the farm, almost all, now that they were actually committed to the adventure, felt dread and apprehension. They had heard enough about Efrafa to daunt the stoutest heart. But before reaching it—or wherever they were going—they had to expect two days on the open down. Foxes, stoats, weasels—any of these might be encountered, and the only recourse would be flight above ground. Their progress was straggling and broken, slower than that which Holly had made with his picked band of three. Rabbits strayed, took alarm, stopped to rest. After a time Hazel divided them into groups, led by Silver, Bigwig and himself. Yet still they moved slowly, like climbers on a rock face, first some and then others taking their turn to cross the same piece of ground.

But at least the cover was good. June was moving toward July and high summer. Hedgerows and verges were at their rankest and thickest. The rabbits sheltered in dim green sun-flecked caves of grass, flowering marjoram and cow parsley; peered round spotted hairy-stemmed clumps of viper's bugloss, blooming red and blue above their heads; pushed between towering stalks of yellow mullein. Sometimes they scuttled along open turf, colored like a tapestry meadow with self-heal, centaury and tormentil. Because of their anxiety about elil and because they were nose to ground and unable to see far ahead, the way seemed long.

Had their journey been made in years gone by, they would have found the downs far more open, without standing crops, grazed close by sheep; and they could hardly have hoped to go far unobserved by enemies. But the sheep were long gone and the tractors had plowed great expanses for wheat and barley. The smell of the green, standing corn was round them all day. The mice were numerous and so were the kestrels. The kestrels were disturbing, but Hazel had been right when he guessed that a healthy, full-grown rabbit was too large a quarry for them. At all events, no one was attacked from above.

Some time before ni-Frith, in the heat of the day, Silver paused in a little patch of thorn. There was no breeze and the air was full of the sweet, chrysanthemum-like smell of the flowering compositae of dry uplands—corn chamomile, yarrow and tansy. As Hazel and Fiver came up and squatted beside him, he looked out across the open ground ahead.

"There, Hazel-rah," he said, "that's the wood that Holly didn't like."

Two or three hundred yards away and directly across their line, a belt of trees ran straight across the down, stretching in each direction as far as they could see. They had come to the line of the Portway—only intermittently a road—which runs from north of Andover, through St. Mary Bourne with its bells and streams and watercress beds, through Bradley Wood, on across the downs and so to Tadley and at last to Silchester—the Romans' Calleva Atrebatum. Where it crosses the downs, the line is marked by Caesar's Belt, a strip of woodland as straight as the road, narrow indeed but more than three miles long. In this hot noonday the trees of the Belt were looped and netted with darkest shadow. The sun lay outside, the shadows inside the trees. All was still, save for the grasshoppers and the falling finch song of the yellowhammer on the thorn. Hazel looked steadily for a long time, listening with raised ears and wrinkling his nose in the unmoving air.

"I can't see anything wrong with it," he said at last. "Can you, Fiver?"

"No," replied Fiver. "Holly thought it was a strange kind of wood and so it is, but there don't seem to be any men there. All the same, someone ought to go and make sure, I suppose. Shall I?"

The third group had come up while Hazel had been gazing at the Belt, and now all the rabbits were either nibbling quietly or resting, with ears laid flat, in the light green sun-and-shade of the thorn thicket.

"Is Bigwig there?" asked Hazel.

Throughout the morning Bigwig had seemed unlike himself—silent and preoccupied, with little attention for what was going on around him. If his courage had not been beyond question, it might have been thought that he was feeling nervous. During one long halt Bluebell had overheard him talking with Hazel, Fiver and Blackberry, and later had told Pipkin that it sounded for all the world as though Bigwig were being reassured. "Fighting, yes, anywhere," he had heard him say, "but I still reckon that this game is more in someone else's line than mine." "No," replied Hazel, "you're the only one that can do it: and remember, this isn't sport, if the farm raid was. Everything depends on it." Then, realizing that Bluebell could hear him, he added, "Anyway, keep on thinking about it and try to get used to the idea. We must get on now." Bigwig had gone moodily down the hedgerow to collect his group.

Now he came out of a nearby clump of mugwort and flowering thistle and joined Hazel under the thorn.

"What do you want?" he asked abruptly.

"King of Cats" (Pfeffa-rah), answered Hazel, "would you like to go and have a look in those trees? And if you find any cats or men or anything like that, just chase them off, would you, and then come and tell us it's all right?"

When Bigwig had slipped away, Hazel said to Silver, "Have you any idea how far the Wide Patrols go out? Are we inside their range yet?"

"I don't know, but I'd guess that we are," said Silver. "As I understand it, the range is up to the patrol. Under a pushing sort of captain, a patrol may go out a long way, I believe."

"I see," said Hazel. "Well, I don't want to meet a patrol if it can possibly be helped, and if we do, not one of them must get back to Efrafa. That's one reason why I brought so many of us. But by way of avoiding them, I'm going to try to make use of this wood. Perhaps they don't fancy it any more than Holly did."

"But surely it doesn't run the way we want to go?" said Silver.

"We're not going to Efrafa, though," said Hazel. "We're going to find somewhere to hide, as near to it as we can safely get. Any ideas?"

"Only that it's terribly dangerous, Hazel-rah," said Silver. "You *can't* get near Efrafa safely and I don't know how you can begin to look for somewhere to hide. And then the patrol—if there is one—they'll be cunning brutes. They might very well spot us and not show themselves at all—simply go and report."

"Well, here comes Bigwig back again," said Hazel. "Is it all right,

Bigwig? Good—let's get them into the wood and go down the length of it a little way. Then we must slip out on the other side and make sure that Kehaar finds us. He's coming to look for us this afternoon and at all costs we mustn't miss him."

Less than half a mile to the west, they came upon a spinney adjoining the southern edge of Caesar's Belt. To the west again was a shallow, dry downland combe, perhaps four hundred yards across and overgrown with weeds and rough, yellowing summer tussocks. There, well before sunset, Kehaar, flying westward down the Belt, spotted the rabbits lying up, all among the nettles and goose grass. He sailed down and alighted near Hazel and Fiver.

"How's Holly?" asked Hazel.

"'E sad," said Kehaar. "'E say you no come back." Then he added, "Mees Clover, she ready for mudder."

"That's good," said Hazel. "Is anyone doing anything about it?"

"Ya, ya, ees all to fight."

"Oh, well, I suppose it'll sort itself out."

"Vat you do now, Meester 'Azel?"

"This is where you start helping, Kehaar. We need a place to hide, as near the big warren as we can safely get—somewhere where those other rabbits won't find us. If you know the country well enough, perhaps you can suggest something."

"Meester 'Azel, 'ow close you vant?"

"Well, no further away than Nuthanger Farm is from the Honeycomb. In fact, that's really about the limit."

"Ees only von t'ing, Meester 'Azel. You go udder side river, den dey not find you."

"Over the river? You mean we swim across?"

"Na, na, rabbit no sveem dis river. Ees peeg, ees deep, go queek. But ees pridge, den udder side plenty place for hide. Ees close to varren, like you say."

"And you think that's the best we can do?"

"Ees plenty trees und ees river. Udder rabbits no find you."

"What do you think?" said Hazel to Fiver.

"It sounds better than I'd hoped for," said Fiver. "I hate to say it, but I think we ought to go straight there as fast as we can, even if it makes everyone exhausted. We're in danger all the time we're on the down, but once we get off it we can rest."

"Well, I suppose we'd better go on by night, if they'll do

it—we've done it before—but they must feed and rest first. Start fu Inlé? There'll be a moon."

"Oh, how I've come to loathe those words 'start' and 'fu Inlé,' " said Blackberry.

However, the evening feed was peaceful and cool and after a time everyone felt refreshed. As the sun was sinking, Hazel brought them all together, under close cover, to chew pellets and rest. Although he did his best to appear confident and cheerful, he could feel that they were on edge, and after parrying one or two questions about the plan, he began to wonder how he could distract their thoughts and get them to relax until they were ready to set off again. He remembered the time, on the first night of his leadership, when they had been forced to rest in the wood above the Enborne. At least it was good to see that no one was exhausted now: they were as tough a bunch of hlessil as ever raided a garden. Not a blade of grass to choose between them, thought Hazel: Pipkin and Fiver looked as fresh as Silver and Bigwig. Still, a little entertainment would be all to the good and raise their spirits. He was just going to speak up when Acorn saved him the trouble.

"Will you tell us a story, Dandelion?" he asked.

"Yes! yes!" said several others. "Come on! Make it a stunner while you're at it!"

"All right," said Dandelion. "How about 'El-ahrairah and the Fox in the Water'?"

"Let's have 'The Hole in the Sky,' " said Hawkbit.

"No, not that," said Bigwig suddenly. He had spoken very little all the evening and everyone looked round. "If you're going to tell a story, there's only one I want," he went on. " 'El-ahrairah and the Black Rabbit of Inlé.' "

"Perhaps not that one," said Hazel.

Bigwig rounded on him, snarling. "If there's going to be a story, don't you think I've got as good a right as anyone to choose it?" he asked.

Hazel did not reply and after a pause, during which no one else spoke, Dandelion, with a rather subdued manner, began.

The Story of El-ahrairah and the Black Rabbit of Inlé

The power of the night, the press of the storm,
    The post of the foe;
Where he stands, the Arch Fear in a visible form,
    Yet, the strong man must go.

                    Robert Browning, *Prospice*

"Sooner or later, everything leaks out and animals get to hear what others think about them. Some say that it was Hufsa who told King Darzin the truth about the trick with the lettuces. Others say that Yona the hedgehog went gossiping in the copses. But, however it was, King Darzin got to know that he had been made a fool when he delivered his lettuces to the marshes of Kelfazin. He did not call his soldiers out to fight—not yet. But he made up his mind that he would find an opportunity to get his own back on El-ahrairah. El-ahrairah knew this and he warned all his people to be careful, especially when they went about alone.

"Now late one afternoon in February, Rabscuttle led some of the rabbits out to a rubbish heap on the edge of a garden, some way away from the warren. The evening came on cold and misty, and well before twilight a fog came down thick. They set off for home, but they got lost: and then they had trouble with an owl and became confused over their direction. Anyway, Rabscuttle got separated from the others, and after wandering about for some time, he strayed into the guards' quarters outside King Darzin's city; and they caught him and took him up to the King.

"King Darzin saw his chance to spite El-ahrairah. He put Rabscuttle into a special prison hole and every day he was brought out and made to work, sometimes in the frost, digging and tunneling. But El-ahrairah swore he would get him out somehow. And so he did, for he and two of his does spent four days digging a tunnel from the wood into the back of the bank where Rabscuttle had been set to work. And in the end this tunnel came near to the hole in the bank down which Rabscuttle had been sent. He was supposed to be digging to turn the hole into a storeroom and the guards were watching outside while he worked. But El-ahrairah reached him, for he could hear him scratching in the dark; and they all slipped away down the tunnel and escaped through the wood.

"When the news reached King Darzin, he became very angry indeed, and he determined that this time he would start a war and finish El-ahrairah once and for all. His soldiers set out in the night and went to the meadows of Fenlo; but they couldn't get down the rabbit holes. Some tried, to be sure, but they soon came out again, because they met El-ahrairah and the other rabbits. They were not used to fighting in narrow places in the dark and they got bitten and scratched until they were glad to come out tail-first.

"But they didn't go away: they sat outside and waited. Whenever any of the rabbits tried to silflay they found their enemies ready to jump on them. King Darzin and his soldiers couldn't watch all the holes—there were too many—but they were quick enough to dash off wherever they saw a rabbit show his nose. Very soon El-ahrairah's people found that it was all they could do to snatch a mouthful or two of grass—just enough to keep alive—before they had to bolt underground again. El-ahrairah tried every trick he could think of, but he couldn't be rid of King Darzin or get his own people away. The rabbits began to become thin and miserable underground and some of them fell ill.

"At last El-ahrairah felt quite desperate and one night, when he had been risking his life again and again to bring down a few mouthfuls of grass for a doe and her family whose father had been killed the day before, he called out, 'Lord Frith! I would do anything to save my people! I would drive a bargain with a stoat or a fox—yes, or with the Black Rabbit of Inlé!'

"Now, as soon as he had said this, El-ahrairah realized in his heart that if there was one creature anywhere who might have the will and certainly had the power to destroy his enemies, it was the Black Rabbit of Inlé. For he was a rabbit, and yet more powerful than King Darzin a thousand times over. But the thought made El-ahrairah sweat and shudder, so that he had to crouch down where he was in the run. After a time he went to his own burrow and began to think of what he had said and what it meant.

"Now, as you all know, the Black Rabbit of Inlé is fear and everlasting darkness. He *is* a rabbit, but he is that cold, bad dream from which we can only entreat Lord Frith to save us today and tomorrow. When the snare is set in the gap, the Black Rabbit knows where the peg is driven; and when the weasel dances, the Black Rabbit is not far off. You all know how some rabbits seem just to throw their lives away between two jokes and a theft: but the truth is that their foolishness comes from the Black Rabbit, for it is by his will that they do not smell the dog or see the gun. The Black Rabbit brings sickness, too. Or again, he will come in the night and call a rabbit by name: and then that rabbit must go out to him, even though he may be young and strong to save himself from any other danger. He goes with the Black Rabbit and leaves no trace behind. Some say that the Black Rabbit hates us and wants our destruction. But the truth is—or so they taught me—that he, too, serves Lord Frith and does no more than his appointed task—to bring about what must be. We come into the world and we have to go: but we do not go merely to serve the turn of one enemy or another. If that were so, we would all be destroyed in a day. We go by the will of the Black Rabbit of Inlé and only by his will. And though that will seems hard and bitter to us all, yet in his way he is our protector, for he knows Frith's promise to the rabbits and he will avenge any rabbit who may chance to be destroyed without the consent of himself. Anyone who has seen a gamekeeper's gibbet knows what the Black Rabbit can bring down on elil who think they will do what they will.

"El-ahrairah spent the night alone in his burrow and his thoughts were terrible. As far as he knew, no rabbit had ever tried to do what he had in mind. But the more he thought about it—as well as he could for hunger and fear and the trance that comes upon rabbits face to face with death—the more it seemed to him that there was at least a chance of success. He would seek out the Black Rabbit and offer him his own life in return for the safety of his people. But if, when he offered his life, he did not mean the offer to be accepted, it would be better not to go near the Black Rabbit at all. The Black Rabbit might not accept his life: yet still, perhaps, he might get a chance to try something else. Only, there could be no cheating the Black Rabbit. If his people's safety were to be had, by whatever means, the price would be his life. So unless he failed, he would not return. He would therefore need a companion to bring back whatever it was that was going to overthrow King Darzin and save the warren.

"In the morning, El-ahrairah went to find Rabscuttle and they talked far into the day. Then he called his Owsla together and told them what he meant to do.

"Later that evening, in the last of the twilight, the rabbits came out and attacked King Darzin's soldiers. They fought very bravely and some of them were killed. The enemy thought they were trying to break out of the warren and did everything they could to surround them and force them back into their holes. But the truth was that all the fighting was simply to distract King Darzin's attention and keep his soldiers busy. As darkness set in, El-ahrairah and Rabscuttle slipped out from the other end of the warren and made off down the ditch, while the Owsla fell back and King Darzin's soldiers jeered at them down the holes. As for King Darzin, he sent a message to say that he was ready to talk to El-ahrairah about terms of surrender.

"El-ahrairah and Rabscuttle set out on their dark journey. What way they went I don't know and no rabbit knows. But I always remember what old Feverfew—d'you remember him?—used to say when he told this story. 'They didn't take long,' he said. 'They took no time at all. No. They limped and stumbled through a bad dream to that terrible place they were bound for. Where they were traveling, the sun and moon mean nothing and winter and summer less. But you will never know'—and then he used to look all round at us—'you will never know, and neither do I, how far El-ahrairah went on his journey into the dark. You see the top of a great stone sticking out of the ground. How far is it to the middle? Split the stone. Then you'll know.'

"At last they came to a high place where there was no grass. They scrambled upward, over splinters of slate, among gray rocks bigger than sheep. Mist and icy rain swirled about them and there was no sound but the trickling of water and sometimes, from far above, the cry of some great, evil bird on the wing. And these sounds echoed, for they were between black cliffs of stone, taller than the tallest trees. The snow lay in patches all about, for the sun never shone to melt it. The moss was slippery, and whenever they pushed out a pebble, it rattled down and down behind them in the gullies. But El-ahrairah knew the way and on he went, until the mist grew so thick that they could see nothing. Then they kept close to the cliff and little by little, as they went, it overhung them until it made a dark roof above their backs. Where the cliff ended was the mouth of a tunnel, like a huge rabbit hole. In the freezing cold and silence, El-ahrairah stamped and flashed his tail to Rabscuttle. And then, as they were about to go into the tunnel, they realized that what they had thought, in the gloom, to be a part of the rock was not rock. It was the Black Rabbit of Inlé, close beside them, still as lichen and cold as the stone."

"Hazel," said Pipkin, staring into the dusk and trembling, "I don't like this story. I know I'm not brave—"

"It's all right, Hlao-roo," said Fiver, "you're not the only one." In fact he himself seemed composed and even detached, which was more than could be said for any other rabbit in the audience: but Pipkin was hardly to realize this. "Let's go out there for a bit and watch the spiders catching moths, shall we?" said Fiver. "I think I can remember where I left a patch of vetch—it must be somewhere this way." Still talking quietly, he led Pipkin out into the overgrown combe. Hazel turned to make sure of the direction they had taken and as he did so Dandelion hesitated, uncertain whether to resume.

"Go on," said Bigwig, "and don't leave anything out."

"I think many things are left out, if only the truth could be known," said Dandelion, "for no one can say what happens in that country where El-ahrairah went of his own accord and we do not. But, as I was told, when they first became aware of the Black Rabbit, they fled down the tunnel—as needs they must, for there was nowhere else to run. And this they did although they had come on purpose to encounter him and all depended on their doing so. They did no differently from all of us; and the end, too, was no different, for when they had done slipping and tripping and falling along the tunnel, they found themselves in a vast stone burrow. All was of stone: the Black Rabbit had dug it out of the mountain with his claws. And there they found, waiting for them, him from whom they had fled. There were others in that burrow also—shadows without sound or smell. The Black Rabbit has his Owsla, too, you know. I would not care to meet them.

"The Black Rabbit spoke with the voice of water that falls into pools in echoing places in the dark.

" 'El-ahrairah, why have you come here?'

" 'I have come for my people,' whispered El-ahrairah.

"The Black Rabbit smelled as clean as last year's bones and in the dark El-ahrairah could see his eyes, for they were red with a light that gave no light.

" 'You are a stranger here, El-ahrairah,' said the Black Rabbit. 'You are alive.'

" 'My lord,' replied El-ahrairah, 'I have come to give you my life. My life for my people.'

"The Black Rabbit drew his claws along the floor.

" 'Bargains, bargains, El-ahrairah,' he said. 'There is not a day or a night but a doe offers her life for her kittens, or some honest captain of Owsla his life for his Chief Rabbit's. Sometimes it is taken, sometimes it is not. But there is no bargain, for here what is is what must be.'

"El-ahrairah was silent. But he thought, 'Perhaps I can trick him into taking my life. He would keep a promise, as Prince Rainbow kept his.'

" 'You are my guest, El-ahrairah,' said the Black Rabbit. 'Stay in my burrow as long as you wish. You may sleep here. And you may eat here, and they are few indeed who can do as much. Let him eat,' he said to the Owsla.

" 'We will not eat, my lord,' said El-ahrairah, for he knew that if he ate the food which they gave him in that burrow, his secret thoughts would become plain and there would be an end of tricks.

" 'Then at least we must entertain you,' said the Black Rabbit. 'You must feel at home, El-ahrairah, and make yourself comfortable. Come, let us play bob-stones.' *

" 'Very well,' said El-ahrairah, 'and if I win, my lord, perhaps you will be so good as to accept my life in return for my people's safety.'

" 'I will,' said the Black Rabbit. 'But if I win, El-ahrairah, you shall give me both your tail and your whiskers.'

"The stones were brought and El-ahrairah sat down in the cold

---

* Bob-stones is a traditional game of rabbits. It is played with small stones, fragments of stick or the like. Fundamentally it is a very simple kind of gambling, on the lines of "Odds or Evens." A "cast" of stones on the ground is covered by the player's front paw. The opponent must then hazard some sort of surmise about its nature—e.g., one or two, light or dark, rough or smooth.

and the echoes to play against the Black Rabbit of Inlé. Now, as you may suppose, El-ahrairah knew how to play bob-stones. He could play as well as any rabbit that ever covered a cast. But there—in that dreadful place, with the Black Rabbit's eyes upon him and the Owsla who made no sound—try as he would, his wits deserted him and even before he cast, he felt that the Black Rabbit knew what was down. The Black Rabbit showed never the least haste. He played as the snow falls, without sound or change, until at last El-ahrairah's spirit failed him and he knew that he could not win.

" 'You can pay your stakes to the Owsla, El-ahrairah,' said the Black Rabbit, 'and they will show you a burrow to sleep in. I shall return tomorrow and if you are still here I will see you. But you are free to leave whenever you wish.'

"Then the Owsla took El-ahrairah away and cut off his tail and pulled out his whiskers; and when he came to himself, he was alone with Rabscuttle in a hollow stone burrow, with an opening to the mountain outside.

" 'Oh, master,' said Rabscuttle, 'what will you do now? For Frith's sake let us go away. I can feel for both of us in the dark.'

" 'Certainly not,' said El-ahrairah. He still hoped to get what he wanted from the Black Rabbit somehow and he felt sure that they had been put into this burrow so that they would be tempted to steal away. 'Certainly not. I can make do very well with some willow herb and clematis. Go out and get some, Rabscuttle, but make sure you come back before tomorrow evening. You had better try to bring some food, too, if you can.'

"Rabscuttle went out as he was told and El-ahrairah was left alone. He slept very little, partly for the pain and partly for the fear that never left him; but chiefly because he was still searching for some trick that would serve his turn. The next day Rabscuttle returned with some pieces of turnip, and after El-ahrairah had eaten them, Rabscuttle helped him to patch himself up with a gray tail and whiskers made from the winter drift of clematis and ragwort. In the evening he went to meet the Black Rabbit as though nothing had happened.

" 'Well, El-ahrairah,' said the Black Rabbit—and he did not wrinkle his nose up and down when he sniffed, but thrust it forward, as a dog does—'my burrow cannot be what you are used to: but perhaps you have done your best to make yourself comfortable?'

" 'I have, my lord,' said El-ahrairah. 'I am glad that you allow me to stay.'

" 'Perhaps we will not play bob-stones tonight,' said the Black Rabbit. 'You must understand, El-ahrairah, that I have no wish to make you suffer. I am not one of the Thousand. I repeat, you may stay or leave as you please. But if you are going to remain, perhaps you would care to hear a story; and to tell one yourself, if you like.'

" 'Certainly, my lord,' said El-ahrairah. 'And if I can tell a story as good as yours, perhaps you will accept my life and grant the safety of my people.'

" 'I will,' said the Black Rabbit. 'But if not, El-ahrairah, you will have to forfeit your ears.' He waited to see whether El-ahrairah would refuse the wager, but he did not.

"Then the Black Rabbit told such a tale of fear and darkness as froze the hearts of Rabscuttle and El-ahrairah where they crouched on the rock, for they knew that every word was true. Their wits turned. They seemed to be plunged in icy clouds that numbed their senses; and the Black Rabbit's story crept into their hearts like a worm into a nut, leaving them shriveled and empty. When at last that terrible story was ended, El-ahrairah tried to speak. But he could not collect his thoughts and he stammered and ran about the floor, like a mouse when the hawk glides low. The Black Rabbit waited silently, with no sign of impatience. At last it was clear that there would be no story from El-ahrairah, and the Owsla took him and put him into a deep sleep: and when he woke, his ears were gone and only Rabscuttle was beside him in the stone burrow, crying like a kitten.

" 'Oh, master,' said Rabscuttle, 'what good can this suffering bring? For the sake of Lord Frith and the green grass, let me take you home.'

" 'Nonsense,' said El-ahrairah. 'Go out and get me two good, big dock leaves. They will do very well for ears.'

" 'They will wither, master,' said Rabscuttle, 'and I am withered now.'

" 'They will last long enough,' said El-ahrairah grimly, 'for what I have to do. But I cannot find the way.'

"When Rabscuttle was gone, El-ahrairah forced himself to think clearly. The Black Rabbit would not accept his life. Also, it was plain that he himself would never be able to win any sort of wager against him: he might as well try to run a race across a sheet of ice. But if the Black Rabbit did not hate him, why did he inflict these sufferings upon him? To destroy his courage and make him give up and go away. But why not simply send him away? And why wait, before hurting him, till he himself proposed a wager and lost it? The answer came to him suddenly. These shadows had no power either to send him away or to hurt him, except with his own consent. They would not help him, no. They would seek possession of his will and break it if they could. But supposing that he could find among them something that would save his people, could they stop him from taking it away?

"When Rabscuttle came back, he helped El-ahrairah to disguise his horrible, maimed head with two dock leaves in place of ears, and after a while they slept. But El-ahrairah kept dreaming of his starving rabbits waiting in the runs to push back King Darzin's soldiers and placing all their hopes on him: and at last he woke, cold and cramped, and wandered out into the runs of the stone warren. As he limped along, trailing the dock leaves on either side of his head—for he could not raise or move them like the ears he had lost—he came to a place from which several narrow runs led down deeper into the ground; and here he found two of the ghastly, shadowy Owsla moving about some dark business of their own. They turned and stared, to make him afraid, but El-ahrairah was past being afraid and he stared back at them, wondering what they had in mind to persuade him to lose.

" 'Turn back, El-ahrairah,' said one at last. 'You have no business here, in the pit. You are alive; and have suffered much already.'

" 'Not as much as my people,' replied El-ahrairah.

" 'There is enough suffering here for a thousand warrens,' said the shadow. 'Do not be stubborn, El-ahrairah. In these holes lie all the plagues and diseases that come to rabbits—fever and mange and the sickness of the bowels. And here, too, in this nearest hole, lies the white blindness, that sends creatures hobbling out to die in the fields, where even the elil will not touch their rotting bodies. This is our task, to see that all these are ready for the use of Inlé-rah. For what is is what must be.'

"Then El-ahrairah knew that he must give himself no time to think. He pretended to go back, but suddenly turned, rushed upon the shadows and plunged into the nearest hole faster than a raindrop into the ground. And there he lay, while the shadows flickered and gibbered about the entrance, for they had no power to move him, except by fear. After a time they went away and El-ahrairah was left alone, wondering whether he would be able to reach King Darzin's army in time without the use of whiskers or ears.

"At last, when he was sure that he must have stayed in the hole long enough to be infected, El-ahrairah came out and began to make his way back along the run. He did not know how soon the disease would appear or how long he would take to die, but plainly he ought to return as quickly as he could—if possible, before there was any sign of illness on him. Without going near Rabscuttle, he must tell him to hurry ahead, reach the rabbits in the warren and warn them to block all the holes and stay inside until King Darzin's army was destroyed.

"He blundered into a stone in the dark, for he was shivering and feverish and in any case he could feel little or nothing without his whiskers. At that moment a quiet voice said, 'El-ahrairah, where are you going?' He had heard nothing, but he knew that the Black Rabbit was beside him.

" 'I am going home, my lord,' he replied. 'You said that I might go when I wished.'

" 'You have some purpose, El-ahrairah,' said the Black Rabbit. 'What is it?'

" 'I have been in the pit, my lord,' answered El-ahrairah. 'I am infected with the white blindness and I am going to save my people by destroying the enemy.'

" 'El-ahrairah,' said the Black Rabbit, 'do you know how the white blindness is carried?'

"A sudden misgiving seized upon El-ahrairah. He said nothing.

" 'It is carried by the fleas in rabbits' ears,' said the Black Rabbit. 'They pass from the ears of a sick rabbit to those of his companions. But, El-ahrairah, you have no ears and fleas will not go to dock leaves. You can neither catch nor carry the white blindness.'

"Then at last El-ahrairah felt that his strength and courage were gone. He fell to the ground. He tried to move, but his back legs dragged along the rock and he could not get up. He scuffled and then lay still in the silence.

" 'El-ahrairah,' said the Black Rabbit at last, 'this is a cold warren: a bad place for the living and no place at all for warm hearts and brave spirits. You are a nuisance to me. Go home. I myself will save your people. Do not have the impertinence to ask me when. There is no time here. They are already saved.'

"In that moment, while King Darzin and his soldiers were still jeering down the holes of the warren, confusion and terror came upon them in the falling darkness. The fields seemed full of huge rabbits with red eyes, stalking among the thistles. They turned and fled. They vanished in the night; and that is why no rabbit who tells the tales of El-ahrairah can say what kind of creatures they were or what they looked like. Not one of them has ever been seen, from that day to this.

"When at last El-ahrairah was able to rise to his feet, the Black Rabbit was gone and Rabscuttle was coming down the run, looking for him. Together they went out to the mountainside and made their way down the stone-rattling gully in the mist. They did not know where they were going, except that they were going away from the Black Rabbit's warren. But after a time it became plain that El-ahrairah was ill from shock and exhaustion. Rabscuttle dug a scrape and there they stayed for several days.

"Later, when El-ahrairah began to get better, they wandered on, but they could not find their way back. They were confused in their wits and had to beg help and shelter of other animals whom they met. Their journey home lasted three months, and many adventures they had. Some of these, as you know, are stories in themselves. Once they lived with a lendri and found pheasants' eggs for him in the wood. And once they barely escaped from the middle of a hayfield when the hay was cutting. All the time, Rabscuttle looked after El-ahrairah, brought him fresh dock leaves and kept the flies from his wounds until they healed.

"At last, one day, they came back to the warren. It was evening, and as the sun stretched out all the hills, they could see any number of rabbits at silflay, nibbling in the grass and playing over the ant heaps. They stopped at the top of the field, sniffing the gorse and herb robert on the wind.

" 'Well, they look all right,' said El-ahrairah. 'A healthy lot, really. Let's just slip in quietly and see whether we can find one or two of the Owsla captains underground. We don't want a lot of fuss.'

"They made their way along the hedgerow, but could not altogether get their bearings, because apparently the warren had grown bigger and there were more holes than before, both in the bank and in the field. They stopped to speak to a group of smart young bucks and does sitting under the elder bloom.

" 'We want to find Loosestrife,' said Rabscuttle. 'Can you tell us where his burrow is?'

" 'I never heard of him,' answered one of the bucks. 'Are you sure he's in this warren?'

" 'Unless he's dead,' said Rabscuttle. 'But surely you must have heard of Captain Loosestrife? He was an officer of the Owsla in the fighting.'

" 'What fighting?' asked another buck.

" 'The fighting against King Darzin,' replied Rabscuttle.

" 'Here, do me a favor, old fellow, will you?' said the buck. 'That fighting—I wasn't born when it finished.'

" 'But surely you know the Owsla captains who were?' said Rabscuttle.

" 'I wouldn't be seen dead with them,' said the buck. 'What, that white-whiskered old bunch? What do we want to know about them?'

" 'What they did,' said Rabscuttle.

" 'That war lark, old fellow?' said the first buck. 'That's all finished now. That's got nothing to do with us.'

" 'If this Loosestrife fought King What's-His-Name, that's his business,' said one of the does. 'It's not our business, is it?'

" 'It was all a very wicked thing,' said another doe. 'Shameful, really. If nobody fought in wars, there wouldn't be any, would there? But you can't get old rabbits to see that.'

" 'My father was in it,' said the second buck. 'He gets on about it sometimes. I always go out quick. "They did this and then we did that" and all that caper. Makes you curl up, honest. Poor old geezer, you'd think he'd want to forget about it. I reckon he makes half of it up. And where did it get him, tell me that?'

" 'If you don't mind waiting a little while, sir,' said a third buck to El-ahrairah, 'I'll go and see if I can find Captain Loosestrife for you. I don't actually know him myself, but then it's rather a big warren.'

" 'That's good of you,' said El-ahrairah, 'but I think I've got my bearings now and I can manage by myself.'

"El-ahrairah went along the hedgerow to the wood and sat alone under a nut bush, looking out across the fields. As the light began to fail, he suddenly realized that Lord Frith was close beside him, among the leaves.

" 'Are you angry, El-ahrairah?' asked Lord Frith.

" 'No, my lord,' replied El-ahrairah, 'I am not angry. But I have learned that with creatures one loves, suffering is not the only thing for which one may pity them. A rabbit who does not know when a gift has made him safe is poorer than a slug, even though he may think otherwise himself.'

" 'Wisdom is found on the desolate hillside, El-ahrairah, where none comes to feed, and the stony bank where the rabbit scratches a hole in vain. But, speaking of gifts, I have brought a few trifles for you. A pair of ears, a tail and some whiskers. You may find the ears slightly strange at first. I put a little starlight in them, but it is really quite faint: not enough, I am sure, to give away a clever thief like you. Ah, there is Rabscuttle coming back. Good, I have something for him, too. Shall we—' "

"Hazel! Hazel-rah!" It was Pipkin's voice from behind a clump of burdock on the edge of the little circle of listeners. "There's a fox coming up the combe!"

32

Across the Iron Road

Some people have the idea that rabbits spend a good deal of their time running away from foxes. It is true that every rabbit fears the fox and will bolt if it smells one. But many rabbits go all their lives without seeing a fox and probably only a few actually fall victim to an enemy who smells strongly and cannot run as fast as they can. A fox trying to catch a rabbit usually creeps upwind under cover—perhaps through a patch of woodland to the edge. Then, if he succeeds in getting close to where the rabbits are at silflay along the bank or in the field, he lies still and watches his chance for a quick snatch. It is said that sometimes he fascinates them, as the weasel does, by rolling and playing in the open, coming closer little by little until he can make a grab. However this may be, it is certain that no fox hunts rabbits by going openly up a combe at sunset.

Neither Hazel nor any of the rabbits who had been listening to Dandelion's story had ever seen a fox. Nevertheless, they knew that a fox in the open, plain to be seen, is not dangerous as long as it is spotted in time. Hazel realized that he had been careless to allow everyone to gather round Dandelion and to have failed to post even one sentry. What wind there was was from the northeast and the fox, coming up the combe from the west, might have broken in upon them without warning. But from this danger they had been saved by Fiver and Pipkin going into the open. Even in his flash of alarm as Pipkin spoke, it crossed Hazel's mind that Fiver, no doubt reluctant to advise him in front of the others, had probably seized the opportunity provided by Pipkin's fear to post himself as a sentry.

Hazel thought quickly. If the fox were not too close, all they had to do was run. There was woodland nearby and they could vanish into it, keeping more or less together, and simply continue on their way. He pushed through the burdocks.

"How close is it?" he asked. "And where's Fiver?"

"I'm here," replied Fiver, from a few yards away. He was squatting under the long briars of a dog rose and did not turn his head as Hazel came up beside him. "And there's the fox," he added. Hazel followed his gaze.

The rough, weed-covered ground of the combe sloped away below them, a long dip bounded on the north by Caesar's Belt. The last of the setting sun shone straight up it through a break in the trees. The fox was below them and still some way off. Although it was almost directly downwind and therefore must be able to smell them, it did not look as though it were particularly interested in rabbits. It was trotting steadily up the combe like a dog, trailing its white-tipped brush. In color it was sandy brown, with dark legs and ears. Even now, though obviously not hunting, it had a crafty, predatory look that made the watchers among the dog roses shiver. As it passed behind a patch of thistles and disappeared from view, Hazel and Fiver returned to the others.

"Come on," said Hazel. "If you've never seen a fox, don't bother to go and look now. Just follow me."

He was about to lead the way up the south side of the combe when suddenly a rabbit shouldered him roughly aside, pushed past Fiver and was gone into the open. Hazel stopped and looked round in amazement.

"Who was that?" he asked.

"Bigwig," answered Fiver, staring.

Together they went quickly back to the briars and once more looked into the combe. Bigwig, in full view, was loping warily downhill, straight toward the fox. They watched him, aghast. He drew near, but still the fox paid no attention.

"Hazel," said Silver from behind, "shall I—?"

"No one is to move," said Hazel quickly. "Keep still, all of you."

At about thirty yards' distance the fox saw the approaching rabbit. It paused for a moment and then continued to trot forward. It was almost upon him before Bigwig turned and began to limp up the north slope of the combe toward the trees of the Belt. The fox hesitated again and then followed him.

"What's he up to?" muttered Blackberry.

"Trying to draw it off, I suppose," replied Fiver.

"But he didn't have to! We should have got away without that."

"Confounded fool!" said Hazel. "I don't know when I've been so angry."

The fox had quickened its pace and was now some distance away from them. It appeared to be overtaking Bigwig. The sun had set and in the failing light they could just make him out as he entered the undergrowth. He disappeared and the fox followed. For several moments all was quiet. Then, horribly clear across the darkening, empty combe, there came the agonizing squeal of a stricken rabbit.

"O Frith and Inlé!" cried Blackberry, stamping. Pipkin turned to bolt. Hazel did not move.

"Shall we go, Hazel?" asked Silver. "We can't help him now."

As he spoke, Bigwig suddenly broke out of the trees, running very fast. Almost before they could grasp that he was alive, he had recrossed the entire upper slope of the combe in a single dash and bolted in among them.

"Come on," said Bigwig, "let's get out of here!"

"But what—what— Are you wounded?" asked Bluebell in bewilderment.

"No," said Bigwig, "never better! Let's go!"

"You can wait until I'm ready," said Hazel in a cold, angry tone. "You've done your best to kill yourself and acted like a complete fool. Now hold your tongue and sit down!" He turned and, although it was rapidly becoming too dark to see any distance, made as though he were still looking out across the combe. Behind him, the rabbits fidgeted nervously. Several had begun to feel a dream-like sense of unreality. The long day above ground, the close, overgrown combe, the frightening story in which they had been absorbed, the sudden appearance of the fox, the shock of Bigwig's inexplicable adventure—all these, following one upon another, had flooded their spirits and left them dull and bemused.

"Get them out, Hazel," whispered Fiver, "before they all go tharn."

Hazel turned at once. "Well, no fox," he said cheerfully. "It's gone and we'll go, too. For goodness' sake keep close together, because if anyone gets lost in the dark we may not find him again. And remember, if we come upon any strange rabbits, you're to attack them at once and ask questions afterward."

They skirted the side of the wood that lay along the southern edge of the combe and then, in ones and twos, slipped across the empty road beyond. Little by little their spirits cleared. They found themselves in open farmland—indeed, they could both smell and hear the farm, not far away on the evening side—and the going was easy: smooth, wide pasture fields, sloping gently downhill and divided not by hedges but by broad, low banks, each as wide as a lane and overgrown with elder, dogwood and spindle. It was true rabbit country, reassuring after the Belt and the tangled, goose-grassed combe; and when they had covered a good distance over the turf—halting continually to listen and sniff and running, now one and now another, from each piece of cover to the next—Hazel felt safe in giving them a rest. As soon as he had sent out Speedwell and Hawkbit as sentries, he led Bigwig to one side.

"I'm angry with you," he said. "You're the one rabbit we're not going to be able to do without and you have to go and run a silly risk like that. It wasn't necessary and it wasn't even clever. What were you up to?"

"I'm afraid I just lost my head, Hazel," replied Bigwig. "I've been strung up all day, thinking about this business at Efrafa—got me really on edge. When I feel like that I have to do something—you know, fight or run a risk. I thought if I could make that fox look a fool I wouldn't feel so worried about the other thing. What's more, it worked—I feel a lot better now."

"Playing El-ahrairah," said Hazel. "You duffer, you might have thrown your life away for nothing—we all thought you had. Don't try it again, there's a good chap. You know everything's going to depend on you. But tell me, whatever happened in the trees? Why did you cry like that, if you were all right?"

"I didn't," said Bigwig. "It was very queer, what happened, and bad, too, I'm afraid. I was going to lose the homba in the trees, you see, and then come back. Well, I went into the undergrowth, and I'd just stopped limping and was starting to run really fast when suddenly I found myself face to face with a bunch of rabbits—strangers. They were coming toward me, as if they were going out into the open combe. Of course, I didn't have time to get a good look at them, but they seemed to be big fellows. 'Look out—run!' I said as I dashed up to them, but all they did was try to stop me. One of them said, 'You stay here!' or something like that, and then he got right in my way. So I knocked him down—I had to—and raced off, and the next thing I heard was this dreadful squealing. Of course, I went even faster then and I got clear of the trees and came back to you."

"So the homba got this other rabbit?"

"It must have. After all, I led it right onto them, even though I didn't mean to. But I never saw what actually happened."

"What became of the others?"

"I've no idea. They must have run, I suppose."

"I see," said Hazel thoughtfully. "Well, perhaps it's all for the best. But look here, Bigwig, no more fancy tricks until the proper time—there's too much at stake. You'd better stay near Silver and me—we'll keep you in good heart."

At that moment Silver came up to them.

"Hazel," he said, "I've just realized where we are and it's a lot too close to Efrafa. I think we ought to make off as soon as we can."

"I want to go right round Efrafa—wide," said Hazel. "Do you think you can find the way to that iron road Holly told us about?"

"I think so," replied Silver. "But we can't make too big a circle or they'll be completely exhausted. I can't say I know the way, but I can tell the direction all right."

"Well, we'll just have to take the risk," said Hazel. "If only we can get there by early morning, they can rest at the other end."

They met with no more adventures that night, moving quietly along the edges of the fields under the dim light of a quarter-moon. The half-darkness was full of sounds and movement. Once Acorn put up a plover, which flew round them, calling shrilly, until at length they crossed a bank and left it behind. Soon after, somewhere near them, they heard the unceasing bubbling of a nightjar—a peaceful sound, without menace, which died gradually away as they pushed on. And once they heard a corncrake calling as it crept among the long grass of a path verge. (It makes a sound like a human fingernail drawn down the teeth of a comb.) But elil they met none and although they were continually on the watch for signs of an Efrafan patrol, they saw nothing but mice, and a few hedgehogs hunting for slugs along the ditches.

At last, as the first lark rose toward the light that was still far up in the sky, Silver, his pale fur sodden dark with dew, came limping back to where Hazel was encouraging Bluebell and Pipkin.

"You can pluck up your spirits, Bluebell," he said. "I think we're close to the iron road."

"I wouldn't care about my spirits," said Bluebell, "if my legs weren't so tired. Slugs are lucky not to have legs. I think I'll be a slug."

"Well, I'm a hedgehog," said Hazel, "so you'd better get on!"

"You're not," replied Bluebell. "You haven't enough fleas. Now, slugs don't have fleas, either. How comforting to be a slug, among the dandelions so snug—"

"And feel the blackbird's sudden tug," said Hazel. "All right, Silver, we're coming. But where *is* the iron road? Holly said a steep, overgrown bank. I can't make out anything like that."

"No, that's away up by Efrafa. Down here it runs in a sort of combe of its own. Can't you smell it?"

Hazel sniffed. In the cool damp, he picked up at once the unnatural smells of metal, coal smoke and oil. They went forward and in a very short time found themselves looking down from among the bushes and undergrowth on the edge of the railway cutting. All was quiet, but as they paused at the top of the bank, a tussling pack of six or seven sparrows flew down to the line and began to peck about between the sleepers. Somehow, the sight was reassuring.

"Are we to cross, Hazel-rah?" asked Blackberry.

"Yes," said Hazel, "at once. Put it between us and Efrafa: then we'll feed."

They went rather hesitantly down into the cutting, half expecting the fiery, thundering angel of Frith to appear out of the twilight; but the silence remained unbroken. Soon they were all feeding in the meadow beyond, too tired to pay attention to concealment or to anything but the ease of resting their legs and nibbling the grass.

From above the larches Kehaar sailed down among them, alighted and folded his long, pale gray wings.

"Meester 'Azel, vat you do? You no stay 'ere?"

"They're tired out, Kehaar. They've got to have a rest."

"Ees not to rest 'ere. Ees rabbits come."

"Yes, but not just yet. We can—"

"Ya, ya, ees coming for find you! Ees close!"

"Oh, curse these confounded patrols!" cried Hazel. "Come on, all of you, get down the field into that wood! Yes, you, too, Speedwell, unless you want to have your ears chewed off in Efrafa. Come on, move!"

They tottered over the pasture to the woodland beyond and lay completely exhausted on flat, bare ground under fir trees. Hazel and Fiver consulted Kehaar again.

"It's no good expecting them to go any further, Kehaar," said Hazel. "They've been going all night, you know. We'll have to sleep here today. Did you actually see a patrol?"

"Ya, ya, come all along by udder side iron road. Yoost in time you go."

"Well, then, you saved us. But look, Kehaar, could you go and see where they are now? If they're gone, I'm going to tell our lot to go to sleep—not that they need telling: look at them!"

Kehaar returned with the news that the Efrafan patrol had turned back without crossing the iron road. Then he offered to keep watch himself until the evening and Hazel, greatly relieved, at once told the rabbits to sleep. One or two had already fallen asleep, lying on their sides on the open ground. Hazel wondered whether he ought to wake them and tell them to get under thicker cover, but as he was thinking about it he fell asleep himself.

The day came on hot and still. Among the trees the wood pigeons called drowsily and from time to time a late cuckoo stammered. In the fields, nothing moved except the constantly swishing tails of the cows gathered flank to flank in the shade.

The Great River

Never in his life had he seen a river before—this sleek, sinuous,
full-bodied animal. . . . All was a-shake and a-shiver—glints and gleams
and sparkles, rustle and swirl, chatter and bubble.
                              Kenneth Grahame, *The Wind in the Willows*

When Hazel woke, he started up at once, for the air
around him was full of the sharp cries of some creature hunting. He
looked quickly round, but could see no signs of alarm. It was
evening. Several of the rabbits were already awake and feeding on
the edge of the wood. He realized that the cries, urgent and
startling though they were, were too small and shrill for any kind of
elil. They came from above his head. A bat flittered through the
trees and out again without touching a twig. It was followed by
another. Hazel could sense that there were many all about, taking
flies and moths on the wing and uttering their minute cries as they
flew. A human ear would hardly have heard them, but to the
rabbits the air was full of their calls. Outside the wood, the field was
still bright with evening sunshine, but among the firs the light was
dusky and here the bats were coming and going thickly. Mixed
with the resinous scent of the firs there came another smell, strong
and fragrant, yet sharp—the perfume of flowers, but of some kind
unknown to Hazel. He followed it to its source at the edge of the
wood. It came from several thick patches of soapwort growing
along the edge of the pasture. Some of the plants were not yet in
bloom, their buds curled in pink, pointed spirals held in the pale
green calices, but most were already star-flowering and giving off
their strong scent. The bats were hunting among the flies and
moths attracted to the soapwort.

Hazel passed hraka and began to feed in the field. He was
disturbed to find that his hind leg was troubling him. He had
thought that it was healed, but the forced journey over the downs
had evidently proved too much for the muscle torn by the shotgun
pellets. He wondered whether it was far to the river of which
Kehaar had spoken. If it was, he was in for trouble.

"Hazel-rah," said Pipkin, coming up from among the soapwort, "are you all right? Your leg looks queer—you're dragging it."

"No, it's all right," said Hazel. "Look, Hlao-roo, where's Kehaar? I want to talk to him."

"He's flown out to see if there's a patrol anywhere near, Hazel-rah. Bigwig woke some time ago and he and Silver asked Kehaar to go. They didn't want to disturb you."

Hazel felt irritated. It would have been better to be told at once which way to go, rather than to wait while Kehaar looked for patrols. They were going to cross a river and, as far as he was concerned, they could not do it too soon. Fretting, he waited for Kehaar. Soon he had become as tense and nervous as he had ever been in his life. He was beginning to believe that after all he might have been rash. It was clear that Holly had not underrated their danger near Efrafa. He had little doubt that Bigwig, by sheer chance, had led the fox onto a Wide Patrol which had been following their trail. Then, in the morning, again by luck and the help of Kehaar, they had evidently just missed another at the crossing of the iron road. Perhaps Silver's fear was well founded and a patrol had already spotted and reported them without their knowing? Had General Woundwort got some sort of Kehaar of his own? Perhaps a bat was at this moment talking to him? How was one to foresee and guard against everything? The grass seemed sour, the sunshine chilly. Hazel sat hunched under the firs, worrying dismally. He felt less annoyed, now, with Bigwig: he could understand his feelings. Waiting was bad. He fidgeted for some kind of action. Just as he had decided to wait no longer, but to collect everyone and go immediately, Kehaar came flying from the direction of the cutting. He flapped clumsily down among the firs, silencing the bats.

"Meester 'Azel, ees no rabbits. I t'ink maybe dey no like for go across iron road."

"Good. Is it far to the river, Kehaar?"

"Na, na. Ees close, in vood."

"Splendid. We can find this crossing in daylight?"

"Ya, ya. I show you pridge."

The rabbits had gone only a short distance through the wood when they sensed that they were already near the river. The ground became soft and damp. They could smell sedge and water.

Suddenly, the harsh, vibrating cry of a moor hen echoed through the trees, followed by a flapping of wings and a watery scuttering. The rustling of the leaves seemed also to echo, as though reflected distantly from hard ground. A little further on, they could distinctly hear the water itself—the low, continuous pouring of a shallow fall. A human being, hearing from a distance the noise of a crowd, can form an idea of its size. The sound of the river told the rabbits that it must be bigger than any they had known before— wide, smooth and swift. Pausing among the comfrey and ground elder, they stared at each other, seeking reassurance. Then they began to lollop hesitantly forward into more open ground. There was still no river to be seen, but in front they could perceive a flicker and dance of mirrored light in the air. Soon afterward Hazel, limping ahead with Fiver near him, found himself on a narrow green path that divided the wilderness from the riverbank.

The path was almost as smooth as a lawn and clear of bushes and weeds, for it was kept cut for fishermen. Along its further side the riparian plants grew thickly, so that it was separated from the river by a kind of hedge of purple loosestrife, great willow herb, fleabane, figwort and hemp agrimony, here and there already in bloom. Two or three more of the rabbits emerged from the wood. Peering through the plant clumps, they could catch glimpses of the smooth, glittering river, evidently much wider and swifter than the Enborne. Although there was no enemy or other danger to be perceived, they felt the apprehension and doubt of those who have come unawares upon some awe-inspiring place where they themselves are paltry fellows of no account. When Marco Polo came at last to Cathay, seven hundred years ago, did he not feel—and did his heart not falter as he realized—that this great and splendid capital of an empire had had its being all the years of his life and far longer, and that he had been ignorant of it? That it was in need of nothing from him, from Venice, from Europe? That it was full of wonders beyond his understanding? That his arrival was a matter of no importance whatever? We know that he felt these things, and so has many a traveler in foreign parts who did not know what he was going to find. There is nothing that cuts you down to size like coming to some strange and marvelous place where no one even stops to notice that you stare about you.

The rabbits were uneasy and confused. They crouched on the

grass, sniffing the water smells in the cooling, sunset air: and moved closer together, each hoping not to see in the others the nervousness he felt in himself. As Pipkin reached the path a great, shimmering dragonfly, four inches long, all emerald and sable, appeared at his shoulder, hovered, droning and motionless, and was gone like lightning into the sedge. Pipkin leaped back in alarm. As he did so there came a shrill, vibrant cry and he caught sight, between the plants, of a brilliant azure bird flashing past over the open water. A few moments later there came, from close behind the plant hedge, the sound of a fairly heavy splash: but what creature might have made it there was no telling.

Looking round for Hazel, Pipkin caught sight of Kehaar, a little way off, standing in a patch of shallow water between two clumps of willow herb. He was stabbing and snapping at something in the mud and after a few moments pulled out a six-inch leech and swallowed it whole. Beyond him, some distance down the path, Hazel was combing the goose grass out of his coat and evidently listening to Fiver as they sat together under a rhododendron. Pipkin ran along the bank and joined them.

"There's nothing wrong with the place," Fiver was saying. "There's no more danger here than anywhere else. Kehaar's going to show us where to get across, isn't he? The thing to do is to get on with it before it gets dark."

"They'll never stop here," replied Hazel. "We can't stay and wait for Bigwig in a place like this. It's unnatural for rabbits."

"Yes, we can—calm down. They'll get used to it quicker than you think. I tell you, it's better than one or two other places we've been in. Not all strange things are bad. Would you like *me* to take them over? Say it's because of your leg."

"Fine," said Hazel. "Hlao-roo, can you get everyone along here?"

When Pipkin had gone, he said, "I feel troubled, Fiver. I'm asking so much of them, and there are so many risks in this plan."

"They're a better lot than you give them credit for," replied Fiver. "If you were to—"

Kehaar called raucously across, startling a wren out of the bushes.

"Meester 'Azel, vat for you vait?"

"To know where to go," answered Fiver.

"Pridge near. You go on, you see."

Where they were, the undergrowth stood close to the green path, but beyond—downstream, as they all intuitively felt—it gave way to open parkland. Out into this they went, Hazel following Fiver.

Hazel did not know what a bridge was. It was another of Kehaar's unknown words that he did not feel up to questioning. Despite his trust in Kehaar and his respect for his wide experience, he felt still more disturbed as they came into the open. Clearly, this was some sort of man place, frequented and dangerous. A short way ahead was a road. He could see its smooth, unnatural surface stretching away over the grass. He stopped and looked at it. At length, when he was sure that there were no men anywhere near, he went cautiously up to the verge.

The road crossed the river on a bridge about thirty feet long. It did not occur to Hazel that there was anything unusual in this. The idea of a bridge was beyond him. He saw only a line of stout posts and rails on either side of the road. Similarly, simple African villagers who have never left their remote homes may not be particularly surprised by their first sight of an airplane: it is outside their comprehension. But their first sight of a horse pulling a cart will set them pointing and laughing at the ingenuity of the fellow who thought of that one. Hazel saw without surprise the road crossing the river. What worried him was that where it did so there were only very narrow verges of short grass, offering no cover. His rabbits would be exposed to view and unable to bolt, except along the road.

"Do you think we can risk it, Fiver?" he asked.

"I can't see why you're bothered," answered Fiver. "You went into the farmyard and the shed where the hutch rabbits were. This is much less dangerous. Come on—they're all watching while we hesitate."

Fiver hopped out on the road. He looked round for a moment and then made his way to the nearer end of the bridge. Hazel followed him along the verge, keeping close beside the rail on the upstream side. Looking round, he saw Pipkin close behind. In the middle of the bridge Fiver, who was perfectly calm and unhurried, stopped and sat up. The other two joined him.

"Let's put on a bit of an act," said Fiver. "Make them inquisitive. They'll follow us just to see what we're looking at."

There was no sill along the edge of the bridge: they could have walked off it into the water three feet below. From under the lowest rail they looked out, upstream, and now, for the first time, saw the whole river plainly. If the bridge had not startled Hazel, the river did. He remembered the Enborne, its surface broken by gravel spits and plant growth. The Test, a weed-cut, carefully tended trout stream, seemed to him like a world of water. A good ten yards wide it was, fast-flowing and smooth, spangling and dazzling in the evening sun. The tree reflections on the even current were unbroken as on a lake. There was not a reed or a plant to be seen above the water. Close by, under the left bank, a bed of crowfoot trailed downstream, the wheel-like leaves all submerged. Darker still, almost black, were the mats of water moss, their thick masses motionless on the bed of the river and only the trailing fronds waving slowly from side to side. Waving, too, were the wider expanses of pale green cressweed; but these rippled with the current, lightly and quickly. The water was very clear, with a bed of clean yellow gravel, and even in the middle was hardly four feet deep. As the rabbits stared down they could discern, here and there, a very fine scour, like smoke—chalk and powdered gravel carried along by the river as dust is blown on the wind. Suddenly, from under the bridge, with a languid movement of its flat tail, swam a gravel-colored fish as long as a rabbit. The watchers, immediately above, could see the dark, vivid spots along its sides. Warily it hung in the current below them, undulating from side to side. It reminded Hazel of the cat in the yard. As they stared, it swam upward with a lithe flicker and stopped just below the surface. A moment later its blunt nose thrust clear of the stream and they saw the open mouth, pure white inside. Rhythmically, without haste, it sucked down a floating sedge fly and sank back under water. A ripple spread outward in subsiding circles, breaking both the reflections and the transparency. Gradually the stream grew smooth and once more they saw the fish below them, waving its tail as it held its place in the current.

"A water hawk!" said Fiver. "So they hunt and eat down there, too! Don't fall in, Hlao-roo. Remember El-ahrairah and the pike."

"Would it eat me?" asked Pipkin, staring.

"There may be creatures in there that could," said Hazel. "How do we know? Come on, let's get across. What would you do if a hrududu came?"

"Run," said Fiver simply, "like this." And he scurried off the further end of the bridge into the grass beyond.

On this far side of the river, undergrowth and a grove of great horse chestnuts extended almost down to the bridge. The ground was marshy, but at least there was plenty of cover. Fiver and Pipkin began at once on some scrapes, while Hazel sat chewing pellets and resting his injured leg. Soon they were joined by Silver and Dandelion, but the other rabbits, more hesitant even than Hazel, remained crouching in the long grass on the right bank. At last, just before darkness fell, Fiver re-crossed the bridge and coaxed them to follow him back. Bigwig, to everyone's surprise, showed considerable reluctance, and only crossed in the end after Kehaar, returning from another flight over Efrafa, had asked whether he would like him to go and fetch a fox.

The night that followed seemed to all of them disorganized and precarious. Hazel, still conscious of being in man country, was half expecting either a dog or a cat. But although they heard owls more than once, no elil attacked them and by the morning they were in better spirits.

As soon as they had fed, Hazel set them to exploring the surroundings. It became even more plain that the ground near the river was too wet for rabbits. Indeed, in places it was almost bog. Marsh sedge grew there, pink, sweet-scented valerian and the drooping water avens. Silver reported that it was drier up in the woodland away from the bank, and at first Hazel had the idea of picking a fresh spot and digging again. But presently the day grew so hot and humid that all activity was quenched. The faint breeze vanished. The sun drew up a torpid moisture from the watery thickets. The smell of water mint filled all the hydrophanic air. The rabbits crept into the shade, under any cover that offered. Long before ni-Frith, all were drowsing in the undergrowth.

It was not until the dappled afternoon began to grow cool that Hazel woke suddenly, to find Kehaar beside him. The gull was strutting from side to side with short, quick steps and pecking impatiently in the long grass. Hazel sat up quickly.

"What is it, Kehaar? Not a patrol?"

"Na, na. Ees all fine for sleep like bloody owls. Maybe I go for Peeg Vater. Meester 'Azel, you getting mudders now soon? Vat for vait now?"

"No, you're right, Kehaar, we must start now. The trouble is, I can see how to start but not how to finish."

Hazel made his way through the grass, roused the first rabbit he found—who happened to be Bluebell—and sent him to fetch Bigwig, Blackberry and Fiver. When they came, he took them to join Kehaar on the short grass of the riverbank.

"This is the problem, Blackberry," he said. "You remember that when we were under the down that evening I said we should have to do three things: get the does out of Efrafa, break up the pursuit and then get right away so that they wouldn't find us. This plan you've thought up is clever. It'll do the first two things, all right, I'm sure of that. But what about the last one? The Efrafan rabbits are fast and savage. They'll find us if we're to be found and I don't believe we can run away faster than they can follow—especially with a lot of does who've never been out of Efrafa. We couldn't possibly stand and fight them to a finish—we're too few. And on top of that, my leg seems to be bad again. So what's to be done?"

"I don't know," answered Blackberry. "But, obviously, we shall need to disappear. Could we swim the river? No scent then, you know."

"It's too swift," said Hazel. "We'd be carried away. But even if we *did* swim it, we couldn't count on not being followed. From what I've heard of these Efrafans, they'd certainly swim the river if they thought *we* had. What it comes to is that, with Kehaar to help us, we can break up a pursuit while we're getting the does out, but they'll know which way we've gone and they won't leave it at that. No, you're right, we've got to vanish without a trace, so that they can't even track us. But how?"

"I don't know," said Blackberry again. "Shall we go up the river a little way and have a look at it? Perhaps there's somewhere we could use for a hiding place. Can you manage that, with your leg?"

"If we don't go too far," replied Hazel.

"Can I come, Hazel-rah?" asked Bluebell, who had been waiting about, a little way off.

"Yes, all right," said Hazel good-naturedly, as he began to limp along the bank upstream.

They soon realized that the woodland on this left bank was lonely, thick and overgrown—denser than the nut copses and bluebell woods of Sandleford. Several times they heard the drumming of a great woodpecker, the shyest of birds. As Blackberry was suggesting that perhaps they might look for a hiding place somewhere in this jungle, they became aware of another sound—the falling water which they had heard on their approach the day before. Soon they reached a place where the river curved round in a bend from the east, and here they came upon the broad, shallow fall. It was no more than a foot high—one of those artificial falls, common on the chalk streams, made to attract trout. Several were already rising to the evening hatch of fly. Just above the fall a plank footbridge crossed the river. Kehaar flew up, circled the pool and perched on the hand rail.

"This is more sheltered and lonely than the bridge we crossed last night," said Blackberry. "Perhaps we could make some use of it. You didn't know about this bridge, Kehaar, did you?"

"Na, not know, not see heem. But ees goot pridge—no von come."

"I'd like to go across, Hazel-rah," said Blackberry.

"Well, Fiver's the rabbit for that," replied Hazel. "He simply loves crossing bridges. You carry on. I'll come behind, with Bigwig and Bluebell here."

The five rabbits hopped slowly along the planks, their great, sensitive ears full of the sound of the falling water. Hazel, who was not sure of his footing, had to stop several times. When at length he reached the further side, he found that Fiver and Blackberry had already gone a little way downstream below the fall and were looking at some large object sticking out from the bank. At first he thought that it must be a fallen tree trunk, but as he came closer he saw that, although it was certainly wooden, it was not round, but flat, or nearly flat, with raised edges—some man thing. He remembered how once, long ago, sniffing over a farm rubbish heap with Fiver, he had come upon a similar object—large, smooth and flat. (That had, in fact, been an old, discarded door.) It had been of no use to them and they had left it alone. His inclination was to leave this alone, too.

One end of the thing was pressed into the bank, but along its length it diverged, sticking out slightly into the stream. There were ripples round it, for under the banks the current was as swift as in midstream, on account of weed-cutting and sound camp-sheeting. As Hazel came nearer, he saw that Blackberry had actually scrambled on the thing. His claws made a faint hollow sound on the wood, so there must be water underneath. Whatever it might be, the thing did not extend downward to the bottom: it was lying on the water.

"What are you after, Blackberry?" he said rather sharply.

"Food," replied Blackberry. "Flayrah. Can't you smell it?"

Kehaar had alighted on the middle of the thing, and was snapping away at something white. Blackberry scuttered along the wood toward him and began to nibble at some kind of greenstuff. After a little while Hazel also ventured out on the wood and sat in the sunshine, watching the flies on the warm, varnished surface and sniffing the strange river smells that came up from the water.

"What is this man thing, Kehaar?" he asked. "Is it dangerous?"

"Na, no dangerous. You not know? Ees poat. At Peeg Vater is many, many poat. Men make dem, go on vater. Ees no harm."

Kehaar went on pecking at the broken pieces of stale bread. Blackberry, who had finished the fragments of lettuce he had found, was sitting up and looking over the very low side, watching a stone-colored, black-spotted trout swim up into the fall. The "boat" was a miniature punt, used for reed-cutting—little more than a raft, with a single thwart amidships. Even when it was unmanned, as now, there were only a few inches of freeboard.

"You know," said Fiver from the bank, "seeing you sitting there reminds me of that other wooden thing you found when the dog was in the wood and you got Pipkin and me over the river. Do you remember?"

"I remember shoving you along," said Bigwig. "It was jolly cold."

"What puzzles me," said Blackberry, "is why this boat thing doesn't go along. Everything in this river goes along, and fast, too—see there." He looked out at a piece of stick floating down on the even two-mile-an-hour current. "So what's stopping this thing from going?"

Kehaar had a short-way-with-landlubbers manner which he sometimes used to those of the rabbits that he did not particularly like. Blackberry was not one of his favorites: he preferred straightforward characters such as Bigwig, Buckthorn and Silver.

"Ees rope. You like bite heem, den you go damn queek, all de vay."

"Yes, I see," said Fiver. "The rope goes round that metal thing where Hazel's sitting: and the other end's fixed on the bank here. It's like the stalk of a big leaf. You could gnaw it through and the leaf—the boat—would drop off the bank."

"Well, anyway, let's go back now," said Hazel, rather dejectedly. "I'm afraid we don't seem to be any nearer to finding what we're looking for, Kehaar. Can you possibly wait until tomorrow? I had the idea that we might all move to somewhere a bit drier before tonight—higher up in the wood, away from the river."

"Oh, what a pity!" said Bluebell. "Do you know, I'd quite decided to become a water rabbit."

"A what?" asked Bigwig.

"A water rabbit," repeated Bluebell. "Well, there are water rats and water beetles and Pipkin says that last night he saw a water hawk. So why not a water rabbit? I shall float merrily along—"

"Great golden Frith on a hill!" cried Blackberry suddenly. "Great jumping Rabscuttle! That's it! That's it! Bluebell, you *shall* be a water rabbit!" He began leaping and skipping about on the bank and cuffing Fiver with his front paws. "Don't you see, Fiver? Don't you see? We bite the rope and off we go: and General Woundwort doesn't know!"

Fiver paused. "Yes, I *do* see," he replied at length. "You mean on the boat. I must say, Blackberry, you're a clever fellow. I remember now that after we'd crossed that other river you said that that floating trick might come in handy again sometime."

"Here, wait a moment," said Hazel. "We're just simple rabbits, Bigwig and I. Do you mind explaining?"

Then and there, while the black gnats settled on their ears, by the plank bridge and the pouring waterfall, Blackberry and Fiver explained.

"Could you just go and try the rope, Hazel-rah?" added Blackberry, when he had finished. "It may be too thick."

They went back to the punt.

"No, it's not," said Hazel, "and it's stretched tight, of course, which makes it much easier to gnaw. I can gnaw that, all right."

"Ya, ees goot," said Kehaar. "You go fine. But you do heem

queek, ya? Maybe somet'ing change. Man come, take poat—you know?"

"There's nothing more to wait for," said Hazel. "Go on, Bigwig, straightaway, and may El-ahrairah go with you. And remember, you're the leader now. Send word by Kehaar what you want us to do; we shall all be here, ready to back you up."

Afterward, they all remembered how Bigwig had taken his orders. No one could say that he did not practice what he preached. He hesitated a few moments and then looked squarely at Hazel.

"It's sudden," he said. "I wasn't expecting it tonight. But that's all to the good—I hated waiting. See you later."

He touched his nose to Hazel's, turned and hopped away into the undergrowth. A few minutes later, guided by Kehaar, he was running up the open pasture north of the river, straight for the brick arch in the overgrown railway embankment and the fields that lay beyond.

34

General Woundwort

Like an obelisk towards which the principal streets of a town converge, the strong will of a proud spirit stands prominent and commanding in the middle of the art of war.

Clausewitz, *On War*

Dusk was falling on Efrafa. In the failing light, General Woundwort was watching the Near Hind Mark at silflay along the edge of the great pasture field that lay between the warren and the iron road. Most of the rabbits were feeding near the Mark holes, which were close beside the field, concealed among the trees and undergrowth bordering a lonely bridle path. A few, however, had ventured out into the field, to browse and play in the last of the sun.

Further out still were the sentries of the Owsla, on the alert for the approach of men or elil and also for any rabbit who might stray too far to be able to get underground quickly if there should be an alarm.

Captain Chervil, one of the two officers of the Mark, had just returned from a round of his sentries and was talking to some of the does near the center of the Mark ground when he saw the General approaching. He looked quickly about to see whether anything was at fault. Since all seemed to be well, he began nibbling at a patch of sweet vernal with the best air of indifference that he could manage.

General Woundwort was a singular rabbit. Some three years before, he had been born—the strongest of a litter of five—in a burrow outside a cottage garden near Cole Henley. His father, a happy-go-lucky and reckless buck, had thought nothing of living close to human beings except that he would be able to forage in their garden in the early morning. He had paid dearly for his rashness. After two or three weeks of spoiled lettuces and nibbled cabbage plants, the cottager had lain in wait and shot him as he came through the potato patch at dawn. The same morning the man set to work to dig out the doe and her growing litter. Woundwort's mother escaped, racing across the kale field toward the downs, her kittens doing their best to follow her. None but Woundwort succeeded. His mother, bleeding from a shotgun pellet, made her way along the hedges in broad daylight, with Woundwort limping beside her.

It was not long before a weasel picked up the scent of the blood and followed it. The little rabbit cowered in the grass while his mother was killed before his eyes. He made no attempt to run, but the weasel, its hunger satisfied, left him alone and made off through the bushes. Several hours later a kind old schoolmaster from Overton, walking through the fields, came upon Woundwort nuzzling the cold, still body and crying. He carried him home to his own kitchen and saved his life, feeding him with milk from a nasal dropper until he was old enough to eat bran and greenstuff. But Woundwort grew up very wild and, like Cowper's hare, would bite when he could. In a month he was big and strong and had become savage. He nearly killed the schoolmaster's cat, which had found him at liberty in the kitchen and tried to torment him. One night, a week later, he tore the wire from the front of his hutch and escaped to the open country.

Most rabbits in his situation, lacking almost all experience of wild life, would have fallen victim at once to the elil: but not Woundwort. After a few days' wandering, he came upon a small warren and, snarling and clawing, forced them to accept him. Soon he had become Chief Rabbit, having killed both the previous Chief and a rival named Fiorin. In combat he was terrifying, fighting entirely to kill, indifferent to any wounds he received himself and closing with his adversaries until his weight overbore and exhausted them. Those who had no heart to oppose him were not long in feeling that here was a leader indeed.

Woundwort was ready to fight anything except a fox. One evening he attacked and drove off a foraging Aberdeen puppy. He was impervious to the fascination of the mustelidae, and hoped someday to kill a weasel, if not a stoat. When he had explored the limits of his own strength, he set to work to satisfy his longing for still more power in the only possible way—by increasing the power of the rabbits about him. He needed a bigger kingdom. Men were the great danger, but this could be circumvented by cunning and discipline. He left the small warren, taking his followers with him, and set out to look for a place suited to his purpose, where the very existence of rabbits could be concealed and extermination made very difficult.

Efrafa grew up round the crossing point of two green bridle paths, one of which (the east-to-west) was tunnel-like, bordered on both sides by a thick growth of trees and bushes. The immigrants, under Woundwort's direction, dug their holes between the roots of the trees, in the undergrowth and along the ditches. From the first the warren prospered. Woundwort watched over them with a tireless zeal that won their loyalty even while they feared him. When the does stopped digging, Woundwort himself went on with their work while they slept. If a man was coming, Woundwort spotted him half a mile away. He fought rats, magpies, gray squirrels and, once, a crow. When litters were kindled, he kept an eye on their growth, picked out the strongest youngsters for the Owsla and trained them himself. He would allow no rabbit to leave the warren. Quite early on, three who tried to do so were hunted n and forced to return.

As the warren grew, so Woundwort developed his system to keep it under control. Crowds of rabbits feeding at morning and evening were likely to attract attention. He devised the Marks, each controlled by its own officers and sentries, with feeding times changed regularly to give all a share of early morning and sunset—the favorite hours for silflay. All signs of rabbit life were concealed as closely as possible. The Owsla had privileges in regard to feeding, mating and freedom of movement. Any failure of duty on their part was liable to be punished by demotion and loss of privileges. For ordinary rabbits, the punishments were more severe.

When it was no longer possible for Woundwort to be everywhere, the Council was set up. Some of the members came from the Owsla, but others were selected solely for their loyalty or their cunning as advisers. Old Snowdrop was growing deaf, but no one knew more than he about organizing a warren for safety. On his advice, the runs and burrows of the various Marks were not connected underground, so that disease or poison, if they came, would spread less readily. Conspiracy would also spread less readily. To visit the burrows of another Mark was not allowed without an officer's permission. It was on Snowdrop's advice, too, that Woundwort at length ordered that the warren was not to extend further, on account of the risk of detection and the weakening of central control. He was persuaded only with difficulty, for the new policy frustrated his restless desire of power after power. This now needed another outlet, and soon after the warren had been stopped from growing he introduced the Wide Patrols.

The Wide Patrols began as mere forays or raids, led by Woundwort, into the surrounding country. He would simply pick four or five of the Owsla and take them out to look for trouble. On the first occasion they were lucky enough to find and kill a sick owl that had eaten a mouse that had eaten poison-dressed seed corn. On the next, they came upon two hlessil whom they compelled to return with them to join the warren. Woundwort was no mere bully. He knew how to encourage other rabbits and to fill them with a spirit of emulation. It was not long before his officers were asking to be allowed to lead patrols. Woundwort would give them tasks—to search for hlessil in a certain direction or to find out whether a particular ditch or barn contained rats which could later be attacked in force and driven out. Only from farms and gardens were they ordered to keep clear. One of these patrols, led by a certain Captain Orchis, discovered a small warren two miles to the east, beyond the Kingsclere-Overton road, on the outskirts of Nutley Copse. The General led an expedition against it and broke it up, the prisoners being brought back to Efrafa, where a few of them later rose to be Owsla members themselves.

As the months went on, the Wide Patrols became systematic; during summer and early autumn there were usually two or three out at a time. There came to be no other rabbits for a long way round Efrafa and any who might wander into the neighborhood by chance were quickly picked up. Casualties in the Wide Patrols were high, for the elil got to know that they went out. Often it would take all a leader's courage and skill to complete his task and bring his rabbits—or some of his rabbits—back to the warren. But the Owsla were proud of the risks they ran: and, besides, Woundwort was in the habit of going out himself to see how they were getting on. A patrol leader, more than a mile from Efrafa, limping up a hedgerow in the rain, would come upon the General squatting like a hare under a tussock of darnel, and find himself required then and there to report what he had been doing or why he was off his route. The patrols were the training grounds of cunning trackers, swift runners and fierce fighters, and the casualties—although there might be as many as five or six in a bad month—suited Woundwort's purpose, for numbers needed keeping down and there were always fresh vacancies in the Owsla, which the younger bucks did their best to be good enough to fill. To feel that rabbits were competing to risk their lives at his orders gratified Woundwort, although he believed—and so did his Council and his Owsla—that he was giving the warren peace and security at a price which was modest enough.

Nevertheless, this evening, as he came out from among the ash trees to talk to Captain Chervil, the General was feeling seriously concerned about several things. It was less and less easy to keep the size of the warren under control. Overcrowding was becoming a grave problem, and this despite the fact that many of the does were re-absorbing their litters before birth. While their doing so was all to the good in itself, some of them were growing restive and hard to manage. Not long ago a group of does had come before the Council and asked to leave the warren. They had been peaceable at first, offering to go as far away as the Council wished: but when it had become plain that their request was not going to be granted on any terms, they had become first petulant and then aggressive and the Council had had to take strong measures. There was still a good deal of bad feeling over the business. Then, in the third place, the Owsla had lately lost a certain amount of respect among the rank and file.

Four wandering rabbits—giving themselves out to be some kind of embassy from another warren—had been held and impressed into the Right Flank Mark. He had intended, later, to find out where they had come from. But they had succeeded in playing a very simple trick, bamboozling the Mark commander, attacking his sentries and escaping by night. Captain Bugloss, the officer responsible, had, of course, been demoted and expelled from the Owsla, but his disgrace, though very proper, only added to the General's difficulties. The truth was that Efrafa had become, for the moment, short of good officers. Ordinary Owsla—sentries—were not too hard to find, but officers were another matter and he had lost three in less than a month. Bugloss was as good as a casualty: he would never hold rank again. But, worse, Captain Charlock—a brave and resourceful rabbit—while leading the pursuit of the fugitives, had been run down on the iron road by a train: a further proof, if any were needed, of the wicked malice of men. Worst of all, only two nights ago a patrol which had been out to the north had returned with the shocking news that its leader, Captain Mallow, an officer of exceptional prestige and experience, had been killed by a fox. It was an odd business. The patrol had picked up the scent of a fairly large party of rabbits evidently coming toward Efrafa from the north. They had been following it but had not yet sighted their quarry when suddenly a strange rabbit had burst in upon them as they were nearing the edge of some woodland. They had, of course, tried to stop him and at that moment the fox, which had apparently been following him closely, had come from the open combe beyond and killed poor Mallow in an instant. All things considered, the patrol had come away in good order and Groundsel, the second in command, had done well. But nothing more had been seen of the strange rabbit; and the loss of Mallow, with nothing to show for it, had upset and demoralized the Owsla a good deal.

Other patrols had been sent out at once, but all that they had established was that the rabbits from the north had crossed the iron road and disappeared southward. It was intolerable that they should have passed so close to Efrafa and gone their way without being apprehended. Even now they might possibly be caught, if only there were a really enterprising officer to put in charge of the search. It would certainly need an enterprising officer—Captain Campion perhaps—for patrols seldom crossed the iron road, and the wet country beyond—the country near the river—was only partly known. He would have gone himself, but with the recent disciplinary troubles in the warren he could not take the risk; and Campion could hardly be spared just now. No—infuriating as it was, the strangers were best forgotten for the moment. The first thing was to replace the Owsla losses—and preferably with rabbits who knew how to deal ruthlessly with any further signs of dissension. They would simply have to promote the best they had got, draw their horns in for a time and concentrate on training until things got back to normal.

Woundwort greeted Captain Chervil rather abstractedly and went on turning the problem over in his mind.

"What are your sentries like, Chervil?" he asked at length. "Do I know any of them?"

"They're a good lot, sir," replied Chervil. "You know Marjoram: he's been on patrol with you as a runner. And I think you know Moneywort."

"Yes, I know them," said Woundwort, "but they wouldn't make officers. We need to replace Charlock and Mallow: that's what I'm getting at."

"That's difficult, sir," said Chervil. "That sort of rabbit doesn't hop out of the grass."

"Well, they've got to hop from somewhere," said Woundwort. "You'd better think about it and tell me any ideas that occur to you. Anyway, I want to go round your sentries now. Come with me, will you?"

They were about to set off when a third rabbit approached—none other than Captain Campion himself. It was Campion's principal duty to search the outskirts of Efrafa at morning and evening and to report anything new—the tire marks of a tractor in mud, the droppings of a sparrow hawk or the spreading of fertilizer on a field. An expert tracker, he missed little or nothing and was one of the very few rabbits for whom Woundwort felt a genuine respect.

"Do you want me?" said Woundwort, pausing.

"Well, I think so, sir," replied Campion. "We've picked up a hlessi and brought him in."

"Where was he?"

"Down by the arch, sir. Just this side of it."

"What was he doing?"

"Well, sir, he says he's come a long way on purpose to join Efrafa. That's why I thought you might like to see him."

"*Wants* to join Efrafa?" asked Woundwort, puzzled.

"That's what he says, sir."

"Why can't the Council see him tomorrow?"

"Just as you like, sir, of course. But he strikes me as being a bit out of the ordinary. I'd say, a distinctly useful rabbit."

"H'm," said Woundwort, considering. "Well, all right. I haven't got long, though. Where is he now?"

"At the Crixa, sir." Campion meant the crossing point of the two bridle paths, which was about fifty yards away, among the trees. "Two of my patrol are with him."

Woundwort made his way back to the Crixa. Chervil, being on duty with his Mark, remained where he was. Campion accompanied the General.

At this hour the Crixa was all green shade, with red gleams of sun that winked through the moving leaves. The damp grass along the edges of the paths was dotted with spikes of mauve bugle, and the sanicles and yellow archangels flowered thickly. Under an elder bush, on the far side of the track, two Owslafa, or Council police, were waiting; and with them was the stranger.

Woundwort saw at once what Campion had meant. The stranger was a big rabbit, heavy but alert, with a rugged, seasoned appearance and the look of a fighter. He had a curious thick growth of fur—a kind of topknot—on the crown of his head. He stared at Woundwort with a detached, appraising air which the General had not encountered for a very long time.

"Who are you?" said Woundwort.

"My name is Thlayli," replied the stranger.

"Thlayli, *sir*," prompted Campion.

The stranger said nothing.

"The patrol brought you in, I'm told. What were you doing?"

"I've come to join Efrafa."

"Why?"

"I'm surprised you ask. It's your warren, isn't it? Is there anything odd about someone wanting to join?"

Woundwort was nonplused. He was no fool and it was, he could not help feeling, extremely odd that any right-minded rabbit should choose to walk into Efrafa of his own accord. But he could hardly say so.

"What can you do?"

"I can run and fight and spoil a story telling it. I've been an officer in an Owsla."

"Fight, can you? Could you fight him?" said Woundwort, looking at Campion.

"Certainly, if you wish." The stranger reared up and aimed a heavy cuff at Campion, who leaped back just in time.

"Don't be a fool," said Woundwort. "Sit down. Where were you in an Owsla?"

"Far off. The warren was destroyed by men, but I escaped. I've been wandering some time. It won't surprise you that I heard of Efrafa. I've come a long way to join it. I thought you might have some use for me."

"Are you alone?"

"I am now."

Woundwort considered again. It was likely enough that this rabbit had been an officer in an Owsla. Any Owsla would want him. If he was speaking the truth, he had had wits enough to escape the destruction of his warren and survive a long journey through open country. It must have been a very long journey, for there was no warren within the normal range of the Efrafan patrols.

"Well," he said at length, "I dare say we might be able to find some use for you, as you put it. Campion here will look after you tonight, and tomorrow morning you'll come before the Council. Meanwhile, don't start fighting, do you see? We can give you plenty to do without that."

"Very well."

The following morning, after the Council had discussed the predicament of the warren due to the recent losses, General

Woundwort proposed that, for a start, they might do worse than try the big newcomer as an officer in the Near Hind Mark, under the instruction of Captain Chervil. The Council, having seen him, agreed. By ni-Frith Thlayli, still bleeding from the Mark gash inflicted in his left haunch, had taken up his duties.

3 5

Groping

This world, where much is to be done, and little known . . .

Dr. Johnson

"And then before the Mark silflay," said Chervil, "I always have a look at the weather. The previous Mark send a runner, of course, to say when they're going down, and he reports on the weather, but I always go and have a look for myself as well. In moonlight we put the sentries fairly close in and keep on the move ourselves to make sure no one goes too far. But in rain or darkness we send the Mark up in small groups, one after the other, and each group has a sentry in charge. In absolutely desperate weather we ask the General's permission to postpone the silflay."

"But do they often try to run away?" asked Bigwig. During the afternoon he had been up and down the runs and crowded burrows with Chervil and Avens, the other Mark officer, and had thought to himself that never in his life had he seen such a cheerless, dispirited lot of rabbits. "They don't strike me as a very difficult bunch."

"Most of them are no trouble, it's true," said Avens, "but you never know when trouble's coming. For instance, you'd have said there wasn't a more docile lot in Efrafa than the Right Flank. And then one day they get four hlessil wished on them by the Council, and the next evening Bugloss isn't very quick in the uptake for some reason, and suddenly these hlessil play a trick on him and bunk. And that's the end of him—to say nothing of poor old

Charlock, killed on the iron road. When something like that happens, it happens like lightning and it isn't always planned: sometimes it's more like a frenzy. A rabbit tears away on impulse and if you don't knock him over quick, the next thing you know three more will be off after him. The only safe way is to watch all the time when they're above ground and do your own relaxing when you can. After all, that's what we're here for—that and the patrols."

"Now, about burying hraka," said Chervil, "you can't be too strict. If the General finds any hraka in the fields he'll stuff your tail down your throat. They always try to dodge burying, though. They want to be natural, the anti-social little beasts. They just don't realize that everyone's good depends on everyone's cooperation. What I do is to set three or four of them to dig a new trough in the ditch every day, as a punishment. You can nearly always find someone to punish if you try hard enough. Today's squad fills up yesterday's trough and digs another. There are special runs leading into the bottom of the ditch and the Mark have got to use those and no others when they go out to pass hraka. We keep a hraka sentry in the ditch to make sure they come back."

"How do you check them in after silflay?" asked Bigwig.

"Well, we know them all by sight," replied Chervil, "and we watch them go down. There are only two entrance holes for the Mark and one of us sits at each hole. Every rabbit knows which hole he has to use and I should certainly miss any of mine who didn't go down. The sentries come in last of all—I only call them in when I'm quite sure that all the Mark are down. And once they're down, of course, they can't very well get out, with a sentry at each hole. Digging I should hear. You're not allowed to dig in Efrafa without permission from the Council. The only really dangerous time is when there's an alarm—say, a man or a fox. Then we all bolt for the nearest hole, of course. So far, it doesn't seem to have occurred to anyone that he could bolt the other way and have quite a long start before he was missed. Still, no rabbit will bolt toward elil, and that's the real safeguard."

"Well, I admire your thoroughness," said Bigwig, thinking to himself that his secret task seemed to be even more hopeless than he had expected. "I'll get the hang of it all as soon as I can. When do we have the chance of a patrol?"

"I expect the General will take you on patrol himself, to begin with," said Avens. "He did me. You may not be so keen when you've had a day or two with him—you'll be worn out. Still, I must admit, Thlayli, you're a fine size, and if you've been living rough for some time you'll probably manage it all right."

At this moment a rabbit with a white scar across his throat came down the run.

"The Neck Mark's just going down, Captain Chervil, sir," he said. "It's a beautiful evening: I should make the most of it."

"I was wondering when you were going to show up," replied Chervil. "Tell Captain Sainfoin I'm bringing my Mark up at once."

Turning to one of his own sentries who was close by, Chervil told him to go round the burrows and send everyone up for silflay.

"Now," he said, "Avens, you go to the further hole as usual, and Thlayli can join me on the nearer one. We'll send four sentries out to the line, to start with, and when the Mark have all gone out we'll add four more and keep two in reserve. I'll see you in the usual place, by the big flint in the bank."

Bigwig followed Chervil along the run, down which came the scents of warm grass, clover and hop trefoil. He had found most of the runs closer and stuffier than he was used to, no doubt because there were so few holes into the open air. The prospect of an evening silflay, even in Efrafa, was pleasant. He thought of the beech leaves rustling above the far-off Honeycomb, and sighed. "I wonder how old Holly's getting on," he thought, "and whether I'll ever see him again: or Hazel either, for the matter of that. Well, I'll give these blighters something to think about before I've finished. I do feel lonely, though. How hard it is to carry a secret by yourself!"

They reached the mouth of the hole and Chervil went outside to look round. When he returned, he took up station at the top of the run. As Bigwig found a place alongside, he noticed for the first time, in the opposite wall of the run, a kind of recess like an open cave. In this, three rabbits were squatting. Those on either side had the tough, stolid look of members of the Owslafa. But it was at the one in the middle that he stared. This rabbit had very dark fur—almost black. But this was not the most remarkable thing about him. He was dreadfully mutilated. His ears were nothing but shapeless shreds, ragged at the edges, seamed with ill-knit scars and beaded here and there with lumps of proud, bare flesh. One eyelid was misshapen and closed askew. Despite the cool, exciting air of the July evening, he seemed apathetic and torpid. He kept his gaze fixed on the ground and blinked continually. After a time he lowered his head and rubbed his nose on his forepaws in a listless manner. Then he scratched his neck and settled down in his former drooping position.

Bigwig, his warm, impulsive nature stirred by curiosity and pity, went across the run.

"Who are you?" he asked.

"My name is Blackavar, sir," replied the rabbit. He did not look up and spoke without expression, as though he had answered this question many times before.

"Are you going to silflay?" said Bigwig. No doubt, he thought, this was some hero of the warren, wounded in a great fight and now infirm, whose past services merited an honorable escort when he went out.

"No, sir," answered the rabbit.

"Why ever not?" said Bigwig. "It's a lovely evening."

"I don't silflay at this time, sir."

"Then why are you here?" asked Bigwig, with his usual directness.

"The Mark that has the evening silflay, sir," began the rabbit. "The Mark that has—they come—I—" He hesitated and fell silent.

One of the Owslafa spoke. "Get on with it," he said.

"I come here for the Mark to see me," said the rabbit in his low, drained voice. "Every Mark should see how I have been punished as I deserve for my treachery in trying to leave the warren. The Council were merciful—the Council were merciful—the Council— I can't remember it, sir, I really can't," he burst out, turning to the sentry who had spoken. "I can't seem to remember anything."

The sentry said nothing. Bigwig, after staring in shocked silence for a few moments, rejoined Chervil.

"He's supposed to tell everybody who asks," said Chervil, "but he's getting sort of stupid after half a month of it. He tried to run away. Campion caught him and brought him back and the Council ripped up his ears and said he had to be shown at every morning and evening silflay, as an example to the others. But if you ask me, he won't last much longer. He'll meet a blacker rabbit than himself one of these nights."

Bigwig shuddered, partly at Chervil's tone of callous indifference and partly at his own memories. The Mark were filing up now and he watched as they went past, each darkening the entrance for a moment before hopping out under the hawthorn. It was clear that Chervil prided himself on knowing his rabbits by name. He spoke to most of them and was at pains to show that he had some knowledge of their personal lives. It seemed to Bigwig that the answers he got were not particularly warm or friendly, but he did not know whether to put that down to dislike of Chervil or merely to the lack of spirit that seemed to be common to the rank and file in Efrafa. He was closely on the watch—as Blackberry had advised him to be—for any signs of disaffection or rebellion, but he could see little grounds for hope in the expressionless faces that went by. At the end came a little group of three or four does, talking among themselves.

"Well, are you getting on all right with your new friends, Nelthilta?" said Chervil to the first, as she passed him.

The doe, a pretty, long-nosed rabbit not more than three months old, stopped and looked at him.

"You'll get on yourself one day, Captain, I dare say," she replied. "Like Captain Mallow—he got on, you know. Why don't you send some does on Wide Patrol?"

She paused for Chervil to reply, but he made no answer and did not speak to the does who followed Nelthilta out into the field.

"What did she mean by that?" asked Bigwig.

"Well, there's been trouble, you know," said Chervil. "A bunch of does in the Near Fore started a row at a Council meeting. The General said they must be broken up and we had a couple sent to us. I've been keeping an eye on them. They're no trouble themselves, but Nelthilta's taken up with them and it seems to have made her cheeky and resentful: sort of thing you saw just now. I don't really mind that—it shows they feel the Owsla's on top. If the young does became quiet and polite I should be much more worried: I should wonder what they were up to. All the same, Thlayli, I'd like you to do what you can to get to know those particular does and bring them a bit more into line."

"Right," said Bigwig. "By the way, what are the rules about mating?"

"Mating?" said Chervil. "Well, if you want a doe, you have one—any doe in the Mark, that is. We're not officers for nothing, are we? The does are under orders and none of the bucks can stop you. That just leaves you and me and Avens; and we shall hardly quarrel. There are plenty of does, after all."

"I see," said Bigwig. "Well, I'll silflay now. Unless you've got any other ideas, I'll go and talk to some of the Mark and then go round the sentries and get the lie of the land. What about Blackavar?"

"Leave him," said Chervil. "He's none of our business. The Owslafa will keep him here until the Mark come back and after that they'll take him away."

Bigwig made his way into the field, conscious of the wary glances of the rabbits he passed. He felt perplexed and apprehensive. How was he to begin his dangerous task? Begin he must, in one way or another, for Kehaar had made it clear that he was not ready to wait. There was nothing for it but to take a chance and trust somebody. But whom? A warren like this must be full of spies. Probably only General Woundwort knew who the spies were. Was there a spy watching him now?

"I shall just have to trust my feelings," he thought. "I'll go round the place a bit and see if I can make any friends. But I know one thing—if I *do* succeed in getting any does out of here, I'll take that poor wretched Blackavar with me as well. Frith on a bridge! It makes me angry just to think of him being forced to sit there like that. General Woundwort indeed! A gun's too good for him."

Nibbling and pondering, he moved slowly over the open meadow in the evening sun. After a while he found that he was approaching a small hollow, much like the one on Watership Down where he and Silver had found Kehaar. In this hollow there were four does, with their backs to him. He recognized them as the little group who had gone out last. They had evidently finished the hungry, intent stage of feeding and were browsing and talking at leisure, and he could see that one of them had the attention of the other three. Even more than most rabbits, Bigwig loved a story and now he felt attracted by the prospect of hearing something new in this strange warren. He moved quietly up to the edge of the hollow just as the doe began to speak.

At once he realized that this was no story. Yet he had heard the like before, somewhere. The rapt air, the rhythmic utterance, the intent listeners—what was it they recalled? Then he remembered the smell of carrots, and Silverweed dominating the crowd in the great burrow. But these verses went to his heart as Silverweed's had not.

Long ago
The yellowhammer sang, high on the thorn.
He sang near a litter that the doe brought out to play,
He sang in the wind and the kittens played below.
Their time slipped by all under the elder bloom.
But the bird flew away and now my heart is dark
And time will never play in the fields again.

Long ago
The orange beetles clung to the rye-grass stems.
The windy grass was waving. A buck and doe
Ran through the meadow. They scratched a hole in the bank,
They did what they pleased all under the hazel leaves.
But the beetles died in the frost and my heart is dark;
And I shall never choose a mate again.

The frost is falling, the frost falls into my body.
My nostrils, my ears are torpid under the frost.
The swift will come in the spring, crying "News! News!
Does, dig new holes and flow with milk for your litters."
I shall not hear. The embryos return
Into my dulled body. Across my sleep
There runs a wire fence to imprison the wind.
I shall never feel the wind blowing again.

The doe was silent and her three companions said nothing: but their stillness showed plainly enough that she had spoken for all of them. A flock of starlings passed overhead, chattering and whistling, and a liquid dropping fell into the grass among the little group, but none moved or startled. Each seemed taken up with the same melancholy thoughts—thoughts which, however sad, were at least far from Efrafa.

Bigwig's spirit was as tough as his body and quite without sentimentality, but, like most creatures who have experienced hardship and danger, he could recognize and respect suffering when he saw it. He was accustomed to sizing up other rabbits and deciding what they were good for. It struck him that these does were not far from the end of their powers. A wild animal that feels that it no longer has any reason to live reaches in the end a point when its remaining energies may actually be directed toward dying. It was this state of mind that Bigwig had mistakenly attributed to Fiver in the warren of the snares. Since then his judgment had matured. He felt that despair was not far from these does; and from all that he had heard of Efrafa, both from Holly and from Chervil, he could understand why. He knew that the effects of overcrowding and tension in a warren show themselves first in the does. They become infertile and aggressive. But if aggression cannot mend their troubles, then often they begin to drift toward the only other way out. He wondered what point on this dismal path these particular does had reached.

He hopped down into the hollow. The does, disturbed from their thoughts, looked at him resentfully and drew back.

"I know you're Nelthilta," said Bigwig to the pretty young doe who had retorted to Chervil in the run. "But what's your name?" he went on, turning to the doe beside her.

After a pause, she answered reluctantly, "Thethuthinnang, sir." *

"And yours?" said Bigwig, to the doe who had spoken the verses.

She turned to him a look of such wretchedness, so full of accusation and suffering, that it was all he could do not to beg her then and there to believe that he was her secret friend and that he hated Efrafa and the authority which he represented. Nelthilta's rejoinder to Chervil in the run had been full of hatred, but this doe's gaze spoke of wrongs beyond her power to express. As Bigwig stared back at her, he suddenly recalled Holly's description of the great yellow hrududu that had torn open the earth above the destroyed warren. "That might have met a look like this," he thought. Then the doe answered, "My name is Hyzenthlay, sir."

"Hyzenthlay?" said Bigwig, startled out of his self-possession. "Then it was you who—" He stopped. It might be dangerous to ask whether she remembered speaking to Holly. But whether she did or

* Thethuthinnang: "Movement of Leaves." The first and last syllables are stressed, as in the phrase "Once in a way."

not, here, evidently, was the rabbit who had told Holly and his companions about the troubles of Efrafa and the discontent of the does. If he remembered Holly's story rightly, she had already made some sort of attempt to leave the warren. "But," he thought, as he met once more her desolate eyes, "what is she good for now?"

"May we have permission to go, sir?" asked Nelthilta. "The company of officers absolutely overpowers us, you see: we find a little of it goes an awfully long way."

"Oh—yes—certainly—by all means," replied Bigwig in confusion. He remained where he was as the does hopped away, Nelthilta raising her voice to remark, "What a great oaf!" and half looking round in the evident hope that he would take her up.

"Oh, well, there's one of them with some spirit left, anyway," he thought, as he made his way out to the sentries.

He spent some time talking to the sentries and learning how they were organized. It was a depressingly efficient system. Each sentry could reach his neighbor in a matter of moments; and the appropriate stamping signal—for they had more than one—would bring out the officers and the reserves. If necessary, the Owslafa could be alerted in almost no time at all and so could Captain Campion, or whatever officer might be patrolling the outskirts of the warren. Since only one Mark fed at a time, there could hardly be any confusion about where to go if an alarm were given. One of the sentries, Marjoram, told him about the attempted escape by Blackavar.

"He pretended to feed his way out as far as he could," said Marjoram, "and then he made a dash. He actually managed to knock down two sentries who tried to stop him; and I doubt whether anyone on his own has ever done as much as that. He ran like mad, but Campion had got the alarm, you see, and he simply moved round and intercepted him further down the fields. Of course, if he hadn't smashed up the sentries, the Council might have let him off more lightly."

"Do you like the warren life?" asked Bigwig.

"It's not too bad now I'm in the Owsla," answered Marjoram, "and if I can get to be an officer it'll be better still. I've done two Wide Patrols now—they're the thing for getting yourself noticed. I can track and fight as well as most, but of course they want more than that from an officer. I think our officers are a strong bunch, don't you?"

"Yes, I do," said Bigwig with feeling. It struck him that Marjoram evidently did not know that he himself was a newcomer to Efrafa. At any rate, he showed neither jealousy nor resentment. Bigwig was beginning to realize that in this place nobody was told more than was good for him, or got to know much except what was before his nose. Marjoram probably supposed that he, Bigwig, had been promoted out of another Mark.

As darkness fell, just before the end of the silflay, Captain Campion came up the field with a patrol of three and Chervil ran out to meet him on the sentry line. Bigwig joined them and listened to the talk. He gathered that Campion had been out as far as the iron road but had found nothing unusual.

"Don't you ever go beyond the iron road?" he asked.

"Not very often," answered Campion. "It's wet, you know—bad rabbit country. I have been there, but on these ordinary circuit patrols I'm really looking nearer home. My job is partly to notice anything new that the Council ought to know about, and partly to make sure we pick up anyone who bolts. Like that miserable Blackavar—and he gave me a bite I shan't forget, before I got him down. On a fine evening like this, I generally go down as far as the bank of the iron road and then work along this side of it. Or sometimes I go out in the other direction, as far as the barn. It all depends what's wanted. By the way, I saw the General earlier this evening and I rather think he means to take you on patrol in two or three days' time, as soon as you've settled down and your Mark have come off the dawn and evening silflay."

"Why wait for that?" said Bigwig with all the enthusiasm he could assume. "Why not sooner?"

"Well, a Mark generally keeps a full Owsla when it's on dawn and evening silflay. The rabbits are more lively at those times, you see, and need more supervision. But a Mark that's on ni-Frith and fu-Inlé silflay can generally spare Owsla for a Wide Patrol. Now I'll leave you here. I've got to take my lot to the Crixa and report to the General."

As soon as the Mark had gone underground and Blackavar had been taken away by his escort, Bigwig excused himself to Chervil and Avens and went to his own burrow. Although the rank and file were cramped underground, the sentries had two large, roomy burrows to themselves, while each officer had a private burrow. By himself at last, Bigwig settled down to think over his problem.

The difficulties were bewildering. He was fairly certain that with Kehaar's help he himself could escape from Efrafa whenever he wished. But how in the world was he to bring a bunch of does out—supposing that any were ready to try it? If he took it upon himself to call the sentries in during a silflay, Chervil would see in a matter of moments what he had done. The only possibility, then, was to make the break-out during the day: to wait until Chervil was asleep and then order a sentry to leave his post at the mouth of one of the holes. Bigwig considered. He could see no flaw in this idea. Then the thought came to him, "And what about Blackavar?" Blackavar presumably spent the day under guard in some special burrow. Probably hardly anyone knew where—no one knew anything in Efrafa—and certainly no one would tell. So he would have to leave Blackavar: no realistic plan could include him.

"I'll be jiggered if I leave him," muttered Bigwig to himself. "I know Blackberry would say I was a fool. Still, he's not here and I'm doing this myself. But suppose I wreck the whole thing because of Blackavar? Oh, Frith in a barn! What a business!"

He thought until he realized that he was thinking in circles. After a time, he fell asleep. When he woke, he could tell that it was moonlight outside, fine and still. It occurred to him that perhaps he might start his venture from the other end—by persuading some of the does to join him and working out a plan afterward, perhaps with their help. He went down the run until he came upon a young rabbit sleeping as best he could outside an overcrowded burrow. He woke him.

"Do you know Hyzenthlay?" he asked.

"Oh, yes, sir," replied the rabbit, with a rather pathetic attempt to sound brisk and ready.

"Go and find her and tell her to come to my burrow," said Bigwig. "No one else is to come with her. Do you understand?"

"Yes, sir."

When the youngster had scurried off, Bigwig returned to his burrow, wondering whether there would be any suspicion. It seemed unlikely. From what Chervil had said, it was common enough for Efrafan officers to send for does. If he were questioned he had only to play up. He lay down and waited.

In the dark, a rabbit came slowly up the run and stopped at the entrance to the burrow. There was a pause.

"Hyzenthlay?" said Bigwig.

"I am Hyzenthlay."

"I want to talk to you," said Bigwig.

"I am in the Mark, sir, and under your orders. But you have made a mistake."

"No, I haven't," replied Bigwig. "You needn't be afraid. Come in here, close beside me."

Hyzenthlay obeyed. He could feel her fast pulse. Her body was tense: her eyes were closed and her claws dug into the floor.

"Hyzenthlay," whispered Bigwig in her ear, "listen carefully. You remember that many days ago now, four rabbits came to Efrafa in the evening. One had very pale gray fur and one had a healed rat bite in his foreleg. You talked with their leader—his name was Holly. I know what he told you."

She turned her head in fear. "How do you know?"

"Never mind. Only listen to me."

Then Bigwig spoke of Hazel and Fiver; of the destruction of the Sandleford warren and the journey to Watership Down. Hyzenthlay neither moved nor interrupted.

"The rabbits who talked to you that evening," said Bigwig, "who told you about the warren that was destroyed and of how they had come to ask for does from Efrafa—do you know what became of them?"

Hyzenthlay's reply was no more than the faintest murmur in his ear.

"I know what I heard. They escaped the next evening. Captain Charlock was killed pursuing them."

"And was any other patrol sent after them, Hyzenthlay? The next day, I mean?"

"We heard that there was no officer to spare, with Bugloss under arrest and Charlock dead."

"Those rabbits returned to us safely. One of them is not far away now, with our Chief Rabbit and several more. They are cunning and resourceful. They are waiting for me to bring does out of Efrafa—as many as I can get to come. I shall be able to send them a message tomorrow morning."

"How?"

"By a bird—if all goes well." Bigwig told her about Kehaar. When he had finished, Hyzenthlay made no reply and he could not tell whether she was considering all that he had said or whether fear and disbelief had so troubled her that she did not know what to say. Did she think he was a spy trying to trap her? Did she perhaps wish only that he would let her go away? At last he said,

"Do you believe me?"

"Yes, I believe you."

"Might I not be a spy sent by the Council?"

"You are not. I can tell."

"How?"

"You spoke of your friend—the one who knew that that warren was a bad place. He is not the only such rabbit. Sometimes I can tell these things, too: but not often now, for my heart is in the frost."

"Then will you join me—and persuade your friends as well? We need you: Efrafa doesn't need you."

Again she was silent. Bigwig could hear a worm moving in the earth nearby and faintly down the tunnel came the sound of some small creature pattering through the grass outside. He waited quietly, knowing that it was vital that he should not upset her.

At last she spoke again, so low in his ear that the words seemed barely more than broken cadences of breathing.

"We can escape from Efrafa. The danger is very great, but in that we can succeed. It is beyond that I cannot see. Confusion and fear at nightfall—and then men, men, it is all things of men! A dog—a rope that snaps like a dry branch. A rabbit—no, it is not possible!—a rabbit that rides in a hrududu! Oh, I have become foolish—tales for kittens on a summer evening. No, I cannot see as I did once: it is like the shapes of trees beyond a field of rain."

"Well, you'd better come and meet this friend of mine," said Bigwig. "He talks just like that, and I've come to trust him, so I trust you, too. If you feel we're going to succeed, that's fine. But what I'm asking is whether you'll bring your friends to join us."

After another silence, Hyzenthlay said,

"My courage—my spirit: it's so much less than it was. I'm afraid to let you rely on me."

"I can tell that. What is it that's worn you down? Weren't you the leader of the does who went to the Council?"

"There was myself and Thethuthinnang. I don't know what's happened to the other does who were with us. We were all in the Right Fore Mark then, you know. I've still got the Right Fore mark, but I've been marked again since. Blackavar—you saw him?"

"Yes, of course."

"He was in that Mark. He was our friend and encouraged us. Only a night or two after the does went up to speak to the Council, he tried to run away, but he was caught. You've seen what they did to him. That was the same evening that your friends came: and the next night they escaped. After that, the Council sent for us does once more. The General said that no one else would have the chance to run away. We were to be split up among the Marks, no more than two to each Mark. I don't know why they left Thethuthinnang and me together. Perhaps they didn't stop to think. Efrafa's like that, you know. The order was 'Two to each Mark,' so as long as the order was carried out it didn't particularly matter which two. Now I'm frightened and I feel the Council are always watching."

"Yes, but *I'm* here now," said Bigwig.

"The Council are very cunning."

"They'll need to be. We've got some rabbits who are far more cunning, believe me. El-ahrairah's Owsla, no less. But tell me—was Nelthilta with you when you went to the Council?"

"Oh, no, she was born here, in the Near Hind. She's got spirit, you know, but she's young and silly. It excites her to let everyone see that she's a friend of rabbits who are thought of as rebels. She doesn't realize what she's doing or what the Council are really like. It's all a kind of game to her—to cheek the officers and so on. One day she'll go too far and get us into trouble again. She couldn't be trusted with a secret, on any account."

"How many does in this Mark would be ready to join an escape?"

"Hrair. There's a great deal of discontent, you know. But,

Thlayli, they mustn't be told until a very short time before we run—not just Nelthilta, but all of them. No one can keep a secret in a warren and there are spies everywhere. You and I must make a plan ourselves and tell no one but Thethuthinnang. She and I will get enough does to come with us when the time comes."

Bigwig realized that he had stumbled, quite unexpectedly, upon what he needed most of all: a strong, sensible friend who would think on her own account and help to bear his burden.

"I'll leave it to you to pick the does," he said. "I can make the chance to run if you'll have them ready to take it."

"When?"

"Sunset will be best, and the sooner the better. Hazel and the others will meet us and fight any patrol that follows. But the main thing is that the bird will fight for us. Even Woundwort won't be expecting that."

Hyzenthlay was silent again and Bigwig realized with admiration that she was going over what he had said and searching for flaws.

"But how many can the bird fight?" she said at last. "Can he drive them *all* away? This is going to be a big break-out and, make no mistake, Thlayli, the General himself will be after us with the best rabbits he has. We can't go on running away forever. They won't lose track of us and sooner or later they'll overtake us."

"I told you our rabbits were more cunning than the Council. I don't think you'd really understand this part, however carefully I explained. Have you ever seen a river?"

"What is a river?"

"Well, there you are. I can't explain. But I promise you we shan't have to run far. We shall actually disappear before the Owsla's eyes—if they're there to see. I must say I'm looking forward to that."

She said nothing and he added, "You must trust me, Hyzenthlay. Upon my life, we're going to vanish. I'm not deceiving you."

"If you were wrong, those who died quickly would be the lucky ones."

"No one's going to die. My friends have prepared a trick that El-ahrairah himself would be proud of."

"If it is to be at sunset," she said, "it must be tomorrow or the next night. In two days the Mark loses the evening silflay. You know that?"

"Yes, I'd heard. Tomorrow, then. Why wait longer? But there is one other thing. We're going to take Blackavar."

"Blackavar? How? He is guarded by Council police."

"I know. It adds very much to the risk, but I've decided that I can't leave him behind. What I mean to do is this. Tomorrow evening, when the Mark silflay, you and Thethuthinnang must keep the does near you—as many as you've got together—ready to run. I shall meet the bird a little way out in the meadow and tell him to attack the sentries as soon as he sees me go back into the hole. Then I shall come back and deal with Blackavar's guards myself. They won't be expecting anything of the sort. I'll have him out in a moment and join you. There'll be complete confusion and in that confusion we'll run. The bird will attack anyone who tries to follow us. Remember, we go straight down to the great arch in the iron road. My friends will be waiting there. You've only to follow me—I'll lead the way."

"Captain Campion may be on patrol."

"Oh, I do hope he is," said Bigwig. "I really do."

"Blackavar may not run at once. He will be as startled as the guards."

"Is it possible to warn him?"

"No. His guards never leave him and they take him out to silflay alone."

"For how long will he have to live like that?"

"When he has been to every Mark in turn, the Council will kill him. We all feel sure of that."

"Then that settles it. I *won't* go without him."

"Thlayli, you are very brave. Are you cunning, too? All our lives will depend on you tomorrow."

"Well, can you see anything wrong with the plan?"

"No, but I am only a doe who has never been out of Efrafa. Suppose something unexpected happens?"

"Risk is risk. Don't you want to get out and come and live on the high downs with us? Think of it!"

"Oh, Thlayli! Shall we mate with whom we choose and dig our own burrows and bear our litters alive?"

"You shall: and tell stories in the Honeycomb and silflay whenever you feel like it. It's a fine life, I promise you."

"I'll come! I'll run any risk."

"What a stroke of luck that you should be in this Mark," said Bigwig. "Before this talk with you tonight, I was at my wits' end, wondering whatever I was going to do."

"I'll go back to the lower burrows now, Thlayli. Some of the other rabbits are bound to wonder why you sent for me. It's not mating time with me, you see. If I go now, we can say you made a mistake and were disappointed. Don't forget to say that."

"I won't. Yes, go now, and have them ready at silflay tomorrow evening. I shan't fail you."

When she had gone, Bigwig felt desperately tired and lonely. He tried to hold in his mind that his friends were not far off and that he would see them again in less than a day. But he knew that all Efrafa lay between himself and Hazel. His thoughts broke up into the dismal fancies of anxiety. He fell into a half-dream, in which Captain Campion turned into a seagull and flew screaming over the river, until he woke in panic: and dozed again, to see Captain Chervil driving Blackavar before him toward a shining wire in the grass. And over all, as big as a horse in a field, aware of all that passed from one end of the world to the other, brooded the gigantic figure of General Woundwort. At last, worn out with his apprehensions, he passed into a deep sleep where even his fear could not follow, and lay without sound or movement in the solitary burrow.

36

Approaching Thunder

We was just goin' ter scarper
When along comes Bill 'Arper,
So we never done nuffin' at all.

Music Hall Song

Bigwig wavered gradually up from sleep, like a bubble of marsh gas from the bed of a still stream. There was another rabbit beside him in the burrow—a buck. He started up at once and said, "Who is it?"

"Avens," replied the other. "Time for silflay, Thlayli. Larks have gone up. You're a sound sleeper."

"I dare say," said Bigwig. "Well, I'm ready." He was about to lead the way down the run, but Avens' next words brought him to a halt.

"Who's Fiver?" said Avens.

Bigwig grew tense. "What did you say?"

"I said, who's Fiver?"

"How should I know?"

"Well, you were talking in your sleep. You kept saying, 'Ask Fiver, ask Fiver.' I wondered who he was."

"Oh, I see. A rabbit I knew once. He used to foretell the weather and so on."

"Well, he could do it now, then. Can you smell the thunder?"

Bigwig sniffed. Mixed with the scents of grass and cattle came the warm, thick smell of a heavy cloud mass, still far off. He perceived it uneasily. Almost all animals are disturbed by the approach of thunder, which oppresses them with its mounting tension and breaks the natural rhythm by which they live. Bigwig's inclination was to go back to his burrow, but he had little doubt that no mere trifle like a thundery morning would be allowed to interfere with the timetable of an Efrafan Mark.

He was right. Chervil was already at the entrance, squatting opposite Blackavar and his escort. He looked round as his officers came up the run.

"Come on, Thlayli," he said. "Sentries are out already. Does the thunder worry you?"

"It does rather," replied Bigwig.

"It won't break today," said Chervil. "It's a long way off yet. I'd give it until tomorrow evening. Anyway, don't let the Mark see it affects you. Nothing's to be altered unless the General says so."

"Couldn't wake him up," said Avens, with a touch of malice. "There was a doe in your burrow last night, Thlayli, wasn't there?"

"Oh, was there?" said Chervil. "Which one?"

"Hyzenthlay," replied Bigwig.

"Oh, the marli tharn," * said Chervil. "Funny, I didn't think she was ready."

---

* *Marli*—a doe. *Tharn*—stupefied, distraught. In this particular context, the nearest translation might be "the maiden all forlorn."

"She wasn't," said Bigwig. "I made a mistake. But if you remember, you asked me to do what I could to get to know the awkward squad and bring them a bit more under control, so I kept her talking for a time, just the same."

"Get anywhere?"

"Hard to say, really," said Bigwig, "but I'll keep at it."

He spent the time while the Mark went out in deciding upon the best and quickest way to enter the hole and attack Blackavar's escort. He would have to put one of them out of action in no time at all and then go straight for the other, who would be that much less unprepared. If he had to fight him, it would be better to avoid doing it between Blackavar and the mouth of the hole, for Blackavar would be as bewildered as the rest and might bolt back down the run. If he was going to bolt anywhere he must bolt outward. Of course, with any luck, the second guard might make off underground without fighting at all, but one could not count on that. Efrafan Owslafa were not given to running away.

As he went out into the field, he wondered whether he would be spotted by Kehaar. The arrangement had been that Kehaar would find him whenever he might come above ground on the second day.

He need not have worried. Kehaar had been over Efrafa since before dawn. As soon as he saw the Mark come up, he alighted a little way out in the field, halfway between the undergrowth and the sentry line, and began pecking about in the grass. Bigwig nibbled his way slowly toward him and then settled down to feed without a glance in his direction. After a while, he sensed that Kehaar was behind him, a little to one side.

"Meester Pigvig, I t'ink ees not goot ve talk much. Meester 'Azel, 'e say vat you do? Vat you vant?"

"I want two things, Kehaar—both at sunset tonight. First, our rabbits must be down by the big arch. I shall come through that arch with the does. If we're pursued, you and Hazel and the rest must be ready to fight. The boat thing, is it still there?"

"Ya, ya, men no take heem. I tell Meester 'Azel vat you say."

"Good. Now listen, Kehaar, this is the second thing, and it's terribly important. You see those rabbits out beyond us, in the field? They're the sentries. At sunset, you meet me here. Then I shall run back to those trees and go down a hole. As soon as you see me go in, attack the sentries—terrify them, drive them away. If they won't run, hurt them. They *must* be driven off. You'll see me come out again almost at once and then the does—the mothers—will start running with me and we'll go straight down to the arch. But we may very well be attacked on the way. If that happens, can you pile in again?"

"Ya, ya. I fly at dem—dey no stop you."

"Splendid. That's it, then. Hazel and the others—are they all right?"

"Fine—fine. Dey say you damn good fella. Meester Pluebell, 'e say to pring one mudder for everyone else and two for 'im."

Bigwig was trying to think of some appropriate reply to this when he saw Chervil running across the grass toward him. At once, without speaking again to Kehaar, he took a few hops in Chervil's direction and began biting busily at a patch of clover. As Chervil came up, Kehaar flew low above their heads and disappeared over the trees.

Chervil looked after the flying gull and then turned to Bigwig. "Aren't you afraid of those birds?" he asked.

"Not particularly," answered Bigwig.

"They sometimes attack mice, you know, and rabbit kittens, too," said Chervil. "You were taking a risk, feeding there. Why were you so careless?"

For answer, Bigwig sat up and gave Chervil a playful cuff, hard enough to roll him over.

"That's why," he said.

Chervil got up with a sulky air. "All right, so you're heavier than I am," he said. "But you've got to learn, Thlayli, that there's more than weight to being an Efrafan officer. And it doesn't alter the fact that those birds can be dangerous. Anyway, it's not the season for them and that's odd, for a start. It'll have to be reported."

"Whatever for?"

"Because it's unusual. Everything unusual has to be reported. If we don't report it and someone else does, nice fools we shall look when we have to say we saw it. We couldn't say we didn't—several of the Mark have seen it. In fact, I shall go and report it now. Silflay's nearly over, so if I'm not back in time, you and Avens had better see the Mark underground yourselves."

As soon as Chervil had left him, Bigwig went to look for

Hyzenthlay. He found her in the hollow with Thethuthinnang. Most of the Mark did not appear to be unduly affected by the thunder, which was still distant, as Chervil had said. The two does, however, were subdued and nervous. Bigwig told them what he had arranged with Kehaar.

"But will this bird really attack the sentries?" asked Thethuthinnang. "I've never heard of anything like that."

"It will, I promise you. Get the does together as soon as silflay begins this evening. When I come out with Blackavar, the sentries will be running for cover."

"And which way do we run?" asked Thethuthinnang.

Bigwig took them well out into the field, so that they could see the distant arch in the embankment about four hundred yards away.

"We're bound to meet Campion," said Thethuthinnang. "You know that?"

"I believe he had some trouble stopping Blackavar," replied Bigwig. "So I'm sure he won't be good enough for me and the bird. Look, there's Avens bringing in the sentries—we'll have to go. Now, don't worry. Chew your pellets and get some sleep. If you can't sleep, sharpen up your claws: you may need them."

The Mark went underground and Blackavar was taken away by the escort. Bigwig returned to his burrow and tried to put the coming evening out of his mind. After some time he gave up the idea of spending the day alone. He made a round of the lower burrows, joined a game of bob-stones, heard two stories and told one himself, passed hraka in the ditch and then, on an impulse, went to Chervil and obtained his consent to visit another Mark. He wandered across the Crixa, found himself in the middle of the ni-Frith silflay with the Left Flank Mark and went underground with them. Their officers shared a single large burrow and here he met some experienced veterans and listened with interest to their stories of Wide Patrols and other exploits. In the mid-afternoon he came back to the Near Hind relaxed and confident, and slept until one of the sentries woke him for silflay.

He went up the run. Blackavar was already slumped in his alcove. Squatting beside Chervil, Bigwig watched the Mark go out. Hyzenthlay and Thethuthinnang passed him without a glance. They looked tense but steady. Chervil followed the last rabbit.

Bigwig waited until he was sure that Chervil had had time to get well away from the hole. Then, with a last, quick look to where Blackavar was sitting, he went out himself. The bright sunset dazzled him and he sat up on his hind legs, blinking and combing the fur along one side of his face as his eyes got accustomed to the light. A few moments later he saw Kehaar come flying across the field.

"This is it, then," he said to himself. "Here we go."

At that moment a rabbit spoke from behind him.

"Thlayli, I want a few words with you. Just come back under the bushes, will you?"

Bigwig dropped on his front paws and looked round.

It was General Woundwort.

3 7

The Thunder Builds Up

You k'n hide de fier, but w'at you gwine do wid de smoke?
        Joel Chandler Harris, *Proverbs of Uncle Remus*

Bigwig's first impulse was to fight Woundwort on the spot. He realized immediately that this would be futile and would only bring the whole place round his ears. There was nothing to do but obey. He followed Woundwort through the undergrowth and into the shade of the bridle path. Despite the sunset, the evening seemed heavy with cloud and among the trees it was sultry and gray. The thunder was building up. He looked at Woundwort and waited.

"You were out of the Near Hind burrows this afternoon?" began Woundwort.

"Yes, sir," replied Bigwig. He still disliked addressing Woundwort as "sir," but since he was supposed to be an Efrafan officer, he could not very well do otherwise. However, he did not add that Chervil had given him permission. He had not been accused of anything as yet.

"Where did you go?"

Bigwig swallowed his annoyance. No doubt Woundwort knew perfectly well where he had been.

"I went to the Left Flank Mark, sir. I was in their burrows."

"Why did you go?"

"To pass the time and learn something from listening to the officers."

"Did you go anywhere else?"

"No, sir."

"You met one of the Left Flank Owsla—a rabbit named Groundsel."

"Very likely. I didn't learn all their names."

"Have you ever seen that rabbit before?"

"No, sir. How could I?"

There was a pause.

"May I ask what this is all about, sir?" said Bigwig.

"I'll ask the questions," said Woundwort. "Groundsel has seen *you* before. He knew you by the fur on your head. Where do you think he saw you?"

"I've no idea."

"Have you ever run from a fox?"

"Yes, sir, a few days ago, while I was coming here."

"You led it onto some other rabbits and it killed one of them. Is that correct?"

"I didn't intend to lead it onto them. I didn't know they were there."

"You didn't tell us anything about this?"

"It never occurred to me. There's nothing wrong in running from a fox."

"You've caused the death of an Efrafan officer."

"Quite by accident. And the fox might have got him anyway, even if I'd not been there."

"It wouldn't," said Woundwort. "Mallow wasn't the rabbit to run onto a fox. Foxes aren't dangerous to rabbits who know their business."

"I'm sorry the fox got him, sir. It was a stroke of very bad luck."

Woundwort stared at him out of his great, pale eyes.

"Then one more question, Thlayli. That patrol was on the track of a band of rabbits—strangers. What do you know about them?"

"I saw their tracks too, about that time. I can't tell you any more than that."

"You weren't with them?"

"If I'd been with them, sir, would I have come to Efrafa?"

"I told you I'd ask the questions. You can't tell me where they might have gone?"

"I'm afraid I can't, sir."

Woundwort stopped staring and sat silent for some time. Bigwig felt that the General was waiting for him to ask if that was all and whether he could now go. He determined to remain silent himself.

"Now there's another thing," said Woundwort at last. "About this white bird in the field this morning. You're not afraid of these birds?"

"No, sir. I've never heard of one hurting a rabbit."

"But they have been known to, for all your wide experience, Thlayli. Anyway, why did you go near it?"

Bigwig thought quickly. "To tell you the truth, sir, I think I may have been trying to make an impression on Captain Chervil."

"Well, you could have a worse reason. But if you're going to impress anyone, you'd better start with me. The day after tomorrow I'm taking out a Wide Patrol myself. It will cross the iron road and try to pick up traces of those rabbits—the rabbits Mallow would have found if you hadn't gone and blundered into him. So you'd better come along and show us how good you are then."

"Very well, sir; I shall be glad to."

There was another silence. This time Bigwig decided to make as if to go. He did so, and immediately a fresh question stopped him short.

"When you were with Hyzenthlay, did she tell you why she was put into the Near Hind Mark?"

"Yes, sir."

"I'm not at all sure the trouble's over there, Thlayli. Keep an eye on it. If she'll talk to you, so much the better. Perhaps those does are settling down and perhaps they aren't. I want to know."

"Very well, sir," said Bigwig.

"That's all," said Woundwort. "You'd better get back to your Mark now."

Bigwig made his way into the field. The silflay was almost over, the sun had set and it was growing dark. Heavy clouds dimmed the afterlight. Kehaar was nowhere to be seen. The sentries came in and the Mark began to go underground. Sitting alone in the grass, he waited until the last rabbit had disappeared. There was still no sign of Kehaar. He hopped slowly to the hole. Entering, he knocked into one of the police escort, who was blocking the mouth to make sure that Blackavar did not try to bolt as he was taken down.

"Get out of my way, you dirty little tale-bearing blood-sucker," said Bigwig. "Now go and report that," he added over his shoulder, as he went down to his burrow.

*   *   *

As the light faded from the thick sky, Hazel slipped once more across the hard, bare earth under the railway arch, came out on the north side and sat up to listen. A few moments later Fiver joined him and they crept a little way into the field, toward Efrafa. The air was close and warm and smelled of rain and ripening barley. There was no sound close by, but behind and below them, from the water meadow on the nearer bank of the Test, came faintly the shrill, incessant fussing of a pair of sandpipers. Kehaar flew down from the top of the embankment.

"You're sure he said tonight?" asked Hazel for the third time.

"Ees bad," said Kehaar. "Maybe dey catch 'im. Ees finish Meester Pigvig. You t'ink?"

Hazel made no reply.

"I can't tell," said Fiver. "Clouds and thunder. That place up the field—it's like the bottom of a river. Anything could be happening in there."

"Bigwig's there. Suppose he's dead? Suppose they're trying to make him tell them—"

"Hazel," said Fiver. "Hazel-rah, you won't help him by staying here in the dark and worrying. Quite likely there's nothing wrong. He's just had to sit tight for some reason. Anyway, he won't come tonight—that's certain now—and our rabbits are in danger here. Kehaar can go up tomorrow at dawn and bring us another message."

"I dare say you're right," said Hazel, "but I hate to go. Just suppose he were to come. Let Silver take them back and I'll stay here."

"You couldn't do any good by yourself, Hazel, even if your leg was all right. You're trying to eat grass that isn't there. Why don't you give it a chance to grow?"

They returned under the arch and as Silver came out of the bushes to meet them, they could hear the other rabbits stirring uneasily among the nettles.

"We'll have to give it up for tonight, Silver," said Hazel. "We must get them back over the river now, before it's completely dark."

"Hazel-rah," said Pipkin, as he slipped by, "it—it is going to be all right, isn't it? Bigwig will come tomorrow, won't he?"

"Of course he will," said Hazel, "and we'll all be here to help him. And I'll tell you something else, Hlao-roo. If he doesn't come tomorrow, I'm going into Efrafa myself."

"I'll come with you, Hazel-rah," said Pipkin.

*   *   *

Bigwig crouched in his burrow, pressed against Hyzenthlay. He was trembling, but not with cold: the stuffy runs of the Mark were dense with thunder; the air felt like a deep drift of leaves. Bigwig was close to utter nervous exhaustion. Since leaving General Woundwort, he had become more and more deeply entangled in all the age-old terrors of the conspirator. How much had Woundwort discovered? Clearly, there was no information that failed to reach him. He knew that Hazel and the rest had come from the north and crossed the iron road. He knew about the fox. He knew that a gull, which should have been far away at this time of year, was hanging round Efrafa and that he, Bigwig, had deliberately been near it. He knew that Bigwig had made a friend of Hyzenthlay. How long could it be before he took the final step of fitting all these things together? Perhaps he had already done so and was merely waiting to arrest them in his own time?

Woundwort had every advantage. He sat secure at the junction of all paths, seeing clearly down each, while he, Bigwig, ludicrous in his efforts to measure up to him as an enemy, clambered clumsily and ignorantly through the undergrowth, betraying himself with every movement. He did not know how to get in touch with Kehaar again. Even if he managed to do so, would Hazel be able to bring the rabbits a second time? Perhaps they had already been spotted by Campion on patrol? To speak to Blackavar would be suspect. To go near Kehaar would be suspect. Through more holes than he could possibly stop, his secret was leaking—pouring —out.

There was worse to come.

"Thlayli," whispered Hyzenthlay, "do you think you and I and Thethuthinnang could get away tonight? If we fought the sentry at the mouth of the run, we might be able to get clear before a patrol could start after us."

"Why?" asked Bigwig. "What makes you ask that?"

"I'm frightened. We told the other does, you see, just before the silflay. They were ready to run when the bird attacked the sentries, and then nothing happened. They all know about the plan—Nelthilta and the rest—and it can't be long before the Council find out. Of course we've told them that their lives depend on keeping quiet and that you're going to try again. Thethuthinnang's watching them now: she says she'll do her best not to sleep. But no secret can be kept in Efrafa. It's even possible that one of the does is a spy, although Frith knows we chose them as carefully as we could. We may all be arrested before tomorrow morning."

Bigwig tried to think clearly. He could certainly succeed in getting out with a couple of resolute, sensible does. But the sentry—unless he could kill him—would raise the alarm at once and he could not be sure of finding the way to the river in the dark. Even if he did, it was possible that the pursuit might follow him over the plank bridge and into the middle of his unprepared, sleeping friends. And at the best he would have come out of Efrafa with no more than a couple of does, because his nerve had failed. Silver and the others would not know what he had had to endure. They would know only that he had run away.

"No, we mustn't give up yet," he said, as gently as he could. "It's the thunder and the waiting that make you feel so much upset. Listen, I promise you that by this time tomorrow you'll be out of Efrafa forever and the others with you. Now go to sleep here for a little while and then go back and help Thethuthinnang. Keep thinking of those high downs and all that I told you. We'll get there—our troubles won't last much longer."

As she fell asleep beside him, Bigwig wondered how on earth he was going to fulfill this promise and whether they would be woken by the Council police. "If we are," he thought, "I'll fight until they tear me to bits. They'll make no Blackavar out of me."

*   *   *

When he woke, he found that he was alone in the burrow. For a moment he wondered whether Hyzenthlay had been arrested. Then he felt sure that the Owslafa could not have removed her while he slept. She must have woken and slipped back to Thethuthinnang without disturbing him.

It was a little before dawn, but the oppression in the air had not lessened. He slipped up the run to the entrance. Moneywort, the sentry on duty, was peering uneasily out of the mouth of the hole, but turned as he approached.

"I wish it would rain, sir," he said. "The thunder's enough to turn the grass sour, but not much hope of it breaking before the evening, I'd say."

"It's bad luck for the Mark's last day on dawn and evening," replied Bigwig. "Go and wake Captain Chervil. I'll take your place here until the Mark come up."

When Moneywort had gone, Bigwig sat in the mouth of the hole and sniffed the heavy air. The sky seemed as close as the tops of the trees, covered with still cloud and flushed on the morning side with a lurid, foxy glow. Not a lark was up, not a thrush singing. The field before him was empty and motionless. The longing to run came over him. In less than no time he could be down to the arch. It was a safe bet that Campion and his patrol would not be out in weather like this. Every living creature up and down the fields and copses must be muted, pressed down as though under a great, soft paw. Nothing would be moving, for the day was unpropitious and instincts were blurred and not to be trusted. It was a time to crouch and be silent. But a fugitive would be safe. Indeed, he could not hope for a better chance.

"O Lord with the starlight ears, send me a sign!" said Bigwig.

He heard movement in the run behind him. It was the Owslafa bringing up the prisoner. In the thundery twilight, Blackavar looked more sick and dejected than ever. His nose was dry and the whites of his eyes showed. Bigwig went out into the field, pulled a mouthful of clover and brought it back.

"Cheer up," he said to Blackavar. "Have some clover."

"That's not allowed, sir," said one of the escort.

"Oh, let him have it, Bartsia," said the other. "There's no one to see. It's hard enough for everyone on a day like this, let alone the prisoner."

Blackavar ate the clover and Bigwig took up his usual place as Chervil arrived to watch the Mark go out.

The rabbits were slow and hesitant and Chervil himself seemed unable to rise to his usual brisk manner. He had little to say as they passed him. He let both Thethuthinnang and Hyzenthlay go by in silence. Nelthilta, however, stopped of her own accord and stared impudently at him.

"Under the weather, Captain?" she said. "Brace up, now. You may have a surprise soon, who knows?"

"What do you mean?" answered Chervil sharply.

"Does might grow wings and fly," said Nelthilta, "and before very much longer, too. Secrets go faster than moles underground."

She followed the other does into the field. For a moment Chervil looked as though he were going to call her back.

"I wonder whether you could have a look at my off hind foot?" said Bigwig. "I think I've got a thorn in it."

"Come on, then," said Chervil, "outside. Not that we'll be able to see much better there."

But whether because he was still thinking about what Nelthilta had said, or for some other reason, he did not make a particularly thorough search for the thorn—which was perhaps as well, for there was no thorn there.

"Oh, confound it!" he said, looking up, "there's that dratted white bird again. What's it keep coming here for?"

"Why does it worry you?" asked Bigwig. "It's not doing any harm—only looking for snails."

"Anything out of the ordinary is a possible source of danger," replied Chervil, quoting Woundwort. "And you keep away from it today, Thlayli, d'you see? That's an order."

"Oh, very well," said Bigwig. "But surely you know how to get rid of them? I thought all rabbits knew that."

"Don't be ridiculous. You're not suggesting attacking a bird that size, with a beak as thick as my front paw?"

"No, no—it's a sort of charm thing that my mother taught me. You know, like 'Ladybird, ladybird, fly away home.' That works and so does this—or it always used to with my mother."

"The ladybird thing only works because all ladybirds crawl to the top of the stem and then fly."

"Well, all right," said Bigwig, "have it your own way. But you don't like the bird and I've offered to get rid of it for you. We had a lot of these charms and sayings in my old warren. I only wish we'd had one to get rid of men."

"Well, what is the charm?" said Chervil.

"You say,

"O fly away, great bird so white,
And don't come back until tonight.

"Of course, you have to use hedgerow talk. No use expecting them to understand Lapine. Let's have a go, anyway. If it doesn't work, we're none the worse, and if it does, the Mark will think it was you who drove the bird away. Where's it got to? I can hardly see anything in this light. Oh, there it is, look, behind those thistles. Well, you run like this. Now you have to hop to this side, then to the other side, scratch with your legs—that's right, splendid—cock your ears and then go straight on until—ah! Here we are; now then:

"O fly away, great bird so white,
And don't come back until tonight.

"There you are, you see. It *did* work. I think there's more than we know to some of these old rhymes and spells. Of course, it might have been just going to fly away anyway. But you must admit it's gone."

"Probably all that prancing about as we came up to it," said Chervil sourly. "We must have looked completely mad. What on earth will the Mark think? Anyway, now we're out here, we may as well go round the sentries."

"I'll stop and feed, if you don't mind," said Bigwig. "I didn't get much last night, you know."

*   *   *

Bigwig's luck was not altogether out. Later that morning, quite unexpectedly, he came upon a chance to talk to Blackavar alone. He had been through the sweltering burrows, finding everywhere quick breathing and feverish pulses; and he was just wondering whether he could not plausibly go and press Chervil to ask the Council's permission for the Mark to spend part of the day in the bushes above ground—for that might very well bring some sort of opportunity with it—when he began to feel the need to pass hraka. No rabbit passes hraka underground: and, like schoolchildren who know that they cannot very well be refused a request to go to the lavatory as long as it is not too soon after the last time, the Efrafan rabbits used to slip into the ditch for a breath of air and a change of scene. Although they were not supposed to be allowed to go more often than was necessary, some of the Owsla were easier than others. As Bigwig approached the hole that led into the ditch, he found two or three young bucks loitering in the run and, as usual, set himself to act his part as convincingly as he could.

"Why are you hanging about here?" he asked.

"The prisoner's escort are up at the hole and they turned us back, sir," answered one. "They're not letting anyone out for the moment."

"Not to pass hraka?" said Bigwig.

"No, sir."

Indignant, Bigwig made his way to the mouth of the hole. Here he found Blackavar's escort talking to the sentry on duty.

"I'm afraid you can't go out for the moment, sir," said Bartsia. "The prisoner's in the ditch, but he won't be long."

"Neither shall I," said Bigwig. "Just get out of the way, will you?" He pushed Bartsia to one side and hopped into the ditch.

The day had become even more lowering and overcast. Blackavar was squatting a little way off, under an overhanging plume of cow parsley. The flies were walking on his shreds of ears, but he seemed not to notice them. Bigwig went along the ditch and squatted beside him.

"Blackavar, listen," he said quickly. "This is the truth, by Frith and the Black Rabbit. I am a secret enemy of Efrafa. No one knows this but you and a few of the Mark does. I'm going to escape with them tonight and I'm going to take you as well. Don't do anything yet. When the time comes I'll be there to tell you. Just brace up and get yourself ready."

Without waiting for an answer, he moved away as though to find a better spot. Even so, he was back at the hole before Blackavar, who evidently meant to stay outside for as long as the escort—clearly in no hurry themselves—would allow.

"Sir," said Bartsia, as Bigwig came in, "that's the third time, sir, that you've disregarded my authority. Council police can't be treated in this way. I'm afraid I shall have to report it, sir."

Bigwig made no reply and returned up the run.

"Wait a bit longer if you can," he said as he passed the bucks. "I don't suppose that poor fellow will get out again today."

He wondered whether to go and look for Hyzenthlay, but decided that it would be prudent to keep away from her. She knew what to do, and the less they were seen together the better. His head ached in the heat and he wanted only to be alone and quiet. He went back to his burrow and slept.

3 8

The Thunder Breaks

Why, now, blow wind, swell billow and swim bark!
The storm is up and all is on the hazard!

Shakespeare, *Julius Caesar*

Late in the afternoon it came on dark and very close. It was plain that there would be no true sunset. On the green path by the riverbank, Hazel sat fidgeting as he tried to imagine what might be going on in Efrafa.

"He told you he wanted you to attack the sentries while the rabbits were feeding, didn't he," he said to Kehaar, "and that he'd bring the mothers out in the confusion?"

"Ya, say dis, but not 'appen. Den 'e say go away, come again tonight."

"So that's still what he means to do. The question is, when *will* they be feeding? It's getting dark already. Silver, what do you think?"

"If I know them, they won't alter anything they usually do," said Silver. "But if you're worried in case we're not there in time, why not go now?"

"Because they're always patrolling. The longer we wait up there, the greater the risk. If a patrol finds us before Bigwig comes, it won't be just a matter of getting ourselves away. They'll realize we're there for some purpose and give the alarm, and that'll be the end of any chance he's got."

"Listen, Hazel-rah," said Blackberry. "We ought to reach the iron road at the same time as Bigwig and not a moment before. Why don't you take them all over the river now and wait in the undergrowth, near the boat? Once Kehaar's attacked the sentries, he can fly back and tell us."

"Yes, that's it," answered Hazel. "But once he's told us, we must get up there in no time at all. Bigwig's going to need us as well as Kehaar."

"Well, *you* won't be able to dash up to the arch," said Fiver, "with your leg. The best thing you can do is to get on the boat and have the rope gnawed half through by the time we come back. Silver can look after the fighting, if there's going to be any."

Hazel hesitated. "But some of us are probably going to get hurt. I can't stay behind."

"Fiver's right," said Blackberry. "You *will* have to wait on the boat, Hazel. We can't risk your being left to be picked up by the Efrafans. Besides, it's very important that the rope should be half gnawed—that's a job for someone sensible. It mustn't break too soon or we're all finished."

It took them some time to persuade Hazel. When at last he agreed, he was still reluctant.

"If Bigwig doesn't come tonight," he said, "I shall go and find him, wherever he is. Frith knows what may have happened already."

As they set off up the left bank, the wind began to blow in fitful, warm gusts, with a multifoliate rustling through the sedges. They had just reached the plank bridge when there came a rumble of thunder. In the intense, strange light, the plants and leaves seemed magnified and the fields beyond the river very near. There was an oppressive stillness.

"You know, Hazel-rah," said Bluebell, "this really is the funniest evening I've ever gone looking for a doe."

"It's going to get a lot funnier soon," said Silver. "There'll be lightning and pouring rain. For goodness' sake, all of you, don't panic, or we'll never see our warren again. I think this is going to be a rough business," he added quietly to Hazel. "I don't like it much."

*   *   *

Bigwig woke to hear his name repeated urgently.

"Thlayli! Thlayli! Wake up! *Thlayli!*"

It was Hyzenthlay.

"What is it?" he said. "What's the matter?"

"Nelthilta's been arrested."

Bigwig leaped to his feet.

"How long ago? How did it happen?"

"Just now. Moneywort came down to our burrow and told her to come up to Captain Chervil at once. I followed them up the run. When she got to Chervil's burrow, there were two Council police waiting just outside and one of them said to Chervil, 'Well, as quick as you can, and don't be long.' And then they took her straight out. They must have gone to the Council. Oh, Thlayli, what shall we do? She'll tell them everything—"

"Listen to me," said Bigwig. "There's not a moment to lose. Go and get Thethuthinnang and the others and bring them up to this burrow. I shan't be here, but you must wait quietly until I come back. It won't be long. Quick now! Everything depends on it."

Hyzenthlay had hardly disappeared down the run when Bigwig heard another rabbit approaching from the opposite direction.

"Who's there?" he said, turning swiftly.

"Chervil," answered the other. "I'm glad you're awake. Listen, Thlayli, there's going to be a whole lot of trouble. Nelthilta's been arrested by the Council. I was sure she would be, after my report to Vervain this morning. Whatever it was she was talking about, they'll get it out of her. I dare say the General will be here himself as soon as he knows what's what. Now look here, I've got to go over to the Council burrow at once. You and Avens are to stay here and get the sentries on duty immediately. There'll be no silflay and no one is to go outside for any reason whatever. All the holes are to be double-guarded. Now, you understand these orders, don't you?"

"Have you told Avens?"

"I haven't time to go looking for Avens; he's not in his burrow. Go and alert the sentries yourself. Send someone to find Avens and someone else to tell Bartsia that Blackavar won't be wanted this evening. Then sit on those holes—and the hraka holes, too—with every sentry you've got. For all I know, there may be some plot to make a break-out. We arrested Nelthilta as quietly as we could, but the Mark are bound to realize what's happened. If necessary you're to get rough, do you see? Now I'm off."

"Right," said Bigwig. "I'll get busy at once."

He followed Chervil to the top of the run. The sentry at the hole was Marjoram. As he stood clear to let Chervil pass, Bigwig came up behind him and looked out into the overcast.

"Did Chervil tell you?" he said. "Silflay's early tonight, on account of the weather. The orders are that we're to get on with it at once."

He waited for Marjoram's reply. If Chervil had already told him that no one was to go out, it would be necessary to fight him. But after a moment Marjoram said, "Have you heard any thunder yet?"

"Get on with it at once, I said," answered Bigwig. "Go down and get Blackavar and the escort up, and be quick, too. We'll need to get the Mark out immediately if they're to feed before the storm breaks."

Marjoram went and Bigwig hurried back to his own burrow. Hyzenthlay had lost no time. Three or four does were crammed into the burrow itself and nearby, in a side run, Thethuthinnang was crouching with several more. All were silent and frightened and one or two were close to the stupefaction of terror.

"This is no time to go tharn," said Bigwig. "Your lives depend on doing as I say. Listen, now. Blackavar and the police guards will be up directly. Marjoram will probably come up behind them and you must find some excuse to keep him talking. Soon after, you'll hear fighting, because I'm going to attack the police guards. When you hear that, come up as fast as you can and follow me out into the field. Don't stop for anything."

As he finished speaking, he heard the unmistakable sound of Blackavar and the guards approaching. Blackavar's weary, dragging gait was like that of no other rabbit. Without waiting for the does to reply, Bigwig returned to the mouth of the run. The three rabbits came up in single file, Bartsia leading.

"I'm afraid I've brought you up here for nothing," said Bigwig. "I've just been told that silflay's canceled for this evening. Have a look outside and you'll see why."

As Bartsia went to look out of the hole, Bigwig slipped quickly between him and Blackavar.

"Well, it looks very stormy, certainly," said Bartsia, "but I shouldn't have thought—"

"*Now,* Blackavar!" cried Bigwig, and leaped on Bartsia from behind.

Bartsia fell forward out of the hole with Bigwig on top of him. He was not a member of the Owslafa for nothing and was reckoned a good fighter. As they rolled over on the ground, he turned his head and sank his teeth in Bigwig's shoulder. He had been trained to get a grip at once and to hold it at all costs. More than once in the past this had served him well. But in fighting a rabbit of Bigwig's strength and courage it proved a mistake. His best chance would have been to keep clear and use his claws. He retained his hold like a dog, and Bigwig, snarling, brought both his own back legs forward, sank his feet in Bartsia's side and then, ignoring the pain in his shoulder, forced himself upward. He felt Bartsia's closed teeth come tearing out through his flesh and then he was standing above him as he fell back on the ground, kicking helplessly. Bigwig leaped clear. It was plain that Bartsia's haunch was injured. He struggled, but could not get up.

"Think yourself lucky," said Bigwig, bleeding and cursing, "that I don't kill you."

Without waiting to see what Bartsia would do, he jumped back into the hole. He found Blackavar grappling with the other guard. Just beyond them, Hyzenthlay was coming up the run with Thethuthinnang behind her. Bigwig gave the guard a tremendous cuff on the side of the head, which knocked him clear across the run and into the prisoner's alcove. He picked himself up, panting, and stared at Bigwig without a word.

"Don't move," said Bigwig. "There'll be worse to come if you do. Blackavar, are you all right?"

"Yes, sir," said Blackavar, "but what do we do now?"

"Follow me," said Bigwig, "all of you. Come on!"

He led the way out again. There was no sign of Bartsia, but as he looked back to make sure that the others were following, he caught a glimpse of the astonished face of Avens peering out of the other hole.

"Captain Chervil wants you!" he called, and dashed away into the field.

As he reached the clump of thistles where he had spoken to Kehaar that morning, a long roll of thunder sounded from across the valley beyond. A few great, warm drops of rain were falling. Along the western horizon the lower clouds formed a single purple mass, against which distant trees stood out minute and sharp. The upper edges rose into the light, a far land of wild mountains. Copper-colored, weightless and motionless, they suggested a glassy fragility like that of frost. Surely, when the thunder struck them again they would vibrate, tremble and shatter, till warm shards, sharp as icicles, fell flashing down from the ruins. Racing through the ocher light, Bigwig was impelled by a frenzy of tension and energy. He did not feel the wound in his shoulder. The storm was his own. The storm would defeat Efrafa.

He was well out into the great field and looking for a sight of the distant arch when he felt along the ground the first stamping thuds of the alarm. He pulled up and looked about him. There did not seem to be any stragglers. The does—however many there were— were well up with him, but scattered to either side. Rabbits in flight tend to keep away from each other, and the does had opened out as they left the hole. If there was a patrol between him and the iron road they would not get past it without loss unless they came closer together. He would have to collect them, despite the delay. Then another thought came to him. If they could get out of sight, their pursuers might be puzzled, for the rain and the failing light would make tracking difficult.

The rain was falling faster now and the wind was rising. Over on the evening side, a hedge ran down the length of the field toward the iron road. He saw Blackavar nearby and ran across to him.

"I want everyone the other side of that hedge," he said. "Can you get hold of some of them and bring them that way?"

Bigwig remembered that Blackavar knew nothing except that they were on the run. There was no time to explain about Hazel and the river.

"Go straight to that ash tree in the hedge," he said, "and take all the does you can pick up on the way. Get through to the other side and I'll be there as soon as you are."

At this moment Hyzenthlay and Thethuthinnang came running toward them, followed by two or three other does. They were plainly confused and uncertain.

"The stamping, Thlayli!" panted Thethuthinnang. "They're coming!"

"Well, run, then," said Bigwig. "Keep near me, all of you."

They were better runners than he had dared to hope. As they made for the ash tree, more does fell in with them and it seemed to him that they ought now to be a match for a patrol, unless it were a very strong one. Once through the hedge he turned south and, keeping close beside it, led them down the slope. There, ahead of him, was the arch in the overgrown embankment. But would Hazel be there? And where was Kehaar?

*   *   *

"Well, and what was to happen after that, Nelthilta?" asked General Woundwort. "Make sure you tell us everything, because we know a good deal already. Let her alone, Vervain," he added. "She can't talk if you keep cuffing her, you fool."

"Hyzenthlay said—oh! oh!—she said a big bird would attack the Owsla sentries," gasped Nelthilta, "and we would run away in the confusion. And then—"

"She said a *bird* would attack the sentries?" interrupted Woundwort, puzzled. "Are you telling the truth? What sort of a bird?"

"I don't—I don't know," panted Nelthilta. "The new officer—she said he had told the bird—"

"What do *you* know about a bird?" said Woundwort, turning to Chervil.

"I reported it, sir," replied Chervil. "You'll not forget, sir, that I reported the bird—"

There was a scuffling outside the crowded Council burrow and Avens came pushing his way in.

"The new officer, sir!" he cried. "He's gone! Taken a crowd of the Mark does with him. Jumped on Bartsia and broke his leg, sir! Blackavar's cut and run, too. We never had a chance to stop them. Goodness knows how many have joined him. Thlayli—it's Thlayli's doing!"

"Thlayli?" cried Woundwort. "Embleer Frith, I'll *blind* him when I catch him! Chervil, Vervain, Avens—yes and you two as well—come with me. Which way has he gone?"

"He was going downhill, sir," answered Avens.

"Lead the way you saw him take," said Woundwort.

As they came out from the Crixa, two or three of the Efrafan officers checked at the sight of the murky light and increasing rain. But the sight of the General was more alarming still. Pausing only to stamp the escape alarm, they set out behind him toward the iron road.

Very soon they came upon traces of blood which the rain had not yet washed away, and these they followed toward the ash tree in the hedge to the west of the warren.

*　　*　　*

Bigwig came out from the further side of the railway arch, sat up and looked round him. There was no sign either of Hazel or of Kehaar. For the first time since he had attacked Bartsia he began to feel uncertain and troubled. Perhaps, after all, Kehaar had not understood his cryptic message that morning? Or had some disaster overtaken Hazel and the rest? If they were dead—scattered—if there was no one left alive to meet him? He and his does would wander about the fields until the patrols hunted them down.

"No, it shan't come to that," said Bigwig to himself. "At the worst we can cross the river and try to hide in the woodland. Confound this shoulder! It's going to be more nuisance than I thought. Well, I'll try to get them down to the plank bridge at least. If we're not overtaken soon, perhaps the rain will discourage whoever's after us; but I doubt it."

He turned back to the does waiting under the arch. Most of them looked bewildered. Hyzenthlay had promised that they were to be

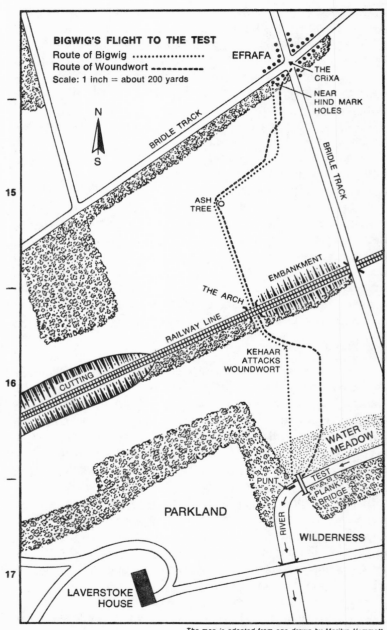

BIGWIG'S FLIGHT TO THE TEST
Route of Bigwig ....
Route of Woundwort ----------
Scale: 1 inch = about 200 yards

EFRAFA

THE CRIXA

NEAR HIND MARK HOLES

N
S

BRIDLE TRACK

BRIDLE TRACK

15

ASH TREE

EMBANKMENT

THE ARCH

RAILWAY LINE

CUTTING

16

KEHAAR ATTACKS WOUNDWORT

WATER MEADOW

PUNT

TEST

PLANK BRIDGE

PARKLAND

RIVER

WILDERNESS

17

LAVERSTOKE HOUSE

The map is adapted from one drawn by Marilyn Hemmett

protected by a great bird and that the new officer was going to work a secret trick to evade the pursuit—a trick which would defeat even the General. These things had not happened. They were wet through. Runnels of water were trickling through the arch from the uphill side, and the bare earth was beginning to turn into mud. Ahead of them there was nothing to be seen but a track leading through the nettles into another wide and empty field.

"Come on," said Bigwig. "It's not far now and then we'll all be safe. This way."

All the rabbits obeyed him at once. There was something to be said for Efrafan discipline, thought Bigwig grimly, as they left the arch and met the force of the rain.

Along one side of the field, beside the elms, farm tractors had pounded a broad, flat path downhill toward the water meadow below—that same path up which he had run three nights before, after he had left Hazel by the boat. It was turning muddy now—unpleasant going for rabbits—but at least it led straight to the river and was open enough for Kehaar to spot them if he should turn up.

He had just begun to run once more when a rabbit overtook him.

"Stop, Thlayli! What are you doing here? Where are you going?"

Bigwig had been half expecting Campion to appear and had made up his mind to kill him if necessary. But now that he actually saw him at his side, disregarding the storm and the mud, self-possessed as he led his patrol, no more than four strong, into the thick of a pack of desperate runaways, he could feel only what a pity it was that the two of them should be enemies and how much he would have liked to have taken Campion with him out of Efrafa.

"Go away," he said. "Don't try to stop us, Campion. I don't want to hurt you."

He glanced to his other side. "Blackavar, get the does to close up. If there are any stragglers the patrol will jump on them."

"You'd do better to give in now," said Campion, still running beside him. "I shan't let you out of my sight, wherever you go. There's an escape patrol on the way—I heard the signal. When they get here you won't stand a chance. You're bleeding badly now."

"Curse you!" cried Bigwig, striking at him. "You'll bleed too, before I've done."

"Can I fight him, sir?" said Blackavar. "He won't beat me a second time."

"No," answered Bigwig, "he's only trying to delay us. Keep running."

"Thlayli!" cried Thethuthinnang suddenly, from behind him. "The General! The General! Oh, what shall we do?"

Bigwig looked back. It was indeed a sight to strike terror into the bravest heart. Woundwort had come through the arch ahead of his followers and was running toward them by himself, snarling with fury. Behind him came the patrol. In one quick glance Bigwig recognized Chervil, Avens and Groundsel. With them were several more, including a heavy, savage-looking rabbit whom he guessed to be Vervain, the head of the Council police. It crossed his mind that if he were to run, immediately and alone, they would probably let him go as he had come, and feel glad to be so easily rid of him. Certainly the alternative was to be killed. At this moment Blackavar spoke.

"Never mind, sir," he said. "You did your very best and it nearly came off. We may even be able to kill one or two of them before it's finished. Some of these does can fight well when they're put to it."

Bigwig rubbed his nose quickly against Blackavar's mutilated ear and sat back on his haunches as Woundwort came up to them.

"You dirty little beast," said Woundwort. "I hear you've attacked one of the Council police and broken his leg. We'll settle with you here. There's no need to take you back to Efrafa."

"You crack-brained slave-driver," answered Bigwig. "I'd like to see you try."

"All right," said Woundwort, "that's enough. Who have we got? Vervain, Campion, put him down. The rest of you, start getting these does back to the warren. The prisoner you can leave to me."

"Frith sees you!" cried Bigwig. "You're not fit to be called a rabbit! May Frith blast you and your foul Owsla full of bullies!"

At that instant a dazzling claw of lightning streaked down the length of the sky. The hedge and the distant trees seemed to leap forward in the brilliance of the flash. Immediately upon it came the thunder: a high, tearing noise, as though some huge thing were being ripped to pieces close above, which deepened and turned to enormous blows of dissolution. Then the rain fell like a waterfall. In a few seconds the ground was covered with water and over it, to a height of inches, rose a haze formed of a myriad minute splashes. Stupefied with the shock, unable even to move, the sodden rabbits crouched inert, almost pinned to the earth by the rain.

A small voice spoke in Bigwig's mind.

"Your storm, Thlayli-rah. Use it."

Gasping, he struggled up and pushed Blackavar with his foot. "Come on," he said, "get hold of Hyzenthlay. We're going."

He shook his head, trying to blink the rain out of his eyes. Then it was no longer Blackavar who was crouching in front of him but Woundwort, drenched in mud and rain, glaring and scrabbling in the silt with his great claws.

"I'll kill you myself," said Woundwort.

His long front teeth were bared like the fangs of a rat. Afraid, Bigwig watched him closely. He knew that Woundwort, with all the advantage of weight, would jump and try to close with him. He must try to avoid him and rely on his claws. He shifted his ground uneasily and felt himself slipping in the mud. Why did Woundwort not jump? Then he realized that Woundwort was no longer looking at him, but staring over his head at something beyond, something that he himself could not see. Suddenly, Woundwort leaped backward and in the same moment, through the all-enveloping sound of the rain, there sounded a raucous clamor.

"Yark! Yark! Yark!"

Some big white thing was striking at Woundwort, who was cowering and guarding his head as best he could. Then it was gone, sailing upward and turning in the rain.

"Meester Pigvig, ees rabbits come!"

Sights and feelings swirled through Bigwig as though in a dream. The things that were happening no longer seemed connected by anything except his own dazed senses. He heard Kehaar screaming as he dived again to attack Vervain. He felt the rain pouring cold into the open gash in his shoulder. Through the curtain of rain he glimpsed Woundwort dodging among his officers and urging them back into the ditch on the edge of the field. He saw Blackavar striking at Campion and Campion turning to run. Then someone beside him was saying, "Hullo, Bigwig. Bigwig! Bigwig! What do you want us to do?" It was Silver.

"Where's Hazel?" he said.

"Waiting at the boat. I say, you're wounded! What—"

"Then get these does down there," said Bigwig.

All was confusion. In ones and twos the does, utterly bemused and scarcely able to move or to understand what was said to them, were urged into getting up and stumbling their way down the field. Other rabbits began to appear through the rain: Acorn, clearly frightened, but determined not to run; Dandelion encouraging Pipkin; Speedwell and Hawkbit making toward Kehaar—the only creature visible above the ground haze. Bigwig and Silver brought them together as best they could and made them understand that they were to help to get the does away.

"Go back to Blackberry, go back to Blackberry," Silver kept repeating. "I left three of our rabbits in different places to mark the way back," he explained to Bigwig. "Blackberry's first, then Bluebell, then Fiver—he's quite near the river."

"And there *is* Blackberry," said Bigwig.

"You did it, then, Bigwig," said Blackberry, shivering. "Was it very bad? Good heavens, your shoulder—"

"It's not finished yet," said Bigwig. "Has everyone passed you?"

"You're the last," said Blackberry. "Can we go? This storm's terrifying me!"

Kehaar alighted beside them.

"Meester Pigvig," he said, "I fly on dose damn rabbits, but dey no run, dey get in ditch. I no catch 'em in dere. Dey coming all along beside you."

"They'll never give up," said Bigwig. "I warn you, Silver, they'll be at us before it's done. There's thick cover in the water meadow—they'll use that. Acorn, come back, keep away from that ditch!"

"Go back to Bluebell! Go back to Bluebell!" repeated Silver, running from side to side.

They found Bluebell by the hedge at the bottom of the field. He was white-eyed and ready to bolt.

"Silver," he said, "I saw a bunch of rabbits—strangers, Efrafans, I suppose—come out of the ditch over there and slip across into the water meadow. They're behind us now. One of them was the biggest rabbit I've ever seen."

"Then don't stay here," said Silver. "There goes Speedwell. And who's that? Acorn and two does with him. That's everyone. Come on, quick as you can."

It was only a short distance now to the river, but among the sodden patches of rushes, the bushes and sedge and deep puddles, they found it next to impossible to tell their direction. Expecting to be attacked at any moment, they scuttered and floundered through the undergrowth, finding here a doe and there one of their own rabbits and forcing them on. Without Kehaar they would certainly have lost all touch with each other and perhaps never reached the river. The gull kept flying backward and forward along the direct line to the bank, only alighting now and then to guide Bigwig toward some straggling doe whom he had spotted going the wrong way.

"Kehaar," said Bigwig, as they waited for Thethuthinnang to struggle up to them through a half-flattened clump of nettles, "will you go and see whether you can spot the Efrafans? They can't be far away. But why haven't they attacked us? We're all so scattered that they could easily do us a lot of harm. I wonder what they're up to?"

Kehaar was back in a very short time.

"Dey hiding at pridge," he said, "all under pushes. I come down, dat peeg fella 'e make for fight me."

"Did he?" said Bigwig. "The brute's got courage, I'll give him that."

"Dey t'ink you got to cross river dere or else go all along pank. Dey not know heem poat. You near poat now."

Fiver came running through the undergrowth.

"We've been able to get some of them on the boat, Bigwig," he said, "but most of them won't trust me. They just keep asking where *you* are."

Bigwig ran behind him and came out on the green path by the bank. All the surface of the river was winking and plopping in the rain. The level did not appear to have risen much as yet. The boat was just as he remembered it—one end against the bank, the other a little way out in the stream. On the raised part at the near end Hazel was crouching, his ears drooping on either side of his head and his flattened fur completely black with rain. He was holding the taut rope in his teeth. Acorn, Hyzenthlay and two more were crouching near him on the wood, but the rest were huddled here and there along the bank. Blackberry was trying unsuccessfully to persuade them to get out on the boat.

"Hazel's afraid to leave the rope," he said to Bigwig. "Apparently he's bitten it very thin already. All these does will say is that you're their officer."

Bigwig turned to Theththinnang.

"This is the magic trick now," he said. "Get them over there, where Hyzenthlay's sitting, do you see? All of them—quickly."

Before she could reply, another doe gave a squeal of fear. A little way downstream, Campion and his patrol had emerged from the bushes and were coming up the path. From the opposite direction Vervain, Chervil and Groundsel were approaching. The doe turned and darted for the undergrowth immediately behind her. Just as she reached it, Woundwort himself appeared in her way, reared up and dealt her a great, raking blow across the face. The doe turned once more and ran blindly across the path and onto the boat.

Bigwig realized that since the moment when Kehaar had attacked him in the field, Woundwort had not only retained control over his officers but had actually made a plan and put it into effect. The storm and the difficult going had upset the fugitives and disorganized them. Woundwort, on the other hand, had taken his rabbits into the ditch and then made use of it to get them down to the water meadow, unexposed to further attack from Kehaar. Once there, he must have gone straight for the plank bridge—which he evidently knew about—and set an ambush under cover. But as soon as he had grasped that for some reason the runaways were not making for the bridge after all, he had instantly sent Campion to make his way round through the undergrowth, regain the bank downstream and cut them off; and Campion had done this without error or delay. Now Woundwort meant to fight them, here on the bank. He knew that Kehaar could not be everywhere and that the bushes and undergrowth provided enough cover, at a pinch, to dodge him. It was true that the other side had twice his numbers, but most of them were afraid of him and none was a trained Efrafan officer. Now that he had them pinned against the river, he would split them up and kill as many as possible. The rest could run away and come to grief as they might.

Bigwig began to understand why Woundwort's officers followed him and fought for him as they did.

"He's not like a rabbit at all," he thought. "Flight's the last thing he ever thinks of. If I'd known three nights ago what I know now, I don't believe I'd ever have gone into Efrafa. I suppose he hasn't realized about the boat, too? It wouldn't surprise me." He dashed across the grass and jumped on the planking beside Hazel.

The appearance of Woundwort had achieved what Blackberry and Fiver could not. Every one of the does ran from the bank to the boat. Blackberry and Fiver ran with them. Woundwort, following them close, reached the edge of the bank and came face to face with Bigwig. As he stood his ground, Bigwig could hear Blackberry just behind him, speaking urgently to Hazel.

"Dandelion's not here," said Blackberry. "He's the only one."

Hazel spoke for the first time. "We shall have to leave him," he answered. "It's a shame, but these fellows will be at us in a moment and we can't stop them."

Bigwig spoke without taking his eyes from Woundwort. "Just a few more moments, Hazel," he said. "I'll keep them off. We can't leave Dandelion."

Woundwort sneered up at him. "I trusted you, Thlayli," he said. "You can trust me now. You'll either go into the river or be torn to pieces here—the whole lot of you. There's nowhere left to run."

Bigwig had caught sight of Dandelion looking out of the undergrowth opposite. He was plainly at a loss.

"Groundsel! Vervain!" said Woundwort. "Come over here beside me. When I give the word, we'll go straight into them. As for that bird, it's not dangerous—"

"There it is!" cried Bigwig. Woundwort looked up quickly and leaped back. Dandelion shot out of the bushes, crossed the path in a flash and was on the boat beside Hazel. In the same moment the rope parted and immediately the little punt began to move along the bank in the steady current. When it had gone a few yards, the stern swung slowly outward until it was broadside on to the stream. In this position it drifted to the middle of the river and into the southward bend.

Looking back, the last thing Bigwig saw was the face of General Woundwort staring out of the gap in the willow herb where the boat had lain. It reminded him of the kestrel on Watership Down which had pounced into the mouth of the hole and missed the mouse.

PART IV

Hazel-rah

39

The Bridges

Boatman dance, boatman sing,
Boatman do most anything,
Dance, boatman, dance.
　　Dance all night till the broad daylight,
　　Go home with the girls in the morning.
Hey, ho, boatman row,
　　Sailing down the river on the Ohio.

American Folk Song

On almost any other river, Blackberry's plan would not have worked. The punt would not have left the bank or, if it had, would have run aground or been fouled by weeds or some other obstruction. But here, on the Test, there were no submerged branches and no gravel spits or beds of weed above the surface at all. From bank to bank the current, regular and unvaried, flowed as fast as a man strolling. The punt slipped downstream smoothly, without any alteration of the speed which it had gained within a few yards of leaving the bank.

Most of the rabbits had very little idea of what was happening. The Efrafan does had never seen a river and it would certainly have been beyond Pipkin or Hawkbit to explain to them that they were on a boat. They—and nearly all the others—had simply trusted Hazel and done as they were told. But all—bucks and does alike—realized that Woundwort and his followers had vanished. Wearied by all they had gone through, the sodden rabbits crouched without talking, incapable of any feeling but a dull relief and without even the energy to wonder what was going to happen next.

That they should feel any relief—dull or otherwise—was remarkable in the circumstances and showed both how little they understood their situation and how much fear Woundwort could inspire, for their escape from him seemed to be their only good fortune. The rain was still falling. Already so wet that they no longer felt it, they were nevertheless shivering with cold and weighted with their drenched fur. The punt was holding over half an inch of rainwater. There was one small, slatted floorboard and this was floating. Some of the rabbits, in the first confusion of boarding the punt, had found themselves in this water, but now all had got clear of it—most either to bows or stern, though Thethuthinnang and Speedwell were hunched on the narrow thwart, amidships. In addition to their discomfort, they were exposed and helpless. Finally, there was no way of controlling the punt and they did not know where they were going. But these last were troubles beyond the understanding of everyone but Hazel, Fiver and Blackberry.

Bigwig had collapsed beside Hazel and lay on his side, exhausted. The feverish courage which had brought him from Efrafa to the river had gone and his wounded shoulder had begun to hurt badly. In spite of the rain and the throbbing pulse down his foreleg, he felt ready to sleep where he was, stretched upon the planking. He opened his eyes and looked up at Hazel.

"I couldn't do it again, Hazel-rah," he said.

"You haven't got to," replied Hazel.

"It was touch and go, you know," said Bigwig. "A chance in a thousand."

"Our children's children will hear a good story," answered Hazel, quoting a rabbit proverb. "How did you get that wound? It's a nasty one."

"I fought a member of the Council police," said Bigwig.

"A what?" The term "Owslafa" was unknown to Hazel.

"A dirty little beast like Hufsa," said Bigwig.

"Did you beat him?"

"Oh, yes—or I shouldn't be here. I should think he'll stop running. I say, Hazel-rah, we've got the does. What's going to happen now?"

"I don't know," said Hazel. "We need one of these clever rabbits to tell us. And Kehaar—where's he gone? He's supposed to know about this thing we're sitting on."

Dandelion, crouching beside Hazel, got up at the mention of

"clever rabbits," made his way across the puddled floor and returned with Blackberry and Fiver.

"We're all wondering what to do next," said Hazel.

"Well," said Blackberry, "I suppose we shall drift into the bank before long and then we can get out and find cover. There's no harm, though, in going a good long way from those friends of Bigwig's."

"There is," said Hazel. "We're stuck here in full view and we can't run. If a man sees us we're in trouble."

"Men don't like rain," said Blackberry. "Neither do I, if it comes to that, but it makes us safer just now."

At this moment Hyzenthlay, sitting just behind him, started and looked up.

"Excuse me, sir, for interrupting you," she said, as though speaking to an officer in Efrafa, "but the bird—the white bird—it's coming toward us."

Kehaar came flying up the river through the rain and alighted on the narrow side of the punt. The does nearest to him backed away nervously.

"Meester 'Azel," he said, "pridge come. You see 'im pridge?"

It had not occurred to any of the rabbits that they were floating beside the path up which they had come earlier that evening before the storm broke. They were on the opposite side of the hedge of plants along the bank and the whole river looked different. But now they saw, not far ahead, the bridge which they had crossed when they first came to the Test four nights before. This they recognized at once, for it looked the same as it had from the bank.

"Maybe you go under 'im, maybe not," said Kehaar. "But you sit dere, ees trouble."

The bridge stretched from bank to bank between two low abutments. It was not arched. Its underside, made of iron girders, was perfectly straight—parallel with the surface and about eight inches above it. Just in time Hazel saw what Kehaar meant. If the punt did pass under the bridge without sticking, it would do so by no more than a claw's breadth. Any creature above the level of the sides would be struck and perhaps knocked into the river. He scuttered through the warm bilgewater to the other end and pushed his way up among the wet, crowded rabbits.

"Get down in the bottom! Get down in the bottom!" he said.

"Silver, Hawkbit—all of you. Never mind the water. You, and you—what's your name? Oh, Blackavar, is it?—get everyone into the bottom. Be quick."

Like Bigwig, he found that the Efrafan rabbits obeyed him at once. He saw Kehaar fly up from his perch and disappear over the wooden rails. The concrete abutments projected from each bank, so that the narrowed river ran slightly faster under the bridge. The punt had been drifting broadside on, but now one end swung forward, so that Hazel lost his bearings and found that he was no longer looking at the bridge but at the bank. As he hesitated, the bridge seemed to come at him in a dark mass, like snow sliding from a bough. He pressed himself into the bilge. There was a squeal and a rabbit tumbled on top of him. Then a heavy blow vibrated along the length of the punt and its smooth movement was checked. This was followed by a hollow sound of scraping. It grew dark and a roof appeared, very low above him. For a moment Hazel had the vague idea that he was underground. Then the roof vanished, the punt was gliding on and he heard Kehaar calling. They were below the bridge and still drifting downstream.

The rabbit who had fallen on him was Acorn. He had been struck by the bridge and the blow had sent him flying. However, though dazed and bruised, he seemed to have escaped injury.

"I wasn't quick enough, Hazel-rah," he said. "I'd better go to Efrafa for a bit."

"You'd be wasted," said Hazel. "But I'm afraid there's someone at the other end who hasn't been so lucky."

One of the does had held back from the bilgewater, and the upstream girder under the bridge had caught her across the back. It was plain that she was injured, but how badly Hazel could not tell. He saw Hyzenthlay beside her and it seemed to him that since there was nothing he could do to help, it would probably be best to let them alone. He looked round at his bedraggled, shivering comrades and then at Kehaar, spruce and brisk on the stern.

"We ought to get back on the bank, Kehaar," he said. "How can we do it? Rabbits weren't meant for this, you know."

"You not stop poat. But again is nudder pridge more. 'E stop 'im."

There was nothing to be done but wait. They drifted on and came to a second bend, where the river curved westward. The current did not slacken and the punt came round the bend almost in the middle of the stream, revolving as it did so. The rabbits had been frightened by what had happened to Acorn and to the doe, and remained squatting miserably, half in and half out of the bilge. Hazel crept back to the raised bow and looked ahead.

The river broadened and the current slackened. He realized that they had begun to drift more slowly. The nearer bank was high and the trees stood close and thick, but on the further bank the ground was low and open. Grassy, it stretched away, smooth as the mown gallops on Watership Down. Hazel hoped that they might somehow drop out of the current and reach that side, but the punt moved quietly on, down the very center of the broad pool. The open bank slipped by and now the trees towered on both sides. Downstream, the pool was closed by the second bridge, of which Kehaar had spoken.

It was old, built of darkened bricks. Ivy trailed over it and the valerian and creeping mauve toadflax. Well out from either bank stood four low arches—scarcely more than culverts, each filled by the stream to within a foot of the apex. Through them, thin segments of daylight showed from the downstream side. The piers did not project, but against each lay a little accumulation of flotsam, from which driftweed and sticks continually broke away to be carried through the bridge.

It was plain that the punt would drift against the bridge and be held there. As it approached, Hazel dropped back into the bilgewater. But this time there was no need. Broadside on, the punt struck gently against two of the piers and stopped, pinned squarely across the mouth of one of the central culverts. It could go no further.

They had floated not quite half a mile in just over fifteen minutes.

Hazel put his forepaws on the low side and looked gingerly over upstream. Immediately below, a shallow ripple spread all along the waterline, where the current met the woodwork. It was too far to jump to the shore and both banks were steep. He turned and looked upward. The brickwork was sheer, with a projecting course halfway between him and the parapet. There was no scrambling up that.

"What's to be done, Blackberry?" he asked, making his way to the bolt fixed on the bow, with its ragged remnant of painter. "You got us on this thing. How do we get off?"

"I don't know, Hazel-rah," replied Blackberry. "Of all the ways we could finish up, I never thought of this. It looks as though we'll have to swim."

"Swim?" said Silver. "I don't fancy it, Hazel-rah. I know it's no distance, but look at those banks. The current would take us down before we could get out: and that means into one of these holes under the bridge."

Hazel tried to look through the arch. There was very little to be seen. The dark tunnel was not long—perhaps not much longer than the punt itself. The water looked smooth. There seemed to be no obstructions and there was room for the head of a swimming animal between the surface of the water and the apex of the arch. But the segment was so narrow that it was impossible to see exactly what lay on the other side of the bridge. The light was failing. Water, green leaves, moving reflections of leaves, the splashing of the raindrops and some curious thing that appeared to be standing in the water and to be made of vertical gray lines—these were all that could be made out. The rain echoed dismally up the culvert. The hard, ringing noise from under the soffit, so much unlike any sound to be heard in an earth tunnel, was disturbing. Hazel returned to Blackberry and Silver.

"This is as bad a fix as we've been in," he said. "We can't stay here, but I can't see any way out."

Kehaar appeared on the parapet above them, flapped the rain out of his wings and dropped down to the punt.

"Ees finish poat," he said. "Not vait more."

"But how can we get to the bank, Kehaar?" said Hazel.

The gull was surprised. "Dog sveem, rat sveem. You no sveem?"

"Yes, we can swim as long as it's not very far. But the banks are too steep for us, Kehaar. We wouldn't be able to stop the current taking us down one of these tunnels and we don't know what's at the other end."

"Ees goot—you get out fine."

Hazel felt at a loss. What exactly was he to understand from this? Kehaar was not a rabbit. Whatever the Big Water was like, it must be worse than this and Kehaar was used to it. He never said much in any case and what he did say was always restricted to the simplest, since he spoke no Lapine. He was doing them a good turn because they had saved his life but, as Hazel knew, he could not help despising them for timid, helpless, stay-at-home creatures who could not fly. He was often impatient. Did he mean that he had looked at the river and considered it as if he were a rabbit? That there was slack water immediately below the bridge, with a low, shelving bank where they could get out easily? That seemed too much to hope for. Or did he simply mean that they had better hurry up and take a chance on being able to do what he himself could do without difficulty? This seemed more likely. Suppose one of them did jump out of the boat and go down with the current—what would that tell the others, if he did not come back?

Poor Hazel looked about him. Silver was licking Bigwig's wounded shoulder. Blackberry was fidgeting on and off the thwart, strung up, able to feel only too clearly all that Hazel felt himself. As he still hesitated, Kehaar let out a squawk.

"Yark! Damn rabbits no goot. Vat I do, I show you."

He tumbled clumsily off the raised bow. There was no gap between the punt and the dark mouth of the culvert. Sitting low in the water like a mallard, he floated into the tunnel and vanished. Peering after him, Hazel could at first see nothing. Then he made out Kehaar's shape black against the light at the far end. It floated into daylight, turned sideways and passed out of the restricted view.

"What does that prove?" said Blackberry, his teeth chattering. "He may have flown off the surface or put his great webbed feet down. It's not he that's soaked through and shivering and twice as heavy with wet fur."

Kehaar reappeared on the parapet above.

"You go now," he said shortly.

Still the wretched Hazel hung back. His leg had begun to hurt again. The sight of Bigwig—Bigwig of all rabbits—at the end of his tether, half unconscious, playing no part in this desperate exploit, lowered his courage still more. He knew that he had not got it in him to jump into the water. The horrible situation was beyond him. He stumbled on the slippery planking and, as he sat up, found Fiver beside him.

"I'll go, Hazel," said Fiver quietly. "I think it'll be all right."

He put his front paws on the edge of the bow. Then, on the

instant, all the rabbits froze motionless. One of the does stamped on the puddled floor of the punt. From above came the sounds of approaching footsteps and men's voices, and the smell of a burning white stick.

Kehaar flew away. Not a rabbit moved. The footsteps grew nearer, the voices louder. They were on the bridge above, no further away than the height of a hedge. Every one of the rabbits was seized by the instinct to run, to go underground. Hazel saw Hyzenthlay looking at him and returned her stare, willing her with all his might to keep still. The voices, the smell of men's sweat, of leather, of white sticks, the pain in his leg, the damp, chuckling tunnel at his very ear—he had known them all before. How could the men not see him? They must see him. He was lying at their feet. He was wounded. They were coming to pick him up.

Then the sounds and smells were receding into the distance, the thudding of the footsteps diminished. The men had crossed the bridge without looking over the parapet. They were gone.

Hazel came to. "That settles it," he said. "Everyone's got to swim. Come on, Bluebell, you say you're a water rabbit. Follow me." He got on the thwart and went along it to the side.

But it was Pipkin that he found next to him.

"Quick, Hazel-rah," said Pipkin, twitching and trembling. "I'll come, too. Only be quick."

Hazel shut his eyes and fell over the side into the water.

As in the Enborne, there was an instant shock of cold. But more than this, and at once, he felt the pull of the current. He was being drawn away by a force like a high wind, yet smooth and silent. He was drifting helplessly down a suffocating, cold run, with no hold for his feet. Full of fear, he paddled and struggled, got his head up and took a breath, scrabbled his claws against rough bricks underwater and lost them again as he was dragged on. Then the current slackened, the run vanished, the dark became light and there were leaves and sky above him once more. Still struggling, he fetched up against something hard, bumped off it, struck it again and then for a moment touched soft ground. He floundered forward and found that he was dragging himself through liquid mud. He was out on a clammy bank. He lay panting for several moments and then wiped his face and opened his eyes. The first thing he saw was Pipkin, plastered with mud, crawling to the bank a few feet away.

Full of elation and confidence, all his terrors forgotten, Hazel crawled over to Pipkin and together they slipped into the undergrowth. He said nothing and Pipkin did not seem to expect him to speak. From the shelter of a clump of purple loosestrife they looked back at the river.

The water came out from the bridge into a second pool. All round, on both banks, trees and undergrowth grew close. There was a kind of swamp here and it was hard to tell where water ended and woodland began. Plants grew in clumps both in and out of the muddy shallows. The bottom was covered with fine silt and mud that was half water and in this the two rabbits had made furrows as they dragged themselves to shore. Running diagonally across the pool, from the brickwork of the bridge near the opposite bank to a point a little below them on their own side, was a grating of thin, vertical iron rods. In the cutting season the river weed, drifting in tangled mats from the fishing reaches above, was held against this grating and raked out of the pool by men in waders, who piled it to be used as compost. The left bank was a great rubbish heap of rotting weed among the trees. It was a green, rank-smelling place, humid and enclosed.

"Good old Kehaar!" said Hazel, gazing with satisfaction round the fetid solitude. "I should have trusted him."

As he spoke, a third rabbit came swimming out from under the bridge. The sight of him, struggling in the current like a fly in a spider's web, filled them both with fear. To watch another in danger can be almost as bad as sharing it. The rabbit fetched up against the grating, drifted a little way along it, found the bottom and crawled out of the turbid water. It was Blackavar. He lay on his side and seemed unaware of Hazel and Pipkin when they came up to him. After a little while, however, he began to cough, vomited some water and sat up.

"Are you all right?" asked Hazel.

"More or less," said Blackavar. "But have we got to do much more tonight, sir? I'm very tired."

"No, you can rest here," said Hazel. "But why did you risk it on your own? We might already have gone under, for all you knew."

"I thought you gave an order," replied Blackavar.

"I see," said Hazel. "Well, at that rate you're going to find us a sloppy lot, I'm afraid. Was there anyone else who looked like coming when you jumped in?"

"I think they're a bit nervous," answered Blackavar. "You can't blame them."

"No, but the trouble is that anything can happen," said Hazel, fretting. "They may all go tharn, sitting there. The men may come back. If only we could tell them it's all right—"

"I think we can, sir," said Blackavar. "Unless I'm wrong, it's only a matter of slipping up the bank there and down the other side. Shall I go?"

Hazel was disconcerted. From what he had gathered, this was a disgraced prisoner from Efrafa—not even a member of the Owsla, apparently—and he had just said that he felt exhausted. He was going to take some living up to.

"We'll both go," he said. "Hlao-roo, can you stay here and keep a lookout? With any luck, they'll start coming through to you. Help them if you can."

Hazel and Blackavar slipped through the dripping undergrowth. The grass track which crossed the bridge ran above them, at the top of a steep bank. They climbed the bank and looked out cautiously from the long grass at the verge. The track was empty and there was nothing to be heard or smelled. They crossed it and reached the end of the bridge on the upstream side. Here the bank dropped almost sheer to the river, some six feet below. Blackavar scrambled down without hesitation, but Hazel followed more slowly. Just above the bridge, between it and a thorn bush upstream, was a ledge of turf which overhung the water. Out in the river, a few feet away, the punt lay against the weedy piers.

"Silver!" said Hazel. "Fiver! Come on, get them into the water. It's all right below the bridge. Get the does in first, if you can. There's no time to lose. The men may come back."

It was no easy matter to rouse the torpid, bewildered does and make them understand what they had to do. Silver went from one to another. Dandelion, as soon as he saw Hazel on the bank, went at once to the bow and plunged in. Speedwell followed, but as Fiver was about to go Silver stopped him.

"If all our bucks go, Hazel," he said, "the does will be left alone and I don't think they'll manage it."

"They'll obey Thlayli, sir," said Blackavar, before Hazel could reply. "I think he's the one to get them started."

Bigwig was still lying in the bilgewater, in the place he had taken up when they came to the first bridge. He seemed to be asleep, but when Silver nuzzled him he raised his head and looked about in a dazed manner.

"Oh, hello, Silver," he said. "I'm afraid this shoulder of mine's going to be a bother. I feel awfully cold, too. Where's Hazel?"

Silver explained. Bigwig got up with difficulty and they saw that he was still bleeding. He limped to the thwart and climbed on it.

"Hyzenthlay," he said, "your friends can't be any wetter, so we'll get them to jump in now. One by one, don't you think? Then there'll be no risk of them scratching or hurting each other as they swim."

In spite of what Blackavar had said, it was a long time before everyone had left the boat. There were in fact ten does altogether— though none of the rabbits knew the number—and although one or two responded to Bigwig's patient urging, several were so much exhausted that they remained huddled where they were, or looked stupidly at the water until others were brought to take their place. From time to time Bigwig would ask one of the bucks to give a lead and in this way Acorn, Hawkbit and Bluebell all scrambled over the side. The injured doe, Thrayonlosa, was clearly in a bad way and Blackberry and Thethuthinnang swam through together, one in front of her and one behind.

As darkness closed in, the rain stopped. Hazel and Blackavar went back to the bank of the pool below the bridge. The sky cleared and the oppression lifted as the thunder moved away eastward. But it was fu Inlé before Bigwig himself came through the bridge with Silver and Fiver. It was as much as ever he could do to keep afloat, and when he reached the grating he rolled over in the water, belly uppermost, like a dying fish. He drifted into the shallows and, with Silver's help, pulled himself out. Hazel and several of the others were waiting for him, but he cut them short with a flash of his old bullying manner.

"Come on, get out of the way," he said. "I'm going to sleep now, Hazel, and Frith help you if you say I'm not."

"That's how *we* go on, you see," said Hazel to the staring Blackavar. "You'll get used to it after a bit. Now, let's look for somewhere dry that no one else has found and then perhaps we can sleep, too."

Every dry spot among the undergrowth seemed to be crowded with exhausted, sleeping rabbits. After searching for a time they found a fallen tree trunk, from the underside of which the bark had pulled away. They crept beneath the twigs and leaves, settled themselves in the smooth, curved trough—which soon took on some of the warmth of their bodies—and slept at once.

40

The Way Back

> Dame Hickory, Dame Hickory,
> Here's a wolf at your door,
> His teeth grinning white,
> And his tongue wagging sore!
> "Nay," said Dame Hickory, "Ye False Faerie!"
> But a wolf t'was indeed, and famished was he.
>
> Walter de la Mare, *Dame Hickory*

The first thing that Hazel learned the next morning was that Thrayonlosa had died during the night. Thethuthinnang was distressed, for it was she who had picked Thrayonlosa as one of the more sturdy and sensible does in the Mark and persuaded her to join in the escape. After they had come through the bridge together, she had helped her ashore and fallen asleep beside her in the undergrowth, hoping that she might have recovered by the next day. But she had woken to find Thrayonlosa gone and, searching, had found her in a clump of reeds downstream. Evidently the poor creature had felt that she was going to die and, in the manner of animals, had slipped away.

The news depressed Hazel. He knew that they had been lucky to get so many does out of Efrafa and to escape from Woundwort without having to stand and fight. The plan had been a good one, but the storm and the frightening efficiency of the Efrafans had nearly defeated it. For all the courage of Bigwig and of Silver, they would have failed without Kehaar. Now Kehaar was going to leave them, Bigwig was wounded, and his own leg was none too good. With the does to look after, they would not be able to travel in the open as fast or as easily as they had on the way down from Watership. He would have liked to stay where they were for a few days, so that Bigwig could recover his strength and the does find their feet and get used to life outside a warren. But the place, he realized, was hopelessly inhospitable. Although there was good cover, it was too wet for rabbits. Besides, it was evidently close to a road busier than any they had known. Soon after daylight they began to hear and smell hrududil passing, not so far away as the breadth of a small field. There was continual disturbance and the does in particular were startled and uneasy. Thrayonlosa's death made matters worse. Worried by the noise and vibration and unable to feed, the does kept wandering downstream to look at the body and whisper together about the strange and dangerous surroundings.

He consulted Blackberry, who pointed out that probably it would not be long before men found the boat; then very likely several would be close by for some time. This decided Hazel that they had better set out at once and try to reach somewhere where they could rest more easily. He could hear and smell that the swamp extended a long way downstream. With the road lying to the south, the only way seemed to be northward, over the bridge, which was in any case the way home.

Taking Bigwig with him, he climbed the bank to the grass track. The first thing they saw was Kehaar, picking slugs out of a clump of hemlock near the bridge. They came up to him without speaking and began to nibble the short grass nearby.

After a little while Kehaar said, "Now you getting mudders, Meester 'Azel. All go fine, eh?"

"Yes. We'd never have done it without you, Kehaar. I hear you turned up just in time to save Bigwig last night."

"Dis bad rabbit, pig fella, 'e go fight me. Plenty clever, too."

"Yes. He got a shock for once, though."

"Ya, ya. Meester 'Azel, soon is men come. Vat you do now?"

"We're going back to our warren, Kehaar, if we can get there."

"Ees finish here now for me. I go to Peeg Vater."

"Shall we see you again, Kehaar?"

"You go back hills? Stay dere?"

"Yes, we mean to get there. It's going to be hard going with so many rabbits, and there'll be Efrafan patrols to dodge, I expect."

"You get dere, later on ees vinter, plenty cold, plenty storm on Peeg Vater. Plenty bird come in. Den I come back, see you vere you live."

"Don't forget, then, Kehaar, will you?" said Bigwig. "We shall be looking out for you. Come down suddenly, like you did last night."

"Ya, ya, frighten all mudders und liddle rabbits, all liddle Pigvigs run avay."

Kehaar arched his wings and rose into the air. He flew over the parapet of the bridge and upstream. Then he turned in a circle to the left, came back over the grass track and flew straight down it, skimming just over the rabbits' heads. He gave one of his raucous cries and was gone to the southward. They gazed after him as he disappeared above the trees.

"Oh, fly away, great bird so white," said Bigwig. "You know, he made me feel I could fly, too. That Big Water! I wish I could see it."

As they continued to look in the direction where Kehaar had gone, Hazel noticed for the first time a cottage at the far end of the track, where the grass sloped up to join the road. A man, taking care to keep still, was leaning over the hedge and watching them intently. Hazel stamped and bolted into the undergrowth of the swamp, with Bigwig hard on his heels.

"You know what he's thinking about?" said Bigwig. "He's thinking about the vegetables in his garden."

"I know," replied Hazel. "And we shan't be able to keep this lot away from them once they get the idea into their heads. The quicker we push on the better."

Shortly afterward the rabbits set out across the park to the north. Bigwig soon found that he was not up to a long journey. His wound was painful and the shoulder muscle would not stand hard use. Hazel was still lame and the does, though willing and obedient, showed that they knew little about the life of hlessil. It was a trying time.

In the days that followed—days of clear sky and fine weather— Blackavar proved his worth again and again, until Hazel came to rely on him as much as on any of his veterans. There was a great deal more to him than anyone could have guessed. When Bigwig had determined not to come out of Efrafa without Blackavar, he had been moved entirely by pity for a miserable, helpless victim of Woundwort's ruthlessness. It turned out, however, that Blackavar, when not crushed by humiliation and ill-treatment, was a good cut above the ordinary. His story was an unusual one. His mother had not been born an Efrafan. She had been one of the rabbits taken prisoner when Woundwort attacked the warren at Nutley Copse. She had mated with an Efrafan captain and had had no other mate. He had been killed on Wide Patrol. Blackavar, proud of his father, had grown up with the resolve to become an officer in the Owsla. But together with this—and paradoxically—there had come to him from his mother a certain resentment against Efrafa and a feeling that they should have no more of him than he cared to give them. Captain Mallow, to whose Mark—the Right Fore—he had been sent on trial, had praised his courage and endurance but had not failed to notice the proud detachment of his nature. When the Right Flank needed a junior officer to help Captain Chervil, it was Avens and not Blackavar who had been selected by the Council. Blackavar, who knew his own worth, felt convinced that his mother's blood had prejudiced the Council against him. While still full of his wrongs he had met Hyzenthlay and made himself a secret friend and adviser of the discontented does in the Right Fore. He had begun by urging them to try to get the Council's consent to their leaving Efrafa. If they had succeeded they would have asked for him to be allowed to go with them. But when the does' deputation to the Council failed, Blackavar turned to the idea of escape. At first he had meant to take the does with him, but his nerve, strained to the limit, as Bigwig's had been, by the dangers and uncertainties of conspiracy, had given way and in the end he had simply made a dash on his own, to be caught by Campion. Under the punishment inflicted by the Council his mercurial spirit had fallen low and he had become the apathetic wretch the sight of whom had so much shocked Bigwig. Yet at the whispered message in the hraka pit this spirit had flickered up again where another's might well have failed to do so, and he had been ready to set all on the hazard and have another shot. Now, free among these easy-going strangers, he saw himself as a trained Efrafan using his skill to help them in their need. Although he did all that he was told, he did not hesitate to make suggestions as well, particularly when it came to reconnoitering and looking for signs of danger. Hazel, who was ready to accept advice from anybody when he thought it was good, listened to most of what he said and was content to leave it to Bigwig—for whom, naturally, Blackavar entertained a tremendous respect—to see that he did not overreach himself in his warm-hearted, rather candid zeal.

After two or three days of slow, careful journeying, with many halts in cover, they found themselves, late one afternoon, once more in sight of Caesar's Belt, but further west than before, close to a little copse at the top of some rising ground. Everyone was tired and when they had fed—"evening silflay every day, just as you promised," said Hyzenthlay to Bigwig—Bluebell and Speedwell suggested that it might be worthwhile to dig some scrapes in the light soil under the trees and live there for a day or two. Hazel felt willing enough, but Fiver needed persuasion.

"I know we can do with a rest, but somehow I don't altogether like it, Hazel-rah," he said. "I suppose I've got to try to think why?"

"Not on my account," answered Hazel. "But I doubt you'll shift the others this time. One or two of these does are 'ready for mudder,' as Kehaar would say, and that's the real reason why Bluebell and the rest are prepared to be at the trouble of digging scrapes. Surely it'll be all right at that rate, won't it? You know what they say—'Rabbit underground, rabbit safe and sound.'"

"Well, you may be right," said Fiver. "That Vilthuril's a beautiful doe. I'd like a chance to get to know her better. After all, it's not natural to rabbits, is it?—on and on day after day."

Later, however, when Blackavar returned with Dandelion from a patrol they had undertaken on their own initiative, he came out more strongly against the idea.

"This is no place to stop, Hazel-rah," he said. "No Wide Patrol would bivouac here. It's fox country. We ought to try to get further before dark."

Bigwig's shoulder had been hurting him a good deal during the afternoon and he felt low and surly. It seemed to him that Blackavar was being clever at other people's expense. If he got his way they would have to go on, tired as they were, until they came to somewhere which was suitable by Efrafan standards. There they would be as safe—no more and no less—than they would have been if they had stayed at this copse; but Blackavar would be the clever fellow who had saved them from a fox that had never existed outside his own fancy. His Efrafan scoutcraft act was getting to be a bore. It was time someone called his bluff.

"There are likely to be foxes anywhere about the downs," said Bigwig sharply. "Why is this fox country more than anywhere else?"

Tact was a quality which Blackavar valued about as much as Bigwig did; and now he made the worst possible reply.

"I can't exactly tell you why," he said. "I've formed a strong impression, but it's hard to explain quite what it's based on."

"Oh, an impression, eh?" sneered Bigwig. "Did you see any hraka? Pick up any scent? Or was it just a message from little green mice singing under a toadstool?"

Blackavar felt hurt. Bigwig was the last rabbit he wanted to quarrel with.

"Ye think I'm a fool, then," he answered, his Efrafan accent becoming more marked. "No, there was neether hraka ner scent, but I still think that this is a place where a fox comes. On these patrols we used to do, ye know, we—"

"Did *you* see or smell anything?" said Bigwig to Dandelion.

"Er—well, I'm not really quite sure," said Dandelion. "I mean, Blackavar seems to know an awful lot about patrolling and he asked me whether I didn't feel a sort of—"

"Well, we can go on like this all night," said Bigwig. "Blackavar, do you know that earlier this summer, before we had the benefit of your experience, we went for days across every kind of country— fields, heather, woods, downs—and never lost one rabbit?"

"It's the idea of scrapes, that's all," said Blackavar apologetically. "New scrapes get noticed; and digging can be heard a surprisingly long way, ye know."

"Let him alone," said Hazel, before Bigwig could speak again. "You didn't get him out of Efrafa to bully him. Look, Blackavar, I suppose I've got to decide this. I think you're probably right and there is a certain amount of risk. But we're at risk all the time until we get back to our warren and everyone's so tired that I think we might just as well stop here for a day or two. We shall be all the better for it."

Enough scrapes were finished by soon after sunset and next day, sure enough, all the rabbits felt a great deal better for a night underground. As Hazel had foreseen, there was some mating and a scuffle or two, but no one was hurt. By the evening a kind of holiday spirit prevailed. Hazel's leg was stronger and Bigwig felt fitter than at any time since he went into Efrafa. The does, harassed and bony two days before, were beginning to look quite sleek.

On the second morning, silflay did not begin until some time after dawn. A light wind was blowing straight into the north bank of the copse, where the scrapes had been dug, and Bluebell, when he came up, swore he could smell rabbits on it.

"It's old Holly pressing his chin glands for us, Hazel-rah," he said. "A rabbit's sneeze on the morning breeze sets homesick hearts aglow—"

"Sitting with his rump in a chicory clump and longing for a nice plump doe," replied Hazel.

"That won't do, Hazel-rah," said Bluebell. "He's got two does up there."

"Only hutch does," replied Hazel. "I dare say they're fairly tough and fast by now, but all the same they'll never be quite like our own kind. Clover, for instance—she'd never go far from the hole on silflay, because she knew she couldn't run as fast as we can. But these Efrafan does, you see—they've been kept in by sentries all their lives. Yet now there aren't any, they wander about quite happily. Look at those two, right away under the bank there. They feel they can— Oh, great Frith!"

As he spoke a tawny shape, dog-like, sprang out of the overhanging nut bushes as silently as light from behind a cloud. It landed between the two does, grabbed one by the neck and dragged her up the bank in a flash. The wind veered and the reek of fox came over the grass. With stamping and flashing of tails every rabbit on the slope dashed for cover.

Hazel and Bluebell found themselves crouched with Blackavar. The Efrafan was matter-of-fact and detached.

"Poor little beast," he said. "You see, their instincts are weakened by life in the Mark. Fancy feeding under bushes on the windward side of a wood! Never mind, Hazel-rah, these things happen. But look, I tell you what. Unless there are two hombil, which would be very bad luck, we've got till ni-Frith at least to get away. That homba won't be hunting any more for some time. I suggest we all move on as soon as we can."

With a word of agreement, Hazel went out to call the rabbits together. They made a scattered but swift run to the northeast, along the edge of a field of ripening wheat. No one spoke of the doe. They had covered more than three quarters of a mile before Bigwig and Hazel halted to rest and to make sure that no one had fallen behind. As Blackavar came up with Hyzenthlay, Bigwig said,

"You told us how it would be, didn't you? And I was the one who wouldn't listen."

"Told you?" said Blackavar. "I don't understand."

"That there was likely to be a fox."

"I don't remember, I'm afraid. But I don't see that any of us could possibly have known. Anyway, what's a doe more or less?"

Bigwig looked at him in astonishment, but Blackavar, apparently unconcerned either to stress what he had said or to break off the talk, simply began to nibble the grass. Bigwig, puzzled, moved away and himself began to feed a little distance off, with Hyzenthlay and Hazel.

"What's he getting at?" he asked after a while. "You were all there when he warned us, two nights ago, that there was likely to be a fox. I treated him badly."

"In Efrafa," said Hyzenthlay, "if a rabbit gave advice and the advice wasn't accepted, he immediately forgot it and so did everyone else. Blackavar thought what Hazel decided; and whether it turned out later to be right or wrong was all the same. His own advice had never been given."

"I can believe that," said Bigwig. "Efrafa! Ants led by a dog! But we're not in Efrafa now. Has he really forgotten that he warned us?"

"Probably he really has. But whether or not, you'd never get him to admit that he warned you or to listen while you told him he'd been right. He could no more do that than pass hraka underground."

"But you're an Efrafan. Do you think like that, too?"

"I'm a doe," said Hyzenthlay.

*   *   *

During the early afternoon they began to approach the Belt and Bigwig was the first to recognize the place where Dandelion had told the story of the Black Rabbit of Inlé.

"It was the same fox, you know," he said to Hazel. "That's almost certain. I ought to have realized how likely it was that—"

"Look here," said Hazel, "you know very well what we owe to you. The does all think El-ahrairah sent you to get them out of Efrafa. They believe no one else could have done it. As for what happened this morning, it was my fault as much as yours. But I never supposed we *would* get home without losing some rabbits. In fact we've lost two and that's better than I expected. We can get back to the Honeycomb tonight if we press on. Let's forget about the homba now, Bigwig—it can't be altered—and try to— Hello, who's this?"

They were coming to a thicket of juniper and dog roses, tangled at ground level with nettles and trails of bryony on which the berries were now beginning to ripen and turn red. As they stopped to pick a line into the undergrowth, four big rabbits appeared out of the long grass and sat looking down at them. One of the does, coming up the slope a little way behind, stamped and turned to bolt. They heard Blackavar check her sharply.

"Well, why don't you answer his question, Thlayli?" said one of the rabbits. "Who am I?"

There was a pause. Then Hazel spoke.

"I can see they're Efrafans because they're marked," he said. "Is that Woundwort?"

"No," said Blackavar, at his shoulder. "That's Captain Campion."

"I see," said Hazel. "Well, I've heard of you, Campion. I don't know whether you mean us any harm, but the best thing you can do is to let well alone. As far as we're concerned, our dealings with Efrafa are finished."

"You may think that," replied Campion, "but you'll find it's otherwise. That doe behind you must come with us; and so must any others that are with you."

As he spoke, Silver and Acorn appeared lower down the slope, followed by Thethuthinnang. After a glance at the Efrafans, Silver spoke quickly to Thethuthinnang, who slipped back through the burdocks. Then he came up to Hazel.

"I've sent for the white bird, Hazel," he said quietly.

As a piece of bluff it was effective. They saw Campion look upward nervously and another of the patrol glanced back to the cover of the bushes.

"What you're saying is stupid," said Hazel to Campion. "There are a lot of us here and unless you've got more rabbits than I can see, we're too many for you."

Campion hesitated. The truth was that for once in his life he had acted rashly. He had seen Hazel and Bigwig approaching, with Blackavar and one doe behind them. In his eagerness to have something really worthwhile to show on his return to the Council, he had jumped to the conclusion that they were alone. The Efrafans usually kept fairly close together in the open and it had not occurred to Campion that other rabbits might straggle more widely. He had seen a golden opportunity to attack—perhaps kill—the detestable Thlayli and Blackavar, together with their one companion—who seemed to be lame—and bring the doe back to the Council. This he could certainly have done; and he had decided to confront rather than ambush them, in the hope that the bucks would surrender without fighting. But now, as more rabbits began to appear in ones and twos, he realized that he had made a mistake.

"I have a great many more rabbits," he said. "The does must stay here. The rest of you can go. Otherwise we shall kill you."

"Very well," said Hazel. "Bring your whole patrol into the open and we'll do as you say."

By this time a considerable number of rabbits was coming up the slope. Campion and his patrol looked at them in silence but made no move.

"You'd better stay where you are," said Hazel at length. "If you try to interfere with us it will be the worse for you. Silver and Blackberry, take the does and go on. The rest of us will join you."

"Hazel-rah," whispered Blackavar, "the patrol must be killed—all of them. They mustn't report back to the General."

This had also occurred to Hazel. But as he thought of the dreadful fight and the four Efrafans actually torn to pieces—for that was what it would mean—he could not find it in his heart to do it. Like Bigwig, he felt a reluctant liking for Campion. Besides, it would take some doing. Quite probably some of his own rabbits would be killed—certainly wounded. They would not reach the Honeycomb that night and they would leave a fresh blood trail wherever they went. Apart from his dislike of the whole idea, there were disadvantages that might be fatal.

"No, we'll let them alone," he replied firmly.

Blackavar was silent and they sat watching Campion as the last of the does disappeared through the bushes.

"Now," said Hazel, "take your patrol and go the same way that you saw us come. Don't speak—go."

Campion and the patrol made off downhill and Hazel, relieved to be rid of them so easily, hurried after Silver, with the others close behind.

Once through the Belt, they made excellent progress. After the rest of a day and a half the does were in good shape. The promise of an end to the journey that night and the thought that they had escaped both the fox and the patrol made them eager and responsive. The only cause of delay was Blackavar, who seemed uneasy and kept hanging about in the rear. At last, in the late afternoon, Hazel sent for him and told him to go ahead, on the line of the path they were following, and look out for the long strip of the beech hanger in the dip on the morning side. Blackavar had not been gone very long before he came racing back.

"Hazel-rah, I've been quite close to that wood you spoke of," he said, "and there are two rabbits playing about on a patch of short grass just outside it."

"I'll come and see," said Hazel. "Dandelion, you come, too, will you?"

As they ran down the hill to the right of the track, Hazel fairly skipped to recognize the beech hanger. He noticed one or two yellow leaves and a faint touch of bronze here and there in the green boughs. Then he caught sight of Buckthorn and Strawberry running toward them across the grass.

"Hazel-rah!" cried Buckthorn. "Dandelion! What happened? Where are the others? Did you get any does? Is everyone all right?"

"They'll be here very soon," said Hazel. "Yes, we've got a lot of does and everyone who went has come back. This is Blackavar, who's come out of Efrafa."

"Good for him," said Strawberry. "Oh, Hazel-rah, we've watched at the end of the wood every evening since you went. Holly and Boxwood are all right—they're back at the warren: and what do you think? Clover's going to kindle. That's fine, isn't it?"

"Splendid," said Hazel. "She'll be the first. My goodness, we've had a time, I can tell you. And so I will—what a story!—but it must wait a bit. Come on—let's go and bring the others in."

By sunset the whole party—twenty rabbits all told—had made their way up the length of the beech hanger and reached the warren. They fed among the dew and the long shadows, with twilight already fallen in the fields below. Then they crowded down into the Honeycomb to hear Hazel and Bigwig tell the story of their adventures to those who had waited so eagerly and so long to hear it.

As the last rabbits disappeared underground the Wide Patrol, which had followed them from Caesar's Belt with superlative skill and discipline, veered away in a half-circle to the east and then turned for Efrafa. Campion was expert at finding a night's refuge in the open. He planned to rest until dawn and then cover the three miles back by evening of the following day.

41

The Story of Rowsby Woof and the Fairy Wogdog

Be not merciful unto them that offend of malicious wickedness. They grin like a dog and run about through the city. But thou, O Lord, shalt have them in derision. Thou shalt laugh all the heathen to scorn.

Psalm 59

Now came the dog days—day after day of hot, still summer, when for hours at a time light seemed the only thing that moved; the sky—sun, clouds and breeze—awake above the drowsing downs. The beech leaves grew darker on the boughs and fresh grass grew where the old had been nibbled close. The warren was thriving at last and Hazel could sit basking on the bank and count their blessings. Above and under ground, the rabbits fell naturally into a quiet, undisturbed rhythm of feeding, digging and sleeping. Several fresh runs and burrows were made. The does, who had never dug in their lives before, enjoyed the work. Both Hyzenthlay and Thethuthinnang told Hazel that they had had no idea how much of their frustration and unhappiness in Efrafa had been due simply to not being allowed to dig. Even Clover and Haystack found that they could manage pretty well and boasted that they would bear the warren's first litters in burrows that they had dug for themselves. Blackavar and Holly became close friends. They talked a great deal about their different ideas of scouting and tracking, and made some patrols together, more for their own satisfaction than because there was any real need. One early morning they persuaded Silver to come with them and traveled over a mile to the outskirts of Kingsclere, returning with a tale of mischief and feasting in a cottage garden. Blackavar's hearing had weakened since the mutilation of his ears; but Holly found that his power of noticing and drawing conclusions from anything unusual was almost uncanny and that he seemed to be able to become invisible at will.

Sixteen bucks and ten does made a happy enough society for a warren. There was some bickering here and there, but nothing serious. As Bluebell said, any rabbits who felt discontented could always go back to Efrafa; and the thought of all that they had faced together was enough to take the sting out of anything that might have made a real quarrel. The contentment of the does spread to everyone else, until one evening Hazel remarked that he felt a perfect fraud as Chief Rabbit, for there were no problems and hardly a dispute to be settled.

"Have you thought about the winter yet?" asked Holly.

Four or five of the bucks, with Clover, Hyzenthlay and Vilthuril, were feeding along the sunny west side of the hanger about an hour before sunset. It was still hot and the down was so quiet that they could hear the horses tearing the grass in the paddock of Cannon Heath Farm, more than half a mile away. It certainly did not seem a time to think of winter.

"It'll probably be colder up here than any of us have been used to," said Hazel. "But the soil's so light and the roots break it up so much that we can dig a lot deeper before the cold weather comes. I think we ought to be able to get below the frost. As for the wind, we can block some of the holes and sleep warm. Grass is poor in winter, I know; but anyone who wants a change can always go out with Holly here and try his luck at pinching some greenstuff or cattle roots. It's a time of year to be careful of the elil, though. Myself, I shall be quite happy to sleep underground, play bob-stones and hear a few stories from time to time."

"What about a story now?" said Bluebell. "Come on, Dandelion. 'How I Nearly Missed the Boat.' What about that?"

"Oh, you mean 'Woundwort Dismayed,' " said Dandelion. "That's Bigwig's story—I wouldn't presume to tell it. But it makes a change to be thinking about winter on an evening like this. It reminds me of a story I've listened to but never tried to tell myself. So some of you may know it and perhaps some won't. It's the story of Rowsby Woof and the Fairy Wogdog."

"Off you go," said Fiver, "and lay it on thick."

"There was a big rabbit," said Dandelion. "There was a small rabbit. There was El-ahrairah; and he had the frost in his fine new whiskers. The earth up and down the runs of the warren was so hard that you could cut your paws on it, and the robins answered each other across the bare, still copses, 'This is my bit here. You go and starve in your own.'

"One evening, when Frith was sinking huge and red in a green sky, El-ahrairah and Rabscuttle limped trembling through the frozen grass, picking a bite here and there to carry them on for another long night underground. The grass was as brittle and tasteless as hay, and although they were hungry, they had been making the best of the miserable stuff so long that it was as much as they could do to get it down. At last Rabscuttle suggested that they might take a risk for once in a way and slip across the fields to the edge of the village, where there was a big vegetable garden.

"This particular garden was bigger than any of the others round about. The man who worked in it lived in a house at one end and he used to dig or cut great quantities of vegetables, put them into a hrududu and drive them away. He had put wire all round the garden to keep rabbits out. All the same, El-ahrairah could usually find a way in if he wanted to; but it was dangerous, because the man had a gun and often shot jays and pigeons and hung them up.

" 'It isn't only the gun we'd be risking, either,' said El-ahrairah, thinking it over. 'We'd have to keep an eye open for that confounded Rowsby Woof as well.'

"Now, Rowsby Woof was the man's dog; and he was the most objectionable, malicious, disgusting brute that ever licked a man's hand. He was a big, woolly sort of animal with hair all over his eyes and the man kept him to guard the vegetable garden, especially at night. Rowsby Woof, of course, did not eat vegetables himself and anyone might have thought that he would be ready to let a few hungry animals have a lettuce or a carrot now and then and no questions asked. But not a bit of it. Rowsby Woof used to run loose from evening till dawn the next day; and not content with keeping men and boys out of the garden, he would go for any animals he found there—rats, rabbits, hares, mice, even moles—and kill them if he could. The moment he smelled anything in the nature of an intruder he would start barking and kicking up a shine, although very often it was only this foolish noise which warned a rabbit and enabled him to get away in time. Rowsby Woof was reckoned to be a tremendous ratter and his master had boasted about this skill of his so often and showed him off so much that he had become revoltingly conceited. He believed himself to be the finest ratter in the world. He ate a lot of raw meat (but not in the evening, because he was left hungry at night to keep him active) and this made it rather easier to smell him coming. But even so, he made the garden a dangerous place.

" 'Well, let's chance Rowsby Woof for once,' said Rabscuttle. 'I reckon you and I ought to be able to give him the slip if we have to.'

"El-ahrairah and Rabscuttle made their way across the fields to the outskirts of the garden. When they got there, the first thing they saw was the man himself, with a white stick burning away in his mouth, cutting row after row of frosted cabbages. Rowsby Woof was with him, wagging his tail and jumping about in a ridiculous manner. After a time the man piled as many of the cabbages as he could into a wheel thing and pushed them away to the house. He came back several times and when he had taken all the cabbages to the door of the house he began carrying them inside.

" 'What's he doing that for?' asked Rabscuttle.

" 'I suppose he wants to get the frost out of them tonight,' replied El-ahrairah, 'before he takes them away in the hrududu tomorrow.'

" 'They'd be much better to *eat* with the frost out of them, wouldn't they?' said Rabscuttle. 'I wish we could get at them while they're in there. Still, never mind. Now's our chance. Let's see what we can do up this end of the garden while he's busy down there.'

"But hardly had they crossed the top of the garden and got among the cabbages than Rowsby Woof had winded them and down he came, barking and yelping, and they were lucky to get out in time.

" 'Dirty little beasts,' shouted Rowsby Woof. 'How—how! How—how dare you come snou—snou—snouting round here? Get out—out! Out—out!'

" 'Contemptible brute!' said El-ahrairah, as they scurried back to the warren with nothing to show for all their trouble. 'He's really annoyed me. I don't know yet how it's going to be done, but, by Frith and Inlé, before this frost thaws, we'll eat his cabbages inside the house and make him look a fool into the bargain!'

" 'That's saying too much, master,' said Rabscuttle. 'A pity to throw your life away for a cabbage, after all we've done together.'

" 'Well, I shall be watching my chance,' said El-ahrairah. 'I shall just be watching my chance, that's all.'

"The following afternoon Rabscuttle was out, nosing along the top of the bank beside the lane, when a hrududu came by. It had doors at the back and these doors had somehow come open and were swinging about as the hrududu went along. There were things inside wrapped up in bags like the ones men sometimes leave about the fields; and as the hrududu passed Rabscuttle, one of these bags fell out into the lane. When the hrududu had gone Rabscuttle, who hoped that the bag might have something to eat inside, slipped down into the lane to have a sniff at it. But he was disappointed to find that all it contained was some kind of meat. Later he told El-ahrairah about his disappointment.

" 'Meat?' said El-ahrairah. 'Is it still there?'

" 'How should I know?' said Rabscuttle. 'Beastly stuff.'

" 'Come with me,' said El-ahrairah. 'Quickly, too.'

"When they got to the lane the meat was still there. El-ahrairah dragged the bag into the ditch and they buried it.

" 'But what good will this be to us, master?' said Rabscuttle.

" 'I don't know yet,' said El-ahrairah. 'But some good it will surely be, if the rats don't get it. Come home now, though. It's getting dark.'

"As they were going home, they came on an old black wheel-covering thrown away from a hrududu, lying in the ditch. If you've ever seen these things, you'll know that they're something like a huge fungus—smooth and very strong, but pad-like and yielding too. They smell unpleasant and are no good to eat.

" 'Come on,' said El-ahrairah immediately. 'We have to gnaw off a good chunk of this. I need it.'

"Rabscuttle wondered whether his master was going mad, but he did as he was told. The stuff had grown fairly rotten and before long they were able to gnaw off a lump about as big as a rabbit's head. It tasted dreadful, but El-ahrairah carried it carefully back to the warren. He spent a lot of time that night nibbling at it and after morning silflay the next day he continued. About ni-Frith he woke Rabscuttle, made him come outside and put the lump in front of him.

" 'What does that look like?' he said. 'Never mind the smell. What does it *look* like?'

"Rabscuttle looked at it. 'It looks rather like a dog's black nose, master,' he answered, 'except that it's dry.'

" 'Splendid,' said El-ahrairah, and went to sleep.

"It was still frosty—very clear and cold—that night, with half a moon, but fu Inlé, when all the rabbits were keeping warm underground, El-ahrairah told Rabscuttle to come with him. El-ahrairah carried the black nose himself and on the way he pushed it well into every nasty thing he could find. He found a—"

"Well, never mind," said Hazel. "Go on with the story."

"In the end," continued Dandelion, "Rabscuttle kept well away from him, but El-ahrairah held his breath and still carried the nose somehow, until they got to the place where they had buried the meat.

" 'Dig it up,' said El-ahrairah. 'Come on.'

"They dug it up and the paper came off. The meat was all bits joined together in a kind of trail like a spray of bryony, and poor Rabscuttle was told to drag it along to the bottom of the vegetable garden. It was hard work and he was glad when he was able to drop it.

" 'Now,' said El-ahrairah, 'we'll go round to the front.'

"When they got to the front, they could tell that the man had gone out. For one thing, the house was all dark but, besides, they could smell that he had been through the gate a little while before. The front of the house had a flower garden and this was separated from the back and the vegetable garden by a high, close-boarded fence that ran right across and ended in a big clump of laurels. Just the other side of the fence was the back door that led into the kitchen.

"El-ahrairah and Rabscuttle went quietly through the front garden and peeped through a crack in the fence. Rowsby Woof was sitting on the gravel path, wide awake and shivering in the cold. He was so near that they could see his eyes blink in the moonlight. The kitchen door was shut, but nearby, along the wall, there was a hole above the drain where a brick had been left out. The kitchen floor was made of bricks and the man used to wash it with a rough broom and sweep the water out through the hole. The hole was plugged up with an old cloth to keep out the cold.

"After a little while El-ahrairah said in a low voice,

" 'Rowsby Woof! O Rowsby Woof!'

"Rowsby Woof sat up and looked about him, bristling.

" 'Who's there?' he said. 'Who are you?'

" 'O Rowsby Woof!' said El-ahrairah, crouching on the other side of the fence. 'Most fortunate, most blessed Rowsby Woof! Your reward is at hand! I bring you the best news in the world!'

" 'What?' said Rowsby Woof. 'Who's that? None of your tricks, now!'

" 'Tricks, Rowsby Woof?' said El-ahrairah. 'Ah, I see you do not know me. But how should you? Listen, faithful, skillful hound. I am the Fairy Wogdog, messenger of the great dog spirit of the East, Queen Dripslobber. Far, far in the East her palace lies. Ah, Rowsby Woof, if only you could see her mighty state, the wonders of her kingdom! The carrion that lies far and wide upon the sands! The manure, Rowsby Woof! The open sewers! Oh, how you would jump for joy and run nosing all about!'

"Rowsby Woof got to his feet and looked about in silence. He could not tell what to make of the voice, but he was suspicious.

" 'Your fame as a ratter has come to the ears of the Queen,' said El-ahrairah. 'We know you—and honor you—as the greatest ratter in the world. That is why I am here. But poor, bewildered creature! I see you are perplexed, and well you may be. Come here, Rowsby Woof! Come close to the fence and know me better!'

"Rowsby Woof came up to the fence and El-ahrairah pushed the rubber nose into the crack and moved it about. Rowsby Woof stood close, sniffing.

" 'Noble rat-catcher,' whispered El-ahrairah, 'it is indeed I, the Fairy Wogdog, sent to honor you!'

" 'Oh, Fairy Wogdog!' cried Rowsby Woof, dribbling and piddling all over the gravel. 'Ah, what elegance! What aristocratic distinction! Can that really be decayed cat that I smell? With a delicate overtone of rotten camel! Ah, the gorgeous East!' "

("What on earth's 'camel'?" said Bigwig.

"I don't know," replied Dandelion. "But it was in the story when I heard it, so I suppose it's some creature or other.")

" 'Happy, happy dog!' said El-ahrairah. 'I must tell you that Queen Dripslobber her very self has expressed her gracious wish that you should meet her. But not yet, Rowsby Woof, not yet. First you must be found worthy. I am sent to bring you both a test and a proof. Listen, Rowsby Woof. Beyond the far end of the garden there lies a long rope of meat. Aye, real meat, Rowsby Woof, for though we are fairy dogs, yet we bring real gifts to noble, brave animals such as you. Go now—find and eat that meat. Trust me, for I will guard the house until you return. That is the test of your belief.'

"Rowsby Woof was desperately hungry and the cold had got into his stomach, but still he hesitated. He knew that his master expected him to guard the house.

" 'Ah, well,' said El-ahrairah, 'never mind. I will depart. In the next village there lives a dog—'

" 'No, no,' cried Rowsby Woof. 'No, Fairy Wogdog, do not leave me! I trust you! I will go at once! Only guard the house and do not fail me!'

" 'Have no fear, noble hound,' said El-ahrairah. 'Only trust the word of the great Queen.'

"Rowsby Woof went bounding away in the moonlight and El-ahrairah watched him out of sight.

" 'Are we to go into the house now, master?' asked Rabscuttle. 'We shall have to be quick.'

" 'Certainly not,' said El-ahrairah. 'How could you suggest such double-dealing? For shame, Rabscuttle! We will guard the house.'

"They waited silently and after a while Rowsby Woof returned, licking his lips and grinning. He came sniffing up to the fence.

" 'I perceive, honest friend,' said El-ahrairah, 'that you found the meat as swiftly as though it had been a rat. The house is safe and all is well. Now hark. I shall return to the Queen and tell her of all that has passed. It was her gracious purpose that if you showed yourself worthy tonight, by trusting her messenger, she would herself send for you and honor you. Tomorrow night she will be passing through this land on her way to the Wolf Festival of the North and she means to break her journey in order that you may appear before her. Be ready, Rowsby Woof!'

" 'Oh, Fairy Wogdog!' cried Rowsby Woof. 'What joy it will be to grovel and abase myself before the Queen! How humbly I shall roll upon the ground! How utterly shall I make myself her slave! What menial cringing will be mine! I will show myself a true dog!'

" 'I do not doubt it,' said El-ahrairah. 'And now, farewell. Be patient and await my return!'

"He withdrew the rubber nose and very quietly they crept away.

"The following night was, if anything, still colder. Even El-ah-rairah had to pull himself together before he could set out over the fields. They had hidden the rubber nose outside the garden and it took them some time to get it ready for Rowsby Woof. When they had made sure that the man had gone out, they went cautiously into the front garden and up to the fence. Rowsby Woof was padding up and down outside the back door, his breath steaming in the frosty air. When El-ahrairah spoke, he put his head on the ground between his front paws and whined for joy.

" 'The Queen is coming, Rowsby Woof,' said El-ahrairah from behind the nose, 'with her noble attendants, the fairies Postwiddle and Sniffbottom. And this is her wish. You know the crossroads in the village, do you not?'

" 'Yes, yes!' whined Rowsby Woof. 'Yes, yes! Oh, let me show how abject I can be, dear Fairy Wogdog. I will—'

" 'Very well,' said El-ahrairah. 'Now, O fortunate dog, go to the crossroads and await the Queen. She is coming on the wings of night. It is far that she must come, but wait patiently. Only wait. Do not fail her and great blessing will be yours.'

" 'Fail her? No, no!' cried Rowsby Woof. 'I will wait like a worm upon the road. Her beggar am I, Fairy Wogdog! Her mendicant, her idiot, her—'

" 'Quite right, most excellent,' said El-ahrairah. 'Only make haste.'

"As soon as Rowsby Woof had gone, El-ahrairah and Rabscuttle went quickly through the laurels, round the end of the fence and along to the back door. El-ahrairah pulled the cloth out of the hole above the drain with his teeth and led the way into the kitchen.

"The kitchen was as warm as this bank and at one end was a great pile of vegetables ready for the hrududu in the morning— cabbages, brussels sprouts and parsnips. They were thawed out and the delicious smell was quite overpowering. El-ahrairah and Rabscuttle began at once to make amends for the past days of frozen grass and tree bark.

" 'Good, faithful fellow,' said El-ahrairah with his mouth full. 'How grateful he will be to the Queen for keeping him waiting. He will be able to show her the full extent of his loyalty, won't he? Have another parsnip, Rabscuttle.'

"Meanwhile, down at the crossroads, Rowsby Woof waited eagerly in the frost, listening for the coming of Queen Dripslobber. After a long time he heard footsteps. They were not the steps of a dog but of a man. As they came near, he realized that they were the steps of his own master. He was too stupid to run away or hide, but merely remained where he was until his master—who was returning home—came up to the crossroads.

" 'Why, Rowsby Woof,' said his master, 'what are you doing here?'

"Rowsby Woof looked foolish and nosed about. His master was puzzled. Then a thought came to him.

" 'Why, good old chap,' he said, 'you came to meet me, did you? Good fellow, then! Come on, we'll go home together.'

"Rowsby Woof tried to slip away, but his master grabbed him by the collar, tied him by a bit of string he had in his pocket and led him home.

"Their arrival took El-ahrairah by surprise. It fact, he was so busy stuffing cabbage that he heard nothing until the doorhandle rattled. He and Rabscuttle had only just time to slip behind a pile of baskets before the man came in, leading Rowsby Woof. Rowsby Woof was quiet and dejected and did not even notice the smell of rabbit, which anyway was all mixed up with the smell of the fire and the larder. He lay on the mat while the man made some sort of drink for himself.

"El-ahrairah was watching his chance to dash out of the hole in the wall. But the man, as he sat drinking and puffing away at a white stick, suddenly looked round and got up. He had noticed the draft coming in through the open hole. To the rabbits' horror, he picked up a sack and plugged the hole up very tightly indeed. Then he finished his drink, made up the fire and went away to sleep, leaving Rowsby Woof shut in the kitchen. Evidently he thought it too cold to turn him out for the night.

"At first Rowsby Woof whined and scratched at the door, but after a time he came back to the mat by the fire and lay down. El-ahrairah moved very quietly along the wall until he was behind a big metal box in the corner under the sink. There were sacks and old papers here, too, and he felt fairly sure that Rowsby Woof could not manage to see behind it. As soon as Rabscuttle had joined him, he spoke.

" 'O Rowsby Woof!' whispered El-ahrairah.

"Rowsby Woof was up in a flash.

" 'Fairy Wogdog!' he cried. 'Is that you I hear?'

" 'It is indeed,' said El-ahrairah. 'I am sorry for your disappointment, Rowsby Woof. You did not meet the Queen.'

" 'Alas, no,' said Rowsby Woof: and he told what had happened at the crossroads.

" 'Never mind,' said El-ahrairah. 'Do not be downhearted, Rowsby Woof. There was good reason why the Queen did not come. She received news of danger—ah, great danger, Rowsby Woof!—and avoided it in time. I myself am here at the risk of my own safety to warn you. You are lucky indeed that I am your friend, for otherwise your good master must have been stricken with mortal plague.'

" 'With plague?' cried Rowsby Woof. 'Oh, how, good fairy?'

" 'Many fairies and spirits there are in the animal kingdoms of the East,' said El-ahrairah. 'Some are friends and there are those—may misfortune strike them down—who are our deadly enemies. Worst of them all, Rowsby Woof, is the great rat spirit, the giant of Sumatra, the curse of Hamelin. He dares not openly fight our noble Queen, but he works by stealth, by poison, by disease. Soon after you left me, I learned that he has sent his hateful rat goblins through the clouds, carrying sickness. I warned the Queen; but still I remained here, Rowsby Woof, to warn you. If the sickness falls—and the goblins are very near—it will harm not you, but your master it will slay—and me, too, I fear. You can save him, and you alone. I cannot.'

" 'Oh, horror!' cried Rowsby Woof. 'There is no time to be lost! What must I do, Fairy Wogdog?'

" 'The sickness works by a spell,' said El-ahrairah. 'But if a real dog of flesh and blood could run four times round the house, barking as loudly as he could, then the spell would be broken and the sickness would have no power. But alas! I forgot! You are shut in, Rowsby Woof. What is to be done? I fear that all is lost!'

" 'No, no!' said Rowsby Woof. 'I will save you, Fairy Wogdog, and my dear master, too. Leave it to me!'

"Rowsby Woof began to bark. He barked to raise the dead. The windows shook. The coal fell in the grate. The noise was terrifying. They could hear the man upstairs, shouting and cursing. Still Rowsby Woof barked. The man came stamping down. He flung open the window and listened for thieves, but he could hear nothing, partly because there was nothing to hear and partly because of the ceaseless barking. At last he picked up his gun, flung open the door and went cautiously out to see what was the matter. Out shot Rowsby Woof, bellowing like a bull, and tore around the house. The man followed him at a run, leaving the door wide.

" 'Quick!' said El-ahrairah. 'Quicker than Wogdog from the Tartar's bow! Come on!'

"El-ahrairah and Rabscuttle dashed into the garden and disappeared through the laurels. In the field beyond they paused for a moment. From behind came the sounds of yelping and woofing, mixed with shouts and angry cries of 'Come 'ere, damn you!'

" 'Noble fellow,' said El-ahrairah. 'He has saved his master, Rabscuttle. He has saved us all. Let us go home and sleep sound in our burrow.'

"For the rest of his life Rowsby Woof never forgot the night when he had waited for the great Dog Queen. True, it was a disappointment, but this, he felt, was a small matter, compared with the recollection of his own noble conduct and of how he had saved both his master and the good Fairy Wogdog from the wicked rat spirit."

42

News at Sunset

You will be sure to prove that the act is unjust and hateful to the gods? Yes, indeed, Socrates; at least, if they will listen to me.

Plato, *Euthyphro*

As he came to the end of his story, Dandelion remembered that he was supposed to be relieving Acorn as sentry. The post was a little way away, near the eastern corner of the wood, and Hazel—who wanted to see how Boxwood and Speedwell were getting on with a hole they were digging—went with Dandelion along the foot of the bank. He was just going down the new hole when he noticed that some small creature was pattering about in the grass. It was the mouse that he had saved from the kestrel. Pleased to see that he was still safe and sound, Hazel turned back to have a word with him. The mouse recognized him and sat up, washing his face with his front paws and chattering effusively.

"Is a good a days, a hot a days. You like? Plenty for eata, keepa warm is a no trouble. Down in a bottom a hill is a harvest. I go for a corn a, but is a long a way. I tink a you go away, is a not a long a you come a back, yes?"

"Yes," said Hazel, "a lot of us went away, but we found what we were looking for and now we've come back for good."

"Is a good. Is a lots of rabbits a now, keepa grass a short."

"What difference does it make to him if the grass is short?" said Bigwig, who, with Blackavar, was lolloping and nibbling close by. "He doesn't eat it."

"Is a good a for get about, you know?" said the mouse in a familiar tone which made Bigwig shake his ears with irritation. "Is a run along the queek—but is a no seeds a from a short a grass. Now is a warren a here and now a today is a new a rabbits a come, soon is another warren a more. New rabbits is a your friends a too?"

"Yes, yes, all friends," said Bigwig, turning away. "There was something I wanted to say, Hazel, about the newborn rabbits, when they're ready to come above ground."

Hazel, however, had remained where he was, looking intently at the mouse.

"Wait a moment, Bigwig," he said. "What did you say, mouse, about another warren? Where is there going to be another warren?"

The mouse was surprised. "You not a know? Not a your friends?"

"I don't know until you tell me. What did you mean about new rabbits and another warren soon?" His tone was urgent and inquisitive.

The mouse became nervous and, after the manner of his kind, began to say what he thought the rabbits would like to hear.

"Maybe is a no warren. Is a plenty good a rabbits 'ere, is all a my friends. Is a no more rabbits. Not a for want other rabbits."

"But what other rabbits?" persisted Hazel.

"No, sir. No, sir, no other rabbits, is a not a go for soon a rabbits, all stay 'ere are my friends, a save a me a very good a my life, zen 'ow can I if a she mek me?" twittered the mouse.

Hazel considered this lot briefly, but it beat him.

"Oh, come on, Hazel," said Bigwig. "Let the poor little beast alone. I want to talk to you."

Hazel ignored him. Going close to the mouse, he bent his head and spoke quietly and firmly.

"You've often said you're our friend," he said. "If you are, tell me, and don't be afraid, what you know about other rabbits coming."

The mouse looked confused. Then he said, "I not see other rabbits, sir, but a my brother 'e say yellowhammer say is a new rabbits, plenty, plenty rabbits, come to combe over on a morning side. Maybe is a lots a rubbish. I tell you a wrong, you no like a mouse for more, not a friend a more."

"No, that's all right," said Hazel. "Don't worry. Just tell me again. Where did the bird say these new rabbits were?"

" 'E say is a come just a now on a morning side. I not a see."

"Good fellow," said Hazel. "That's very helpful." He turned back to the others. "What d'you make of this, Bigwig?" he asked.

"Not much," answered Bigwig. "Long-grass rumors. These little creatures say anything and change it five times a day. Ask him again fu Inlé—he'll tell you something else."

"If you're right, then I'm wrong and we can all forget it," said Hazel. "But I'm going to get to the bottom of this. Someone must go and see. I'd go myself, but I've got no speed with this leg."

"Well, leave it for tonight, anyway," said Bigwig. "We can—"

"Someone must go and see," repeated Hazel firmly. "A good patroller, too. Blackavar, go and get Holly for me, will you?"

"I'm here, as it happens," said Holly, who had come along the top of the bank while Hazel was speaking. "What's the trouble, Hazel-rah?"

"There's a rumor of strangers on the down, on the morning side," replied Hazel, "and I wish I knew more. Can you and Blackavar run over that way—say, as far as the top of the combe—and find out what's going on?"

"Yes, of course, Hazel-rah," said Holly. "If there really are some other rabbits there, we'd better bring them back with us, hadn't we? We could do with a few more."

"It depends who they are," said Hazel. "That's what I want to find out. Go at once, Holly, will you? Somehow it worries me not to know."

Holly and Blackavar had hardly set off when Speedwell appeared above ground. He had an excited, triumphant look which attracted everyone's attention immediately. He squatted in front of Hazel and looked round him in silence, to make sure of his effect.

"You've finished the hole?" asked Hazel.

"Never mind the hole," answered Speedwell. "I didn't come up to say that. Clover's had her litter. All good, healthy kittens. Three bucks and three does, she says."

"You'd better go up in the beech tree and sing that," said Hazel. "See that everybody knows! But tell them not to go crowding down disturbing her."

"I shouldn't think they would," said Bigwig. "Who'd be a kitten again, or even want to see one—blind and deaf and no fur?"

"Some of the does may want to see them," said Hazel. "They're excited, you know. But we don't want Clover disturbed into eating them or anything miserable like that."

"It looks as though we really are going to live a natural life again at last, doesn't it?" said Bigwig, as they browsed their way along the bank. "What a summer it's been! I keep dreaming I'm back in Efrafa, you know; but it'll pass off, I suppose. One thing I brought back out of that place, though, and that's the value of keeping a warren hidden. As we get bigger, Hazel, we ought to take care of that. We'll do better than Efrafa, though. When we've reached the right size, rabbits can be encouraged to leave."

"Well, don't *you* leave," said Hazel, "or I'll tell Kehaar to bring you back by the scruff of the neck. I'm relying on you to produce us a really good Owsla."

"It's certainly something to look forward to," said Bigwig. "Take a pack of young fellows across to the farm and chase the cats out of the barn to get an appetite. Well, it'll come. I say, this grass is as dry as horsehair on barbed wire, isn't it? What about a run down the hill to the fields—just you and I and Fiver? Corn's been cut, you know, and there should be good pickings. I expect they're going to burn off the field, but they haven't done it yet."

"No, we must wait a bit," said Hazel. "I want to hear what Holly and Blackavar have to say when they come in."

"That needn't keep you long," replied Bigwig. "Here they come already, unless I'm much mistaken. Straight down the open track, too! Not bothered about keeping hidden, are they? What a rate they're going!"

"There's something wrong," said Hazel, staring at the approaching rabbits.

Holly and Blackavar reached the long shadow of the wood at top speed, as though they were being pursued. The watchers expected them to slow down as they came to the bank, but they kept straight on and appeared actually to be going to run underground. At the last moment Holly stopped, looked about him and stamped twice. Blackavar disappeared down the nearest hole. At the stamping, all the rabbits above ground ran for cover.

"Here, wait a minute," said Hazel, pushing past Pipkin and Hawkbit as they came across the grass. "Holly, what's the alarm? Tell us something, instead of stamping the place to pieces. What's happened?"

"Get the holes filled in!" gasped Holly. "Get everyone underground! There's not a moment to lose." His eyes rolled white and he panted foam over his chin.

"Is it men, or what? There's nothing to be seen, heard or smelled. Come on, tell us something and stop gibbering, there's a good chap."

"It'll have to be quick, then," said Holly. "That combe—it's full of rabbits from Efrafa."

"From Efrafa? Fugitives, do you mean?"

"No," said Holly, "not fugitives. Campion's there. We ran right into him and three or four more that Blackavar recognized. I believe Woundwort's there himself. They've come for us—don't make any mistake about that."

"You're sure it's more than a patrol?"

"I'm certain," answered Holly. "We could smell them; and we heard them, too—below us in the combe. We wondered what so many rabbits could be doing there and we were going down to see when we suddenly came face to face with Campion. We looked at him and he looked at us and then I realized what it must mean and we turned and ran. He didn't follow us—probably because he'd had no orders. But how long will it take them to get here?"

Blackavar had returned from underground, bringing Silver and Blackberry.

"We ought to leave at once, sir," he said to Hazel. "We might be able to get quite a long way before they come."

Hazel looked about him. "Anyone who wants to go can go," he said. "I shan't. We made this warren ourselves and Frith only knows what we've been through on account of it. I'm not going to leave it now."

"Neither am I," said Bigwig. "If I'm for the Black Rabbit, there's one or two from Efrafa will come with me."

There was a short silence.

"Holly's right to want to stop the holes," went on Hazel. "It's the best thing to do. We fill the holes in, good and thorough. Then they have to dig us out. The warren's deep. It's under a bank, with tree roots all through it and over the top. How long can all those rabbits stay on the down without attracting elil? They'll have to give it up."

"You don't know these Efrafans," said Blackavar. "My mother used to tell me what happened at Nutley Copse. It would be better to go now."

"Well, go on, then," answered Hazel. "I'm not stopping you. And I'm not leaving this warren. It's my home." He looked at Hyzenthlay, heavy with young, who was sitting in the mouth of the nearest hole and listening to the talk. "How far do you think *she'll* get? And Clover—do we leave her or what?"

"No, we must stay," said Strawberry. "I believe El-ahrairah will save us from this Woundwort; and if he doesn't, I'm not going back to Efrafa, I'll tell you that."

"Fill in the holes," said Hazel.

As the sun set, the rabbits fell to clawing and scrabbling in the runs. The sides were hard with the hot weather. It was not easy to get started, and when the soil began to fall, it was light and powdery and did little to block the holes. It was Blackberry who hit upon the idea of working outward from inside the Honeycomb itself, scratching down the ceilings of the runs where they came into the meeting hall and blocking the holes by breaking the underground walls into them. One run, leading up into the wood, was left open for coming and going. It was the one where Kehaar used to shelter and the lobby at the mouth was still cluttered with guano. As Hazel passed the place, it occurred to him that Woundwort did not know that Kehaar had left them. He dug out as much of the mess as he could and scattered it about. Then, as the work went on below, he squatted on the bank and watched the darkening eastern skyline.

His thoughts were very sad. Indeed, they were desperate. Although he had spoken resolutely in front of the others, he knew only too well how little hope there was of saving the warren from the Efrafans. They knew what they were doing. No doubt they had their methods of breaking into a closed warren. It was the faintest of chances that elil would disperse them. Most of the Thousand hunted rabbits for food. A stoat or a fox took a rabbit and took no more until it was ready to hunt again. But the Efrafans were accustomed to a death here and there. Unless General Woundwort himself were killed, they would stay until the job was done. Nothing would stop them, short of some unexpected catastrophe.

But suppose that he himself were to go and talk to Woundwort? Might there not just possibly be a chance of getting him to see sense? Whatever had happened at Nutley Copse, the Efrafans could not fight to the finish against rabbits like Bigwig, Holly and Silver without losing lives—probably a good many lives. Woundwort must know this. Perhaps it might not be too late, even now, to persuade him to agree to a new plan—a plan that would be as good for one warren as the other.

"And perhaps it might be," thought Hazel grimly. "But it's a possible chance and so I'm afraid the Chief Rabbit has got to take it. And since this savage brute is probably not to be trusted, I suppose the Chief Rabbit must go alone."

He returned to the Honeycomb and found Bigwig.

"I'm off to talk to General Woundwort, if I can get hold of him," he said. "You're Chief Rabbit until I come back. Keep them at it."

"But, Hazel," said Bigwig, "wait a moment. It's not safe—"

"I shan't be long," said Hazel. "I'm just going to ask him what he's up to."

A moment later he was down the bank and limping up the track, pausing from time to time to sit up and look about him for an Efrafan patrol.

43

The Great Patrol

What is the world, O soldiers?
It is I.
I, this incessant snow,
This northern sky;
Soldiers, this solitude
Through which we go
Is I.

Walter de la Mare, *Napoleon*

When the punt floated down the river in the rain, part of General Woundwort's authority went with it. He could not have appeared more openly and completely at a loss if Hazel and his companions had flown away over the trees. Until that very moment he had shown up strongly, a most formidable adversary. His officers had been demoralized by Kehaar's unexpected attack. He had not. On the contrary, he had kept up the pursuit in spite of Kehaar and had actually carried out a scheme to cut off the fugitives' retreat. Cunning and resourceful in adversity, he had nearly succeeded in hurting the gull when he leaped at him out of the close cover by the plank bridge. Then, when he had his quarry cornered in a place where Kehaar could not have done a great deal to help them, they had suddenly shown their own cunning greater than his, and left him bewildered on the bank. He had overheard the very word—tharn—spoken by one of his officers to another as they returned to Efrafa through the rain. Thlayli, Blackavar and the does of the Near Hind had vanished. He had tried to stop them and he had conspicuously failed.

For a great part of that night Woundwort remained awake, considering what was best to be done. The following day he called a Council meeting. He pointed out that it would be no good taking an expedition down the river to look for Thlayli unless it were strong enough to defeat him if it found him. That would mean taking several officers and a number of the Owsla. There would be the risk of trouble at home while they were away. There might be another break-out. The odds were that they would not find Thlayli at all, for there would be no trail and they did not know where to search for him. If they did not find him, they would look even bigger fools when they came back.

"And fools we look now," said Woundwort. "Make no mistake about that. Vervain will tell you what the Marks are saying—that Campion was chased into the ditch by the white bird and Thlayli called down lightning from the sky and Frith knows what besides."

"The best thing," said old Snowdrop, "will be to say as little about it as possible. Let it blow over. They've got short memories."

"There's one thing I think worth doing," said Woundwort. "We know now that there was one place where we *did* find Thlayli and his gang, only nobody realized it at the time. That was when Mallow was after them with his patrol, just before he was killed by the fox. Something tells me that where they were once, there they'll be again, sooner or later."

"But we can hardly stay out there with enough rabbits to fight them, sir," said Groundsel, "and it would mean digging in and living there for some time."

"I agree with you," replied Woundwort. "A patrol will be stationed there continuously until further notice. They'll dig scrapes and live there. They'll be relieved every two days. If Thlayli comes, he's to be watched and followed secretly. When we know where he's taken the does, then we may be able to deal with him. And I'll tell you this," he ended, glaring round at them with his great, pale eyes. "If we *do* find out where he is, I shall be ready to go to a great deal of trouble. I told Thlayli I'd kill him myself. He may have forgotten that, but I haven't."

Woundwort led the first patrol in person, taking Groundsel to show him where Mallow had picked up the strangers' southward trail. They dug scrapes among the scrub along the edge of Caesar's Belt and waited. After two days their hopes were lower. Vervain relieved Woundwort. He was relieved two days later by Campion. By this time there were captains in the Owsla who said privately to each other that the General was in the grip of an obsession. Some way would have to be found of getting him to drop it before it went too far. At the Council meeting the next evening it was suggested that the patrol should be discontinued in two days' time. Woundwort, snarling, told them to wait and see. An argument began, behind which he sensed more opposition than he had ever encountered before. In the middle of this, with a dramatic effect that could not have been better timed from the General's point of view, Campion and his patrol came in, dead beat, with the report that they had met Thlayli and his rabbits exactly where Woundwort had said they would. Unseen, they had followed them to their warren, which, though a long way off, was not too distant to be attacked, especially since no time would have to be spent in searching for it. It did not appear to be very large and could probably be surprised.

The news put an end to all opposition and brought both Council and Owsla back under Woundwort's undisputed control. Several of the officers were for starting at once, but Woundwort, now that he was sure of his followers and his enemy, took his time. Having learned from Campion that he had actually come face to face with Thlayli, Blackavar and the rest, he decided to wait some little while, in case they might be on their guard. Besides, he wanted time both to reconnoiter the way to Watership and to organize the expedition. His idea was that, if possible, they should make the journey in one day. This would forestall any possible rumors of their approach. To satisfy himself that they could do this and still be fit to fight when they arrived, he took Campion and two others, and himself covered the three and a half miles to the down east of Watership. Here, he grasped at once the best way to approach the beech hanger without being seen or smelled. The prevailing wind was westerly, as at Efrafa. They would arrive at evening and then assemble and rest in the combe south of Cannon Heath Down. As soon as twilight fell and Thlayli and his rabbits had gone underground, they would come along the ridge and attack the warren. With luck, there would be no warning whatever. They would be safe for the night in the captured warren and the following day he himself and Vervain would be able to return to

Efrafa. The remainder, under Campion, could have a day's rest and then make their way back with the does and any other prisoners there might be. The whole thing could be finished in three days.

It would be best not to take too many rabbits. Anyone not strong enough to go the distance and then fight would only be a nuisance. In the event, speed might turn out to be everything. The slower the journey, the more dangerous it would be, and stragglers would attract elil and discourage the rest. Besides, as Woundwort very well knew, his leadership was going to be vital. Every rabbit would need to feel that he was close to the General; and if he felt himself one of a picked band as well, that would be all to the good.

The rabbits to go were chosen most carefully. There were in fact about twenty-six or -seven of them, half Owsla and the rest promising youngsters recommended by their Mark officers. Woundwort believed in emulation and he let it be known that there would be plenty of chances to win rewards. Campion and Chervil were kept busy taking out endurance patrols, and tussles and training fights were organized at morning silflay. The members of the expedition were excused all sentry duties and allowed to silflay whenever they wished.

They started before dawn one clear August morning, going due north in groups along the banks and hedges. Before they had reached the Belt, Groundsel's party was attacked by a pair of stoats, one old and the other a yearling. Woundwort, hearing the squealing from behind him, covered the distance in a few moments and set upon the veteran stoat with slashing teeth and great kicks from his needle-clawed back paws. With one of its forelegs ripped to the shoulder, it turned and made off, the younger one following.

"You ought to be able to see to these things yourself," said Woundwort to Groundsel. "Stoats aren't dangerous. Come on."

Shortly after ni-Frith, Woundwort went back to pick up stragglers. He found three, one injured by a piece of glass. He stopped the bleeding, brought the three up to rejoin their groups and then called a halt to rest and feed, himself keeping a watch round about. It was very hot and some of the rabbits were showing signs of exhaustion. Woundwort formed these into a separate group and took charge of it himself.

By the early evening—about the same time as Dandelion was beginning the story of Rowsby Woof—the Efrafans had skirted an enclosure of pigs east of Cannon Heath Farm and were slipping into the combe south of Cannon Heath Down. Many were tired and, in spite of their tremendous respect for Woundwort, there was a certain feeling that they had come a long way from home. They were ordered to take cover, feed, rest and wait for sunset.

The place was deserted, except for yellowhammers and a few mice pattering about in the sun. Some of the rabbits went to sleep in the long grass. The slope was already in shadow when Campion came running down with the news that he had come face to face with Blackavar and Holly in the upper part of the combe.

Woundwort was annoyed. "What made them come traipsing over here, I wonder?" he said. "Couldn't you have killed them? Now we've lost surprise."

"I'm sorry, sir," said Campion. "I wasn't really alert at the time and I'm afraid they were a bit too quick for me. I didn't pursue them because I wasn't sure whether you'd want me to."

"Well, it may not make much difference," said Woundwort. "I don't see what they can do. But they'll try to do something, I suppose, now they know we're here."

As he went among his rabbits, looking them over and encouraging them, Woundwort considered the situation. One thing was clear—there was no longer the chance of catching Thlayli and the rest off their guard. But perhaps they were already so much frightened that they would not fight at all? The bucks might give up the does to save their own lives. Or they might already be on the run, in which case they must be followed and caught at once, for they were fresh and his own rabbits were tired and could not pursue them far. He ought to find out quickly. He turned to a young rabbit of the Neck Mark who was feeding close at hand.

"Your name's Thistle, isn't it?" he asked.

"Thistle, sir," answered the rabbit.

"Well, you're the very fellow I want," said Woundwort. "Go and find Captain Campion and tell him to meet me up there by that juniper—do you see where I mean?—at once. You'd better come there, too. Be quick: there's no time to lose."

As soon as Campion and Thistle had joined him, Woundwort took them up to the ridge. He meant to see what was happening over at the beech hanger. If the enemy were already in flight, Thistle could be sent back with a message to Groundsel and

Vervain to bring everyone up immediately. If they were not, he would see what threats could do.

They reached the track above the combe and began to make their way along it with some caution, since the sunset was in their eyes. The light west wind carried a fresh smell of rabbits.

"If they *are* running, they haven't gone far," said Woundwort. "But I don't think they *are* running. I think they're still in their warren."

At that moment a rabbit came out of the grass and sat up in the middle of the track. He paused for a few moments and then moved toward them. He was limping and had a strained, resolute look.

"You're General Woundwort, aren't you?" said the rabbit. "I've come to talk to you."

"Did Thlayli send you?" asked Woundwort.

"I'm a friend of Thlayli," replied the rabbit. "I've come to ask why you're here and what it is you want."

"Were you on the riverbank in the rain?" said Woundwort.

"Yes, I was."

"What was left unfinished there will be finished now," said Woundwort. "We are going to destroy you."

"You won't find it easy," replied the other. "You'll take fewer rabbits home than you brought. We should both do better to come to terms."

"Very well," said Woundwort. "These are the terms. You will give back all the does who ran from Efrafa and you will hand over the deserters Thlayli and Blackavar to my Owsla."

"No, we can't agree to that. I've come to suggest something altogether different and better for us both. A rabbit has two ears; a rabbit has two eyes, two nostrils. Our two warrens ought to be like that. They ought to be together—not fighting. We ought to make other warrens between us—start one between here and Efrafa, with rabbits from both sides. You wouldn't lose by that, you'd gain. We both would. A lot of your rabbits are unhappy now and it's all you can do to control them, but with this plan you'd soon see a difference. Rabbits have enough enemies as it is. They ought not to make more among themselves. A mating between free, independent warrens—what do you say?"

At that moment, in the sunset on Watership Down, there was offered to General Woundwort the opportunity to show whether he was really the leader of vision and genius which he believed himself to be, or whether he was no more than a tyrant with the courage and cunning of a pirate. For one beat of his pulse the lame rabbit's idea shone clearly before him. He grasped it and realized what it meant. The next, he had pushed it away from him. The sun dipped into the cloud bank and now he could see clearly the track along the ridge, leading to the beech hanger and the bloodshed for which he had prepared with so much energy and care.

"I haven't time to sit here talking nonsense," said Woundwort. "You're in no position to bargain with us. There's nothing more to be said. Thistle, go back and tell Captain Vervain I want everyone up here at once."

"And this rabbit, sir," asked Campion. "Shall I kill him?"

"No," replied Woundwort. "Since they've sent him to ask our terms, he'd better take them back.—Go and tell Thlayli that if the does aren't waiting outside your warren, with him and Blackavar, by the time I get down there, I'll tear the throat out of every buck in the place by ni-Frith tomorrow."

The lame rabbit seemed about to reply, but Woundwort had already turned away and was explaining to Campion what he was to do. Neither of them bothered to watch the lame rabbit as he limped back by the way he had come.

44

A Message from El-ahrairah

The enforced passivity of their defence, the interminable waiting, became insupportable. Day and night they heard the muffled thud of the picks above and dreamt of the collapse of the grotto and of every ghastly eventuality. They were subject to "castle-mentality" in its most extreme form.

Robin Fedden, *Crusader Castles*

"They've stopped digging, Hazel-rah," said Speedwell. "As far as I can tell, there's no one in the hole."

In the close darkness of the Honeycomb, Hazel pushed past three or four of his rabbits crouching among the tree roots and reached the higher shelf where Speedwell lay listening for sounds from above. The Efrafans had reached the hanger at early twilight and at once begun a search along the banks and among the trees to find out how big the warren was and where its holes were. They had been surprised to find so many holes in such a small area, for not many of them had had experience of any warren but Efrafa, where very few holes served the needs of many rabbits. At first they had supposed that there must be a large number of rabbits underground. The silence and emptiness of the open beechwood made them suspicious, and most kept outside, nervous of an ambush. Woundwort had to reassure them. Their enemies, he explained, were fools who made more runs than any properly organized warren needed. They would soon discover their mistake, for every one would be opened, until the place became impossible to defend. As for the droppings of the white bird, scattered in the wood, it was plain that they were old. There were no signs whatever that the bird was anywhere near. Nevertheless, many of the rank and file continued to look cautiously about them. At the sudden cry of a peewit on the down, one or two bolted and had to be brought back by their officers. The story of the bird which had fought for Thlayli in the storm had lost nothing in the telling up and down the burrows of Efrafa.

Woundwort told Campion to post sentries and keep a patrol

round about, while Vervain and Groundsel tackled the blocked holes. Groundsel set to work along the bank, while Vervain went into the wood, where the mouths of the holes lay between the tree roots. He came at once upon the open run. He listened, but all was quiet. Vervain (who was more used to dealing with prisoners than with enemies) ordered two of his rabbits to make their way down it. The discovery of the silent, open run gave him the hope that he might be able to seize the warren by a sudden dash to the very center. The wretched rabbits, obeying his orders, were met by Silver and Buckthorn at a point where the run opened out. They were cuffed and mauled and barely got out with their lives. The sight of them did nothing to encourage Vervain's party, who were reluctant to dig and made little headway during the darkness before moonrise.

Groundsel, who felt that he ought to set an example, himself dug his way into the loose, fallen soil of one of the bank runs. Plowing over the soft earth like a fly on summer butter and holding his head clear, he suddenly found himself face to face with Blackavar, who sank his front teeth into his throat. Groundsel, with no freedom to use his weight, screamed and kicked out as best he could. Blackavar hung on and Groundsel—a heavy rabbit, like all the Efrafan officers—dragged him forward a short distance before he could rid himself of his grip. Blackavar spat out a mouthful of fur and jumped clear, clawing with his front paws. But Groundsel had already gone. He was lucky not to have been more severely wounded.

It became clear to Woundwort that it was going to be extremely difficult, if not impossible, to take the warren by attack down the defended runs. There would be a good chance of success if several runs could be opened and then tackled at the same time, but he doubted whether his rabbits would attempt it, after what they had seen. He realized that he had not given enough thought, earlier on, to what he would have to do if he lost surprise and had to force an entry: he had better give it some thought now. As the moon rose, he called Campion in and talked it over with him.

Campion's suggestion was that they should simply starve the warren out. The weather was warm and dry and they could easily stay two or three days. This Woundwort rejected impatiently. In his own mind, he was not altogether certain that daylight might not bring the white bird down upon them. They ought to be under-ground by dawn. But, apart from this secret anxiety, he felt that his reputation depended on a fighting victory. He had brought his Owsla to get at these rabbits, knock them down and beat them. A siege would be a miserable anti-climax. Also, he wanted to get back to Efrafa as soon as he could. Like most warlords, he was never very confident about what was going on behind his back.

"If I remember rightly," he said, "after the main part of the warren at Nutley Copse was taken and the fighting was as good as over, there were a few rabbits who shut themselves into a smaller burrow where it was difficult to get at them. I said they were to be dealt with and then I went back to Efrafa with the prisoners. How *were* they dealt with and who did it, do you know?"

"Captain Mallow did it," said Campion. "He's dead, of course; but I expect there's someone here who was with him. I'll go and find out."

He returned with a heavy, stolid Owsla sentry named Ragwort, who at first had some difficulty in understanding what it was that the General wanted to know. At last, however, he said that when he had been with Captain Mallow, more than a year ago, the Captain had told them to dig a hole straight down into the ground. In the end the earth had given way under them and they had fallen down among some rabbits, whom they had fought and beaten.

"Well, that's about the only way it *can* be done," said Wound-wort to Campion. "And if we get them all onto it, relieving each other in shifts, we should have a way into the place before dawn. You'd better get your sentries out again—not more than two or three—and we'll make a start at once."

Soon after, Hazel and his rabbits, below in the Honeycomb, heard the first sounds of scratching above. It was not long before they realized that the digging was going on at two points. One was at the north end of the Honeycomb, above the place where the tree roots formed a kind of cloister in the burrow. Here the roof, latticed through and through with fine roots, was very strong. The other seemed to be more or less above the open center of the Honeycomb, but rather nearer to the south end, where the hall broke up into bays and runs with columns of earth between. Beyond these runs lay several of the warren's burrows. One, lined with fur torn from her own belly, contained Clover and the pile of grass and leaves, covered over with earth, in which her newborn litter were sleeping.

"Well, we seem to be putting them to a great deal of trouble," said Hazel. "That's all to the good. It'll blunt their claws and I should think they'll be tired out before they've done. What do you make of it, Blackberry?"

"I'm afraid it's a bad lookout, Hazel-rah," replied Blackberry. "It's true they're in trouble up at the top end. There's a lot of ground above us there and the roots will hold them up for a long time. But down this end it's easier for them. They're bound to dig through fairly soon. Then the roof will come in; and I can't see that we can do anything to stop them."

Hazel could feel him trembling as he spoke. As the sounds of digging continued, he sensed fear spreading all through the burrow. "They'll take us back to Efrafa," whispered Vilthuril to Thethuthinnang. "The warren police—"

"Be quiet," said Hyzenthlay. "The bucks aren't talking like that and why should we? I'd rather be here now, as we are, than never have left Efrafa."

It was bravely said, but Hazel was not the only one who could tell her thoughts. Bigwig remembered the night in Efrafa when he had calmed her by talking of the high downs and the certainty of their escape. In the dark, he nuzzled Hazel's shoulder and pressed him over to one side of the wide burrow.

"Listen, Hazel," he said, "we're not finished yet. Not by a long way. When the roof breaks, they'll come down into this end of the Honeycomb. But we can get everybody back into the sleeping burrows behind and block the runs that lead to them. They'll be no better off."

"Well, if we do that, it'll last a bit longer," said Hazel. "But they'll soon be able to break into the sleeping burrows, once they're in here."

"They'll find me there when they do," said Bigwig, "and one or two more besides. I shouldn't wonder if they didn't decide to go home."

With a kind of wry envy, Hazel realized that Bigwig was actually looking forward to meeting the Efrafan assault. He knew he could fight and he meant to show it. He was not thinking of anything else.

The hopelessness of their chances had no important place in his thoughts. Even the sound of the digging, clearer already, only set him thinking of the best way to sell his life as dearly as he could. But what else was there for any of them to do? At least Bigwig's preparations would keep the others busy and perhaps do something to dispel the silent fear that filled all the warren.

"You're quite right, Bigwig," he said. "Let's prepare a little reception. Will you tell Silver and the others what you want and get them started?"

As Bigwig began to explain his plan to Silver and Holly, Hazel sent Speedwell to the north end of the Honeycomb to listen to the digging and keep reporting what he could make out about its progress. As far as he could see, it would make little difference whether the roof-fall came there or in the center, but at least he ought to try to show the others that he was keeping his wits about him.

"We can't break these walls down to stop the run between, Bigwig," said Holly. "They hold the roof up at this end, you know."

"I know that," answered Bigwig. "We'll dig into the walls of the sleeping burrows behind. They'll need to be bigger anyway, if we're all going to get in there together. Then kick the loose earth back into the spaces between the columns. Stop the whole thing right up."

Since he had come out of Efrafa, Bigwig's standing was very high. Seeing him in good heart, the others set aside their fear as best they could and did as he told them, enlarging the burrows beyond the south end of the Honeycomb and piling up the soft earth in the entry runs until what had been a colonnade began to become a solid wall. It was during a pause in this work that Speedwell reported that the digging above the north end had stopped. Hazel went and crouched beside him, listening for some time. There was nothing to be heard. He went back to where Buckthorn sat guarding the foot of the single open run—Kehaar's run, as it was called.

"You know what's happened?" he said. "They've realized they're all among the beech roots up there, so they've chucked it. They'll be going harder at the other end now."

"I suppose so, Hazel-rah," replied Buckthorn. After a little he said, "D'you remember the rats in the barn? We got out of that all right, didn't we? But I'm afraid we shan't get out of this. It's a pity, after all we've done together."

"Yes, we shall," said Hazel, with all the conviction he could muster. But he knew that if he stayed he would not be able to keep up the pretense. Buckthorn—a decent, straightforward fellow if ever there was one—where would he be by ni-Frith tomorrow? And he himself—where had he led them, with all his clever schemes? Had they come over the common, among the shining wires, through the thunderstorm, the culverts on the great river, to die at the claws of General Woundwort? It was not the death they deserved; it was not the right end of the clever track they had run. But what could stop Woundwort? What could save them now? Nothing, he knew—unless some tremendous blow were to fall upon the Efrafans from outside: and of that there was no chance. He turned away from Buckthorn.

Scratch, scratch: scratch, scratch came the sound of the digging above. Crossing the floor in the dark, Hazel found himself beside another rabbit, who was crouching silently on the near side of the new-piled wall. He stopped, sniffing. It was Fiver.

"Aren't you working?" he asked listlessly.

"No," replied Fiver. "I'm listening."

"To the digging, you mean?"

"No, not the digging. There's something I'm trying to hear—something the others can't hear. Only I can't hear it either. But it's close. Deep. Leaf-drift, deep. I'm going away, Hazel—going away." His voice grew slow and drowsy. "Falling. But it's cold. Cold."

The air in the dark burrow was stifling. Hazel bent over Fiver, pushing the limp body with his nose.

"Cold," muttered Fiver. "How—how. How—how cold!"

There was a long silence.

"Fiver?" said Hazel. "Fiver? Can you hear me?"

Suddenly a terrible sound broke from Fiver; a sound at which every rabbit in the warren leaped in dreadful fear; a sound that no rabbit had ever made, that no rabbit had the power to make. It was deep and utterly unnatural. The rabbits working on the far side of the wall crouched terrified. One of the does began to squeal.

"Dirty little beasts," yelped Fiver. "How—how dare you? Get out—out! Out—out!"

Bigwig burst through the piled earth, twitching and panting.

"In the name of Frith, stop him!" he gasped. "They'll all go mad!"

Shuddering, Hazel clawed at Fiver's side.

"Wake! Fiver, wake!"

But Fiver was lying in a deep stupor.

In Hazel's mind, green branches were straining in the wind. Up and down they swayed, thresh and ply. There was something—something he could glimpse between them. What was it? Water he sensed; and fear. Then suddenly he saw clearly, for an instant, a little huddle of rabbits on the bank of a stream at dawn, listening to the sound of yelping in the wood above and the scolding of a jay.

"If I were you, I shouldn't wait until ni-Frith. I should go now. In fact, I think you'll have to. There's a large dog loose in the wood. There's a large dog loose in the wood."

The wind blew, the trees shook their myriads of leaves. The stream was gone. He was in the Honeycomb, facing Bigwig in the dark, across the motionless body of Fiver. The scratching from above was louder and closer.

"Bigwig," said Hazel, "do as I say at once, there's a good fellow. We've got hardly any time. Go and get Dandelion and Blackberry and bring them to me at the foot of Kehaar's run, quickly."

At the foot of the run Buckthorn was still in his place. He had not moved at Fiver's cry, but his breath was short and his pulse very quick. He and the other three rabbits gathered about Hazel without a word.

"I've got a plan," said Hazel. "If it works, it'll finish Woundwort for good and all. But I've no time to explain. Every moment counts now. Dandelion and Blackberry, you come with me. You're to go straight up out of this run and through the trees to the down. Then northward, over the edge and down to the fields. Don't stop for anything. You'll go faster than I shall. Wait for me by the iron tree at the bottom."

"But Hazel—" said Blackberry.

"As soon as we've gone," said Hazel, turning to Bigwig, "you're to block this run and get everyone back behind the wall you've made. If they break in, hold them up as long as you can. Don't give in to them on any account. El-ahrairah has shown me what to do."

"But where are you going, Hazel?" asked Bigwig.

"To the farm," said Hazel, "to gnaw another rope. Now, you two, follow me up the run: and don't forget, you stop for nothing until you're down the hill. If there are rabbits outside, don't fight—run."

Without another word he dashed up the tunnel and out into the wood, with Blackberry and Dandelion on his heels.

45

Nuthanger Farm Again

Cry Havoc! And let slip the dogs of war.

Shakespeare, *Julius Caesar*

At that moment General Woundwort, out on the open grass below the bank, was facing Thistle and Ragwort in the checkered yellow moonlight of the small hours.

"You weren't put at the mouth of that run to listen," he said. "You were put there to stop anyone breaking out. You had no business to leave it. Get back at once."

"I give you my word, sir," said Thistle querulously, "there's some animal down there that is not a rabbit. We both heard it."

"And did you smell it?" asked Woundwort.

"No, sir. No tracks or droppings either. But we both heard an animal and it was no rabbit."

Several of the diggers had left their work and were gathered nearby, listening. A muttering began.

"They had a homba that killed Captain Mallow. My brother was there. He saw it."

"They had a great bird that turned into a shaft of lightning."

"There was another animal that took them away down the river."

"Why can't we go home?"

"Stop that!" said Woundwort. He went up to the group. "Who

said that? You, was it? Very well, go home. Go on, hurry up. I'm waiting. That's the way—over there."

The rabbit did not move. Woundwort looked slowly round.

"Right," he said. "Anyone else who wants to go home can get on with it. It's a nice long way and you'll have no officers, because they'll all be busy digging, including myself. Captain Vervain, Captain Groundsel, will you come with me? You, Thistle, go out there and fetch Captain Campion. And you, Ragwort, get back to the mouth of that run you had no business to leave."

Very soon the digging was resumed. The hole was deep now—deeper than Woundwort had expected and still there was no sign of a fall. But all three rabbits could sense that not far below them there lay a hollow space.

"Keep at it," said Woundwort. "It won't take long now."

When Campion came in, he reported that he had seen three rabbits running away over the down to the north. One appeared to be the lame rabbit. He had been about to pursue them but had returned in response to the order brought by Thistle.

"It doesn't matter," said Woundwort. "Let them go. There'll be three less when we get in. What, you again?" he snapped, as Ragwort appeared beside him. "What is it this time?"

"The open run, sir," said Ragwort. "It's been broken in and stopped from down below."

"Then you can start doing something useful," said Woundwort. "Get that root out. No, that one, you fool."

The digging continued, as the first streaks of light began to come into the east.

* * *

The great field at the foot of the escarpment had been reaped, but the straw had not yet been burned and lay in long pale rows upon the darker stubble, tenting over the bristling stalks and the weeds of harvest—knotgrass and pimpernel, fluellen and speedwell, heartsease and persicary—colorless and still in the old moonlight. Between the lines of straw the expanse of stubble was as open as the down.

"Now," said Hazel, as they came out from the belt of hawthorn and dogwood where the pylon stood, "are you both sure you understand what we're going to do?"

"It's a tall order, isn't it, Hazel-rah?" answered Dandelion. "But we've got to try it, that's certain. There's nothing else that'll save the warren now."

"Come on, then," said Hazel. "The going's easy, anyway—half as far now the field's been cut. Don't bother about cover—just run in the open. Keep with me, though. I'll go as fast as I can."

They crossed the field easily enough, Dandelion running ahead. The only alarm came when they startled four partridges, which whirred away over the hedge to the west and sailed down, spread-winged, into the field beyond. Soon they reached the road and Hazel halted among the quickset on top of the nearer bank.

"Now, Blackberry," he said, "this is where we leave you. Lie close and don't move. When the time comes, don't break too soon. You've got the best head of any of us. Use it—and keep it, too. When you get back, go to ground in Kehaar's run and stay there till things are safe. Have you got your line clear?"

"Yes, Hazel-rah," replied Blackberry. "But, as far as I can see, I may have to run from here to the iron tree without a check. There's no cover."

"I know," said Hazel. "It can't be helped. If the worst comes to the worst, you'll have to turn for the hedge and then keep popping in and out of it. Do whatever you like. There's no time for us to stay and work it out. Only make sure you get back to the warren. It all depends on you."

Blackberry burrowed his way into the moss and ivy round the base of the thorn. The other two crossed the road and made uphill toward the sheds beside the lane.

"Good roots they keep there," said Hazel, as they passed them and reached the hedge. "Pity we've no time just now. When this is over we'll have a nice, quiet raid on the place."

"I hope we do, Hazel-rah," said Dandelion. "Are you going straight up the lane? What about cats?"

"It's the quickest way," said Hazel. "That's all that matters now."

By this time the first light was clear and several larks were up. As they approached the great ring of elm trees, they heard once more the quick sighing and rustling above them and one yellow leaf came spinning down to the edge of the ditch. They reached the top of the slope and saw before them the barns and the farmyard.

Birdsong was breaking out all round and the rooks were calling from high in the elms, but nothing—not even a sparrow—moved on the ground. Straight in front, on the other side of the farmyard, close to the house, stood the dog kennel. The dog was not to be seen, but the rope, tied to the eye bolt on the flat roof, trailed over the edge and disappeared across the straw-covered threshold.

"We're in time," said Hazel. "The brute's still asleep. Now, Dandelion, you mustn't make any mistake. You lie in the grass just there, opposite the kennel. When the rope's gnawed through you'll see it fall. Unless the dog's ill or deaf, it'll be alert by then; probably before, I'm afraid, but that's my lookout. It's up to you to attract it and make it chase you all the way down to the road. You're very fast. Take care it doesn't lose you. Use the hedges if you want to; but remember it'll be trailing the rope. Get it down to Blackberry. That's all that matters."

"If we ever meet again, Hazel-rah," said Dandelion, as he took cover in the grass verge, "we ought to have the makings of the best story ever."

"And you'll be the chap to tell it," said Hazel.

He moved away in a half-circle to the morning side and reached the wall of the farmhouse. Then he began to hop cautiously along the wall, in and out of the narrow flower bed. His head was a tumult of smells—phlox in bloom, ashes, cow dung, dog, cat, hens, stagnant water. He came to the back of the kennel, reeking of creosote and of rank straw. A half-used bale of straw stood against it—no doubt clean bedding which, in the dry weather, had not been put back under cover. Here at least was one piece of luck, for he had expected to have trouble in getting on the roof. He scrambled up the straw. Across part of the felted roof lay a torn piece of old blanket, wet with dew. Hazel sat up, sniffing, and put his forepaws on it. It did not slip. He pulled himself up.

How much noise had he made? How strong was his scent over the tar and straw and farmyard? He waited, tense to jump, expecting movement below. There was no sound. In a terrible miasma of dog smell, which gripped him with fear and called "Run! Run!" down every nerve, he crept forward to where the eye bolt was screwed into the roof. His claws scraped slightly and he stopped again. Still there was no movement. He crouched down and began to nibble and gnaw at the thick cord.

It was easier than he had thought it would be. It was a good deal easier than the cord on the punt, though about as thick. The punt cord had been drenched through with rain, pliant, slippery and fibrous. This, though dewy on the outside, was dry-cored and light. In very little time the clean inside was showing. His chisel-like foreteeth bit steadily and he felt the dry strands rip. The cord was as good as half through already.

At that moment he felt the heavy weight of the dog move beneath him. It stretched, shuddered and yawned. The rope moved a little and the straw rustled. The foul smell of it came strong, in a cloud.

"It doesn't matter if it hears me now," thought Hazel. "If only I can get the rope bitten through quickly, it doesn't matter. The dog'll go to Dandelion, if only I can be quick enough to make sure that the rope breaks when it begins to tug."

He ripped at the cord again and sat back for a quick breath, looking across the track to where Dandelion was waiting. Then he froze and stared. A short distance behind Dandelion, in the grass, was the white-chested tabby, wide-eyed, tail lashing, crouching. It had seen both himself and Dandelion. As he watched, it crept a length nearer. Dandelion was lying still, watching the front of the kennel intently, as he had been told. The cat tensed itself to spring.

Before he knew what he was doing, Hazel stamped on the hollow roof. Twice he stamped and then turned to leap to the ground and run. Dandelion, reacting instantly, shot out of the grass to the open gravel. In the same moment, the cat jumped and landed exactly where he had been lying. The dog gave two quick, sharp barks and rushed out of the kennel. It saw Dandelion at once and ran to the full extent of the rope. The rope went taut, held for an instant and then parted at the point where Hazel had gnawed it to a thread. The kennel jerked forward, tilted, fell back and struck the ground with a jolt. Hazel, already off balance, clawed at the blanket, missed his footing and fell over the edge. He landed heavily on his weak leg and lay kicking. The dog was gone.

Hazel stopped kicking and lay still. There was a spurt of pain along his haunch, but he knew that he could move. He remembered the raised floor of the barn across the farmyard. He could limp the short distance, get under the floor and then make his way to the ditch. He raised himself on his forelegs.

On the instant he was knocked sideways and felt himself pressed down. There was a light but sharp pricking beneath the fur across his back. He lashed out with his hind legs, but struck nothing. He turned his head. The cat was on him, crouched half across his body. Its whiskers brushed his ear. Its great green eyes, the pupils contracted to vertical black slits in the sunshine, were staring into his own.

"Can you run?" hissed the cat. "I think not."

4 6

Bigwig Stands His Ground

Hard pounding this, gentlemen. Let's see who will pound longest.
                    The Duke of Wellington (at Waterloo)

Groundsel scrambled up the steep slope of the shaft and rejoined Woundwort in the pit at the top.

"There's nothing left to dig, sir," he said. "The bottom will fall in if anyone goes down there now."

"Can you make out what's below?" asked Woundwort. "Is it a run or a burrow we shall be into?"

"I'm fairly sure it's a burrow, sir," answered Groundsel. "In fact, it feels to me as though there's an unusually big space underneath."

"How many rabbits are in it, do you think?"

"I couldn't hear any at all. But they may be keeping quiet and waiting to attack us when we break in."

"They haven't done much attacking up to now," said Woundwort. "A poor lot, I'd say—skulking underground, and some of them running away in the night. I don't fancy we'll have much trouble."

"Unless, sir—" said Groundsel.

Woundwort looked at him and waited.

"Unless the—the animal attacks us, sir," said Groundsel. "Whatever it is. It's not like Ragwort to imagine anything. He's very stolid. I'm only trying to think ahead," he added, as Woundwort still said nothing.

"Well," said Woundwort at last, "if there *is* an animal, it'll find out that *I'm* an animal, too." He came out on the bank, where Campion and Vervain were waiting with a number of the other rabbits.

"We've done all the hard work now," he said. "We'll be able to take our does home as soon as we've finished down below. The way we'll go about it is this. I'm going to break the bottom of the hole in and go straight down into the burrow underneath. I want only three others to follow, otherwise there'll be complete confusion and we shall all be fighting each other. Vervain, you come behind me and bring two more. If there's any trouble we'll deal with it. Groundsel, you follow. But you're to stay in the shaft, understand? Don't jump down until I tell you. When we know where we are and what we're doing, you can bring a few more in."

There was not a rabbit in the Owsla but had confidence in Woundwort. As they heard him preparing to go first into the depths of the enemy warren as calmly as though he were looking for dandelions, his officers' spirits rose. It seemed to them quite likely that the place would be given up without any fighting at all. When the General had led the final assault at Nutley Copse he had killed three rabbits underground and no more had dared to oppose him, although there had been some hard tussles in the outer runs the day before.

"Very well," said Woundwort. "Now, I don't want anyone straying away. Campion, you see to that. As soon as we get one of the blocked runs opened from inside, you can fill the place up. Keep them together here till I let you know and then send them in fast."

"Best of luck, sir," said Campion.

Woundwort jumped into the pit, flattened his ears and went down the shaft. He had already decided that he was not going to stop to listen. There was no point, since he meant to break in at once whether there was anything to be heard or not. It was more important that he should not seem to hesitate or cause Vervain to do so; and that the enemy, if they were there, should have the shortest possible time in which to hear him coming. Below, there would be either a run or a burrow. Either he would have to fight immediately or else there would first be a chance to look round and sense where he was. It did not matter. What mattered was finding rabbits and killing them.

He came to the bottom of the shaft. As Groundsel had said, it was plainly thin—brittle as ice on a puddle—chalk, pebbles and light soil. Woundwort scored it across with his foreclaws. Slightly damp, it held a moment and then fell inward, crumbling. As it fell, Woundwort followed it.

He fell about the length of his own body—far enough to tell him that he was in a burrow. As he landed he kicked out with his hind legs and then dashed forward, partly to be out of Vervain's way as he followed and partly to reach the wall and face about before he could be attacked from behind. He found himself against a pile of soft earth—evidently the end of a blocked run leading out of the burrow—and turned. A moment later Vervain was beside him. The third rabbit, whoever he was, seemed to be in difficulties. They could both hear him scrabbling in the fallen soil.

"Over here," said Woundwort sharply.

The rabbit, a powerful, heavy veteran by the name of Thunder, joined them, stumbling.

"What's the matter?" asked Woundwort.

"Nothing, sir," answered Thunder, "only there's a dead rabbit on the floor and it startled me for a moment."

"A dead rabbit?" said Woundwort. "Are you sure he's dead? Where is he?"

"Over there, sir, by the shaft."

Woundwort crossed the burrow quickly. On the far side of the rubble that had fallen in from the shaft was lying the inert body of a buck. He sniffed at it and then pressed it with his nose.

"He's not been dead long," he said. "He's nearly cold but not stiff. What do you make of it, Vervain? Rabbits don't die underground."

"It's a very small buck, sir," answered Vervain. "Didn't fancy the idea of fighting us, perhaps, and the others killed him when he said so."

"No, that won't do. There's not a scratch on him. Well, leave him, anyway. We've got to get on, and a rabbit this size isn't going to make any difference, dead or alive."

He began to move along the wall, sniffing as he went. He passed the mouths of two blocked runs, came to an opening between thick tree roots and stopped. The place was evidently very big—bigger than the Council burrow at Efrafa. Since they were not being attacked, he could turn the space to his own advantage by getting some more rabbits in at once. He went back quickly to the foot of the shaft. By standing on his hind legs he could just rest his forepaws on the ragged lip of the hole.

"Groundsel?" he said.

"Yes, sir?" answered Groundsel from above.

"Come on," said Woundwort, "and bring four others with you. Jump to this side"—he moved slightly—"there's a dead rabbit on the floor—one of theirs."

He was still expecting to be attacked at any moment, but the place remained silent. He continued to listen, sniffing the close air, while the five rabbits dropped one by one into the burrow. Then he took Groundsel over to the two blocked runs along the eastern wall.

"Get these open as quick as you can," he said, "and send two rabbits to find out what's behind the tree roots beyond. If they're attacked you're to go and join in at once."

"You know, there's something strange about the wall at the other end, sir," said Vervain, as Groundsel began setting his rabbits to work. "Most of it's hard earth that's never been dug. But in one or two places there are piles of much softer stuff. I'd say that runs leading through the wall have been filled up very recently—probably since yesterday evening."

Woundwort and Vervain went carefully along the south wall of the Honeycomb, scratching and listening.

"I believe you're right," said Woundwort. "Have you heard any movement from the other side?"

"Yes, sir, just about here," said Vervain.

"We'll get this pile of soft earth down," said Woundwort. "Put two rabbits on it. If I'm right and Thlayli's on the other side, they'll run into trouble before long. That's what we want—to force him to attack them."

As Thunder and Thistle began to dig, Woundwort crouched silently behind them, waiting.

*   *   *

Even before he heard the roof of the Honeycomb fall in, Bigwig knew that it could be only a matter of time before the Efrafans found the soft places in the south wall and set to work to break through one of them. That would not take long. Then he would have to fight—probably with Woundwort himself; and if Woundwort closed with him and used his weight, he would have little chance. Somehow he must manage to hurt him at the outset, before he expected it. But how?

He put the problem to Holly.

"The trouble is this warren wasn't dug to be defended," said Holly. "That was what the Slack Run was for, back at home, so the Threarah once told me. It was made so that if we ever had to, we could get down beneath an enemy and come up where he wasn't expecting us."

"That's it!" cried Bigwig. "That's the idea! Look, I'm going to dig myself into the floor of the run just behind this blocked opening. Then you cover me with earth. It won't be noticed—there's so much digging and mess in the place already. I know it's a risk, but it'll be better than just trying to stand up in front of a rabbit like Woundwort."

"But suppose they break through the wall somewhere else?" said Holly.

"You must try to make them do it here," replied Bigwig. "When you hear them on the other side, make a noise—do a bit of scratching or something—just above where I am. Anything to get them interested. Come on, help me to dig. And, Silver, get everyone back out of the Honeycomb now and close this wall completely."

"Bigwig," said Pipkin, "I can't wake Fiver. He's still lying out there in the middle of the floor. What's to be done?"

"I'm afraid there's nothing we can do now," replied Bigwig. "It's a great pity, but we'll have to leave him."

"Oh, Bigwig," cried Pipkin, "let me stay out there with him! You'll never miss me, and I can go on trying—"

"Hlao-roo," said Holly as kindly as he could, "if we lose no one but Fiver before this business is ended, then the Lord Frith himself will be fighting for us. No, I'm sorry, old chap, not another word. We need you, we need everyone. Silver, see that he goes back with the others."

When Woundwort dropped through the roof of the Honeycomb,

Bigwig was already lying under a thin covering of soil on the other side of the south wall, not far from Clover's burrow.

*   *   *

Thunder sank his teeth into a piece of broken root and pulled it out. There was an instant fall of earth and a gap opened where he had been digging. The soil no longer reached to the roof. It was only a broad pile of soft earth, half filling the run. Woundwort, still waiting silently, could smell and hear a considerable number of rabbits on the far side. He hoped that now they might come into the open burrow and try to attack him. But they made no move.

When it came to fighting, Woundwort was not given to careful calculation. Men, and larger animals such as wolves, usually have an idea of their own numbers and those of the enemy and this affects their readiness to fight and how they go about it. Woundwort had never had any need to think like this. What he had learned from all his experience of fighting was that nearly always there are those who want to fight and those who do not but feel they cannot avoid it. More than once he had fought alone and imposed his will on crowds of other rabbits. He held down a great warren with the help of a handful of devoted officers. It did not occur to him now—and if it had, he would not have thought it mattered—that most of his rabbits were still outside; that those who were with him were fewer than those on the other side of the wall and that until Groundsel had got the runs open they could not get out even if they wanted to. This sort of thing does not count among fighting rabbits. Ferocity and aggression are everything. What Woundwort knew was that those beyond the wall were afraid of him and that on this account he had the advantage.

"Groundsel," he said, "as soon as you've got those runs open, tell Campion to send everyone down here. The rest of you, follow me. We'll have this business finished by the time the others get in to join us."

Woundwort waited only for Groundsel to bring back the two rabbits who had been sent to search among the tree roots at the north end of the burrow. Then, with Vervain behind him, he climbed the pile of fallen earth and thrust his way into the narrow run. In the dark he could hear and smell the rustling and crowding of rabbits—both bucks and does—ahead of him. There were two bucks directly in his path, but they fell back as he plowed through the loose soil. He plunged forward and felt the ground suddenly turn beneath him. The next moment a rabbit started up from the earth at his feet and sank his teeth in the pit of his near foreleg, just where it joined the body.

Woundwort had won almost every fight of his life by using his weight. Other rabbits could not stop him and once they went down they seldom got up. He tried to push now, but his back legs could get no purchase in the pile of loose, yielding soil behind him. He reared up and, as he did so, realized that the enemy beneath him was crouching in a scooped-out trench the size of his own body. He struck out and felt his claws score deeply along the back and haunch. Then the other rabbit, still keeping his grip under Woundwort's shoulder, thrust upward with his hind legs braced against the floor of the trench. Woundwort, with both forefeet off the ground, was thrown over on his back on the earth pile. He lashed out, but the enemy had already loosed his hold and was beyond his reach.

Woundwort stood up. He could feel the blood running down the inside of his near foreleg. The muscle was wounded. He could not put his full weight on it. But his own claws, too, were bloody and this blood was not his.

"Are you all right, sir?" asked Vervain, behind him.

"Of course I'm all right, you fool," said Woundwort. "Follow me close."

The other rabbit spoke from in front of him.

"You told me once to start by impressing you, General. I hope I have."

"I told you once that I would kill you myself," replied Woundwort. "There is no white bird here, Thlayli." He advanced for the second time.

Bigwig's taunt had been deliberate. He hoped that Woundwort would fly at him and so give him a chance to bite him again. But as he waited, pressed to the ground, he realized that Woundwort was too clever to be drawn. Always quick to size up any new situation, he was coming forward slowly, keeping close to the ground himself. He meant to use his claws. Afraid, listening to Woundwort's approach, Bigwig could hear the uneven movement of his fore-paws, almost within striking distance. Instinctively he drew back and as he did so the thought came with the sound: "The near forepaw's dragging. He can't use it properly." Leaving his right flank exposed, he struck out on his near side.

His claws found Woundwort's leg, ripping sideways; but before he could draw back, Woundwort's whole weight came down on him and the next moment his teeth had met in his right ear. Bigwig squealed, pressed down and thrashing from side to side. Woundwort, feeling his enemy's fear and helplessness, loosed his hold of the ear and rose above him, ready to bite and tear him across the back of the neck. For an instant he stood above the helpless Bigwig, his shoulders filling the run. Then his injured foreleg gave way and he lurched sideways against the wall. Bigwig cuffed him twice across the face and felt the third blow pass through his whiskers as he sprang back. The sound of his heavy breathing came plainly from the top of the earth pile. Bigwig, the blood oozing from his back and ear, stood his ground and waited. Suddenly he realized that he could see the dark shape of General Woundwort faintly outlined where he crouched above him. The first traces of daylight were glimmering through the broken roof of the Honeycomb behind.

47

The Sky Suspended

Ole bull he comes for me, wi's head down. But I didn't flinch . . . I went for 'e. 'Twas him as did th' flinchin'.

Flora Thompson, *Lark Rise*

When Hazel stamped, Dandelion leaped instinctively from the grass verge. If there had been a hole he would have made for it. For the briefest instant he looked up and down the gravel. Then the dog was rushing upon him and he turned and made for the raised barn. But before he reached it he realized that he must not take refuge under the floor. If he did, the dog would check: very likely a man would call it back. He had to get it out of the farmyard and down to the road. He altered direction and raced up the lane toward the elms.

He had not expected the dog to be so close behind him. He could hear its breath and the loose gravel flying under its paws.

"It's too fast for me!" he thought. "It's going to catch me!" In another moment it would be on him and then it would roll him over, snapping his back and biting out his life. He knew that hares, when overtaken, dodge by turning more quickly and neatly than the pursuing dog and doubling back on their track. "I shall have to double," he thought desperately. "But if I do, it will hunt me up and down the lane and the man will call it off, or else I shall have to lose it by going through the hedge: then the whole plan will fail."

He tore over the crest and down toward the cattle shed. When Hazel had told him what he was to do, it had seemed to him that his task would consist of leading the dog on and persuading it to follow him. Now he was running simply to save his life, and that at a speed he had never touched before, a speed he knew he could not keep up.

In actual fact Dandelion covered three hundred yards to the cattle shed in a good deal less than half a minute. But as he reached the straw at the entrance it seemed to him that he had run forever. Hazel and the farmyard were long, long ago. He had never done anything in his life but run in terror down the lane, feeling the dog's breath at his haunches. Inside the gate a big rat ran across in front of him and the dog checked at it for a moment. Dandelion gained the nearest shed and went headlong between two bales of straw at the foot of a pile. It was a narrow place and he turned round only with some difficulty. The dog was immediately outside, scratching eagerly, whining and throwing up loose straw as it sniffed along the foot of the bales.

"Sit tight," said a young rat, from the straw close beside him. "It'll be off in a minute. They're not like cats, you know."

"That's the trouble," said Dandelion, panting and rolling the whites of his eyes. "It mustn't lose me; and time's everything."

"What?" said the rat, puzzled. "What you say?"

Without answering, Dandelion slipped along to another crack, gathered himself a moment and then broke cover, running across the yard to the opposite shed. It was open-fronted and he went straight through to the boarding along the back. There was a gap under the broken end of a board and here he crept into the field beyond. The dog, following, thrust its head into the gap and pushed, barking with excitement. Gradually the loose board levered open like a trapdoor until it was able to force its way through.

Now that he had a better start, Dandelion kept in the open and ran down the field to the hedge beside the road. He knew he was slower, but the dog seemed slower, too. Choosing a thick part, he went through the hedge and crossed the road. Blackberry came to meet him, scuttering down the further bank. Dandelion dropped exhausted in the ditch. The dog was not twenty feet away on the other side of the hedge. It could not find a big enough gap.

"It's faster than ever I thought," gasped Dandelion, "but I've taken the edge off it. I can't do any more. I must go to ground. I'm finished."

It was plain that Blackberry was frightened.

"Frith help me!" he whispered. "I'll never do it!"

"Go on, quick," said Dandelion, "before it loses interest. I'll overtake you and help if I can."

Blackberry hopped deliberately into the road and sat up. Seeing him, the dog yelped and thrust its weight against the hedge. Blackberry ran slowly along the road toward a pair of gates that stood opposite each other further down. The dog stayed level with him. As soon as he was sure that it had seen the gate on its own side and meant to go to it, Blackberry turned and climbed the bank. Out in the stubble he waited for the dog to reappear.

It was a long time coming; and when at last it pushed its way between the gatepost and the bank into the field, it paid him no attention. It nosed along the foot of the bank, put up a partridge and bounced after it and then began to scratch about in a clump of dock plants. For some time Blackberry felt too terrified to move. Then, in desperation, he hopped slowly toward it, trying to act as though he had not noticed that it was there. It dashed after him, but almost at once seemed to lose interest and returned to its nosing and sniffing over the ground. Finally, when he was utterly at a loss, it set off over the field of its own accord, padding easily along beside one of the rows of threshed straw, trailing the broken cord and pouncing in and out at every squeak and rustle. Blackberry, sheltering behind a parallel row, kept level with it. In this manner they covered the distance to the pylon line, halfway to the foot of the down. It was here that Dandelion caught up with him.

"It's not fast enough, Blackberry! We *must* get on. Bigwig may be dead."

"I know, but at least it's going the right way. I couldn't get it to move at all, to start with. Can't we—"

"It's got to come up the down at speed or there'll be no surprise. Come on, we'll draw it together. We'll have to get ahead of it first, though."

They ran fast through the stubble until they neared the trees. Then they turned and crossed the dog's line in full view. This time it pursued instantly and the two rabbits reached the undergrowth at the bottom of the steep with no more than ten yards to spare. As they began to climb they heard the dog crashing through the brittle elders. It barked once and then they were out on the open slope with the dog running mute behind them.

*   *   *

The blood ran over Bigwig's neck and down his foreleg. He watched Woundwort steadily where he crouched on the earth pile, expecting him to leap forward at any moment. He could hear a rabbit moving behind him, but the run was so narrow that he could not have turned even if it had been safe to do so.

"Everyone all right?" he asked.

"They're all right," replied Holly. "Come on, Bigwig, let me take your place now. You need a rest."

"Can't," panted Bigwig. "You couldn't get past me here—no room—and if I go back that brute'll follow—next thing you'd know he'd be loose in the burrows. You leave it to me. I know what I'm doing."

It had occurred to Bigwig that in the narrow run even his dead body would be a considerable obstacle. The Efrafans would either have to get it out or dig round it and this would mean more delay.

In the burrow behind him he could hear Bluebell, who was apparently telling the does a story. "Good idea," he thought. "Keep 'em happy. More than I could do if I had to sit there."

"So then El-ahrairah said to the fox, 'Fox you may smell and fox you may be, but I can tell your fortune in the water.' "

Suddenly Woundwort spoke.

"Thlayli," he said, "why do you want to throw your life away? I can send one fresh rabbit after another into this run if I choose. You're too good to be killed. Come back to Efrafa. I promise I'll give you the command of any Mark you like. I give you my word."

"Silflay hraka, u embleer rah," replied Bigwig.

" 'Ah ha,' said the fox, 'tell my fortune, eh? And what do you see in the water, my friend? Fat rabbits running through the grass, yes, yes?' "

"Very well," said Woundwort. "But remember, Thlayli, you yourself can stop this nonsense whenever you wish."

" 'No,' replied El-ahrairah, 'it is not fat rabbits that I see in the water, but swift hounds on the scent and my enemy flying for his life.' "

Bigwig realized that Woundwort also knew that in the run his body would be nearly as great a hindrance dead as alive. "He wants me to come out on my feet," he thought. "But it's Inlé, not Efrafa, that I shall go to from here."

Suddenly Woundwort leaped forward in a single bound and landed full against Bigwig like a branch falling from a tree. He made no attempt to use his claws. His great weight was pushing, chest to chest, against Bigwig's. With heads side by side they bit and snapped at each other's shoulders. Bigwig felt himself sliding slowly backward. He could not resist the tremendous pressure. His back legs, with claws extended, furrowed the floor of the run as he gave ground. In a few moments he would be pushed bodily into the burrow behind. Putting his last strength into the effort to remain where he was, he loosed his teeth from Woundwort's shoulder and dropped his head, like a cart horse straining at a load. Still he was slipping. Then, very gradually it seemed, the terrible pressure began to slacken. His claws had a hold of the ground. Woundwort, teeth sunk in his back, was snuffling and choking. Though Bigwig did not know it, his earlier blows had torn Woundwort across the nose. His nostrils were full of his own blood, and with jaws closed in Bigwig's fur he could not draw his breath. A moment more and he let go his hold. Bigwig, utterly exhausted, lay where he was. After a few moments he tried to get up, but a faintness came over him and a feeling of turning over and over in a ditch of leaves. He closed his eyes. There was silence and then, quite clearly, he heard Fiver speaking in the long grass. "You are closer to death than I. You are closer to death than I."

"The wire!" squealed Bigwig. He jerked himself up and opened his eyes. The run was empty. General Woundwort was gone.

*   *   *

Woundwort clambered out into the Honeycomb, now dimly lit down the shaft by the daylight outside. He had never felt so tired. He saw Vervain and Thunder looking at him uncertainly. He sat on his haunches and tried to clean his face with his front paws.

"Thlayli won't give any more trouble," he said. "You'd better just go in and finish him off, Vervain, since he won't come out."

"You're asking *me* to fight him, sir?" asked Vervain.

"Well, just take him on for a few moments," answered Woundwort. "I want to start them getting this wall down in one or two other places. Then I'll come back."

Vervain knew that the impossible had happened. The General had come off worst. What he was saying was, "Cover up for me. Don't let the others know."

"What in Frith's name happens now?" thought Vervain. "The plain truth is that Thlayli's had the best of it all along, ever since he first met him in Efrafa. And the sooner we're back there the better."

He met Woundwort's pale stare, hesitated a moment and then climbed on the earth pile. Woundwort limped across to the two runs, halfway down the eastern wall, which Groundsel had been told to get open. Both were now clear at the entrances and the diggers were out of sight in the tunnels. As he approached, Groundsel backed down the further tunnel and began cleaning his claws on a projecting root.

"How are you getting on?" asked Woundwort.

"This run's open, sir," said Groundsel, "but the other will take a bit longer, I'm afraid. It's heavily blocked."

"One's enough," said Woundwort, "as long as they can come

down it. We can bring them in and start getting that end wall down."

He was about to go up the run himself when he found Vervain beside him. For a moment he thought that he was going to say that he had killed Thlayli. A second glance showed him otherwise.

"I've—er—got some grit in my eye, sir," said Vervain. "I'll just get it out and then I'll have another go at him."

Without a word Woundwort went back to the far end of the Honeycomb. Vervain followed.

"You coward," said Woundwort in his ear. "If my authority goes, where will yours be in half a day? Aren't you the most hated officer in Efrafa? That rabbit's *got* to be killed."

Once more he climbed on the earth pile. Then he stopped. Vervain and Thistle, raising their heads to peer past him from behind, saw why. Thlayli had made his way up the run and was crouching immediately below. Blood had matted the great thatch of fur on his head, and one ear, half severed, hung down beside his face. His breathing was slow and heavy.

"You'll find it much harder to push me back from here, General," he said.

With a sort of weary, dull surprise, Woundwort realized that he was afraid. He did not want to attack Thlayli again. He knew, with flinching certainty, that he was not up to it. And who was? he thought. Who could do it? No, they would have to get in by some other way and everyone would know why.

"Thlayli," he said, "we've unblocked a run out here. I can bring in enough rabbits to pull down this wall in four places. Why don't you come out?"

Thlayli's reply, when it came, was low and gasping, but perfectly clear.

"My Chief Rabbit has told me to defend this run and until he says otherwise I shall stay here."

"His Chief Rabbit?" said Vervain, staring.

It had never occurred to Woundwort or any of his officers that Thlayli was not the Chief Rabbit of his warren. Yet what he said carried immediate conviction. He was speaking the truth. And if he was not the Chief Rabbit, then somewhere close by there must be another, stronger rabbit who was. A stronger rabbit than Thlayli. Where was he? What was he doing at this moment?

Woundwort became aware that Thistle was no longer behind him.

"Where's that young fellow gone?" he said to Vervain.

"He seems to have slipped away, sir," answered Vervain.

"You should have stopped him," said Woundwort. "Fetch him back."

But it was Groundsel who returned to him a few moments later.

"I'm sorry, sir," he said, "Thistle's gone up the opened run. I thought you'd sent him or I'd have asked him what he was up to. One or two of my rabbits seem to have gone with him—I don't know what for, I'm sure."

"I'll give them what for," said Woundwort. "Come with me."

He knew now what they would have to do. Every rabbit he had brought must be sent underground to dig and every blocked gap in the wall must be opened. As for Thlayli, he could simply be left where he was and the less said about him the better. There must be no more fighting in narrow runs, and when the terrible Chief Rabbit finally appeared he would be pulled down in the open, from all sides.

He turned to re-cross the burrow, but remained where he was, staring. In the faint patch of light below the ragged hole in the roof, a rabbit was standing—no Efrafan, a rabbit unknown to the General. He was very small and was looking tensely about him—wide-eyed as a kitten above ground for the first time—as though by no means sure where he might be. As Woundwort watched, he raised a trembling forepaw and passed it gropingly across his face. For a moment some old, flickering, here-and-gone feeling stirred in the General's memory—the smell of wet cabbage leaves in a cottage garden, the sense of some easy-going, kindly place, long forgotten and lost.

"Who the devil's that?" asked General Woundwort.

"It—it must be the rabbit that's been lying there, sir," answered Groundsel. "The rabbit we thought was dead."

"Oh, is that it?" said Woundwort. "Well, he's just about your mark, isn't he, Vervain? That's one of them you might be able to tackle, at all events. Hurry up," he sneered, as Vervain hesitated, uncertain whether the General were serious, "and come on out as soon as you've finished."

Vervain advanced slowly across the floor. Even he could derive˙

little satisfaction from the prospect of killing a tharn rabbit half his own size, in obedience to a contemptuous taunt. The small rabbit made no move whatever, either to retreat or to defend himself, but only stared at him from great eyes which, though troubled, were certainly not those of a beaten enemy or a victim. Before his gaze, Vervain stopped in uncertainty and for long moments the two faced each other in the dim light. Then, very quietly and with no trace of fear, the strange rabbit said,

"I am sorry for you with all my heart. But you cannot blame us, for you came to kill us if you could."

"Blame you?" answered Vervain. "Blame you for what?"

"For your death. Believe me, I am sorry for your death."

Vervain in his time had encountered any number of prisoners who, before they died, had cursed or threatened him, not uncommonly with supernatural vengeance, much as Bigwig had cursed Woundwort in the storm. If such things had been liable to have any effect on him, he would not have been head of the Owslafa. Indeed, for almost any utterance that a rabbit in this dreadful situation could find to make, Vervain was unthinkingly ready with one or other of a stock of jeering rejoinders. Now, as he continued to meet the eyes of this unaccountable enemy—the only one he had faced in all the long night's search for bloodshed—horror came upon him and he was filled with a sudden fear of his words, gentle and inexorable as the falling of bitter snow in a land without refuge. The shadowy recesses of the strange burrow seemed full of whispering, malignant ghosts and he recognized the forgotten voices of rabbits done to death months since in the ditches of Efrafa.

"Let me alone!" cried Vervain. "Let me go! Let me go!"

Stumbling and blundering, he found his way to the opened run and dragged himself up it. At the top he came upon Woundwort, listening to one of Groundsel's diggers, who was trembling and white-eyed.

"Oh, sir," said the youngster, "they say there's a great Chief Rabbit bigger than a hare; and a strange animal they heard—"

"Shut up!" said Woundwort. "Follow me, come on."

He came out on the bank, blinking in the sunlight. The rabbits scattered about the grass stared at him in horror, several wondering whether this could really be the General. His nose and one eyelid were gashed and his whole face was masked with blood. As he limped down from the bank his near foreleg trailed and he staggered sideways. He scrambled into the open grass and looked about him.

"Now," said Woundwort, "this is the last thing we have to do, and it won't take long. Down below, there's a kind of wall." He stopped, sensing all around him reluctance and fear. He looked at Ragwort, who looked away. Two other rabbits were edging off through the grass. He called them back.

"What do you think you're doing?" he asked.

"Nothing, sir," replied one. "We only thought that—"

All of a sudden Captain Campion dashed round the corner of the hanger. From the open down beyond came a single, high scream. At the same moment two strange rabbits, running together, leaped the bank into the wood and disappeared down one of the blocked tunnels.

"Run!" cried Campion, stamping. "Run for your lives!"

He raced through them and was gone over the down. Not knowing what he meant or where to run, they turned one way and another. Five bolted down the opened run and a few more into the wood. But almost before they had begun to scatter, into their midst bounded a great black dog, snapping, biting and chasing hither and thither like a fox in a chicken run.

Woundwort alone stood his ground. As the rest fled in all directions he remained where he was, bristling and snarling, bloody-fanged and bloody-clawed. The dog, coming suddenly upon him face to face among the rough tussocks, recoiled a moment, startled and confused. Then it sprang forward; and even as they ran, his Owsla could hear the General's raging, squealing cry, "Come back, you fools! Dogs aren't dangerous! Come back and fight!"

48

Dea ex Machina

And as I was green and carefree, famous among the barns
About the happy yard and singing as the farm was home,
In the sun that is young once only . . .

Dylan Thomas, *Fern Hill*

When Lucy woke, the room was already light. The curtains were not drawn and the pane of the open casement reflected a gleam of sun which she could lose and find by moving her head on the pillow. A wood pigeon was calling in the elms. But it was some other sound, she knew, that had woken her—a sharp sound, a part of the dream which had drained away, as she woke, like water out of a washbasin. Perhaps the dog had barked. But now everything was quiet and there was only the flash of sun from the windowpane and the sound of the wood pigeon, like the first strokes of a paint brush on a big sheet of paper when you were still not sure how the picture was going to go. The morning was fine. Would there be any mushrooms yet? Was it worth getting up now and going down the field to see? It was still too dry and hot—not good mushroom weather. The mushrooms were like the blackberries—both wanted a drop of rain before they'd be any good. Soon there'd be damp mornings and the big spiders would come in the hedges—the ones with a white cross on their backs. Jane Pocock running off to the back of the schoolbus when she brought one in a matchbox to show Miss Tallant.

> Spider, spider on the bus,
> Soppy Jane that made a fuss,
> Spider got th' eleven-plus.

Now she couldn't catch the reflection in her eyes any more. The sun had moved. What was going to happen today? Thursday— market day in Newbury. Dad would be going in. Doctor was coming to see Mum. Doctor had funny glasses that pinched on his nose. They'd made a mark each side. If he wasn't in a hurry he'd talk to her. Doctor was a bit funny-like when you didn't know him, but when you did he was nice.

Suddenly there was another sharp sound. It ripped through the still, early morning like something spilled across a clean floor—a squealing—something frightened, something desperate. Lucy jumped out of bed and ran across to the window. Whatever it was, it was only just outside. She leaned well out, with her feet off the floor and the sill pressing breathlessly across her stomach. Tab was down below, right by the kennel. He'd got something: rat it must be, squealing like that.

"Tab!" called Lucy sharply. "Tab! Wha' you got?"

At the sound of her voice the cat looked up for a moment and immediately looked back again at its prey. 'T'weren't no rat, though; 't'was a rabbit, layin' on its side by the kennel. It looked proper bad. Kicking out an' all. Then it squealed again.

Lucy ran down the stairs in her nightdress and opened the door. The gravel made her hobble and she left it and went on up the flower bed. As she reached the kennel the cat looked up and spat at her, keeping one paw pressed down on the rabbit's neck.

"Git out, Tab!" said Lucy. "Crool thing! Let'n alone!"

She cuffed the cat, which tried to scratch her, ears laid flat. She raised her hand again and it growled, ran a few feet and stopped, looking back in sulky rage. Lucy picked up the rabbit. It struggled a moment and then held itself tense in her firm grip.

" 'Old still!" said Lucy. "I ain't goin' 'urtcher!"

She went back to the house, carrying the rabbit.

"What you bin up to, eh?" said her father, boots scratch-scratch over the tiles. "Look at yore feet! En I told you— Wha' got there, then?"

"Rabbit," said Lucy defensively.

"In yer nightdress an' all, catch yore bloomin' death. Wha' want with 'im, then?"

"Goner keep 'im."

"You ain't!"

"Ah, Dad. 'E's nice."

" 'E won't be no bloomin' good t'yer. You put 'im in 'utch 'e'll only die. You can't keep woild rabbit. 'N if 'e gets out 'e'll do all manner o' bloomin' 'arm."

"But 'e's bad, Dad. Cat's bin at 'im."

"Cat was doin' 'is job, then. Did oughter've let 'im finish be roights."

"I wanner show 'im to Doctor."

"Doctor's got summin' better to do than bide about wi' old rabbit. You jus' give 'im 'ere, now."

Lucy began to cry. She had not lived all her life on a farm for nothing and she knew very well that everything her father had said was right. But she was upset by the idea of killing the rabbit in cold blood. True, she did not really know what she could do with it in the long run. What she wanted was to show it to Doctor. She knew that Doctor thought of her as a proper farm girl—a country girl. When she showed him things she had found—a goldfinch's egg, a Painted Lady fluttering in a jam jar or a fungus that looked exactly like orange peel—he took her seriously and talked to her as he would to a grown-up person. To ask his advice about a damaged rabbit and discuss it with him would be very grown-up. Meanwhile, her father might give way or he might not.

"I on'y just wanted to show 'im to Doctor, Dad. I won't let 'im do no 'arm, honest. On'y it's nice talking to Doctor."

Although he never said so, her father was proud of the way Lucy got on with Doctor. She was proper bright kid—very likely goin' to grammar school an' all, so they told him. Doctor had said once or twice she was real sensible with these things she picked up what she showed him. Comin' to somethin', though, bloody rabbits. All same, would'n' 'urt, long's she didn' let 'un go on the place.

"Why don' you do somethin' sensible," he said, " 'stead o' bidin' there 'ollerin' and carryin' on like you was skimmish? You wants go'n get some cloze on, then you c'n go'n put 'im in that old cage what's in shed. One what you 'ad for they budgies."

Lucy stopped crying and went upstairs, still carrying the rabbit. She shut it in a drawer, got dressed and went out to get the cage. On the way back she stopped for some straw from behind the kennel. Her father came across from the long barn.

"Did y'see Bob?"

"Never," said Lucy. "Where's 'e gone, then?"

"Bust 'is rope an' off. I know'd that old rope were gett'n on like, but I didn't reckon 'e could bust 'im. Anyways, I go' go in to Newbury s'mornin'. 'F'e turns up agen you'd best tie 'im up proper."

"I'll look out fer 'im, Dad," said Lucy. "I'll ge' bi' o' breakfast up to Mum now."

"Ah, that's good girl. I reckon she'll be right's a trivet tomorrer."

Doctor Adams arrived soon after ten. Lucy, who was making her bed and tidying her room later than she should have been, heard him stop his car under the elms at the top of the lane and went out to meet him, wondering why he had not driven up to the house as usual. He had got out of the car and was standing with his hands behind his back, looking down the lane, but he caught sight of her and called in the rather shy, abrupt way she was used to.

"Er—Lucy."

She ran up. He took off his pince-nez and put them in his waistcoat pocket.

"Is that your dog?"

The Labrador was coming up the lane, looking decidedly tired and trailing its broken rope. Lucy laid hold of it.

" 'E's bin off, Doctor. 'Bin ever so worried 'bout 'im."

The Labrador began to sniff at Doctor Adams' shoes.

"Something's been fighting with him, I think," said Doctor Adams. "His nose is scratched quite badly, and that looks like some kind of a bite on his leg."

"What d'you reckon t'was, then, Doctor?"

"Well, it might have been a big rat, I suppose, or perhaps a stoat. Something he went for that put up a fight."

"I got a rabbit s'mornin', Doctor. Woild one. 'E's aloive. I took 'un off o' the cat. On'y I reckon e's 'urt. Joo like see 'im?"

"Well, I'd better go and see Mrs. Cane first, I think." (Not "your mother," thought Lucy.) "And then if I've got time I'll have a look at the chap."

Twenty minutes later Lucy was holding the rabbit as quiet as she could while Doctor Adams pressed it gently here and there with the balls of two fingers.

"Well, there doesn't seem to be much the matter with him, as far as I can see," he said at last. "Nothing's broken. There's something funny about this hind leg, but that's been done some time and it's more or less healed—or as much as it ever will. The cat's scratched him across here, you see, but that's nothing much. I should think he'll be all right for a bit."

"No good to keep 'im, though, Doctor, would it? In 'utch, I mean."

"Oh, no, he wouldn't live shut up in a box. If he couldn't get out he'd soon die. No, I should let the poor chap go—unless you want to eat him."

Lucy laughed. "Dad'd be ever s'woild, though, if I was to let 'im go anywheres round 'ere. 'E always says one rabbit means 'undred an' one."

"Well, I'll tell you what," said Doctor Adams, taking his thin fob watch on the fingers of one hand and looking down at it as he held it at arm's length—for he was long-sighted—"I've got to go a few miles up the road to see an old lady at Cole Henley. If you like to come along in the car, you can let him go on the down and I'll bring you back before dinner."

Lucy skipped. "I'll just go'n ask Mum."

On the ridge between Hare Warren Down and Watership Down, Doctor Adams stopped the car.

"I should think this would be as good as anywhere," he said. "There's not a lot of harm he can do here, if you come to think about it."

They walked a short distance eastward from the road and Lucy set the rabbit down. It sat stupefied for nearly half a minute and then suddenly dashed away over the grass.

"Yes, he *has* got something the matter with that leg, you see," said Doctor Adams. "But he could perfectly well live for years, as far as that goes. Born and bred in a briar patch, Brer Fox."

49

Hazel Comes Home

Well, we've been lucky devils both
And there's no need of pledge or oath
To bind our lovely friendship fast,
  By firmer stuff
  Close bound enough.—

Robert Graves, *Two Fusiliers*

Although Woundwort had shown himself at the last to be a creature virtually mad, nevertheless what he did proved not altogether futile. There can be little doubt that if he had not done it, more rabbits would have been killed that morning on Watership Down. So swiftly and silently had the dog come up the hill behind Dandelion and Blackberry that one of Campion's sentries, half asleep under a tussock after the long night, was pulled down and killed in the instant that he turned to bolt. Later—after it had left Woundwort—the dog beat up and down the bank and the open grass for some time, barking and dashing at every bush and clump of weeds. But by now the Efrafans had had time to scatter and hide, as best they could. Besides, the dog, unexpectedly scratched and bitten, showed a certain reluctance to come to grips. At last, however, it succeeded in putting up and killing the rabbit who had been wounded by glass the day before, and with this it made off by the way it had come, disappearing over the edge of the escarpment.

There could be no question now of the Efrafans renewing their attack on the warren. None had any idea beyond saving his own life. Their leader was gone. The dog had been set on them by the rabbits they had come to kill—of this they were sure. It was all one with the mysterious fox and the white bird. Indeed, Ragwort, the most unimaginative rabbit alive, had actually heard it underground. Campion, crouching in a patch of nettles with Vervain and four or five more, met with nothing but shivering agreement when he said that he was sure that they ought to leave at once this dangerous place, where they had already stayed far too long.

Without Campion, probably not one rabbit would have got back to Efrafa. As it was, all his skill as a patroller could not bring home half of those who had come to Watership. Three or four had run and strayed too far to be found and what became of them no one ever knew. There were probably fourteen or fifteen rabbits—no more—who set off with Campion, some time before ni-Frith, to try to retrace the long journey they had made only the previous day. They were not fit to cover the distance by nightfall: and before long they had worse to face than their own fatigue and low spirits. Bad news travels fast. Down to the Belt and beyond, the rumor spread that the terrible General Woundwort and his Owsla had been cut to pieces on Watership Down and that what was left of them was trailing southward in poor shape, with little heart to keep alert. The Thousand began to close in—stoats, a fox, even a tomcat from some farm or other. At every halt yet another rabbit was not to be found and no one could remember seeing what had happened to him. One of these was Vervain. It had been plain from the start that he had nothing left and, indeed, there was little reason for him to return to Efrafa without the General.

Through all the fear and hardship Campion remained steady and vigilant, holding the survivors together, thinking ahead and encouraging the exhausted to keep going. During the afternoon of the following day, while the Off Fore Mark were at silflay, he came limping through the sentry line with a straggling handful of six or seven rabbits. He was close to collapse himself and scarcely able to give the Council any account of the disaster.

Only Groundsel, Thistle and three others had the presence of mind to dart down the opened run when the dog came. Back in the Honeycomb, Groundsel immediately surrendered himself and his fugitives to Fiver, who was still bemused from his long trance, and scarcely restored to his senses sufficiently to grasp what was toward. At length, however, after the five Efrafans had remained crouching for some time in the burrow, listening to the sounds of the dog hunting above, Fiver recovered himself, made his way to the mouth of the run where Bigwig still lay half conscious, and succeeded in making Holly and Silver understand that the siege was ended. There was no lack of helpers to tear open the blocked gaps in the south wall. It so happened that Bluebell was the first through into the Honeycomb; and for many days afterward he was still improving upon his imitation of Captain Fiver at the head of his crowd of Efrafan prisoners—"like a tomtit rounding up a bunch of molting jackdaws," as he put it.

No one was inclined to pay them much attention at the time, however, for the only thoughts throughout the warren were for Hazel and Bigwig. Bigwig seemed likely to die. Bleeding in half a dozen places, he lay with closed eyes in the run he had defended and made no reply when Hyzenthlay told him that the Efrafans were defeated and the warren was saved. After a time, they dug carefully to broaden the run and as the day wore on the does, each in turn, remained beside him, licking his wounds and listening to his low, unsteady breathing.

Before this, Blackberry and Dandelion had burrowed their way in from Kehaar's run—it had not been blocked very heavily—and told their story. They could not say what might have happened to Hazel after the dog broke loose, and by the early afternoon everyone feared the worst. At last Pipkin, in great anxiety and distress, insisted on setting out for Nuthanger. Fiver at once said that he would go with him and together they left the wood and set off northward over the down. They had gone only a short distance when Fiver, sitting up on an anthill to look about, saw a rabbit approaching over the high ground to the west. They both ran nearer and recognized Hazel. Fiver went to meet him while Pipkin raced back to the Honeycomb with the news.

As soon as he had learned all that had happened—including what Groundsel had to tell—Hazel asked Holly to take two or three rabbits and find out for certain whether the Efrafans had really gone. Then he himself went into the run where Bigwig was lying. Hyzenthlay looked up as he came.

"He was awake a little while ago, Hazel-rah," she said. "He asked where you were; and then he said his ear hurt very much."

Hazel nuzzled the matted fur cap. The blood had turned hard and set into pointed spikes that pricked his nose.

"You've done it, Bigwig," he said. "They've all run away."

For several moments Bigwig did not move. Then he opened his eyes and raised his head, pouching out his cheeks and sniffing at the two rabbits beside him. He said nothing and Hazel wondered whether he had understood. At last he whispered, "Ees finish Meester Voundvort, ya?"

"Ya," replied Hazel. "I've come to help you to silflay. It'll do you good and we can clean you up a lot better outside. Come on: it's a lovely afternoon, all sun and leaves."

Bigwig got up and tottered forward into the devastated Honeycomb. There he sank down, rested, got up again and reached the foot of Kehaar's run.

"I thought he'd killed me," he said. "No more fighting for me—I've had enough. And you—your plan worked, Hazel-rah, did it? Well done. Tell me what it was. And how did you get back from the farm?"

"A man brought me in a hrududu," said Hazel, "nearly all the way."

"And you flew the rest, I suppose," said Bigwig, "burning a white stick in your mouth? Come on, tell me sensibly. What's the matter, Hyzenthlay?"

"Oh!" said Hyzenthlay, staring. "Oh!"

"What is it?"

"He did!"

"Did what?"

"He *did* ride home in a hrududu. And I saw him as he came—that night in Efrafa, when I was with you in your burrow. Do you remember?"

"I remember," said Bigwig. "I remember what I said, too. I said you'd better tell it to Fiver. That's a good idea—let's go and do it. And if he'll believe you, Hazel-rah, then I will."

And Last

Professing myself, moreover, convinced that the General's unjust interference, so far from being really injurious to their felicity, was perhaps rather conducive to it, by improving their knowledge of each other, and adding strength to their attachment, I leave it to be settled by whomsoever it may concern. . . .

Jane Austen, *Northanger Abbey*

It was a fine, clear evening in mid-October, about six weeks later. Although leaves remained on the beeches and the sunshine was warm, there was a sense of growing emptiness over the wide space of the down. The flowers were sparser. Here and there a yellow tormentil showed in the grass, a late harebell or a few shreds of purple bloom on a brown, crisping tuft of self-heal. But most of the plants still to be seen were in seed. Along the edge of the wood a sheet of wild clematis showed like a patch of smoke, all its sweet-smelling flowers turned to old man's beard. The songs of the insects were fewer and intermittent. Great stretches of the long grass, once the teeming jungle of summer, were almost deserted, with only a hurrying beetle or a torpid spider left out of all the myriads of August. The gnats still danced in the bright air, but the swifts that had swooped for them were gone and instead of their screaming cries in the sky, the twittering of a robin sounded from the top of a spindle tree. The fields below the hill were all cleared. One had already been plowed and the polished edges of the furrows caught the light with a dull glint, conspicuous from the ridge above. The sky, too, was void, with a thin clarity like that of water. In July the still blue, thick as cream, had seemed close above the green trees, but now the blue was high and rare, the sun slipped sooner to the west and, once there, foretold a touch of frost, sinking slow and big and drowsy, crimson as the rose hips that covered the briar. As the wind freshened from the south, the red and yellow beech leaves rasped together with a brittle sound, harsher than the fluid rustle of earlier days. It was a time of quiet departures, of the sifting away of all that was not staunch against winter.

Many human beings say that they enjoy the winter, but what they really enjoy is feeling proof against it. For them there is no winter food problem. They have fires and warm clothes. The winter cannot hurt them and therefore increases their sense of cleverness and security. For birds and animals, as for poor men, winter is another matter. Rabbits, like most wild animals, suffer hardship. True, they are luckier than some, for food of a sort is nearly always to be had. But under snow they may stay underground for days at a time, feeding only by chewing pellets. They are more subject to disease in winter and the cold lowers their vitality. Nevertheless, burrows can be snug and warm, especially when crowded. Winter is a more active mating season than the late summer and the autumn, and the time of greatest fertility for the does starts about February. There are fine days when silflay is still enjoyable. For the adventurous, garden-raiding has its charms. And underground there are stories to be told and games to be played—bob-stones and the like. For rabbits, winter remains what it was for men in the middle ages—hard, but bearable by the resourceful and not altogether without compensations.

On the west side of the beech hanger, in the evening sun, Hazel and Fiver were sitting with Holly, Silver and Groundsel. The Efrafan survivors had been allowed to join the warren and after a shaky start, when they were regarded with dislike and suspicion, were settling down pretty well, largely because Hazel was determined that they should.

Since the night of the siege, Fiver had spent much time alone and even in the Honeycomb, or at morning and evening silflay, was often silent and preoccupied. No one resented this—"He looks right through you in such a nice, friendly way," as Bluebell put it—for each in his own manner recognized that Fiver was now more than ever governed, whether he would or no, by the pulse of that mysterious world of which he had once spoken to Hazel during the late June days they had spent together at the foot of the down. It was Bigwig who said—one evening when Fiver was absent from the Honeycomb at story time—that Fiver was one who had paid more dearly than even himself for the night's victory over the Efrafans. Yet to his doe, Vilthuril, Fiver was devotedly attached, while she had come to understand him almost as deeply as ever Hazel had.

Just outside the beech hanger, Hyzenthlay's litter of four young rabbits were playing in the grass. They had first been brought up to graze about seven days before. If Hyzenthlay had had a second litter she would by this time have left them to look after themselves. As it was, however, she was grazing close by, watching their play and every now and then moving in to cuff the strongest and stop him bullying the others.

"They're a good bunch, you know," said Holly. "I hope we get some more like those."

"We can't expect many more until toward the end of the winter," said Hazel, "though I dare say there'll be a few."

"We can expect anything, it seems to me," said Holly. "Three litters born in autumn—have *you* ever heard of such a thing before? Frith didn't mean rabbits to mate in the high summer."

"I don't know about Clover," said Hazel. "She's a hutch rabbit: it may be natural to her to breed at any time, for all I know. But I'm sure that Hyzenthlay and Vilthuril started their litters in the high summer because they'd had no natural life in Efrafa. For all that, they're the only two who *have* had litters, as yet."

"Frith never meant us to go out fighting in the high summer, either, if that comes to that," said Silver. "Everything that's happened is unnatural—the fighting, the breeding—and all on account of Woundwort. If he wasn't unnatural, who was?"

"Bigwig was right when he said he wasn't like a rabbit at all," said Holly. "He was a fighting animal—fierce as a rat or a dog. He fought because he actually felt safer fighting than running. He was brave, all right. But it wasn't natural; and that's why it was bound to finish him in the end. He was trying to do something that Frith never meant any rabbit to do. I believe he'd have hunted like the elil if he could."

"He isn't dead, you know," broke in Groundsel.

The others were silent.

"He hasn't stopped running," said Groundsel passionately. "Did you see his body? No. Did anyone? No. Nothing could kill him. He made rabbits bigger than they've ever been—braver, more skillful, more cunning. I know we paid for it. Some gave their lives. It was worth it, to feel we were Efrafans. For the first time ever, rabbits didn't go scurrying away. The elil feared us. And that was on account of Woundwort—him and no one but him. We weren't good enough for the General. Depend upon it, he's gone to start another warren somewhere else. But no Efrafan officer will ever forget him."

"Well, now I'll tell you something," began Silver. But Hazel cut him short.

"You mustn't say you weren't good enough," he said. "You did everything for him that rabbits could do and a great deal more. And what a lot we learned from you! As for Efrafa, I've heard it's doing well under Campion, even if some things aren't quite the same as they used to be. And listen—by next spring, if I'm right, we shall have too many rabbits here for comfort. I'm going to encourage some of the youngsters to start a new warren between here and Efrafa; and I think you'll find Campion will be ready to send some of his rabbits to join them. You'd be just the right fellow to start that scheme off."

"Won't it be difficult to arrange?" asked Holly.

"Not when Kehaar comes," said Hazel, as they began to hop easily back toward the holes at the northeast corner of the hanger. "He'll turn up one of these days, when the storms begin on that Big Water of his. He can take a message to Campion as quickly as you'd run down to the iron tree and back."

"By Frith in the leaves, and I know someone who'll be glad to see him!" said Silver. "Someone not so very far away."

They had reached the eastern end of the trees and here, well out in the open where it was still sunny, a little group of three young rabbits—bigger than Hyzenthlay's—were squatting in the long grass, listening to a hulking veteran, lop-eared and scarred from nose to haunch—none other than Bigwig, captain of a very free-and-easy Owsla. These were the bucks of Clover's litter and a likely lot they looked.

"Oh, no, no, no, no," Bigwig was saying. "Oh, my wings and beak, that won't do! You—what's your name—Scabious—look, I'm a cat and I see you down at the bottom of my garden chewing up the lettuces. Now, what do I do? Do I come walking up the middle of the path waving my tail? Well, do I?"

"Please, sir, I've never seen a cat," said the young rabbit.

"No, you haven't yet," admitted the gallant captain. "Well, a cat is a horrible thing with a long tail. It's covered with fur and has bristling whiskers and when it fights it makes fierce, spiteful noises. It's cunning, see?"

"Oh, yes, sir," answered the young rabbit. After a pause, he said politely, "Er—you lost your tail?"

"Will you tell us about the fight in the storm, sir?" asked one of the other rabbits, "and the tunnel of water?"

"Yes, later on," said the relentless trainer. "Now look, I'm a cat, right? I'm asleep in the sun, right? And you're going to get past me, right? Now then—"

"They pull his leg, you know," said Silver, "but they'd do anything for him." Holly and Groundsel had gone underground and Silver and Hazel moved out once more into the sun.

"I think we all would," replied Hazel. "If it hadn't been for him that day, the dog would have come too late. Woundwort and his lot wouldn't have been above ground. They'd have been down below, finishing what they'd come to do."

"He beat Woundwort, you know," said Silver. "He had him beat before the dog came. That was what I was going to say just now, but it was as well I didn't, I suppose."

"I wonder how they're getting on with that winter burrow down the hill," said Hazel. "We're going to need it when the hard weather comes. That hole in the roof of the Honeycomb doesn't help at all. It'll close up naturally one day, I suppose, but meanwhile it's a confounded nuisance."

"Here come the burrow-diggers, anyway," said Silver.

Pipkin and Bluebell came over the crest, together with three or four of the does.

"Ah ha, ah ha, O Hazel-rah," said Bluebell. "The burrow's snug, it hath been dug, t'is free from beetle, worm and slug. And in the snow, when down we go—"

"Then what a lot to you we'll owe," said Hazel. "I mean it, too. The holes are concealed, are they?"

"Just like Efrafa, I should think," said Bluebell. "As a matter of fact, I brought one up with me to show you. You can't see it, can you? No—well, there you are. I say, just look at old Bigwig with those youngsters over there. You know, if he went back to Efrafa now they couldn't decide which Mark to put him in, could they? He's got them all."

"Come over to the evening side of the wood with us, Hazel-rah?" said Pipkin. "We came up early on purpose to have a bit of sunshine before it gets dark."

"All right," answered Hazel good-naturedly. "We've just come back from there, Silver and I, but I don't mind slipping over again for a bit."

"Let's go out to that little hollow where we found Kehaar that morning," said Silver. "It'll be out of the wind. D'you remember how he cursed at us and tried to peck us?"

"And the worms we carried?" said Bluebell. "Don't forget them."

As they came near the hollow they could hear that it was not empty. Evidently some of the other rabbits had had the same idea.

"Let's see how close we can get before they spot us," said Silver. "Real Campion style—come on."

They approached very quietly, upwind from the north. Peeping over the edge, they saw Vilthuril and her litter of four lying in the sun. Their mother was telling the young rabbits a story.

"So after they had swum the river," said Vilthuril, "El-ahrairah led his people on in the dark, through a wild, lonely place. Some of them were afraid, but he knew the way and in the morning he brought them safely to some green fields, very beautiful, with good, sweet grass. And here they found a warren; a warren that was bewitched. All the rabbits in this warren were in the power of a wicked spell. They wore shining collars round their necks and sang like the birds and some of them could fly. But for all they looked so fine, their hearts were dark and tharn. So then El-ahrairah's people said, 'Ah, see, these are the wonderful rabbits of Prince Rainbow. They are like princes themselves. We will live with them and become princes, too.'"

Vilthuril looked up and saw the newcomers. She paused for a moment and then went on.

"But Frith came to Rabscuttle in a dream and warned him that that warren was enchanted. And he dug into the ground to find where the spell was buried. Deep he dug, and hard was the search, but at last he found that wicked spell and dragged it out. So they all fled from it, but it turned into a great rat and flew at El-ahrairah. Then El-ahrairah fought the rat, up and down, and at last he held it, pinned under his claws, and it turned into a great white bird which spoke to him and blessed him."

"I seem to know this story," whispered Hazel, "but I can't remember where I've heard it."

Bluebell sat up and scratched his neck with his hind leg. The little rabbits turned round at the interruption and in a moment had tumbled up the side of the hollow, squeaking "Hazel-rah! Hazel-rah!" and jumping on Hazel from all sides.

"Here, wait a minute," said Hazel, cuffing them off. "I didn't come here to get mixed up in a fight with a lot of roughs like you! Let's hear the rest of the story."

"But there's a man coming on a horse, Hazel-rah," said one of the young rabbits. "Oughtn't we to run into the wood?"

"How can you tell?" asked Hazel. "I can't hear anything."

"Neither can I," said Silver, listening with his ears up.

The little rabbit looked puzzled.

"I don't know how, Hazel-rah," he answered, "but I'm sure I'm not mistaken."

They waited for some little time, while the red sun sank lower. At last, just as Vilthuril was about to go on with the story, they heard hooves on the turf and the horseman appeared from the west, cantering easily along the track toward Cannon Heath Down.

"*He* won't bother us," said Silver. "No need to run: he'll just go by. You're a funny chap, though, young Threar, to spot him so far off."

"He's always doing things like that," said Vilthuril. "The other day he told me what a river looked like and said he'd seen it in a dream. It's Fiver's blood, you know. It's only to be expected with Fiver's blood."

"Fiver's blood?" said Hazel. "Well, as long as we've got some of that I dare say we'll be all right. But, you know, it's turning chilly here, isn't it? Come on, let's go down, and hear the rest of that story in a good, warm burrow. Look, there's Fiver over on the bank now. Who's going to get to him first?"

A few minutes later there was not a rabbit to be seen on the down. The sun sank below Ladle Hill and the autumn stars began to shine in the darkening east—Perseus and the Pleiades, Cassiopeia, faint Pisces and the great square of Pegasus. The wind freshened, and soon myriads of dry beech leaves were filling the ditches and hollows and blowing in gusts across the dark miles of open grass. Underground, the story continued.

Epilogue

> He did look far
> Into the service of the time, and was
> Discipled of the bravest: he lasted long,
> But on us both did haggish age steal on,
> And wore us out of act. . . .
>> Shakespeare, *All's Well That Ends Well*

> He was part of my dream, of course—but then I was part of his dream, too.
>> Lewis Carroll, *Through the Looking-Glass*

"And what happened in the end?" asks the reader who has followed Hazel and his comrades in all their adventures and returned with them at last to the warren where Fiver brought them from the fields of Sandleford. The wise Mr. Lockley has told us that wild rabbits live for two or three years. He knows everything about rabbits: but all the same, Hazel lived longer than that. He lived a tidy few summers—as they say in that part of the world—and learned to know well the changes of the downs to spring, to winter and to spring again. He saw more young rabbits than he could remember. And sometimes, when they told tales on a sunny evening by the beech trees, he could not clearly recall whether they were about himself or about some other rabbit hero of days gone by.

The warren prospered and so, in the fullness of time, did the new warren on the Belt, half Watership and half Efrafan—the warren that Hazel had first envisaged on that terrible evening when he set out alone to face General Woundwort and try to save his friends against all odds. Groundsel was the first Chief Rabbit; but he had Strawberry and Buckthorn to give him advice and he had learned better than to mark anyone or to order more than a very occasional Wide Patrol. Campion readily agreed to send some rabbits from Efrafa and the first party was led by none other than Captain Avens, who acted sensibly and made a very good job of it.

General Woundwort was never seen again. But it was certainly true, as Groundsel said, that no one ever found his body, so it may perhaps be that, after all, that extraordinary rabbit really did wander away to live his fierce life somewhere else and to defy the elil as resourcefully as ever. Kehaar, who was once asked if he would look out for him in his flights over the downs, merely replied, "Dat damn rabbit—I no see 'im, I no vant I see 'im." Before many months had passed, no one on Watership knew or particularly cared to know whether he himself or his mate was descended from one or two Efrafan parents or from none at all. Hazel was glad that it should be so. And yet there endured the legend that somewhere out over the down there lived a great and solitary rabbit, a giant who drove the elil like mice and sometimes went to silflay in the sky. If ever great danger arose, he would come back to fight for those who honored his name. And mother rabbits would tell their kittens that if they did not do as they were told, the General would get them—the General who was first cousin to the Black Rabbit himself. Such was Woundwort's monument: and perhaps it would not have displeased him.

One chilly, blustery morning in March, I cannot tell exactly how many springs later, Hazel was dozing and waking in his burrow. He had spent a good deal of time there lately, for he felt the cold and could not seem to smell or run so well as in days gone by. He had been dreaming in a confused way—something about rain and elder bloom—when he woke to realize that there was a rabbit lying quietly beside him—no doubt some young buck who had come to ask his advice. The sentry in the run outside should not really have let him in without asking first. Never mind, thought Hazel. He raised his head and said, "Do you want to talk to me?"

"Yes, that's what I've come for," replied the other "You know me, don't you?"

"Yes, of course," said Hazel, hoping he would be able to remember his name in a moment. Then he saw that in the darkness of the burrow the stranger's ears were shining with a faint silver light. "Yes, my lord," he said. "Yes, I know you."

"You've been feeling tired," said the stranger, "but I can do something about that. I've come to ask whether you'd care to join my Owsla. We shall be glad to have you and you'll enjoy it. If you're ready, we might go along now."

They went out past the young sentry, who paid the visitor no attention. The sun was shining and in spite of the cold there were a few bucks and does at silflay, keeping out of the wind as they nibbled the shoots of spring grass. It seemed to Hazel that he would not be needing his body any more, so he left it lying on the edge of the ditch, but stopped for a moment to watch his rabbits and to try to get used to the extraordinary feeling that strength and speed were flowing inexhaustibly out of him into their sleek young bodies and healthy senses.

"You needn't worry about them," said his companion. "They'll be all right—and thousands like them. If you'll come along, I'll show you what I mean."

He reached the top of the bank in a single, powerful leap. Hazel followed; and together they slipped away, running easily down through the wood, where the first primroses were beginning to bloom.

Lapine Glossary

Bob-stones A traditional game among rabbits. (*See* footnote on page 246.)

Crixa, the The center of Efrafa, at the crossing point of two bridle paths.

Efrafa The name of the warren founded by General Woundwort.

El-ahrairah The rabbit folk hero. The name (Elil-hrair-rah) means "Enemies-Thousand-Prince" = the Prince with a Thousand Enemies.

Elil Enemies (of rabbits). (*See* footnote on page 4.)

Embleer Stinking, e.g. the smell of a fox.

Flay Food, e.g. grass or other green fodder.

Flayrah Unusually good food, e.g. lettuce.

Frith The sun, personified as a god by rabbits. Frithrah! = the lord Sun—used as an exclamation.

Fu Inlé After moonrise.

Hlao Any dimple or depression in the grass, such as that formed by a daisy plant or thistle, which can hold moisture. The name of a rabbit. (*See* page 16.)

Hlao-roo "Little Hlao." An affectionate diminutive of the name of Hlao, one of the rabbits in the story.

Hlessi A rabbit living above ground, without a regular hole or warren. A wandering rabbit, living in the open. (Plural, hlessil.)

Homba A fox. (Plural, hombil.)

Hrair A great many; an uncountable number; any number over four. U Hrair = The Thousand (enemies). (*See* footnote on page 4.)

Hrairoo "Little Thousand." The name of Fiver in Lapine. (*See* footnote on pages 4–5.)

Hraka Droppings, excreta.

Hrududu A tractor, car or any motor vehicle. (Plural, hrududil.)

Hyzenthlay Literally, "Shine-dew-fur" = Fur shining like dew. The name of a doe.

Inlé Literally, the moon; also moonrise. But a second meaning carries the idea of darkness, fear and death.

Lendri A badger.

Marli A doe. Also carries the meaning "mother."

M'saion "We meet them."

Narn Nice, pleasant (to eat).

Ni-Frith Noon.

Nildro-hain "Blackbird's Song." The name of a doe.

Owsla The strongest rabbits in a warren, the ruling clique. (*See* footnote on page 5.)

Owslafa The Council police (a word found only in Efrafa).

Pfeffa A cat.

Rah A prince, leader or chief rabbit. Usually used as a suffix. E.g. Threarah = Lord Threar.

Roo Used as a suffix to denote a diminutive. E.g. Hrairoo.

Sayn Groundsel.

Silf Outside, that is, not underground.

Silflay To go above ground to feed. Literally, to feed outside. Also used as a noun.

Tharn Stupefied, distraught, hypnotized with fear. But can also, in certain contexts, mean "looking foolish," or again "heartbroken" or "forlorn."

Thethuthinnang "Movement of Leaves." The name of a doe.

Thlay	Fur.
Thlayli	"Fur-head." A nickname.
Threar	A rowan tree, or mountain ash.
Vair	To excrete, pass droppings.
Yona	A hedgehog. (Plural, yonil.)
Zorn	Destroyed, murdered. Denotes a catastrophe.